POLITICAL MEMOIRS
1905-1917

POLITICAL MEMOIRS
1905-1917

by
Paul Miliukov

Edited by Arthur P. Mendel

Translated by Carl Goldberg

Ann Arbor
THE UNIVERSITY OF MICHIGAN PRESS

Introduction

PAUL MILIUKOV, THE ACKNOWLEDGED LEADER of Russian liberalism and one of Russia's most distinguished prerevolutionary historians, began these memoirs in Vichy, France, in 1940, having waited, he said, until there was nothing else of value for him to do. By then, he had completed the prolonged revision of *Outlines of the History of Russian Civilization*, his finest achievement as an historian, and the seizure by the Nazis of his Paris library ended further scholarship. The Nazi occupation of Paris also brought an end to the émigré journal he had edited since 1921 and, thereby, to his lifelong career as a political analyst. But what, in any case, could he have written about current affairs at that time? Russia, still his ultimate concern and still the cherished homeland he could defend in spite of Stalinism, had been for a year the ally of Nazi Germany, the embodiment of everything he most hated. The shock and shame of the alliance were partly purged by the German invasion the following year, only to be replaced, however, by an ever-deepening pessimism and dejection as the Nazis swept on toward Moscow. "The gigantic experiment," he now judged, "has ended in gigantic catastrophe." So, he gave the final two years of his life to the past, spending his days on the memoirs and his evenings in following despondently the news of the terrible decimation of his country. He died on March 3, 1943, at eighty-four years of age. Although he had not finished his memoirs, he had lived just long enough for an event, no doubt, far more important to him: on February 2, the German Sixth Army surrendered at Stalingrad.

The Odyssey of this remarkable man is also that of modern Russia, for if the victory at Stalingrad occurred at the end of his life, its beginning, in 1859, was marked by the Crimean debacle and by the first efforts to eradicate the causes of that humiliation—efforts that were to continue, with halts and regressions, now slowly, now precipitously, until our own time. Miliukov's whole life's struggle, all that he suffered and sacrificed, comes to a single question whose meaning is at least as vital today as it was in his time: Do political freedom and representative government have parts to play in the drama of social and economic reformation? Or were Miliukov's life and the lives of countless others who struggled to create a free Russia just so much waste for History's bulging dustbins—futile antics of no relevance for this gargantuan transformation that could only progress, as it did in fact progress, from one tyranny to another?

There are distinguished scholars of Russian history who argue the latter case, who believe that there was "no chance for a liberal constitutional Russia whatsoever." Others argue that "Russia on the eve of the war (World War I) was well advanced on the path of evolution toward a modern democratic state." As for Miliukov, he was convinced not merely of the possibility of Russia moving toward a Western European form of parliamentary, constitutional government and open society, but almost of its inevitability. He was himself a product of the social transformation and an illustration of its impact on political thought and action. His origins were typically middle class—his father was an architect and, later, a bank appraiser; his secondary school interests fused a traditional study of the Classics with an eager enthusiasm for modern positivism, for the exhilarating new field of sociology and its luminaries, Comte, Spencer, and Marx; and his social consciousness had matured enough to win him a year-long suspension from Moscow University. There was nothing at all unusual in this simultaneous commitment to scholarship and politics: few self-respecting Russian university students would have thought of doing otherwise. But what was remarkable, and, as time went on, increasingly extraordinary, was Miliukov's ability to achieve so much in both.

In 1886, at the age of twenty-seven, he published his first article, on Russian historiography, and at the same time began six years of archival research for his master's thesis. During this period he provided for himself and his wife, whom he married in 1889, by assisting at the University and teaching history at two secondary schools. To all appearances a conventional, scholarly analysis of documents relating to the Russian economy under Peter the Great, his thesis reflected clearly the political and social values that were to remain with Miliukov to the end of his life and to inspire all his political goals and tactics. The central argument of the study, he later wrote, was that the "Europeanization of Russia is not a product of borrowing, but the inevitable result of an internal evolution, which is in principle identical in Russia and Europe, but only held back by surrounding conditions."

Had Miliukov followed the customary career, he would have gone on to other specialized and largely technical analyses, preferably in social or economic history, which in Russia, as in Europe at the time, were the most prestigious themes for aspiring historians. Showing from the outset an unusual independence of mind and strength of will, however, Miliukov rejected this familiar and expected direction, and in 1892, as soon as he had completed his economic study, he turned to a broad, general, and humanistic study of Russian culture. Inspired by Guizot's *Histoire de la civilisation en France* and intent on preparing a meaningful series of lectures for a new course on Russian culture, he began work on *Outlines of the History of Russian Civilization*. Initially published in three volumes during 1896–1903, and widely translated, the work was revised in the 1930's and supplemented at that time by a section covering the earliest centuries of Russian history. Lost for a time, then requiring long editorial preparation, this concluding section of the supplementary volume did not appear in print until 1964.

To this day, Miliukov's *Outlines* continue to serve as the best single comprehensive survey of Russian culture from its beginnings through the nineteenth century. Here again, as in his study of the Russian economy, Miliukov's scholarship is imbued throughout with his political values. In the words of Michael Karpovich, editor of the English translation of the *Outlines*, and one of the two editors of the original memoirs, Miliukov tried in this great work "to join past to present and build a foundation on which to foresee the future." Through it all is the essential conviction that also underlies his work on Peter—that Russia was neither fully Western, as doctrinaire "Westerners" in Russia argued, nor radically different from the West, as no less one-sided Slavophiles maintained, but rather a synthesis of both, European in the long run and in its general contours, but distinguished by a variety of particular attributes resulting from Russia's relative backwardness, its slower tempo of development, and the various special conditions that necessarily molded its developing thought and institutions.

It was this same conviction that guided Miliukov's entire political life, inspired his endless stream of programs, rationalized for him and others innumerable shifts in strategy and tactics, and, as much as any other factor, caused his and his party's ultimate failure. It was also, it seems, this fusion of Europe and Russia that, at the turn of the century, drove him from scholarship to revolutionary politics. Few scholars have enjoyed a more promising beginning for an illustrious academic career. The meticulous care he had taken with his research showed him an undoubtedly committed historian and earned him an envied reputation, rare for one so young. He might even look forward to the time he would replace the illustrious Kliuchevsky as *the* Russian historian. His sudden shift from "scientific," economic history to cultural and intellectual history as well as the unmistakably tendentious, political themes that characterize his first works, however, reflected a growing dissatisfaction with the scholar's life, comfortably ensconced in library and lecture hall, safe from political turmoil. Scholarship alone was not enough, not in Russia in the 1890's, not for a European Russian. It was not enough to write about an inevitable Europeanization of Russia: Miliukov had to do what he could to bring it about.

As it did with so many other talented young men and women of the time, the tsarist bureaucracy helped Miliukov step by step in his transition from a politically innocuous historian to a leader of revolution. The one-year expulsion from Moscow University in 1881 and the unrelieved repression and tedium that distinguished the reign of Alexander III promoted both his continued involvement in student opposition groups and, in the late 1880's, the liberal tone of his university and secondary school lectures and discussions. Then, in 1891–92, while Miliukov was completing his six-year economic study, Russia was overwhelmed by a catastropic famine—a consequence of bureaucratic stagnation and rural exploitation—which abruptly ended the "quiet years" of Alexander's reign and sparked a political resurgence that was to dominate the reign of the last Romanov.

Now the state had no choice but to free what few instruments of social service Russia possessed. The elected, local self-governing Zemstvos, established by Alexander II as part of the Great Reforms of the 1860's, then repeatedly restricted as a threat to autocracy, had now to be allowed full freedom to cope with the famine. And how could the state hold back the throngs of students who now rushed to the countryside to do what they could, in imitation of the great "populist" movement "to the people" twenty years before, a movement that had ended in regicide? But more important than the revival of old opposition groups was the new realization, comparable to the awakening after the Crimean defeat, that stagnation meant disaster, that Russia had to change radically, and that such change could only mean rapid Europeanization. "For thirteen years, I could imperturbably concern myself with scholarship. I can now no longer do this. More and more I am bound fast to politics." In these words, Miliukov announced to a Nizhny-Novgorod student body, at the end of 1894, his choice of politics as his principal commitment.

On January 17, 1895, the new tsar, Nicholas II, took up the challenge of the revived opposition, of the Zemstvo leaders and of the countless young Russians who were then experiencing the same rededication to politics that Miliukov acknowledged in Nizhny-Novgorod. "I will preserve the foundations of autocracy as resolutely and as uncomprisingly as did my late father," Nicholas proclaimed. As for the renewed hopes for political reform, he went on, they were but "senseless dreams." For Miliukov, the effect of this reaction was sharp and swift. Less than a month after the tsar's statement, the minister of education ordered that Miliukov be dismissed from the university and forbidden to teach anywhere, while the Ministry of Internal Affairs decreed his exile from Moscow for two years because of his "harmful influence on students." He went to Riazan, where he spent the two years pleasantly enough, writing his *Outlines*, caring for his garden, and playing violin in a local quartet. The exile completed, Miliukov was given a choice of either a year in prison or two years "exile abroad." After he made his "choice," Miliukov decided on the Balkans as his place of exile, first Bulgaria, at the University of Sofia, then Turkey. During his exile, he kept in close touch with Russian political events, at the same time nurturing a passionate interest in Balkan affairs that was later to have an important influence in his political life and contribute significantly to his final defeat.

Back in St. Petersburg in 1899, he plunged at once into politics, siding with the Marxists, then the most consistent Westerners and the group that had won ascendancy among the radical opposition during Miliukov's exile in Riazan and the Balkans. Still striving for his now familiar balance between extreme Westernism and the more traditional Russian tendencies, however, he maintained his associations with the Populist foes of Russian Marxism and, in the winter of 1900, gave an address at a gathering in honor of Peter Lavrov, a leading Populist theorist who had died that February. The liberal theme of the address was enough to bring police reprisal once again, first, a sentence of six months in prison, then, after six months of restricted freedom— he could not remain in St. Petersburg—another six-month prison sentence. Before undergoing the second sentence, Miliukov was permitted a trip to England, on the promise that he would return to complete the sentence. Miliukov gave his word, spent the winter of 1901–2 in England improving his English, returned to Russia on time, and, pillow in hand, knocked on the prison door. But it was Sunday, and he could not get in. He went home, came back Monday, got in, and spent another six months in reading, writing, and talking politics.

Looking back today through the agonies of total terror, all this seems unbelievably mild. And it is all the more so when we realize that by 1902 the fledgling opposition disdained by Nicholas in 1895 had reached dangerous proportions. The new revolutionary ascent began in 1899–1900 with a series of student and worker strikes and demstrations, caused largely by a sharp economic recession that hit the Russian economy at the time. But far more serious for the state was the revival of revolutionary terror on a scale that recalled the exploits of the Populists twenty years before. In February 1901 the minister of education was assassinated; the following year, the minister of the interior fell victim to the terrorists; and, also in 1902, an attempt was

made on the life of the most illustrious of all reactionaries, Pobedonostsev. Most threatening of all, however, were the peasant disturbances
that broke out sporadically in these first years of the new century.
Partly in response to the rural crisis, and reminiscent of the postfamine
situation a decade earlier, the provincial Zemstvos ignored prohibitions
against inter-Zemstvo meetings and held conferences that were to play
an essential part in the emerging revolution. Finally, in June 1902, the
journal *Osvobozhdenie,* which was to represent the left wing of the
liberal movement, in contrast to the Zemstvo moderates, was founded
in Stuttgart. In recognition of both his wide political knowledge and
his earlier participation in the opposition, Miliukov was asked to edit
the journal. Since this would have required another, and this time
virtually permanent, emigration, he declined, preferring instead to become a principal contributor.

Thus, the man who came to jail that Sunday in 1902 had already
advanced far along the road toward leadership of a burgeoning revolution, as the minister of interior, the dreaded Plehve, indirectly acknowledged when, during a prison interview with Miliukov, he raised the
possibility of Miliukov's appointment as minister of education! Nowhere does Miliukov's justly renowned cool control, audacity, and
pride come out more clearly than in his reply to this extraordinary
suggestion. He would probably turn down such an offer, he said, "because one could not really do anything in this post. But if your honor
were to offer me your position, then I would give it some thought."
Miliukov was understandably anxious about the outcome of this bizarre
exchange with one of the most powerful and reactionary officials in
Russia. But luck was still with him, and he was soon released, with a
warning not to engage in open struggle with the government, but also
with permission to go abroad to give a series of lectures in the United
States on Russian political conditions! Since the authorities must certainly have known the kind of lectures he would give, we are again
left wondering about the character of tsarist repression.

In these 1903 public lectures at the University of Chicago and at
Lowell Institute, Boston, the fusion of politics and scholarship, evident
in Miliukov's earliest works, attains completion, for it was the critical
situation in Russia at the time that guided Miliukov's selection and interpretation of what were for him the principal forces of Russian
history. Upon completion of the series, Miliukov returned to Europe,
first to England and then, once more, to the Balkans, where he gathered material for another series of lectures, this time on Balkan history,
to be given at the University of Chicago in 1904–5.

Considering what was happening in Russia in 1904, it is surprising that Miliukov did, in fact, sail for the United States and start the

course. During the brief period that separated his first series of lectures at the University of Chicago, in the summer of 1903, and his second series, planned for the winter of 1904–5, the nascent struggle that Plehve had warned Miliukov not to enter was rapidly moving toward a full-scale revolution. In July 1904 Plehve himself became its most prominent victim, but not before he had joined others in urging Russia into war with Japan, an "easy" war that, it was hoped, would transform bitter opposition into enthusiastic patriotism and perhaps also end the economic depression that had, since the turn of the century, contributed mightily to the universal discontent. Had the war been the triumphant success that the government understandably expected—after all, Russia was Europe and Japan was the backward East—it might indeed have had this effect on domestic affairs. But it was the Crimea all over again. Incredible ineptitude, treasonable surrenders, ignominious retreats, and tragic-comic disasters piled humiliation upon humiliation, infuriated the already rebellious population, and demoralized the army, crippling it as a force against revolution.

One could hardly imagine more propitious conditions for revolution than those gathered in 1905. All groups and classes were aroused. The peasantry, looking back on a decade that began with calamitous famine and ended in economic depression, were at last rising in vengeance and seemed to be moving toward the great peasant upheaval that revolutionary Populists had long predicted. To this emerging jacquerie, led by the Social Revolutionary party, the heirs of revolutionary Populism, there were now added the more recent opposition forces, planted and nurtured, paradoxically, by the state iself. The Crimean defeat and the famine disaster had pointed toward a single conclusion—economic and social transformation. The hesitant efforts of the state to carry out the implications of such calamities had thrown open the institutes of higher education to all classes, established elected organs of local self-government in town and country, and advanced diverse economic programs that rapidly filled old and new urban centers with a middle class and proletariat. For Russia to progress, to avoid disasters like Crimea and the famine, all this and much, much more in the way of social, economic, political, and cultural change had to be pushed by the government. But the inevitable consequence of such change was the creation of new forces of opposition to the government, vastly more powerful and effective than had ever before challenged the tsar and his bureaucracy. Zemstvo participants, with decades of experience in self-government; a large, concentrated, and rebellious student body, recruited from the antagonized middle and lower classes; an almost entirely new world of professionals (teachers, doctors, lawyers, accountants, agronomists, engineers, and the like); a working class, hastily recruited from the countryside and packed into grotesquely deficient urban quarters—these were the indirect, unwanted, but inevitable by-products of the state's efforts to catch up with the West.

In August 1904, one month after Plehve's assassination, a meeting was held in Paris of liberals and socialists who would channel and further intensify this revolutionary torrent. Miliukov was prominent among them. The following month one decision of that conference was realized in the establishment of the League of Liberation, the organization of left-wing liberalism that appears so persistently and decisively in the memoirs. In November the moderate, Zemstvo liberals held a conference that was as significant as the Paris meeting in August, since it revealed an agreement between the more radical "Liberationists" and the Zemstvo representatives as to the essential goal of the revolution: the establishment of a truly legislative parliament that would effectively share power with the Court and bureaucracy, not merely a consultative body as previous Zemstvo conferences had advocated.

This was the immediate background to Miliukov's Chicago University lectures on Balkan history. Did he really believe that he would be able to stay away? In December the shameful surrender of Port Arthur and in January the still more disgraceful and politically inept "Bloody Sunday" firing on a peaceful and demonstrably loyal workers' procession proved to Miliukov that he had left Europe in the wrong direction. He abruptly cancelled his course, after getting about four or five lectures into it, and remained in the United States only long enough to complete the manuscript of *Russia and Its Crisis*, his 1903 lectures in Chicago and Boston. Characteristically, he dated the foreword to the completed work, "Abraham Lincoln's birthday, 1905."

The part of Miliukov's memoirs published here covers a twelve-year period beginning with his return to Russia in this spring of 1905 and ending in the summer of 1917, shortly after his forced resignation as minister of foreign affairs for the Provisional Government. From any point of view it was one of the most turbulent, dramatic, and phantasmagoric periods in the history of Russia or any other country. The period of just over a decade witnessed two major revolutions—those of 1905 and February 1917—that destroyed tsarism and that led to the eve of another rising that brought the Bolsheviks to power, the painful climax of the Japanese war and the incomparably more brutal and costly three-year conflict with the German and Austro-Hungarian empires, a gargantuan effort to transform the rural economy from the hoary communal system of traditional Russia to the Western system of private property and individual farmsteads, and a veritable explosion of magnificent intellectual and cultural achievements, equal or better than anything in the West, that contributed grandly to universal civilization. It is all too rich and complex, too filled with drama, wonder, and personal shades and moods of experience to be squeezed into a schematicized survey here.

Miliukov was at or near the center of it all. Throughout the revolutionary year 1905 he was among those founding and directing the organizations of the revolution and in other ways mobilizing disparate opposition groups into the victorious united front that won from the state the principal concession, an elected legislative assembly, the Duma. Although excluded by technicalities from participation in the First and Second State Dumas of 1906 and 1907, he remained the principal architect of the liberals' policy both inside and outside the Duma. From November 1907 when he entered the Third State Duma as a delegate from St. Petersburg, he further strengthened his leadership of the liberals and enhanced his prominence and authority throughout Russia by a succession of influential speeches on the urgent issues of the day. When the disasters and scandals of war again provoked intense antagonism against the tsarist Court and bureaucracy, he was once again able to assume leadership in organizing and directing the opposition, this time toward the final overthrow of the autocracy. His dominant role as minister of foreign affairs in the new Provisional Government was, thus, the triumphal climax of a twenty-year struggle. It was also the beginning of the precipitous, total, and tragic defeat both for himself and his cause.

Although it is unnecessary to supplement here Miliukov's own account of this history, one theme that runs through the entire work does warrant comment, since it concerns the vital issue raised at the beginning of this introduction: the place, if any, of Western liberalism —to which Miliukov devoted his life—in countries, like Russia, undergoing rapid transformation from a predominately rural, traditional society. A host of questions comes to mind as we follow Miliukov's and his party's attempts to prove not merely that liberalism has a part to play in this drama, but that it has a leading part. What specific tactics should liberals so placed follow? Should they, as Miliukov at first argued, seek allies on the left, an alliance with workers' and peasants' socialist parties, and thereby attempt an immediate overthrow of the archaic regime? Or should they, as more conservative liberals maintained and as Miliukov also came to believe, reconcile themselves to more gradual progress and more humble goals, goals attainable, if at all, only by cooperation with the more reasonable representatives of the Establishment, with the "right" rather than the "left"? One should keep in mind as these memoirs are read that Russia had only just begun the "great transformation," that the circumstances and conditions that had favored constitutionalism in the West had only begun to emerge in Russia. The heritage of traditional Russia, with all its values and routines, its preferences and antipathies, remained largely intact both at the top, in the all-encompassing bureaucracy and in the Imperial Court, and at the bottom, among the peasant masses and their recent offspring, the nascent urban proletariat. Could a Court and bureaucracy still living in a sixteenth-century milieu be won over by the political reformers? That is, was alliance with the "right" possible? If not, and this is Miliukov's contention in his memoirs, if alliance with the masses on the "left" was indispensable, could the peasants and workers on their socialist leaders be trusted to follow the leadership of the liberals toward achieving liberal goals? Were the freedoms of speech, meeting, and travel, the right of election and effective participation in political affairs, and the rest of the liberals' program also essential desiderata for "the people"? In a society so recently set on the road of "modernization," the liberals in town and country were too few to act alone. Where, under these conditions, should they turn for support?

Given the crisis of war and the consequent demoralization and emasculation of the defense forces, the liberal minority was able to take advantage of mass discontent, first to weaken the autocracy, in 1905, then, in February 1917, to overthrow it. But what followed? When Miliukov returned to Russia in April 1905 he favored a republic. In the chaotic, anarchical days of March 1917, after Tsar Nicholas II had abdicated, Miliukov almost alone among the leaders of the "bourgeois" revolution urged with all the force in him that Nicholas' brother, Michael, continue the Romanov dynasty. The reasons for this change constitute the real drama and, perhaps, the essential meaning for us of the memoirs.

The Bolshevik triumph ended Miliukov's political life in Russia. After October, he joined the anti-Bolshevik forces of Generals Kornilov and Denikin in the south of Russia. To the dismay of many of his liberal friends, he even went to Kiev in mid-1918 in the hope of recruiting support for the anti-Bolshevik cause from the German army, which then occupied the Ukraine. In November 1918, he left Russia for good, going first to the Balkans, then to permanent exile in Western Europe.

If he had antagonized many of his fellow liberals by his negotiations with the Germans, he was to break with others in emigration as he worked his way toward an ambivalent, although for Miliukov characteristic, evaluation of the new Soviet regime. He continued to attack all that was oppressive in it, but he found that he could support the new rulers when they defended what he considered to be Russia's traditional national interests. Moreover, he gradually came to believe that something positive would come of the Soviet experience, or, perhaps more correctly, that notwithstanding all the distortions, absurdities, and monstrosities of Bolshevik rule, the general direction of Soviet policies still followed the line of Europeanization he had charted so long ago in his first book on Peter the Great, the direction to which he had himself dedicated his entire life. Thus, he could support the nationalist Stalin against the internationalist Trotsky, find extenuating circumstances for Russia's invasion of Finland and alliance with Hitler, and even believe that Russia might emerge from the Soviet experience with a part in world history greater than ever before, that of a giant link between East and West, the agent for the synthesis that was his final hope for Russia as it had always been both the expression and meaning of his own life.

The present translation comprises the greater part of the original Russian edition of Miliukov's memoirs, covering, without deletion, the years 1905–17, but excluding the first section of the memoirs, those that concern the earlier period in Miliukov's life summarized in this Introduction. In their preface to the Russian edition of the memoirs, the editors, Michael M. Karpovich and Boris I. Elkin, note their decision not to publish the final pages of the manuscript, about twenty-nine manuscript pages containing the account of events down to the October revolution, because this part was not in finished form. They also decided not to publish several of Miliukov's "harsh judgments of a purely personal nature." The Russian edition was first published in 1955 by the Chekhov Publishing House. Rights to the manuscript are held by the National Board of Young Men's Christian Association, which has kindly granted the permission for this translation.

ARTHUR P. MENDEL

Contents

The Revolution and the
Kadets 1905-7

Home Again

I HAVE OFTEN BEEN REPROACHED for talking too much about politics and too little about myself in that part of my memoirs which was published in *Russkie Zapiski*[1] in 1938–9 and which I will discuss here. My excuse is simply that my life was too tightly interwoven with my political activities to leave much time for my personal affairs. It is true that in the field of politics alone, I could have given more emphasis to my personal role than I did. But others have already spoken too much about that, and not always favorably: they rather blamed me for overemphasizing my personal role. I can say only that this is the way things happened, and that personal vanity never had any influence. I am sure that those who knew me better would agree. Nevertheless, glancing back at the past, I feel that in the course of this historical account I really ought to give more in the way of a self-evaluation. Those who want to compare this account with the printed text of my articles in *Russkie Zapiski* will probably notice the difference. Perhaps they will now reproach me from the other side, saying that I exaggerate my personal role in the course of events. The man who sets himself a definite task, and who accomplishes it to a certain degree cannot, without ceasing to be candid, avoid explaining the facts in terms of the goal which he set for himself. To a certain degree therefore, he must merge events with himself, rather than himself with events. A high correlation between his intentions and his achievements can be considered his personal success; a low correlation, his personal failure. I have nothing to pride myself on in this regard, since I had many more failures than successes. These were due not only to unfavorable circumstances but essentially to the role which, entirely consciously, I chose to play. But, even admitting that my goal turned out to be unrealizable, I would not now, looking back, have chosen a different one.

Reproaches for omissions of personal items from my biography can, of course, also be directed to another aspect of my life. The *biographie romancée* is now in style. I would not say that I have no material for such a biography. Because of my silence on this matter, my future biographer—if there is one—will perhaps substitute anecdotes for facts. I must take the risk, however, because there are other persons involved. I will leave this story to the indiscretions of others.

My wanderings spanned ten years, with five years on each side of the "century line" (1895–1905). These ten years covered that period of life (age 30–40) when one's personality is finally formed, and when the direction and character of one's activity is determined. These years could not pass for me, of course, without important changes. During the first half of the decade, I was involved in my university career, but with my banishment from Moscow this peaceful life in the old Russian capital came to an abrupt end. Thrown at first into provincial Russia (Riazan), then into Europe (Sofia) and finally into the New World, I left behind me a friendly circle of young Russian historians, which has been so well described by A. A. Kizevetter, and a wider circle of students who came to the station to see me off on my way to exile in Riazan. At the farewell dinner of *Russkaia Mysl*, V. A. Goltsev prophetically wished me to become the historian of the fall of the Russian autocracy. At that time I could not imagine that I would not only fulfill his wish but that, to a certain degree, I myself, as a political figure, would turn out to have a part in that fall. My professional comrades from Moscow lamented my departure—and the circumstances which caused it—considering it a "betrayal" of our academic profession. I hope that in the grand total of life this accusation will disappear.

Only now, as I look back over my recollections, can I say definitely what the change was that took place in me. Having lost the reputation as a young historian with which I left Russia, I returned "home" with the reputation of a young politician. The change took place gradually, but it was inevitable in my position. Abroad, I found myself in the role of an observer of the political life and the foreign policy of the democratic states. At home, events were occurring which demanded the application of these observations, and demanded it from me, since such Russian observers were scarce. I have already described how my new role was reflected in the articles of our émigré journal *Osvobozhdenie* and also in various kinds of propaganda concerning the Russian Liberation movement which in auditoriums and at meetings was aimed at American readers and listeners. I in no way tried to transform myself from a historian into a politician, but that is what happened. It was the inexorable demand of the times. And I had reason to be grateful that I could combine observations of life in the advanced democracies with conclusions derived from the study of Russian history. The former pointed to the goal; the latter fixed the limits of possible achievements.

Such was my advantage. My disadvantage lay in the fact that during those ten years, I had been excluded from the circle of observers and participants in Russian life, and during that time, Russian life did not stand still. In my absence, from the very beginning of my wanderings in the middle of the 1890's, a new generation had grown up and had entered cultural and public life. I had left behind the germs of future disagreements with the youth, in cultural as well as in political affairs. It is true that in these disagreements I felt I had an advantage. I could preserve my independence from transitory passions. Perhaps others will judge differently.

Two examples will indicate the character of these disagreements. Let me review first the cultural history of this young generation after 1892, when D. S. Merezhkovsky issued his "manifesto," *The Reasons for the Decline and the New Trends in Contemporary Russian Literature.* I clashed with these men of letters, who had overthrown "old chains" for a "new beauty," precisely when they transferred their decadent attitudes from literature to politics. This occurred when they turned to religious-philosophical "idealism," as in the anthology of 1902, and in the completely open attack on politics by that same circle in the anthology *Vekhi (Signposts)* in 1909. At that time, even persons close to us in politics began to move towards this "idealistic" current: Struve, Berdiaev, Bulgakov, and Novgorodtsev. They viewed with animosity what they considered the "formalism" of the rigorously structured parliamentary system which the older generation steadfastly upheld. They advocated, instead, a return to the ancient formula, "not institutions, but people; not politics, but morals." In Russia ever since the time of Karamzin, this suspicious formula had concealed reactionary attitudes. In the collection *Vekhi*, the group which gathered around Struve came out with a bitter denunciation of the entire Russian intelligentsia, past and present, blaming it for the failure of the revolution of 1905. In a special book,[2] a group led by I. I. Petrunkevich tore apart these attacks in the way deserved. But we are still only approaching the revolution of 1905; we will return in good time to a consideration of the activities of the various participants.

The second result of my wanderings in the decade 1895–1905 had a deeper significance for me. I have in mind events involving the socialist parties which took place during this time. Relying on historical facts, I tried in my American book to demonstrate the possibility of a rapprochement between the Russian liberals and the Russian socialists for the purpose of achieving their common aim of political freedom. After the introduction of the Zemstvos[3] and the appearance of the liberal professions, the aristocratic liberals of the 1860's developed a system of realistic practical politics. For their part, the socialists were convinced that the Russian people were not innately socialists, and that the state would not crumble simply as a result of invoking the spirit of the masses. The state had to be won; political reform had to precede social reform. The knowledge I had gained from studying the history of the Russian revolutionary movement demonstrated the inevitability of the socialists' transition from Utopian to practical politics. The psychology of the defeated and disillusioned revolutionary socialists of the 1880's and 1890's of the last century led to the same conclusion. Thus, for example, Alexander Mikhailov, an early pioneer, condemned to death for his activities in the movement, wrote to his friends from Petropavlovsk Fortress in 1881, in a letter presented at his trial: "All remote and unattainable goals should be temporarily brushed aside. Socialist and federal ideals must be relegated to second place, to plans for the distant future. The Zemstvo Constituent Congress with universal suffrage and freedom of speech, press and assembly must become the slogan of the present." This was, in fact, Herzen's old program. But in the spring of 1880, the Executive Committee of the People's Will party had attached certain qualifications to it. I will pass over the even more restrained demands contained in the famous letter from the Executive Committee to Alexander III in 1881, and refer only to a statement made in that same year by Mezentsev's assassin, Kravchinsky: "Socialism was not and is not an obstacle to the unification of the Russian opposition. The freedom of all Russians is dear to us, regardless of party affiliation. We are ready to defend it in the name of the general, nonclass, feeling of civic solidarity which exists in all advanced countries, and which exists to a greater degree, the more civilized those countries are. Concerning the political question, which is the burning question of the day, our program is exactly the same as the program of the progressive faction of the Russian liberals." Such quotations could be adduced indefinitely. I will add only my personal impressions. The mood described above remained unchanged in 1903 when I became acquainted with the London émigrés, who represented the same attitudes and, to some extent, the same people. During the time I was living at Udelnaia, my neighbor was the poet, Melshin-Yakubovich, a member of the People's Rights party, which had succeeded the People's Will. Here, too, political aims took precedence over social. The early ("legal") Marxists, while combating the utopias of Populism, were undergoing the same evolution before my very eyes. Russia is no different from the other civilized countries, Melshin maintained; before the transition to socialist economics forms can take place, Russia must pass through the stage of developed capitalism. Precisely the same idea was implied in the plea with which Struve ended his prerevolutionary book: "Let us learn from capitalism." My very last impression was the agreement between the constitutional and revolutionary parties in Paris concerning our common political goal, namely, the destruction of the autocracy. And even Lenin, Lenin "himself," looked me over as a possible, a temporary (or, rather, "short-term") fellow traveler on the road from the "bourgeois" revolution to the socialist one. In 1903, at his invitation, I met with him in his miserable room in London. Our conversation turned into an argument over the realism of his views on the tempo of the impending events. The argument was futile. Lenin constantly repeated his position, only with difficulty following the arguments of his opponent. Nevertheless, the idea of a "bourgeois revolution" which was supposed to precede the socialist revolution was firmly implanted in him, and remained so for a long time. I did not notice it then—there was much that I could not know—but in the bosom of "Russian" social democracy other ideas were already developing. I did not pay sufficient attention to the fact that at our joint congress in 1905, only the national minorities factions of the Social Democrats took part. The "Russian" faction was intentionally absent, keeping its hands free. I also missed the meaning of the fact that as far back as his transition from the Black Partition group to his rejected article for *The People's Will* (that is, still in the early 1880's), Plekhanov was ready to replace one overthrown Utopia with another. The old Utopia rested on the belief that the peasantry was inherently socialist. The new Utopia announced the replacement of this fantastic revolutionary role of the peasantry by a more dangerous Utopia: the victory of the working class as the only necessary factor for the immediate introduction of socialism on an international scale, in all civilized countries. Finally, I did not foresee that the blare of the impending revolution would force the "professional" revolutionaries to rouse themselves and retreat from a conciliatory position. The inner workings of the tight circle of Social Democratic émigrés was, at that time, entirely unknown to me.

Such was the situation when I returned to Russia, perfectly confident that I was on a conciliatory mission. I had not yet chosen the exact political stand which I would take. I considered it unquestionable that the revolution could succeed in achieving its immediate goal of political liberty only on the basis of a peaceful agreement between the "liberals" and the "revolutionaries". I thought that the position I had taken in the journal *Osvobozhdenie* was far enough to the "left" to help bring this agreement about. I did not delude myself as to chances of moving our "right-wing" Zemstvoists to the left. Our left-wingers from the League of Liberation seemed to me to be sufficiently prepared and moderate to serve as the center of convergence for the entire front of the developing struggle. Under these conditions, my mission seemed assured of success.

It should not be concluded, however, that my optimism concerning the possibility of a multiparty agreement on tactics was for me the only condition of success in the forthcoming political struggle. I was by no means blind to the role of the government in this struggle. In this respect, the increasing complexity of the situation had become clear to me from my observations abroad of the rapid progress of events in Russia. Documentary evidence of those observations can be found in my American book, *Russia and Its Crisis*. I planned to conclude it with information which I had just received concerning the radical-liberal resolutions of the Zemstvo Congress of November 6-8 (19–21), and the Paris Congress of Opposition and Revolutionary Parties, all of which indicated the harmony between the liberals and the revolutionaries in their combined attack on the state power. This harmony, however, was marred by sharp dissonance after "Bloody Sunday."[4] The event was interpreted as the first popular uprising, and even though it was crushed by the authorities, it was fraught with future consequences. In the text of the book, I spoke of the extreme difficulty, even for an "experienced and authoritative politician," of determining, in view of the shift of the whole antigovernment front to the left, that minimum political program which could still "save the situation" and "satisfy public opinion." Correcting the last proofs before my departure from America, I considered it necessary to add the following comments to the text: "These lines were written before the complications of the Winter of 1904–5. There is now no single government figure who can save the situation. The word belongs to the people's representatives." We can see here already, anticipating the events of the end of 1905 and the beginning of 1906, the later roles of Witte and the Duma.

I should make still another personal reservation regarding the change I foresaw in my own role. It occurs with everyone who exchanges his study for the public arena, and there goes with it an increase both in fame and in the public's expectations, expectations of the most diverse and conflicting kinds. His individual personality is gradually covered over with impressions of his political deeds, which are interpreted in various ways. Returning to Russia with a reputation formed during my wanderings, I should have known that it would be impossible to lose myself in a mass of my like-minded comrades. I desired only to be one of them and to join in common action with them, to walk, so to say, shoulder to shoulder with them. But they looked upon me, a novice in politics, in another way; some looked with curiosity, others with interest, and still others—my friends—with definite expectations. All this was reinforced by the tempo and temperature of the heated struggle which had begun before my arrival. My own personality unwittingly became clouded. I won't say that it became a mask; I could not have gone along with that. Nevertheless, against my will and wishes, my name and myself were separated.

In order to explain this sensation which I, like all others who find themselves in a similar situation, was fated to experience, I will take the liberty of citing from Hessen's memoirs, observations he made of me precisely at the moment when this separation between personality and name began to take place. Hessen met me for the first time at Miakotin's name-day party in Sestroretsk, where friends from the journal *Russkoe Bogatstvo* were gathered. I attracted his interest because, like a stranger, I sat apart from the rest. He struck up a conversation with me, and "did not once sense that unpleasant coldness caused by prejudice, party bias and the tendency to reject everything not found in the Koran." On the way back from the party to the station, he discovered that he had been talking with the author of *Outlines*.[5] This was evidently my "personality." Two years later he met Miliukov, the "Kadet," and recoiled from the "name." About fifteen years later, he finally solved the contradiction: "Miliukov is not a Kadet"; his ability to lead "Kadetism" without himself being a "Kadet" shows that "perhaps he has no genuine political convictions. He is sure that realistic politics can be conducted on that spot occupied by the Kadets. Miliukov can carry out this policy; without him, it would be carried out worse or not at all." The question remains, who "put" the Kadets on that spot? The reader will find the answer to this question later on. In order to "put" someone in a certain "place," a person must himself stand in that place. In order to work out a collective opinion on something, and in order to work with a collective, a person must himself be a member of that collective. It is impossible to give a collective the unity of a "personality". The phrase "Constitutional Democrat" still does not indicate unity. But when the collective is given its "name" from the outside, when it is nicknamed "K. D.," then a certain degree of unity has already been achieved, then the generic traits have been fortified, and the boundary between "K. D.'s" and "non-K. D.'s" has been clearly established. How can Miliukov, without betraying himself, be primarily a "Kadet"? This can be explained only by the process of achieving the given degree of collective unity, by a process which cost great effort to those who took part in it. But this will be discussed later.

During the time of my wanderings, changes also occurred in my personal and family life. First of all, during my absence, the duty of raising the children fell exclusively on my wife. Our third and last child was born during our stay in Bulgaria. Our eldest son was fifteen when I returned. This gives some idea of the quantity and quality of the burden which fell on my wife's shoulders. Just like my scholarly career before, so now my political career could have been realized only with her cooperation. Our life collaboration remained close and harmonious. Above all, during our separation, my wife regained her sense of self-sufficiency and independence, which she had been so afraid of losing in marriage. Her student work, on the Russian women of the pre-Petrine period, remained unfinished. Nevertheless, her interest in the women's movement was reinforced. I think that her acquaintance with Karavelov's wife gave her a great impulse in this direction. Karavelov's wife stood at the head of the movement for the emancipation of Bulgarian women, who were still trapped in the vise of the Turkish family structure. These observations strengthened her interest in the Russian women's movement as well. She died in Paris, having become chairman of the Society of Russian University Women, which she represented also at foreign congresses. To this was added charitable activities in Russia, and later in London and in Paris. Her literary works concentrated on such themes as the relationship of Godwin's daughter to Shelley, or the fate of Herzen's wife. In a word, she developed her own circle of personal and public activity. For my part, I could devote only snatches of time to my family life, which had been interrupted ever since the time of my imprisonments, and still more by my trips abroad. I repeat that all of this in no way altered, but, rather, strengthened our ideological intimacy and our collaboration. Our family ties, however, inevitably loosened; each of us screened off our own sphere of activity.

What I Found in Russia

WAS I TOO LATE in returning to Russia in April of 1905? In this feverish year, from January's "Bloody Sunday" to April, events had hardly been static. They unfolded at an accelerated pace. Still, on the whole, the general character of the political situation remained unchanged, and nothing decisive had happened. In its attempts to meet even the more moderate sector of society halfway, the confused government was still hampered by the "unbending will" of the monarch, who was supported by a handful of close favorites—reactionaries like Pobedonostsev, Prince Meshchersky, and others. The revolutionary movement had not even come close to involving the masses. In place of the masses there was still only the intellectuals' "simulation of revolution," as Obninsky put it. The first attempts by the socialists to form political parties had not succeeded in working out party programs, and they were already split over questions of tactics. The fundamental cleavage occurred between the veterans of the Populist movement, who theoretically sought support among the peasantry, and the young Marxists, who had not yet resolved the arguments between "legal" and "illegal" factions and who were divided even inside the "illegal" group. "Society," in a broad sense, was doubtlessly united by the generally elated mood, but it had not succeeded in organizing itself into more definite groups, and it did not understand the real meaning of the slogans which were becoming more radical all the time. I could have predicted all of this from what I had learned abroad. Personal observations on the spot only confirmed and made more precise what I already knew.

I could reproach myself for arriving late only in one sense—if indeed anything had really depended on my late return, or even on my absence from Russia during these months. I have in mind the rapid shift to the left of the militant political slogans, and, as a result, the divergence between the two wings of the liberation movement, the "Zemstvoists" and the "Liberationists." But with clear conscience I can say that neither I nor anyone else could have prevented it. The

9

roots of this split were contained in the general psychology of the Russian intelligentsia, and its fruits were manifested quite independently of my personal influence and before I could have exerted that influence. On the contrary, my presence in Russia at the beginning of the shift to the left would only have forced me to take part in it. The possibility of my playing that moderating role which I was able to play after the formation of the political trend called "kadetism" would have been weakened, if not wholly eliminated. It was fortunate that, amidst the raging passions, I was able to preserve the independence of my political position. My "wanderings" surely contributed to that fact. From a distance, with what I had learned from my foreign experience, political perspectives were clearer and broader than would have been possible in a "hand-to-hand combat." It is another question, however, what role in general "Kadetism" played in Russian political life, and what role it could have played under different conditions. Although that question transcends the limits of an autobiography, it will be partially clarified later, in the account of events interwoven with the biography.

Coming back to what I found in Russia upon my return, I should emphasize that the process of clarifying political positions had not yet yielded any decisive results. For the public at large, this process had just begun. Nor did I immediately grasp the different shades of political opinions and attitudes. These various shades and disagreements, dependent as they were on the extent of further collaboration or conflict among the different political currents, could come to light only in the course of events.

I have already had occasion to speak about the establishment of my relations with the progressive groups which had existed before the moment of battle. I had friends among all of them, and this in itself indicates the absence of sharp differentiation between them in the actual political struggle. My closest personal friends were among the Populists of *Russkoe Bogatstvo*. V. A. Miakotin even offered me membership in the Central Committee of the Social Revolutionary party, then passing through a crisis. He was quite surprised when I told him that I did not consider myself a socialist. Not to be a socialist in this milieu meant excommunication from the "order" in which each novice was examined on his faith and in which only the "devoted" were accepted. This was an obligatory tradition of the radical Russian intelligentsia.

The cult of the new tradition had not yet had time to form among the young Russian Marxists, and their doctrine itself was only in the early stages of development. This fact was conducive to a certain degree of tolerance among these people who soon turned out to be the most intolerant. As long as service to the masses was considered to be the fundamental task of the "intelligentsia" by the S. D.'s as well as the S. R.'s, my place was with both of them. I was accepted by both the Writers' Union and the Free Economic Society.[6] The former was organized by the Literary Fund where both liberal and Populist democracy were represented by such leaders as K. K. Arsenev and N. F. Annensky. In the latter, the same N. F. Annensky and E. D. Kuskova united the "third element"[7] of the Zemstvoists with the cooperative movement under the protective shield of the chairman, Count Heiden, a liberal conservative of the English type. My centrist position was most favorable, not only as an observation point but also as a means of political self-determination. Self-determination, however, was yet to come.

The first step in that direction, of course, had to be the definition of my relations to the organization that was nearest to me in political outlook and that had retained, at least in principle, the same centrist character. The League of Liberation included representatives of the various currents mentioned above, who, while working for the common cause, had not yet separated from their organizations. There were Zemstvo Constitutionalists as well as a more mixed circle of collaborators from the journal *Osvobozhdenie*. Even Struve had already crossed several divisions of the political spectrum. From my polemic on the pages of *Osvobozhdenie*, it could be seen that a variety of currents, both left-wing and right-wing, found shelter in the columns of this journal. This was possible, of course, only because the process of differentiation had just begun.

In its background, the League of Liberation included two elements which were united in the beginning by a common direction and a minimal program, but which later split over the question of tactics and even over the program itself. I already have mentioned that both elements, the Zemstvoists and the Liberationists, had gone to Switzerland in equal numbers to establish the League. When the League was formed in Russia, the representatives of both groups, again in equal numbers, composed the council of the League. The Zemstvo Constitutionalists were represented by six members: I. I. Petrunkevich (Tver), Prince P. D. Dolgorukov (Moscow), Prince D. I. Shakhovsky (Yaroslavl), N. N. Kovalevsky (Kharkov), I. V. Luchitsky (Kiev), and N. N. Lvov (Samara). The group which defined itself by its adherence to the "intelligentsia" included N. F. Annensky, V. Ya. Bogucharsky, L. I. Lutugin, V. V. Khizhniakov, A. V. Peshekhonov, and S. N. Prokopovich. The names alone indicate that the second group was more tightly bound and would consequently turn out to be the more active. The so-called "Great Petersburg Group," with twelve to fourteen

members, also collaborated on the council. A "technical subgroup,"
including Bogucharsky, Khizhniakov, E. D. Kuskova, Sokolov, Mik-
lashevsky, and Kupriianova, was formed from the Petersburg group
for distributing the journal and for maintaining relations with the provinces. It was tightly unified, enterprising, and capable of taking active
and rapid steps. A closely knit group of "sympathizers" was formed
around it. As can be seen, the League expanded only around its left
wing. All the initiatives came from the left-wing volunteers. Conscious
of their basic differences with the right wing, the "intellectuals" (I will
henceforth refer to them as "Liberationists") had no desire to join
with them in a single "party," and contented themselves, instead, with
a loose "federation" in the League. At the Third Congress of the
League of Liberation as a whole (at the end of March 1905), an attempt was made to convert the League into a party. While the program was being defined, however, the disagreements turned out to be
so great that the majority of the participants in the congress came out
against formation of a party. Therefore, it was explicitly stated that
only those "general points on which all groups agreed" would be included in the program of the League, and that the League's "decisions could be considered binding only insofar as political conditions
remained unchanged." In view of this stipulation, "several decisions
were purposely left open," and others were admitted to be "conditional." This was a very reasonable measure, but a disadvantageous
one for the right wing because "political conditions" were moving at
an ever increasing speed to the left. The stipulation was doubtlessly
made with the inevitable leftward evolution in mind.

The tactics of the League also reflected this leftward evolution. In
fact, no obligatory tactical directives had existed at all. It was precisely in the area of tactics that the predominance of the leftist elements in the League was expressed. After the Zemstvo Congress of
November 1904 and under the pretext of carrying out its decisions,
the League issued the directive to arrange a series of banquets everywhere on these themes. The very word "banquets" recalled that period
in the reign of Louis Philippe when the open struggle began which
led to the overthrow of the July monarchy. The call for the banquets
and the program of the League itself far exceeded the limits of the
Zemstvo Congress' eleven points. In the heated speeches of the banquet orators, both universal suffrage and the Constituent Assembly
were already mentioned. All of this was absorbed, during those
months, by the general, excited mood, which the banquets also
sought to promote. In his book, *Poslednii Samoderzhets,* published
outside Russia, the future left-wing Kadet, Obninsky, very aptly characterized this mood as "cries of tormented people who united various

circles of the population by emotion rather than reason." "An illusion of a complete unanimity of Russian society was created," he wrote. "General hatred for the bureaucracy blended with the unity of political and social ideals." "Society, apparently taking stock of its strength, screwed up its courage." In the initial phases of the struggle, "illusion" and "courage" were perhaps useful and even necessary. But, according to Obninsky's concluding words, "the simulation of the imminence of the revolution, which in reality was only in its embryonic stage," could become dangerous. Continuation of the oratorical excesses in imitation of the era of Louis Philippe could lead to the same grievous results as they had in that era. I do not know how I would have found my place among our banquet orators had I attended the "banquets."

Even before my return, the League had dictated the next step, one much more important for a broad organization of society. Before the November Zemstvo Congress, in a resolution dated October 20, 1904, the League decided "to begin agitation for the formation of unions of lawyers, engineers, professors, writers and others from the liberal professions. Congresses of these unions were to be organized and a permanent bureau was to be elected by each of them. Finally, these bureaus were to be united among themselves as well as with the bureau of Zemstvo and city officials into a single Union of Unions." Because of the lack of division of society into political parties, the idea of organizing it along professional lines was quite successful. Associations of this sort, with a more or less identical political direction, could be formed, of course, only at the time of a rise in general political ferment. Through them the politically amorphous progressive Russian elements were given the opportunity to unite for the first time, not only spiritually but also formally. I could associate myself completely with this method, which represented the initial, transitional stages of political organization, and which I considered an indispensable preliminary condition of free political life. However, the hurried fusion of separate groups into a single "Union of Unions" already concealed an ulterior motive, namely, to centralize the whole movement in Petersburg and to monopolize direction of its activities.

It should be added that in the midst of these diffuse circumstances, the tsar made his first political concession. On February 18, 1905, a few days after Kaliaev's bomb ripped to pieces Moscow's governor-general, the Grand Duke Sergei Alexandrovich, Sviatopolk-Mirsky's successor, Bulygin, published a rescript concerning the convocation of "the most dignified and trustworthy people, elected from the population, to take part in the preliminary formulation and consideration of legislative proposals"—it being understood that "the immutability of the fundamental laws of the Empire shall be preserved." More important for Russian society than that small concession, which did not go beyond earlier similar unrealized attempts, was a secret circular issued by the minister of the interior which stated that "the existing public and class institutions are not to be hindered in their discussions of proposals for advancing the welfare of the nation." The public interpreted this circular as giving permission to discuss publicly questions concerning the political system, and the confused police confirmed this interpretation by temporarily not interfering. Society was thereby granted an opportunity to express itself, no longer "secretly," as had been the practice of the League, but now quasi-legally. In the balance of my impressions of the activities of the League of Liberation, observing its increasing success among those who were prepared to act in resonance with the League's great tuning fork, and noting its rapidly expanding influence and connections, I could not help feeling that political competition would develop faster than political cooperation. In any case, I had no control over the force originating from this center. Rather, I had either to subordinate myself and become assimilated, or to embark upon an open struggle. I still could not ascertain the limit of our mutual agreements, but I gradually felt that this limit was being approached by the Liberationists. In general, the intellectual tone of Petersburg, where the ruling center of the Union of Unions was created, had been and continued to be too far to the left for me, too abstract and too theoretical. My attention unwittingly switched to Moscow, my former native city, where I felt more at home and where I felt freer from outside influences and past decisions. What was Moscow like then? What changes had occurred there during my ten-year absence?

At first, I did not notice any major changes in the university or in the journalistic and political circles which had been closest to me. Our Moscow literary and professional circle, which Andrei Bely had so unjustly and hostilely caricatured, was then rather deserted. As before, the university, the journals, the newspapers and scholarship occupied the first place in the life of Moscow. In Petersburg, on the other hand, the top rank belonged to the Court, the high officials, and the military. This self-containment, one might say, of Moscow gave the Moscow intelligentsia a self-assurance, spiritual balance, and a greater calm, in contrast to the eternal anxiety, nervousness, and bustle of Petersburg. Even the traditional Moscow spirit of opposition to the government did not acquire that sharp character which proximity to government power gave to the Petersburg intelligentsia. The social strata of Moscow, the merchants and the aristocracy, stood

closer to each other as well as to their intellectuals. Thus, Moscow
society enjoyed more cultural and political unity than did Petersburg
or the other outlying districts of Russia. The workers' movement
played an ever increasing political role in Petersburg, where its leading ideological circles were located. In Moscow, the elements of unrest manifested themselves chiefly in student agitation, which had already become a tradition and had even acquired a position of leadership in Russia. In Petersburg, political programs were worked out.
In Moscow, legislative projects were elaborated scientifically and systematically, projects which—and Moscow firmly believed this—would
be realized at some future time through radical, but reasonable and
peaceful, reforms. Moscow did not like to be disturbed too early.

During the ten years of my wanderings, I was not in Moscow even
once—except for passing through from one depot to another, from one
exile to another, on my way from Riazan to Bulgaria. Moscow had
been so built-up during that time that, passing through from Nikolaevsky Station to Nikita Gates, where I was given shelter by the
lawyer, M. Mandelshtam (my future political opponent from the
left), I could hardly recognize parts of the city. Thanks to the merchant class, a striking new trend was introduced in Moscow archi-
tecture. Amidst the old aristocratic mansions in the Empire style,
there arose along the boulevards and sidestreets the most fastidious
imitations of European architectural achievements of various eras. The
futile efforts to create a native, national style were abandoned. In
their place arose the cosmopolitan "World of Art."[8] The new generation of merchant art patrons chose from this "World" all sorts of
styles. The Tarasovsky mansion on Spiridonovka, for example, reflected the antique classicism of Palladio. Also on Spiridonovka, Ivan
Abramovich Morozov built a castle in Gothic style; while on Pre-
chistenka, he built a palace in the style of the Portuguese Renaissance.
On Zubovsky Boulevard, his brother, Mikhail, erected his palace with
a Classic facade and finished each room in a different historic style.
I came to know these last two palaces in connection with my political
activity. In the "Portuguese" castle reigned Varvara Alexeevna Morozova, a lady well-known to the Moscow intelligentsia. She was a
person of amazing energy and readiness to serve the social cause in
the spirit of the 1870's. Everything about her, from her modest appearance and unassuming dress to her personal entourage, created
amidst surrounding splendor, attested to her profound faith in the
immutable ideal of social progress and in the necessity of sowing
the seeds of "everlasting reason and goodness." Her mentor and friend
was V. M. Sobolevsky, editor since 1881 and later the copublisher of
Russkie Vedomosti, the Moscow "professors' " paper which was closest

to me. People of our type, already old-fashioned, felt at home here. All sorts of "liberal" organizations held their meetings and found true assylum at V. A. Morozova's. I will speak about the palace of the other Morozov later.

Even before my arrival, political work was being carried out very energetically in Moscow. After their failure to create a "party" within the framework of the League of Liberation, the Zemstvo Constitutionalists undertook more freely the formation of their own party. When D. N. Shipov's group left,[9] those who remained felt themselves closer in their political convictions, and that much more able to fill in the gaps, omissions, vaguenesses, and misunderstandings in the program of the League of Liberation. In Moscow I found this separatist political work going on in the political circle whose views were nearest my own, and I associated myself with it eagerly. Here at last I was "myself."

First of all, I was introduced into the circle—or committee—of Russian jurists who were busy reworking the text of a constitution for the future party, which had earlier been published abroad by the editors of *Osvobozhdenie*. Authoritative professors, such as M. M. Kovalevsky and S. A. Muromtsev and others, also took part. The working force was provided by the young professors-jurists of the new generation. Here I met F. F. Kokoshkin, P. I. Novgorodtsev, and others for the first time, and we immediately started polemics on the question of a bicameral versus a unicameral system. I detected a conservative ulterior motive in the bicameral system: to restrict the people by class representation. Bulgaria taught me the advantages of a single chamber. But Kokoshkin shook me down from my position. In addition to all his other incomparable virtues, he was an amazing debator. He not only guessed the mood of his opponent but he actually formulated his opponent's thought more clearly. Then he crushed his opponent in such a soft and friendly manner that his opponent willingly admitted defeat. The agility of his mind was equalled only by the firmness of his basic convictions. He understood the meaning of political compromise, but he also recognized its limitations. With a dose of personal doctrinarism, he defended the collective decision once it had been made. I can remember no other case where my mutual understanding with someone went as far as to enable me to anticipate a common train of thought on any given question. Our editorials— mine in *Rech* and his in *Russkie Vedomosti*—frequently coincided in both theme and argument. The Bolsheviks' barbaric murder of Kokoshkin brought me profound grief. One soldier's bullet is all it takes to annihilate a fragile and delicate organization, but how many generations were needed to create it! Archimedes and the barbarians. History repeats itself.

We did not argue over the other fundamental question concerning universal suffrage, as that question had been decided beforehand in the affirmative. My Bulgarian experience taught me that there is not only nothing frightening in universal suffrage but that such a system serves as a guarantee against many evils of other systems. Direct elections from large districts, better than anything else, assure the election of an intelligent and politically mature representative. Two-stage or multistage elections may bind the representative more closely to his village, but then he will be not a representative, but an agent, susceptible to influence and bribery. Kokoshkin resolved this question on principle; I, in practice. But we both resolved it in exactly the same way.

In addition to political reforms, it was absolutely necessary to place one of the social questions on the agenda and to find a reasonable solution for it—namely, the agrarian question. Of course, we all knew that we were treading on dangerous ground where class interests clash and where a struggle was already being waged with no respect for the law or authorities. How was it possible to find a just solution while working amidst the landowning nobility, even if they were Zemstvo Constitutionalists? Our Zemstvoists who joined the political group of Constitutionalists, although they were few in number, fortunately viewed the land question with a striking degree of selflessness and readiness for sacrifice. But even they could not escape reproaches for harboring a class-oriented party spirit. Our solution to the agrarian problem always remained a target of attack for our class adversaries.

There were members of our committees, at any rate, whom it was impossible to suspect of serving class interests. To these members belonged the professional element, represented by V. E. Yakushkin, whose agrarian radicalism was a family tradition stretching all the way back to the Decembrists. The "third element" was represented by a confirmed philanthropist, a Zemstvo agronomist, Chernenkov, for whom it was painful to make even the slightest deviation from his wholehearted views on the task of agrarian reform. The radicalism of our agrarian project was manifested, better than anything else, by the fierce attack it provoked against itself in aristocratic and, then, in government circles.

In those days, finally, we were forced to touch upon the nationality question, in connection with the strivings of the Poles for autonomy. We decided that question after a series of conferences with the Poles, who gathered at the residence of the lawyer, A. P. Lednitsky.

Several days later, after the November Zemstvo Congress, the first
Russian-Polish agreement was reached there with the participation of
eminent Poles as well as the Russians, Muromtsev, Skalon, Goltsev,
Nikolai Guchkov, and Prince Peter D. Dolgorukov. The Russian-
Polish Congress followed, in Moscow on April 7 (20), 1905. "The Poles
in the Polish Kingdom are unanimous in their striving for autonomy,"
declared Lednitsky, "but they are equally unanimous in their understanding of the need to preserve State unity with Russia, and to fix the
borders of the Polish Kingdom within the existing limits." It was
necessary to take advantage of this conciliatory mood and to strengthen
it through a friendly Russian response. However, when the question
was brought up at the conference in Morozov's "Portuguese" mansion,
A. I. Guchkov came out sharply against Polish autonomy. I answered
him no less sharply and heatedly. Our argument created a sensation
in Moscow. The question of Polish autonomy later served as a watershed between the Octobrists and the Kadets. Guchkov referred to the
"organic integrity" of his "well-grounded" conviction in contrast to my
"bookishness." The general sympathy, of course, was on my side. This
was not the last of my clashes with my former university comrade, who
had since become a dangerous political rival.

Beyond the range of my direct observations in Moscow was a
secret circle of aristocratic pioneers of the Moscow opposition. This
circle was later colorfully and lovingly portrayed by V. A. Maklakov,
who contrasted its moderate character with the invasion by the "liberation movement" from the "street." This circle, which bore the name
Besedy, consisted of marshals of the nobility and other distinguished
Moscovites. By the time I arrived, however, it was already too late to
busy oneself with peaceful discussions. Some of the members of this
circle (e.g., Pavel D. Dolgorukov) went over to more active organizations, including the Zemstvo Constitutionalists. Even V. A. Maklakov
himself was forced into sin by defending, as a lawyer, the right of
universal suffrage.

The influence of the liberation movement on Zemstvo circles was
at its height. While I was still in Moscow, the Second Zemstvo Congress, which met April 22–26, 1905, in Yu. N. Novosiltsev's mansion on
Nikitskaia Boulevard, testified to this fact.

The participants in the first Congress, November 1904, had reason
to think of their meeting as "accidental" and of the opinions expressed
there as "personal." By the time of the April Congress, however, such
expressions were wholly inappropriate. This time the composition of
the congress was for the most part sanctioned by the Zemstvo boards
and meetings. By April, the opinions and decisions of November had
not only been welcomed but had been far surpassed in their radical-

ism by speeches at Zemstvo meetings and by resolutions of the professional congresses at the end of 1904 and beginning of 1905. This
was no doubt due to the influence of the League of Liberation and
their banquets. The April Congress was supposed to sum up all that
had been achieved by the six-month evolution of public opinion.
Such questions as universal suffrage with all four "tails",[10] the unicameral versus the bicameral system, single-stage versus multistage
elections, and finally, the question of the Constituent Assembly—all of
these issues were on the agenda for discussion. The most disturbing
question was whether or not the April Congress would be able to hold
up under this great, additional political burden.

Here, through my Moscow friends, I met for the first time some
of the leading Zemstvo activists who had received their political training since the time of the Zemstvo struggles with Plehve. But I had no
formal right to stand in their ranks myself. To preserve the authoritative character of the congress, the members permitted no outsiders to
attend. Together with several members and friends of the Novosiltsev
family, I was given the opportunity to follow the course of the debates
at the congress, through a half-open door in an adjoining room, an
observation point that afforded little opportunity for personal contact.
We shared the anxiety of our hosts for a satisfactory outcome of the
debates in the next room.

Through the crack in the door, we could hear the disunity of the
speakers when it came to delicate topics. There is M. V. Rodzianko
arguing against universal suffrage by pointing to the ignorance of the
masses and their slavelike subordination to the authorities. M. A.
Stakhovich also does not believe that the masses are politically mature.
But the fiery N. N. Lvov tears from his place and takes a position
which subsequently would be so untypical of him. With passion and
conviction he poses the question of principle: Yes or no? Do you believe in the people or do you not? The entire political stand of democracy depends on the answer. A deafening applause accompanies his
speech. The majority is with him. But the debates are not finished;
the vote will be taken tomorrow. Will the effect last until then? D. N.
Shipov's changed status gives cause for hope. We witnessed his great
moral weight at the November Congress. In April, he somehow faded
into the background, keeping quiet in the back rows. He responded
only when called on, and his impotent answers were heard in silence.

The influence of the liberationists triumphed. Universal suffrage
was adopted and two-stage elections were rejected. True, an upper
chamber was also adopted—to be comprised of representatives from
the Zemstvos, after their reorganization. Concerning the Constituent
Assembly, which was disguised as "the first representative assembly,"

a lower chamber was adopted, and its task was defined as "not so much legislation on particular questions, as the establishment of State law and order". Later on, this formula was made even more precise: "not organic legislation, but the formulation of fundamental laws as well as a constitution." A new political record was thus set in April. All of us rejoiced, myself included. But since the time of my arrival, I had been only a detached onlooker in this first great political turn of events. My personal, responsible appearances were still to come.

First Steps On My Conciliatory Mission

ACCORDING TO CONTEMPORARY WITNESSES, my reputation as an "inveterate revolutionary" preceded me—at least in this milieu. The risk involved in my first public appearance was thus increased for those who would decide to arrange it without permission from the authorities. However, the interest—or curiosity—in listening to the traveling political artist won out. I was obliged above all to the young ensign, Igor Platonovich Demidov, Novosiltsev's trusted friend and his daughter's fiancé, who himself had only just returned from the Far East. Our acquaintance developed into a friendly collaboration, which ended only by the final catastrophe of war sweeping us in different directions. As it turned out, the risk of police interference actually sharpened the interest in political speeches, which became fashionable in the best homes.

"All of Moscow," it was said, showed up for the lecture. "Extreme leftists" like Doctor Zhbankov, Vikhliaev, and Bleklov were there, along with the titled nobility represented by Prince V. M. Golitsyn, the mayor of Moscow, and the family of Prince Peter Nikolaevich Trubetskoy, marshal of the nobility in the Moscow Province. There was even someone from the "Samara" conservative circle. Some of the Moscow merchants were likewise present. The center was composed of various members of the Zemstvo Congress who had just passed resolutions in this same hall. The Moscow intelligentsia was represented by lawyers, professors, editors, and journalists from *Russkie Vedomosti* and *Russkaia Mysl*. The flanks of public opinion which came together here usually avoided each other at other times. The student youth was absent: students tried in vain to break into the meeting hall, where they were rebuffed by the master of ceremonies, that same Demidov, who stoically bore their reproaches for "contemptibly" carrying out police functions, and "for not understanding the freedom of public expression." But it could not have been otherwise: the hall sat only three hundred to five hundred persons and was already filled to overflowing. I could not help recalling the festive hall of a meeting between the Nizhnii Novgorod gentry, the governor, and the bishop. At that meeting in 1894, I had announced the dawn of the new "constitutional" reign of Nicholas II, thereby opening for myself a direct route to exile in provincial Russia and abroad. Now, ten years later, a further step had to be taken: the "constitution" had to be reconciled with the "revolution"—and that turned out to be more acceptable and more feasible! The tempo of history was increasing, and the future "historian of the fall of the autocracy" began a new chapter in his narrative.

Success, of course, was assured by the demonstrative character of the speech, the festive surroundings, and the select makeup of the audience. I flattered myself in thinking that the content of the speech itself played a significant role. The possibility of a reconciliation was evidently both accepted and desired by the various political shades which had gathered here. It could hardly have appeared as feasible to the others as it did to me, with my incomplete knowledge of all that had happened in Russia during the ten-year period. At any rate, it was intriguing to hear a conciliatory speech from an "inveterate revolutionary" who, in addition, adduced "revolutionary" evidence of this conciliatory attitude among the extremists. The speech also helped to change the opinion which the audience had formed of the speaker himself. My fine friend, the ensign, uttered a greeting appropriate for the occasion, and presented me with a tremendous bouquet of mimosa. The moment of my "official acceptance" into the ranks of the select Moscow community passed successfully.

This appearance, of course, was soon followed by others. The Moscow youth, who were not allowed to enter Novosiltsev's mansion, claimed first rights to me. It was with special pleasure that I accepted the invitation from that circle, whose friendship with me had led to my exile from Moscow. With the cooperation of N. V. Shilovskaia, a lady acquaintance of mine from Riazan and at this time a student in Moscow, a "tea" was arranged in the democratic quarter of the city. The room resembled a garret, and already by the start of my talk it was filled with thick tobacco smoke. There was no platform in the room; instead, the speaker was placed on a simple wooden table, around which the listeners bunched up together in a tight ring. It was terribly hot, and towards the end it became difficult to breathe. The place was crammed. The reception was simple and friendly; I was accepted as one of them, as if we had never been separated. My theme was the same as at Novosiltsev's mansion, but here I spoke more freely and I probably colored my presentation somewhat differently. On such occasions, an argument usually follows the lecture, but this time I felt no psychological resistance at all from my listeners.

They accepted my facts and conclusions without criticism, and looked at me, evidently, as at an authoritative teacher. Later on, all this was to change, but at the end of April and the beginning of May, the political differentiation had not yet occurred. My speech satisfied the mood of the moment.

My third appearance in Moscow created a lasting impression in my memory. After the aristocratic mansion and the students' garret, I was invited to give a talk at the merchant's palace on Zubovsky Boulevard. I was scheduled to speak to the guests of the hostess, Marguerite Kirillovna, who was the widow of Mikhail Morozov, the prematurely deceased amateur historian. The invitation confirmed the success I had already achieved in Moscow. The surroundings were entirely different here than in Novosiltsev's mansion. The magnificent hall, finished in the Classical style, the spectacular stage, the elegant, well-dressed ladies in gilded armchairs, the colors, the lines—all of it cried to be captured in a "historical" painting. In fact, a painting was decided upon, either—I am not certain—by the hostess or the artist. Pasternak began to draw sketches and pretty well tired me out as his figure for the orator on stage. Beneath the stage in the foreground, the portraits of the hostess and her guests were supposed to appear. The picture was not painted, however, probably because the big event shrunk in size before later historical pictures, and the novelty wore off.

The charming hostess showed some interest in becoming acquainted, all the more so as she was interested in the speaker personally. Several days later, I received a visit from her companion who brought a donation of several thousand rubles for the formation of a political party. I had addressed my lecture in her palace precisely to this question, which had been renewed with fresh material after our work on a program in April under Liberationist influences. Also, I was asked to help orient the hostess in the labyrinth of political arguments which she found so strange. From time to time, I noticed Marguerite Kirillovna's presence at our political meetings. At last she invited me to converse with her personally. Our talks began, far surpassing the limits of politics, and assuming a direction which I had not at all expected. I was met face to face by the new trends in literature and art among the Moscow merchant Maecenas. In its own way, this was a sort of examination on modern trends in the culture of the latest generation.

Marguerite Kirillovna was the exact opposite of Varvara Alexeevna Morozova whom I mentioned earlier. Young, "taken for her beauty," as the merchants say, and widowed early, she thirsted for new impressions and followed the latest word in fashion. She faithfully reflected the attitudes of the youth who had grown up while I was away

and whom I now found strange. Our conversations were very instructive for me, and we eventually touched upon all aspects of the
new trends. I was forced throughout, not merely to "pass," but to
oppose. It began, of course, from a common philosophical "outlook."
The German word *Weltanschauung* had long since become traditional
in our intellectual circles, but it had a different sense, depending on the
prevailing philosophical system. My "positivism" and my "criticism"
were left far behind now. The ethical and religious views of Vladimir
Solovev had been developed by his young followers. I still tried to
protect myself against metaphysics with the aid of F. Lange, but my
interlocutress began immediately with references to Schopenhauer.
She was especially interested in that mystical element of metaphysics
by which I was especially repulsed.

We did not stick to philosophy for long, but soon switched over
to the latest literary trends. In the center of M. K.'s wildly enthusiastic
generation was Andrei Bely. She was especially intrigued by Bely's
deliberate religious solemnity. Bely did not walk, but fluttered about
in the air, like some celestial being, barely touching the floor, all the
time executing some sort of undulatory, wing-like motions with his
arms, which M. K. touchingly reproduced. Bely did not speak: he
prophesied, and his works were mysterious like the aphorisms of the
Sibyls. His words hid secrets, inaccessible to the layman. I had seen
Bely as a child in his family, and all his artificial affectations, which
others also observed without worship, evoked in me a sense of extreme
distaste.

From literature we turned to music. I was overjoyed to learn that
M. K. was a pianist, and in all sincerity I offered her my services as a
violinist acquainted with chamber music. I realized my naïveté when
I learned that M. K.'s interest was concentrated on music lessons
which she was taking from Scriabin. I had no idea at that time of the
female company surrounding Scriabin, which so harmfully influenced
the latest directions of his work and which was reflected in his impotent
attempts to express in music some sort of mystical-erotic cosmogony.
M. K. was attracted here, too, by the element of mysticism and the
charm of secrets not accessible to the uninitiated.

We did not speak much of the visual arts. The wide corridor of
the Morozov Palace presented an entire art gallery, and I lingered
there with envy. I do not remember whether or not modernism prevailed in the selection of paintings there. It seems to me that the enthusiasm of the Moscow art patrons for the new trends in art began
some years later.

There was one subject which we did not touch upon at all. This
was politics, a subject which the new trends regarded either neutrally

or negatively. I had absolutely no reason to consider myself her mentor. I was rather an examinee, and one who failed the exam at that. Marguerite Kirillovna's interest in our conversations weakened, as the antithetical natures of our ideological positions became apparent. As a result, the absorbing tête-à-têtes in the Egyptian room of the palace ceased as abruptly as they had begun.

It was then time to carry my propagandistic missions from the capital to the provinces, where, as I recall, the provincial sections of the League of Liberation helped me to organize a tour. My theme was still the same: a rapprochement between the "liberals" and the "revolutionaries." I deeply regret that very few recollections remain from this tour. I remember only that I was impressed by the contrast between the North and the South. In general, in the North, neither my historical references, my political conclusions, nor my explanations of the program met with resistance, but were accepted sympathetically. In the Southern centers of the old leftist organizations, however, political passions were already running high. Such was the case, for example, in Kursk. And in Kharkov, I got into a real battle with my listeners. The harmony of my historical constructs was utterly demolished by opposing assertions. Our arguments were furious. I argued with my well-versed opponents literally the whole night long without interruption. In the rays of the rising sun, we parted, exhausted and unreconciled.

This first political tour of mine was highly beneficial to me. It was not the same as speaking before American clubs or giving lectures to a more or less prepared audience. Here I had to address crowds whose level and political sympathies were uncertain and probably very mixed. The rules of public speaking before the masses took shape by themselves, and they had to be followed in the future. Although the rules are very elementary, they can be learned only from experience, and few people, according to my observations, hold to them. The first of these rules is to speak in such a way that the whole audience can hear. I found out that I possessed the necessary strong voice for speaking to a crowd without shouting. Otherwise, the listeners will become inattentive and restless; they will begin to cough and to make noise; and some of them will simply leave. The second rule is to speak understandably and intelligibly to all, taking into account those who are least advanced. Now comes a double requirement which is difficult to unite in a single speaker. Some speeches affect the emotions of the listeners; other speeches, their reason. The more numerous the audience, the easier it is for the speaker to evoke the desired emotions. This demands a special ability from the orator. He must provide a graphic demonstration of personal passions and feelings through the use of dramatic gestures and inflections of the voice. The content of the speech recedes into the background and is replaced by a flight of oratorical inspiration amidst poetic confusion. In this way, demagogs are created who are capable of swaying large masses, of calling them to action and of leading them.

I had no trouble convincing myself that I could not have taken this road even if I had wanted to do so. Another road was open to me: calm reasoning, not with the aim of enthralling my listeners, but with the aim of persuading them. Other devices were required to accomplish this, the most important of which was a reasonable simplification of the arguments, making them comprehensible to the general audience. I had mastered this pedagogical device early in my teaching career. Then, after catching the listeners' attention, it is necessary to hold it. In order to do this, the thread of reasoning must always be in the listeners' consciousness. Any complications, digressions, or extra details will immediately distract their attention; the thread will be lost, and the untrained listener will not be able to pick it up again. From this follows the necessity of coherence, of a definite plan which the listeners can follow in order to understand where in the train of reasoning they are, and not lose sight of the whole. This requirement is most important for holding the attention of an audience to the end. Arriving unprepared, leaving the train of thought to the inspiration of the moment, would be just as erroneous as bringing a prepared text and reading from it. The speech should be lively. The speaker should be constantly checking its effect on the audience's attention, changing and directing the course of his argument accordingly. Otherwise, the loss of attention will be irretrievable. The last rule is not to ignore the opponents' objections. On the contrary, the speaker must pay them the fullest attention and assure himself of the last word in their analysis, either for agreement or for dispute. Otherwise, the meeting would have been for nothing, the opponents would be left unsatisfied and offended, and this feeling would be shared by the audience which would then find itself thrown into a half-way position. On the other hand, a detailed analysis of the objections helps to establish among the listeners, if not total unity of mind, then at least some kind of compromise with the speaker which is acceptable to all. Leaving the meeting, the listener feels that he is coming away with something new. This is better than ending the meeting with a vote on a previously prepared resolution thereby dividing the audience into majority and minority. It is only in a strictly party struggle that this last action may be necessary. It is better to leave doubt than to force a choice.

I do not mean to imply that I followed all these rules to the letter after the first round. But, consciously or unconsciously, they were put into practice before large audiences after my first appearance. My conciliatory mission was directed to this end, even in the content of my talks.

From a political point of view, too, I derived a new and useful conclusion. I began to realize that in my formulations, the last chronological link was missing. I have already said something about this. From the extreme leftist position, people of our kind could not be collaborators, or even "fellow travelers." We were, rather, competitors and potential enemies. It was possible, perhaps, to achieve victory in league with us, but by no means was it possible to stay together after the victory. Our supposed "class" interest contradicted the interest of, in their view, the only truly revolutionary class—the working proletariat. Only the proletariat's legal representatives, the S. D.'s, could be true revolutionaries. Our "liberal democracy," and even the "revolutionary democracy" of the socialist Populists were identically assigned to the category of "petit-bourgeois" parties. No matter how far we moved to the left, we still could not escape from the S. D.'s category. It was precisely in the years 1904–5 that the doctrines and tactics of this S. D. implacability came to light in articles by contributors to *Iskra*. But for the time being, things had not yet gone from the doctrine to practice. The doctrine itself was still in the process of being formed. Its infallibility had yet to be proven in practice, and this could be accomplished only as the future revolution unfolded, and only as a result of the struggle against us and the Populists for influence over the masses. May, June, and even part of July still allowed me to hang on to my conciliatory views. But my hopes for an agreement, and with them my hopes for the success of the whole revolutionary movement, gradually but constantly faded.

The professional unions which were started by the resolution of the League of Liberation at the end of 1904 still remained as the connecting link between the "liberals" and the "revolutionaries." The unions, like the League itself, were soon to serve as the arena for the ideological and organizational struggle. My attention now shifted to them.

From Words to Deeds

My work in Moscow on the preparation of the program for the future party, as well as my "conciliatory" lectures and speeches in both Moscow and the provinces still did not, of course, represent genuine political activity. Fulfillment of the directives originating in the left wing of the League of Liberation undoubtedly did represent such activity, even in the period of "simulated revolution." One could characterize as political activity the agitation through the banquet campaign, developed according to the decision of the League. It should be mentioned here that the campaign achieved its aim. The second directive of the League, carried out with the aid of sympathizers but through the direct participation of the League, was the organization of a series of professional unions. This project was undertaken simultaneously with the banquets. It, too, achieved its goal in March and April of 1905, just before my return to Russia. This first organizational step had great political significance because, until that time, the progressive Russian community had not been organized at all. It coincided completely with my plans. Since the introduction of a constitutional system was proclaimed as the fundamental political task, it was necessary to prepare society for carrying out constitutional functions. Above all, groups united by common political goals had to be formed immediately. The preparatory work for the creation of a "Constitutional Democratic" party was only a part of this general task. The task as a whole could be fulfilled only when other political currents, as well, were organized into political parties. A system of political parties was the other side of constitutionalism—and the Russian public had to be trained for this.

But it required time, and that did not suit the tactics of the left wing of the League of Liberation. In the interests of centralization (or for the "simulation" of revolution) they decided to speed up preparatory work. On the very day of "Bloody Sunday" (January 9), in anticipation of future events, several of the radically inclined unions met in the lodgings of the Free Economic Society and founded the Central

Bureau of the Union of Unions. The second half of the directive of October 20, 1904, was thereby realized. The obvious aim of this hasty step was to keep the leadership of the political organization of society in their hands. This fictitious Bureau of the Union of Unions immediately undertook its first active measure: it sent a well-known delegation to Witte,[11] but without success. Only later did this arbitrary Bureau of the Union of Unions become somewhat official through the co-optation of two representatives (of course, holding the same political views) from each union. It lasted in that state until May 8-9 when the First Congress of the Union of Unions met in Moscow, comprising sixty delegates from fourteen organizations.

I viewed the organizational task begun by the League of Liberation more seriously. I understood, of course, that the formation of political parties was no easy matter, and that the unions could play only the temporary role of party surrogates. As early as April, I came out in print in defense of the idea of the unions against sharp attacks from both right and left. The Social Democrats, especially, who tried to grab a monopoly on public organization, condemned the unions for doing precisely what, in my opinion, gave them their chief value, becoming obviously political instead of remaining strictly professional. The S. D.'s wanted the unions to remain neutral soil so that they could sow their own crops. I told them in reply that there was enough room in the unions for everyone, and that their absence from the unions would lead to the creation of a moderate, centrist mood which would spread to the masses. This is exactly what the S. D.'s feared. As the union movement grew, the S. D.'s became more suspicious. They made me their personal scapegoat, because I wanted to pull the unions up to the level of the most moderate of the political trends, namely, constitutional democracy. Trotsky expanded his attack from me to the whole of the Union of Unions. In his opinion, this organization "represented the organizational apparatus for leading the mixed intellectual opposition into political subordination to Zemstvo liberalism, the most backward and inert of all the currents." For Trotsky, this was a "Zemstvo bridle, slipped on the democratic intelligentsia by the Liberationists." The S. D.'s displayed special zeal when they noticed that several unions, by their very nature, were linked to the masses (for example, the Peasant Union, then still in its embryonic stage and affiliated with the Union of Unions). In the June 21 issue of *Iskra*, an article appeared asserting that "half-way democracy is not only organizing its intellectual avant-garde without our cooperation, but even more, it intends to compete with us in our natural political domains, among the popular masses, and in particular the proletariat."

From their point of view, the S. D.'s would have been perfectly

correct if what they so feared was indeed happening, instead of the
exact opposite. I genuinely expected—and told them so—that "alongside of the extreme and uncompromising voices, more moderate and
practical voices would soon be heard" among the masses. I considered
this not only possible but desirable, in view of the fact that the political direction and the role of the unions were still questions to be
decided. Radical attitudes, in general, dominated in the unions, but
the degree of radicalism and the content of the platforms were extremely diversified. The powers of the central organ, too rapidly
monopolized by the Petersburg Bureau and in reality very extensive,
remained formally undefined. A more suitable organization of the
Union of Unions was absolutely necessary in order to return to the
unions themselves full independence in choosing their political direction. I was not entirely sure that this could have been achieved, that
the unions could dissociate themselves not only from the leadership
claims of the socialist parties but also from the intentions of their
closest, like-minded comrades in the League of Liberation. At any
rate, my political task—and this time it was truly my personal task—
was very clearly drawn. It was hardly what the Petersburg center
would have predicted. Be that as it may, when preparations for convoking the "Bulygin" Duma[12] became unavoidable, and when, for this
purpose, the Second Congress of the Union of Unions (which had the
character of a Constituent Congress), convened on May 24, I was
unanimously elected chairman of the Union. Before I go into my role
as chairman, it is necessary to say something about the prevailing
mood and attitude when the congress met in Moscow. These were the
"Days of Tsushima."

On May 14–15 (27–28), the Second Russian Squadron, made up
of old ships of various sorts and sent to certain destruction in the
Japanese waters, was annihilated by the Japanese in the Tsushima
Straits. This war, into which the adventurists, with protection from
above, had dragged Russia for their own material gain, was extremely
unpopular in Russian society. The continuous defeats and retreats of
Kuropatkin, the surrender of Port Arthur, the annihilation of the first
squadron—all of this struck painfully on the national self-esteem.
Tsushima demonstrated the complete incompetence of the government
not only to govern but even to wage a war in defense of Russia's
national interests. The revolution, which Plehve wanted to extinguish
by means of a "small, victorious war," gained new strength.

I was in Petersburg during those days, and I received an invitation from the League of Liberation to take part in the first public protest of the defeat at Tsushima. It was impossible to refuse the invitation, even though the protest was one of those "simulations" of revolu-

tion which held little attraction for me. Sometime in the next few days we were supposed to meet at a concert in Pavlovsk, and there, during the intermission, a speaker would be put forward who would explain to the public the significance of popular protest. The good V. V. Vodovozov, who was always ready for battle, consented to be the speaker. The demonstration, however, was a deplorable failure. That part of the public which did not have time to leave the hall, scattered as soon as it learned that it was being drawn into politics. The police were rushed in and began their work immediately. We barely managed to hide the speaker in our tiny group since he stood out like a sore thumb because of his clothes, his dishevelled hair and his great sheepskin hat. This frivolous gesture at such a serious time made a grim impression on me and cured me forever of such "simulations."

I went to Moscow after this incident and found myself in the midst of preparations for a patriotic demonstration of another kind, one that was capable of genuinely expressing at least the national, if not the "popular" indignation. Simultaneously, a large group of the Zemstvo minority held a conference in Moscow for the purpose of clarifying their position vis-à-vis the forthcoming election to the "Bulygin" Duma. In the name of the Bureau of Congresses, the representative of the majority from the Zemstvo congresses, F. A. Golovin, proposed to D. N. Shipov, who in view of the seriousness of the situation had brushed aside the disagreements that had divided the Zemstvoists, to meet together at a general, "Coalition" Congress on May 24. With some hesitation this proposal was accepted, but immediately there arose deep-seated disagreements as to the goal of unification. While the minority came to the congress with the aim of "supporting the government authority" at this difficult time, the majority wanted to win from the government a "change in the State structure." In this spirit, the congress drew up a project for an "address-petition" to be presented to the tsar. The sharp tone of the project was softened for the benefit of the minority, but Shipov still refused to become a member of the delegation. The majority then softened the address to the tsar even further. As the delegation's speaker for the introductory remarks, they chose a man who was acceptable to the minority but who enjoyed unquestioned moral authority among all—Prince S. N. Trubetskoi.

It must be admitted, that Sergei Nikolaevich fully justified his election. If it was, in general, necessary or possible to address the tsar at this time, in the name of the congress, then it could have been done only in the tone chosen by this patriotic orator, in the moving tone of sincere suffering for one's native land. I was among a small group of

friends who met in the Hotel France on Morskaia Street for the purpose of "rehearsing" Trubetskoi's speech before the departure of the
delegation to Peterhof. Later, we heard the impressions of the delegation after its return to the hotel. I can vouch for the satisfaction that
we all felt with Trubetskoi's address to the tsar, which he gave in the
spirit of a "fatherly" reprimand. The immediate aim of the task could
be considered attained. For the first time, the tsar was genuinely
moved by a voice from the other world. For the first time, we heard
from his lips words resembling a sincere promise of reform, and, as it
were, an understanding of the necessity of reform.

It goes without saying that this political move could arouse only
expressions of discontent from the left. The "Coalition Congress" was
subjected to savage denunciation for the very idea of uniting the
majority and the minority in a single political move, for the form of
the address to the tsar, and for particular phrases in Trubetskoi's
speech, such as the word "sedition." After Tsushima, other actions
had to be taken. Even Trubetskoi's brother, Evgenii, wrote in *Pravo*:
"This mockery of public opinion must sooner or later be stopped. Only
vilification will greet future attempts by our guardians to take care of
us. . . . Step aside, gentlemen, and make way for the people's representatives. . . ."

Amidst the aroused mood of the various political groups, the
Second Congress of the Union of Unions met in Moscow on May 24–
26. Its theme, one that it shared with the other congresses, was how to
deal with the "Bulygin" Duma. But the congress also had its own
business to handle. The resolutions of the first congress of May 8–9
were inconclusive: they had to be discussed in the various unions. The
unions now brought back their decisions to the Second Congress. Although until this time the Union of Unions was formally only an organ
of reciprocal information, it was in fact "an autonomous body on federal principles," according to the strange formula which cloaked its
active independence. The decisions of the Union could be carried out
(again, formally) only with the authorization through their delegates
of the individual unions. In reality, of course, the Union of Unions
functioned without waiting for authorization, and uninhibited by the
lack of such authorization.

These ambiguous relationships had to be regulated, and I, as
chairman, had the opportunity of choosing one path or another. The
Petersburg Bureau, of course, wanted the congress to legalize its independence. I agreed that the central organ should not be hindered
by requiring it to obtain special authorization in each case. On the
other hand, I proposed to restrict its freedom of decision, once and for
all, within definite political limits. These limits were predetermined

by the platforms of the individual unions, that is, by those points which the unions had in common. I proposed that these common points be adopted as the limits of the lawful powers of the central bureau. It was, of course, difficult to object to that proposal. But when the limits were fixed in this way, it turned out that the only formula which was common to each union and which consequently was binding on the Union of Unions itself was the following: "A struggle for the political liberation of Russia on the principle of democracy." The left-wingers rightly considered this formula too vague, and it was developed further into a concrete demand: "The necessity of the immediate convocation of a Constituent Assembly of the people's representatives, elected by universal, direct and secret ballot." Incidentally, it had been proposed that this sacremental formula be included in the petition to the tsar which was worked out by the "Coalition Congress." According to the memoirs of D. N. Shipov, it was also proposed that the whole congress, that is, more than two hundred persons, go before the tsar. It was the minority which insisted on replacing the two hundred persons by a delegation and on rewording our formula from "elected," etc., to "chosen for the assembly, on terms of equality and without distinction by all your subjects."

This "betrayal," in the view of the leftists, defined the relationship of the Union of Unions Congress to the "Coalition Congress." The congress of the Union of Unions rejected a proposal to express sympathy with the "Coalition Congress." On the other hand, it also rejected the opposite proposal, namely, to issue a "protest" against the delegation to the tsar. The congress, in a way, adopted a position of benevolent neutrality. I think that my chairmanship was significant in this respect, although the Union of Unions chose its own path. The congress considered as obligatory for all its members a fait accompli manner of action, that is, a de facto freedom of the press, speech, unions, meetings, and arrangement of demonstrations for various occasions. In the event of persecution, each member was required to declare openly his membership in the Union, and an organization for their judicial defense was established. Instead of addressing the tsar, the congress decided to go to society and the people by adopting the appeal which I had written. I had used very sharp expressions in its composition, but these expressions corresponded both to my personal mood and to the mood of those gathered at the congress. What in other circumstances would have appeared as demagogy and rhetoric was here a frank expression of the general feeling. In direct opposition to the hope expressed in the "Coalition Congress" declaration, the appeal stated that "the hope that they will listen to us is gone". "Each person should act according to his knowledge, his ability and his political convictions. . . . All means may now be legitimately used against the terrible danger (E. Trubetskoi had said "catastrophe") latent in the continued existence of the present government. . . . We appeal to everything in the people that is alive and capable of answering crude blows, and we say: 'with all forces, with all means, achieve the immediate elimination of the bandit gang that has seized power, and put in its place the Constituent Assembly . . . so that as quickly as possible, it can put an end to the war and to the political regime which has dominated until now.' "

As can be seen, my appeal was filled with echoes of the events of the moment. What was going on behind the scenes in the Japanese War, the role of the imperially approved knights of profit, was well known to me. For all these Bezobrazovs and Alexeevs, the term "bandit gang" was not merely rhetoric. The "shock" of Tsushima too strongly struck the body of Russia. This "bandit gang" also played a role in dividing the political currents. In certain circles, I had been taken for a "conciliator" from the right, but this reputation was now destroyed. The boundary between myself and the "right" became clearer: it passed between me and A. I. Guchkov. The Zemstvo Constitutionalists were also to the left of this boundary. How far to the left with respect to the League of Liberation and the Union of Unions? That depended on further clarification in the policies of the Petersburg organs. Petersburg could hardly be satisfied with my chairmanship of the Union of Unions. They had probably intended an honorary role for me, but I assumed an active one, and I tried to restrict their political independence within definite limits. Of course, they paid no attention to my efforts or to my title of chairman (see below). I was, by chance, absent from the Third Congress of the Union of Unions held in Petersburg-Terioki on July 1–3. The Union of Zemstvo Constitutionalists was also absent. The fundamental question concerning participation in the elections to the "Bulygin" Duma was there decided negatively by nine of the unions that voted against participation, contrary to my point of view. Three unions, however, came out for participation: the Writers, Professors, and High School Teachers. Four unions abstained: Peasants, Equal Rights for Jews, Veterinarians, and Elementary School Teachers. The four abstaining unions declared that "to answer this question, positively or negatively, is impossible at the present time." They proposed that the decision be postponed until the next congress "after and depending upon the result of the proposed protest" (that is, the protest against a Duma having only consultative powers and being based on the curia system of indirect and restricted elections). And so we see that by

July the unions had still not shifted very far to the left; some of them continued to waver.

In the meantime, because of the participation of the socialist parties, the revolutionary movement had spread to the masses and the whole picture began to change. Our political current was, as it were, cut off from this process. During those months, news about the internal evolution taking place at the core of the socialist parties, especially the S. D.'s, reached us both sparsely and late. We discovered the results of these secret developments only after they began to be expressed in the course of our political struggle. I will return to them at that time.

Each morning we read in the newspapers about workers' strikes in various Russian cities, and railroad employees, small artisans' groups, and unions from all sorts of professions were beginning to affiliate with the striking workers. The strikes were ever more frequently being described as "general." Alongside of the workers, the peasant movement also flared up—especially in the black-earth regions. Armed detachments of S. R.'s, now here, now there, committed acts of terrorism, directing their blows at all levels of the administration, from governors to neighborhood and village police forces, at all ranks of the state police and gendarmes. One's eyes became used to the daily repetition of the same headlines, but it was difficult to perceive the dynamic of the revolution or to feel it from newspaper excerpts. Only later when these same facts were sorted out and classified in books was it possible to grasp the whole force of the revolutionary wave. The general meaning of the revolutionary outbursts was obscured by the absence of both a clearly expressed political direction and a unifying aim that would draw together various revolutionary outbursts motivated by the class demands of the workers, the local needs of the peasants, and so on. The socialist parties preferred to propagate general slogans rather than set concrete tasks. Systematic leadership from the center was not yet in evidence. According to the most revolutionary parties, the revolution was developing "spontaneously." The S. D.'s still put the problem of "unleashing" the revolution before the problem of its "organization." Under such conditions, the traditional influence of the Populists had still not been forced out by S. D. agitation, and among the peasantry, populist influence was unquestionably predominant. There was still the possibility of instilling more moderate "bourgeois" political tendencies in the masses. This was confirmed even by the jealousy of the S. D.'s toward potential competition from the "Zemstvoists," as they indiscriminately labeled their opponents at that time. The genuine Zemstvo Constitutionalists specifically included in their political calculations the possibility of propaganda among the masses.

It was precisely this last group that came more and more into its own as the political currents separated. With all the defections to the right, its composition still remained, rather indefinitely, on the left. This must be judged in the context of a general displacement of the political struggle in that direction. It must not be forgotten that we were concerned with the creation, not of a revolutionary party, but of a constitutional one, whose task would be to carry on the struggle with parliamentary means. In the spectrum of political parties which had sprung up, the parliamentary place had yet to be filled, and it was up to us to fill it. Unless it was filled, it would have been impossible even to think of establishing a constitutional regime in Russia. To place this special task before the future party became more and more my personal task, and my activities among those elements which displayed a tendency to join our future party were increasingly devoted to it.

The immediate issue to be decided was, then, the question of participation or nonparticipation in the elections to the "Bulygin" Duma, which served as a touchstone for choosing one road or the other—revolution or constitution. We saw that, on this question, vacillation persisted even in the leftist groups. Even *Iskra* wrote with reference to the decision of the Terioki Congress of the Union of Unions: "The Union of Unions decided to boycott the elections, but is that correct?" The answer to that question belonged first of all to the constitutionalists, and, hence, it became urgent to convene a new Zemstvo Congress. For this reason, the "Coalition Congress" was regarded in "our" circle not only as an annoying distraction but also as a dangerous delay, and the trip to the tsar was judged as a mistaken step backward. Above all, the new congress was supposed to dissociate itself from this incorrect course and return the contingent of the future party to the path already indicated by the unified majority from the Zemstvo congresses. The goals of the Zemstvo Congress which met together with representatives from the cities on July 6–8 were to verify the unity of views of the majority, to correct and supplement the sections of the future program accordingly, and, finally, to begin building the party. During the following few days, July 9–10, the Zemstvo Constitutionalist group was to draw its conclusions from the decisions of the Congress. This time I took direct part in their conferences and associated myself closely with the work of the congress. The half-open door through which I observed the Zemstvoists in Novosiltsev's mansion was opened wider for me now, although I still was not able to cross its threshold.

From the superficial view of the congress, and from the outcome of the clash there with police carrying out the will of the ministry, one could see at once how much the political situation had changed during the interval between May and July. This time we met in the tremendous home of Prince Pavel Dmitrievich Dolgorukov, in the neglected garden on Znamensky Lane, the same house where the host's late elder brother, Nikolai, and myself had once studied for the gymnasium exams. Someone no doubt still remembers the photograph of the numerous (235) members of this congress in the foreground of the princely palace. Assistant Minister Trepov declared beforehand that the decisions of the congress would be illegal. To the police who came to disperse the congress, the presidium simply referred to the "tsar's will"; that is, to convey the promise of the tsar "to all friends living on the land and in the cities." The Bureau of the Congresses carefully prepared the work of the congress, and in place of the Bulygin project, which the congress had rejected, it offered its own project of "a fundamental law," which had been published on the opening day of the congress in *Russkie Vedomosti*. The bureau's project was adopted "on the first reading." V. D. Nabokov then proposed "to defend the natural rights," as stated in the resolutions of the November Congress of 1904, "by all peaceful means, not excluding disobedience of the orders of the authorities which violate these rights." In accordance with a proposal of the brothers Pavel and Peter Dolgorukov, it was decided "to maintain the closest contact with the broad masses" in order to "evaluate the impending reforms together with the people," "to win the freedom necessary to carry out the reforms," and "to work out at the local level the problems of putting into practice the electoral system devised by the general Zemstvo Congress." The extremely daring formulation of these barely masked resolutions can be properly appreciated when one remembers that they implied the introduction of a Constitutional Assembly and universal elections virtually without the permission of the authorities. The congress adopted the text of the address to the people which the bureau prepared, but it showed itself extremely cautious when the question arose as to distributing this appeal among the masses. Several speakers considered the address to the people as much "too revolutionary a means." When the discussions came around to the main specific task—the elections to the Bulygin Duma—the congress, after stormy debates, displayed still more caution and left the question open. The scope of the congress was thus defined, from the adoption of semirevolutionary principles to a realistic political movement, given the prevailing circumstances.

For a unified party, this scope was too broad. Still, the attitudes of the future members were clarified, if not the extent of their preparedness. But the work on the political unification of the party had only begun.

The ambiguity of the congress's position between the right and the left came out more clearly in the Zemstvo Constitutionalist conferences on July 10–11, after the close of the congress. The Zemstvo Constitutionalists sharply dissociated themselves from the delegation to the tsar, which "did not represent an act of the Zemstvo Constitutionalists, but an act of the Coalition Congress, and the results of that delegation do not obligate us in any way." The League of Liberation was still considered a necessary constituent of the party, and in order to secure a definite agreement with that group, it was decided to include in the party program "statements concerning economic, financial, provincial and nationality questions." These were precisely the issues which could give rise to disagreements even within a "broad circle of like-minded men." On the other hand, the question of the party's attitude towards the Union of Unions, in whose name I spoke, evoked stormy debates and an exasperated rejoinder from me, which somebody painstakingly recorded, and which I will reproduce here almost in its entirety. "If the members of our group behave so delicately towards physical means of struggle, then I am afraid that our plans for organizing a party will be fruitless. It is difficult, you know, to rely on peaceful solutions to the urgent questions of governmental reorganization at a time when a revolution is already taking place around us. Or perhaps you are counting on someone else's physical force, hoping in your hearts for a certain outcome but refusing to take part personally in acts of physical coercion? But this would be hypocrisy, and such a hypocritical position on this question would be intolerable to a civic conscience. In your hearts you all no doubt rejoice over certain acts of physical violence which you all expected beforehand and whose historical significance is immense. . . . In general, after all that I have heard here, I have doubts, not about whether or not we should join with the Union of Unions, but about whether or not the Union of Unions itself will refuse the honor of maintaining comradely relations with us." The meeting was moved by my reproach and decided to participate in the Union of Unions. At that time, I did not foresee that I myself would soon be forced to leave that organization in the course of later political differentiation. Not only were the political attitudes of the party not defined but neither were my own. Entrance into the party on the eve of its formation was left open from both ends, although more from the left than from the right.

In spite of such indefiniteness, the July Congress concluded that all the elements for the formation of a party were well enough prepared for the congress to undertake its first executive measure. Twenty members were elected and authorized to enter agreements at their own discretion with groups of similar political inclinations. Primarily, they had in mind, of course, the League of Liberation, but they also looked toward the Union of Unions. Together with persons authorized by the other groups, they were to form a temporary committee of the party and begin to undertake the necessary measures for the party's organization. The bureau, together with these twenty authorized members, was to continue its work on the unfinished sections of the program, and the next congress of Zemstvo Constitutionalists was scheduled to meet "immediately" after the promulgation of the law for the Bulygin Duma. Circumstances, however, changed all these plans and created an entirely new situation, a situation in which the party's political self-determination was completed.

The Bulygin Duma and Prison

SINCE S. E. KRYZHANOVSKY'S MEMOIRS were published, it has no longer been a secret who composed all of the "constitutional" and "electoral" acts of that period. Kryzhanovsky was not a "high official," but among the faithful elders who surrounded the tsar, he was the only young man who remembered his university course on constitutional law. At the university, he was a friend of our D. I. Shakhovsky. Now, the two men traveled along opposite roads. Kryzhanovsky's knowledge of law came in handy for helping the government manufacture cleverly drafted acts of illegality. In the words of the author, who was secretly offended at his insignificance in front of those honored ignoramuses, the "enfeebled elders" spent whole months helplessly chewing on themes which were way beyond them. At last the project emerged from its hiding place virtually unchanged, that is, not improved politically. It was still uncertain exactly when this "tsar's will" would be carried out, or indeed, whether it would be carried out at all. It was only by accident that I became acquainted with the subsequent history of the Bulygin Duma.

In the second half of July, the tsar convened a conference, under his chairmanship, in Peterhof, consisting of five grand dukes plus all the ministers and high officials. Because of his intimacy with the tsar's family, Professor Kliuchevsky was also included in the conference. It was here, in deepest secrecy that the fate of the Bulygin project was to be decided. After his arrival in Petersburg, V. O. Kliuchevsky sent his son, Boris, to bring me the material he had received and to ask my help in orienting him in the political situation of the northern capital. I was extremely pleased by this invitation, since it took up again the thread of our relations, which had been interrupted after I defended my dissertation. I had always esteemed and loved my former university teacher, and his turning to me now showed that he retained some kind feelings towards me, too, inspite of my "betrayal" of our discipline. We struck up daily contacts in his hotel on Pushkin Street. In the course of the entire week while the conference was going on, I spent all my evenings with Kliuchevsky, listening to his detailed account of what was taking place at Peterhof and discussing the next day's program with him.[13]

V. O. [Kliuchevsky] had been invited through the initiative of the rightist clique, which hoped to find in him a reliable ally. During the first few days, the rightists disclosed all their secret plans to him. With a characteristic slyness, V. O. Kliuchevsky let them keep their delusions. It was in this way that I learned about the backstage political struggle at the conference. The object of the struggle was not so much the Duma itself as it was the key to controlling the Duma by means of the electoral law, Kryzhanovsky's chef d'oeuvre. The project preserved, only in an extremely limited way, of course, the beginnings of classless elections. The conspirators favored direct elections based on class. "Otherwise, people of the Zemstvo type would wind up in the Duma, people to whom the age-old Russian principles are not dear," reasoned one of the leaders, Stishinsky, who defended the organization of the "League of the Fatherland." These opponents of the government project were stubborn, and to the very end of the conference they refused to give in. The tsar, worked over by the rightists, apparently wavered. Kliuchevsky was in the advantageous position of having spoken in favor of the government project. Twice he came out against elections based on class. His statement, which reminded the tsar of Trubetskoy's exhortation, created a strong impression. Class-based elections, he said, "can be interpreted as a defense of the interests of the nobility. Then the sombre spectre of a class Tsar will arise in the people's imagination. May God preserve us from the consequences." At Peterhof, the nobility was definitely not at its best. Grand Duke Vladimir Alexandrovich, crying sedition, openly attacked the various Petrunkeviches and Dolgorukovs. Great hopes were placed on the "grey" muzhik. It is true that to a certain degree, Kliuchevsky's lectures supported this attitude toward the nobility and the peasantry. Kliuchevsky was true only to himself.

When at last the Duma project became law (August 6), I had an opportunity to write a background article in *Pravo* concerning the place of the present act in the series of previous attempts at political reform. Kryzhanovsky's secret documents which Kliuchevsky had passed on to me, served as material for the article. The fundamental inadequacies of the law were self-evident, as were also its advantages over previous abortive proposals. The next day another article of mine appeared in *Syn Otechestva* in which I came out categorically against the boycott of the Bulygin Duma. With it, I said, the Rubicon, before which the Russian political struggle had been stopped for half a century, was finally crossed. From the act of August 6, it followed that the existence of political parties was conceded, and, therefore, that those "freedoms" which are necessarily tied to elections of the people's representatives were also recognized. No matter how imperfect the Duma may have been, it was a new arena for carrying out the open parliamentary struggle that characterized our political movement. Incidentally, these statements of mine gave Trotsky the chance to shift his political gunsights from Struve to me.

On the same day that my article appeared (August 7), the government went out of its way to strengthen Trotsky's argument. It decided, upon publication of the Duma Act, to withdraw the only "freedom" which the ukase of February 18 had permitted, namely the freedom of public discussion concerning the reformation of the old order. Consequently, retroactive prosecution could be directed at those who had taken advantage of that freedom. By an irony of fate, I was the one chosen as the target for attack.

That morning the delegates from the Union of Unions gathered at my rooms in Udelnaia Station for the purpose of considering the attitude which the Union should take toward the Bulygin Duma. This was, of course, a private meeting. Nevertheless, because of the government's badly informed judgment that the Union of Unions was the most dangerous organization, it was the first to suffer. My rooms were surrounded by the police, who arrested all the visitors gathered there. They loaded us on several cabs and took us off to jail. True, they had to search for a jail, since the raid was so sudden that places for us had not been prepared beforehand. With pillows and nightclothes under our arms, we passed by the puzzled public, across the Neva from "Kresty" to Shpalernaia and then back from Shpalernaia to "Kresty" where they finally took us in. Our reception was extremely respectful, since our little group contained two state councilors, delegates from the Union of Engineers, and Professors A. A. Brandt and Ya. I. Gordeenko. Thus began my third and last jail term.

The government apparently realized its stupidity. At least, during the whole month that we spent in jail, they did not disturb us even once with interrogations. The new trends were, in general, reflected also in the penal system. The director of the prison exhibited all the symptoms of liberalism. He acquainted me with the prison system and discussed with me ways of organizing the prisoners' labor and entertainment and of running the prison library. During my wife's visits, we were no longer separated by a double wire screen; they gave us a special room, and my wife freely handed me the latest issues of illegal literature. Once a week, my friend, A. V. Timofeev, the director of St. Nicholas' Hospital, came to visit me from Udelnaia. The prison director led us into his study where we buried ourselves in a chess game, unrestricted by any time limit. In between moves, I learned about the most important events of the week. This time, I decided to use my leisure for reading and rereading Populist literature. The prison library was not a bad one, having grown with the donations from former intellectual prisoners. I read quite a bit during the month. I reread in chronological order all of Gleb Uspensky and was struck by the forceful talent of this remarkable writer and by the precision of his sociological observations on the degeneration of the Russian city and the Russian village in the postreform years. Here was a veritable storehouse of information for the historian of the era of the "great reforms" of Alexander II. It is too bad that Uspensky has been unjustly forgotten by the public. I reread Levitov who is even more forgotten than Uspensky, and to my surprise, I saw in him the legitimate predecessor of Gorky. With difficulty I waded through Reshetnikov's style, and he revealed to me a clear picture of the neglected early stages of Russian colonization. I could not get through Zlatovratsky; the saccharine enthusiasm of this new Homer sickened me as before. Saltykov repaid me with interest; for the first time I reread all of his works in chronological order. The colors of great satirists necessarily fade with time, and it is almost necessary to read them with a scholarly commentary. What force there was in Saltykov's concentrated sarcasm! What knowledge of the old ways of life and of the ephemeral heroes, exactly as if he pulled them out of Gogol's collection! What delicate sensitivity in observing this series of commonplace scoundrels and "bureaucratic babes" which replaced each other almost monthly on the surface of the social scum! For a parallel to Uspensky, I read through the series by Rugunov-Makarov Zol, but it was a stale swamp compared to Uspensky's broad Russian flood, sweeping up the chips of our past. Yes, indeed, I could be thankful for this peaceful backwater of a prison which sheltered me for a month from another flood—that of the swollen Russian tidal wave. In prison I had time to rest and to think. I was late for the Zemstvo Constitutionalist Congress which was supposed to convene "immediately" upon publication of the law for the Bulygin Duma. My kind friends, however, decided to postpone the congress until my release from jail. There was really no sense in prolonging our stay in jail. They released us just as they had arrested us, without interrogation and without any apparent reason. After I was freed, the last All-Zemstvo and City Congress before the formation of the party took place on September 12–15.

From Bulygin to Witte:
Formation of the Party

As I HAVE ALREADY MENTIONED, the July Congress of Zemstvo and city delegates was, in general, radically inclined and considered the formation of a political party as the urgent issue. In an agreement between the Liberationists and the Zemstvoists (who made up about one-third of the membership of the League of Liberation), the August Congress of the League defined this task as "the transition of the League of Liberation from a secret society to an open political party in the European sense of the word." As we shall see, this definition was more suitable for us than for the Liberationists. Also, I considered such a formula to be the best definition of the task which I had set for myself personally. But precisely for this reason, the formula already contained the grain of future serious disagreements which were to make impossible the formation of a unified political party from, on the one side, Liberationists and the Zemstvoists and, on the other, the urban representatives.

The basic disagreements did not concern the program. The inadequate sections of our program, which dealt with agrarian and workers' problems, were lifted almost bodily from the March program of the League of Liberation. The program on the nationality question (Polish autonomy and decentralization) was specially prepared by F. F. Kokoshkin. The disagreements were over tactics, and especially over the attitude toward elections to the Bulygin Duma.

Our congress, which convened late compared to the August Liberationist Congress, was scheduled for September 12–15, after my release from jail. As can be seen from what had been said, my personal role in these congresses grew, and I now assumed formally a leading role. Together with Professor M. M. Kovalevsky, I was elected as a member of the organizational bureau of the congress. The mood of the congress, which had been delayed to this late date, had changed significantly during the interval. Somewhere I have said that the

September Congress "met under gloomy omens, in the glow of the agrarian fire, during the first manifestations of Black Hundred reaction in the provincial cities." We had reason to be afraid that ordinary, basic fear would effect part of the delegates to the congress, and we were not entirely mistaken. True, our usual majority remained united, but, after Shipov's group left, a new right-wing minority sprang up numbering thirty-one to thirty-nine persons, out of a total of 193 delegates. (The whole congress consisted of 130 Zemstvoists plus sixty-three representatives from the cities.) The new minority kept quiet during the meetings, but behind the scenes one could hear accusations of "despotism" against the Bureau of Congresses, and of "irresponsibility" and "radicalism" against the majority of the congress. It was not the social part of the program, but the nationality section, so carefully and painstakingly worked out by Kokoshkin, which was subjected to special attack at the congress. Representatives from the non-Zemstvo (i.e., Western) provinces were present at the congress, and after heated arguments between A. I. Guchkov and the lawyer Vrublevsky, Polish autonomy was passed with only one dissenting vote (under the conditions that the integrity of the Russian empire be maintained and that autonomy apply only to the ethnically Polish territories). The resolution for the "decentralization" of Russia, however, did not win approval, even though Kokoshkin attached all sorts of qualifications to it. It was postponed by the bureau until "after civil rights are instituted and a regular popular representative body for the whole empire is established." In addition, "decentralization" was not to be applied everywhere at once, but "according to the needs of the local population and the natural borders of the autonomous regions." Even with all these qualifications, it was understood that there must first be "an opening of a legal path for establishing local autonomy." We deliberately said nothing about the relations of the autonomous territories to the nationalities. This section of the project was passed by a majority of seventy-eight, with thirty-seven delegates voting against it. Evidently, this minority was the kernel of the competing party, which later took the name "Party of the 17th of October." The first chairman of the congresses, Count P. A. Heiden, was the first to put his signature to its "proclamation" although it was A. I. Guchkov who moved into the leadership position of that party by objecting to Polish autonomy.

Reflecting the change in the general mood by the middle of September, the position on the principal tactical question—the elections to the Bulygin Duma—also changed. The militant, offensive attitude which had prevailed in July no longer prevailed. With all its negative aspects, the Bulygin Duma was an accomplished fact. The attitude toward it still remained unquestionably negative, but there were no longer any speeches about agreements with the "people" against the Duma. A position on the elections had to be defined, even though the elections were based on an unacceptable electoral law. The double-edged formula adopted in July was repeated in September: on the one hand, "a united group" of like-minded men, having entered the Duma, was "to serve as a focus and a fulcrum for the social movement"; on the other hand, the aim was "to achieve by means of the Duma a guarantee of personal and public liberty and a regular, popular representative body." Here was the embryo of a conflict between two opposing tactics: a struggle from without and a struggle from within the Duma. The two could be brought together only in strong hands. Having fallen into various hands, both tactics interfered with and weakened each other.

I was elected to the "Central Electoral Committee" in Petersburg, but the "question of active participation of the committee in the election campaign" was "left open." Events were surging forward so rapidly towards a radicalization of the social movement that all our preparations risked being left on the drawing board. Already in September, the strike movement had taken on a "general" character, drawing into itself elements which usually remained aloof from politics. After the universities were proclaimed autonomous (this was a concession by the government to S. N. Trubetskoy), the university buildings became inaccessible to the police, and their auditoriums were used for daily meetings (not only of students) which repeated the radical slogans of the day and made them universal. In such a situation, the government's former concessions were clearly inadequate. Having retreated somewhere into the fog, the Bulygin Duma ceased to occupy the center of interest. How far the government would go in granting new concessions, and how much could be done against its will, remained unclear. The limits stretched to infinity. The very name "Constitutional Democratic" party was already a hindrance. The demands were now for a "democratic republic" resulting from an "armed uprising" and the seizure of power by a "provisional government" according to the prescription of the Third (Bolshevik) Socialist Congress. In the light of such moods and events, the task of the party congress became extraordinarily complicated. The leftist temperament of the majority of the party gained strength precisely at a time when the Bureau of Congresses and the group which united around it wanted to uphold the line of the July and September congresses, without retreating backwards like the September minority but also without meeting the heightened demands of the moment. The question centered around the preservation or alteration of the personality of the party which had only just begun to take shape. The situation was complicated by the fact that, as it was taking shape, the party deviated ever more from its "Liberationist" origins.

The Constituent Congress was fixed for October 12. But as this date approached, the situation became more and more alarming. The strike at the railroad junctions was the last straw. By making all movement impossible, it brought the activity of all branches of government and public life to a standstill. The government was completely at a loss. The Portsmouth Peace had just been concluded, but the troops had still not returned from the front. Witte, the "hero" of Portsmouth, returned to Petersburg, and all eyes turned to him as the only possible restorer of internal peace.

The cessation of transportation services threatened the very existence of the congress. The road to Moscow was cut off for almost three-fourths of our members. To what extent could the congress, meeting under such conditions, be considered legitimate? The tempo of events, however, became so feverish that it was politically unavoidable and urgent to respond to them, and this could be done only in the name of an existing party. Since all the preparations had been made for the formal launching of the party, the bureau decided not to pay attention to the obstacles.

I was entrusted with delivering the introductory address to the congress, in line with the decisions just mentioned. My task was made somewhat easier by the fact that many of the Petersburg members of the League of Liberation were absent. Had they been present, they certainly would have introduced an element of implacability. Their absence made my task especially crucial. What I have termed the "personality" of the party too obviously coincided with my own political personality, and I already knew what they thought about that in Petersburg (see also below). By predetermining, in my introductory remarks, the character of the party which had been formed, I also definitively prescribed my own future behavior. Of course, I foresaw that a battle was impending and that, apart from the formulated party decisions, I would have to throw my personal weight into the struggle—and the responsibility would be my own. This was, in its way, an entrance exam for leadership.

That opinion be united and party discipline obligatory were the two basic conditions for the transition from a "League" to a "party." In reality, however, there were two irreconcilable currents here. The limits of disagreement had to be fixed widely enough to accommodate them, but it was not clear how much these limits would be forced to expand even further as a result of the surge of revolutionary feelings, on the one hand, and the resoluteness of the leaders to preserve the "personality" of the party, on the other. I tried to proceed from the one point which we all accepted, and which had already been incorporated in the name of the party itself.

A "constitutional" party need not be "republican"; that is its first limitation. A "democratic" party need not be "socialist"; that is the second limitation. We had to fight for these limitations. To the right of us were the industrialists and the landowners who had already revealed their class aspirations. On this side, the boundary was clear. It was less clear on the left, where we had "not opponents, but allies." I was forced to permit the maximum possible disagreement, while still remaining within the limits of a single party. Responding to the slogans of a democratic republic and the socialization of the means of production, I said, "some of us do not associate ourselves with these slogans, some because they consider them totally unacceptable; others, because they consider such aims to be outside the limits of practical politics." "Obstacles of this sort are not insuperable if you do not consider the party to be an eternal union." But, "in spite of our different motives, the party can act as a single unit as long as it is possible to move together towards a common goal. Any attempt to emphasize the goals just mentioned and to incorporate them into the program will result in an immediate schism." Foreseeing the possibility of this result (which in fact occurred), I called upon the members of the congress to display "political foresight and wisdom," and I pointed out that "our program is the most left wing of all analogous political groups in Western Europe." For Russia, I continued, "this is the first attempt to convert intellectual ideals into feasible political demands, taking everything from the literary declarations which can be incorporated into a political program." I even regretfully envisaged that "this characteristic of our program might not be properly appreciated at a time of such high social tension such as we are now experiencing; but without doubt it will be so appreciated afterward." This appeal to the court of posterity was not without risk; the verdict might have turned out less favorable than we expected.

Nevertheless, the bureau did all that it could. "The debates at the congress were stormy," according to contemporary recollections. Personally, I do not remember whether or not they actually were. The virtually complete absence of Liberationists from the congress lowered the tone of the debates. The points concerning social legislation which they considered important were incorporated into our program, closely following the text of the March Liberation Congress; we only added precision and detail. The unexpected "storm" arose from the wrangling between me and my wife over the question of extending suffrage rights to women. In vain I tried to persuade the congress that the program was already overloaded without that. The whole cargo might sink to the bottom; and besides, the question of women's suffrage was not an urgent one. (I was later to defend it myself in the Fourth Duma.) In spite of support from the bureau, I wound up in the minority, which was permitted to consider itself "not bound" by either this decision or by the "difference of opinion" over "a unicameral or bicameral system." The much more important questions of principle such as republic versus monarchy, the formation of a general land fund from "nationalized" lands, the use to be made of this fund, and so on, were either avoided or pushed into the background. Solutions to these problems were put off for the future. It was with this comparative success that we emerged from the arguments over the program.

More important at that moment, however, was the question of tactics. It was still the same question of the stand the party should take on the elections to the (Bulygin) Duma and on the activity of the party members in the Duma itself. I was entrusted as well with delivering the report on this part of the work of the congress. But this time the obstacles were insurmountable. When my report was ready, events were unfolding rapidly, creating a new situation every day. In those days, the paramount question was the party's attitude toward the general strike. For three days before the appearance of the manifesto of October 17, dark rumors were circulating that something important was being prepared at the summit. Waiting for an explanation, the congress twice had to postpone the report on tactics; and twice I was forced to rewrite the report. In this period of anxious expectation, I had to restrict myself to the most general phrases. Then, on the last day, at the end of the drawn-out congress, a journalist from a friendly newspaper burst breathlessly into the hall waving a crumpled proofsheet still wet with ink. It was the text of the Manifesto of October 17.

None of us had expected this unparalleled sensation. No one was prepared for it. The bureau itself learned of the contents of the manifesto for the first time when it was read to the congress. Given our generally excited mood, the manifesto created a vague and unsatisfactory impression on us. On the one hand, there were the all-too-common phrases of "disturbances and troubles which have filled the royal heart with heavy sorrow" and which in the name of the "exalted vow of imperial devotion," have evoked the "adoption of measures for the immediate cessation of the dangerous disturbances." On the other hand, these "measures" were seen as promises to grant firm foundations for genuine personal inviolability and "civil liberty," "in order to pacify the country as speedily as possible." But most important, we heard the sacred words: "no law without the approval of the Duma," "genuine participation in the supervision" of state power, participation in the Duma elections by those classes of the population that had been entirely deprived of electoral rights, and finally (only prospectively, it is true), "further development of general suffrage by the newly established legislative system (through the Duma?)!" What was this? Another cunning ruse and delay, or genuinely serious intentions? Should we believe it or not?

At any rate, there was no time to lose, especially now. It was already the end of the congress, and we had to announce the existence of the new party. Also, in the name of the new party, we had to congratulate those who were undeniably the heroes of the day: the participants in the general strike! We considered the strike a "peaceful" and "organized" means of struggle which was in accord with our own views.

Directly after the close of the congress, we all made our way to a previously arranged banquet in the Literary Circle on Great Dmitrovka. The banquet was supposed to be a farewell celebration in honor of the participants in the congress, but now the main concern was the exchange of opinions on the still unpublished document. There was no time to come to an agreement and take the pulse of public opinion on it.

Established by M. K. Morozova, this "Literary Circle" was a strange institution with a purely Muscovite atmosphere. Briusov reigned on the stage in the main hall, along with that generation of new decadent youth about whom I had talked with Marguerite Kirillovna. Here, literary reports were delivered on the latest themes. The spectators' hall itself was a gambling casino, the revenue from which went to the upkeep of the establishment. We had to pass through the lower gambling hall in order to get to the upper dining room where a long table had been set for the members of the congress and for other distinguished Moscow guests. Down below, the public was mixed. They also had heard about the important event of the evening and were preparing to celebrate it in their own way. Upon our arrival, the usual visitors of the hall abandoned their gaming tables and crowded around us; in addition to them, the hall was filled by the public swarming around the light. The crowd was ecstatic; they were ready to celebrate both the manifesto and us. And the hero of this celebration turned out to be me. They hoisted me onto their arms, carried me over to a table in the middle of the hall, set me on the table, and thrust a glass of champagne in my hands. Several of the more enthusiastic ones scrambled onto the table to embrace me in Moscow style and, with not very steady movements, thoroughly doused me with the sparkling beverage. When things had calmed down a little, the crowd bunched up tightly around the table and insisted that I give them a speech on the issue which had so excited everyone. My speech, evidently, was supposed to reflect the festive mood.

I found myself placed in a difficult position. After a more careful reading of the text of the manifesto, my own mood was not at all festive. Paying no attention to the elated mood of the public which surrounded me, I threw cold water on their merrymaking. I do not recall the exact words of my agitated improvization, but I remember its general content clearly. Yes, I told them, the victory is won, and it is not a small one. But, you see, this victory is not the first one; it is only a new link in the chain of our victories. How many are already behind us! And will this be our last and final triumph? If only to hang on to what we have already won, we must not forsake the battle stations. We must continue to struggle for our liberty each day in order to be worthy of it. There are few "heroes" here. We need the support of the man in the street; and I call upon him to support "heroic" deeds. Such a speech could hardly have pleased them. They carried me off noisily, but it seemed to me that the send-off was not as warm as the moment when they placed me on the table. At least, crawling down from the table and making my way to the upper hall turned out to be easier than making my way to this improvised rostrum.

In the upper hall, too, the animation was considerable, though the mood was more serious. Here, as well, I had to speak first. Among my own crowd and friends, my speech was more intimate. I gave a detailed analysis of what had occurred in order to draw an outline, however rough, of our attitude toward these events. A skeptical note was dominant. I do not believe that by this time I had seen the text of Witte's report which accompanied the manifesto. Witte's report, however, contained some indefinite qualifications that indicated an improved understanding of the public frame of mind which had made the concessions necessary. In the light of previous, similar imperial acts, the evasiveness of the expressions in the manifesto itself was perfectly obvious. True, Pobedonostsev's hand was not felt behind the manifesto, but it was still material from the same factory. I analyzed what had been promised as well as what had been left unsaid in the manifesto.

Why did the manifesto speak of "sorrow" and "vow" the immediate cessation of disturbances by measures of the authorities, when these "disturbances" were supposed to be stopped peacefully? Why were the promises stated in the present tense, while their fulfillment is left for the future to a "unified" cabinet? What sort of cabinet would this be? And what did "unified" mean? Why was it necessary to strengthen the promises for "firm bases" with the word "genuine"?

Why, especially, did the elections to the Duma "not remain" in accord with the old law, and why were new elements of the population to participate in the elections only "as far as possible," in a situation of artificially created haste? Why is the "development of the principle of general suffrage" postponed until the introduction of "the newly established legislative system"? Why these three words "development," "principle," and "general" instead of a direct proclamation of "universal" suffrage? It was all well and good that the Duma was at last drawn into the legislative process, but why did the manifesto speak only of "approval"? Why, in the new legislative regime, was there a humble silence on the other legislative house, the State Council? What were the guarantees "of genuine participation of the people's delegates" in the supervision over "state power"? And why the word "supervision" instead of "control"? Why, too, was it further qualified by saying that the activities of the authorities must be "in conformity with the law" without mentioning the efficacy of those activities? Why was it stressed that the powers were "established by us" as if they were unalterable? Why were the deputies referred to in the old way as "delegates"?

All these objections suggested themselves after a careful reading of the text which I had in my mind. They all underscored the obvious ambiguity of the promises given in the manifesto, and instead of an accomplished stage, they again created some sort of a transitional phase. The party had to accommodate itself to the new situation, but to do so, other facts were needed which were not available. In addition, the hasty proclamation of the existence of the party together with the inadequate composition of the congress, in which the Moscow attitudes predominated over those of Petersburg, made it necessary to schedule a new congress as a supplement to our "Constituent Congress." It could hardly be denied, however, that the appearance of the first political party was most timely, having come precisely at the moment when political parties were necessary for an open and legal struggle within the representative body which had been granted legislative powers. The fundamental question which had been left "open" and controversial was thus decided; namely, the question of the party's participation in the elections. Nevertheless, the question could not be "closed" without a decree from a new congress.

I did not have to wait long for my pessimism to be clearly confirmed. After several days of tense and nervous efforts, after debates and the unexpected outcome, I was exhausted. I stayed at home the whole next morning and part of the afternoon. Some friends came to see me and told me about the demonstrations in the streets in honor of the manifesto. Our dear V. V. Vodovozov scrambled onto a barrel and delivered an animated speech to the "people." But when I went out for a walk the next day, those same "people" behaved differently. In the morning on Malaia Nikitskaya, I met a crowd which stretched all the way from Okhotny Riad to the Nikitsky Gates. They were dressed in visored caps and knee-length "kaftans." After that we referred to them as "okhotnoriadtsy," by which term we meant the very dull man-in-the-street who inclined toward the Black Hundreds. In the front of the crowd, the standard-bearers carried a large portrait of the tsar and some other figures or icons which I could not make out. The crowd shouted something and sang—I do not think it was a hymn—and knocked the caps off bystanders who did not have time to bare their heads. I confess that I was afraid for my intelligentsia derby hat, and I turned into the nearest side street. The crowd, which seemed rather thin, passed by. This was one of the first, comparatively innocent manifestations of Trepov's "strong-arm" response to the imperial manifesto.

Witte and the Kadets

WITTE'S APPEARANCE in the public arena created an entirely new political situation. Our naive and hostile opponents reproached the Kadets, and especially me personally, for not knowing how to take advantage of this situation and, thereby, for leading Russia to revolution. In our critics' opinion, the political struggle ended with the publication of the October Manifesto; henceforth, the strategy was to collaborate with the powers that be. The Kadets, they said, rejected collaboration and continued the struggle, thereby undermining the good intentions of the tsarist government and provoking its resistance and reaction.

The whole history of events, both before and after, serves as a clear refutation of this view. It was no accident that this view arose from the attitude of that circle of moderate-liberal Muscovite old-timers which bore the name *Besedy* (Discussions). A young member, V. A. Maklakov, gave the circle a friendly description in an entire book of memoirs which was devoted precisely to this central question of the Kadet (and especially Miliukov's) responsibility for losing the opportunity to achieve peaceful political evolution. The role which they ascribe to me is very flattering, and I cannot and do not want to deny the position which serves as a target for my opponent's arrows. It is true that I played a certain role in determining the Kadet policy, and if my opponents consider that role significant, then I can only derive moral satisfaction from that fact. Maklakov's detailed criticism follows our ("my") behavior step by step and takes up hundreds of pages. Obviously I cannot answer it here with an equally detailed polemic. I did devote an entire article to it in *Sovremennye Zapiski* and several satirical columns in *Poslednie Novosti*. I can only set forth the facts here as they relate to me personally. It will not be out of place, however, to mention several facts which dominated the situation. In the first place, reconciling ourselves with the tsarist government by no means meant leading it or even changing its intentions. Even if the first favorite, Witte, would have agreed to this, the tsar was still there, be-

54

hind him, and the tsar's "immutable will" concerning his regime, and his treatment of his leading "Moors," are only too well known. In the second place, the experiment which they demanded that we perform (if indeed they did demand it of us at that time), and which they now condemn us for neglecting, was performed by those same critics of ours in their struggle against us. I considered it our special merit that Russian society followed our example and rushed to organize itself into political parties. At that time, the nearest party to the right of us was the party of the "October Manifesto." The "Octobrists" set for themselves precisely that task which they insisted that we carry out; namely, to come to an agreement with the tsarist government and lend it "support."[14] Indeed, could the Octobrists themselves carry out their own task? And if not, then what were the obstacles? Were they not the same ones that stood—or would have arisen—in our own path? They answered us: but it was you who had the authority over public opinion, and you should have exerted your influence in it. Our answer was obvious: our authority was a consequence of our political stand, and it would have fallen immediately to the level of the "Octobrists" had we adopted their policy. I am ready to admit that the political demands of many of my colleagues were greatly excessive. It was possible to influence them in the direction of moderation, however, only through political education and experience. In fact, I made this my personal task, as will be seen later. Such education required time and especially the experience which was rapidly being piled up by events. We could decide the limits of compromise only at the given moment. No matter how rapidly these "moments" followed one another, at the end of 1905 they only began to affect political tactics. They required a reciprocal movement from the other side. When such response was not forthcoming, Russia had to travel that same road by which she had just arrived at the October Manifesto, namely, by the combination of liberal tactics with the threat of revolution. Witte was appointed for the purpose of suppressing the "sedition," while we were supposed to use ourselves for that purpose. What was supposed to happen, did in fact happen: through their own fault, the "sedition" of the leftists was crushed, without our help.

From what has been said, it is apparent why we ended up to the left of Witte in 1905, not only by our temperament but also by reasoned calculation. In the next section I will explain why we ended up to the right of the leftists. It was between these two limits that we at last found our identity; we became that group, which, through no choice of ours, was given the appropriate nickname "Kadets." Henceforth, we were recognized by our own passport. We shall see later that even this level of political maturity was not achieved right away.

We guided ourselves by reality. Our critics were clutching a phantom, and history left them behind.

Before all else, however, we must get to know Witte, the dominant figure of the time. I will speak about this powerful man in the way I myself understood him. He was a rare Russian genius with all the merits of and the great defects of his type. He stood head and shoulders above the whole ruling clique, through which he had to clear his own path to action. Action was the first demand of his nature. Like all natural geniuses, Witte was an encyclopedist. He could undertake anything; he learned through practice and disdained bookish affectations. With his great common sense he immediately distinguished the primary from the secondary and went directly toward the goal which he had set. He knew how to save everything useful which he found along the way; and he cast away everything that he knew was unnecessary: people, knowledge, advice, backstage intrigues, all those who were faithless, envious, or hostile. He had a wonderful knack for finding those people who were needed at any time, and he could organize their efforts, make them work for him and for his goal of that particular moment. He must have possessed great ability, because the deeds he undertook were on a large scale. His self-confidence grew with his successes; he assumed a commanding tone, and he strengthened his resistance to everything alien or inimical. In the event of failure, he became impassioned and unjust. Witte never blamed himself; he slandered people and hated his enemies. If he ran into an obstacle which he could not overcome, he immediately became discouraged, the ground began to slip from under him and he threw himself into some devious path, ready to commit unseemly acts. In the end, he stepped down, offended, piling up incriminating material for posterity. Witte was never at a loss when it came to justifying himself.

The Court milieu in which Witte was forced not so much to act as to find support for his actions, had always been ill-disposed towards him. In those circles, they looked upon Witte—and Witte even considered himself—as a stranger and newcomer from a more democratic land, and, therefore, as a suspicious and even dangerous person. For his part, Witte treated this official circle of dignitaries with a hardly concealed contempt, to which they in turn responded with forced politeness (while Witte was in favor) and concealed animosity. Under Alexander III, Witte's favorable position was helped by his particular characteristics. Witte's crude manner and coarse speech impressed the emperor and suited his simple mentality. Witte's simplified explanations were comprehensible to Alexander, his persistence was convincing, and the originality and boldness of his financial and economic

policies were justified by obvious successes. All this changed under
Nicholas II, especially because of the tsarina. The tsar's weak will
and the tsarina's evil will clashed with Witte's determined character
and resolute action. The clarity of Witte's goals and his readiness to
achieve them oppressed and embarrassed the emperor's eternally unprepared and timid mind. The pressure began to be felt as coercion
and evoked a growing resistance. The tsar became impatient, his face
and eyes turned into an impenetrable mask. Finally, influenced by
the fortuitous intuition of some genuinely "privy" councilor, the tsar
decided everything with a sudden refusal, in writing, to cooperate
with yesterday's favorite. In his bills of indictment for posterity, Witte
painstakingly, with documentation, traced all the secret passages
which led to the tsar's passivity. Witte himself was not averse to
using the same methods. In his *Memoirs*, when there was already
nothing left to hope for, Witte threw caution to the winds, and, without the slightest hesitation heaped choice words of abuse on this main
culprit of his unsteady rises and falls.

Witte's third and next rise came in September and October of
1905, under the most urgent circumstances. They summoned him
again, because it was impossible to do otherwise. He had just concluded an honorable peace which put an end to the "childish" and
"criminal" (his words) war against the "macaques" which had been
undertaken against his resolute resistance. This time he was summoned to tame the revolution. In the eyes of the "camarilla," his
"left-wing" reputation made him some sort of an expert on revolutionary secrets. Ill-wishers even rumored that he was planning to
shove the tsar aside so that he could become the president of a Russian republic. As though he were a monopolist, Witte could fix his own
conditions; his previous successful rises taught him to be cautious
and to secure his rear while taking the most resolute steps. He could
afford to make bold proposals: either I or a dictatorship—because
there were no candidates available for a dictatorship. As is already
known, the grand duke, Nikolai Nikolaevich with a revolver in his
hand, forced the tsar to sign the October Manifesto.[15] In those days,
with equal haste and urgency, Witte openly flaunted the word "constitution" before the tsar—a word which in normal times was inad-
missible. Witte was prepared to take it upon himself to carry out the
imperial promises in case the tsar, according to his habit, would refuse to do so. Witte would proclaim these promises in the form of his
own "most humble report," and with the tsar's approval, he would have
it published. In the report, the mission of carrying out the tsar's
promises would be entrusted to a "unified cabinet" which would place
the premier above the rivalry of his colleagues. If the tsar should

change his mind, then his servant would take the blame. Unexpectedly for Witte, however, the tsar detected a cunning, vile trick in Witte's ministerial humility. Witte wanted to take credit himself for the merits of the imperial concessions: better that the credit should go directly to the tsar. The tsar, himself, would immediately turn the promises into facts by giving the people what had been promised; the servant's "report" would be replaced by the emperor's "manifesto."

Such advice, no doubt, was given to Nicholas II by D. N. Trepov. I suspect that this is so, because Trepov subsequently gave the same advice to me. This curious contest between the minister's "caution" and the emperor's "magninimity" lasted for five whole days. Of course, the tsar's will was victorious. The victors had hoped to outwit Witte by throwing out of the prepared manifesto the reference to the "legislative power" of the state Duma, for in the term "legislative power" was hidden the term "constitution." Here Witte took a firm stand. True, this promise was not put into the manifesto project by him, but by Prince Obolensky, who "caught fire" easily and who knew better than Witte the basic demands of society. In Witte's own report, "constitution" was veiled by the phrase "the ascertained political views of the majority of Russian society."

Witte was victorious in his ultimatum; there were no longer any obstacles from above. But his political amateurism was shown by the fact that he completely failed to foresee the obstacles from below, from the public itself. When his previous rises had been frustrated from above, he was accustomed to receiving the fullest cooperation from below, from those public figures to whom he turned for help. It was worth their while to "nod to the caliph for an hour," and they showed themselves completely ready to serve his aims. It is true that their help turned out to be useless after the reorganizations outlined in the Manifesto of December 12, 1904,[16] went into effect. Moreover, the work of the agricultural committees which Witte had created in order to investigate the needs of the agrarian industry acquired a political significance in the hands of his colleagues that turned out to be dangerous for him. The Zemstvo Constitutionalists even used the committees' findings for one of their important publications. But this time, there was no such danger. All the same, "politics" was the order of the day, and it seemed to Witte that the cooperation of public figures in carrying out the "political views of the majority" was merely a matter of course. Obviously, the limits of cooperation were defined by the scope of the "report," by the procedure indicated in the report, and by the limits permitted in the tsar's manifesto. However, Witte met with a series of surprises, proving that he was unaware of the public mood at the time: it was not at all the same as it was when

Witte had freely used the professional knowledge of professors and other experts.

In his *Memoirs* Witte gave a detailed account of how he gathered his information about political attitudes and demands before October 17. The motley composition of his random informants was enough to show how far he was from the centers of Russian political life. The most important in this series of informants was the military professor Kuzmin-Karavaev, an ambitious man who proved his worth by his intrigues in the Tver Zemstvo. Next came the modernistic journalist, M. O. Menshikov, who, though a Judas, was endowed with a great flair for his work. Third on the list was the reactionary Prince Meshchersky, who had served as an influential advisor to Alexander III and who published the state-subsidized *Grazhdanin*, the indispensable newspaper of the tsars. It is significant that such diversely selected informants arrived at one and the same conclusion: Russia demands a constitution. At first, Witte did not follow this route. On the contrary, he summoned D. N. Shipov, surely aware that since the congress of November 1904, Shipov had declared himself against granting a constitution. Witte also summoned A. I. Guchkov, who had recently split with the majority of the Zemstvo-City Congress. In Shipov, Witte came upon an honest man who explained to him that together with Guchkov they were preparing a minority party (the future Octobrists), and that he, Shipov, would only join a ministry which genuinely represented all of public opinion and only when he would be given a more responsible post than that of state comptroller, which he had been offered. Guchkov was not so much repulsed by these ideological considerations as he was by the possible scandal which might result if such a discredited figure as P. N. Durnovo were appointed the head of the police in Witte's cabinet. Shipov showed Witte where he should turn: to the Bureau of Zemstvo Congresses. Shipov then named the candidates for the respective posts: S. A. Muromtsev for minister of justice; I. I. Petrunkevich for minister of the interior; and Prince G. E. Lvov for minister of agriculture. Concerning Moromtsev and Lvov, an old friend of Shipov's, the information was good and Witte summoned them by wire from Moscow, where the Bureau of Congresses was scheduled to meet precisely at that time.

The bureau had not yet come together when the telegram arrived. Those members who were present hastened to take advantage of the invitation and immediately sent a delegation. Petrunkevich was absent; his place was taken by Prince Lvov, a leader in the Zemstvo and a person who, though silent in difficult situations, was nobody's fool. The second member of the delegation, just as reticent but unbending in his political convictions, was F. A. Golovin, the future chairman of the Second Duma. The third member was F. F. Kokosh-kin, the party ideologist. The role of speaker for the delegation was given tc him. S. A. Muromtsev was intentionally avoided, and not without reason, because of his complaisance. With such members, the delegation did not represent the ministerial candidates which Witte had expected; rather they were the consultants sent to prepare a pre-liminary report to the Zemstvo "bureau" concerning Witte's intentions and proposals. The delegates were authorized to do no more than to inform Witte about the political program of the Zemstvo Constitution-alists. Kokoshkin clearly stated the provisions which at that time were generally accepted: a Constituent Assembly elected by "four-tail" elec-tions and empowered to work out the "Fundamental Law" of the state. The situation was ambiguous, since two of the delegates were, in effect, already members of a party, but the party as such had not passed such resolutions. Kokoshkin's declaration corresponded com-pletely to the spirit of the party as it was defined in an editorial in the first issue of Osvobozhdenie, with an amendment in No. 13 for universal suffrage. October 17, however, had created a new situation and the party had not yet had time to react. In order to shift the responsibility from themselves, the delegates stipulated that a report of their declaration to Witte be published in Russkie Vedomosti. When this was, indeed, done, their mission came to an end. I was present in F. A. Golovin's apartment in Moscow when the delegation was hur-riedly appointed. I can testify that even though the haste and the very election of the delegates itself was beyond the competence of those few gathered there, the question of authorization did not arise. To that extent, everyone understood that the delegation was not carrying some sort of "ultimatum" and that the summons did not mean the be-ginning of negotiations about ministerial posts. Rather, it was under-stood that the delegation had the simple aim of gathering information for a report to the Bureau of Congresses. If you prefer, the hasty election of the delegation did have an ulterior motive: not to allow obligations to be assigned prematurely and not to make any promises, in view of the uncertainty of the situation and the probability that Witte, the temporary master of the situation, had ulterior motives of his own.

Witte was not sure precisely whom he was addressing and he had no idea about the party affiliation of the members of the delegations or about party currents and programs in general. He, therefore, under-stood Kokoshkin's statement in the only way he could: as something new, which was neither in the "manifesto" nor in his "most humble report"; consequently, it did not suit him at all. The declarations un-tied his hands: one alternative at least was excluded, and Witte returned to his starting place—another summons to Shipov and Guchkov. But again Witte met with disappointment. Shipov repeated in writing his previous arguments against accepting a ministerial post in spite of the fact that Witte had already obtained the tsar's approval for the appointment. As if that were not enough, Shipov was granted a personal audience with the tsar, without Witte's knowledge, in order to explain to Nicholas in person his reasons for refusing the post. The tsar admitted that Shipov was "right," and with that, Witte's whole manuever fell through. His stockpile of available ministers was exhausted; and he had to look elsewhere for members of his "unified cabinet."

Witte also conducted interviews with the representatives of the press, to whom he had turned once before, on the occasion of his mission to America.[17] But here, too, a surprise was in store for him. It was only during the interview with the Petersburg press that Witte learned of the existence of the "unions" and that the entire press was united in one of them. Witte also learned that the press was already carrying out the decisions of the "union" regarding unauthorized activity—without censorship. These statements, made by Propper, the owner of *Birzhevki*, were confirmed by the silence of all those who showed up for the interview. Instead of listening to Witte, Propper presented him with "insolent demands, the wrong demands, the wrong statements" and in an unduly familiar tone which immediately outraged Witte. Whoever knew Propper can easily picture the premier's indignation. The publisher of *Birzhevki* began straight away, "We do not believe the government one bit." He then presented "demands," which were in no way within the particular competence of the press, summarized the general program of the left-wing groups, called for the removal of the troops from the capital and their replacement by a militia, universal amnesty, and Trepov's discharge. ("In order not to appear weak," Witte recalled, "I was forced to let him go for two weeks.") Witte concluded that the press was "demoralized," that it had gone mad; "it was impossible to rely on it." It was even worse than the delegation from the Zemstvo Bureau. This source too was now closed; the entire press was written off as belonging to the enemy's camp.

There was one more recourse: the liberal professors with whom Witte was generally on friendly terms. It is only by chance that we know of Witte's encounter in those early days with Professor Petrazhitsky and I. V. Hessen, the editor of *Pravo*. After midnight on October 24, both of these men called on Witte at his home in order to gain assurance that the bloodshed of January 9 would not be repeated at the Technological Institute, where a demonstration had already been started. Witte greeted his late visitors in his nightshirt, reprimanded them for their inopportune visit, and informed them that he had already obtained some concessions from Trepov. Having assumed his share of responsibility himself, he then turned to theirs, and was most embarrassed when he found out that the extremist parties themselves had called off the demonstration. It followed, therefore, that their authority was more effective than the dictator's mediation.

There then followed a discussion on political topics, from which the visitors concluded that Witte was "swallowed up by the events of the day" and that "he completely failed to realize that the focus of the struggle will be the question of the competence of the State Duma." To Witte's naive answer that this was the business of the Duma itself, they explained that "in such case the Duma will be converted into a Constituent Assembly." Hearing this, Witte immediately became aroused "as if he had just regained his senses." (This was after his meeting with the delegation from the Bureau of Congresses.) Then something totally unexpected happened. Jurists had come to him, and it was sufficient for him to ask them "to compose a draft of the fundamental laws for him." Only Witte's motives, however, were unexpected; his goal was clear, and typical of him. The proposal was consistent with Witte's "report." On October 24, 1905, Witte already foresaw February and April of 1906. What he did not foresee was that the "Fundamental Laws" (a deliberate rephrasing of the term "constitution") would be drafted without his participation and by specialists of a different kind. For their part, Petrazhitsky and Hessen were aware of the "delicate position" in which Witte's proposition had placed them; they declined the offer and hurriedly took their leave.

Returning to Petersburg, I managed to take part in one episode of Witte's search for public figures to fill his cabinet. My role was connected with the invitation to E. N. Trubetskoy to become Minister of Public Education. Upon arriving in Petersburg, Trubetskoy turned to the circle around Pravo to discuss his candidacy. Evidently, he wanted to accept the offer, and he looked to us for approval. I came out strongly against it, not only because I considered Trubetskoy unsuitable for this role but also, I admit, because his acceptance would be a violation of the general political line which we had taken. Moreover, Witte himself came to the same conclusion because of the candidate's personality. "I need a minister," he said, "and they sent me some sort of a Hamlet."

By the end of October and beginning of November 1905, the general negative attitude (not only that of our party) toward cooperation with Witte's "constitutionalism" could be considered perfectly clear. I, too, got my turn to talk to Witte in those days. He did not invite me as a prospective candidate for his cabinet; rather, he wanted some sort of expert advice on the general political situation and the possible ways out of it. I considered myself bound to accept the invitation as well as to express myself with complete frankness. Independent of the party's struggle, I had formed a mixed judgment of Witte. With all his inexperience and conceit, he was still the greatest of all the Russian Government officials. In my opinion he was the only one who was capable of viewing objectively the difficulties of his own position. I felt sorry for him, because I sensed that he could not get the better of those difficulties and that he would turn out to be a "caliph for an hour" just as the others had.

My story of our conversation was printed in 1921 and evoked a captious criticism from V. A. Maklakov. I cannot avoid returning to it now, both because I consider it important for my overall political conceptions and because, while writing these memoirs, my own earlier account again came to my attention. I had written that version at the request of a foreign press agency (*Correspondance Russe*) not fifteen years, but one and a half months after the actual conversation. Naturally, it was less intimate than the later version I wrote for "my own people." Nevertheless, it conveys more fully and clearly the course and content of the conversation. Reconstructing the conversation now, I will make use of both sources, which complement each other quite well.

Witte received me on the main floor of the Winter Palace, where the windows faced out on the Neva, in a room that seemed more like a vast hallway. Our talk began in the same way that Propper had begun his "insolent" discussion. "Why don't the leading public figures come to Witte?" My answer, of course, was the same as Propper's: "They do not come because they do not believe." What can be done so that they will believe? The government must not limit itself to promises; it must carry them out immediately. The first steps can be taken without waiting for society's cooperation. Pick out as ministers those who are serious and not discredited in the eyes of the public; or choose other members from the administration. Form a temporary, "working" cabinet from them, and begin work at once. This idea had already been expressed during the hasty discussion of tactics at our Constituent Congress; it was nothing new, and it demanded no special wisdom. Witte had, in effect, already started in this direction by inviting N. N. Kutler, a future member of our party, to be his deputy minister of agriculture and to draw up a "Kadet" agrarian project. I will return later to the consequences of this invitation.

On hearing my words about a "working cabinet" as a temporary substitute for the "public cabinet," Witte was suddenly transformed;

he jumped out of his chair, extended his clumsy hand and, shaking mine which I had extended to him in some bewilderment, loudly exclaimed: "At last I hear the first intelligent word. I'll do it!"

As the discussion continued, however, it became apparent that each of us had understood something different although we had used the same words. It was still not clear just what this "working cabinet" should do in order to merit the public's confidence. Here, too, I wanted to come as close as possible to the realistic possibilities. As to the problem of what should be done, I answered: If I were to speak to you as a party member, I would have to repeat what Kokoshkin told you in the name of the delegation from the Bureau of Congresses. I will not do this, however, because I realize that the path which the party recommends would be too involved and time consuming for you. "Given the present critical situation, it would be much too risky to bring Russia back to normalcy by means of three-stage elections: (1) A defective (in our opinion) election of a Duma which would then draw up a correct (in the sense of universal suffrage) electoral law; (2) the election of a Constituent Assembly on the basis of this law; (3) the election of a normal legislative body based on a charter to be promulgated by the Constituent Assembly." Of course, not even one of these three stages, by which the party hoped to lead Russia to constitutionalism, was in Witte's mind. I agreed that such a path was "fraught with jolts and catastrophes," thereby admitting that it was unacceptable to the government (and dangerous for us). However, once the government had decided to give Russia a constitution, then "it would be best to announce this openly and directly and to grant immediately a charter liberal enough to satisfy society at large." I pointed out to Count Witte that the Bulgarian constitution, which was clearly acceptable to the Russian people, might serve as a model for such a charter, or if not the Bulgarian, then perhaps the Belgian or some other constitution guaranteeing universal suffrage. I also pointed out that "the draft of such a constitution has already been worked out by the Zemstvo Congress." Dramatizing and simplifying my words, I expressed myself graphically: "Call in somebody today and order him to translate into Russian either the Belgian or, better yet, the Bulgarian constitution. Tomorrow, present the translation to the Tsar for his signature; and the day after tomorrow, publish it." I was sharply reproved by my critics for this "simplification." Of course, Witte understood what I meant by "today," "tomorrow," and "the day after." Instead of giving me a direct answer, he started to oppose my views by the most twisted and mutually contradictory arguments. First, "society will no longer be satisfied with a constitution handed down from above." I did not know it then, but it was the preparation of just such "fundamental laws" which Witte wanted to entrust to Professor Petrazhitsky and I. Hessen. Witte turned out to be more radical than I was. I reassured him: "Society will not be satisfied because, above all, society does not believe that the bureaucracy would grant such a liberal constitution. If, however, such a constitution were granted, society would make noise for a while and then calm down." Then Witte made exactly the opposite objection: "The people do not want a constitution!" This, at least, was more sincere. I have already spoken of the government's intentions to create a representative body dominated by a majority of obedient peasants. That was, in reality, the persistent ulterior motive in drafting the electoral laws for the Duma. We know this from the memoirs of Kryzhanovsky, the man who drafted those electoral laws. Although I was struck by Witte's vagaries (these lines were written in 1905),[18] I did not tell him that by using such arguments he was undoing everything that he had done and that he was creating doubts as to his intentions. I merely objected that the matter at hand was still the same as what he had called a constitution "by legal means" in his "report" to the tsar. If Witte really did have such a constitution in mind, and if the people were really so much accustomed to the rule of the tsar, then, obviously, the people would be more easily reconciled to a constitution given by the tsar, than to a charter issued by a restricted and improperly elected Duma. Assuming that Witte really wanted to grant Russia a constitution, he would have no objections to the above argument. But this was yet to be clarified. Just after he visited Witte, my old friend, Paul Boyer, told me the reason for Witte's evasiveness. Witte frankly admitted to Boyer that the tsar did not want a constitution. He told the same thing to Petrunkevich, but the situation had changed since that time by the publication of the manifesto. I wanted a direct answer from Witte, and I asked him point blank: "If your power is sufficient to do so, then why do you refuse to utter the decisive word 'constitution'?" Witte was already cooled by my proposals and he answered me in a disappointed tone, tersely and dryly, but equally directly: "I cannot because the Tsar does not wish it." This was what I had been waiting for—the short point of all the long speeches. I ended our talk with words which I still remember clearly: "Then it is useless for us to talk. I cannot give you any sensible advice."

My critics severely reproached me for placing so much stress on the "word" when its "content" had already been conceded. But that was precisely the point: the content had not been conceded, and the refusal to utter the "word" plus all the subsequent events were evidence of this fact. The stubborn reluctance to utter this irrevocable "word" showed that behind the alleged concession, the hope—and not only the hope but the certainty—was hidden that when the revolutionary tornado subsided, it would then be possible to get rid of both the concessions and their author. Another "word" would then be loudly proclaimed, a word which under one pretext or another had been preserved in the "Fundamental Laws": the word, "autocrat." In both cases, the question involved more than a mere sound, more than mere vibrating waves of air. There are some words which sound like magic and which chill the blood; and there are other words, the same kind of word-symbols, which cause blood to flow, civil wars to be fought, and regimes to arise and be shattered. When our opponents, who by then had become everyone's enemies, began to use word-shibboleths which charmed the masses, simple words like peace, land, rights of labor, class struggle, we had nothing to oppose to them. Our words were taken from us: constitution, rights, law, equality. There was no "constitution"; "revolution" had come instead. The "revolution" was a fact, while the "constitution" was only the un-realized hope of the hated "class." We had nothing with which "to entice" the blood, so the transition from one form of violence to another naturally occurred. That is why I so stubbornly insisted on uttering the "word." Its content was the aim of my political struggle. Without it, the struggle became a senseless game. Convinced that the "word" was not going to be spoken, I told Witte essentially the same thing I told Plehve three years before. *Hic Rhodus, hic salta!* If not, then not: if you cannot, you simply cannot! The struggle will continue; but, alas, the weapons have been knocked from our hands.

V. A. Maklakov, who witnessed my "scolding" of the October Manifesto at the Literary Circle banquet, reproachfully recalled the final sentence of my speech: "Nothing has changed; the war continues." I did not remember the words, but I could well have spoken them, expressing as they do, not only my own feelings at the time but also that of a great many people. Yes, the war continued; but whom could we lean on for support? Those who did not believe the war had ended, naturally turned to that force which had led to the October Manifesto itself. The words of the Latin poet became an everyday expression: *flectere si nequeo superos Acheronta movebo,* if I cannot budge the gods, I shall move Acheron. The term "Acheron," which signified the revolutionary masses, was in great use at that time as a way of avoiding the attention of the censors. The born swimmers of the Acheron continued to pursue their own aims, but the question was still whether or not to cooperate with them, even though I considered such cooperation to be a guarantee of our mutual success. As can be seen from my conversation with Witte, I considered that, as far as we

were concerned, tactics should be less uncompromising, if we wanted
to continue the struggle by peaceful means—the only means available
to us. With this in mind, I took part in the next Zemstvo-City Congress,
which convened on November 7, 1905, the anniversary of the November Congress of 1904.

I already mentioned the ambiguous mood of the preceding (September) congress which passed thoroughly revolutionary resolutions,
but displayed extreme caution when it came to means for carrying
them out. That congress finally adopted a temporizing stand, but now
the situation was more definite. Once and for all, the congress had to
define its attitude toward Witte's policy. Witte himself provided the
occasion for this when he turned to the congress, as if appealing to
the declaration of the "bureau's" delegation. Witte seemed to indicate
by this move that he still needed public support, and he knew from
Shipov that another party was being formed from the members of
the congress, a party which lay to the right of the Kadets. What he
did not know was that the Kadet party had retained its majority at
the congress. He also did not know that the November Congress, which
had a mixed political composition, was the last one before such
congresses were definitely replaced by distinct political parties. Witte
hoped that this time the Zemstvoists would send more conservative
representatives to the congress. He even proposed that the congress be
held in Petersburg (just as Sviatopolk-Mirsky had done), and he expected the Zemstvo Congress to give the government's policy a vote
of confidence. Evidently, some of the members of the congress had
made such promises to him, and those promises were supposed to be
fulfilled at the congress itself. The newspaper *Rus* even expressed the
wish that the congress would be transformed into something like a
provisional government under Witte. From the other side, the S. D.'s,
as well, demanded that the "liberals" of the congress declare themselves to be a provisional "coalition" government. Such was the great
muddle of political ideas just a few months before the convocation of
the First State Duma.

Contrary to Witte's expectations and the intentions of the minority,
the November Congress upheld its established tradition. First of all,
it met in Moscow, not in Petersburg, and thereby underscored its
independence. The new participants, very few in number even including those from Petersburg, were able to form a majority with
other delegates at the congress. They only succeeded in reinforcing
the attitudes of the right-wing minority. The majority preserved its
party unity. The congress might have had doubts about the unauthorized delegation from its "bureau"; but instead of repudiating it,
the congress confirmed the delegation's purely informative role, as

indeed it should have. For its part, the congress adopted several decisions consistent with the current situation and aimed at facilitating an agreement with the state should negotiations with Witte be continued. This, in essence, was the political significance of the congress.

I took an active part in preparing these decisions. I managed to incorporate my point of view into them, and I could therefore view these decisions as a personal success in my efforts to make the party's tactics more realistic. It is true that my success was far from complete, since, in fact, even my personal opinions had not yet become sufficiently realistic. Thus, the decisions of the congress were not destined to acquire practical significance. Still, these decisions for the first time revealed the political face of the party and contributed to the party's self-identification.

The congress offered several decisions which tended to soften the sharper and purely theoretical edges of the party's tactics. In some sense, this was a continuation of my conversation with Witte. Most important of all, the congress decided to combine a "proper and logical application of the constitutional principles of the Manifesto with (1) the immediate publication of an act on the applicability of universal, direct, equal and secret elections in the convocation of the (first) representative body; and (2) with the formal transfer of constituent functions to this first gathering of the people's representatives for the purpose of drafting, with the Tsar's confirmation, the constitution of the Russian Empire." By this somewhat veiled formula, several important concessions were made, retreats from positions taken in Kokoshkin's statements. Of the three-stage elections of which I had spoken so disapprovingly to Witte, only one part remained. The preliminary convocation of a representative body elected according to Kryzhanovsky's electoral law was eliminated; but, on the other hand, a separate Constitutional Assembly was also rejected, and a republican character of this assembly was precluded by the demand for the "Tsar's confirmation" of the constitutional project worked out by the assembly. In addition, the chance of any purely constituent character for the assembly, elected on the basis of universal suffrage, was removed by the decision to entrust it with "the establishment of the basic principles of land reform and the enactment of necessary labor legislation." In other words, this assembly was entrusted with what was then called, "organic work." The assembly thus amounted to a normal, ordinary legislative body. As we shall see, the changes were quite radical. Of all this, the essential and most immediate issue of disagreement with the government was the application of universal suffrage to Russia's first and only elections. This proposal was shared even by the Kadets' right-wing rivals.

The subsequent proposals of the congress pursued a course that would not contradict the government's own views about the limits of its authority. "For the purpose of calming the country," the congress recommended that the government, "without waiting for the people's representatives" (even though this would be, in effect Witte's "working" cabinet), "should busy itself immediately with carrying out, within legislative norms, all the fundamental principles of political liberty" proclaimed in the October Manifesto. It was thereby recognized that legislative authority was in no way suspended while waiting for the Duma to be convoked. Next on the list of projects for immediate enactment came the abolitions of all exceptional, administrative legal procedures and capital punishment, amnesty, replacement of the old administration which had not been affected by the new principles, and, in particular, investigation of the pogroms which had sullied the days of popular rejoicing. The congress demanded that the administration and the police (as well as all public officials) be forced to answer for their guilt in the pogroms. A special delegation consisting of those persons whom Shipov had named on October 18 (Muromtsev and Petrunkevich, with Kokoshkin as the third) was supposed to explain and justify these proposals to Witte. If the government were favorably inclined there should have been, it would seem, no obstacles in the way of renewing negotiations with this delegation even on the basis of these proposals.

True, the right-wing minority was not satisfied. They introduced a specific proposal asking the congress to express its confidence in Witte. Even this proposal, which was defended by M. A. Stakhovich, was not defeated by the congress, but after all the debates and decisions, it took on a conditional meaning. "The government can rely on the support of the Zemstvo workers" the congress declared, "only in so far as it carries out the constitutional principles of the Manifesto correctly and consistently. The Zemstvo and City circles will meet any deviation from these principles with resolute opposition." Witte's personal telegram to Petrunkevich, appealing to the "patriotism" of public figures, did not help; nor did the efforts of Prince Pavel D. Dolgorukov, who considered it "necessary to lend Witte a helping hand." This was the voice from Besedy[19]—the voice of yesterday. The majority of the congress could not go that far without losing face.

The conciliatory character of the congress' decisions was emphasized and, of course, also condemned by the other side, that is, by the Social Democrats. Their delegation submitted a resolution to the congress which stated that "the only way out of the situation is to overthrow the government by means of an armed uprising and the convocation of a Constituent Assembly for the establishment of a democratic republic." The S. D. Committee considered the congress' attempt to enter negotiations with the government as a "shameful deal between the bourgeoisie and the government at the expense of the people's rights." Here was the voice of "Acheron" blaring at us and helping us find our own identity. Here, for the first time, the political boundary between us was definitely drawn.

But how was our attempt at self-identification met from Witte's side? His tactics were already far removed from those of the early October days. I had no doubt that our efforts had come too late and that, in spite of all our restraint, our proposals would prove to be insufficiently moderate. At any rate, we could not compete with our minority, and Witte could not help being irritated by the failure of that minority's proposals at the congress. I resolutely opposed sending a delegation, for fear that it would run into a direct refusal and be placed in a humiliating position. It turned out even worse. Witte simply refused to see the delegates and sent us a strong reprimand through the Council of Ministers. The government refused to "leave the path" charted in the manifesto. It was now impossible, he said, to publish the "laws"; only "temporary rules" could be issued. As for the "conditions of supporting the government by one party or another," the government "in the given situation is interested only" in society itself "taking into account the consequences of its reluctance to co-operate with the State in carrying out the principles of the Manifesto and preserving order." This is how the peaceful intentions of the congress were interpreted. This is how the hand extended to Witte was crudely thrust aside. Thus had the distance covered in one month been marked off, from the "attempt to realize the principles" with society's cooperation, to the true meaning of Witte's "maintenance of order." He could not have put it more clearly: we no longer need you.

Specifically, Witte not only no longer needed us but we actually became dangerous for him. He hoped to find support elsewhere. A kind of "countercongress" was undertaken which would finally express the "true" attitudes of the Zemstvos and cities and which would grant Witte that "confidence" on credit which would save him from the growing distrust from above. The self-government boards received an official invitation from Witte which had the force of a command. Witte instructed them to elect four representatives each and to hold them in readiness in case they should be called. The newspaper Rus had already begun agitation for such a congress under Witte's leadership. However, the refusal of several of the Zemstvos to elect representatives together with the approaching elections to the Duma and the organization of the government party of October 17 prompted Witte to give up this all-too-obvious masquerade.

After our conversation, I met Witte only once again, one evening at a certain public meeting. He had been in retirement for some time and had fallen into disfavor. Noticing me, he made his way through the crowd toward me. He greeted me, recalled our first meeting, and spoke several words to me which I cannot help remembering. "It's too bad that I did not know you well then. Events might have gone differently." I would have been greatly flattered by this belated confession—if I had not known Witte's egocentrism. He lived the entire rest of his life in a passionate dream of returning to power in order to redo "in a second edition" that historical moment when, in his own words, they took him on "as a stop-gap" and cast him off, treating him "worse than a household servant." He wanted so much to finish what they had kept him from accomplishing (as he thought), or what he was never capable of doing (as others thought). In his declining years, the past must have appeared to him as a variant of the maxim: *"Si jeunesse savait; si vieillesse pouvait."* It is true that he lacked the knowledge; but he lacked the power as well.

The Kadets and the Leftists

IF THE LAST MONTHS of 1905 do not represent the denouement of the first Russian revolutionary drama, they at least bring it to the threshold of that denouement. The curve of revolutionary activity, brought artificially to its highest point, began to descend after December—to the unattentive eye imperceptibly at first, then ever more sharply. On the surface it seemed that the revolutionary movement was celebrating its first tangible successes. The supporters of the Acheron thought that they had gained a new arena for their struggle in the new representative body. At first, they carried on the struggle openly, but after the failure of the First Duma experiment, they worked clandestinely, although taking full advantage of the Second Duma. On the surface, flirtation with our "friends on the left" continued, but it gradually cooled as our "friends" became more and more our "friendly enemies." My hopes for collaboration between the constitutional and revolutionary movements, as a condition of mutual success, turned out to be an unrealizable dream, and together with that dream perished also the cause of our common struggle. I have had attributed to me the following proposal to our left-wing competitors, which I supposedly made during the preelection polemics: "You make the thunder and lightening backstage, and we will carry out the struggle for both of us on stage." This, of course, was a caricature of our tactics. The situation was rather the reverse: the thunder and ligthening were made by them on stage, and while they were mere playful noises, they undermined the struggle for real achievements.

It is the concern of history to describe in detail how all this happened. However, since my autobiography is so closely intertwined with events, I will be forced in places to touch upon not only their general traits but also their details. We are approaching one of the most important moments in modern Russian history, and the testimony of one of the participants will not be superfluous.

I have already spoken about our Kadet attitude to the government of October 17. At that time, it was up to us to choose our political stance vis-à-vis the government. For the reasons mentioned above, we consciously let that moment slip by. One might argue, as do our political opponents on the right, that we made a mistake. But while our opponents, who did not make our "mistake," ended their game in a draw and paid for it with their political reputation, we finished the year with an offer of honorable compromise. Witte crudely repulsed our offer. Rather than rely on the uncertain prospects of conscientious collaboration with the real Russian public, Witte preferred to fight for the preservation of his personal position "at the top"—a goal which in the end turned out to be no less uncertain. As for our relationship with the leftists, the choice of political stance was theirs, not ours. They were the ones who chose to end the year with a sharp refusal to cooperate with us. As a result, their tactics met with a crushing defeat. Our recent allies from the League of Liberation and its branches played no small role in creating the abyss between us and the leftists. But the main reason for the abyss was the ideological changes that had taken place among the socialists themselves.

I spoke before about the polemics between us and the monopolists of the proletariat from the new anti-Leninist *Iskra*. At that time I had not yet learned about the appearance of another, even more irreconcilable trend, the Leninist "Jacobins" who were striving to wrest the leadership from the "Girondists-neo-Iskraists." I knew nothing of the London "Third Congress" in May, the first all-Bolshevik congress. At that congress the general front of the "Liberationist" movement adopted the slogans of universal suffrage and the Constituent Assembly, and then, with the Mensheviks absent, went on to outline the next step—the complete victory of the "democratic worker-peasant dictatorship." This dictatorship was supposed to come about as the result of a successful armed uprising which would overthrow the autocracy, with its nobility and officials, and replace it by a democratic republic, with a revolutionary "Provisional Government" at the helm. The S. D.'s would join this government in order to "pressure" it not only from the "bottom" but also from the "top." It would still be a bourgeois-democratic state, but, together with the necessary cooperation of the world revolution, its existence would facilitate the transition to socialism in Russia. Here, in embryonic form, was the whole Leninist program of 1917. It radically opposed the bourgeois "treachery" and the destruction and restriction of the revolution by an "atrophied constitution," especially when the adamant government was reluctant even to consider that constitution. Given such a left-wing position, "bourgeois democracy" not only refused to approve further cooperation but, on the contrary, rejected cooperation on principle in order "not to tie our hands" to extreme leftist tactics.

It must be admitted that the simplified projection of Leninist geometric lines into a political vacuum, because of their general comprehensibility and the absolute form of their assertions and demands, was to have a much more powerful effect on the masses than the tortuous resolutions, filled with bourgeois reservations, which the Mensheviks meeting in Geneva counterposed to the decisions of the Third Congress in London. The subtleties of this internecine struggle among the S. D.'s simply did not reach us in time. Only at the end of July did Lenin publish his comments comparing the Bolshevik and Menshevik resolutions in a sensational pamphlet called *Two Tactics*. The disagreement over the "two tactics" had managed to smooth over somewhat by October. The chief difference was not so much in their slogans, but in the means to be used in their realization. What Lenin already in May had boldly placed first on the agenda, the Mensheviks had left beyond the horizon of practical politics. By October and November, these slogans had not only shown themselves to be realistic but, with Trotsky's assistance, were even surpassed. He credited himself with the ideological innovation stating that a "provisional government" with a predominance of S. R.'s should be formed not after the victorious armed uprising, but in the very process of that uprising in order to guide it. In fact, this innovation became the cornerstone of the tactics of the Workers' Soviet, as Trotsky conceived it.

How could our "Liberationists" champion this new tactic which was formally opposed to the parliamentary tactics we had decided upon at our November Congress?

The League of Liberation consisted of very diverse political elements. This fact, as we know, not only hindered it from becoming a party itself but also from permitting the formation of a party from within its ranks. In the end, the six delegates from the Zemstvo Constitutionalists who were elected to the Council of the League (see above), all turned out to be the most faithful Kadets. For all practical purposes, they did not take part in the activities of the other half of the delegates, the "intellectuals." The group of "intellectuals" concentrated its activity in the Petersburg "Big Group" of the League of Liberation, which included the intermediaries who passed on current socialist party slogans to the League. In that way, the socialists managed to grab control of such Petersburg organizations as the Imperial Technical Society ("Salt Town") and the Imperial Free Economic Society, which subsequently became an arena for the S. D.'s. The "Big Group" spread its influence also to those professional unions of which its members were chairmen. In addition, the "Big

Group" had the controlling influence on the Union of Unions, after the latter created a separate Petersburg Union of Unions, which then merged with the Central Bureau of the All-Russian Union of Unions during the decisive October Days. In a word, this gemmation of the League of Liberation, together with assistance from groups of "sympathizers," spread its influence very wide, and, at the same time, contributed to its rapid leftward movement. The confirmed "Liberationists" themselves were divided into "reasonable" and "rash." Advocating preliminary "organization" of the revolution, the "reasonable" group struggled against the increasing leftward list and against efforts by the socialist party to introduce extremist revolutionary agitation among the workers. To the "reasonable" group belonged such figures as Prokopovich-Kuskova, Annensky, Bogucharsky, and Khizhniakov. The transitional role between the "reasonable" and the "rash" was played by the talented and highly gifted orator-"vulgarist," mining engineer, and organizer of large meetings, L. I. Lutugin. At "home" in the League of Liberation, he behaved "cleverly," like a shrewd politician; but when he found himself in front of a crowd (which he referred to as "lop-eared") he suddenly flared up and, transforming himself into a people's tribune, summoned the crowd to an immediate charge against the "strongholds." He ridiculed himself and his listeners in front of his intellectual allies, but he understood the significance of the "lop-eared" crowd and he forecast a bitter fate to his intellectual friends: "They'll crack your heads, comrades, and that'll be the end of you. Only your mouths will water." Here was the secret of this double role which he so talentedly and cleverly performed. A different role was played by such fanatics as the dull, limited, and narrow party lawyer, N. D. Sokolov, who faithfully transmitted the S. D. party commands to the League and the unions. And then there were the "sympathizers," like the silent Charnolussky with his eternal conspirator's face, and his inseparable friend, that intolerable windbag and liar, Falbork. (They were the ones who dragged me into the demonstration at Pavlovsk.) There were all kinds of people.

When the Constitutional Democratic party was formed in October (unexpectedly even for its own members), the motley union became extraordinarily agitated. The Kadets themselves thought that, due to the strike, the October Constituent Congress in Moscow was incomplete and that its decisions should be reexamined by the next congress. This, however, did not satisfy those who opposed the party's formation. As early as the end of October, there appeared in *Russkie Vedomosti* a communique announcing that the entire group of Moscow "Liberationists" was leaving the newly formed party. The Petersburg group acted no less decisively. With an expanded membership, the

"Big Group" convened after the Moscow Congress, intending to limit itself to an annulment of the decisions we had just passed. But after stormy debates, it rejected a simple postponement and decided not to join the party at all. The Zemstvo members of the league then had two talks with three "delegates" from the "Liberationist Secessionists." I took part in one of those talks, which was held in V. D. Nabokov's apartment, and according to I. V. Hessen's memoirs, I even took the role of the spokesman. It is interesting to note that Hessen wrote about me from his Petersburg point of view. He had never seen, he said, a more confused, a "more bitter and prejudiced attitude among our erstwhile comrades-in-arms." For Hessen, as chairman, "it was not easy to restrain raging passions." Perhaps, the real reason for this stormy state of affairs, he noted, was "the fact that the speaker was Miliukov, and that even at that time, his leading role appeared as tutelage, and he had thus become a barrier between the party and public opinion." Evidently, by "public opinion" Hessen meant the leftist Petersburg opinion from which the party wanted to separate itself. But the assertion that it was I who was the "barrier" because of my "tutelage" shows that they blamed me personally for what could be considered the rightward shift of the party. In the interests of the "leftward shift" and "charged with a high voltage current, the Petersburg members did not wish to break down the barrier between us." I do not want to deny that I was against this "current" and that I played a certain role in erecting this "barrier." From the opposite side, it was no coincidence that Witte regretted that he "did not know me very well" at that time. Both statements pointed in the same direction. I really did want to create a self-sufficient constitutional party, not dependent on anybody, which could play a worthy role in the Russian parliament, and without which a "parliament" could not exist. If my opponents exaggerated my successes, that was their business.

But what did they themselves want, pouncing on me for my "leading role"? Many mutually contradictory objections were raised at that same stormy meeting. Some demanded that the Kadets adjust their "parliamentary tactics" to fit their "revolutionary program." Others, on the contrary, preferred that the party move to the right, leaving its place to the leftists. Still others accused us of trying to occupy ministerial posts. I. I. Petrunkevich objected: "He is a soldier who does not want to be a general." I added, more moderately: "Well, that is still a long way off." The S. D.'s reserved the generals' posts for themselves in the armed uprising, just as they did the "seizure of power."

The more serious objections against the Kadet party centered around the fact that the party core was "Zemstvoist" and "bourgeois,"

that a more "popular party" should have arisen from the League of
Liberation. The protestors themselves knew that the formation of such
a party was impossible as long as we all represented a staff without
an army, and especially at a time when preliminary preparation of
worker and peasant cadres was still needed. The Kadets strove for
just such preparation; but even the "reasonable" ones cut the party
off from the possibility of penetrating into the popular depths by
considering these depths to be their own monopoly. Also, the immediate creation of a "purely popular party," "without socialism" but
with a Constitutional Democratic coloring, directly contradicted the
role which our leftist opponents were forced to play. "Don't go to the
Kadets," insisted Lutugin in his role as tribune-"vulgarizer." "They
rustle ballot sheets, but there are no ballot boxes," he quipped. I was
harshly rebuffed for using this "catchword" expression in one of my
articles, where I opposed the rustling of "ballots" to the force of
weapons. "Is it worth it to waste one's soul on fruitless parliamentarism? Come on, better sign up with the literacy committee." For the
Committee of Political Literacy, this would have been a still more
roundabout path.

Thus ended our ties with the League of Liberation. The League
followed ever more closely the line of the Petersburg Union of Unions
and even (by a misunderstanding, as I chose to believe) the road of
the Soviet of Workers' Deputies. Here and there, its direct participation
in the very creation of these organizations cannot be doubted, but a
formal split between us did not occur.

My own ties with the Union of Unions came to an abrupt end
at that meeting where the police took us from my apartment at
Udelnaia to Kresty. My very title of chairman was both inconvenient
and dubious. Was I elected chairman only for the Moscow Congress,
or was I "really" chairman? Of course, I did not object to either of
these interpretations. After my release from jail, the situation had
already changed so much, that, for me, cooperation with the Petersburg Union of Unions was completely out of the question. The S. D.'s
became dominant once and for all, and the joint sessions of the Central
Committee with the newly emerged Central Bureau (whose decisions
were binding only for Petersburg) lasted from October 21 to November 15. Several Liberationists were attracted to that group, but no
members of the Kadet party. I have before me now a packet of
Bulletins of this unified organization from the end of the year, containing all the fruits of their paper activity: "resolutions," "appeals,"
"proclamations"—most of which were totally unacceptable to us. They
were all about the same, and their content testified to the sad fact
of their loss of influence. No matter how hard the organization tried

to adapt itself to the tone and content of the revolutionary slogans, no matter how generously it promised the S. D.'s its sympathy and cooperation, its active role came too late and was pushed into the background. Meanwhile, the most extreme organization, the Soviet of Workers' Deputies, which guided the revolutionary movement of 1905, rose to its height. They simply stopped paying any attention to the Union of Unions in its final form, to its salutations, greetings, and adherence.

This was black ingratitude. A few people know that the Soviet of Workers' Deputies owed its very origin to that same League of Liberation and its Petersburg group, and not at all to Trotsky and the Mensheviks who claimed the role of founder. As they had done with the idea of the "banquets" and the idea of the Union of Unions, so did the Liberationists, after "Bloody Sunday," push forward and realize the idea of the Soviet of Workers' Deputies. For this purpose they made use of Shidlovsky's government committee, which had been appointed to conduct a study on the needs and demands of the workers. One of the workers' deputies who landed on the commission, Khrustalev, transferred his mandate to the intellectual Nosar. "Intellectual" speeches were heard in the committee; the officials noticed at once that "the deputies were controlled by the revolutionaries." The committee was consequently dissolved, and Nosar was banished from Petersburg. Nevertheless, the Liberationists brought him back and hid him. Some of the committee deputies who had been spared, then formed the "Soviet," and by the spring of 1905 they had expanded their membership to fifty or sixty. Meeting in the League of Liberation's illegal printing house or in private apartments of the members of the "Big Group," the Soviet of Workers' Deputies existed in this form until October. The first appeal to the factory and plan workers concerning the convocation of the new Soviet was printed in this printing house. At that point Nosar, who had hid himself in an empty railroad car and had spent the nights at the homes of the Liberationists, emerged from his hiding place and took the lead of the Soviet. The Soviet took over the lodgings of the Free Economic Society where the Liberationists had long since assumed a dominant position.

Together with the Mensheviks, the "liberal bourgeoisie" continued to consider the Soviet "an organ of revolutionary self-government." A. S. Suvorin knew better when he began to tease Witte in *Novoe Vremia,* saying that a "second government" stood near him. We have seen that this is just what Trotsky had planned. Trotsky himself came up with an explanation as to why the enterprise failed. It seems that Lenin "delayed his arrival from abroad," and without him, the Bolsheviks were "helpless." But Trotsky also had another explanation:

"All the elements of the victorious revolution were present, but these elements had not yet ripened." This was closer to the truth; but after he drew the conclusion from this admission that the "unripened" revolution could not be "victorious," Trotsky retreated to his final position: Maybe so, but the revolution is "permanent"; and if it still does not win, then it will establish new records, it will carry out "dress rehearsals," and sometime in the future it will win.

At last Lenin returned to Petersburg. Anonymously present in the galleries of the Free Economy, he saw immediately that "this is a talking shop," a "workers' parliament." We need an organ of power; we need a Bolshevik party organ to guide the impending revolutionary denouement. So the "battle organization" of the party undertook the preparation of the armed uprising.

How did the Kadets regard all of this? I already mentioned that there was much that we did not know. In particular, we did not notice that the leadership of the Soviet of Workers' Deputies was going over to the Bolsheviks. The Soviet's demand on the day after the publication of the October Manifesto that the "troops be removed from the city" and that "arms be distributed to the proletariat" seemed simply naive to us. The fiasco of the November strike for the eight-hour workday evoked our disapproval of further strikes, and the Mensheviks could still condemn their own left-wingers for "breaking with the bourgeoisie." The failure of the second, "political" strike—against the trial of the rebellious Kronstadt sailors and against introducing martial law into Poland—induced I. I. Petrunkevich to send a telegram to Witte requesting an end to martial law. Witte conceded. But we had to fix the limits of our "collaboration" somewhere because, with the Bolsheviks persistently preparing an armed uprising, such "collaboration" became more and more ambiguous. Among the youth, the slogan of an armed uprising now became just as compelling and was accepted in just as much a matter of course as the previous slogans of the Constituent Assembly and universal suffrage had been. I remember one small incident at one of the business sessions of the Free Economic Society. The very correct Count Heiden was chairman. The hall was filled with young people. An intellectual-looking derby hat traveled along the rows of the audience and, without the slightest embarrassment was passed on to the presidium on stage. Count Heiden took the hat, assumed an impenetrable gaze and passed it on to N. F. Annensky. Annensky's face lit up with one of his most joyous smiles. He passed the hat on to me. I spied a crumpled scrap of paper in the bottom of the hat, with the laconic inscription in pencil: "to a.u." Annensky leaned over and explained to me in a whisper: "This means, to the armed uprising!" I passed on the empty hat. Our presidium, which consisted of an Octobrist, a Kadet, and a Socialist Revolutionary, expressed their attitude differently, but in general they expressed something like friendly neutrality. A whole collection of such head pieces had been made at the factories.

And so what? Were we for it or against it? This time I got the opportunity to express myself personally and in print, and I thank my stars for this opportunity. By December, the time of the armed uprising in Moscow, I had become a journalist and an editor of a newspaper. During these months, newspapers appeared without prior approval, without any permission from above, and the interference from the censors was minimal. The reader may recall Propper's "arrogant tone" and the demands which he made to Witte concerning the removal of the troops and the formation of a popular militia. (This was the demand of the Soviet of Workers' Deputies.) Propper owned three newspapers which in common parlance were called *Birzhevki* (stockbrokers)—a morning paper, an evening paper, and a provincial paper. He was an entrepreneur with a flair, and he prided himself on the fact that he had gone "to Witte." He somehow felt that the wind was blowing in the direction of the Kadets, and he decided to place a stake on us by putting the least profitable of the three *Birzhevki* (the morning one) at our complete disposal. The leadership of the paper was to go to me, I. V. Hessen, and M. I. Ganfman. Only Ganfman was at that time a genuine newspaperman; we had to study still more. I boldly undertook the work. With Propper's consent, we fired all the old workers and staff. I was forced to spend the first few days (or rather nights) in those empty rooms standing by the type case, working as the maker-up, scanning piles of reported material which were brought in and checking the galley proofs. During the spare moments, I would sit myself down at the corner of the table to write an editorial or fill in the lacunae with brief articles and remarks on all possible topics. It was a hard school, but it served as my initiation into journalism. I added this third profession to my other two: historian and politician. My main teacher was M. I. Ganfman, a man of great knowledge in the journalistic world and incorruptible honor. He was more left-wing than we were, but he was not a party man, and in his professional work he put his own views to the side.

The newspaper existed only for a short time. At first it was called *Narodnaia Svoboda,* the same name as the party. Later, the paper was closed down for printing the financial-economic "manifesto" of the Soviet of Workers' Deputies. The paper reappeared under the name *Svobodnyi Narod,* and finally, on December 20, it was closed for the second time. Propper admitted that his experiment with us had failed, and he returned to his morning *Birzhevka.* Under the influence of the Sebastopol sailors' mutiny, Witte managed in these short weeks first to arrest Khrustalev-Nosar on November 26 and then, on December 3, the whole Soviet of Workers' Deputies in the lodgings of the Free Economic Society, amounting to 267 members. The leaders of the Soviet answered with an armed uprising in Moscow (December 9–20), but it was quickly crushed by government troops on the very day our paper was shut down for the last time.

Given the mood of the leftists, there was, of course, no way whatsoever for us to prevent the armed uprising at that time. Nevertheless, we did make our political stand completely clear. In this critical moment, I already felt myself secure enough in the saddle to be able to differ with the party, and I could speak about the tragic Moscow days in the name of our whole political movement. For several days before the beginning of the uprising, I warned in the most insistent words of its inevitable defeat and of the great danger to the course of the whole revolutionary movement which would result from the leftists' failure. We still had not yet separated ourselves from this common cause. Let me reproduce here a few original exerpts from the first few issues of our newspaper. In the very first issue of *Narodnaia Svoboda* I wrote: "We thoroughly understand and willingly admit the supreme right of revolution, as a factor in the creation of future rights, in the open struggle with the obsolete political system and its historic rights. But we do not deify the revolution; we do not make a fetish out of it. We remember equally well that revolution is only a method, a means of struggle, and not a goal in itself. The method is bad if it harms the cause which it is supposed to serve. Both the goals and the means of the Russian revolutionary movement should be subjected to serious and independent public criticism. . . . To engage in such criticism in no way weakens that revolutionary mood to which we are all bound by so many important victories." Furthermore, I pointed out (alas, I was mistaken with regard to the Bolsheviks, whom I still did not consider a separate group) that the revolutionary organizations themselves "are gradually ceasing to overestimate their own forces." I only expressed the misgiving that it is more difficult to change "official revolutionary jargon than the convictions of individual persons." Nevertheless, I expressed the hope that "sooner or later they will admit . . . that their hope of overcoming the technical forces of the State by means of a direct armed uprising, and their hope of immediately transforming Russia into a democratic republic were based on a very large dose of overestimation of their own strength." I recalled that "there is a certain limit, beyond which the creative and constructive force of revolutionary propaganda becomes destructive, and beyond which yesterday's friend and ally can become tomorrow's bitter enemy. We come very close to that limit if we resort to such powerful tactical measures as the political strike too often and too easily. We come very close if we resort to means which rely on revolutionary enthusiasm and which destroy the normal course of the country's life to a greater or lesser degree." "The fate of the Russian revolution depends to a significant degree on the attitude of the neutral elements." "From the depths, from the grass roots come the pogroms and the agrarian conflagrations. . . . We must go there in order to have the right to prophesy about the future of the Russian revolution."

The Soviet of Workers' Deputies was arrested, and when the attempt to answer the arrest with a general strike to be followed by an armed uprising in Petersburg failed, the Bolshevik agitators turned their attention to Moscow, which had just organized its own Soviet of Workers' Deputies and which had not yet tasted defeat. The Bolsheviks also turned their attention to the provincial branches of the Soviet, where the mood was higher pitched. Accordingly, I changed my arguments from general statements to "pleas" directed at "all those on whom the decision depends, to reconsider before it is too late." "The top officers must be certain that they are leading their soldiers to victory, not to the slaughterhouse. If they are not convinced of this, then the decision to call a political strike is wrong. In October the political strike was a heroic civilian feat. It was doubtlessly a political mistake in November. Now, a political strike could turn out to be a crime—a crime against the revolution!" On December 9 I repeated my arguments again. I argued against the optimism of *Severnyi Golos* which continued to assert that a strike would result in the surrender of the government to the revolution, that the revolution would create its "Provisional Government," which would then summon the Constituent Assembly. I compared this absurd belief with the cold interview which Witte gave to Dillon, the correspondent from the *Daily News*. Witte maintained that "Russian society is insufficiently inspired by the instinct for self-preservation and must be taught a good lesson. Let society burn itself; then it will come on its own to the government for help." This smacked of conscious provocation and two months later a report from Pierre Leroux in *Matin* confirmed that this is precisely what it was. "Weren't you warned?" (about the impending uprising), he asked Admiral Dubasov. "The police and the government knew," answered Dubasov. "Then what can we conclude from that?" said the Frenchman in surprise. After a little hesitation and with some embarrassment, his excellency uttered the four words: "on a laissé faire."

Of course, my warning, too, turned out to be in vain. That same day that I printed an article about Witte's provocation in Petersburg, the strike was already going full steam in Moscow. The Executive Committee had hastily prepared the uprising. Already during the day, detachments of armed workers appeared on the streets and began skirmishes with the troops. By evening, the strike had become an open uprising, with barricades and all. For five whole days, this small handful of workers fought from behind these defensive barricades against the troops which happened to be on hand in Moscow. On the sixth day, the Smolensky Guards Regiment arrived from Petersburg. The entrenched daredevils on Presnaia Street—two or three hundred in all—continued the battle against the Smolensky Guards for another five days until the uprising was finally crushed once and for all. The suppression cost the destruction of an entire city block and the lives of hundreds of random passers-by who fell into the no less random shooting. Through such means, the pacification of the unrest made a much stronger impression than the uprising itself. Some of the Bolshevik members of the S. D.'s had long expected precisely such an effect and, as it became known later, had planned it that way. On December 14, I began my editorial in an excited tone. "Incredible events are taking place in the ancient Russian capital. They are shelling Moscow with cannons. They are shooting with even more fury, more insistence and more accuracy than they had shown against the Japanese troops. What has happened? Where is the enemy?"

I described the volleys fired across the facades of houses and the iron signboards of the barricades, which were built during the day and abandoned at night, and I asked, "What is this? Moscow is living through days which make the Napoleonic days of 1812 look pale. Yet officially, everything is calm in Moscow! . . . What is the explanation of the government's total impotence in the face of this violent explosion?" I answered, "If order can be restored only by placing an armed soldier at the side of every ordinary citizen, and by placing a cannon in front of every house, it means that the soldiers and the cannons are not protecting those whom they should. If everyone is against the government, that means that the government is against everyone. . . . That is why the government must use all its force in order to undertake even the smallest action. That is why it places its cannons on an empty square and fires for hours along empty streets. That is why it cannot control a man without destroying the house where he lives with cannon balls." Even Montesquieu had a parable to explain the meaning of this: "A man wants to get an apple. To do this he chops down the tree. There you have the definition of despotism."

Recollections of the Moscow destruction did not disappear quickly. If Witte had intended to teach society a lesson by this action, then the lesson had worked in reverse. Here are my own observations which I made at the time: "The mistakes of our revolutionaries divided society, pushing its moderate elements to the right. The government's indiscriminate reaction can again restore the unity of the revolutionary mood and push the middle elements to the left. The bloody pacification of the Moscow uprising was the first of such government mistakes, and it may not be the last."

Both my diagnosis and prognosis proved correct very soon afterward. As a result of the mistaken government reaction the unity of the antigovernment front was restored (only to a certain degree, of course). The Kadets, above all, gained from the restoration of unity. But, alas, the common struggle for political liberty failed. As I have already noted, the curve of success in the struggle against the government declined from this point. The main reason for this sudden change was the final split between our tactics and those of the leftists. The Moscow uprising, thoughtlessly undertaken and doomed beforehand, placed an insurmountable barrier between us and the socialists.

Our Dubious Victory: The First Duma

THE GENERAL FEATURE which distinguished 1906 from 1905 was the appearance of open political parties in the political arena, and the corresponding appearance—more or less without government permission—of political literature, journals, pamphlets, and especially newspapers. There was no longer a "simulated" revolution, concealing a united front of public opinion. The revolution now acted in its own name, and a large spectrum of political parties arose from it, including parties that were friendly, neutral, or hostile to it. The "party" supplanted the "unions," which had broken up into party groups, retaining only their professional nucleus. In this sense I considered my aim—or my prognosis—achieved. Next in line came that task which for a parliamentary political party was the most important one: the elections to the popular representative body. All of the public's attention was now necessarily focused on this task. The "rustle of ballot sheets" became a reality. The "ballot boxes," whose absence Lutugin exploited, now appeared. How were these ballot boxes used by the government, the voters, the liberals, the opposition, and the revolution?

Witte, who still held the decisive authority in his hands, lost his chance to use the elections for a national plebiscite in favor of the autocracy. In Kryzhanovsky's words, he "vacillated long and agonizingly over this question." Universal suffrage was by no means demanded only by the "leftists." The same Kryzhanovsky recounted in his *Memoirs* how he came to be present at Witte's conference and how even such moderate figures as M. A. Shakhovich, E. N. Trubetskoy, and D. N. Shipov tried to persuade the all-powerful premier to agree to universal suffrage. S. A. Muromtsev even presented his own project for an electoral law. Unfortunately, because of his secretiveness in these "extra rounds," we do not know whether or not this was the same project that the Kadets had worked out with Muromtsev's participation. In any case, Witte charged Kryzhanovsky with the task of rendering Muromtsev's project harmless, while Guchkov and Shipov defended the project in the Council of Ministers. In the end,

Kryzhanovsky, the magician and wizard of constitutional law, won. His project for a curia system with multistaged elections, which was originally intended for the Bulygin Duma, was incorporated together with a few liberal-leaning amendments into the election statutes published on December 11. The voters gained time to recover from the fright of the government's reaction, to gather together and debate the issues two, three, or four times before the final "ballot box." The election dragged out.

In such a situation, and given the mood of the public, excited by the experience of the December catastrophe in Moscow and still more strongly aroused afterward—it was fairly certain that no defects in the electoral stature of December 11 would prevent the public mood from expressing itself in the elections. The electoral campaign itself served as a powerful means for gaining political influence over the masses. Nevertheless, the leftist parties again displayed their doctrinarism by announcing a boycott of the elections.

This act left me greatly disappointed in the political wisdom of my closest friends from the Socialist Revolutionary Populist group around *Russkoe Bogatstvo*. I simply could not understand such people as Annensky or Miakotin. On the agrarian question, the Populist ideology gushed into our party ranks, so that our adversaries' accusations of our being "socialist" were, in this respect, not entirely groundless. Through the Populists' cooperation, we could count on the understanding and sympathy of the peasants toward us. This was a way to widen and deepen the electoral struggle. But at the same time, my friends displayed a total lack of understanding of the situation by retreating to the sidelines, away from the impending battle, in the name of some persisting illusions.

Compared with the Populists, the S. D.'s and especially the Mensheviks still behaved fairly intelligently. Some of the Menshevik arguments were quite serious, paralleling our own. During these months I even praised Plekhanov for his articles in "Diary of a Social Democrat." Their attitude toward the Duma boycott was far from unconditional. They were ready to admit their mistakes and to change their tactics, even while preserving the integrity of their goals. While one could understand the situation, it was still impossible to regain time lost by the error.

In any case, this time we were "fortunate in having such comrades." Their exit from the electoral arena left us a free hand. The elections were the only struggle accessible to the average man, and we were left as the most "leftist" party, the only leftist party, in that struggle. The average citizen could express his opposition sentiments only through us. The appearance of government and "ministerial" parties, hastily tacked together, did not count; while the rightists and their truly antipopular goals were too transparent and their electoral means too violent.

What sort of party was ours, a party which thanks to the role it had taken for itself, had ended up in such a favorable position? Without doubt, the most conscious political elements of the Russian intelligentsia joined the Kadets. Not for nothing was it called the "professors' party." The party's most active elements in the country were the progressive Zemstvo and urban activists, who were the only group of people experienced in the social struggle and who never restricted themselves to the narrow confines of technical work in the Zemstvos. They were also bound to the popular grass roots, especially through the so called "third element," the professional personnel in the Zemstvo establishments—the physicians, agronomists, teachers, etc. It was to the party's credit that all its predictions concerning the failure of extreme revolutionary tactics were born out in fact. In accordance with the decision of the Kharkov Congress, the provincial branches of the party, which were already organized in 1904, worked energetically to spread the party's views. Sympathy for the party was reflected in the rapid growth of its supporters. Before the elections in January 1906 the party numbered about 100,000 registered members. The party of the people's freedom could thus be considered the most widely organized, the most politically prepared of all the parties since it combined the principles of a democratic movement with a businesslike approach to the political struggle. Its chances for victory in a purely parliamentary struggle were very great, but was the struggle a "purely parliamentary" one? Apart from its dangerous competitors on the left and its harmless ones on the right, what was going on in its own midst?

In spite of the fact that the "left-wing" Liberationists had left the party at the very time of its formation, the party was still not a unified whole. It was to become unified in the process of real struggle, but that was still in the future. Several of the leaders of the Russian intelligentsia, like K. K. Arsenev, M. M. Kovalevsky, and others, did not join the party even though they did much of the preparatory work on the party's ideology. Whether it was because they were not accustomed to collective action and mutual ideological concessions, or whether it was because of their individual personalities, lifetime habits, and views, whatever the reason may have been, these public figures broke up into small groups and formed a string of closed political clubs which could not possibly have had any influence on the course of political life in the country. To some of them, the "Kadets" seemed too moderate; to others, we were too radical. They continued to observe and criticize events—from the sidelines.

Those who joined the party brought with them, not so much different views, as different attitudes. Of course, the lack of political experience was felt above all; for there had been no place in Russia to acquire such experience. Our party also had reflected the aroused mood of the country. For me, personally, the failure of the revolutionary movement in December 1905 signaled a general fall in the curve of the social struggle. I was even then inclined to consider a sad outcome of this first open political conflict between society and the government as inevitable. The majority of my colleagues who shared my political views thought differently. And, in fact, the elated mood triggered by the elections did genuinely represent a new source of strength. It was only necessary to know how to manage it. Oh, if only I had really been the "tutor" the Petersburg members thought I was! And if only Witte had been in fact the ally that he in words portrayed himself as being at our last meeting! But, alas, neither the one nor the other was true.

Because of the incompleteness of the October Congress, even the formation of the party was not yet finished. The final decisions on the questions of tactics, ideology, and party organization were supposed to be taken at the Second Party Congress on January 5-11, 1906. In agreement with the Central Committee, I was given the task of preparing the report on tactics for the congress. My aim, of course, was to pull both extreme flanks toward the center so that the party could acquire a distinct character. Without this, it was impossible even to establish the party's attitude toward the forthcoming elections. Meeting the party leftists halfway, I decided, first of all, to treat the question of the elections as a separate topic in itself, apart from the question of the party's behavior in the Duma. The latter issue was naturally more complex than the first because we already knew how the elections would go and in what quality and quantity we would take part in the Duma. Even in the event of an electoral defeat, I said, we would still play the "advantageous role of political opposition." I showed, however, that our chances for success were by no means dismal. Regardless of government pressure, the very postponement of the elections, the inability of the government to take advantage of their December victory, and the discrediting of the right-wing parties all made our success easier. Finally, in addition to these arguments against the boycott—and, specifically, in view of the possible success—I still had to adapt our program to the real conditions of legal struggle in the parliament. In other words, we had to continue what the November Congress of 1905 had partly achieved, in defiance of the thunder and lightning of our leftist friends and enemies. This was perhaps the most difficult part of my task.

In November we had resolved that the "constituent" work must have the "tsar's approval." Now we elaborated on that formula: "Russia should become a constitutional and parliamentary monarchy." The struggle for a democratic republic was once and for all stricken from the party program. Even in November, "Constituent Assembly" had been replaced by a "Duma with constituent functions." I explained that "in any case, by introducing the optional term Constituent Assembly we did not have in mind an assembly with complete and sovereign authority." This interpretation did away with the amendment introduced at the January Congress, which recalled the demand for the Constituent Assembly instead of the Duma. That amendment was rejected by 137 to 80, a vote that disclosed a compact majority at the congress. In order to satisfy the minority, local groups were given "freedom in using the terminology" (but not the sense) of the Constituent Assembly.

Next came the definition of the "constituent" activity of the Duma. Included were a mandatory change in the electoral statute and a strengthening by law of civil liberties promised in the October Manifesto. (Witte had agreed to replace them only by "temporary rules" while waiting for the Duma's "legislative action"!) But should the Duma, having confined itself to passing on the "constituent" issues, go on to demand its own dissolution as many people believed? As early as the November Congress we had embarked upon another road; we wanted to broaden the Duma's powers to the point implied by the suspect term "organic work." However, the Duma was then transformed into "a normal legislative institution" and our congress rejected such "organic work." But it was immediately thereafter forced (ninety-five to four, with seven abstentions) to expand the agenda of Duma business "to include, in addition to the electoral law, any legislative enactments of an unconditionally urgent character necessary for the pacification of the country." Of course, this meant the agrarian question above all, for it was this question alone which brought the peasants to the Duma. Nevertheless, much more than that could have been implied, so the question was raised: Should these urgent tasks be spelled out? The congress answered negatively with a majority of seventy-three votes. Then followed Struve's and Rodichev's roundabout proposal: "While working toward its main goal, the party cannot avoid placing in its program those reforms whose crying necessity is indicated by life itself. These include labor and land reform and the satisfaction of the just demands of the national minorities." The congress was induced to adopt such a proposal, but Kokoshkin, the guardian of our principles, introduced his own amendment, which distinguished between commitments to the voters to accomplish the main task (after which the Duma was to be dispersed and new elections held) and the plans for future activity. This was an attempt to bring the congress back to the doctrinaire declarations which had been presented to Witte. This was the fight waged in the course of voting between the various tendencies within the party. This was also reflected in the statements of my co-speaker, M. M. Vinaver: "The party derives all its strength from the organization of the public's consciousness by all manner of propaganda and agitation." The aim of this last point was the "restoration of faith in that force which, since November 1904, had helped to activate the whole wave of the liberating movement; faith that awakening the minds and strengthening the will of the broad masses was a cause and not merely a word; faith which, influenced by the mood of the moment, seemed to be dying." This eloquence was a verbal concession to left-wing sentiments. Everyone knew, of course, what force had raised the "wave": it was none other than the "Acheron." During this time, Struve, on the other hand, still appealed to an "agreement between the monarch and the nation" through the creation of a "public ministry"! Neither the one nor the other, neither Struve's idyll nor Vinaver's utopia, suited the given moment. Struve developed his idyll in his personal newspaper *Poliarnaia Zvezda,* while Vinaver's bow in the direction of the leftists evoked only the irony of Count Landau and the implacable cries of Count Pavel Tolstoy in the paper of the Liberationist Secessionists, *Bez Zaglaviia.* In my concluding words, without nodding to either side, I decided to stress that, not withstanding the Central Committee's misgivings, the party, at its Second Congress, turned out to be united behind the views of the majority and confident and businesslike in its basic decisions. "The party found itself, and felt within its bosom the presence of a collective thought and will. . . . This feeling of solidarity and the consciousness of the value of belonging to a large whole emerged as a new feeling at the congress, a feeling which we have long and anxiously awaited and which we now greet with rapture." I even compared this feeling with Kipling's "christening a ship" in full confidence that the creaking in the grooves strengthened our whole structure, and that the Kadet "ship" could boldly embark upon an expedition, strewn with many underwater boulders.

I no longer recall whether I really believed what I said or whether I wanted to instill this faith in others. Both were probably true. At any rate, I was sure that experience would teach us what bare faith lacked.

The electoral campaign began in circumstances which were in no way favorable for our party. We were persecuted from the right and assailed from the left. News about the government's violent measures was coming in ever more frequently from our provincial organizations.

One after another our fellow members fell victim to these government actions. We discovered that the provincial authorities were receiving their orders from the center, but we got only evasive explanations in response to our protests. Witte declared in print that the view ascribed to him concerning the "necessity of paralyzing the activity of the Kadet party is entirely without foundation." Nevertheless, the persecution continued. At best, this meant that Witte himself was no longer in a position to influence the elections. But if not Witte, then who? Durnovo? Trepov?

After February 1906 we got the opportunity to pose these questions in print. At last the newspaper of the party and its followers appeared: *Rech*. The paper received solid financial backing from the engineer, Bak. This was no longer Propper with his *Birzhevka*. Bak did not speculate on the Kadets; he was motivated by purely ideological considerations. He believed in us, and he did not interfere in the financial or even in the editorial business of the paper. I. I. Petrunkevich became our treasurer, while I. V. Hessen and myself were editors. Our assistant was the irreplacable M. I. Ganfman. I became almost the permanent editor-in-chief. My political articles written during those months were collected in a book called *God Borby*. Whoever wants to feel the feverish pulse beat of that year may reread those articles now. They were not a history, but a daily record that took the place of a diary.

I cannot go into detail here about how the political scenery of the elections changed from day to day, unexpectedly even for us. Things grew worse for us, and the government persecutions could hardly fill us with optimism. It was only with heavy heart that we entered in our chronicle the battle feats of Generals Rennenkampf or Riman, Admirals Chukhnin, Abramov, and Zhdanov, the censor Sokolov, and so on. Then, after March, the police began to receive "alarming news" from the provinces. What I had spoken about many times since December 1905 had come to pass. The "fear of revolution disappeared" from the average man. True, the first meetings at which the peasants' and workers' representatives were elected were conducted sluggishly and with large absenteeism. Neither government influence nor leftist party propaganda had yet reached these grass roots. It was at this stage that the accusation could be leveled against Witte that "he was not capable" of organizing elections. The workers paid little attention to the S. D. decrees to boycott the elections. The peasants, however, already knew what they wanted. Even the curia of small landowners reacted weakly; they preferred to elect "their own," especially clergymen. By the middle of March, this picture began to change. The political complexion of the elections was determined even before any party influence could take effect; it was determined, on the one hand, by the general opposition sentiments of the masses and, on the other, by the all-too-obvious government pressure. At the next stage, at the meetings of the electors where the struggle over party lists began, new attitudes in favor of the Kadets could be felt.

Witte's semiofficial paper *Russkoe Gosudarstvo* then tried to change course and began to discuss favorably the possibility of a Kadet victory. The arguments for creating a "ministerial party" were brushed aside. In the second half of March, when the Kadets achieved a brilliant victory in the Moscow and Petersburg elections, the semi-official newspaper even resorted to flattery. *Russkoe Gosudarstvo* congratulated us on the "approaching Spring"; they showered us with lyrical appeals "to love" and "to forget the past"; they greeted us as "desired guests" in the Duma—"if the guests come without any revolutionary intentions." They continued to ignore our genuine intentions, however. Beginning in early April after all these outpourings had met with a cold reception from us, frankly threatening tones were heard from the columns of this semiofficial paper. They gave us a choice: "either the Kadet representatives shift somewhat to the right" and betray their program, or else. . . . Then there followed gloating predictions about what would happen if the Duma were to discredit itself by radicalism. But the left-wing parties had already threatened us—if the Duma were to discredit itself by moderation! We only repeated: "The struggle cannot stop. It is up to the government to carry out that struggle in a civilized manner." We reminded the government that the October Manifesto left the future development of electoral law to the judgment of the Duma. We wrote that Witte himself admitted that only the Duma could issue "laws" concerning civil liberties, in place of the "temporary regulations" then in force. This was, in fact, our "constituent" work.

At the same time, however, in the secret recesses of the government, not merely a "law" but a "constitutional act" from above was already being prepared in anticipation of the Duma's attempt to carry it through by parliamentary means. The editors of *Rech* got a hold of this project of "Fundamental Laws" straight from the printers and published it with severe criticisms. As a result of our criticism, the government did make some small changes; but one week before the Duma was to meet, Witte's government fell. He was no longer needed—after the government, thanks to him, had managed to float a loan in Paris and after the troops had returned from Manchuria. The government's military and material forces were now sufficient for the government no longer to fear the Duma. Witte's place was taken by I. L. Goremykin who was instructed, as we found out later, to dissolve the Duma, if the Duma should desire to pass its agrarian legislation. Together with this, all the preparations for giving the Duma a half-decent reception crumbled. Apparently, it had been decided to conquer the Duma in a war of attrition.

The threat of conflict with the tsarist government, thus, already hung over the Duma even before it convened. While such a conflict still did not seem inevitable, especially to our provincial members, the party leaders fully understood its seriousness. Our third party congress met under this overhanging threat and found itself in a strange position: the party had a majority, but the government refused to give in. Although I was not a member of the Duma, I was again supposed to speak at the congress in the name of the Central Committee on the most difficult question of the moment—the question of party tactics.

The fundamental question, which was supposed to have been treated first but which I postponed until the end of my report, was: "Given the present situation, should the people's representatives rely on revolutionary or parliamentary forms of activity?" Essentially, this meant: Is the revolution in Russia continuing or has it ended? I suggested leaving the question unanswered—not because I could not make up my own mind, but because, "given the possibility of two different answers in our own group, there was a chance that no common answer would be found." This meant that I already felt that the party, under the influence of its electoral success, would not be anywhere near as monolithic when it came to the Duma as it was three months before when it was preparing for the elections. The delegates to the congress from the provinces, above all, came with the notion that the elections bound them to represent not only their own party but also the attitudes of their provinces—those attitudes which had elected them and which were transferred to them as a result of the aloofness of the leftist parties. These attitudes were perfectly natural, but they in no way suited the more sober appraisal of the situation at our center.

With this in mind, the party Central Committee tried to restrain its parliamentary faction from an unequal struggle by directing its attitudes along channels decided upon at the January Congress. Let the conflict threaten; let it even be inevitable. We must create the most favorable conditions possible for that conflict. The country had to be given the necessary material in time in order to judge the meaning of the conflict. To do this, it was necessary not only to "be in the Duma" but to remain there for a more or less prolonged period. During this time, we would have to avoid sharp clashes which would give the initiative in the conflict to the government. Consequently, we had to begin with issues that were the least dangerous for us. In my opinion, these centered on our legislative drafts concerning universal suffrage and "liberties." According to the Struve-Rodichev-Kokoshkin resolution, our party obligations consisted precisely of these goals; but after attaining these goals, other problems would arise, namely, the most difficult ones. It was impossible, however, to hide the fact either from ourselves or from the assembly that the painful issues lay elsewhere. In the immediate future we faced a bitter settling of accounts with the government and clashes over the legal stipulations restricting the rights of the people's representatives. These restrictions, introduced by the Act of February 20, were binding on the Duma. We intended to carry out our legislative work within the limits of this act and to treat in the same way those "displays of public indignation" which had piled up in abundance against the old administration. Our argument was that the old officials had already left, while the new cabinet had not yet done anything. This meant of course, ignoring the political significance of Witte's retirement and his replacement by Goremykin. It was no less of a mistake, we felt, to maintain that the first steps toward carrying out our agrarian project would not in themselves provoke a conflict. Given its new attitudes, the parliamentary faction could not accept our "limits." Our proposals simply did not correspond to the situation which had come about just before the Duma opened.

The debates exposed the complete divergence between the congress and the cautious tone of my report with its "cold calculation" of the plan of action for the Duma. Their response to me was that since it was the "aroused mood of the people" and "not the party program" which had won at the elections, we are bound "to go all the way," "calmly and confidently," that then "the people will support us." We have no reason to fear a conflict; the conflict "already exists." The conflict will begin "from the first day," and therefore it follows that we should ignore the government, ignore the laws issued after October 17, ignore the State Council and pass all of our legislative program in the form of an "ultimatum" or "declaration." If the government does not give way, then we will turn to the people with an "appeal" for support. If necessary, we "will die for liberty." The peasants had instructed their elected representatives: "Go and die there with glory; or else you will die here with shame." Rodichev encouraged us with his fiery speech: "The Duma cannot be dissolved; the voice of the people is with us." The strength of the Duma is its "daring"; and "those who clash with the people will be pushed aside by the force of the people, into the abyss." A. A. Kizevetter echoed Rodichev at the congress, where he, too, won stormy applause: "If they dissolve the Duma, then it will be the last act of that government; they will cease to exist." Obviously, given such attitudes, it was absolutely impossible to draw up any concrete plan of action for the Duma. We could do nothing but leave the course of events to fate—and to the decisions of our parliamentary faction. At the congress it was still somehow possible to control the oratorical passions, and my report was adopted with minor changes. But it was clear that those same attitudes would be carried over into the Duma. The omens were of the worst. Then, in the last minute, while still absorbed in the congress, we were stunned by an "event of extraordinary importance." The above-mentioned project of a constitution "granted from above," which Witte had already outlined and which had been printed in *Rech* in accordance with *lex ferenda,* was now issued in the form of a "Fundamental Law," placing new fetters on the people's legislative powers. With this act, the government placed "all government policies under the extra-ordinary safeguards" of legislative norms "inviolable by the Duma" and "shielded everything that hindered the expression of the will of the people's representatives." When I made that statement I should also have confessed to the congress that, with the approval of the Central Committee, I had thrown out of my report a section which dealt precisely with such an encroachment on the people's rights. "Now we have the right to be harsh" I said very excitedly. "We must immediately answer this fraud against the people." The Central Com-mittee hurriedly drafted a resolution which ended with the statement that "no obstacles created by the government will restrain the people's elected representatives from fulfilling the tasks entrusted to them by the people." This resolution set the tone for the First Duma. But from the ranks of the congress, exclamations of protest rang out: "Too weak; it must be sharper; it does not express our mood." Only at Rodichev's insistence did the congress adopt our resolution unanimously.

Conflicts Among the Duma Deputies

IF EVEN AMONG OURSELVES it was difficult to change discord into harmony, then among the Duma deputies gathered together from different political currents it was simply impossible. Our electoral victory did not turn out to be nearly as complete as it had seemed to us in the heat of the elections. The Kadets comprised only one-third of the Duma membership—34 percent. (Initially we had 153 members; later this figure increased to 179, or 37.4 percent.) A group calling itself "labor" gradually formed to our left. Together we could command a majority—if only they would not be too disunified and if only their leaders would not pull in different directions. However, out of their 107 members, only twenty stood "closer to the Kadets," while an equal number leaned toward the S. R.'s and the S. D.'s. Consequently, the Duma majority was unpredictable and unstable. The issue was decided each time by a center core of forty-eight "Trudoviks," who either designated themselves as "nonpartisan" or declined any designation whatever. These were the progressive elements of the peasant deputies, and between our two factions there was a constant struggle for their support. There were other peasants in the Duma who were especially fearful of any leadership and who never did officially affiliate with definite parties. The government tried in vain to lure them into a special boardinghouse which was run by a certain Erogin and which was known by the mocking nickname *Zhivopyrni*. Through their reserved and secretive behavior, however, these peasants succeeded in hiding their real views. The government's plan—and Witte's—of obtaining a Duma of "dullards" and of making a ministerial party out of them clearly did not succeed. And there were no other ministerial parties in the Duma either.

A small handful of Octobrists sat to our right. They, too, deceived Witte's expectations. Included in their group were several cultured persons who were embarrassed by their party name and renamed themselves the Party of "Peaceful Reconstruction." They were joined by several members from the group of "democratic reforms." Both groups generally voted with us. Sometimes, however, they amazed us with their political tricks, usually very inopportune. Further to the right came the dark reaction—cachectic and impotent. The most influential leaders from the Black Hundreds did not make it to the Duma. Instead they sent registered telegrams to the government from the outside demanding that the Duma be dissolved. Their telegrams were hospitably printed in *Pravitelstvennyi Vestnik*.

Much more serious and dangerous were our so-called "friends on the left." Because of the futile boycott tactics, their representation, too, was weak and undistinguished. The Social Democrats from the Caucasus arrived only toward the end, and, cudgels in hand, began to carry out their tactics. But their hands were tied, both by their small mandate and by the narrow limits of the Duma Acts themselves. Their instructions were received from the outside, developed at their meeting and in the press, and were directed primarily against our Duma faction. Their influence was weakened, however, by internal discord. The failure of revolutionary tactics at the end of 1905 forced them to arrange a Conciliatory Congress in April 1906. The congress resulted not in "unification," but in renewed disagreements between the vanquished Bolsheviks and their Menshevik critics. Such leaders as Axelrod and Plekhanov conclusively demonstrated the fundamental impracticability of tactics calling for the seizure of power by the proletariat through a victorious revolution. They continued to argue that only "bourgeois-democratic" revolution was possible in Russia; hence, it was necessary not to fight the "liberals" and the "capitalists," but to support them. Their position was so clearly vindicated by the December failure that the Mensheviks prevailed at the congress. Nevertheless, Bolshevik tactics continued to be applied in practice. As before, the Bolsheviks answered the Mensheviks' reasoning with demagogic appeals to the primitive instincts of the masses. As a result of such propaganda, the Mensheviks were driven back almost to the position of the Kadets. We even found some support in their newspapers. Support for us was also reflected in their attitude towards the Duma. At their meetings, the Menshevik Central Committee proposed replacement of the government by a cabinet from the Duma majority. They considered the Kadets and the Laborites as a single unit, and they expected the Duma to prepare "the next stage in the struggle." The Petersburg Bolsheviks, on the contrary, considered the Duma "impotent" and proposed to split the Laborites from the "liberal parties" by sharpening the conflicts within the Duma and then "demanding that the Duma turn directly to the people." In vain Plekhanov explained to them that by discrediting the Duma they would in effect be supporting the government, which, rather than wait for the people to come to the Duma's rescue, would simply dissolve the Duma. The Bolsheviks repeated their own argument: "the people must take everything by themselves; we want a decisive struggle outside the Duma." This meant a return to the tactics of December 1905, and more than anything else, of course, the introduction of these ideas into the Duma was responsible for its catastrophic end. The Bolsheviks managed to palm off on the Trudoviks a proposal "to organize committees in the provinces elected by universal suffrage for the purpose of discussing the agrarian question." "We must create a force in the country which will give us the possibility of victory. We want to give the Russian people such momentum that they will be impossible to stop." In these words did the Laborite leader Aladin candidly argue in defense of the Bolshevik proposal which the Trudoviks disconcertedly introduced as early as May 26.

Such was the situation that emerged after the elections to the First Duma. My attitude was determined above all by the fact that I personally was not a member of the Duma. The government had revoked the apartment qualifications which I had tried to arrange.[20] On the memorable day of April 27 at the gates of the Taurida Palace, I met the deputies who were returning along the Neva from the Winter Palace to the old palace of Potemkin. Kryzhanovsky expressed his regrets over my (second) interpretation; in his opinion, I was "more harmful outside the Duma than inside it." He as well as others were sure that I "was directing the Duma from the snack bar." I cannot deny that I did have a certain influence in the Duma. As a member of the party's Central Committee, I could participate most intimately in the activities of our parliamentary faction. We had a common table in the "snack bar" where during breakfast we hurriedly discussed the current questions of the day in view of the overload of Duma work. During the sessions themselves I could follow the course of the debates not only from the top, from the gallery, but also from below, from the journalists' box to the left of the speaker's platform. From that spot I could maintain constant contact with the deputies. Nevertheless, not only could I not control the whole Duma but I could not even begin to control our own Duma faction. I could not have controlled them even if I had been a Duma member. I have already spoken about the attitudes and moods of our Duma faction (and party) immediately after the elections, and about the difficulty of leading that faction given the dominant mood of those months. Even less, therefore, could I bear the responsibility for the behavior of the whole Duma.

My role was determined primarily by my personal intimacy with the leaders of our party who were elected to the Duma, my colleagues from the Central Committee, Petrunkevich, Vinaver, Kokoshkin, and

Rodichev. Petrunkevich stood over us all, as the "patriarch" of our political movement and as the living conscience of our party. However, neither he nor our entire Duma faction could follow the kaleidoscope of the daily, usually stormy, events in the conference hall. Someone had to be on the alert all the time, to make decisions on the spot, and three of us, more or less inadvertently, came to this role: Vinaver, Kokoshkin, and myself. But Kokoshkin was often ill, and he concentrated on general matters of principle. Two of us were left, and with our different approaches, we, in a way, complemented each other. In a biographical sketch of Vinaver, I noted that he approached the Duma work as a jurist, while I approached it as a historian. Vinaver's powerful and agile mind immediately grasped the peculiarities of a situation and embodied them in a clear and concise formula, which obscured sharp corners and smoothed out contradictions. While his formula did not always settle the question, it was usually acceptable to everyone. His heightened and rather rhetorical tone reflected his literary talent and admirably suited the grand style of the resolutions of the First Duma. Vinaver's brilliant pamphlet *Conflicts in the First Duma* clearly explained how his diplomatic influence managed to reconcile the clashes which arose almost every day between the various groups and how he succeeded in dragging the creaky Duma wagon from one swampy hole in the road to the next. This helped to "drag out" the Duma's work as our pre-Duma report had demanded; but it in no way contributed to changing the Duma's general political direction. As a method of resolving conflicts, it was rather like Penelope's weaving or the labor of Sisyphus.

I was more interested in the connection between the daily events within the Duma and their general relationship to what was going on outside of the Duma. In the next section I will come back to this sort of "conflict" which so frequently occurred outside the Duma as a result of the Duma's behavior. In fact, the reason for the Duma tragedy lay precisely in this parallel between conflicts inside the Duma and those occurring outside. If it would have been possible for me to "direct" the Duma, then my "direction" would have consisted of removing the common source of both conflicts by means of moderating the Duma's political temperament and increasing the government's political wisdom. But neither the one nor the other—and especially not a combination of the two—was possible, whether for myself or for anyone else.

Opposed to us three—Vinaver, Kokoshkin, and myself—stood the three Trudovik "leaders," Aladin, Zhilkin, and Anikin. I knew only the first one personally; we met in London, where he played a rather pitiable role among the Russian emigrants. I remember how at meet-

ings in the home of Z. D. Shklovskaia, the wife of I. V. Shklovsky, the
hostess and I made fun of Aladin's haughty seriousness, which accompanied his inner insignificance. Aladin defended himself clumsily in a
bear-like fashion. He was a very small man who earned his bread
honestly by keeping books for petty shopkeepers in Whitechapel. I
would never have imagined that I would meet him in Petersburg in the
role of a Trudovik leader and in the pose of the least restrained speaker
in the First Duma. His speeches were fluent but as crude, arrogant, and
provocative as could be. After one of his first appearances he came to
me, and, sprawling out on the couch, asked, in a tone which brooked
no opposition: "Well, how'd you like it?" I answered him in the same
tone: "Very poor!" Aladin was not at all embarrassed: "You don't
understand. It must be that way now. You will see what is still to
come." And, soon, he did in fact become famous all over Russia. The
other two Trudoviks were conscientious and modest persons, with
whom one could talk seriously. But they rather kept to the background,
and were incapable of leading.

On the whole, we had the most friendly relations with the Trudovik group—especially at the beginning, before they came under the
influence of outside forces. During the most critical period when we
met together to decide on the first steps to be taken in the Duma, they
elected me chairman of our joint sessions. Preliminary discussions on
the Duma's answer to the "king's speech" was carried on jointly between our two "troikas." On the question of expressing our lack of
confidence in the ministry, I again chaired a united session and deliberately bent the gathering towards the Trudoviks' formula. At another
time, during a joint discussion regarding steps to be taken after the
tsar refused to see the Duma delegations sent to him with an address,
the Trudovik group agreed to accept our more moderate Kadet formula. Once, to my great pride, our faction sent me to the peasants to
defend the Kadet agrarian project. I cannot hide the pleasure I felt
when I subsequently read the peasants' answer in Vinaver's *Conflicts*.
In his words, I "was popular among the Trudovik group, and the
peasants even expressed regrets at not having anyone who could argue
so clearly and sensibly." We had peasants even in our own faction;
they amounted to 6 percent of our group and were all solid, businesslike people from the northern provinces.

The first stage of friendly contact passed quickly, however, after
the intellectuals of their party began to influence the Trudoviks.
Systematic attacks on the Kadets then took place at their meetings.
But, apparently, the peasants did not like this tone, and their favorable
inclination toward us became even greater after the Social Democrats
from the Caucasus arrived and began advocating revolutionary struggle

outside the Duma. In the end, the peasants could no longer tolerate such leadership and decided to leave the Trudovik group. With their forty members, they formed a separate "peasants' faction." This promised to change the whole face of the Duma, and perhaps even to give us the majority. But precisely because of the "appeal to the people" (this was on the eve of the Duma's dissolution), the Kadet majority utterly collapsed. In Minister Shvanenbakh's words, the government preferred to call the Duma "a new Soviet of Workers' Deputies or a Union of Unions." Vinaver recorded that on the very day of the dissolution, Zhilkin turned to him with the words, "Now we will follow you," to which Vinaver answered curtly, "Too late."

Of course, there were demagogic thrusts even from among our Kadet circles. Professor Guerrier, who, following Taine, taught us our views about the French revolution, issued a scholarly pamphlet during those years in which he collected a whole bouquet of such Kadet speeches. I read this tendentious book with irritation. Did we really say such things? His citations were professorially precise, all carefully fished out of the Duma's stenographic reports. We had to admit it even to ourselves: yes, we really had said those things; we really were guilty. If we had made such speeches more often, we would have been scolded less from the left. . . .

I recall also my attitude toward the unification of the independent, national "autonomists" into a parliamentary group. The basic nucleus of this group was very compact. Out of sixty-three members, forty-three belonged to the Polish Kolo and to the representatives from the northwestern and southwestern provinces. These were well-to-do people, some of whom were great landowners. Lithuanians, Latvians, and Ukrainians made up another sixteen members of the nucleus. By merging with members of other factions, the nucleus doubled its size.

I did not join this group and I behaved towards it with caution. I explained my reasons for this in print. The national questions, by their very existence, threatened to complicate the social and constitutional questions which were our main problems. Moreover, the different desires and demands of the various nationalities would have been fused into general formulas, and I already understood that this was a means of asserting the demands of those nationalities who were least prepared for "autonomy." The Poles, represented by A. P. Lednitsky, were the most prepared. They addressed me in print with their own particular question as to why we kept silent on Polish autonomy in the Duma's answer to the tsar's speech. I answered them, also in print, that nothing had changed in the party's attitude towards the Polish question. I did not bother to remind them that for their part, the Kolo had introduced a legislative draft which was in disagreement with

our general assumptions. The same A. P. Lednitsky remarked, however, that "only in the Kadet party" can all the non-Russian nationalities "find genuine backing and support." He also mentioned the
numerous speeches of the Kadet faction on the nationality question.

The basic question which divided us from our chief adversaries,
the Bolsheviks, remained the same as it had been before: through the
Duma, or outside the Duma? In contrast to the Mensheviks, they
argued two extremes at the same time. At one time—"the Duma is
impotent"; at another, the contrary—it is so strong that it could fire
the ministers and decree all the necessary laws. Now, "mobilization of
nationwide opinion and will" is only a means of exerting "extraparliamentary pressure" on the Duma; now, on the contrary, the Duma
itself is a means for organizing the extraparliamentary will of the
people. In the Duma itself, they treated the Trudoviks both as "petty
bourgeois" and as "a revolutionary element."

This time I took a decisive stand. "Our roads part here," I repeated
to our erstwhile "friends on the left." "We do not believe in the
possibility of an organized action of the masses at the present time,
and, therefore, we do not in the least want to "raise hell," or to help
our friends carry out those preparatory measures which, in their
opinion, might help them achieve their aim. No matter how flimsy the
cloth of constitutional legality may be at the beginning, we want to
strengthen that cloth, and not return to the spontaneous force of the
Acheron."

It seemed that this position was clear enough. Did the government
pay any attention to it? Here we come to the issue which divided the
ministers and high officials into two opposing groups: for and against
the continued existence of the Duma. I must admit that now, knowing
the details of this conflict inside the government and high circles, I
am inclined to ascribe a greater significance to the efforts of those
who wanted to preserve the Duma than I thought at that time, when
my judgments were based on the course of events as they appeared on
the surface. Of course, the question was in itself serious enough, but it
was still more so for the supporters of the old monarchy: There is
nothing surprising in the fact that precisely those supporters of the
monarchy who were more thoughtful and farsighted, came out in
word and deed in favor of preserving the Duma. The advocates of the
Duma's dissolution, on the other hand, turned out to be the bureaucrats, who were guided not only by passive faithfulness to tradition but
also by personal pride and ambition.

The decisive factors in this conflict among the ministers and high
officials were, on the one hand, the tsar's immovable will and, on the
other, the utopianism of the leftist currents in the State Duma.

Conflict Among the Ministers
Outside the Duma: "Ministry of
Confidence" or Dissolution?

THE BASIC CONFLICT between the Duma and the government—that same conflict which we met earlier ("the conflict already exists," as stated at our pre-Duma congress) and which the leftists were striving for—did not come to light immediately. It was preceded by the short interval of our "idyll," when we had still not given up hope of carrying out our plans within the strictly "parliamentary" framework of the Duma. But it was precisely our "parliamentarism" which brought on more quickly the conflict with Goremykin's ministry. Because of his position, our chairman, S. A. Muromtsev, considered himself to be the second person in the state after the tsar. Like Rodzianko in the later Third Duma, so Muromtsev did not want to enter into personal relations with the tsar without being "summoned" to come with a "most humble report." We were therefore cut off from all but parliamentary contact with the government. In his capacity as chairman of the Duma, Muromtsev also behaved "pompously," remaining apart from the course of business. In his passive, reserved grandeur, he waited for the deputies themselves to take the first steps and make the first formal addresses. It should be said that as a result of his formally remote relations to our faction, he was not able to keep track of the Duma's real work. Not far from the Taurida Palace, he attended the opening of the Kadet club for the last time as a member of the faction. There he warned us that after his election as chairman, he would have to leave the faction in order to be outside party groupings. I must say that our chairman's majestic pose was regarded by all as a personification of the grandeur of the institution itself, and it gained him tremendous popularity. The Duma was thus left to its own resources, and we were deprived of the natural mediator in the inevitable conflicts with the government.

M. M. Vinaver also "behaved pompously" in the Duma, lending

parliamentary style to his Duma speeches. It was through these attitudes that we viewed the tsar's greetings to the deputies in the Winter
Palace as a "speech from the throne." The answer to it was to be an
"address" which a special delegation elected from the Duma was to
deliver to the tsar in a personal audience. As in a parliamentary
regime, this was supposed to be the only instance in which the people's
representatives directly addressed the monarch. Consequently, in
composing this "address," we intended to use this unique opportunity
to include all our aims and desires. We made a strict division in the
address between what we considered the rights of the Duma and the
prerogatives of the monarch. Our "intentions," our own actions, made
up the first section, while what we "desired" from the monarch was
contained in the second section of the address. In the latter section,
we included a request to the tsar for a complete amnesty, and we
pointed out the impossibility of the Duma's working with the State
Council. We indicated the necessity of abolishing the limitations on
the scope of the Duma's legislative activity, which had just been
imposed by the "Fundamental Laws." We placed special stress in the
second part of the address, on the necessity of creating a "cabinet
which has the confidence of a majority of the Duma" in order that the
responsibility before the people would be "transferred" from the
monarch to his ministers.

The three of us composed this address: Kokoshkin provided basic
material, which had already passed through our party and our Duma
faction. Vinaver was responsible for the style. Only a few individual
phrases from my draft were left in the address. We were very proud
of this document, and in case the Duma failed, as we expected, we
believed that the address would serve as the Duma's last will, towards
a realization in the future of everything outlined in it. But our business concerned the present, not the future.

First of all, the cabinet decided to ignore all our parliamentary
devices. The tsar did not receive our delegations, and the answer to
our "address" came not from the tsar, but from that very cabinet
which we considered unworthy of our confidence. In the government's
answer, the two parts of our "address" were first mixed into one whole,
and then, from the confusion, was picked the criminal aspect of the
"address": our alleged interference in the tsar's prerogatives. They
considered it some sort of "insult to his majesty." According to V. N.
Kokovtsov's memoirs, "there were no disagreements" in the Council
of Ministers. "Giving in to an assault from the Duma cannot be allowed." Kokovtsov formulated three propositions which especially
"could not be allowed": "abolition of the right of private property by
means of forced alienation" (this was our agrarian project), "abolition

of the fundamental laws, with a transition to ministerial responsibility",
and "seizure of all governmental power by the people's representatives." Obviously, the Duma in no way intended to "abolish private
property" or to "seize all power." On the contrary, the Duma re-
affirmed both private property and the separation of powers, preserving the emperor's prerogative. These hasty assertions, made by a
frightened bureaucrat, testified to the anxiety roused by the Duma's
declarations. This anxiety was further intensified from outside: again
according to V. N. Kokovtsov, the reports from the district governors
to the minister of internal affairs, P. A. Stolypin, spoke unanimously
about "the revolutionary upsurge and lack of means to struggle against
it." "The government is thoroughly discredited," they reported, "and
the attention of all is focused on the Duma alone." Goremykin and
Stolypin regularly communicated these reports from the provinces to
the tsar. It would seem that these same voices from the provinces
pointed to the Duma as a means for opposing the "revolutionary upsurge." But this was precisely what the bureaucracy feared, and more
so than they feared the "revolutionary upsurge" itself, which they had
just finished handling in their own way. In a word, the campaign
against the Duma was decided upon in the Council of Ministers. It
was V. I. Gurko, that *enfant terrible* of the reactionaries, who, in a
militant spirit, composed the ministerial declaration responding to the
Duma's "address." The ministers preferred his text to the more softly
worded draft composed by Shcheglovitov. Then, even the tsar apparently hesitated. He even said that he did not like the idea of the
ministers' statement. Should not he personally address the Duma, as
several of his court intimates "urged"? According to Gurko, A. P.
Izvolsky was one of those who "urged" this, suggesting as well the
form of the tsar's speech from the "throne." This would have represented a continuation of the Duma's "parliamentary style," albeit in a
rather peculiar way. Evidently for this reason, Stolypin and Kokovtsov resolutely objected to the tsar's personal intervention. Here already was a symptom of internal disagreement among the ministers,
with the tsar's will in the end favoring resistance to the Duma. The
tsar not only refused to deliver his statement before the Duma but
even regretted that the ministers' declaration was not firm enough.

On May 13, in a "scarcely audible" voice, Goremykin read this
declaration, sent to the Duma, not from the tsar, but from the ministers, without even a mention of the tsar's authority. The declaration
was crude in form and weakly argued in content. The absolutely illegal statement that the Duma's agrarian proposal was "inadmissable"
evoked a veritable storm among the deputies. Not only the Kadets
and the Trudoviks but also M. M. Kovalevsky and Count Heiden

mounted the tribune and proved the unconstitutionality of the declaration, and, with a single voice, they ended their speeches by demanding that the government be dismissed and replaced with a responsible ministry. Goremykin succeeded only in uniting the Duma on the basic demand of the Kadets. A statement of "no confidence" in the government was unanimously accepted by the Duma. The gauntlet, thrown down from above, was thus picked up, and the Duma "idyll" was finished. May 13 became the date which marked the beginning of open struggle.

The struggle, however, did not follow immediately, and the reason for this must be sought in the increasing conflict among the ministers. True, the Council of Ministers decided by the next day that the Duma must be dissolved. Opinion, however, was divided on the question of dissolving the Duma immediately or waiting awhile "to see what kind of turn the sessions would take" and, in particular, "what tactics the leading party (Kadets) would adopt. Only Izvolsky objected against dissolving the Duma. It was finally decided, in the first place, "to keep a vigilant watch over the Duma's activities," and, in the second place, "to obtain the Tsar's authorization in advance" (for dissolution). The first part reflected a compromise with those who were against immediate dissolution and placed that compromise alongside the prepared decision of Goremykin, Kokovtsov, and Stolypin, who expected nothing from the Duma anyway. Goremykin's tactics were evident in his policy of completely ignoring or, as they then said, "boycotting" the Duma. By leaving the Duma to its own resources, with insufficient rights and without the cooperation of the government, it was expected that the Duma would "wither on the vine." Nevertheless, when the Duma somehow put in order its part of the "preparatory legislative programs," it created a good impression and strengthened the position of those among the ministers and high officials surrounding the tsar who were in favor of preserving the Duma.

Thus, another month passed after the Goremykin declaration of May 13. The "vigilant watch" over the Duma continued until the middle of June. There was even a special bureaucrat, Kumanin, who gave daily reports on the Duma's behavior to the authorities. Goremykin buried himself in silence, evidently scheming and biding his time until the appropriate moment. Gurko interpreted his silence as follows: "Keep jabbering as long as you like; I will act when I find it necessary." Stolypin still felt like a novice in Petersburg, and kept stubbornly silent at the ministers' conferences, waiting for his hour to come. The tsar continued in his indecision, hiding his real opinion, as was his habit, or, perhaps, not yet having formed an opinion. In one of his regular reports, Kokovtsov expressed surprise at the tsar's words that "from various sides he hears that things are not so bad" in the Duma, that the Duma "is gradually getting used to its work." In support, the tsar referred to the "echoes of the Duma conversations," echoes that had spread rather far. In the English Club,[21] the Grand Duke Nikolai Mikhailovich expressed himself in a similar manner. The court minister, Baron Fredericks, who was both loved and respected by the tsar and had direct contact with him, told Nicholas the opinion of D. F. Trepov, who had been put in charge of the palace guards. Kokovtsov was alarmed, and advised Stolypin "to keep a closer eye on both of them." As early as the beginning of May, he had had a curious conversation with Trepov at the palace. Trepov had asked him: "What is your attitude towards the idea of a cabinet responsible to the Duma and made up of people enjoying the public confidence?" In response to Kokovtsov's objections, Trepov then asked, staring him in the eye: "Do you consider ministerial responsibility equivalent to a complete seizure of power or the removal of power from the hands of the monarch, converting the monarchy into a mere decoration?" Such was, of course, the opinion of those who favored dissolving the Duma, as one can see from the above quotations. Kokovtsov, probably angry, went even further than that in his reply. He "assumed that it meant still more, namely, the replacement of the monarchy by an entirely different form of state system," that is, evidently, by a republic. Since the public was standing around, this interesting exchange of opinion was unfortunately cut short.

Kokovtsov and Stolypin sensed trouble. Trepov, in fact, out of his own fear, had begun preliminary reconnaissance. He was supported by his brother-in-law, General A. A. Mosolov, an intelligent and observant person who clearly saw the weak sides of the regime and who subsequently disclosed his gloomy forecasts to the public. As an émigré, V. N. Kokovtsov himself published two volumes of memoirs which could serve as a strong indictment against both the tsar and his close associates. But when in a series of eight articles in *Poslednie Novosti* I extracted documentary evidence for that indictment from his memoirs, the scrupulous and conscientious bureaucrat, the faithful servant of unlimited monarchy was seemingly surprised and displeased; he had not meant it that way at all! He was only testifying conscientiously. This was a strange man, this minister of finance, who had come to be premier because of those same qualities of scrupulousness and conscientiousness, exercised within the limits of the service he had undertaken, and had protected the state treasure chest from outside encroachment, including encroachment by the tsar. All of us considered warranted his reputation as an "honest bookkeeper." He guarded from encroachment those interests which his patron entrusted to him; he did not consider himself in any way a "politician," but merely a faithful servant of the throne.

Trepov was a man of another type. He also was the tsar's faithful servant, but he interpreted his job more broadly, saw further, and did not hide what he saw. He, also, was in no way a "politician." However, as a military man, he understood that it is necessary at times to be decisive and to go beyond the limits of one's authority—and even of one's knowledge. Demonstrating precisely these attributes, he began scouting for candidates for a "responsible cabinet." Mosolov knew that Trepov had turned to Muromtsev, to me, and to "other prominent Kadets." At that time, I did not know that Trepov had turned to anyone but me. I found out later that he had also turned to I. I. Petrunkevich and that a meeting had been carefully arranged and even imposed; but our "patriarch" had refused to attend, claiming that he had no right to enter negotiations with the government without the party's permission. Petrunkevich never told me about this rejected offer. Trepov then turned to me with the same offer through the same go-between, that unimportant English correspondent, the "noseless" Lamark, who apparently had carried out many backstage assignments in influential circles.

I agreed without hesitation. It was clearly hopeless to ask for permission from our faction. I considered it impossible to shun the meeting when the matter dealt with our main demand and when there were no other alternatives except the dissolution of the Duma. At that time I was unaware of the "omnipotence" of the palace commandant, of his intimacy with the tsar, or of any practical proposals that he might make to the tsar. I assumed that our talk would be limited to a mutual exchange of information and that, in any case, it would not be at all binding. I told no one about this meeting until the time of the Third Duma. In 1909, I published a detailed account of my talk with Trepov in *Rech*, and I deeply regret that I do not have this issue (February 17) before me now, because my memory simply has not retained all the details of that conversation. I consider this meeting more important than all those that followed later, and I will try to recall all that I can.

Our talk took place in the Restaurant Kiuba. (I was badgered about this restaurant for a long time afterwards by know-it-all newspaper reporters.) Our talk was conducted in very polite tones. Of the two of us, I was much more cautious. Trepov got right down to business and offered me the opportunity of taking part in the formation of a "ministry of confidence." I told him in reply what I had been forced to repeat many times during those months, both in articles and speeches—that it was impossible to select personnel until after the political direction had been chosen. "You cannot enter private negotiations, taking what you like from a prepared program while throwing away the parts which do not suit you." "You must take it alive, as it is, or not at all. . . . There must be no deception here; anyone trying it, would only deceive himself. . . . We are not interested in a superficial rehabilitation of the government while preserving its internal essence; we want decisive and irrevocable change in the whole course." I am taking these quoted phrases from my printed answer to a later interview with Trepov, and it was with these introductory explanations that I began our conversation. I was surprised, actually, that our meeting did not end right there. I do not remember whether or not Trepov raised the question of a so-called "coalition" ministry, but he realized that my above-mentioned views precluded such a ministry. (Later, he called for precisely a "Kadet" ministry.) The rest of our talk, therefore, concerned the "program," not the "persons." Without thinking long, Trepov took a notebook out of his pocket and in a businesslike manner asked me what conditions the Kadets would impose before joining the cabinet. He did not merely note down points of the program with which he already was familiar from the Duma's "address," but at each point went into a special discussion. I am especially sorry that I am not able to reproduce exactly this most interesting part of our talk.

There were, I think, about seven points, including the basic condition, namely, the formation of a responsible ministry from the Duma majority. Regarding the question of "compulsory expropriation," the point in our agrarian program that had so angered Goremykin, Kokovtsov, and Stolypin, Trepov to my amazement immediately answered with complete agreement. Evidently, he had thought this question over beforehand and had made his decision. But—also, evidently, the result of forethought—he accompanied his agreement on the substance of the question with an extraordinarily typical stipulation. Let the tsar do it, not the Duma. Let the peasants receive their additional allotment from the hands of the tsar, by way of an imperial manifesto. I could not help recalling the imperial manifesto of October 17, which had been promulgated in addition to the promises Witte had made in his "report," and I did not care even to object to this statement of the problem. When we got to the question of amnesty, however, the general balked. "The Tsar will never pardon the regicides!" I tried in vain to convince him that this was a thing of the past, a matter of history, that a total amnesty was necessary in order to bring about a corresponding shift in the public mood, that "regicides" were varieties, disappearing along with the change in the conditions which had created them. Finally, I tried to convince him that a demonstration of the tsar's will was needed precisely on this issue, since his was the only power which had the right to grant such an amnesty, and that the gratitude of society consequently would be directed entirely to the tsar himself. It was all in vain. Evidently, Trepov knew better than I the psychology of the tsar and the tsarina, in which personal and dynastic judgments dominated over political. His decision on this question, too, was made beforehand, but he noted it down in his book all the same. As could be expected, universal suffrage met no resistance whatever from him. Indeed, it had been half-promised; and Witte's electoral statute of December 11, with its "grey" peasants and clergy, deceived all expectations and was cursed at all meetings. Neither a revision of the "Fundamental Laws," nor a new constitution created by the Duma's constituent authority (but "with the Tsar's approval"), nor the abolition of the State Council—none of these governmental, juridical matters terrified this general, a stranger to all such legal affairs. He simply took all these things into account and, without objecting, noted them down in his book. At any rate, Trepov's general impressions of our conversation did not preclude further talks. As a sign of the mutual trust which had arisen between us, Trepov gave me his telephone number in Peterhof when we parted and suggested that I contact him soon. I did not find it necessary, however, to take advantage of his kindness. That Trepov's scouting efforts did not remain unknown to the tsar, was clear from one sentence which the tsar later spoke to Kokovtsov, in which the tsar hinted at people who "are somewhat naive in their understanding of State affairs, but who conscientiously search for ways out of a difficult situation." Thus, through direct instructions from the tsar, the talks about ministerial responsibility were transferred from the light touch of Trepov to someone else's less "dilettante" hands. I learned only later, I should add, about the connection between Trepov's first attempt and these future talks.

The first of these talks took place on S. A. Muromtsev's invitation to meet, at his own apartment, the minister of agriculture, Ermolov. I did not know at that time that Muromtsev had also had a meeting with Trepov. Muromtsev told me that Ermolov wanted to get to know me as one of the possible candidates. Ermolov himself began the conversation by announcing that he was speaking with me "on the Tsar's instructions." Our talk followed general political lines and was carried on in a good-humored spirit. Ermolov did not dwell on details, and, for that reason, I do not remember the content of our talk. Evidently, he was supposed to get a general impression of the person rather than the political program. Muromtsev, who had remained silent the whole time, told me later that the impression was favorable. This could also be seen from the fact that sometime later I received an invitation, "on the instructions of the Tsar," to talk with Stolypin himself at his summer home on Aptekar Island. But by the time of the meeting (which according to Kokovtsov's chronology took place on one of the four days between the nineteenth and the twenty-fourth of June), both the purpose and the tone of the meeting with one of the chief advocates of the Duma's dissolution had become entirely different from those of the earlier meetings.

Conversations with me and other Kadets by no means exhausted D. F. Trepov's efforts in this matter, and the Duma opponents were keeping a "vigilant watch" not only on the Duma but also on those who favored preserving it. Stolypin tried to speak with the old man Fredericks. However, "there was such confusion in his head, that it was simply impossible to understand him," Stolypin told Kokovtsov. He promised Kokovtsov to speak to Trepov "without fail," "in view of Trepov's influence on the Tsar." Apparently, nothing came of it. Trepov continued his own way. As a result of his reconnaisance, he had already managed to draw up a rough list of members for his ministry of confidence, which included myself (without my knowledge, of course). He brought this list to the attention of the tsar, and Nicholas passed this "curious document" on to Kokovtsov without naming its author. Here is that document as it was published in Kokovtsov's memoirs:

Chairman of the Council of Ministers—Muromtsev
Minister of the Interior—Miliukov or Petrunkevich
Minister of Justice—Nabokov or Kuzmin-Karavaev
Minister of Foreign Affairs—Muliukov or A. P. Izvolsky
Minister of Finance—Hertsenstein
Minister of Agriculture—N. N. Lvov
State Controller—D. N. Shipov
Ministers of the Army, the Navy and the Court—"to be chosen at His Majesty's discretion."

It is significant that the names of the two chief conspirators against the Duma, Kokovtsov and Stolypin, were not included in the list, and this, of course, strengthened their negative attiude toward Trepov's enterprise. It was almost a "Kadet" list. N. N. Lvov had been a member of our party but had left it because of our agrarian program. He had known Stolypin in Saratov, where he was a Zemstvo leader, and had enjoyed Stolypin's sympathies. The peasant uprisings and the burning of the gentry's estates had made a deep impression on him. A passionate, hot, and nervous orator, and eloquent when he became fired up, he infected people with his firm conviction—to the point of fanaticism. I had agreed that three ministers were to be

chosen "at the discretion" of the tsar already in my conversation with
Trepov, since, even for the Kadets, this was the inviolable territory of
the tsar's prerogative.

The tsar's very presentation of Trepov's list (without even naming
the author) to Kokovtsov was a rather insidious step on Nicholas'
part; for of course he knew about their disagreements over the fate of
the Duma, about the opposing views of Trepov and Kokovtsov. He
wanted to bring them into conflict, retaining the freedom of decision
for himself. He almost told Kokovtsov just that. "I do not immediately
reject what they tell me, although it is very painful for me to hear
views that shatter the fondest dreams of my whole life. But, believe
me, I will not make a decision that goes against my conscience, and,
of course, I will weigh everything you have told me and tell you what
I have decided. Until that time, do not believe, even should they tell
you so, that I have taken such a leap into the unknown." In his
Memoirs, V. N. Kokovtsov always presents the tsar's own words in
quotation marks; but in his account they usually take on a sluggishness
and style peculiar to that memoirist. One cannot doubt the essence of
what the tsar said, however. What the tsar was searching for and
what advice he wanted to receive from his advisor are all too clearly
expressed. And he received just the advice he wanted. "Gripped with
emotion," Kokovtsov gave Nicholas an improvised lecture, which did
not take very much account of the science of state law, but which was
quite well geared to the tsar's mood and comprehension. "Unknown
persons," desiring to gain power, have their own opinion about the
"extent of the monarch's power," an opinion which does not correspond to that of the sovereign. After transferring power to them,
the tsar will only be able to "keep control of the executive organs that
head the government by what has come to be called a coup d'etat."
The tsar turned the conversation to the practical problems of the
moment: "What can we do to set a limit to what is going on in the
Duma and to direct its work along a peaceful path?" Kokovtsov
answered with precisely such a program for a "coup d'etat." "Prepare
for the dissolution of the Duma and the inevitable revision of the
electoral law." This is exactly what the Council of Ministers had decided long ago, and it coincided with the insistent demands of the
gentry and the Black Hundreds organizations, which were approved
of and secretly listened to by the sovereign. "The sovereign stood
silent before me for a long time," Kokovtsov narrated, then "firmly
grasped my hand" and let it go with the parting words mentioned
above. Kokovtsov personally thought that the tsar "did not have a
clearly formed idea of allowing government power to be given over
to the hands of a Kadet ministry." This is a very modest conclusion,

to say the least. It was clear that the question was the reverse: how not to allow this transfer of power. In any case, Kokovtsov continued to fear that the tsar "would allow it." Stolypin himself, in Kokovtsov's opinion, "was far from the only one who liked the idea of a ministry of people enjoying the public confidence"—provided, of course, that he would be included in that ministry. The conspirators already suspected each other. As for Stolypin, Kokovtsov was almost right. These, like Kokovtsov himself, "devoted and no mere flatterers" could be counted on one hand.

After the tsar handed over Trepov's secret to Kokovtsov, that is, after June 15-20, the intrigue against the Duma went forward at full speed. Right after returning from his report to the tsar, Kokovtsov received a visit from D. F. Trepov's brother, Alexander, who was already carrying on the struggle against his brother's policies. He had come "straight from Goremykin," who had refused to heed his alarm, repeating in the same tired voice, "that's all nonsense." Goremykin "had decided not to talk" with Stolypin, since, you never could tell, Stolypin himself might have "taken part" in the Trepov intrigue. A. F. Trepov begged Kokovtsov "to open the Tsar's eyes to the catastrophic danger of this madman's venture" (his brother's). He did not know, of course, that this had already almost been done. According to General Mosolov's memoirs, this role had been played by still another of D. F. Trepov's brothers, Vladimir. Four days passed and again A. F. Trepov came to Kokovtsov, this time completely calm. "His brother (D.F.) had called him to Peterhof. D. F. was very gloomy," and had told him that "he had heard from Stolypin's associates that his whole plan had sunk into oblivion since the dissolution of the Duma was becoming more and more imminent." If we subtract four days from the time of Kokovtsov's report to the tsar, then this shift falls between the nineteenth and the twenty-fourth of June. Let us remember these dates; they will turn out to be historically significant.

D. F. Trepov, however, in spite of the bad news from the camp of the victors, still did not lay down his arms. He gave an interview to Reuter's Press Agency which was published in London. My answer, which has been partially reproduced above, was printed in the June 27 issue of *Rech*. In his interview, Trepov categorically affirmed—and completely correctly—that "neither a coalition ministry nor a ministry organized outside the Duma will appease the country." It was necessary to form a ministry "from the Kadets, because they are the strongest party in the Duma." He admitted that the Kadets "allow the Trudoviks freedom of action in order to scare the government by the proximity of the revolutionary danger"; but this union "will be torn apart when the center is called to take power." Of course, the situation was more complicated than I have presented it here. Even Trepov agreed that a Kadet ministry would entail great risks. The situation of the country was such, however, that the risk had to be taken. As he put it to me at our meeting: When your house is burning, you have to jump out, even from the fifth floor. This "dilettante" was evidently the most farsighted of the official politicians. "Only then— he continued—if even this does not help, will we have to turn to more extreme measures." Trepov's opponents understood this remark as meaning Trepov's own dictatorship; they maintained that Trepov had conceived of the Kadet ministry only as a preparatory maneuver. To such people, it seemed incredibly "crazy" that it was even possible to talk seriously about a Kadet ministry. From Trepov's and Fredericks' future behavior, it is apparent that they talked and thought about it quite seriously.

In this interview, however, I saw Trepov's answer to my conditions. Evidently, he did not think that these conditions were the Kadets' last word. This time he "unconditionally rejected the principle of expropriation," and, as before, he found it impossible to speak of a "complete amnesty." I had to answer him in print that the party could not abandon these positions without losing face. Its task "is not to erect new fortifications on a position already lost," but to "disarm the revolution, having fostered its interest in preserving the new order." Stolypin's semiofficial paper, *Rossiia,* and Suvorin's *Novoe Vremya* said in reply that the party "is scheming," that it is "two-faced," that it "is powerless to restrain the leftists from even more grandiose performances." *Rossiia* occupied itself with an examination of the reasons "for the government's indecision and slowness" in changing its composition. The very words, however, showed that both the opponents and the supporters of Trepov's plan did not consider the struggle ended.

The whole picture of the situation, as it is presented here, was unknown to me when I received Stolypin's invitation "on the instructions of the Tsar." I do not remember the exact date, but, evidently, it took place in those same "four days" when the fate of Trepov's list was decided (June 19–24). For Stolypin, the question was decided no later than the twenty-fourth, and, as we shall see, he had already taken preparatory action. His talk with me pursued a single aim: to find new evidence from my explanations—which he could predict—for the correctness of his tactics.

I found A. P. Izvolsky at Stolypin's place, as if in the role of a delegate from the other camp. But Izvolsky had no influence in the Council of Ministers; he was present only as an honorable witness. He kept quiet the whole time during my conversation with Stolypin. Stolypin had no intention of giving me the chance to express myself on the substantive issues. He was only hunting up material for his indictment. He did not say directly whether the new ministry was to be a "coalition" or "purely Kadet." He soon made it apparent, although indirectly, that Izvolsky might possibly take part in the new ministry, but that his own participation as premier or minister of the interior was unconditionally excluded. I remember his ironical questions: Do I understand that the minister of the interior is at the same time the chief of the gendarmes, and that consequently he carries out functions to which the Kadets are not accustomed? Also half-ironically I replied that the elementary government functions are perfectly well known to the Kadets, but that the manner of fulfilling these functions might differ from what then existed, depending on the general direction of government activity. I added that the behavior of the Kadets in the government should not be prejudged by their role in the opposition. In this connection I. V. Hessen ascribes to me the words: "If I were to give them five kopecks, society would take it as a ruble; but if you were to give them a ruble, they wouldn't consider it worth five kopecks." I could hardly have spoken so cynically to Stolypin.

Stolypin paused only fleetingly on the questions of program, although he was interested in whether or not I would include the ministers of the army, the navy, and the Court among those which should be nominated by the Kadets. I told him the same thing I told Trepov: that we did not intend to interfere with the monarch's prerogatives.

The result of this talk was just what I had expected. According to a later official announcement, "this conversation was immediately reported to His Majesty together with the judgment of the minister of the interior that the fulfillment of the wishes of the Kadet party could affect Russia's interests only in the most disastrous way, a judgment approved by His Majesty in its entirety." It was evidently for this that I had been invited "on instructions from the sovereign" and the wishes of Stolypin.

Apparently, it was not by accident that A. P. Izvolsky came down with me from the top floor of Stolypin's summerhouse, where the conversation had taken place, and offered to give me a lift in his carriage. On the way, he managed to tell me that he understood Stolypin, who was not familiar with European political systems, but that he himself appreciated the significance of the progressive circles' political demands, that he did not share Stolypin's views, and that he felt much closer to our opinions on the necessity of radical political reforms which would bring us closer to Europe and would facilitate the mission of the minister of foreign affairs abroad. I had nothing against the liberal minister's *profession de foi*. The short "white night" had come to an end. It was already light, and the shoppers were hurrying down the streets with their packages. When we got to the Neva, I pointed out to the minister how inconvenient it would be for him to be recognized in the company of such a dangerous person. Izvolsky agreed, remarking only that the same danger also threatened his Kadet traveling companion. I thanked him and we parted.

Stolypin would not be allowed to forget his part in our conversation on the topic of a Kadet ministry. When I mentioned it in the Third Duma, he was stung, and the "Information Bureau" immediately printed a denial. They stated that "the chairman of the Council of Ministers had never had any negotiations whatsoever, not even preliminary ones, with P. N. Miliukov concerning the formation of a Kadet ministry or the offer of ministerial portfolios to members of the Kadet party. In June of 1906, P. N. Miliukov was invited to the minister of the interior, Stolypin, according to the emperor's instructions, for the sole purpose of explaining the plans and desires of the Kadet party, which at that time was the dominant party in the Duma. During his conversation with the minister, P. N. Miliukov explained his views on the state of affairs in detail," and so on. Then there followed the report to the tsar on the result of the conversation which was cited above. In my printed answer to Stolypin, I explained the real situation, pointing out all the preceding serious talks about our ministry as well as the fact that a substantive "discussion" of this, and not simply an information exchange, had taken place at Stolypin's dacha. I also mentioned Trepov's list and the "obstacles" which arose over my refusal to "retain several of the members of the existing cabinet." To deny all this was impossible.

One week later, after the tsar's conversation with Kokovtsov which was cited above, (that is between June 22 and 27, and closer to the 27) the sovereign was already able to "reassure him." "I can tell you now that I never intended to venture into the remote unknown which people were advising me to test. I did not tell this to those who, with the best of intentions, of course, suggested the idea to me. . . . I wanted to verify my own thoughts. . . . What you have told me, I have been told by almost everybody with whom I spoke during that time, and I have no longer any doubts—nor indeed did I ever have any doubts, since I do not have the right to repudiate what has been willed to me by my ancestors and what I must bequeath for safekeeping to my son." As we know now, this fateful notion never left the tsar; this was but a repetition of "the fondest dream of my whole life." But then, what did all this really mean, all this comedy of negotiations about a Kadet cabinet, and the whole serious "conflict" among the ministers and the high officials over this question?

The Outcome of Two Conflicts:
Dissolution of the First Duma

I AM NOW COMING to the most fateful fact of that fateful year, 1905–6: the tragic outcome of the two conflicts, inside and outside the Duma. Inside, the conflict developed between the parliamentary and revolutionary tendencies; while on the outside it was between the tendency to preserve the people's representative body in its "constitutional" form and the tendency to dissolve the Duma and restore as far as possible the entire, unlimited authority of the monarch. I mentioned earlier that I had not expected so strong a current among the high officials, against dissolving the Duma. Nevertheless, I had no doubts about the final outcome. This explains my skeptical attitude towards the talks about a Kadet cabinet. As far as I was concerned, the tsar's will was the decisive factor. I found full corroboration of my (and not only my) assessment when I read the two volumes of V. N. Kokovtsov's memoirs after I had already emigrated from Russia. A scrupulous and conscientious bureaucrat and a monarchist by tradition, the author, to the end of his days it seems, never realized that he committed an act of treason against the memory of his beloved monarch by making public his photographically precise descriptions of his intimate conversations with the tsar.

Nicholas II was doubtlessly an honest person and a good family man, but he was by nature extremely weak-willed. He had never prepared himself to reign, nor did he like it when this burden fell upon him. He, as well as his wife, hated court etiquette and did not conform to it. After conscientiously hearing out the usual reports of his ministers, that so bored him, he would run out of the conferences into the open air to chop wood, his favorite pastime.

As often happens with weak-willed people—like Alexander I, for example—Nicholas was afraid of being influenced by a strong will. Struggling against such influence, he used the same means as Alexander I had used, the only means available to him—cunning and duplicity. We have just seen a clear example of how he was able to conceal his real thoughts while maneuvering among the influences of those who surrounded him. I do not know what the situation would have been, had there not been near him that other strong will, a will to which he completely, though unconsciously, subordinated himself: the will of his wife. The tsarina was by nature obstinate and vain. From the very beginning she felt isolated in a strange country,[22] fenced off from all except a tight circle of her like-minded companions. Both husband and wife had come to the same view of their life's goal: to transfer the paternal inheritance intact to their son. We saw this immutable formula in Kokovtsov's report. They could not help knowing that they were going against the current, but thanks to the empress—"the only one wearing the pants," as she later said of herself in one of her letters to Nicholas—they began the struggle against this current as best they could. This led to a close and careful selection of "family friends," the majority of whom were on an extremely low cultural level. Outside of this intimate circle, there were only ill-wishers and "enemies." They formed an impenetrable fortress, which could be reached only through the aid of that "transcendent world," through those divine fools and mystics skilled in the art of magic.

What else, besides what actually happened, could one have expected from this royal psychology, so poor in ideas and rich only in its faith that Providence had predetermined their fate? In that critical moment of its history, Russia could find no others capable of setting the country on a new road of development. . . .

My story of this decisive moment will be especially detailed since it is based not only on the knowledge of events which I had at that time but also on everything which was published later. Nevertheless, I will not go beyond the autobiographical framework, for I personally continued to be involved, although most of the time only passively.

The story begins on the twenty-fourth of June, 1906. This date should be remembered because it explains much that has remained unclear. As of that date, as has been noted above, P. A. Stolypin had the tsar's authorization in his hands for dissolving the Duma. This circumstance, above all, does away with V. I. Gurko's assertion— Gurko is an untrustworthy witness anyway—that Stolypin did not want to dissolve the Duma. It is true only that he wanted the most "liberal" dissolution possible, and that later he received the tsar's permission to remove the most reactionary ministers from his cabinet (Stishinsky and Shirinsky-Shakhmatov) while bringing in several public figures. From D. N. Shipov's memoirs, we know that Stolypin's "liberalism" went even further. He wanted to use Shipov as a cover by placing him at the head of the cabinet. Shipov received this incredible offer first from N. N. Lvov and then later, on June 26–27, from Stolypin personally. Stolypin wanted to confront Shipov with a fait accompli. He told Shipov that "the dissolution of the Duma should be carried out by a renovated government headed by some public figure who enjoys the confidence of the society at large." The tsar had accepted this plan, and on the twenty-eighth, Shipov was invited to have an audience.

As one might have expected, Shipov reacted sharply to this attempt to use him for Stolypin's intrigues. He stated that he considered the dissolution of the Duma not only inexpedient and "unconstitutional" but downright "criminal," and he did not hide his opinion from the Petersburg public. Stolypin then had to fall back on his second plan. At his meeting with Shipov, in the presence of N. N. Lvov and A. P. Izvolsky, Stolypin had begun to speak not of dissolving the Duma, but of creating a "coalition" cabinet under Shipov's chairmanship, with himself and Izvolsky also taking part. Shipov repeated what he had said earlier. Since the Kadet party is dominant in the Duma, the formation of such a "coalition" cabinet is impossible; the cabinet must be entrusted to "one of the Kadet leaders." Stolypin then had to admit that he "had already received and had spoken with P. N. Miliukov about the probable change in the cabinet, and that P. N. Miliukov had let it be known that he would not shun the task of forming a cabinet were such an offer made to him." My report of my conversation with Stolypin shows how he misconstrued both the aim and the content of our talk. Izvolsky, however, took advantage of this turn in the conversation and expressed the hope that Shipov "would succeed in persuading the Kadets to join a coalition cabinet." By thus recalling my conversation with Stolypin, he hit right at Stolypin's sore spot. "Regarding our (Izvolsky and Stolypin) participation, we should leave this question completely to the free decision of Dmitry Nikolaevich." This did not at all fit Stolypin's plans. According to Shipov, he "feigned the appearance of accepting A. P. Izvolsky's last words." This did not last, however, and he put his cards on the table: Kadet participation in the cabinet was "impossible and too risky." He "insists on the necessity of dissolving the Duma." He did not admit, of course, that the decision to dissolve the Duma had already been made; he only stressed that "the question of forming a new cabinet can be decided only by the Tsar." In other words, he left the question open.

With this retreat back to the original theme, the conversation naturally came to an end. Stolypin, however, could not help but mention that "there is a proposal to grant Shipov an audience tomorrow at Peterhof." He did not know that the tsar had already invited Shipov, and that his whole plan was going to be exposed, since the conversation with the tsar would take a different turn from what Stolypin had counted on.

Preparing for his audience with the tsar, Shipov contacted me through Count P. A. Heiden and had a long conversation with Muromtsev. I remember that Count Heiden, coming up to me in the Duma, asked my opinion of a "coalition cabinet" and even suggested one of the grand dukes for one of the posts belonging to the tsar's prerogative. However, from the snatches he got from our brief chat, he wrongly concluded that I "considered the matter (the rejection of a coalition cabinet) as already determined" and that I "was ready to take upon myself the formation of a cabinet as soon as I would be entrusted with the task." Of course, I never said that, nor even thought it, since I assumed that my conversation with Stolypin had settled the question of my participation. In his memoirs, Shipov discussed his conversation with Muromtsev in more detail. He "spared no efforts to secure Muromtsev's help" in forming a coalition cabinet, but he excluded from that cabinet "the participation of the bureaucratic element, and in particular of P. A. Stolypin." Muromtsev himself was to be the chairman. This was already unrealistic, and Muromtsev, it seems, understood this when he stated that he approved of Shipov's refusal and would do the same himself. The considerations which motivated his refusal are interesting. In the first place, he said, "under the present conditions, no ministry, regardless of its composition, can count on peaceful and productive governmental activity in the near future, nor can it hope to retain its position for a more or less extended time." In other words, no cabinet could control the situation and any cabinet would soon be dismissed. This is precisely what the right-wing press had been saying. In the second place, Muromtsev explained, turning from the matter of principle to his own personal point of view, it was impossible to talk with the Kadets about a "coalition" cabinet because "P. N. Miliukov already thinks of himself as premier." This apparently widespread opinion about my personal intentions roused a feeling of competition in Muromtsev which was also connected to the lack of trust that our Kadet faction felt toward Muromtsev, himself.

Shipov, however, did not give up. On the same day of his very cordial reception at the tsar's palace, he continued to develop his views on the necessity of forming a Kadet cabinet. He could now do it with impunity because he had shifted from practice to principle. The tsar gave Shipov the chance to explain his position when he asked him directly, why he had a negative attitude toward dissolving the Duma. Shipov's answer was deeply thought out and, politically, thoroughly honest. Nobody had spoken with the tsar like that before, and if the bearer of supreme authority could, in fact, be affected by beliefs of this sort, if his stubbornness could, in fact, be explained by a lack of knowledge of the real situation, then everything that needed to be said was said there, openly and honestly.

Shipov frankly pointed out to the tsar the ambiguity of the "constitutional" manifesto of October 17. He also stressed the abnormality of the relations between the government and the people's representatives. Under such conditions, an appeal to the voters (after dissolving the Duma) offered no hope whatsoever that the voter would stand on the side of the government. On the contrary, inevitably and indubitably the voters would send "much more leftist representatives" to the next Duma. (Shipov turned out to be right, but he apparently did not suspect that this was precisely the argument which the opponents of the Duma used in advocating a forced change in the electoral law.) There is another way out, Shipov continued: reconciliation with the present Duma. Such reconciliation required a sincere readiness to work with the Duma and to return to an honest implementation of the October Manifesto. Reconciliation of the Duma with the government, however, would be impossible with a "coalition" cabinet. Consequently, it was necessary to create a cabinet from the Duma majority, and it was entirely probable that, under such conditions, the Kadets would soften their tactics once in power. Shipov even took it upon himself to defend cautiously the basic principles of the Kadet program—including the agrarian project.

Such was the logic of Shipov's speech. He carried the question far beyond Stolypin's plan, which had already been approved by the tsar. Nevertheless, the conversation continued in the spirit of Shipov's views, and shifted naturally enough to the question of personnel. Of the two candidates for premier, Shipov, of course, favored Muromtsev. But he also did justice to Miliukov, who was "the most influential member" of the party. Shipov gave "due tribute to his abilities, his talents and his scholarly erudition." But . . . Miliukov was "too autocratic." Uttering this word in front of the autocrat, he immediately regretted the phrase that he had "thoughtlessly thrown out." Then he continued to describe Miliukov's dark side. "In his basic view of life, Miliukov is above all a rationalist, a positivist historian. His religious consciousness is only weakly developed." Were he placed at the head, he "would hardly base his actions on the demands of moral duty, and his policy could hardly contribute to the necessary spiritual elevation of the country's population." It would be better to give him the post of minister of internal affairs or minister of foreign affairs. That would be "very useful and even necessary." He then proceded to describe Muromtsev. S. A. Muromtsev "is a man of high moral stature." He "enjoys a generally recognized authority," and his appointment as premier "will be welcomed by society at large." At the same time, Muromtsev "is noted for his great tact and gentleness of character." He would "assure the necessary independence to all members of the cabinet, and under his leadership, P. N. Miliukov's participation in the cabinet would be especially useful."

Hearing these character descriptions, the tsar politely summed up his interlocutor's thoughts with the kind phrase: "Yes, in that way the correct relationship between the mental and the spiritual forces may be established"; and with that, the tsar "made it evident that the audience was over."

Did the serious content and sincere tone of Shipov's speech make an impression on the tsar, given his personal disinterestedness? In the court circles at least, they knew that the tsar's impression of the conversation was favorable. Or was this only Nicholas' defensive hypocrisy? Sometime later, V. O. Kliuchevsky told me how the tsar, upon returning home after the audience, told his family: "Well now, that Shipov is a smart fellow. I questioned him about everything, but I told him nothing." Since, Kliuchevsky was close to the tsar's family and its milieu, he could have known this. . . .

Be that as it may, Shipov "felt himself in a bold mood" after returning from the audience, and in this mood immediately went to see Muromtsev and tell him about the conversation. When it came to the talk of the premiership, Muromtsev grew excited. "What right do you have to discuss a question which ought to be decided by the political party itself?" Shipov said something about the "welfare of the country." Muromtsev then expressed himself more clearly: he "expressed doubts about his joint participation with Miliukov in the cabinet." "It is difficult for two bears to get along together in one den."

It was not until I read Shipov's *Memoirs* that I found out about the audience, about his conversation with the tsar, and about his recommendations. I cannot help comparing this to my own episode with Muromtsev. During one of the Duma sessions, the Duma guard came up to me in the press box and said: "The chairman of the Duma asks you to see him in his office immediately." I went. Muromtsev rose from his chair to meet me and, without any preliminary comments, asked me straight away, "Which one of us is going to be premier?" Perhaps he thought that I was more informed about the course of the negotiations. For me this was so unexpected and so amusing that I could not help laughing. I answered him: "In my opinion, neither of us will be premier." Muromtsev apparently thought that I was refusing to answer the question, and he continued to insist. Maybe I would have avoided answering, had I thought that there were serious chances for a Kadet cabinet. I knew that our faction would hardly have chosen Muromtsev. The official part of my answer was, "If the matter has reached such an important stage as a Kadet ministry, then the question of the premiership is only a secondary detail which the party will decide." I felt that this answer was just the one which would dissatisfy Muromtsev; so I continued, "As for myself, I would refuse the premiership with pleasure and leave it to you." These last words had a quite unexpected effect on him. Muromtsev could not hide the joy he felt, and he expressed it by gestures more like a ballerina's entrechat than the reactions of a Duma chairman. With this pirouette our talk ended. Muromtsev had found out what he needed to know, and I hurried back to the conference hall. Evidently, he was seriously waiting at the time for an invitation from Peterhof. Only later, in an offended tone, he wrote his famous phrase in the archaic style of a strict parliamentarian: "The chairman was not summoned."

Meanwhile, as they say in the melodramas, "the enemy was not to be caught napping." Stolypin, to whom Shipov had told the substance of his conversation with the tsar on the very day of his audience, could not "hide the displeasure which filled his whole being." He had already heard that "what Shipov had said created a favorable impression and was greeted sympathetically." This could mean the ruin of all his plans! Saying good-bye to Shipov, he dropped a comment in which his concealed alarm was mixed with a threat: "Now we shall see what follows." I can imagine the chilling tone in which this was said.

The back-stage work had to be continued. In the court circles, they knew that the "favorable attitude" toward Shipov's report "lasted exactly one week." A. P. Izvolsky, who was personally interested, told Shipov that it had continued precisely "until July 5, but on that day the situation changed, and, as you see, the probability of S. A. Muromtsev being invited to Peterhof is diminishing." In answer to the question "What caused this change?" Izvolsky told Shipov, on perfectly good grounds, that "Stolypin's influence can be felt here."

We shall see in fact that on July 5, Stolypin got a new trump in his game, a trump he had been waiting for and of which he skillfully took advantage. After June 24, July 5 is the second historic date in the preparations for dissolving the Duma.

Through mutual friends, knowledge about the "favorable" turn on the issue of a Kadet cabinet finally reached our Kadet circles. They were even assuring each other of a positive outcome. I still did not believe this, but, nevertheless, I felt that I had to tell our faction about my personal role in the negotiations. Until that time I had carried out this whole business on my own, without letting anyone in on it. Now, even our political neighbors knew about the negotiations. I hastily called a special meeting of our faction for the third of July, in order to obtain its instructions, whichever way the question was finally decided. At the meeting I gave a general outline of those conditions, consistent with our program and tactics, which we would have to set in case the government seriously turned to us. They gave me their none-too-friendly sanction.

To our "left-wing" Kadets, a Kadet cabinet seemed a dangerous political venture, verging on a suspicious compromise. In such an atmosphere, the question of allowing a coalition cabinet could not even be posed. There was no discussion of particular Kadet ministers either. Our faction was much more aroused by the question of dissolving the Duma, should a Kadet cabinet not be realized. This outcome seemed to be far more probable, and understandably so, and it was the subject of more than one heated discussion. The speeches of all the members of our faction could be brought down to one question: How should the Duma react to its being dissolved? The most fantastic suggestions were offered. Should they remain seated in their places? Appeal to the country for support? In any case, they should remain together and be ready for anything. I remember that the respected, greybearded old V. I. Dolzhenkov, a school teacher by profession and a fiery, confirmed, and passionate Kadet to the point of fanaticism, was particularly adamant, ready to "die on the spot." The only thing we did not foresee was the form of dissolution that Stolypin so insidiously and maliciously chose. We still had not given up our belief in the Duma's inviolability and in the government's fear of its dissolution, never imagining how far the premier's gubernatorial tactics would go in disregarding the rights of the Duma and the persons of the deputies. Moreover, once the basic conflict with the government really got underway and the question raised as to the very existence of the Duma, then concern about preventing particular conflicts with the government receded into the background. Stolypin was only waiting for an excuse, and we gave it to him in the form of the most controversial of all questions: the agrarian question. And we gave him the pretext precisely during the days of decisive negotiations concerning the formation of a cabinet from the Duma majority, at a time when, in fact, there was no such majority. How could this happen?

The first pretext was not given by the Duma. On July 20, a government announcement appeared, bearing all the marks of provocation. The government "appeased" the population by announcing that the Duma's agrarian reform would not be put into effect. This announcement, of course, was absolutely illegal. It contradicted even those legislative rights of the Duma which were already restricted by the fundamental laws. In a session of the Agrarian Committee, Deputy Kuzmin-Karavaev, a vain and stupid man, an inveterate intriguer and muddle-headed politician, suggested the publication of a "counter-announcement" in the name of the Duma as a reply to the government's announcement. I have already said that the Duma's turning directly to the people was a Trudovik tactic which masked revolutionary aspirations. At that particular time, it would have been more dangerous for the Duma than ever before. Nevertheless, the proposal passed the committee, and on July 4 (I emphasize that date) the finished draft of the agrarian announcement was placed on the agenda of the Duma's plenary session. The party "leaders," myself included, found ourselves faced by a fait accompli, since none of us had followed the course of the draft through the committee, and we had made no decision whatsoever as to how we should regard that draft. The best informed person of all turned out to be—P. A. Stolypin! On that day, July 4, he appeared in the Duma, where he was a rare guest, and sat through the entire session in the minister's box, painstakingly noting down the discussions. In the corridors people were whispering that the reason for this unexpected attention to the Duma was precisely the Duma's agrarian address to the people. Stolypin had the opportunity of hearing the sharpest arguments of the left-wing speakers, and apparently he intended to use the material he collected for a report to the tsar. Our faction suspected nothing, and during the evening meeting, nothing was said about it. We let slip the opportunity of holding back discussion of the project by formal motions.

Only on the morning of July 5 (remember Izvolsky's report) did I finally receive information about what had happened. I immediately sounded the alarm, rushed over to see Petrunkevich and explained to him the danger of the Duma's appeal, which had already been adopted by our faction. I insisted on the necessity of at least preventing a distorted interpretation of the appeal. That evening at our faction's meeting, and on the morning of July 6, in the editorial article of *Rech*, I called attention to Stolypin's threat that in case of agrarian disturbances, Austro-German troops would intervene. I pleaded with them "not to take a single step" which might be interpreted as unconstitutional. "We are perhaps on the eve of terrible decisions," I wrote. "The final days during which it is still possible to establish an agreement between the legislative and executive powers are passing quickly, and preparations for extreme measures are growing on both sides just as quickly. . . . The whole psychology of the issue (a Duma cabinet) has rapidly changed. . . . People who were inclined favorably towards a Duma cabinet recoiled from it in the last minute." Stolypin's *Rossiia* spoke openly: "It is unthinkable to believe that the liberal bourgeoisie can control the extremist currents without repression." "Better to use repressive measures" than to agree to "an extremist program." I pleaded with the Duma "to be especially cautious in view of the highly tense situation."

Our faction, which had grown hostile and suspicious of me after my report about the cabinet on July 3, responded unfavorably to my warnings. My doubts about the "appropriateness of the appeal" evoked grumbles and shouts of anger. The overwhelming majority (all except five) came out for unconditionally preserving the stand which had already been taken. After all, so they said, we were only inviting the population to wait "peacefully and calmly" for the end of the Duma's work! This seemed to be—and in fact was—as far as our moderation would allow our faction to go, and the Trudoviks, in fact, refused to support the statement. I was able to convince Petrunkevich to review the text which had already been adopted and to render it as harmless as possible. Our faction, however, voted down the greater part of the changes which we suggested. G. E. Lvov then repudiated the report, while Petrunkevich was forced to an impromptu defense of the remaining four amendments. The leftists took skillful advantage of the situation. With the assistance of the rightists and the Poles, they abstained from the voting—or voted against the appeal. A strange situation was thus created: only the Kadets had taken the step which placed the whole Duma in jeopardy for being revolutionary. And because of this, a Kadet majority in the Duma could not be found!

The consequences were just what I had foreseen. In Stolypin's report to the tsar on July 4, according to what Stolypin later told Kokovtsov, the question of dissolving the Duma was "touched upon," apparently with direct reference to Stolypin's report on the Duma session. On July 5, while they were dining at Countess Kleinmikhel's, Count Joseph Pototsky informed Kokovtsov that "the day for dissolving the Duma had been set for Sunday" (July 9). Kokovtsov was thunderstruck. Apparently, Stolypin had been playing his game in secret, without the knowledge of his accomplice, the minister of finance. In answer to Kokovtsov's questions, Stolypin merely said that the subject had been "touched on," although he added that by July 7, the sovereign "desires to know the government's opinion." Actually, this opinion had been formed long ago, and the business at hand concerned only the adoption of the particular means that Stolypin had prepared. On July 7, Stolypin arrived at Tsarskoe Selo not only with a detailed plan for dissolving the Duma on July 9 but with documents requiring only the signatures of the other ministers. Evidently, the decision had been taken behind the scenes of the government institutions, in private between the tsar and Stolypin. Apparently, Stolypin was already on July 7 expecting to be appointed to the cabinet in Goremykin's place. Stolypin described this Godunov-like scene to Kokovtsov: He had alluded to his "insufficient experience" and the tsar blessed him with an icon; whereupon Stolypin read the tsar his thoroughly prepared report on military measures for preventing the disorders which could be expected on Sunday! This all sounded like a poorly written comedy, when in reality what was being prepared was a tragedy. Everyone except the former governor felt that a great event was about to take place, perhaps an irreparable one. . . .

At the last moment, this awareness was reflected in another zig-zag of sentiments among the supporters of the Duma at the top and a new act of perfidy that Stolypin was preparing against the Duma. Both the one and the other must be told, since it was over this matter that I was accused of "shortsightedness" in I. V. Hessen's memoirs. In an editorial published on the very day the Duma was dissolved (July 9), but actually written on the evening of the eighth, I said that "there had again occurred a shift to the left" on the question of a Kadet ministry, and that "it is uncertain at which point the new vacillation will come to rest." Then, on the eve of the dissolution, I "calmed" myself with the thought that the Duma would not be dissolved on Sunday. What was going on?

With new facts in my hands, I can now answer the accusations. "The shift to the left," as it turns out, did in fact take place, not, of course, on Stolypin's part, but on the part of his opponents. On July 7, Stolypin told his own story to the ministers, who were awaiting his return from Tsarskoe Selo where he and Goremykin had gone at the tsar's summons. At Tsarskoe, Stolypin had found Baron Fredericks in complete confusion and panic, after having made a last desperate attempt to prevent the dissolution of the Duma. Fredericks tried to persuade Stolypin that the decision to dissolve the Duma "might be fraught with the most fateful consequences, including even the fall of the monarchy." He maintained that the Duma was "perfectly loyal," and that were the tsar to express his displeasure in a personal message to the Duma, with the threat of using the means available to him in the Fundamental Laws, then the Duma "would get down to peaceful work". Fredericks' actions were apparently provoked by Stolypin's latest denunciation of the Duma, and he responded to Stolypin's objections with a thoroughly candid reference to the opinion "of people who are without doubt devoted to the tsar, that all the trouble lay in the poor choice of ministers" (including Stolypin himself), and that "it should not be so difficult to find new people who would relieve the tsar of responsibility of exercising executive power." Of course, there was nothing "incoherent" in all of this; Fredericks was merely giving the basic outlines of Trepov's and Mosolov's plan. He had "more than once" turned to Goremykin with this plan, but Goremykin "does not want to listen to anything." Gurko added one more interesting fact to this information. After leaving the tsar, following his dismissal, and after having signed the order appointing Stolypin to his place, Goremykin himself met D. F. Trepov, who had apparently been waiting for him. When Trepov found out that the decision to dissolve the Duma had already been made, he exclaimed, "Terrible! Tomorrow all of Petersburg will be here!" Goremykin answered drily: "Those who come, will not return." To this Gurko added: "From Trepov's words, Goremykin concluded, however, that all efforts would be made to induce the Tsar to withdraw his decision before the ukase could be published." Goremykin's fear is very important. It confirms the rumor that Goremykin took measures of his own against the possibility that the tsar might that night reconsider the question. He evidently believed that such a demonstration of royal indecision was quite probable. He gave orders, therefore, that no one should awaken him! According to Kokovtsov's testimony, this rumor "was entirely believed by the Council of Ministers and by a number of persons close to the individual ministers." Moreover, to this rumor was added another; namely, that late on the night of July 9, a package from Tsarskoe Selo was delivered to Goremykin, containing a "small letter from the Tsar with an order to delay carrying out the dissolution ukase which he had signed." If this is true, and it is quite possible, then it means that those who opposed dissolving the Duma did not end their struggle until the ukase was actually published on the morning of July 9. Obscure reports of these goings-on were able to reach the office of *Rech,* which explains the phrase in my editorial cited above.

As for the other manifestation of my "shortsightedness," I shared it with all the members of the Duma. It is based on Stolypin's outright fraud, which we complacently believed. In order to take the Duma unawares and to cut off at the roots all possibility of resistance, Stolypin asked Muromtsev to set aside the Duma session on Monday, July 10, for his personal address. According to M. M. Vinaver's recollection, we left the Duma on Saturday "calmed," and looking forward to the Monday session. That is why on Saturday night and early Sunday morning, while sitting in the offices of *Rech,* I could assure I. V. Hessen that he could go to his summer home in Sestroretsk with his mind at ease, since, according to the latest information, nothing was going to happen on Sunday. But if, in those hours, one could talk only about postponing a decision for a day, the issue involved was obviously balanced on a razor's edge.

Dissolution and the Vyborg Manifesto

At dawn I left the offices of *Rech* with instructions to call me if something new should turn up. Before I had even fallen asleep, they phoned and told me that the manifesto announcing the dissolution of the Duma was already on the press. It later became known that the manifesto had been composed that very night in a conference with Kryzhanovsky. I got on my bicycle, and at about seven o'clock in the morning I made the round of apartments of the Central Committee members, inviting them to come together immediately at Petrunkevich's house. By the time they began to arrive (at about eight o'clock), they had already learned the content of the manifesto from the printers, and we knew that the doors of the Duma had been locked. All our dreams about following the example of the Roman Senate by remaining "seated" and not voluntarily leaving the Duma vanished into dust. We quickly had to think up another means of counteraction. Already in May, because of rumors that the Duma was going to be prorogued "for vacation," our faction had instructed me to write a "manifesto to the population." M. M. Vinaver recalled that at that time I considered such a prorogation entirely legal and that I did not consider it necessary to react to it. This time things were different.

F. F. Kokoshkin, our leading expert on constitutional questions, was of the opinion that we had all the necessary grounds for calling the dissolution a violation of the constitution. His main reason was that in the dissolution manifesto no time limit had been set for elections to the new Duma. Basing his argument on the recent Hungarian example, he found it entirely constitutional to base our protest on the principle of passive resistance: that is, the refusal to pay taxes or furnish recruits to the government. The task of drafting the manifesto on this basis was entrusted to me. As a precaution, they isolated me while I carried out this task, in an adjoining apartment belonging to I. I. Petrunkevich's brother, Mikhail Ilych. As I remember it now, I stood there in the empty room by the piano and on the dusty piano top sketched out a rough draft in pencil. Returning to the Central

Committee meeting, I found about twenty members already gathered. I read my text, listened to the comments and made the appropriate corrections. Petrunkevich's and Kokoshkin's basic idea about passive resistance met with no objections whatever. They all agreed on this as the minimum of necessary protest. Since I was not a Duma member, my position was an odd one: without taking part in the Duma itself, I was calling on it to take actions which entailed criminal consequences. I even tried to object. I asked those present if they understood that the step they were about to take might have undesirable political consequences. I reminded them of the voluntary decision made by the members of the Constituent Assembly in the first French revolution, not to take part in the elections to the next legislative assembly. I pointed out that this act of self-denial lowered the level of the people's representative body by depriving it of a whole series of outstanding political figures. Did our deputies take it into account that should the appeal fail, none of them would return to the Duma even if they wanted to? If they were not prepared to commit this political hara-kiri, then the proposed step should not be taken. M. M. Vinaver recalled I. I. Petrunkevich's answer, which was supported by all those present: "This aspect of the business is clear to everyone and does not raise doubts in anyone."

Vinaver considered my draft of the manifesto too weak. There was no "spontaneous force of indignation" in it. It was necessary that the "shout of indignation ring forth like a streak of lightening, illuminating the population with the true meaning of what has been done." For that reason, Vinaver believed, the concluding call for insubordination on the part of the population "did not attract attention." The entire step seemed to be "that pitiful minimum of the range of action which still remained within our power." Vinaver's criticism, of course, was correct—even more so than he thought; but it was just impossible to write the kind of forceful document he wanted. We had no words at our command which could make the people rise up, because the "true meaning of what had happened" was not comprehensible to them. Our action, requiring as it did Koshoshkin's scholarly commentary, did not in fact "ring out," for it was condemned beforehand to go beyond the comprehension of the "people." Vinaver was probably aware of this also because "after a moment's hesitation" he declined Petrunkevich's suggestion to write another appeal in his own style. For the final composition of the text, we again went over to I. I. Petrunkevich's apartment. Several copies of the appeal were made from dictation, and my rough copy was destroyed on the spot as a precautionary measure.

The party's draft was ready. Now it had to be converted into a decision of the Duma. But it was impossible to gether together for this purpose in Petersburg. Not only the lodgings of the Duma but also our Kadet club on Potemkin Street was cordoned off by the troops and the police. It was not for nothing that they had taken the precaution of lodging the Duma within reach of the barracks. I do not remember who made the suggestion, but everyone agreed that we should go to Vyborg. The Trudoviks also agreed to both the appeal and the trip to Vyborg; it seems that even they could not come up with anything stronger. Then, the socialists joined in, still reserving for themselves, as their own reaction, an attempt at armed uprising. They understood and appreciated the fact that our initiative provided the opportunity for uniting the voice of the whole Duma. Zhilkin said as much to Vinaver: "Lead us."

M. M. Vinaver gave a vivid picture of our sojourn in Vyborg. My personal role there receded into the background. I was not a deputy, and I had neither a formal nor a moral right to participate in the discussions or in the agreement to take a decisive step. The leaders of the other political parties also remained on the sidelines, taking part only in the preliminary conferences of their own factions. No one was allowed in the general meeting hall except the deputies.

The general conferences of the deputies in this meeting hall began that very evening. I arrived later that night and managed to spend the night somewhere on the floor side by side with the others. The "foreigners," that is, party members who were not members of the Duma, were allowed into the general hall only the following day, during the noon break. Until then, we heard only rumors about what was going on there.

Of course, the rumor that Muromtsev opened the conference with the sacred words: "The session (of the Duma) continues" was false. Under the circumstances, the Duma chairman felt very awkward: from waiting for the monarch's call to assume the post of premier to conducting a session with a definite revolutionary tint was a change that could hardly please him. Nevertheless, he could not refuse to accept the chairmanship of this session; it is self-evident that any such a refusal would have undermined the reputation he had built up.

At the beginning, the mood of the gathering was extremely exited. Gradually, however, reason began to assert itself. The "'minimum" of the Kadet Manifesto did not, of course, suit the left-wing "maximalism." Faced with stark reality, it was not difficult to realize the impracticality of any such further verbal gestures. Moreover, everyone recognized that it was important to have a general decision from the whole Duma. The leftists could go as far as they wanted by themselves, but the Kadet draft required action, not words. Entering the general meeting hall, I found our faction's spirits significantly lowered, as a result of these considerations. If the first half of our draft continued to seem insufficiently vivid, even after Vinaver's and Kokoshkin's nocturnal amendments, then the second half, which included the appeal to passive resistance, evoked a whole series of objections. These objections had nothing to do with principle; they were entirely practical objections, and more serious because of it. Not to furnish recruits? Not to pay taxes? But the recruitment would not take place until November, four months later; and in any case the direct taxes made up only a negligible part of the budget! Vinaver added the proposal that interest on loans should not be paid and that a political strike be considered. But nonpayment of loans was merely an empty phrase, and the political strike was rejected unanimously. One central idea of the manifesto remained—an appeal to organized action of the people, but without violence. But what if the "people are not ready"? If even this form of protest were rejected, then the appeal would have only one value, that of a tactical step, necessary at the time as the least risky way out of meeting the general demand for a protest against government force. The appeal could be defended only from this point of view. At the very least, it would be a warning to the government against taking further violent steps. In my opinion, it had exactly this effect (see below). It should be added that the considerations mentioned here, were at that time implicitly understood rather than explicitly stated.

A six-member committee was elected from three party groups to work out the final, accepted text. The committee worked through the entire night. On the morning of the third and last day, still sharper discussions flared up within our faction as to whether such an appeal, by its very nature, was acceptable at all. This criticism threatened to kill what remained of the heroic mood. The second, practical, part of the appeal was rejected by a majority of two votes. Even such reserved and politically mature members of our faction as Hertsenstein and Iollos lost their composure and spoke out passionately at the general meeting which opened later. During the noon break, non-Duma party members were again allowed in, and I decided to speak in defense of the appeal as it was. I was upset by our faction's vacillation and its shift to a minor key. I spoke sharply, forgetting that I bore no personal responsibility for the general decision. I argued that it was too late to retreat and that at such a time, the voice of the whole Duma should ring forth in unison. Otherwise, our initiative would go to others and would lose even its tactical significance.

I do not know what would have been the final decision if a new factor, unexpectedly for all, had not appeared. News about our conferences in the Hotel Belvedere had finally reached Petersburg, and an order was sent from there to the governor of Vyborg to break up the meeting. The perturbed Finns called Muromtsev out of the hall for a talk. We would have done wrong by our Finnish friends if we had taken an adamant stand, and Muromtsev promised the governor to adjourn the meeting. He did so, and, putting on his gloves, left. In the midst of the general excitement, Petrunkevich suggested ending the debates and signing the appeal "as it is." There was really no time to continue the arguments. In addition, this new act of force from Petersburg caused the dying embers to flare up again, uniting all of us. It was proposed that Prince P. Dolgorukov be chairman. Hertsenstein and Iollos were first to sign the manifesto. . . . Once signed by the members, it was printed immediately and smuggled into Petersburg.

Our return to Petersburg was not without incidents. Friends and relatives were afraid that we would all be arrested at the station the moment we returned. This did not happen; in order to bring to trial those Duma members who had signed the manifesto, preliminary political and juridical preparations had to be made. It was not only necessary to define the crime but also to decide to lay hands on the people's elected representatives. More serious, however, was the possibility of violent reprisals against us by the Black Hundreds. On the way back, we found out that they were already preparing to ambush us along the road. In addition to Hertsenstein and Iollos, both Vinaver and myself were on their list of condemned. All this explained why our close friends and relatives were anxiously waiting for us by the railway car exit at the Finland Station. One devoted female Kadet energetically shoved me into a carriage which stood waiting for the train's arrival.

The First State Duma thus entered history. History has still not said its last word about it; the interests and ideas connected with the Duma were too various. In conclusion, perhaps it will not be without interest to compare two judgments about the Duma from two opposing sides. One was a severe appraisal and a gloomy forecast. This was Kryzhanovsky's view, which he expressed while still influenced by the tsar's first meeting with the Duma, the reception in the Winter Palace on April 27. The other judgment was Kliuchevsky's and was expressed while the Duma was in session. If his is not the judgment of history, it is at least the opinion of the most talented and deep-thinking of Russian historians.

S. E. Kryzhanovsky recalls that the tsar's appearance was "decked with all the splendor of court etiquette, which pained the Russian eye, so unaccustomed to it." But the eye of the old regime's faithful servant was also pained by the "crowd of long-haired, unwashed deputies in jackets, Russian-style blouses, and long-waisted coats," so out of place against the background of regal splendor. The intelligent bureaucrat immediately concluded from this contrast, so rich with meaning, that "it will hardly be possible to build a bridge between the old and the new Russia." As to his own feelings, he expressed them with the exclamation: "How horrible! . . . It was a gathering of savages! . . ."

Giving his opinion of the Duma's activity in a letter to A. F. Kon, V. O. Kliuchevsky said, "I must admit two things which I did not expect. The first is the rapidity with which the people formed their opinion of the Duma as the most dependable organ of legislative power. Second, I must acknowledge the incontestable moderation of the dominant attitudes displayed in the Duma. The attitudes of this institution, which has authority among the people, are more moderate than the revolutionary wave which is beginning to engulf us. The existence of the Duma is the lowest price that must be paid for a bloodless pacification of the country."

If you like, everything was included in the First Duma. There were even "savages" dragged from backwoods Russia by the government itself, through its law of December 11. There was also the "revolutionary wave," which continued to inundate Russia. Finally, there was the "moderation" displayed by Russia's most educated and cultured element. It was this moderation which gave hope of "pacifying the country," under the condition, of course, that the Duma would enjoy a prolonged existence. In general, it was a complex and precious instrument—the only one that the intelligentsia tradition and the barely awakened popular will could have created in Russia at the time. To operate this instrument, however, an understanding of the situation and a skillful leadership were needed. When Rodichev compared this rare institution to an icon which the government would not raise its hand to destroy, he made a cruel mistake. It was destroyed by the hand of the real "savages" at the top. The "revolutionary wave" ebbed back, as it were, before this crude coercion. But it was only a respite given to the government—and the last one. V. O. Kliuchevsky himself, going against his own sentiments, reached a prophetic conclusion about what had happened: "The Dynasty will cease; Alexei will not reign." It was difficult at the time to believe in the truth of this historian's prediction; but it happened just that way, and only eleven or twelve years after the events described above.

The Revolution Extinguished (1906-7)

THE DISSOLUTION OF THE FIRST STATE DUMA drew a sharp line in Russian political life, dividing what had gone before from what followed. The first symptom of this fundamental shift was the ever more rapid extinction of the revolution. As far as I was concerned, the high point in the revolutionary explosion was the armed uprising in Moscow in December 1905, and its inevitable collapse. After that, the revolutionary curve fell rapidly, and in spite of remnants of revolutionary events that had outlived their time, the direction of this process was unmistakeably and, for me, perfectly clear. How far in the past was the "conciliatory mission" which I undertook when I returned to Russia! I had hoped to direct the Russian revolution along the path of our "friendly enemies," on whose support our mutual success depended. Now, however, the camp of these "friendly enemies" had been shattered into tiny groups, all implacably opposed to our methods of struggle. Following their lead, the French journalists were comparing me to Thiers—not to Thiers, the minister of Louis Philippe, but to Thiers, the president of the Republic, Thiers of Versailles, who shot down the Paris Commune. The political reputation of my old S. R. friends fell quickly, as political terror passed from them to the hands of a new type of terrorist, the "maximalists," who used political terror only as a means of obtaining money through "expropriations" of one kind or another. The traditional sphere of activity of the old S. R.'s was the peasantry, but it was clearly impossible to organize this gigantic, politically amorphous mass, and the first attempts to create "peasant unions" were more or less fictitious. The only expressions of peasant discontent were peasant disturbances that, for various reasons, flared up now here, now there, sometimes engulfing whole provinces, but they were chaotic, impotent, and lacked any program. Their only political consequence was to throw the landowning class into the camp of the reactionaries and to tighten the nobility's organizations. Our plan for peaceful peasant reform remained a red flag for the gentry diehards and a target for government attacks. Even our "friendly enemies" set the peasants against us by promising them a black repartition, socialization, nationalization, and municipalization of the land, anything they pleased, except a peaceful compromise "according to a just appraisal" with the participation of the state.

In the other camp of Russian socialism, the Social Democrats, the situation was more favorable but more complex. The main schism in their ranks occurred between the Bolsheviks and the Mensheviks, and we saw that the more reasonable Menshevik current viewed the situation pretty much as we did. They came to tactical conclusions which were so close to ours that it almost seemed possible to carry on our joint activities with them. It only seemed that way, however, because each instance of such cooperation gave rise to accusations within their party of intimacy with the "bourgeoisie," whereupon the guilty party members were called to order and fell back to their orthodox position. For their part, the Bolsheviks in no way kept to their party line. Their revolutionary line was irreconcilably extreme, "Blanquist," to use foreign jargon. This was the line of the "permanent" revolution, as Trotsky presented it. It aimed not so much at victory in the present as on bench marks for the future; for the present, it was merely supposed to "keep the vestments white." Just as the extreme reactionaries snuffed out the Russian revolution from the right, so did these people diligently snuff it out from the left. The reactionaries, at least, understood what they were doing, and were consciously striving to achieve their aim, namely, a full restoration of the autocracy. The Bolsheviks, on the other hand, stubbornly assailed what was then considered a Utopia, and just as eagerly cleared the path for the reactionaries. The de facto convergence of these two extremes was fatal for a peaceful outcome.

There was also another current of, so to say, semisocialism. These were our former allies from the left wing of the League of Liberation. Their social base was more substantial than the peasantry of the S. R.'s but less so than the working class of the S. D.'s. They relied for support on those active in promoting the village cooperatives, on the lower level, Zemstvo workers (the third element), and on a part of the radical intelligentsia. Their bonds were exclusively ideological; it was difficult to organize them and impossible to bring them out into the streets. Some of these elements even overflowed into our group. They more or less shared our social goals, but they differed in political goals and absolutely rejected our tactics. Understanding (as did the Mensheviks) that the outcome of the revolution in its present stage could be only bourgeois, they grew angry with us, in the end, because our tactics were not moderate enough under the given circumstances, while our program was far too radical. At the time, I formulated this position in an article as follows: "Become Octobrists once and for all, so that we can become Kadets." A contradiction did exist, of course, between our (initial) program and our (party) tactics; but all of Russia suffered from this contradiction which, as it turned out, was impossible to resolve peacefully. It was for that reason that the Bolshevik solution became possible.

How did the government behave, having just won in the person of Stolypin an almost bloodless victory? Its situation was also rather complex. The fact was that it did not win a victory for itself, that is, for the aims of the state, even in the sense that the government understood them. Behind the government stood other forces, which pushed it irresistibly along a path which it had not chosen. The first of these forces was the nobility, the second was the "Black Hundreds." The nobility sensed danger as soon as the tsar announced the convening of "the most worthy people" in the Manifesto of February 18, 1905. And the question arose as to their own elections to this body. At first, this was the idyll of the liberal marshals of the nobility, like Prince P. N. Trubetskoy, the elder brother of Sergei and Eugene. They wanted a representative body of the "propertied classes," somewhat more broadly defined. Behind them, however, stood the whole "estate" which rushed to organize itself and dispatch its scouts to the commission on the Bulygin Duma and "to the Court." S. N. Trubetskoy's statements at the June delegation and V. O. Kliuchevsky's comments at the Peterhof conference concerning "the specter of a class Tsar" had turned Nicholas II against the nobility-class principle. (In general, at Peterhof the nobility was suspected of liberalism.) By a peculiar misunderstanding, the law of August 6 guaranteed peasant representation instead of "nobility" representation. However, when Witte came forward after the October Manifesto, broadened suffrage rights somewhat by the law of December 11th, and entrusted N. N. Kutler with drawing up a project for agrarian reform which included "forced alienation," the true nobility roused themselves and began to organize their "congresses of united nobles' associations." Kutler was immediately dismissed, and the failure of the government in its gamble on the peasantry in the elections to the First Duma put an end to Witte himself. The "Permanent Council" of the nobility's congresses then went into action and played its role in the dissolution of the State Duma. It hindered the realization of Stolypin's plan to create a "dissolution cabinet" from moderate political figures. However, the efforts the nobility took to change immediately the electoral law were not crowned with success: the electoral law remained as before. Whether it was the tsar's wish not to violate the fundamental laws which he himself had sanctioned; or the resistance of the liberal high officials or the remains of Stolypin's own "liberalism"; or the fear of the revolutionary sentiments in the country which had not yet been wiped out; or all of these together—whatever the reason may have been, the coup d'etat after the dissolution of the First Duma did not take place.

There was also another force at hand, a force which was created not only with the assistance of that same "united" nobility but under the supreme protection of the "Court." This force was called the "Black Hundreds." Its history goes back to the reign of Alexander III, when, for the struggle against the revolution, highly placed persons had organized the famous *Holy Brigades*, whose activities were based on terror. At that time, nothing came of the efforts of these fine court gentlemen. Now, however, there appeared new organizers of "white" terrorists, who had fallen to depths where they could be bought and sold. Strengthened by direct support from above, the organizers openly announced in their press that the "highest power in Russia" belonged to their organization. "They did not ask; they demanded," and through the lips of their "future-dictators" they declared that "no exposures could possibly harm them." There even appeared a printed interview with one of these anonymous "future-dictators," who announced that a congress of delegates from the "union" would set up in Petersburg, a "true popular representative body," and that in the future, after the "Jewish question was decided in the provinces" (by means of pogroms), the "bureaucratic cabinet would be replaced by public figures" of that type, and that such a cabinet would act "more resolutely and successfully" not only than the revolutionary assaults but also than the notorious Kadet "siege" (see below). All this might have seemed a hoax, if it were not for that fact that the leaders (Dr. Dubrovin, Purishkevich) and their newspaper *Russkoe Znamia* were in clear view, openly pursuing these ends, arming their "people" for murder (Hertsenstein and Iollos were their victims), and exercising an undoubted influence even over the head of Stolypin himself.

How did Stolypin act in such a situation, armed as he was not only with all the powers of the administration but also with legislative authority provided by the notorious Article 87 of the Russian "constitution," which authorized him to issue measures of legislative character in the absence of the Duma, on condition that he present them to the next Duma within the first two months of its existence?

Stolypin, too, acted extraordinarily resolutely toward the "revolutionary assault." So-called "punitive expeditions" were sent into the most troubled parts of Russia, where they flooded their path with the blood of executions, carried out without trial, leaving behind the most painful memories. On August 12, 1906, an attempt was made on Stolypin's life; and while Stolypin came out unscathed, the bomb destroyed part of his villa on Aptekar Island, wounded his daughter and killed up to thirty people. Within a week, Stolypin gave his answer. Using Article 87, he issued a law establishing "military-field" courts, which were to become another integral feature of the inter-Duma regime. Stolypin's main concern, however, was to struggle against the remnants of the dispersed Duma and to prevent the history of this Duma from repeating itself. The administrative measures poured down on all on the former Duma deputies, but they were carried out with particular speed against the left wing of the Duma. When they made their way home, the police were waiting for them at the stations. For such leaders as Aladin, a half-company of soldiers was assigned. Aladin of course, slipped away. For the peasant deputies, however, this could not be done: the police surrounded their homes, making it absolutely impossible for these deputies to give the voters an account of the Duma's activity. Attempts to break through the blockade resulted in the offender being shot, exiled, or imprisoned. As a result, the population came to the natural conclusion about whom the government was persecuting and why. After a short delay, Stolypin decided to seize the deputies who had signed the Vyborg appeal. The case was begun concerning "distribution" by means of "drafting" (the appeal), and by this charge, 169 possible candidates to the Second Duma, including about 120 members of the Kadet party, were automatically removed from participation in the elections. Those undesirables whom it was impossible to remove legally were removed by senate "interpretations" of the law. In that way, they "interpreted" me, among others. I still lacked the minimum legal residence requirement, but my friends tried to provide me with place-of-work qualifications through the concern that had printed my books. Of course, it was not difficult to arrange this improvised entry into the ranks of "shop assistant." After all these removals and "interpretations," the minister of internal affairs could exclaim in triumph: "The Duma will be headless!" This, it seemed, was the height of success. . . .

It was not enough merely to deprive the future Duma of one group of people. Other people, the desirable ones, had to be brought into the Duma. In August, soon after the dissolution, a conference took place between A. I. Guchkov and Stolypin concerning the formation of a government majority. Naturally, the "Octobrists" were given the first place and were promised support in the elections. But there were not enough "Octobrists," as the elections to the First Duma had shown. The masses has to be mobilized, at least their appearance must be created if not their presence. At this point, a second force, which I mentioned above together with the nobility, was called to the political stage: an unnatural collection from the crude, lower middle class of the towns. There appeared the "union" of the Archangel Michael, the "union of the Russian People," and so on. Guchkov thought up a slogan to link the representatives of the 130,000 landowners with these "Black Hundreds": "flaming patriotism." The "national" banner was hoisted as the common political motto. The "masses," however, now had their own entrance to the "Court," their own "privy councilors" and intermediaries with the tsar, and a sense of being politically independent of the nobility. This was the time when Nicholas II accepted badges from the so-called "Russian people" and even encouraged the cabmen's delegates: Cabmen (or Janitors?) of Russia, unite.

That is how the political situation took shape immediately after the dissolution of the First Duma. How should the People's Freedom party act in such a situation? What conclusion should the party draw from its unsuccessful attempts to act in agreement with the leftist parties? What should its attitude be toward the government which dissolved the Duma? Let us recall that in the summer of 1906 neither the attitude of the government toward the party nor the conditions for calling the next Duma had been clarified. To a certain degree, the party was bound by the act of the Vyborg Manifesto, but the effectiveness of the manifesto depended, formally, on the fixing of a time limit for the next elections and, practically, on the extent of the people's active participation in those sanctions which were supposed to be used as a protest against the government's violations of the law. Moreover, the manifesto was adopted only by the parliamentary faction of the party, leaving the attitude of the whole party toward the manifesto formally undefined. With this last splash, the revolutionary wave quickly rolled into the past. Now it was necessary above all to reappraise the situation in order to untie the party's hands for the immediate future.

For the summer, I moved with my family to a dacha along the Terioki, across the border of Beloostrov. Gerasimov, a member of the first Duma, also settled nearby. This site was chosen deliberately. It was impossible for the members of the party to gather in Petersburg. From this time on, Finland became the place of our more or less conspiratorial political assemblies. In addition, it was impossible to convene a complete congress, so we held our party conferences in Terioki, and our members were supposed to come and go alone. A photograph taken at that time shows our rather crowded gathering at one of the conferences in a pine grove near one of our dachas. Here, we questioned our visitors from various parts of Russia, above all about how ready we should consider the population to carry out the passive resistance proposed in the manifesto. Only Prince Peter Dolgorukov answered this question affirmatively: he knew the attitudes of the peasants of his district (Suzhdansky), and they were "ready." All the rest answered evasively or plainly negatively. We then agreed that the "constitutional" reason for passive resistance would formally disappear when the elections to the Second Duma were fixed. The conclusion followed by itself. Both formally and practically the Vyborg Manifesto lost its force and had to be considered annulled.

We then had to decide what program the party would bring to the elections for the Second Duma. For this purpose, it was not sufficient to convene an incomplete conference like the one at Terioki. A new congress had to be called. It was clearly impossible to do that on Russian territory. Finland remained as a possibility, and the Central Committee settled on Helsinki. The Finns were hospitable to us and gave us the large lodgings of Societetshuset for our meeting. The party members gathered in a significant number, and the congress took on a normal character. Unfortunately, I do not remember the date of the congress;[23] the protocols of the congress could not be printed since the congress had a semiconspiratorial character. Only by my recollections and some later comments can I reconstruct the political significance of the decisions of this congress. I remember only that a rather significant "left-wing" opposition emerged again. Mandelshtam's speeches were especially heated. The party's general tactics had been fixed as early as the Third Congress, before the opening of the First Duma. We considered that the decision of that congress had been carried out in the First Duma as far as circumstances permitted. Now, however, these circumstances had changed greatly and anyone who wanted to follow the line of strict parliamentary activity in the next Duma, would have to go even farther in adapting himself to the new conditions. Our position was all the more unfavorable, since behind us was something that our party considered sacred, that the Duma had accepted, and that had become national: the First Duma's address, which we had passed and which contained all of our previous *desiderata.* On the other hand, the fundamental question and the basic prerequisite of parliamentary activity, as we understood it, had come again in the First Duma and had acquired a certain urgency. This was the question of creating a responsible cabinet, supported by a solid majority in the Duma. Finally, we had to reckon with our legislative drafts through which we expected to put our political and social program into law. The revolution had subsided, no matter how hard we tried to hold our banner high. Given this decrease in revolutionary activity, I viewed both the result of the next elections and the probable atmosphere of parliamentary activity in the Second Duma rather pessimistically. I had no hope of continuing our work even in its old form. Our left wing, however, still retained these hopes. I do not remember whether or not Vinaver's witty remark—that only the "feathers" were left of the party's "wings"—referred to the Helsinki Congress. I remember only that the debates (at the congress) which led to the inevitable operation on the "wings," were very stormy. The operation was a painful one, and it was mainly I who had to carry it out and bear the odium.

We passed the basic principle of a general change in our tactics in a somewhat concealed form: "not an assault, but a well-ordered siege." Strictly speaking, this was not really a change, but merely a more consistent application of what we had done in the First Duma. To state this, however, and to draw a frank conclusion from the "conflicts" in the First Duma was more difficult than to establish the individual facts which together pointed to that conclusion. Once expressed, the principle of repudiating the "storm" was binding. Above all, it obliged us to draw a line once and for all between our tactics and those of the leftists. This was the second decision which, as far as I remember, was outlined at Helsinki. Because of the leftist boycott, leftist voices and attitudes supported us in the elections to the First Duma. Now, as could easily be foreseen, the boycott would be lifted: the leftists would come to the Duma themselves and would act in their own name. The People's Freedom party would now have to show its face in the elections, without fearing the blows of critics and all manner of distortions which had not ceased to pour down on us from both the left and the right.

I do not remember what other conclusions were drawn from these general principles at the congress. The elections were postponed until the beginning of the new year, and the party's tasks could be defined concretely only to the extent that sufficient material had accumulated, that is by autumn. In November (October?) the Central Committee called the representatives of the provincial party committees to Moscow in order to review previous tactical directives. The basic directives of the Helsinki Congress were repeated here, but it was emphasized that the preliminary condition for their realization was the existence of a stable majority in the Duma. Without taking any obligations upon itself before the outcome of the elections was known, the party established in advance the "siege" strategy against the government, assuming the worst possible conditions. The party had no intention whatsoever of reconciling with the government that had dissolved the Duma, but, in the interests of protecting the Duma, with a view towards undertaking the "siege," the party established permitted modes of temporary peaceful coexistence. This meant the elimination of direct conflicts, the refusal to express openly lack of confidence in the cabinet (which would have entailed a legal dissolution), the creation of an "assault-free atmosphere for peaceful legislative work, the immediate selection of legislative projects whose themes coincided with those of the government's legislative projects, participation in the discussion of these projects and of the budget, along with the introduction of specific amendments and strict fiscal control, and so forth. As for the party's own projects which were to be introduced into a Duma with limited legislative powers, the Moscow program decided to review them, in order to make them feasible, not in the future, but in the present. Of these projects, the agrarian project stood at the head of the list. It had been introduced into the First Duma only in the name of a group of party members. In order to strengthen his victory over the people's representatives, Stolypin resorted to Article 87 of the Fundamental Laws on this question too. In his memoirs, S. E. Kryzhanovsky disclosed the theretofore secret fact that there was nothing original in Stolypin's legislative enactments; that he had simply adopted and carried out the suggestions of the nobility. Stolypin's stated intention to give the peasants, once and for all, legal equality with the other estates was to have served as a liberal screen, and it was, of course, acceptable. However, his real aim in all this was to destroy the peasants' separate communal landownership. By means of mobilizing the theretofore inviolable peasants' land strips, Stolypin planned to distract the peasants' attention away from the aim of "forced alienation" of the gentry's lands. In order to oppose this encroachment on the welfare of the great mass of peasants in the interest of one prosperous layer, the party decided to present its own project in a more acceptable form. From the project which it introduced in the First Duma, the party eliminated the "socialist" "after-taste," the creation of a permanent "land fund" from which land would be distributed for use instead of ownership. That project had brought thunder and lightening down on the party for infringing on the holy right of private property. The Central Committee gathered together its best specialists (including N. N. Kutler), set up regional conferences for clarifying local conditions of peasant landownership, and printed a series of their reports. The work lasted all winter, and the party prepared to introduce into the Duma its detailed project concerning this most fundamental of all controversial questions that divided the population from the government. Other legislative projects, prepared for the first Duma by our Moscow jurists, were also reconsidered.

We saw that Stolypin was preparing to convoke the Second Duma in his own way. By the end of the year, his preparations became more energetic and more consistent. For future legislative enactments concerning elections, all political parties were classified either as legalized or unlegalized. To the former belonged the Union of Russian People, the Octobrists, and after some hesitation, those "peaceful reconstructionists" who had refused to participate with Stolypin in his cabinet. The People's Freedom party was proclaimed illegal. This meant that all formal manifestations of its participation in the elections were prohibited. Officials and "civil servants" (in the broadest sense) were forbidden to take part in it. The clergy, on the contrary, according to a ukase of December 12, was "called to active participation" and was obliged to "appear immediately." The curiae of voters were made smaller in every possible way. The instructions issued at the last moment before the elections indicated a whole series of further ruses designed to keep undesirable elements away from the ballot boxes, to assemble those elements protected by the government, and to eliminate both printed and oral agitation by the opposition. It is impossible to enumerate all the devices used.

For their part, the nobility and the Black Hundreds did all they could to elect candidates favoring their interests. More than anything else, they were afraid of what the Kadets were aiming at: a peaceful and proper Duma. If "we can't pick any holes in the Duma's work," they said at a special conference of the nobility on November 24, then "under the shield of authority, won through superficially legal activity, it will pass laws disastrous for the state." "Parliamentarianism will thus be strengthened in Russia and the Duma will become a permanent institution." From this followed Purishkevich's directive: Wherever you cannot elect the rightists, elect the "extreme leftists." "Such is the decision of the Union of Russian People!"

In a word, nothing more could be done without a change in the electoral law. What happened as a result? Here is a comparative table of the composition of the First and Second Dumas:

	FIRST DUMA	SECOND DUMA
Extreme leftists	?	63
Moderate rightists (Octobrists, moderates)	38 (8%)	34 (7%)
Nonpartisan (for the most part concealed reactionaries)	112	22
Kadets	184 (38%)	123 (24%)
Polish deputies	32	39
Trudoviks and generally those "to the left of the Kadets"	85 (18%)	97 (20%)
Socialists (S. D.'s, S. R.'s and Popular Socialists)	26 (5%)	83 (17%)

The government managed to weaken the Duma by depriving it of a stable majority, but it did not succeed in making the Duma its own property. Moreover, notwithstanding the limited franchise and all the attempts at distortion the elections showed the genuine feelings of the overwhelming majority of the Russian population. The Second Duma turned out to be much more leftist than the First Duma. The Kadet votes only in part went over to the leftists and the socialists, who appeared under their own name for the first time. The government got only one-fifth of the Duma membership. This was a brilliant victory for the opposition. For the government's policy, it was an unexpectedly grave and serious failure.

Such was the first impression, but, in fact, the situation was quite different. The extreme rightists achieved their aim. The Duma was divided, not into two, but into three parts. The right and the left, the Black Hundreds and the socialists stood equally apart from parliamentary struggle; both wanted a forceful coup d'etat. Only the Kadet center remained strictly "constitutional." True, during the first month, the national and denominational groups (Poles, Muslims, Cossacks) voted with us. Together, they accounted for 180 to 190 members. Nevertheless, this was still not a majority, and they had no element of stability among them. The cynical and spiteful voting together of the rightists and the leftists could always form a majority.

The Kadet faction itself had changed significantly. The "Vyborgites" had left the ranks, and with them dropped from practical politics the entire layer of Russian citizens who had any experience at all in political struggle. In the main, these were the Zemstvo Constitutionalists, hardened by the struggle between the Zemstvo and Plehve's regime. In their places came people who properly represented the Russian intelligentsia, but who had come out of the ranks and had few ties to political activity. At the head were the ideologists (Struve, Novgorodtsev), the scholars (Kizevetter), the professional jurists (V. A. Maklakov, N. V. Teslenko, V. Hessen), specialists in various fields (N. N. Kutler, Gerasimov), and so on. Our faction continued to represent the highest cultural level in the Duma and its technical work also dominated over that of others. However, it lacked political initiative: it needed leadership from the outside and it followed the decisions of the party and the party's established tradition.

I no longer had the close personal ties with our faction that had bound me with the leaders of the First Duma. I no longer had those hopes which made me harness myself to the Duma chariot. Aware that the revolution was dying, I could not believe that the Duma would be stable or that it could possibly apply the pressure that had been the moral strength of the First Duma. Though no longer standing on the crest of the wave, our faction succeeded by dint of its capacity for work, its knowledge, and its readiness for self-sacrifice. With only a few minor exceptions, our faction was well disciplined and ideologically united. It stoically fulfilled its thankless task of preserving the idea of popular representation and parliamentary tactics.

Nevertheless, I did not abandon the position which I had occupied and for which I had been recognized as a leading spokesman of, and commentator on, our faction's activity. The second collection of my articles from *Rech,* covering the first hundred days of this Duma's existence, show a close observation of our faction's activity and a continual emphasis on—and sometimes criticism of—the political significance of its actions. But there is also here a share of my pessimism regarding the final outcome—a pessimism which, by the way, was widespread, and not only in our ranks, throwing a dark veil over all our work. However, although hope diminished, we did not grow dejected. We did what we had to do, and we did it honorably. We did not yield to the leftists' attack on our impotence, nor did we give in to the persuasions and hints from the rightist circles, concerning the possibility of compromise, nor did we bend under the mockery and malicious gloating of the rightists over our unapproachability. We were content that this time there was no room for mistakes or misinterpretations of our role. We went our own way, we did what we had to do, and we left our lesson behind—if not for the present, then at least for the future.

The Kadets in the Second Duma

"THE LONG-AWAITED DAY has arrived and the seventh-month nightmare of thoughtlessness has come to an end. The representatives of the Russian people return today to the abandoned seats at the Taurida Palace. Will it be for long? That is the universal concern, the black thought which clouds the great joy of this moment. Last year, on the twenty-seventh of April, the people's representative entered this palace like a self-confident youth. It seemed to him that there was no limit to his strength, that everyone and everything would bend before his ardent desire, that the sacred goal would at last be in his hands! The people's representative now returns to the Taurida Palace a mature, experienced man. His step is not so springy, not so self-assured as before. But he goes forward with a firm and calm stride. He has discovered his own strength, and he has learned to control and manage it. He knows that the road is long and that he must conserve his strength. . . . But he knows his way, and he knows that tomorrow he will be closer to his goal than yesterday."

With these words in *Rech*, I greeted the opening of the Second Duma on February 20, 1907. The optimism they express is due entirely to that part of the atmosphere which the Kadets created and which became general among the other segments of the opposition during the elections. The mood was expressed in the slogan "Protect the Duma" which united all the ranks of the opposition in the first days and weeks of the Duma. It was expressed also in the election of the Kadet candidate, F. A. Golovin, as chairman of the Duma, with 350 votes against 100 for the rightist candidates. The same mood was expressed in the general decision to protect the Duma from the sharp conflicts that occurred at the early stages of the First Duma. There was no waiting for the "speech from the throne" and no answer given in the form of an "address" to the tsar. Nor was there any vote of "no confidence"; the first speech from the ministry, concerning the government program, was received in total silence. By that time however, a Bolshevik group of twelve members, on the one hand, and a group of extreme rightists, on the other, had already taken shape. The Duma turned out to be divided not into two but into three groups, each of which pursued its own policy. Over them, a fourth line was pursued— the ministerial line, which, during these early days, wavered between the rightists and the Kadet center, and with which there was still hope for cooperation. In his program speech, Stolypin came out in principle against the Duma's right to express "confidence" in the cabinet, but he sharply distinguished the center from the leftists. To the center, he gave the freedom to express their opinion, even though it might be in opposition, and the freedom to introduce amendments (only partially, it is true) to government legislation. He answered the leftists whose position he summarized with the words "hands up," by the resolute phrase "don't try to scare us." He demonstrated this same attitude, adhering "entirely and in every possible way to Deputy Rodichev" when the Kadet orator refused to violate the authority of the Duma by transferring work on the food question from the Duma committee to provincial "committees," with the aim of creating a "new right" in the provinces, as the Bolshevik speaker, Aleksinsky, put it. The Kadet party remained consistent in spite of the fact that the leftists suspected us of chasing after "portfolios." The Kadets did not summarily refuse to adopt the budget as the leftists did; the Kadets discussed it and sent it to committee. We seriously demonstrated the validity of our views on the agrarian question, thereby forcing Stolypin to recognize, at least in principle, the right of the state to undertake the "forced expropriation" of land, and so on. The war of words that the leftists carried on with the rightists was restricted by a new and stricter procedure composed by the Kadet, V. A. Maklakov: for minor legislative projects and inquiries, two special evenings a week were set aside and fifteen committees were organized whose qualified members discussed their own and government legislative proposals. In a word, the Duma showed itself to be only restrained but also capable of work, without binding itself by any obligatory relationship toward the ministers. As we have seen, it was precisely this that the rightists feared. As it turned out, the leftists also did not like it. Thus the "well-prepared siege" began in the Duma, not against the government, but against the only strictly constitutional party, which had, in fact, from the very nature of the work to be done, obtained a leading position in the Duma.

Let me begin with the leftists. By the end of the very first month, they could no longer stand the comparatively peaceful flow of business in the Duma. They were not prepared for serious committee work. They grew bored in the Duma. There were no dramatic scenes, no gripping effects. Nothing more tragic happened than the collapse of the Duma ceiling before Stolypin's appearance. In their view, the main role of the Duma was forgotten. The Duma should be a tribune, a resonator of the people's emotions, a multiplier of the people's will. Instead, the Duma had turned into a "department of the Ministry of Internal Affairs." It was not the Duma that was "laying siege to Stolypin," but Stolypin who was "laying siege" to the Duma and surrounding it with a "tight blockade." Was it for this that the Duma was worth "protecting"? The slogan "protect the Duma" had now become purely "Kadet." As a result, the tone of the leftist—and especially the extreme leftist—speeches grew more intense; anticonstitutional hints became stronger and more frequent; and in the provinces, attempts were made from the Duma and through the support of the leftist deputies to organize "people's forces." In 1912, the government slipped the spy and provocateur, Malinovsky, into the ranks of the Duma Bolsheviks, and the tsarist secret police prepared his revolutionary speeches for him.

I had to open a campaign against the leftists in *Rech*. In vain I tried to persuade them that "they were subjecting the Duma to danger each minute," that they "were risking not only this Duma, but even the electoral law." I warned them that the "Third Duma will not meet with the same composition" and that "what they are losing now, is not easy to make up." Some answered that the Duma could not be saved by "protecting" it anyway, while others actually undertook to convince the Kadets that they should be consistent and go the whole way and become Octobrists, that they should at least pass even a tiny government bill, in a word, "that they should do something even if only a little bit," instead of just "dawdling around"! We continued to stand our ground, introducing ordinary prose into the spectacle. I answered in *Rech:* "We do not propose to move directly into a period of ordinary, everyday affairs, the heroic period of our parliamentary life. But we must not deceive ourselves; the genuine development and strengthening of the people's representative body will follow that road. The day when the debates in the Taurida Palace will seem just as much an inevitable event of the day as dinner in the afternoon and the theater in the evening; when the daily program will interest one or another particular group; when debates on general policy will become an exception, while the exercise of aimless rhetoric will become practically impossible because there will not be any listeners; that day will be hailed as the day of final triumph of representative government in Russia." But alas! We were so far away from any such copy of Westminster in Petersburg! Our warning, the "protection of the Duma," had now become genuinely only ours, only "Kadet," and more and more pointless. For besides us and the leftists, there were the rightists, both inside the Duma and outside, who in the midst of our strife came onto the stage as victors.

On February 28 (that is, one week after the opening of the Duma), Deputy Purishkevich, the tragic clown of the Second Duma (the role of comic clown was played by Pavel Krupensky), distributed a secret circular to the sections of the Union of Russian People. (I printed that circular, thus exposing the whole business.) The circular "instructed" the sections (Purishkevich said they numbered a "thousand") "to begin sending insistent telegrams to the sovereign emperor and to the Chariman of the Council of Ministers, Stolypin" just as soon as the sign of a cross appeared in the Union's newspaper, *Russkoe Znamia.* In their telegrams, the members of the Union were "to ask insistently and even demand the immediate dissolution of the Duma and a change in the electoral law at all costs." On the day of dissolution, the Union was supposed "to organize a patriotic demonstration with ecclesiastical banners after the church services," in order to show the "peasantry and the troops that they are not alone." The black cross did in fact appear on March 16, and on that same day, the famous editor of *Russkie Vedomosti,* G. B. Iollos, sharing the fate of his friend Hertsenstein, was ambushed and murdered. The circular tried to terrify the people with the warning that "more than 250 terrorists" from the Duma would leave for their summer vacations to "prepare an uprising by Autumn." In answer to my printed accusation that this party "of violent revolution was recognized as the main support of the Russian government," the semiofficial paper limited itself to an ambiguous denial. Running ahead, let me mention that the same Purishkevich announced in the press at the end of May that the task of the semiofficial, right-wing revolutionaries had been completed. "The Duma will be dissolved within two weeks if not within ten days" (it was dissolved within three days). Thus the government subordinated itself to the "demand" of the nobility and the Black Hundreds. Stolypin's line, which I called the "fourth line," dropped off sharply, in response to an obvious decision from above.

It is worth dwelling on this major reversal in Stolypin's line, since it is generally not recognized that Stolypin tried to pursue it differently and to preserve a certain independence from the conspirator's "demands." In order to do this, he strove insistently to get the Duma to utter "the word" which would free it from the groundless accusation of complicity, or at least sympathy, with the murders committed by the leftists. He hoped to rely on this "word" in order to justify his own policy toward the Duma.

Stolypin's efforts began after the middle of March, in connection with the scheduled Duma discussion of the question of abolishing the military field courts which he had created under Article 87. Strictly speaking, this product of inter-Duma legislation fell off by itself about two months after the Duma opened. Apparently, the government deliberately did not put it on the agenda. The Duma discussions on this question took on a very sharp character. In the name of the Kadets, V. A. Maklakov brilliantly argued that the military-field courts beat against the very conception of the state, the conceptions of right and law, that they destroyed the basis of community life and threatened to replace civilized society with a herd of beasts. Stolypin, however, took a firm stand precisely on this question. He began to demonstrate the government's right to undertake extraordinary measures, in view of the fact that the revolution had not stopped, as evidenced by the S. D. and S. R. party resolutions. The condition which he set was transparent enough: you first. This condition was given not only to the incriminated parties but to the whole Duma. Later on, this condition was fixed ever more openly as the *conditio sine qua non* for preserving the Duma. You must express "strong censure and indignation at all revolutionary murder and violence." "Only then will you remove the charge against the Duma that it protects revolutionary terror, that it encourages bomb throwers and tries to provide them with all possible immunity." That is how the government supporters spoke in the Duma. It is clear where this groundless accusation was coming from. It is clear that the demand was made unconditionally and that for Stolypin it had become the condition for continuing his own policy. In order to confront both the Duma and Stolypin with the necessity of new elections once and for all, the rightists introduced a proposal for condemning political murders. "Put this resolution to a vote; what would it cost you? Obviously the Kadets cannot approve of murder." Thus were we advised by intermediaries from the side.

The noose was being tightened. To untie it was extraordinarily difficult, while to cut it required either the overthrow of the cabinet from the right or the success of the rightist plans for dissolving the Duma. Now, with hindsight, I can understand the idea behind Stolypin's unexpected invitation to me to hold confidential talks with him. I accepted the invitation and arrived at the Winter Palace at the appointed time. Kryzhanovsky met me on the first floor, and without directly mentioning the purpose of the visit, he stressed the importance of the impending talks and the necessity of reaching an agreement with the premier. Then they took me to the top floor and led me into Stolypin's office. Stolypin was apparently very nervous, and his eyes caught fire just as they did during the heated arguments in the Duma. The sharp gestures of his broken arm betrayed his agitated state. He stated his condition directly: if the Duma condemns revolutionary murders, he is ready to legalize the People's Freedom party. His approach was unexpected and I was somewhat taken aback. I began to explain that I could not command the party, and that for the party this was a question of political tactics and not an essential point. During a struggle, a party could not retreat from a position it had taken and adopt the position of its enemies, who also, by the way, employed political murder. Stolypin then put the question differently, turning to me, not as a supposed leader of the Duma, but as the author of political articles in the party's journal, *Rech*. "Write an article condemning the murders. I will be satisfied with that." I must admit that I hesitated on this point. It was a personal sacrifice, which did not go against my own convictions, in exchange for cessation of persecution against the party—and it might save the Duma! I set only one condition: that the article would appear without my signature. Stolypin agreed to this too, saying that the style of my articles is well known. I told him that I would accept his offer conditionally, for I had to discuss the matter with the party leaders, without whose consent such an article could not appear in the party's journal. Stolypin consented to this as well, and we agreed that if the article appeared, then his condition would have been met; if not, then not. Recalling this episode now, I understand why Stolypin was so agreeable and so openly cynical. He needed some document or gesture from the leading party in order to strengthen or perhaps even save his own position. Otherwise he would be forced to surrender to the pressure from the right. These were the final moments before his decision would have to be made. At that time I did not fully grasp this maneuver, which now seems even more than probable. The consequences had not yet completely unfolded. At the time, I thought only of strengthening the party, and my sacrifice seemed quite possible. From Stolypin, I went straight to Petrunkevich. Hearing my story, our old leader, who had been gradually stepping aside from party leadership, became terribly excited: "Absolutely not! How could you ever make such a concession, even conditionally? Not only will you ruin your own reputation, but you will drag the whole party down after you. No matter how cautiously you express the idea that is demanded of you, 'the truth will out,' and the semiofficial press will decipher it immediately. No, Never! Better the party be sacrificed than ruined morally. . . ."

After this, of course, the aricle was not written. Stolypin came to the appropriate conclusion, one which, let me repeat, only now do I understand. In the collection of my articles from *Rech*, the reader can see how consistently I argued not only our faction's point of view but also my own, that it was impossible for the party to make the gesture which Stolypin needed by uttering the sacred "word". . . . And even then, I could not help seeing that the fate of the Duma rested on the solution to this question. I zealously began to expose "the conspirators on the right," treating them as the real culprits in the impending dissolution of the Duma and contrasting their semiofficially tolerated murders with murders they wanted us to persuade the Duma to condemn.

For their part, the rightist terrorists gave me their special attention. One fine day, on my way to our editorial offices on Zhukovsky Street, a young chap overtook me on Liteiny Avenue and clobbered me twice on the neck from behind, knocking off my derby and breaking my pince-nez. I quietly bent down to pick up both my hat and glasses and then turned around: before me with widespread arms and a confused expression stood the thick-set young hero of the lower middle class. A crowd had gathered around us, offering to cart him off to the police station and act as witnesses. I immediately suspected a political motive, but not wanting publicity, I asked my attacker, who was flushed and who had obviously pumped himself with vodka for courage, whether or not he knew whom he had hit. Mumbling, he said that he did not. I then let him go, and said nothing about what had happened when I got to the office. You can imagine my surprise when in the evening of the same day our intelligence service informed me that an attempt had been made on my life, that the attacker was hired by Dr. Dubrovin with the instructions to slug me so that I would not get up again, and that when my attacker went back to his client without having carried out the task, Dubrovin scolded him and gave him only a small part of what he had been promised. After this incident, my friends began to notice unmistakeable signs of my being shadowed, and told me that in the window of a house on Ertelevy Lane, just opposite my office window, secret preparations were being made for setting up a gun to shoot me. Later a cabled report from Eidkunen appeared in the papers telling of the arrest at the border of a certain medical assistant, Smirnov. Smirnov was well known to us as an accomplice of the black brigades. The report continued that Smirnov had arrived with instructions to kill Miliukov, Hessen (editor of *Rech*), Gruzenberg (our brilliant defender in political trials), and Sliozberg. I do not remember on whose initiative it was, or whether or not it was in connection with this newspaper report, but several agents came to me, sent by the government, to provide personal protection. For some time, they regularly sat in my kitchen, until I asked that they be relieved of this thankless task.

The Easter vacation came and I decided to give myself a rest from all these troubles by taking a trip abroad. I had already gotten my ticket and passport stamp for the trip. This time I intended to visit

Switzerland, since I had not been there before. On the very eve of my departure, one of my former female students from the Fourth Gymnasium came to see me. She was one of the trio who, after graduation, had studied with me at home and had become quite close to our family. Upset and in tears she told me that she had accidently come upon a circle of Black Hundreds and heard that they had already learned from the police about my stamped passport and about my departure the next day (which she herself did not even know), and that they were going to attack me at the station. I could not but believe this information, which, while coming to me in such a strange manner, was trustworthy beyond doubt. I calmed down my faithful friend, telling her that I would find a way to leave by a route other than the one which they expected me to take. I, in fact, decided not to go to the Finland Station, but to take a cab to Udelnaia instead. I planned to spend the night at Udelnaia with my friend Timofeev, the hospital director, and to leave early the next morning on horseback for the next station, where I could catch the early train to Obo, and from Obo get the boat to Stockholm. A cabled report about my arrival, sent by some unknown person, appeared in the local papers the next morning.

I did not believe, however, that my persecutors were chasing me: I was beyond the limits of their murky horizon. All I wanted was to take a rest, amidst the beauties of nature, from the Sisyphean labor of politics. The ride across the skerries to the picturesque Swedish capital was only the beginning. I stayed for a while in the delightful region around the city, in Salt-sjo and in Djurgârolen'e. Then I prepared a long itinerary for the coming trip—much too long for the short vacation. I made up my mind not to stop anywhere for long, but only to look and to enjoy, selecting those places in Europe which I had not yet visited. At that time it was still possible to take such a fantastic stroll around Europe.

From Stockholm I cut across Sweden to Göteborg, and from there I decided to visit the famous waterfall Trollhättan on the river Elf. I was rewarded for having made this choice: even after Niagara, this colossal stream of water, rushing with tremendous force down the sloping surface, made a strong impression on me. From there I went down to Malmö, crossed the straits to Copenhagen by train (which is transported in its entirety by ferry), and without staying in Denmark, went straight to the interesting and gigantic port of Hamburg. Then I decided to stop in Paris, where the translation of my English book had just appeared under the title La Crise Russe. Herr had written a kind introduction for it, and with my supplementary article, it carried events up to 1907. In Paris, I hurriedly met with Aire and with my translator, and I invited her to travel with me for part of my return trip. She agreed with pleasure, on the one condition that we include Venice, which she had never seen. We devoted only one day to that— enough to carry away a picture of the city on a lagoon and the evening serenades among the gay, multicolored lantern lights of the gondolas. Afterward, we returned to Lake Como, and crossing over its satin surface from Bellagio to Menaggio, we took a postal bus across the Julian Alps, through the Valley of the Bregaglia, around the Bernina Massif, to the little town of Maloja— two names which rang of prehistoric Slavic civilization! From Maloja there opened the huge abyss of the Upper Engadin with its incomparable view of the lakes and the mountains surrounding them. From Sils we rode to Saint-Moritz, stopping at the "Forest House" (Waldhaus) for a day's rest. The horseback ride and the rapid change of scenery pretty well exhausted my traveling companion, and, anyway, it was time to leave. We took the train to Chur, whence she returned to Paris, though I still had time to stop on my way back for a fleeting glance at the Pinakothek in Munich.

I arrived a little late for the opening of the post-Easter session of the Duma. Apparently, everything there was all right and the Kadet tactics had even achieved satisfactory results. The leftists' longwindedness and pranks were kept within bounds by the new strict rules of order. A special time was set aside for purely procedural questions. In the fifteen committees, hard-working members of the Duma energetically prepared draft legislation to be introduced into the general session; this proposed legislation included drafts introduced on the ministers' initiative, together with drafts submitted by the People's Freedom party. The budget was discussed, as were the agrarian project and the projects for judicial and municipal government reform. The committees were also given drafts concerning the food problem, capital punishment, amnesty, etc. Even a modus vivendi with the ministers was worked out, and the Kadets were at last condemned from the left for being a "ministerial party."

In reality, the situation was entirely otherwise. If during the first months of the existence of the Second Duma, the overwhelming majority accepted the tactics of "protecting the Duma"; if during the second month, the leftists rose up against this tactic, proclaiming it "a Kadet tactic," while the government increased its efforts to get the Kadets to condemn the revolutionary murders in order to strengthen its own position against both the rightists and the leftists, then, now, in the third and final month, the picture was totally different. The question of condemning the murders had reached a deadlock, as a result of Kadet resistance, and apparently had ceased to interest the government, which no longer based its attitude toward the Duma on this issue. In the Duma, this issue was somehow unnoticeably done away with by a simple transition to ordinary business. This did not at all mean, however, that the "pacification" issue raised by the government had been settled thereby. The government paper *Rossiia,* together with the Suvorin's *Novoe Vremia,* for which the premier's brother, A. Stolypin wrote, began to argue that it was useless to make concessions to the Kadets, since the Kadets had no "moral authority" over the leftists, and since their desires in no way coincided with the "desires of the people." A surrender to the Kadets, thus, would be a surrender to the socialists. This meant that the choice had been made once and for all between "giving in to the Kadets" and giving in to the nobility and the Black Hundreds. It was characteristic that on one day, in the very end of May, two documents appeared from such disparate sides as Purishkevich and Witte. The former attacked the chairman of the Duma for allowing a leftist deputy to declare that "the autocracy no longer exists in Russia" and for calling Russia a "constitutional state." At the same time our political Proteus, Count Witte, announced in print that "the only judge of his political activity is the Russian autocrat, the Sovereign Emperor, to whom he is and always has been and unto the grave always will be a faithful subject and servant." Evidently, Witte, too, considered himself a candidate for leader of the coup d'etat. We know now that priority was given to P. A. Stolypin and that in the secret recesses of the cabinet, work had already been finished on the electoral law which the rightist revolutionaries were striving for. On May 26, I entitled my editorial "It's already too late" and analyzed the vacillation of the "upper circles" between three alternative slogans: (1) dissolve the Duma immediately; (2) "the Duma will die on the vine"; and (3) the most dangerous alternative for the "130,000" landowners, "we must give the Duma time to grow healthy roots"—anything but that! In essence, the decision to dissolve the Duma had been made after Deputy Zurabov's crude speech against the army, which had been given during my absence.

Stolypin, throwing away his calculation on the "center," trotted out as the slogan for dispersing the Duma, the same one he had used against the leftists: "Don't try to scare us." It was not difficult for the spies and provocateurs to find incriminating evidence in the socialists' tactics which would be impossible to deny; namely, the socialists' efforts in the country and in the army to organize a revolution. A search was made of Deputy Ozol's house. Documents—either genuine or forged—were found, including a soldier's address to the socialist faction, whereupon Stolypin demanded that the Duma revoke the deputy privileges of the entire S. D. faction for its antigovernment activity.

Such a summary demand involved the fundamental question of the deputies' immunity and could not be granted without a prior study of the facts as they concerned each individual deputy. The troubled Kadet faction insisted on passing the demand on to a committee which was to render its decision in the shortest possible time. But the new electoral law was already prepared, and there v. as no need to hide behind such an excuse. Without waiting for the committee's decision, Stolypin dissolved the Duma and carried through his coup d'etat, without even attempting to disguise it, in the form of the electoral "statute" of June 3. The only thing the Kadets could do was to carry through their tactics to the end, to devote the last session to a peaceful discussion of the law[24] and to reject the leftists' suggestion of turning the Duma into a tribune at the last moment by forcefully rejecting the budget and abolishing, by this same "de facto" action, the agrarian legislation of Article 87. In my last editorials, I could do no more than analyze the illegality and the irrationality of Stolypin's demand and emphasize his unwillingness to wait for the Duma's decision. In a private talk, three moderate Kadets, Maklakov, Struve, and Chelnokov (who was at one time the mayor of Moscow), tried to prevail upon Stolypin not to dissolve the Duma. This was exceptionally naive and Stolypin had little difficulty in parrying their objections by offering a sarcastic counterproposal—to protect him against the antigovernment tactics of the leftists. They apparently did not understand that Stolypin himself was caught in the teeth of a powerful and intricate mechanism whose driving belt was controlled by a force which moved it blindly and ineluctably toward that very abyss it desired to escape.

Physiognomy of the Third State Duma

THE FIRST RUSSIAN REVOLUTION ended with the coup d'etat on June 3, 1907. On that day, the new electoral "law" was issued, which we Kadets refused to call a "law," preferring the term "decree" instead. One could not, however, explain this distinction logically, since there was no real boundary between the two terms. If one considered the October Manifesto as such a boundary, then the "Fundamental Laws," issued before the First Duma was even convoked, were in essence a "decree" and not a "law." This had been, in fact, the first "coup d'etat." The forces of the old order, the unlimited monarchy and the landed nobility, were victorious both then and now. At both times their victory was incomplete, and the struggle between the old, obsolete system and the new, embryonic one continued. Now a new curb was placed on the people's representatives: the class electoral law. Even this was only a truce and not a peace. The real victors went much further; they strove for a full restoration of the old order.

Whereas the struggle had been fated earlier to continue in a single direction though along a descending curve, the struggle in this new stage was to take place between the victors themselves. The balance between them which had been achieved by the "decree" of June 3 turned out to be only temporary. Even Stolypin's role in dissolving the Second Duma and in hastily passing the nobility's electoral law sounded a dissonant note in the rightists' victory. The switch from ministerial deals with the "peaceful reconstructionists" to deals with the "Union of Russian People," which was protected by the Court, was too abrupt for Stolypin. In his attempts to create his own party, he inherited Count Witte's alliance with the "Octobrists," whose very name constituted their political program. Naturally enough, the condition for convoking the Third Duma was that Stolypin's allies would come to the Duma as its leaders and as members of a government majority. As a group, however, the Octobrists had been artificially created with the help of the government. Even under the "decree" of June 3, they could not be elected in sufficient numbers without support from the more rightist groups, which were also artificially created for the role of "monarchist" parties. According to the decree of June 3, the elections were still multistaged, but at the first stage of elections, the provincial meetings, the number of electors who could send deputies to the State Duma was so distributed among the various social groups as to give the majority to the landowning nobility.[25] With the additions from the cities, 154 Octobrists were in this way elected to the Duma (out of a total of 442 Duma members). In order to create their majority, the government, using its direct influence, separated a group of seventy "moderate rightists" from the right wing. The result was an unstable majority of 224 members, and the more loosely bound "nationalists" (twenty-six members) had to be added to it, as well as the wholly unbridled Black Hundreds (fifty members). A group of 300 members was thus formed which was ready to obey the wishes of the government and which justified the Third Duma's double nickname: the Duma of "Lords" and "Lackeys". . . . As we can see, the majority was artificially created and far from homogeneous. If, in the Duma's first sessions, Guchkov could say that "the coup d'etat achieved by our monarch is the establishment of a constitutional system," his obligatory ally, Balashov, the leader of the "moderate rightists" could pointedly object: "We do not recognize a constitution and we do not interpret as such the words 'renovated State system.'" Another leader of the same group, Count V. Bobrinsky, who received a salary from the government, declared more frankly that "by the act of June 3 the autocratic sovereign demonstrated his autocratic powers." The other paid deputies, playing the role of scandal-makers—like Purishkevich, P. N. Krupensky, and Markov II—carried on the struggle for complete restoration, relying on the Court circles for support and not considering themselves bound by anything. In an interview for the semiofficial government paper, *Volga*, Stolypin himself declared that the newly established system was "a purely Russian state system corresponding to historical traditions and to the national spirit" and that the Duma had not managed to "snatch away anything from the Tsar's power." The general slogans, accepted by this entire section of the Duma, were Guchkov's "nationalism" and "patriotism."

There was, similarly, in this Duma no unity in the ranks of the conquered—not even to the extent achieved, though just barely, in the first two Dumas. In those Dumas, we could conclude that all "progressive" Russia had been defeated in the struggle against the autocracy. Now, however, we knew that there had been two separate losers, not just a single one. If we fought against the autocracy for constitutional rights, then we had to recognize that we had another adversary in this struggle—revolutionary rights. By conviction and con-

science, we could not help believing that the very word "right" belonged to our group alone. In spite of everything, "right" and "law"
remained the particular aims of our struggle. "Revolution" left the
stage; but for how long? The representatives of the revolution stood
right here next to us. But could we consider them our allies? They did
not consider themselves to be our allies—even temporarily. Their goals
and their means had been and were still different from ours. After the
hard lessons of the first two Dumas, it was impossible not to accept this
fact. I have mentioned that in the Second Duma the Constitutional
Democratic party had already completely freed itself from those
"friendly enemy" relations which had bound it in the First Duma. In
the Third Duma, the separation went even further.

The very conception of the Third Duma excluded the presence
of an opposition, and the government did everything it could at the
elections so that there would be no opposition. The electoral boards
juggled the elections so that the reliable electors would outnumber
the unreliable ones. The undesirable elements and the "unlegalized"
parties were persecuted by the local authorities and were not allowed
to take part in the election. Nevertheless, an opposition did manage
to reach the Duma through a whole series of chinks and cracks which
were left, as if on purpose, in order that some kind of opposition
would be present in the representative body, if only for the sake of
completeness. In the first place, a whole party was available which
Stolypin had legalized but which was not bound to the government
by agreement, as Guchkov's party was. The members of this party
called themselves "Progressives." Its kernel consisted of "Peaceful
Reconstructionists," and it was from them that Stolypin at one time
had chosen his candidates for ministerial posts. They were sincere
constitutionalists, and from time to time they raised the question in
the Duma of organizing a "constitutional center." They did not go the
way of the Octobrists. Soon, in fact, they were drawn in the opposite
direction and were actually joined by some of the politically more
consistent Octobrists who were dissatisfied with their own group, but
who did not want to move as far left as the Kadets. This Progressive
faction was the only one in the Duma to increase its size (from
twenty-three to forty members), but it remained as a result, looser
and all the more undefined and undisciplined. The course of events
gradually brought them together with the Kadets, but this only increased their desire to preserve their independence. Consequently, we
could expect political surprises from them from time to time—including even the desire to "jump right over" the Kadets toward the left.

The role of the real opposition, and one that, given the situation,
was ideologically stable and well organized, was still played by the
People's Freedom party. The very way in which the elections were

conducted made our party's faction a natural spokesman for public opinion. In the five largest Russian cities (Moscow, Petersburg, Kiev, Odessa, and Riga), not only were direct elections retained but the decree of June 3 even extended suffrage rights to apartment tenants. True, even here the electors were distributed unevenly between two curiae: The first curia included the very few, great taxpayers,[26] while the second included the remaining mass of people who could meet the comparatively moderate apartment qualifications. Through these qualifications, at last, even I reached the Duma. This time, they not only did not put up obstacles to my election but, according to rumors which reached me, Kryzhanovsky had decided that it would be better to have me inside the Duma than outside of it (that is, in the capacity of secret inciter, which they had considered me previously). The character of the elections in the second curia made it possible to wage a public electoral campaign and to defend the party's program in open argument with our political adversaries. Our success was so obvious that even the first curia was forced to follow us with the result that, here and there, instead of Octobrists and rightists, our candidates also began to come through.

The political activity of our faction ouside the Duma was not limited to preelection meetings, which had the indirect effect of reviving our party's activities. Both Petersburg and Moscow had been previously divided into districts where district committees were organized to register new party members. Our faction's Duma work gave it vital material for organizing periodic public appearances, with the participation of the "immune" members of our faction. Our meetings were given a particular vitality as a result of our allowing free access to other political currents and because of the controversial character of the debates themselves. To our delight the rightists ignored us and did not bring in their Black Hundreds propaganda, knowing full well that our audiences would not react tolerantly to their presence. Similarly, the official representatives of the left did not come, evidently not wanting to compromise their dignity. On the other hand, there was no end to the rank and file leftist speakers who were ready to do battle with us and who usually filled the list of speakers who were to appear at our meetings. We cannot say that it was difficult to fight them. Our strength lay, above all, in our knowledge of the practical affairs and in the seriousness of our approach to them. The leftists usually went no further than familiarity with pamphlet literature. They brought much passion into the debates and whatever they needed for propaganda purposes, but they could not convince our audience. As an example, let me recall two episodes in which I was personally involved and which later became familiar arguments against the Kadets. Drawing a comparison with a bull fight, I once said that in struggle, one should not wave a red flag in front of opponents. In the leftist interpretation, this meant that I had offended the socialist banner. At another time, I drew upon a well-known fable by La Fontaine, which turned out to be even more risky. I said that one should not, through following outside advice, carry the ass oneself. To "ass," they added the "leftist," and turned out a quite piquant expression: it seems that I called the socialists "leftist asses." From this, of course, they drew the conclusion that I was a "red-baiter." I will relate other incidents later. It was not difficult to carry on such "debates"; they even worked to our advantage, since they entertained the public. Only in one district of Petersburg, the Vyborg workers' quarter, did we meet with strong psychological resistance from the audience. A university student, "Comrade Abram," spoke against us there. Subsequently he became the Soviet "commander-in-chief," Krylenko, who did away with Dukhonin, while still later he was public procurator and predecessor of Vyshinsky. With his light mental baggage, drawn from the cheap pamphlets he had memorized, and with his facile tongue, he beat against our argument with unbelievable aplomb. The working public roared with laughter and our speakers had a difficult time being heard. In general, however, the urban democracy of "business employees" was on our side, and we somehow managed to come out of these battles whole.

Besides those public appearances, our faction energetically acted through the press. After each annual session of the Duma, our faction published a report of its activity. In these reports, I was usually responsible for the section on our faction's tactics in connection with the general political situation, on questions of the constitution and public law, on domestic and foreign policy and on national questions. These were the main themes which I had occasion to speak about in the Duma. The second half of each report included the most important speeches which members of our faction delivered in the Duma. I greatly regret that I do not have these reports with me now in order to develop this part of my memoirs more completely.

I will not dwell upon the role of our paper Rech here. We never formally declared Rech to be a party paper, but its distribution throughout Russia, of course, did more to popularize our views than all the other public activity of our faction combined. Our two reporters, L. M. Nemanov and S. L. Poliakov-Litovtsev, summarized the stenographic reports of the Duma sessions and transmitted their own impressions of the Duma's everyday life. Through their job, they made a name for themselves all over Russia. Our interpretations of the Duma's work, published in the editorials of Rech and in the Moscow "professors'" paper, Russkie Vedomosti, united around us a significant portion of the Russian reading public.

But let us return to other sections of the "opposition" in the Third State Duma. The national groups—the Poles, the Polish-Lithuanians, the Belorussians, and the Moslems—occupied their own peculiar position between the opposition and the government majority. I have already spoken about my cautious attitude toward the national question in the First Duma. At that time, the nationalities expected a general liberation, still linked their own cause with the general Russian cause, and, therefore, distributed themselves among the various Russian political factions. By the Second Duma, they had already become disappointed in the outcome of the Russian political struggle and had moved away somewhat from the general Russian cause, although still remaining democratically inclined. They paid for these democratic leanings by the loss of most of their mandate. The decree of June 3 reduced the number of seats for the Poles from thirty-seven to nineteen, the number for the Asian peoples from forty-four to fifteen and the number for the Caucasians from twenty-nine to ten. This more limited number of seats was filled by more conservatively inclined deputies, who stood in separate groupings, apart from the Russians. They often voted with the opposition, but they (especially the Poles) did not want to break with the government. The Caucasian deputies were a striking exception, especially the Georgians who filled the extreme leftist bench of the Social Democratic faction. Sharing neither the clerical-feudal nor the bourgeois tendencies of the other nationalities, they considered themselves part of Russian social democracy. Together with the Russian S. D.'s, the Georgians took part in the Second International, and precisely because of their international aspirations, were able to carry on a joint struggle with the Russian S. D.'s for the creation of a common "socialist fatherland." (Social Democrats were always opposed to any splintering of large states into small, national units.) All this explains why Gegechkori, Chkheidze, and other Georgians were almost the only representatives of the small (fourteen members), Russian S. D. faction. This also explains their complete isolation from the Russian factions of the Duma opposition and their nonparticipation in the general work of the Duma. Between them and the Kadets, there was an equally small group of "Trudoviks" (fourteen members), who were considered Social Revolutionaries by tradition. In the Third Duma, however, this group was the most colorless of them all and consisted almost exclusively of peasants with either a low or only informal education. The group waited for a leader, a vacant position later to be taken by A. F. Kerensky, who pursued whatever policy happened to please him.

Such were the conditions in which the Kadet faction had to act in the Third Duma.

The Kadets in the Third Duma

I HAD NO DOUBTS, of course, that there was a place for the Kadet faction even in this "Lords" and "Lackeys" Duma of June 3. In this respect, I was the least implacable of all our "leaders." I had advised running for election even for the Bulygin Duma, and later I had fought against the boycott of the First Duma. I always believed that the very idea of popular representation, even though distorted, carried within itself the germ of future internal development. It was clearer to me than it was to many others that the social upheaval of 1905 was only temporary. What, essentially, had changed since then? The movement had ebbed, and together with it, the battle line had been pushed far back. Our previous successes were only apparent, and they masked the real state of affairs only for a short time. The wave fell back, and the State Duma turned out to be an institution crippled by the Fundamental Laws, which had from the beginning in various ways curtailed the rights of the people's representatives, and by the existence of the State Council, which we ourselves called a "bottleneck" and a "cemetery" for the Duma legislation. The struggle now returned to that same impenetrable Chinese wall, and, of necessity, took on more clandestine forms. To the Third Duma, too, we brought with ourselves the shrine of our new testament—the program contained in the First Duma's address. This time, however, we had to deal more cautiously with it. Only in the Fourth Duma did we draw from that address our legislative drafts for civil liberties—and then only as a demonstration. Only then, under the changed conditions, was it possible to begin talking again about changing the electoral law and about the responsibility of the executive authority to the legislature. In anticipation of that time, we had to carry out the dull, boring work of the Third Duma, making sure that at least those rights which the Duma had already obtained would not pass into oblivion and that the political idea behind those rights would not be forgotten. In this sense, then, even the "Lords" Duma, which I have just described, opened several prospects for us. The very instability and diversity of the government majority promised internal shifts. Here too, the truce was only temporary, and none of the sides which had been artificially stuck together could consider its final goal achieved. Nevertheless, the low level of this temporary truce with the government promised a steadfast and protracted struggle more than it did those heights to which we wanted to raise the political achievements of the First Duma. At any rate, in the Third Duma we had won time to reinforce the very existence of the popular representative body, which was something I had always insisted on. Now we had to reconcile ourselves, not to months, but years of further delay. In the meantime, the Duma's activity took on that "humdrum" character which I had described as a first condition for considering the representative body an integral part of Russian reality.

However, the abruptly changed conditions were accompanied, for the third time, by radical changes in the composition as well as in the tactics of the Duma faction of the People's Freedom party. It seemed a long time ago that we had lost the 120 "Vyborgites" who had been deprived of voting rights. The gesture, which, in other circumstances, would have been of historic significance, was already out of place in our congress at Terioki. At the trial, which ended in jail sentences, our old friends did not defend themselves; on the contrary, they came forth as the accusers. The government, however, purposely avoided posing the question as a matter of principle, and both the charges and the sentences were comparatively light. Events quickly erased our sacrifice from memory, and Kadets of another type had gone to the Second Duma: these were the experts and professors, who composed model drafts of constitutional legislation which were never to be realized. Then even this group departed. In the Third Duma sat Kadets who divided among themselves the practical work of the Duma committees. We had always considered such committee work to be the main job of parliamentary activity, but this was the first time that we received the necessary time and material for it. A. I. Shingarev now came into the spotlight for the first time. A former district doctor and Zemstvoist, Shingarev quickly mastered the problems involved in the state budget and became the permanent opponent of V. N. Kokovtsov, the minister of finance. V. A. Stepanov specialized in labor legislation and, as his contribution to the committee work, composed drafts for legislation on vital labor issues, which, however, never got out of the Third Duma. N. V. Nekrasov, another young deputy with a great, though unexpected, future, concentrated on railroad problems. N. N. Kutler, who joined our faction after leaving his minister's bench, consulted with our faction on financial questions. On the most important of all social questions, which Stolypin had solved in a landowner's spirit and had passed originally during the Duma intersession, as extra-Duma legislation, permitted under Article 87, both A. I. Shing-arev and the writer of these lines demonstrated strong opposition (to the government's program). It fell to me as chairman of our faction to speak not only on questions having a constitutional or political character but also on other questions for which sufficiently prepared representatives could not be found. I remember that I even had to give the first speech on the budget, since Kutler refused to do it— perhaps because of his still fresh ties to the government—while Shing-arev had not yet had time to orient himself in this field. I took part in committee work and spoke at general meetings on questions concern-ing the church, the Old Believers, and the sects, on projects for public education and copyrights, on questions of domestic policy, and on nationality questions. My main specialty, however, became foreign policy, and because of the general ignorance in this area which then prevailed, I had no competitors. True, I had highly competent as-sistants, especially F. I. Rodichev and V. A. Maklakov. F. I. Rodichev possessed a truly exceptional gift of eloquence, but his hot temper often carried him beyond the limits permitted both by faction disci-pline and by the political conditions of the moment. In nationality ques-tions he was an inveterate defender of Polish interests, an attitude which was not always warranted by policies of the Poles themselves in the Russian governmental institutions. He likewise did not completely share the views of our faction on the agrarian question. By the subtlety and flexibility of his juridical argumentation, V. A. Maklakov was an incomparable and indispensable orator, but he chose only those speeches which showed him at his best. For its part, the faction could not always entrust him with speaking on the most important political questions, since we knew that he did not always share the Kadet point of view.

As for our tactics in the Third Duma, they are already clear from what has been said. We decided to bury ourselves, with all our strength and knowledge, in the daily governmental activity of the representative institution. We had to learn many things which could be known, understood, and appreciated only by standing at the main-spring of the vast and intricate state machine. It was, thus, impossible to avoid contact with the bureaucracy, the civil servants of the min-istries, who possessed technical knowledge, experience, and routine. The best of them who became acquainted with us in the committees, suffered from the routine themselves. When they understood our good intentions, they came to us on their own for cooperation in their strug-gle against this routine—of course, without the knowledge of their immediate superiors. Shingarev made extensive use of this assistance

in his study of the defects of the Russian budget and auditing department. The same occurred in the area of public education, church, and,
later, naval and foreign policy.

In the first Duma sessions, however, it was still a long way from
this peculiar form of coalescence. First of all, we became the object
of fierce political attack by the government majority, and especially
the rightists. To discredit the opposition—and, specifically, its more
responsible representatives—was both the goal and the justification of
their own victory.

Let me mention Purishkevich's statement that the Kadets were
the most dangerous and undesirable of political elements precisely
because they were the most cautious, intelligent, and politically educated, and the most likely participants in the natural government. It
was natural that the pseudo "constitutionalists" as well as the secret
advocates of autocratic restoration concentrated their most urgent
tactical efforts on discrediting the People's Freedom faction. It was
also natural that I, being the recognized leader of the incriminated
faction, should become the prime target for attack. They considered
us devoid of national and patriotic feelings—which were actually this
Duma's main distinction. They treated us as "antistate" and "revolutionary" elements, ascribing to us all the leftist sins against the representative institution. An insulting gesture towards us committed by
the Duma must be laid to Guchkov's initiative: the refusal to allow
us to join the Duma Committee of State Defense, on the grounds that
we might divulge state secrets to the enemy. The rightists even went
so far as to obstruct our—and especially my—speeches from the Duma's
tribune. When my turn came to speak, P. N. Krupensky passed a note
around to the rightists and nationalists instructing them to "keep
talking"; and they made such noise it was impossible to hear the
speaker. I will not even mention the insulting phrases directed at us
from their benches. Purishkevich. began one of his speeches with a
quotation from Krylov:

Little Paul the Blockhead, that was a proper name,
His gift for telling lies was great, For him t'was just a game.

At another time, during one of his speeches, he noticed a sarcastic
expression on my face, grabbed the glass of water which always stood
on the speakers' tribune, and hurled it at me (I was sitting on the lower
benches in the front of the Duma auditorium). The glass fell at my
feet and shattered. The chairman was forced to exclude Purishkevich
from that session. The high point of these large and small scandals,
however, was the reception given for me by the entire Duma majority

after my return from America for the spring session of 1908. Apparently, the very fact that I took the trip was considered some sort of treason to my homeland, and a demonstration was prepared beforehand for my first Duma speech after my return. As I was getting ready to speak, the members of the majority rose from their seats and walked out of the room. I must admit that my first impression was one of horror. This was, after all, the State Duma, the legal representative institution. I looked at Guchkov and waited to see how my former university comrade sitting at the center would act. When the majority of the auditorium had been emptied, he, too, rose, and with his heavy gait (which was a result of a leg wound received in the Boer War), he headed for the exit. I remained calm and waited silently, not leaving the platform. The chairman ordered an intermission. When the session again resumed, I again went up to the speaker's platform, keeping my turn to speak. The government majority again left the room. The chairman then closed the session. On the next day, I published my "undelivered speech" in *Rech,* and I also expressed my views on the behavior of the meeting. When the next session opened, I again mounted the tribune. There was no sense to further resistance, so the members of the majority remained seated in their places. My speech dealt only with the business of the Duma as it was supposed to, and I did not say a word about the demonstration.

In order not to return to such incidents, let me mention one more clash with Guchkov which occurred much later. At one time I used a rather strong expression about him in one of my speeches, but the expression was entirely "parliamentary" and I had completely forgotten about it. Guchkov, however, seized upon it and sent me his seconds, Rodzianko and Zvegintsev, both members of the Duma and both former military men. He was perfectly well aware of my negative attitude toward duels—an attitude which was shared by the entire intelligentsia at that time—and he probably assumed that I would refuse the duel, thereby lowering myself in the opinion of his like-minded friends. From the time of his Berlin duel (see above), he himself had an established reputation as a rabid duelist. I felt, however, that in the given political situation, I could not refuse the challenge. Guchkov was the leader of the majority and I was considered the leader of the opposition. A refusal would, therefore, be a political act. I accepted the challenge and likewise asked two former military men to be my seconds: a young man, A. M. Koliubakin, a man with a hot temper and sensitive to questions of honor, including military honor; and, as far as I remember, Svechin, a former member of the First Duma. Thus, I showed that I considered this to be a serious matter. I refused to give in to Guchkov's demands. My seconds were greatly dis-

tressed. Come what may, they wanted to rescue me from this pre-
posterous situation, but they had to take into account the rules of the
dueling code as well as my refusal to reconcile. I remember the late
evening of the last conference between the two sides when the conciliatory formula most acceptable to me was worked out. I had no
faith in that formula. I considered the duel inevitable and recalled
Lensky's aria. But . . . my seconds arrived late at night, triumphant
and insistent. They had gotten a compromise which, in their opinion,
I had neither a political nor a moral right to refuse. A refusal would
have shown an incomprehensible stubbornness and obstinacy. Unfortunately, I do not remember either the compromise formula or even
the reason for the original insult to Guchkov, which apparently had
been deliberately exaggerated. I saw that it would have been ridiculous to persist any further so I agreed with my seconds and signed the
paper which they had worked out together with the other side
Guchkov did not succeed either in humiliating me or in forcing me to
fight the duel and, obviously, did not achieve the political aim he was
after.

I will mention, in passing, another "duel," which involved, not me,
but Rodichev. My part in this incident was both unexpected and unpleasant. This has remained my *cas de conscience* until this day, and
I still cannot understand it. Rodichev delivered a very strong speech
against the death penalty, which had been applied even after 1907.
He finished his speech with the phrase "Stolypin's necktie," at which
point he made a gesture with his hands to indicate a noose around
the neck. The impression was so strong that the Duma was dumb
struck for a moment. Then a frantic applause broke loose in honor of
Stolypin, who was sitting in his place; and the whole government
majority stood up. Even I stood up, feeling that it was morally impossible to remain seated. Our faction remained seated, however, and
stared at me in bewilderment. The session broke up. Rodichev was
taken aback. Stolypin left the auditorium and went to the ministers'
quarters. At first I had interpreted my gesture as a protest against
personal insults in a parliamentary speech, but another explanation
immediately appeared. From the ministers' quarters came a report
that Stolypin was deeply shocked, that he did not want to remain
with his children and be known as a "hangman"; and that he had sent
Rodichev his seconds. I was sure that for psychological and other
reasons, it would be impossible for Rodichev to accept the duel. I
told our faction that my action had removed any personal element
from this incident, and that Rodichev had only to excuse himself for
uttering the unfortunate phrase. Still upset and confused, Rodichev
went to offer his apologies, in spite of the opposing opinions which

were expressed. Stolypin used this incident crudely and insultingly. Without offering his hand, he threw out the arrogant phrase at Rodichev: "I forgive you." I felt disgusted with myself. Heated arguments raged in our party's club. In the evening of the same day, our club women reconciled us by bringing a bouquet of flowers to both Rodichev and me. I felt the double sensation of having acted correctly, of not being able to act otherwise, but having placed Rodichev in a humiliating position. The alternatives of accepting the duel or categorically refusing it seem to me, even now, equally impossible for Rodichev.

Three Trips Abroad

BEFORE CONTINUING the story of my Duma activity, I will combine, under this general heading, my three trips abroad in the years 1907–9. All three trips were related to my work in the Duma, though each in a different way. When we compare these differences, we see an interesting curve illustrating a rapid change in the Third Duma's attitude toward me personally and toward our whole faction. I have just described above the point of origin of this curve: the Duma majority's demonstration against me after the first of these trips—to the United States. . . . My second trip (to the Balkans) is closely tied to my speeches in the Duma, not only as a tolerated, but as a more and more recognized expert on foreign policy. The third trip—my participation in the Duma delegation to London—was already equivalent to recognizing that our faction had a legal place in the composition of the State Duma.

My Third Trip to America

My third trip to America was made under different circumstances than my first two trips. First of all, my third trip was entirely in the American style: I stayed in the United States exactly three days. Secondly, and partly for the same reason, it turned into a triumphant procession, prepared for me with the close cooperation, of course, of my friend, Charles Crane. This was, so to say, the zenith of my popularity in America. The occasion for the new invitation was perfectly natural. Both in my lectures and in my book, I foretold the onset of the revolution. My predictions came true; the revolution occurred, and its immediate aims evoked tremendous sympathy in the whole of the civilized world and, particularly, in America. But now the fires of the revolution had burned down, and reaction had set in. The clearest manifestation of reaction was the tsar's violation of the Fundamental Laws and the convocation of the Third Duma, based on a new electoral statute which placed the Russian representative institution under the trusteeship of the government in alliance with the "ruling" class. It is natural that in America people wanted to know what had happened, and to learn it from that same person who had explained the inevitability of the revolutionary denouement. I had, therefore, to offer an explanation, the same one, in fact, which I gave in the supplement to the French translation of my book.

I had received and had accepted the invitation before the electoral campaign had begun and before I was elected to the Duma. After I was elected, my time was no longer my own and I was forced to limit my visit to those three days which were left (after the twelve-days travel time each way across the ocean) before reopening the Duma sessions after the Christmas vacation. For these three days, Crane and my friends made me the focus of a whole series of social demonstrations.

In the center stood the invitation to deliver a report on the new political situation in Russia. This report was placed on the agenda of an influential political organization, the Civic Forum. The aim of this organization's political speeches was to register important aspects of political life, chiefly in the New World, and thereby exert influence on American public opinion. For this purpose, the most influential political figures were invited, including national presidents. Therefore, even to appear under the auspices of the Civic Forum was in itself something like a political event. One of the largest auditoriums in New York at that time, Carnegie Hall, was chosen for the speeches, and the speeches were given under the chairmanship of some influential personage, in my case, Bishop Potter. The speeches were accompanied by public debates which were recorded and distributed for general information and which were followed by a large public vote on a resolution proposed by the chairman.

I delivered my report on the day after the boat arrived. My hosts used the remainder of the first day to arrange meetings with various notables and outstanding public and academic figures of New York. More than six hundred people were invited. I was introduced in the usual American style. I stood on the dias surrounded by my hosts. They led each one of the guests up to me, and spoke his name. I was supposed to utter the sacred words "how do you do," shake their hands, and utter some polite words in case they should speak to me. Among those who greeted me were some persons and names which were familiar to me; it was easier to exchange compliments with them. There were those who only knew my role or, at least, my name; with them it was more difficult. Probably the majority did not know who I was at all; in their case the greetings were limited to the sacramental formula. I was left with a tangible impression from those six hundred, strong American handshakes: my hand was swollen. Here was the kernel of my audience of the next day; they brought with them a ready sympathy for the subject of my talk and scattered themselves on the stage or in the first rows. Behind them was scattered the public, and I was to hear many very left wing and often biting objections from the heights of the auditorium.

The session took place on the next day in festive surroundings. The bishop's introductory speech was devoted to the significance of the events which had occurred in Russia, and to my personal biography. Of course, I had prepared the text of my address beforehand, but I tried to give it a colloquial character. In any case, it was listened to with great attention and interrupted in the appropriate places by the usual salutatory acclaims from the audience. Then, in accord with the chairman's invitation to ask questions but not to enter into polemics, I was met with a barrage of venomous remarks, objections, and questions from the gallery. My description of the conflict between the government and the society seemed much too objective there. They urged me on to more extreme words. I did not want to do this, but, on the contrary, when they shifted from judgments about the government to judgments about Russia, I not only defended myself but took the offensive. The majority of the audience demonstrated their approval, particularly at these points. On the whole, I was quite happy with the impression I had made. In conclusion, the chairman read a statement of approval and asked all those in agreement to utter the archaic word "aye." The "aye" thundered forth loudly, and the meeting was closed.

On the third day, this celebration in my honor reached its high point, although, through my own fault, as we shall see, it was not as high as it might have been. From New York they took me to Washington. There, the program included a reception by the President and a report on Russia to the members of Congress. I prevented the first part of this program from being carried out, because, in order to be introduced to the President I had to have the recommendation of the Russian ambassador, who at that time was Baron Rosen. I had already said in New York that, as a representative of the opposition, I could not turn to the ambassador with this request and that I would run the risk of his refusal. Crane insisted that the ambassador would not refuse and mentioned his personal acquaintance with both the President and the ambassador. (The President at that time was Theodore Roosevelt.) I remained adamant. They tried to change my mind after our arrival in Washington. There, both familiar and unfamiliar intermediaries came to my hotel room and said that the President had expressed the desire to see me. They assured me that the ambassa-

dor's agreement was certain and were amazed by the resistance which
to them was incomprehensible. Afterward, it seemed both strange and
ridiculous even to me. At the time, however, I felt that I was
bound by my political role in Russia. It seemed to me (and it probably was so in reality) that those in Russia who shared my views
would not have understood my turning to the representative of the
Russian government abroad with a request and would have considered such a request a form of betrayal. Let me repeat that things
were that way at that time. In America, at any rate, they evidently
understood that this was not simple stupidity or fanaticism on my
part, but a graphic illustration of what was going on in Russia. They
took me from the hotel to a large building (I do not know if this was
in the Capitol) where the members of both houses of Congress had
gathered. There were neither debates nor reports this time; instead, we had a conversation that was interesting both for me and for
my listeners. The topic, of course, was the same, but this was a gathering of officials and leading political figures. They were interested not
so much in my interpretation of the facts as in the facts themselves.
General knowledge and experience was not, of course, knowledge of
Russia and in this respect I found the gathering rather poorly informed. Nevertheless, they caught the meaning of my words at once.

After the conversation, we had dinner, the group dividing itself
among individual tables. I remember that, among others, Taft (a
judge, and the brother of President Taft) sat down at my table and
the conversation took on a more intimate, but still substantive, character. I returned to New York late at night and the next morning my
boat, "Messageries Maritimes," left for Europe. This was the only time
that, on my trips to America, I took a French boat, and the only time
on my trips that a serious storm came up. Gigantic waves lashed
across the glass tower where the dance hall was located. The spectacle
was fascinating—and frightening. As to my reception upon returning
to the Duma, I have already spoken of this above.

The Balkans and Europe

1908 was the year of my first appearances before the Third Duma.
It was also the year of a serious "Balkan crisis." Of all the Russian
public figures, I turned out to be the only specialist on this question.
My stay in Bulgaria, and my trip through Macedonia and Old Serbia
at the end of the century, together with my trip through the western,
Serbian half of the Balkans in 1904 (these trips are discussed in the
appropriate chapters of these memoirs) acquainted me, not with the
official, but with the internal life of the Slavic peoples of the penin-

sula. I witnessed the rebirth of their national consciousness and their popular struggle against their oppressors, the Turks, and against their guardians, the Austro-Hungarians. All my sympathies were on the side of these liberating aspirations, all the more so since the leadership in that struggle had already shifted from the old "folk-lovers" to a young generation, a newborn, Slavic, democratic intelligentsia.

Nevertheless, the event which had already occurred and those which were about to occur in this small theater had to be considered in the wider European context. Here, in the provinces, one could see quite distinctly that the threads of the intricate fabric of changes occurring in this "windy corner" of Europe led upward to European diplomacy, and through it to the European courts. But for such an outside observer as myself, these threads were lost there, at the summit.

It would not be correct to say, of course, that I was entirely unaware of developments in this area. On the contrary, my views on Europe began to form a long time before, not so much under the influence of facts as under the influence of sentiments and general attitudes. I remember my childhood impressions of the War of 1870 and my youthful experiences during the War of 1877–78, in which I personally took part as a volunteer, although my role was only that of a humble medical orderly in the Caucasus. I was struck at the time by the sharp contrast between the Treaty of San Stefano, arranged right in front of the walls of Constantinople, and Bismarck's "broker's" role at the Berlin Congress, where Russia lost the fruits of her complete victory in Bulgaria, while Austria-Hungary, in reward for her nonparticipation, received the Serbian lands of Bosnia and Herzegovina to "occupy and administer."

Later, the picture was broken up, the main lines lost among the mass of details. The difficulty was increased by the fact that, in the course of events, the shreds of European politics became intertwined. A transitional situation was created, such that even professional diplomacy, and Russian diplomacy in particular, wavered in choosing a direction. Given the mystery which surrounded diplomatic secrets, one either had to be satisfied with the scraps of information which found their way into print or to feed on rumors "from the most reliable sources." I mention this merely in order to explain why I was so far from being completely informed in this area. Meanwhile, my appraisal of events depended on just such sources. In these memoirs, I would like to preserve those shades of my opinion at the time, linked either to my lack of information or to the fact that unfolding events had not reached their final stage.

Subsequently, in historical perspective, it was easy to see that the main axis around which European events revolved toward the turn of the century was William II's accession to the emperor's throne, his antagonism toward Bismarck and his noisy declarations that the German Empire, created by the Iron Chancellor, should be directed toward "world politics." This was in the 1890's. Thus arose the conflict with the democratic powers of England and France over naval construction and the acquisition of colonies. William's intentions, however, were not taken seriously at first, and the open struggle between the uncle (Edward VII) and the nephew did not come to light until somewhat later. In any case, Russia had no relation whatsoever to this contest in the European West. Still, Russian diplomacy had begun to shift away from Germany already under Alexander III. At that time, I did not know the background to the "Three Emperors' League" (Germany, Austria, and Russia), which Bismarck had created in order to gain reinsurance from Russia for his Austrian ally. Concluded in 1884, this alliance was extended in 1887; but after Bismarck's retirement in 1890, it was no longer renewed. It was, however, at precisely this time that the old rivalry between Russian and Austria-Hungary in the Balkans revived. There immediately followed closer ties between Alexander III and France (Kronstadt-Toulon, 1891–93), providing Russian liberalism with the chance to strike up the "Marseillaise" in Petersburg and Moscow. Subsequently I was to witness a diametrically opposed episode, when William II came to visit his cousin and the "Admiral of the Atlantic Ocean" greeted the "Admiral of the Pacific Ocean."[27] Again, I had no way of knowing the contents of the friendly correspondence between "Nicky" and "Willy." Rumors were heard later that William was encouraging "Nicky's" opposition to the Russian social movement and still later to the Duma. There were also rumors that William wanted to distract the tsar's attention away from Europe by turning it toward Asia. Later, we were to learn that this had, in fact, been a means of removing William's rival from the disputed arena in the Balkans, and that he had completely succeeded. We read Nicholas' portentous phrase: "I am not thinking about Constantinople at all now. All my interest and all my attention is focused on China" (1896). This coincided with the beginning of European intervention in the Sino-Japanese struggle, and with the German-Russian-English occupation. England then concluded a separate alliance with Japan (1902), and France demanded the evacuation of Russian troops from Manchuria (1903). The shady dealers at the tsar's Court prevented this—and drew Russia into a war with Japan, ending in the Russian defeat of 1904. Preparing for this war, Russian diplomacy secured itself by a bilateral agreement with Austria-Hungary concerning the mutual preservation of the status quo in the

Balkans (1897). Just before the war, a treaty was concluded in Murzsteg between Nicholas and Franz Josef, concerning Macedonian reforms. Later I learned that William did not lose his influence over Nicholas even after the Russian defeat. During their boat ride in Björkö in 1905, William even added moral coercion to perfidy. Without the knowledge of the Russian foreign minister, William tried to wring out of the tsar an absurd Russo-German treaty which contradicted Russia's Anglo-French orientation. Of course, the fraud was immediately exposed.

Nicholas' attention again turned to the Balkans where threatening signs of Turkish decay were increasing. This time, however, Russia returned to the Balkans in a weakened state, having lost a significant part of her prestige and influence over the Slavic peoples. Austria-Hungary took advantage of this to gain a dominant position for Franz Josef's "crazy quilt" empire by subordinating to itself Slavdom, and especially Serbdom. In the kingdom of Serbia, Austrian influence predominated over King Milan and his heir Alexander. In 1903, the Obrenović dynasty came to an abrupt end with the murder of Alexander and his wife, Dragi. The aged Peter, the Francophile representative of the pro-Russian, Karageorgevich dynasty, ascended the throne. Montenegro was ruled by Nicholas, the Slavic "hero" who enjoyed Russian subsidies and who succeeded in marrying his two daughters, Militsa and Anastasia—both graduates of Petersburg finishing schools —to two Russian grand dukes, Peter and Nikolai Nikolaevich. In Bulgaria, Prince Ferdinand skillfully maneuvered between the Russophile liberal ministers and the opportunist conservatives, concealing for the time being his ties to Austria and Germany. It seemed that Russia still had solid footholds. But it only seemed that way—as long as Russia was strong. After 1906, the situation changed. In October of that year Baron Aehrenthal was appointed Austro-Hungarian foreign minister. During his many years in Petersburg, Aehrenthal made a careful study of the weak points of the Russian regime. He had friends among the Russian right-wing high officials (Shvanebakh), and he followed very closely the revolutionary movement of 1905-6. Under Aehrenthal, there was a marked intensification in Austria's open struggle against the national movement for a "Greater Serbia" and against the independent position (especially economic position) of the Serbian kingdom. The thirty-year "occupation and administration" in Bosnia and Herzegovina—areas which the Serbs considered the cradle of their nationality—served as a convenient point of departure for further seizures.

Germany, of course, stood behind Austria-Hungary, although Austria was strong enough to carry out its Balkan policy independently.

William went ahead with his *Weltpolitik* and, counting on support from Russia, clashed with England and France over his colonial aspirations. After Björkö, however, and especially after his failure in Algeciras, where Russia did not support him, he ceased to believe in the monarchic and dynastic ties which bound him to Nicholas. He openly announced this change himself to our ambassador, Osten-Sacken, in June 1906. The division of Europe into two opposing camps, the Entente and the Triple Alliance, was becoming more and more definite. The antagonism between the two camps centered around the intensified rivalry between the "uncle" and the "nephew," between Edward VII and William. William hated his "uncle," and Edward paid him back with derisive contempt. From 1906 the English king continued to drag Russia into the net of his intricate policies, into the "encirclement" of Germany as William called it. Two different areas of antagonism, Russian-Austrian-Balkan and German-English-Asian, thus merged together. The energetic and talented British ambassador, A. Nicholson, worked in Petersburg, carrying on negotiations with A. P. Izvolsky on the demarcation of spheres of influence in Persia, Afghanistan, and Tibet, where German interests (especially in the Persian Gulf) were beginning to make headway. In 1906, Russia's foreign policy was paralyzed by internal troubles, in which, as we have seen, Izvolsky favored reconciliation with the Duma. But in 1907, Nicholson succeeded in concluding three treaties with Izvolsky, fixing Anglo-Russian relations in the above-mentioned countries. At the same time, England (and Italy) became more vitally interested in the burning Balkan crisis. The old threads were being stretched to the breaking point.

Such was the general picture of the international situation at the beginning of the memorable year of 1908. Let me repeat that not everything in this picture was known to me at that time. The European side of the conflict was much less clear to me than the Balkan side. My own attitude toward events in 1908 was determined precisely by this imbalance.

The year started right off with a harsh dissonance which underlined the Russian-Austrian antagonism in the Balkans. On January 27, Aehrenthal delivered a speech to Austro-Hungarian delegations informing them of a project to build a railroad across the Turkish Sandjak of Novi Pazar. This railroad line would cut off the Serbs in the kingdom from those in Montenegro, Herzegovina, and Bosnia, while it would connect Vienna (by way of Sarajevo) with the road to Salonika. At the same time, it would strengthen for Austria a key strategic point for an advance into the Turkish possessions. Aehrenthal's speech created a tremendous sensation as an obvious manifestation of expansionist politics. Izvolsky hastened to counterpose to the Austrian project a Slavic crossbeam, which would connect the Danube to the Adriatic Sea. This line would assure an access to the sea either across Montenegro or across Dalmatia. Italy, too, was interested in such a line, but across Albania. None of these projects was realized, but the conflict of interests was vividly underscored, and the Balkan conflict quickly grew to a European conflict. From the Russian side, it was declared that Austria had violated the Murzsteg Treaty, while England demanded an extension of direct, general-European influence on Turkey into the Macedonian question. Both Austria and Germany resolutely protested against this. On March 26, in a special note, Izvolsky insisted on appointing a governor-general for Macedonia. On June 9, 1908, a long-planned meeting took place between Edward VII and Nicholas II in Reval, where a new program for Macedonian reform was worked out.

Usually, when Europe exerted special pressure on Turkey in defense of the Christian population, the Turkish sultans would publish some sort of project of their own for introducing self-government in the provinces. When the dangerous moment had passed, all these constitutions, Hatt-i şerif's (1839) and Hatti- Hümayun's (1856), even Mithat's, (1876) and the "laws" of the vilayets (1888), remained on paper. The old Turkish regime, which I knew well, continued to live, as before, with immunity. This time, however, something unexpected happened. The sick man, which Europe had grown accustomed to caring for, suddenly came alive—not the government, but the Turkish people themselves. On demands of the Turkish army, the "bloody" sultan, Abdülhamit, was forced to abdicate. A new liberal era began in Turkey, and on July 24 a new, radical constitution appeared, reinforcing the victory of "Young Turkey." I felt that my knowledge of Turkey was not sufficient, and I decided to take another trip to the Balkans during the vacation of 1908.

I arrived in Constantinople just in time to see the inauguration of the new sultan, Mohamet V, and watched the triumphant procession carrying the sultan to the Great Porte. But there was nothing to be done here. The uprising had come from Salonika where the main leaders of the "Young Turks" were located. I went to the offices of the Turkish opposition paper, where I was greeted as a comrade in arms, a famous Russian radical. We had an animated conversation, and the next day I left for Salonika. Two passengers sat in the compartment across from mine: one a Turk, and the other a Bulgarian. We soon started up a lively conversation which served as a fine introduction for my understanding the new Turkish era. The Turk was dressed in a shabby grey suit, but I soon noticed that each time the train stopped, a deputation was waiting for him and that he went out for a short talk with them. His poor French did not indicate a very advanced education, but that, evidently, did not prevent him from playing some important role among his own people. I gradually learned that by profession he was a postoffice official and that his name was Talaat. He was one of the foremost of the Young Turk leaders—and one trusted by the local population. The Bulgarian was, apparently, a member of the Macedonian revolutionary movement. He welcomed the Young Turk revolt unreservedly, in wildly enthusiastic expressions. Our strife had ended; our struggle has ended; we are all equal now; we are all "Ottomans," all equal citizens without regard to race or religion! For me this was unusual and unexpected. Before me were sitting yesterday's lord and slave, hangman and victim, and I thought to myself, what has become of the customs of age-old domination, on the one hand, and of the submissiveness of the Christian "rayi," on the other? And what would happen if "equality" would be expressed, in say, the loss of that religious protection under which was hidden the real inviolability of the Christian community? Nevertheless, I yielded to the general mood and was inclined to believe that the revolution had worked a miracle.

In Salonika I stayed at the Crystal Palace Hotel and was very pleasantly surprised to find out that my new Turkish acquaintance was rooming and boarding there too. We met every day at the table d'hôte and became involved in long conversations. Talaad questioned me about the Russian revolution and about our struggle against the autocracy, while I questioned him about the causes and the development of the Turkish movement. The Turkish émigrés in Paris served as their ideologists and leaders. Their party was called "Unity and Progress" (Ittihat ve terakki); and their slogan was "a single Ottoman nation." This slogan, by the way, as far as I could understand, had already begun to take on the narrow national meaning of "Turkey for the Turks." In the international sense, this meant, first of all, freedom from foreign guardianship. But it could also mean predominance of the ruling race. I was somewhat taken back when the questions turned not to Paris or Petersburg, but to Berlin. What sort of "constitution" do they have there, and how are civil liberties organized in Germany? Among my new acquaintances, I was especially interested in talking with Hilmi Pasha, the famous inspector general from Macedonia. His interest in Germany had already become completely set. Of the two parts of the slogan "unity and progress," the first evidently dominated. Here was the germ of the entire future history of the dictatorship by the Union et Progrès Committee over the liberal government, and the dictatorship over the committee itself by the military forces. Not for nothing were the leaders impatiently waiting in Salonika for the arrival of Enver Pasha from Asia Minor; not for nothing did they arrange a triumphant reception for him. It goes without saying that at that time it was only possible to guess about all this, but what I had seen was sufficient to allow me to think seriously about the future. My main interest for staying in Salonika had been exhausted, and I could continue on my way. Next on the list was the impending Serbo-Austrian conflict.

I headed for Belgrade and stayed there somewhat longer than previously. I had university friends in the Serbian capital, who introduced me to the young generation of political figures as well as to the young officers. My argument over Bulgarianism, the ruling nationality in Macedonia, had not yet spoiled my relations with the Serbs, and my trip in 1904 through the unliberated Serbian territories together with the beginning rapprochement between this generation and the young Bulgarians, brought us together. As I already mentioned, the struggle for national liberation passed from the generation of influential communal elders to the university youth and acquired thereby a revolutionary character. This time I found that the movement had gone much farther than I had expected, and from the Austro-Hungarian side, it had already evoked a much sharper resistance. To this period belong the famous trial of Masaryk against falsification by the Austrian police, the sensational case of the bomb-throwing spy Nastich, etc. On their side of the struggle, the Serbs organized the underground association "Omladina."

In the tradition of the First Dumas, I continued to stay apart from the official Russian representatives in the Balkans. Knowing of my negative attitude toward Russian Balkan policy, they, in turn, repaid me in kind. This situation inevitably led to somewhat one-sided impressions, gained from contacts with the radical circle of the Balkan nationalities. The Macedonian activist, Rizov, let me in on the secret negotiations which had been going on between the Bulgarian and Serbian political youth since 1904, the year of the "Ilinden" uprising in Macedonia. This fact alone showed that the national movement had already gone beyond the limits of a local, narrowly nationalistic struggle against official Russian trusteeship. But I did not expect that these two areas of conflict had diverged so far. From my contact with Serbian militant youth, I carried away two new impressions. The first was that this youth did not take Russian diplomacy into account at all. The drop in Russian prestige in the Balkans was perfectly evident to me even at that time. My second impression was that this youth undoubtedly greatly overestimated their own forces. Anticipation of war with Austria became an impatient readiness to fight, and victory seemed both easy and certain. Both moods seemed so universal and unquestionable that to get into an argument over these topics would have been totally useless. I could not even dampen the hopes which were stirring within myself. I do not remember how much these impressions were reflected in the reports I sent back to our paper, although I do know that they subsequently came in handy.

In view of the sensational argument over the direction of the railroad—Danube or Salonika—I wanted to acquaint myself with the topography of both routes. On my trip in 1904, I saw only the stony and barren facade of Montenegro—from the Kotor and Cetinje side. With the assistance of Rizov, a former Bulgarian representative in Cetinje, I was able to visit the country's rich plains. Together with our kind guide and commentator, we traveled through southeast Montenegro across Podgorica, then across the picturesque Scutari Lake to Virpazar, the port of Antivari and Ulcinj (Dul'tsino) on the Adriatic. The obstacles which the Austrians had put here were obvious. In passing, I learned many new things about the shady side of Nicholas Chernogorsky's rule (which I spoke about earlier).

I stopped in Sarajevo a second time in order to take the newly constructed railroad from there across the picturesque mountains to the border of the Novi Pazar Sandjak. It was from there that the new section of railroad was supposed to run to Mitrovica, the southern end of the Sandjak which I already knew from my trip to Old Serbia. One could see here the artificiality and difficulty of the engineering task which Aehrenthal had projected. This became evident later when the Sandjak of Novi Pazar was no longer politically necessary, and Aehrenthal returned it to Turkish rule. I also collected supplementary official data on the Austro-Hungarian administration and land taxes, the national and religious composition of the population of Bosnia and Herzegovina, and so on. Finally, on the way back, I stopped at Zagreb, where I met the Croatian participants in the constitutional (as opposed to the revolutionary) struggle and learned about their successes.

I returned to the autumn session of the Duma, armed with many new impressions. Just at that time, however, events of major importance occurred in the Balkans which forced a discussion of Russian policy not only from the Duma rostrum but also in the press.[28]

My personal acquaintance with A. P. Izvolsky was limited to our meeting at Stolypin's place and to our short talk afterward, in which he called himself a liberal and a European. I learned later that he supported the idea of a cabinet formed from the moderate majority of the Duma and defended it not only in the Council of Ministers but also before the tsar himself. In Europe, attitudes toward him were ambiguous. Edward VII met Izvolsky at the liberal court in Copenhagen and took an interest in the diplomatic monocle and the epigrammatic remarks of the future minister. He even called Izvolsky a diplomat in the "grand style." Edward was a keen judge of people, and his impression combined both light irony and a serious judgment. Others thought that Izvolsky was a *poseur,* although they acknowledged the brilliance of his conversations, more the salon than the professional variety, and recognized his erudition and broad views. In his whole manner and appearance, Izvolsky resembled the cultured, ostentatious, Russian "gentleman," with all the positive and negative traits of that type. That is the way he revealed himself in the famous, intimate discussion with Aehrenthal while a guest of the latter's successor, Count Berchtold, in the Buchlau Castle on September 15-16, 1908. Both men later gave different interpretations of the import of this "gentlemanly" talk. Izvolsky maintained that an actual agreement had been made: Aehrenthal would get Bosnia and Herzegovina, and Izvolsky would get a review of the Dardanelles issue at a European conference which he wanted to arrange. Aehrenthal, on the contrary, declared that no agreement of any kind had been reached, that there was merely a promise of friendly support at the conference. While Izvolsky was traveling around the European capitals, trying to carry out his plan, Aehrenthal annexed Bosnia and Herzegovina, and on that same day, October 5, Ferdinand declared Bulgaria independent and himself the "King of the Bulgars." Izvolsky complained bitterly about the duplicity and treachery of the Austro-Hungarian minister. If the information is correct that the talks in Reval concerned not only the Balkans but also the straits, then Izvolsky's hope of receiving support in London becomes understandable, as does his plan to link the annexation of Bosnia with the opening of the Dardanelles for the Russian navy. The objects to be traded, however, were too unequal in value. After the Reichstadt and Berlin treaties, and after thirty years of Austro-Hungarian rule in Bosnia and Herzegovina, the annexation was almost an automatic step, whereas the solution to the Dardanelles question, which had been a European question since 1841, was always linked with a final decomposition and partition of Turkey— something which England had never wanted and which Germany did not want now. Izvolsky found support neither in London nor in Paris, even though he warned Grey that without the straits it would be impossible for him to return to Petersburg, and that he would be replaced by a "reactionary" minister. Not wanting to spoil the impressions made at Reval, Edward VII tried to persuade Grey to give in; but Grey remained firm, and Izvolsky returned empty handed. Aehrenthal, in the meantime, knew that Russia was in a weak position and continued to make use of his success at Serbia's expense. On March 19, 1909, he sent Serbia an ultimatum demanding demobilization of the Serbian army and a change in Serbia's policy regarding Austria-Hungary so that the two countries could live henceforth as good neighbors. When Izvolsky tried to interfere, the German ambassador, Purtales, came to him three days later and demanded the unconditional recognition of the annexation of Bosnia and Herzegovina. For the first time, Germany had come out from behind the scenes. The Council of Ministers decided to concede.

The meeting in Buchlau, the annexation, the Austrian and German ultimatums, and Russia's unconditional concession—this whole series of failures created a tremendous and painful impression on Russian society, regardless of political persuasion. Blame for the failure was concentrated on the person and the policy of Izvolsky. My own stand coincided with the attitudes of the nationalists. Step by step, I followed Izvolsky's failures in *Rech*, unreservedly condemning the minister. I now think that I was unjust to Izvolsky. While this may have been policy in the "grand style," it did not, of course, take into account Russia's weakness at the time, in general and in particular, in the Balkans. Stolypin very aptly described this policy as the "action of a lever without a fulcrum." In any case, if Izvolsky experienced failures (and the failures were repeated by others after him), he was not following his own personal policy, but that of the emperor. The thought of taking the Dardanelles and Constantinople was constantly in Nicholas' mind, and he returned to it more than once. In his inscription on a report of August 30, 1916, we find his words: "We must put an end to Turkey; she has no place in Europe."

In 1908 and afterward I was far from holding these opinions, not only because I maintained a friendly attitude toward the Young Turks and expected them to carry out serious reforms in Turkey but also because my study of the Eastern question had shown me long ago what serious resistance we would meet from Europe if we pursued this path. My articles on the neutralization of the straits, written in 1913, 1915, and the beginning of 1917, can themselves testify to my cautious attitude on the Dardanelles question. It was only our agreement with our allies in 1915 that made me bolder with respect to using the rights which had already been formally presented to us; although even then I did not stop thinking to myself about the difficulties we would face even were we victorious. Liberating the Slavic lands from the Turkish yoke was one thing; banishing the Turks from Europe, however, was a piece of debris from obsolete official tradition. Their voluntary departure, especially in the ideological sphere, became a possibility only after Kemal Atatürk's reforms and after the transfer of the state center to Ankara—something which no one, of course, could foresee at that time.

The Duma Delegation to England

The attitude of the English public toward the Russian Duma throughout its four terms had a noticeable influence on the rapprochement between official England and official Russia. Nevertheless, it caused no small embarrassment to the English Government in its relations with the Russian Government. Specifically, this embarrassment was felt as soon as it was discovered that the convocation of the First Duma was not a sign of reconciliation, but a new stage in the struggle against the old order. Recently (1937), A. P. Izvolsky's correspondence with the Russian ambassador in London, Count Benckendorff, beginning with the year 1906, was published. This correspondence illustrates the growth of internal disagreement in England over the issue of the Duma, and I will make use of several quotations from it as a forward to our visit in 1909. As is already known, the Russian delegation, consisting of members of the Duma (including our Rodichev) and the State Council, arrived in London for a congress of the International World Union of Parliamentarians precisely at the time of the First Duma's dissolution. Premier Campbell-Bannerman used the occasion to utter his famous words: "*La Douma est morte, vive la Douma.*" Count Benckendorff reported the impact made by that speech: "The impression created by his speech among the opposition and even in the Court and in part of his own party (the part which did not like him), was like a hurricane raised against him. . . . It might have led to a ministerial crisis with major parliamentary debates. You can see what might have come from that. I could not let myself be used for that; though I was being pushed into it . . ." (unfortunately the sentence breaks off there in the printed text). At the request of the Russians, the visit of the English squadron to Petersburg was cancelled just before this happened. Then there began an accommodation to the state of affairs that had taken shape in Russia. Benckendorff approved of Stolypin, and after the attempt on the latter's life, he noted a change of public opinion in Stolypin's favor and suggested that the "revolutionary" movement (which implied "reforms") be labeled "terrorist." The leftist currents, however, along with the "writers and naive people" continued making trouble. In the fall, in anticipation of the elections to the Second Duma, they undertook to compose a "memo" or address to the Duma and to send a delegation to Russia. I do not know what happened as a result of this decision—

unless this was the address to Muromtsev which arrived in a beautiful binding, signed by leftist names. After Muromtsev's death in 1910, this document was given to me to forward to his widow (which I did). Apparently, the outcome of the elections to the Second Duma prevented carrying out the plan as it had been conceived. Nevertheless, the project of sending a delegation with the address disturbed the Russian representation in London, all the more so as it coincided with the new pogrom in Siedlce and with a series of appeals to European public opinion concerning the pogrom. One of my interviews reached London and Paris. I do not remember the contents of it, and Count Benckendorff could not find the original text of it either. He only re-called that I "condemned all terroristic means," and then noted that "when such a man as Miliukov and such a party as his carries on a campaign abroad, this shows that, for one reason or another, his party is in a desperate situation (*aux abois*)." He added: "In all of this, I can take seriously only Miliukov; the rest of them are non-entities, without the slightest significance or political influence." Benckendorff believed that "a man like Miliukov could have had a broader response if he would have been able to get down to business," not like the "overt revolutionaries"; but "even then he would have gotten paltry results." However, intending to convince the English, he "committed an error." Benckendorff already had some vague misgivings that the Second Duma would be "worse than the First." He thought, however, that instead of Goremykin, who had taken leave of his senses, Stolypin would be in command, and that although he was a "statesman of limited scope," Stolypin was a strong personality who knew his way and "would go directly to his goal." Benckendorff made only one quali-fication which showed his insight: "Why such particular bitterness against the Kadets, and why this flirtation with the opposite camp? One could slip going down this slope if one lacked strong spirit and decisive will." What Benckendorff did not know, was that this "slip" to the right formed a part of the system. Both correspondents (Benck-endorff and Izvolsky) were very disappointed and were forced to wait for the Third Duma before their hopes could be realized. The king's visit at the beginning of 1907 had to be postponed, and only at Reval in 1908 was a meeting between the sovereigns finally arranged. With instructions from Nicholson, Edward VII spoke with Stolypin at this meeting on the subject of the Third Duma. He was unexpectedly well-informed, and paid Stolypin many compliments on that score. I do not remember whether it was then or somewhat later that it was de-cided to send a delegation of representatives from the Third Duma to England. N. A. Khomiakov, the decorative Duma chairman who was about to leave his post, was placed at the head of the delegation. He was a man of culture and propriety whom Russia was not ashamed to show to Europe. I always remembered him as a member of the Moscow nobility's medical corps, as I met him for the first time in 1878: a lazy gentleman, who shirked his work, lounging on a couch, away from the summer heat of the Caucasus. He was rather inconspicuous in the delegation. The right flank of the delegation was represented by a figure colorful in another sense—Count Bobrinsky; while I was to represent the left flank, for the sake of completeness. Considering Benckendorff's references cited above, it is understandable why they turned to me with this offer. They did not take into account, however, the reputation which I enjoyed among the English leftists. Everything would have gone smoothly if the arrival of the Third Duma's delegation had not been greeted with strong criticism and protest from the leftist press, where the fate of the First Duma had not been forgotten. The members of the delegation decided to publish a reply, and the prepared text of this counterprotest was given to me for signature. Given my relationship to the Third Duma, my personal feelings, and my position with respect to the leftists, I could not sign such a document. My fellow members in the delegation did not want to change the text, and I refused point blank to sign it. This, of course, caused a great sensation: I had not fulfilled the main function for which I had been invited to take part in the delegation in the first place. I remember how our manager, Professor Pares of the University of London and my old friend from 1905 (who had received the title of baronet for his Russian mission), sat for several long hours in my hotel room trying in every possible way to persuade me to sign our declaration. He insisted that I agree and waited, phlegmatically puffing away at his pipe. I did not give in, but offered instead a simple solution. Let Khomiakov sign for the whole delegation; I would not object. Thus the problem was resolved.

Of all the incidents connected with this trip, I remember one of them especially. We were taken to Edinburgh and shown the naval base at Firth of Forth, which had just been constructed. This was their gesture of confidence in their new friends. They showed us the ancient sites and the beauties of this picturesque town, then, after passing under an interminably long bridge, went to a small private banquet that the city had arranged. The bare-legged, Scottish military guard, dressed in traditional plaid kilts, marched past us playing the bagpipes. As a concluding gesture, a pianist sat down at the piano and struck up the English national anthem, as was the custom. All those present stood up, and in a harmonius chorus the Scottish notables sang "God Save the King." Then, in our honor, the pianist played the Russian hymn, but, alas, the two of us, Bobrinsky and myself, were not equal to the occasion. Bobrinsky dragged out an off-key falsetto. I could not stand it and sang out as well as I could, but loudly, "God save the Tsar." A scandal resulted—just the reverse of not signing the delegation's declaration. For a long time afterward, at the party and preelection meetings in Petersburg, I was heaped with abuse for my jingoist patriotism.

I do not recall any other official ceremonies in honor of the delegation. Considering the mixed response from the press, the delegation from the Third Duma clearly did not enjoy a very great success. I met Sir Edward Grey, the minister of foreign affairs, and he made the most favorable impression on me by the simplicity of his manner, his thoughtfulness, his precise way of speaking, and his general appearance of being a sincere and honest man. I had an interesting conversation with Haldane, the minister of war, about his creature, the "territorial troops," which he held in high regard. The young Churchill gave me the impression of an uncorked bottle of champagne. I spent some time with Bryce, for whom I had always had kind feelings, and I met his family. I renewed my acquaintance with some of the leftist political figures and I saw some of my old Russian friends. However, I am afraid of mixing up those meetings and conversations with impressions from my many other trips to England.

"Neo-Slavism" and Pacifism

BEFORE RETURNING to my recollections of the Third Duma's activities, I would like to say something about my relationship to two currents of thought which manifested themselves with particular clarity during these years: "Neo-Slavism" and pacifism. From my Balkan trip, I carried away renewed feelings of sympathy for Progressive Slavic nationalism and its militant orientation. These feelings even began to reconcile my rightist Duma adversaries to me. They found those sentiments counterbalanced, however, by my resistance to "Neo-Slavism" and my pacifist aspirations, both of which I will now discuss.

It seems that Kramář may be considered the inventor of the attractive sounding term "Neo-Slavism." At least he brought the term to us in Petersburg. Without knowing Kramář personally, I had acquired a respect for his name, as the organizer and chief of the Young Czech movement. We had a friendly meeting in Petersburg. Soon, however, this friendly relationship cooled and, later, became somewhat more than reserved. I noticed that in his efforts to create a broad front for "Neo-Slavism," Kramář turned more towards Stolypin and the Poles of the Duma "Kolo" than to us. The aim of his visit, more political than ideological, was revealed: it was to reconcile the Russian Poles with Stolypin, thereby obtaining the votes of the Austrian Poles in the Vienna parliament; there were not enough of them to form the majority which Kramář desired. This aim was disguised by the idea of renewing the Slavic congresses, the first of which was scheduled to be held in Sofia. I knew one old and respected supporter of the idea of Slavic unity in Sofia who published a small journal there. But he represented the old, not the new, Slavism and his views were closer to Russian Slavophilism than to anything else, and rather vague in content. In Russia, it was the debris of old Slavophilism, usually people of conservative political orientation, that rallied around the Kramář's idea. Of course, he was also joined by younger elements, like my enthusiastic and naïve acquaintance, Liaskovsky, who combined the Sofia Congress and the "Neo-Slavism" with the militant aspirations of archaic "Pan-Slavism." Meanwhile, I saw a type that was entirely different from the belated epigone of the era of Kollař and of the younger years of Šafařík, a type represented by the person of Masaryk, the leader of the new, Slavic youth. It was a long way to the ideas of Masaryk from the "Pan-Slavism" of Šafařík, which Palacký had already terminated and whose extremism the Austrian enemies of Slavdom continued to exploit. At that time, I did not know that Masaryk had come out against the fraud of "Neo-Slavism." I do not even recall whether or not I knew of the works of Havlíček, Masaryk's spiritual teacher. Later I did become familiar with them, as well as with Masaryk's book on Havlíček. Nevertheless, I already sensed hypocrisy. I did not go to the congress in Sofia, or to the next one in Prague. In effect, Kramář's propaganda ended with these two congresses. He threw aside this enterprise himself when he saw that the ulterior motive of his policy went unrealized. "Neo-Slavism" soared upward like a rocket, sputtered, and died. The real problems of Slavdom went their own way, passing by this dangerously inflated ideology.

The Society of Slavic Culture, under the chairmanship of Prince Paul Dolgorukov—the same one in which we at one time had sought reconciliation with the Poles—continued to function in Moscow in the spirit of rather moderate Slavism. Later, Prince Paul Dmitrievich organized the Society of Peace, and cultivated a rather immoderate pacifism. During the war he told us half-jokingly, half-seriously, how he had arrived at the battle front by the river which separated the two armies and had pointed out to the German officer on the other shore the advantages of peace. This was probably the only instance of fraternization from the Russian side. I had sympathized with pacifist aspirations for a long time. As early as the First Duma I was a member and vice-chairman of the Parliamentarian Union of Peace, whose figurehead was Lord Werdel, but whose real head was the indefatigable Christian Lange. My hopes, however, were tempered by a sense of reality. I read Bliokh's work, which led Nicholas II to organize the First Hague Conference in 1899, and I carefully followed the Second Hague Conference in 1907, which the Germans opposed. At that time, it seemed to me that the pinnacle of success in the development of international law was the gradual broadening of the content of and the extension of compulsory arbitration. I was really stunned, however, by the appearance of Norman Angell's famous book, *The Great Illusion*. With apparently incontrovertible evidence, the author demonstrated that wars should stop, for the simple reason that they are not profitable. Both the conquerors and the conquered lose equally, and no acquisitions whatever, either material or territorial can bring any profit. Precisely at that time, the Petersburg section of the Society of Peace asked me to deliver a report on pacifism. In the report, I developed Norman Angell's arguments, and, expanding the text somewhat, I published it in 1911 under the title *The Armed World and the Limitations of Armaments.* I do not remember how much my regard for Angell was reflected in that book. Those were idyllic times, when the rules of international law seemed to be as inviolable as some sacred object; when Europe was enjoying prolonged peace; when the colonial struggle had died down for a time; when nationalist ambitions were not fostered; when "imperialism" was almost a dirty word; and when the prospect of eternal peace did not at all seem unattainable. Nevertheless, doubts were stirring within me as to the sanctity of Angell's conclusions. They seemed incontrovertible only by assuming that the entire world, or at least all of Europe, stood on the same cultural level as England. But I knew that this was not so and that William's "world politics" were an obvious refutation of that assumption. In anticipation of a European armed conflict, the great powers were beginning to step up their arms production just at that time. The "great illusion" threatened to become the great disappointment. All this did not come about at once, however, and I must say more about my pacifist role and actions during the Balkan Wars of 1912–13.

My Activities in the Third Duma

THE YOUNG RUSSIAN HISTORIAN B. A. Evreinov, whose premature death
we all mourned, set himself the laborious task of sifting through all
the stenographic records of the Third and Fourth Dumas in order to
compile a list of my speeches from the Duma rostrum, in honor of my
seventieth birthday. From this list, I drew up a table, dividing the
material into five sessions of the Third Duma according to the subject
of the speech and the date it was given (11V—May 11, etc.). I will return to the contents of this table, but first, let me make a few general
remarks concerning the character of my work. The total number of
my speeches was seventy-three in the Third Duma and thirty-seven
in the Fourth Duma. Although these numbers are fairly significant,
they do not in themselves indicate the real quantity of effort that went
into my Duma activities. When I. I. Petrunkevich insisted on publishing my speeches, I made some clippings from the Duma records, and
we ended up with a six hundred to seven hundred page volume in
large format. The edition, however, was never printed. According to
procedural rules, Duma speeches were not supposed to last more than
one hour, but, in order to get around these rules, a member of the
same faction could put his name down to speak after the first speaker
and then yield his place to him in case the first speaker's speech would
go overtime. I was frequently forced to take advantage of this privilege.
In order to deliver such a speech, and in order to get the assembly to
listen to it, many preliminary preparations had to be made. Such
preparations were not limited to work that one did in one's own study,
but presupposed participation on the Duma committee which prepared a report on the given question. The leftist groups in the Duma
usually limited themselves to pronouncements and could thereby free
themselves from the committee phase of this work. Given our views
of the nature of work in the Duma, we could take no such liberty. In
my capacity as faction chairman, I was not only supposed to follow
the general course of Duma business but I also had to familiarize
myself with materials introduced into the Duma by various depart-

ments, materials which often dealt with involved subjects. I was supposed to take part personally in processing materials in these committees, where the preparation of the report took on a political significance (e.g., the budget). Finally I had to undertake specialized
work on those questions for which there were no specialists among
our faction's members. This explains the diversity of themes which I
was forced to speak on during Duma's general sessions; it also explains the quantity of preliminary work which was required for the
preparation of these speeches.

The new direction of our activity inevitably changed the relationship between the party Central Commitee and our Duma faction. Of
course, the Central Committee in Moscow, and its branch in Petersburg, continued to meet with its previous staff of experienced members. Some of the members, however,—and the most important ones
at that—who were sentenced at the Vyborg trial[29] were formally
thrown out of political activity, while the reduction in the scope and
character of political activity itself eliminated, besides the possibility,
also their desire to continue in politics. The policies of the Duma
majority were detestable, while the role of the opposition, especially
at the beginning, seemed fruitless and unimportant. The Duma's work
was shallow and dull, although the rapid tempo of that work precluded either keeping abreast of it or guiding it from the sidelines. Of
necessity my personal role became much more crucial than before, and
a circle of young activists formed around me whose names became well
known to Russia through the press. Our party groups in the provinces,
too, moved far away from us. Their general mood, which had always
been more radical than ours anyhow, did not follow our direction of
evolution. Party congresses were convened even less frequently. (The
eighth and ninth party congresses met under the exceptional conditions of 1917.) Our ties to the provinces were maintained by the
regular publication of our faction's reports concerning its activities
in the Duma, but the response to these reports was very small, and
they usually did not even reach me.

Before turning from these general remarks to a survey of my
activities in the Third Duma, I would like to say something about my
personal affairs during those years (1907–12).

From what has been said, it can be seen that all my attention
during this time was consumed by politics. Almost no time remained
for my private affairs. If my academic friends could ever mourn my
withdrawal from scholarly work, it was precisely during that decade.
I could not even supervise the publication, in new editions, of my
books. My wife opened her own publishing house, corrected the proofs,
contacted the booksellers and kept accounts of the sales. In 1910, V. O.

Kliuchevsky died and I wrote my reminiscences of him. In a way, this was a farewell to my period of scholarly work. During the years before his death, I regularly visited Vasily Osipovich at his home in Zamoskvoreche. Our conversations were limited to politics, which had come to interest Kliuchevsky since the time he ran as a candidate on the Kadet ticket. I reported to him regularly on the course of affairs in the Duma and on the backstage of Russian politics in general. Our views coincided completely.

Even my newspaper work focused on the same themes, these provided by everyday political life. During the time of the plenary and committee sessions, I used to arrive late at the editorial offices. Once there, I would write articles and editorials and would doze off on the editor's famous leather couch while waiting for the proofs and the latest news. I usually did not return home until long after midnight. The only diversion which I did not give up, but, rather, gave more time to, was music. A new chamber group regularly met at my home. A young officer of the guards, and brother of the famous scholar Rostovtsev, played first violin. The cello part was played by a litera- ture teacher, Nelidov, a highly cultured person who later gave up his teaching career to become a writer. My wife played the piano, while I took either the viola or the second violin part. It was also in this musical milieu that during these years I became better acquainted with my future, second wife, N. V. Lavrova. We had first become acquainted a year and a half earlier at a chance meeting in the Velikie Luki rail- road station while waiting for the night train to Petersburg. The pas- sengers were still moving around, the cars were overfilled, the porters were not to be seen, the motley public was sitting about on their luggage or on the floor, and the train was behind schedule. I noticed an attractive young lady sitting near me who apparently was not ac- customed to such commotion. I helped her carry her luggage and get settled in one of the compartments. She was returning from her family in Tomsk to her husband, a construction engineer on the Siberian railroad, while I was finishing one of my preelection trips. When we parted, I gave her my calling card, which for her was simply the card of some unknown person, since she had nothing to do with politics. Her husband told her who I was. He was later killed by workers in some shady affair, and N. V. returned to Petersburg. I re- ceived a note from her inviting me to call on her and "have a dull time over a cup of tea." We did not, however, "have a dull time." Nina Vasilievna turned out to be a fine musician with both a polished technique and a delicate musical sense developed through serious, conservatory studies. She had quit the Petersburg Conservatory at her well-to-do fiancé's insistance just before her final examinations, and she did not regard her musical education as a profession. Nevertheless, teaching music was her favorite pastime, and she hoped that some of her conservatory ties, which she had retained, would help her find private students. Her young daughter, Ksenia, and her magnificent Blutner piano were to follow her to Petersburg. The instrument arrived safely and I began playing duets with my exacting partner, who was accustomed to strict classical music. I had to pull myself together and bone up on Beethoven's Kreutzer Sonata in order not to be left behind. These duets gradually became a custom, while our musical tastes, together with N. V.'s personal qualities, established a firm relationship between us which was destined to continue to the end of my life.

Let me mention another personal trait which appeared during those years, namely, my desire to settle down permanently. My material means increased significantly at this time. My salary as a member of the Duma was supplemented by my pay as editor of *Rech*; and the sales of my *Outlines*, which was still popular, also brought in a constant additional income. I acquired a permanent apartment in one of the cooperative buildings built on the Peski lots, and I moved out of my place on Ertelev Lane. After my first trip to the Crimea, I became attracted to the southern shore. This attraction increased when I. I. Petrunkevich moved there after he broke his leg in an accident while getting off a streetcar in Petersburg. To our great chagrin, he refused once and for all to take any direct part in practical politics. He lived on the estate of his stepdaughter, Countess S. V. Panina, in Gaspre, where Count Tolstoy, during his illness, and Chekhov had earlier enjoyed the hospitality of the hostess. I used to go there on vacations with my wife. A. S. Petrunkevich, Ivan Ilych's wife, was a good musician, who idolized Beethoven. Together with Pol, subsequently a famous music critic, who played the cello part on his viola, we performed the Beethoven trios.

A fortunate occurrence made us owners of a plot of land, which we were able to obtain at a low price, when the area was divided up among the shareholders. Our plot was located between the Aya Cape and the Laspi Bay, which with its fishermen was brilliantly described in a short story by Kuprin. At the top, overlooking the sea, I built a house which cost in all about a thousand rubles and which consisted of four small rooms with eight beds for the children and guests. We spent several of our vacations there.

Later on, we had the opportunity of buying another plot of land in Finland in the area of Iniö, which was then beginning to be settled by summer residents. I had no time for it, but my wife built a large two-story summerhouse there, following plans we had gone over together. The place we chose was at the highest point along the shore, and the upper terrace offered a panoramic view. To the east, the Kronstadt Cupola shone in the rays of the setting sun, while in the southwest, the soft outlines of Fox Nose faded into the mist. It turned out, however, that we did not own this plot for long. One fine day a group of generals and officers arrived on my land. I led them to the terrace to admire the view, and I said in passing: Well, gentlemen, we beg you to come here when Vasily Ivanovich (that is how Emperor William was called) arrives; you will not find a better place for the meeting. The naval officers were of the same opinion, and they soon returned with an obligatory proposal for expropriating this plot of land in order to construct a fort. The expropriation took place; the house was razed and a long-range cannon was placed where my study had once stood. From three points—Kronstadt, Fox Nose and Fort Iniö—cannon fire converged opposite our former dacha, controlling the road to Petersburg.

Our interest in the coastal area of Finland, however, was not exhausted by this first unsuccessful attempt. With the money we received from the expropriation of our dacha, we decided to buy another plot of land beyond the border of the new military zone. We got several offers from local inhabitants and then went searching for a suitable place. While making the rounds, my attention was caught by the picturesque location of one piece of land. Since we could get it for a reasonable price, we decided to take it. A road cut the land into two halves. The upper, hilly part, densely covered with pines, was cut by a gorge with a brook flowing at the bottom. I pictured the prehistoric times when this little brook was a mountain river, washing its way to the sea. The brook continued into the lower part of our land and carried away humus deposits, rare on this sandy shore. A meadow was formed on the gradual slope, ending in a marshy depression which was separated from the shore itself only by a narrow band of willows. Near the entrance to the lower part stood an ancient peasant's hut, solidly constructed from thick logs of red pine—a tree which had long ago disappeared from this area. Behind the hut was a classical quadrangle of half-dilapidated outbuildings. There was a Cyclopean structure of coarse rocks, wooden barns, and at the very entrance, a log cabin which could be converted into a bathhouse.

One could not have found a better combination, in small-scale, of all the Finnish characteristics. We bought the land and I started immediately on the reconstruction. Inside my cabin was one tremendous room, one-quarter of which was occupied by an equally massive ancient oven with wide berths and a bulky flue. I decided to dismantle the oven and replace it by a glazed tile oven similar to the

Balkan or Czech models. I built a bookshelf into the walls, with little doors decorated in imitation mahogany. The room became a large study, and I transferred to it a part of my library, including historical journals source materials, editions of various acts and documents, and a collection of publications of Russian geography. In a word, I brought over everything I did not need for the work I was doing at the time, except books on Russian history. I also transferred my original collection, from my former Moscow library, of old and new classics, which recalled for me my own intellectual growth. The Petersburg part of my library was already supplemented by books connected with my political activities. A single large room was too small, of course, and I made some additions to the house: On the driveway side, we planned a wing with two bedrooms on either side of the hallway. A wide terrace was added to the other end of the house. An upper floor, in light construction, was built over the whole house with bedrooms and a balcony overlooking the terrace. On the side facing the sea, I erected a turret with a small room which could serve as a comfortable study. The outside facade was done in the style of the German Fachwerk, with stone masonry and wooden windows, trimmed in ornamental plaster. This style seemed to me the most suitable for the north. All these additions were made by an experienced Finnish carpenter and his assistant, according to my plans, and all for a reasonable price. The end product was a picturesque little house, and our neighbors, the Leonid Andreev family, came over to take pictures of it. The upper part of our plot had a heavy flow of water located down the slope, and I used it for irrigating the lower part. I located the water source, tapped it and brought water to the house through pipes with a faucet for the kitchen, hoses for the yard and even a reservoir, in the middle of which was a sculptured fountain with rotating streams, when water was not being used for other purposes. I loved this place very much since much of my own labor, including physical labor, had gone into it. Our family of growing children, Sergei and Natalia ("Taka"), spent the summers here and came during the Christmas vacation too, for winter sports. Among the upper pine trees, we selected a place for the Christmas tree; on the lower slope we practiced skiing, and we turned the frozen marsh into a skating pond. Taka made fun of me when I took part in these sports, citing Pushkin's lines: "on delicate webbed feet, a heavy goose," etc. During the summer we cleared and leveled a patch of ground overlooking the road, and used it for a tennis court.

During my years as an émigré, this pastoral idyll met with a sad end. My younger children became victims of the World War and Civil War, while the house was burned by our kind Finnish neighbors in order to induce us to sell them the land. They coveted the meadow very much because it was the only one in the area which was irrigated; they had proposed earlier that I should rent it to them, but I had refused. I saved my books just in time from the attacks of "Vasily Ivanovich" and took them to a Godforsaken village. Later, after the Bolsheviks had taken power, Professor Frank Golder found them and sent them to America, where they arrived, surviving a shipwreck on the way. I had to sell them to Stanford University in California in order to pay the duties and clear a small profit.

But now let me turn to my personal activities in the Duma sessions, following the headings in the table. In the forefront stand the questions of the constitution and state law. Here were introduced the fundamental principles of a state system—the same principles which our party had declared in the first two Dumas. In the Third Duma, however, we had to introduce them more on the basis of what existed, than in accordance with what we desired. The Duma's legislative initiative was generally very limited, and exercising that initiative required the presence of a majority which we did not have. A legislative proposal could be introduced with the signatures of at least thirty Duma members (and we had fifty); but such a proposal could be either rejected immediately or, if not, turned over to committee for a preliminary discussion on its "desirability." Only if it was recognized as desirable could it then be discussed in the Duma session and brought to the attention of the government. Thus, in order not to lose touch with reality, more often than not we were forced to pursue our own views by criticizing the majority's proposals or the government's declarations and bills. In this way we were sometimes even able to obtain a majority or to join with the majority. A typical example of the kind of combinations that could occur is one from the first session of the Duma. On April 24 I spoke in defense of the BudgetCommittee's proposal to form, as part of the Duma's legislative procedure, a commission of inquiry to look into the management of the railroads. Since the time of the First Duma, the government had not permitted any such Duma investigations with the participation of outsiders. Kokovtsov, the minister of finance, in his answer to me, threw out the careless and fighting phrase: "Thank God we have no parliament." He probably meant to say "parliamentarism," that is, a regime based on ministerial responsibility. It would have been impossible to object to that, but to the phrase he actually used, I immediately answered: "Thank God we have a constitution," In print I usually used the expression "false-constitutionalism" or "pseudo-renovated system." In this instance, however, it was absolutely necessary to emphasize the presence of constitutional principles even in the existing Fundamental Laws, since we were waging a struggle to broaden them and were therefore against denying them indiscriminately. On the next day, the Octobrist, Count Uvarov, who was distinguished only by the fact that he wore a white flower in his lapel in imitation of the aged Chamberlain, announced in the name of his faction that the Duma is also a parliament; in a broad sense, he was perfectly correct. The Duma chairman, who at that time was Khomiakov, outdid himself by declaring that Kokovtsov's expression was "out of place." This, of course, Kokovtsov could not tolerate, and the next day, on April 26, apparently on the demand of the government, Khomiakov was forced to take back his words officially and to apologize to the minister from the same chairman's tribune. The Duma, nevertheless, accepted the budget committee's proposal, although in the summer of 1908 there came an imperial decree establishing within the structure of the imperial government, a commission of inquiry which would include members of the Duma and the State Council appointed by the government. And the Octobrists sent their representative. This demonstrated the full scope of the Duma's rights as well as its lack of rights.

Without dwelling here on my other speeches under the first heading (I will return to them later), I will go on to the second: the agrarian question. On the first issue, we were able to form a common front with part of the majority, but on the second, it was impossible, since the very existence of the Third Duma was built on the conflict over the agrarian question. Nevertheless, I would ascribe a special value to our role in this question—not because of the direct results (which were negligible), but because of that echo among the peasantry which we heard in response to our speeches against the Stolypin-nobility legislation.

As is already known, soon after the Second Duma was dissolved, the Decree of November 9, 1906, was issued as a piece of extraordinary, extra-Duma legislation in accordance with Article 87 of the Fundamental Laws. This decree predetermined the direction of agrarian policy in a purely gentry spirit. Kryzhanovsky maintained that Stolypin added nothing of his own to the nobility's project. This was a forced solution to the argument which had long been raging between the rightist and leftist camps of Russian society and which the Kadet party had attempted to solve in the spirit of reasonable compromise. Since the time of the peasant emancipation in 1861, the land allotment, which even then had been given to the peasants in insufficient quantities, had shrunk considerably as a result of the increase in population. "Land-hunger" was recognized as the basic cause of peasant impoverishment. The peasants believed that this cause could be eliminated only by partitioning the private, gentry, state, and court lands among themselves, and they dreamed of obtaining this partition either from the tsarist government or by means of revolution. The nobility wanted to retain not only their lands but also their labor supply; they speculated on the inadequacy of the peasants' land allotments and the high cost to the peasants of renting adjoining plots. The peasants were thus enslaved to the landowner or the local "kulak." Other means of struggling against land-hunger were: buying land from the impoverished and ruined gentry through the nobles' and peasants' land bank, resettling on the free lands of the outlying regions of the country, and raising the productivity of the land by means of improved methods of cultivation, which was impossible in the primitive conditions of communal landownership. However, the sale of the nobility's land quickly weakened the "ruling class," while resettlement had been practiced for a long time, and despite the government's optimism, the supply of the best lands in Siberia had begun to exhaust itself. Only one course remained: the destruction of the commune according to the principle of giving to the rich and taking from the poor. In the first place, this method would distract the peasants' attention away from partitioning the nobility's lands and would drive a wedge between the well-to-do peasants and the poor ones. Second, a class of "strong muzhiks" would be created as candidates for replenishing the diminishing ranks of the "ruling class." Third, the government would acquire the liberal cloak of class reform: private initiative and private property would be freed from the vise in which the peasants had been placed by the liberators of 1861. The left-wing groups in society rejected all these plans of the nobility and defended the inalienability of the allotments in the peasant commune, the preservation of the communes' old procedure of partial and general land redistribution, a reduction of rents, improvement of agricultural productivity by switching to cooperative, mechanized, and intensive cultivation, but above all, in one form or another the forced expropriation of privately owned lands as the immediate and indispensable action to be taken against the fundamental evil of peasant land-hunger. There could be no reconciliation between these two tendencies of aristocracy and democracy; class struggle was being waged, and the government took the side of the ruling class. With this backing, the Third Duma was supposed to decide the question once and for all in favor of the "ruling class." Destruction of the commune and transition to private landownership was supposed to serve as the most practical method of attaining that goal.

As the law demanded, the Decree of November 9 was introduced into the Duma immediately, and the discussion of it lasted from

October 23, 1908, to May 8, 1909. In its desire to speed up the destruction of the commune, the majority went even farther than the government. It made into law the regulation by which all communes which had not been repartitioned within the last 24 years would automatically be considered areas of private-hereditary property, and the plots which its peasants were using at the time the law was issued would be considered their personal property. Nevertheless, as the opposition showed, there were practical difficulties in establishing the fact that land repartition had ceased; and decisions in individual cases were made arbitrarily by the local authorities and land officials.

Our faction organized an energetic fight against this bill. Shingarev was our main speaker; from his personal observation as a district doctor in the Voronezh gubernia, he had acquired a fine knowledge of peasant life. I was armed with my previous studies on the history of the peasant problem before and after the emancipation, and with my knowledge of the current literature. I also had some familiarity with the works of the Russian Zemstvo statisticians from V. I. Pokrovsky's school. The struggle was stubborn, and to my own surprise, I reaped my first serious successes in the opposing camp. They listened to me, and they listened carefully. I spoke for four whole hours, two hours in each of two sessions; it seems this was the only such example in the whole history of the Dumas. For us, however, our success in another area was much more important. The peasants and the clergy in the Third Duma also listened to us. Although they were dependent, they were still a democratic element, and they carried information about our struggle all around Russia. As a result, we were visited by a whole stream of peasant delegates from the most farflung corners of the country. I remember especially one deputation of Siberian peasants; stalwart, mighty, hairy, and wrapped in heavy solid sheepskin coats, these giants from "Zoloto Rein" were as alike as peas in a pod. But, alas, we could neither give nor promise them anything, although much was done to enhance the opposition's reputation in the Third Duma. I will not speak about the substance of our speeches since it was determined entirely by the program of left-wing, Russian economists and by the project of the People's Freedom party. We did not deny the defects in the communal economy; we even recognized the fact of the gradual breaking up of the commune under the influence of individualistic aspirations, which even Gleb Uspensky had spoken about; we even agreed that it ought to be easier for the peasants to leave the commune. Nevertheless, we resolutely protested against the forced destruction of the commune, since it was the only bulwark against the piratical seizures and sale of the commune's land allotments by the powerful elements in the village. We recognized the possibility of the communes evolving in the direction of cooperatives and artels. I knew perfectly well that the commune itself was not an indigenous manifestation of the Russian "spirit" as the Slavophiles and Populists believed; rather, it was the product of the gradual securing of the peasant work force by the landowners and the government.

If, in the agrarian sector of the economy, the nobility was forced to pass radical land reforms in order to protect its interests, then, in the area of government, that same Russian "ruling class" was interested in leaving everything as it had been of old, since the gentry reign of "Mother Catherine (II)." The "red" bureaucrats, under Alexander II, had attempted to introduce a more or less broad system of local self-government (Zemstvo) in Russia, but their attempt remained an unfinished building, a building "without a foundation" (an all-class, self-government in the volost) and "without a roof" (a truly popular representative body). In the subsequent era of reaction under Alexander III, Count Dmitri Tolstoy brought the Zemstvo establishments into harmony with the general aristocratic style of the empire. The Russian provinces continued to be governed by a nobleman—from the old provincial marshal of the nobility to the new "land captains" in the district. As for the central government organs, here, too, the old dictum was still valid, that "the nobility is the dough from which the government bakes its bureaucrats." True, in the various ministries, orders were carried out by flunkies like Kryzhanovsky, by well-trained people with university experience; nevertheless, the spirit of the establishment remained old: it was the spirit of freedom from law and order. Given such a situation, all the efforts of the opposition in the Duma which concerned domestic policy were destined to remain fruitless. It was no accident that a guard of the old "order," the State Council, had been placed over the Duma. I remember my first impression from the hall of the Marinsky Palace, where the members of the Duma were admitted with tickets to the gallery, like the ordinary public. Down below, on quiet velvet armchairs, the elders, with their shiny bald heads, were dozing away. Even some of their names called to mind the epopee of Russian lawlessness and violence. Here, in peace, they were finishing up their destructive careers. These preservers of the "historical principles" and the political traditions of unlimited monarchy formed a solid "partition" between the symbol of the degenerating dynasty and the silent masses. They were fated to play their part not only in extinguishing the auspicious beginnings of the Duma but also as Russia's gravediggers. What a contrast there was between the funereal appearance of this hall and the amphitheater of the Taurida Palace, modeled on the European parliaments, from whose benches came the muffled cries of the party struggle, echoing ever more loudly what was going on beyond those walls in the vast expanses of real Russian life!

It was our faction's lot—and this time together with the leftists—to carry these cries of Russian reality into the Duma—cries which were directed to the Ministry of Internal Affairs, that organ of Russian lawlessness and arbitrary rule. The main form of these addresses was the same as in the first two Dumas, namely, that of interpellation.[30] As before, their force was deadened by the fact that the government could postpone its answer for a month, during which time the interpellation lost a significant portion of its urgency. Of course, the urgency was not lost when these interpellations concerned, not individual violations of the law, but the firmly entrenched practice of Russian rule. In the second session (13, II), it was my turn to defend our factions' interpellation regarding the Azef case. I do not remember whether it was then or a little later that Stolypin gave himself and the Duma rightists the pleasure of exposing (based on Azef's denunciation) my participation in the Paris Congress of constitutional and revolutionary parties in 1905 under the pseudonym of Alexandrov. In that same session (27, V), I spoke about the protection which the ministers of internal affairs and justice gave to the crimes committed by the Union of Russian People. I had occasion to return to these themes in the fifth session of the Duma, in connection with the S. D. interpellation concerning provocations by tsarist police agents among members of the S. D. party and among the revolutionary parties in general (30, XI). Not limiting ourselves to interpellations, we raised in this Duma, fundamental questions concerning the organization of local self-government and the central government's executive and legislative organs. To this subject belongs my speech in the second session (5, III), with its proposal to change the electoral law for the State Council. In this speech, I stressed that our upper chamber was "a bulwark of the old order, an instrument of class interests, and a brake on organic legislation." In the fourth session (19, I), I spoke of government interference in the affairs of the Zemstvo and city self-government. On May 29, 1909, our faction introduced a bill to change the electoral law for the Duma, with the aim of preserving electoral rights for candidates other than those deprived of their rights by courts of law. This was in response to the removal of those rights from the Vyborgites and to the exclusion from the Duma of our party member, A. M. Koliubakin. Of course, these demonstrative speeches were not made with any hope of practical success. The government's violation of the Fundamental Laws had to be spoken about more than once, but I will return to that in a separate section. Having exhausted all the means of struggle against the government's domestic policy, our faction finally decided to resort to an extreme measure: in spite of our faction's rule of voting for the budget, we decided to refuse to confirm the budget for the ministry of internal affairs. In the fourth session (26, II), I based this act of principle on the "complete and irreconcilable contradiction between domestic policy and the fundamental principles of the reorganized state system" as well as on the failures in the area of foreign policy that were a disgrace to the dignity of the nation, a policy that I called "antinationalist and unpatriotic." With suitable changes, this formula was repeated every year when it came time to reject the budget, thus stressing the fact that the Duma was betraying its own mottos and slogans.

One of the most important topics, of course, would have to be finance and economics. In this area, however, my personal participation, which is the subject of this account, appears almost a complete blank. I had always considered that the "power of the purse" should be the fundamental right of the popular representative institution. Every popular representative body in Russia as elsewhere would fight for this right, regardless of its composition or imperfection. I assumed that precisely in the struggle for the budget, the opposition would be able to unite with the majority of the Duma and obtain a certain degree of independence for the people's representatives from the government authority. These expectations were, to a significant degree, fulfilled insofar as this concerns the Duma; they were shattered only by resistance from outside the Duma. As has been mentioned above, our narrowly restricted work on the budget was very quickly monopolized by Shingarev, and I could only be grateful to him for removing this burden from my shoulders, which, on top of all the rest of my Duma work, would have been unbearable. N. N. Kutler busied himself with economic questions which were less closely bound to politics. It was up to me to give speeches only on the budgets of individual ministries; these speeches were often the only means to react politically to one or another aspect of the government's policies. More than anything else, they dealt with foreign policy, since foreign policy was the prerogative of the monarch and, therefore, protected from interference by the Duma. P. N. Krupensky tried to put forward just this view in the last session of the Third Duma. Izvolsky broke this rule, but under Sazonov, the minister's speeches ceased and it was possible to speak about foreign policy in the Duma only when considering the budget of the minister of foreign affairs. This gave me the opportunity to continue my criticism of Sazonov's policy in the third, fourth, and fifth sessions of the Duma. However, since my involvement in foreign policy was not limited to my speeches on the budget, I will devote a

special section to my personal activities in this area during the years
1908–9.

In view of the fact that I was a university graduate and author in
the field of Russian cultural history, questions concerning public education and the church became my specialty in the Duma. Fortune
smiled on questions of public education in this Duma. They were so
widely discussed in the more advanced literature and were so incontestable by their nature that a somewhat cultured, popular representative body could not help putting them on the agenda. True, the
government here, too, began a struggle against the beginnings that
society had already made (mainly the work the Zemstvo had done) by
opposing them with church-parish schools at the bottom and the most
stringent bureaucratic supervision from above. The so-called "monarchist" parties were on the government's leash in this question. The
Octobrist "constitutionalists" vacillated and, avoiding open conflict,
tried to do what they could to promote a solution. Thus, we could
come together on this issue more than on any other.

The chief concern of Russian-educated society and the self-
government bodies was, first, to make the entire population literate,
and second, to acquaint them with their native country. In order to do
this, enough schools would have to be built and a suitable corps of
teachers would have to be created. For both the one and the other,
money was needed, and the Zemstvos did not have enough of it, since
the sources of their budget were seriously cut by the government.
Outstanding Russian pedagogues like Ushinsky, Vodovozov, and Baron
Korf had already thought about a program for teaching reading, writing, and knowledge of the country. Count Tolstoy in his Yasnaia
Poliana popularized the new currents and provided a model for them.
The government, in its fear of enlightening the public, wanted to give
control of the people's school system to the Holy Synod and to teach
Church Slavonic, and church ritual and singing just as in olden times.
Members of the clergy and their unmarried daughters were supposed
to be the teachers. The struggle was at its peak and the people's
representatives were forced to interfere.

The Third Duma, under the direction of the Octobrist center and
the opposition, gave most of its attention, with regard to the budget,
to increasing funds for public education. As early as 1908, the Duma
appropriated more than eight million rubles above the budget to
public education. It did the same in 1909, and in 1910 it raised the
additional appropriations to ten million rubles. During the five years
of the Third Duma's existence, the budget for the ministry of public
education was doubled. In 1910 a bill was introduced for instituting
universal education, which until that time had existed in only a few

counties of Russia, thanks to the efforts of the more progressive Zemstvos. In 1911 that bill was passed by a majority consisting of Octobrists plus the opposition. At the beginning of 1911, against the objections of the minister of finance, the same majority in the Duma passed a financial plan for universal education. Each year for ten years the budget was supposed to be increased by ten million rubles so that by the beginning of the 1920's the material basis for achieving universal literacy would be ready. As for the organization of the public school system, it was, in the first place, turned over to Zemstvo administration. The idea of continuity in the school system, that is, ties between elementary, high school, and higher education, was realized through the creation of the higher public schools, in accordance with the "statute" which the Duma adopted in 1911. In the rural regions where the non-Russian national minorities dominated, the school system was extended to a four-year course in the pupils' native language. Right after this statute was adopted, the Duma nationalists refused to participate in further discussions, thereby admitting defeat.

My personal participation in this area was expressed in committee work as well as in two speeches in the fourth session, in which I criticized the bill on universal education (October 18, 1910) and argued for the right of the national minorities to receive instruction in their native language (November 12, 1910).

The liberalism of the Duma majority did not extend to high schools and colleges. In this area, the government's fight against the very foundations of Russian culture had become a tradition. Ever since Catherine II founded the first properly organized high school at the end of her reign, and ever since Alexander I began the net of Russian universities in the first years of his reign, the newly recreated ministry of "public enlightenment" had worked incessantly against Russian enlightenment, except for the brilliant period of reform under Alexander II. Under the cloak of freedom in science and teaching, the university code of 1863 which had guaranteed academic autonomy was forcibly replaced by the reactionary code of 1884, under the guidance of Minister Delianov. True, life itself prevented the application of the reactionary principles of this code, while in the revolutionary year of 1905, an imperial command had to be issued granting university autonomy. After the revolution was crushed, this decree amounted to nothing, and in 1910 Minister Shvarts introduced a project into the Third Duma for a university code without any autonomy at all. In the same year, however, the new minister, Kasso, took this project back and began to pursue a policy which resembled that of Runich and Magnitsky. His answer came in waves of student agitation such as Russia had not seen since 1906. Then as before, student agitation, in Dr. N. I. Pirogov's widely used phrase, served as a "barometer of social moods" and should have served as a warning to the government. However, also as before, the warning was understood in the opposite sense and served Kasso as an excuse for taking measures which, among a twentieth-century, educated society, gave the impression of a genuine barbarian invasion. The Moscow professors, since the end of the nineteenth century, had been trying to act as intermediates between the government and the student body. In 1911, these attempts led to an extent of havoc in Moscow University unprecedented in academic life. Some of the professors responded to the repressive measures by voluntary resignation. Kasso answered with a general purge: more than one hundred teachers either left or were thrown out, while Kasso filled their places with his own henchmen. Similar events occurred in the Kiev Polytechnic Institute, the Don Institute, and Tomsk University. "Suspect" professors were replaced by "loyal" ones and the level of instruction fell sharply. The most talented and learned teachers left, including all of those whose political views leaned more or less toward the opposition parties. This was the second warning to the government—and one that was just as misunderstood as the first one.

Naturally enough, my speeches in the Duma were predominantly directed against these antisocial manifestations of the government. As early as the first session (1908), I twice criticized the policy of the minister of public education (3, VI and 9, VI). My speeches became especially frequent in the fifth session (February 8 and 15, and March 7 and 14, 1912). Two other speeches of mine (25, X and 16, IV) were devoted to Kasso's policy concerning the high schools. With the aim of isolating the school from society, he abolished the so-called "parents' committees" which had served as just such a link. He likewise did not satisfy the Duma's wishes to allow entrance into the institutions of higher education from the secondary schools (except the gymnasium), and thereby preserved the isolation of the high schools in spite of the above-mentioned concept of educational continuity which prevailed in pedagogical circles.

In questions of church and faith, independently of my world outlook, I shared, as a politician, Cavour's formula: *Chiesa libera nel stato libero*—a free church in a free state. In Russia, ever since ancient times, the church had been enslaved by the state, and since the time of Peter the Great, it had been decapitated. Faith was monopolized by the official creed and was considered not only a matter of personal conscience but also an indispensable characteristic of nationality. Finally, inside of the dominant church itself, the higher bureaucracy of Bishops, centralized in the Holy Synod, enslaved the "white" clergy, clergymen of the urban and rural church democracy. In the opinion of the advanced social circles, all this should give way to a system based on freedom of belief and self-government among the faithful. That faith had become ossified and that church government had been abused were so obvious to everyone that these views penetrated, in a more moderate form, into the midst of the very servants of the church and, through them, to the conservative circles of society. Here, too, extreme rightists carried out commands of a government which had become rigid in its preservation of tradition. Under Alexander III and Nicholas II (until October 17), the most eminent preserver of this tradition was the teacher and councilor of both tsars, that dry and stubborn fanatic who not for nothing had been nicknamed Torquemada—K. P. Pobedonostsev, the high-principled enemy of everything that even resembled freedom and democracy. He is one of those who bear the main responsibility for the destruction of the dynasty.

The Third Duma began its activity concerning religious questions with very promising proposals. The bases of these were three administrative projects introducing the principles of freedom of conscience into this closed sphere. One of these projects even put an end to the monopoly of the dominant church, allowing unrestricted transfer from it to other denominations, including even a change from Christianity to a non-Christian faith. Another bill removed the barriers which severely separated the Old Believers from the official church. Old Believers' communities could be formed without the necessity of obtaining prior permission, requiring only a simple declaration announcing it, and the Old Believer clergy received the right to be called "ministers of divine worship." The third bill removed all restrictions on rights on those leaving (or being ejected from) the spiritual ranks. All of these bills were subjected to substantial changes in the Duma committee, and I took part directly in this work. I spoke on the first and second of those bills at a plenary meeting of the Duma in the second session in 1909 (13, V; 15, V; 23, V). It could be expected, of course, that all these innovations would meet with the most resolute resistance from the State Council where they would be shelved. Concerning the third bill, Nicholas II "with his own hand inscribed: I do not approve" (May 26, 1911). The other two bills got stuck in the State Council. It goes without saying that recognition of a "nondenominational status," that is, not belonging to any positive religion, was quite beyond the horizon of the Third Duma.

Questions which directly concerned the dominant church were, of course, handled in the Holy Synod and in the Council of Ministers, and even the right to bring such questions up in the Duma was disputed—except when new funds were demanded for the budget. The question which, of this sort, was most a matter of principle was the restoration of the complete church organization and hierarchy through the convocation of a landowners' council and the election by it of a new patriarch, after the two-hundred-year interruption. To these two tasks, the progressive part of the clergy added the idea of "renovating" the church, of breathing new life into the numbed body. In the revolutionary year of 1905, the tsar had to come to grips with these aspirations. Together with freedom of conscience and religious toleration, the Decree of April 17, 1905, promised the convocation of the council. The Precouncil Commission began its preparatory work in 1906 but closed its sessions when the First Duma was dissolved. Pobedonostsev was against convening the council, while the conservative part of the clergy seized upon the idea. With the appearance of Pobedonostsev's protégé, Sabler, in the post of Holy Procurator, this movement took definite shape (1911). In this connection I spoke in the fifth session of the Duma (March 4, 1912), trying to bring the question back to the principle of the mutual relations between church and state. In spite of the tsar's promise to decide the question by the time of the Romanov jubilee (1913),[31] the matter was dropped, right up to the time of the revolution.

The same fate met the attempts to revive the church from below, under the pretext of returning to the ancient principles of the Russian Orthodox parish system, wherein the laymen themselves used to elect their candidates for the clergy. The Precouncil Commission of 1906 also dealt with this question, and in December of that same year, the decision to work out a project for organizing the parish was confirmed by the emperor without waiting for the council to be convened. After one year, in December 1907, the project was handed over to the synod by another imperial command and also brought into the Council of Ministers. The right of the laymen to elect their priest and the right of the parish to own property with the rights of a juridical person were accepted as principles. But then the course was reversed. The project was rewritten four times, and finally, when V. K. Sabler assumed the office of holy procurator, in 1911, the project underwent a radical change. The above rights of the laymen were proclaimed incompatible with the Holy Writ and the "spirit of the Orthodox church." Even references to the ancient customs were of no avail, and the project for parish reform was pigeonholed.

It seemed that the other promise of the Decree of 1905 was more likely to be realized: to review the church school system in a liberal spirit. The basic problem here was to make the church school, not a strictly confessional school, but a general educational school which would allow more than just the children of the clergy to study and which would adjust its program to the corresponding levels of the public schools. Here, too, the idea of a continuous chain of education on three levels was accepted: elementary, secondary school, and institutions of higher learning. The education committee of the Holy Synod was ready to convert the four year religious elementary school into a general educational school and even to remake it into a six-year "pre-gymnasium." However, the secondary school of religious seminary was to remain strictly confessional, without any outlet from it into other educational institutions. As Sabler formulated it, it was supposed to serve exclusively for training pastors. The higher level school was a purely theological, religious academy whose rector was supposed to be a bishop, while the majority of teachers were supposed to be persons "of an Orthodox frame of mind" and "preferably members of the holy order." The Duma was able to express its wishes and was supposed to assign the financial means, but on matters of substance, Duma interference in the affairs of church schools was not admissable. At the end of the last session, the tsar addressed the members of the Duma in person and stressed this inadmissability.

As much as we found a point of agreement with the Duma center on questions of self-government, schools, and religion, we had to wage an uninterrupted struggle with them on national questions. Blindly stimulating the growth of separatist aspirations in Russia, the majority of this Duma won fame for its Russian "nationalism" and "national-historic" principles. We warned against this disastrous course, not only as a matter of principle but simply in the name of preserving the unity of the Russian Empire. This domestic policy, which the distorted representative body pursued even farther than the government, already began to bear its poisoned fruits. It was a long way from the time of the First Duma when the Central Committee of the People's Freedom party enjoyed the participation of such outstanding representatives of Russia's national minorities as A. P. Lednitsky (Polish), Ya. Chakste (the future president of the Latvian republic), Ya. Ya. Tennison (the future premier in the Estonian Government), M. S. Adzhemov (Armenian), M. M. Topchibashev (chairman of the Azerbaidzhan Government), I. Ya. Shrag (Ukrainian activist), and others. Now the representatives of the national minority intelligentsias had been deprived of a significant portion of their mandate in the Third Duma; they made their way abroad where they organized propaganda campaigns against Russia, "the prison of peoples". . . .

My main work on the national minority question, as can be seen from the number of my speeches, focused on the Finnish question. Later, when the statement appeared in Markov II's *Zemshchina* that I had been bribed by the Finns, my friend and constant defender, O. O. Gruzenberg, with his fiery temper, insisted that I sue for libel. As could be expected, given the political atmosphere at that time, the court gave an ambiguous verdict acquitting me, the accuser, but not directly indicting the defendents. Now I think that I really was "bribed." My sympathy for this people had suborned me long before the arguments in the Third Duma. As early as the time of Governor-General Bobrikov's crazy policy which had ended so unfortunately in the terrorist act of 1904, I carefully followed the whole struggle of that people, which they carried on within a strict constitutional framework against the Petersburg bureaucracy. At the Paris Congress, we had accepted moral obligations to support the Finns, and the First Duma fulfilled these obligations. The political hospitality of the Finns during the years of our party struggle, my trips to Finland and then my permanent settlement in the peasant backwoods of that country gave me a greater familiarity with the Finnish peasantry. I touched the very source of the national strength of this small people; I discovered the muzhik-like stubborness and determination in the defense of law and order, their fanatical love for their native land, their readiness to make sacrifices, and the conscious partriotism of the peasant masses. I acquired some knowledge of the Finnish language, and, with a dictionary, could make my way through a Finnish book. I learned the short history of the independence of these people, from the time of the ambiguous restoration of their "Fundamental Laws" by Alexander I and the unambiguous reestablishment of the state institutions by Alexander II, who, "while remaining faithful to the constitutional and monarchic principles ratified by the Finnish people," extended their rights by creating the Constitution of 1869 which was approved by the Sejm. I grew fond of this people as I found them, and, yes, I was "suborned" not before, but after I publicly defended their rights and institutions in the Third Duma. I was "suborned" when I awoke one morning in my still unfinished, peasants' cottage and I heard a crowd of them singing near my window. These were peasant lads from the neighboring farm who came with their homespun serenade to greet me as a defender of their homeland. . . . No greetings or expressions of thanks could have given me so much joy as this simple response from the bosom of the people.

When I met and became friends with Mekhelin, the patriarch of the Finnish resistance, at the Paris Congress in 1904, the movement was not restricted to a purely constitutional framework. At that congress I clashed with the representative of the new generation, the "activist," Zilliacus, whom I mentioned earlier. Given the general revolutionary atmosphere, activism had already gone beyond the bounds of the constitutional struggle and aspired to the complete independence of Finland. The behavior of the majority in the Third Duma gave the advantage to this new sentiment. That explains my special persistence in defending Finland's constitutional rights.

Stolypin had no need to think up a plan of struggle against Finnish rights; the plan had already been drawn up by Plehve and partially carried out by Bobrikov. It was necessary simply to make Finland equal to the rest of the Russian provinces. The Duma's rightwing pioneers, in agreement with Stolypin, advanced this aim as a demand of the Russian representative body. Usually, bills hung around the Duma for a long time and then got shelved in the State Council; but this time, the project for imperial legislation tore through the legislative chambers like an express train. On March 17, 1910, it was turned over to committee. On May 23, it was introduced into the plenary meeting and hastily passed in three sessions, breaking all the rules of Duma procedure. The debates were cut off, and, having exhausted all other means, the opposition demonstratively rejected discussing it article by article and even left the room. On May 31, the bill was passed by a majority of the Duma, and on June 17, it was passed unchanged by the State Council and became law. Nevertheless, I did manage to develop my objections both in the preparatory stage and in the discussion stage (in three meetings of the first session and five meetings of the third session). I was well-armed with a knowledge of the specialized literature on the subject, and it was not difficult for me to prove the complete illegality of the actions which both the government and the Duma were about to take. I was not against the principle of establishing a general procedure for passing laws which were valid in both Finland and in Russia; I was protesting against passing these laws by purely Russian legislative bodies, while completely ignoring the corresponding Finnish institutions recognized by the monarch in his capacity as "the Grand Duke of Finland." I recommended a parallel procedure, with specific methods of reaching an agreement in case of discord. The actual content of "all-imperial" legislation was easy to determine on the basis of existing examples which distinguished the most important areas of all-imperial jurisdiction from the remaining area of "local" legislation; this local legislation, again by mutual agreement, should be left to the local Finnish institutions. The Finns had already agreed to this. Nevertheless, when the Russian project became a one-sided law, there was only one way left to paralyze its action. The law established general regulations, but it did not indicate any methods for enforcing them. The law still had to be concretely applied in individual cases. This was done by two bills carried through the Duma by Stolypin in 1911. One of them restored the validity of the decree from Bobrikov's time, which had been issued in 1899 and which had eliminated Finland's miniscule army and replaced it with monetary obligations. This was the main reason for the Finnish resistance at that time. Another bill equalized the rights of Russian citizens (in Finland) with those of the Finns, and this had the appearance of satisfying Russian patriotism. It must be remembered, however, that as against some three million Finns, there were only about eight thousand Russian bureaucrats and summer residents. Most important was the fact that these laws, too, were passed by means of the same one-sided, Russian, imperial legislative procedure. I had occasion again to speak against these bills, three times in the fifth session of the Third Duma, and, of course, just as fruitlessly. Much later, after I had already emigrated, V. A. Maklakov condemned in print my stand on the Finnish question. I answered him with a simple reference to the fact that in those same debates, he, too, took the same position—the only position possible for an experienced jurist as well as for an informed historian. The Finns, of course, took note of my objections and published them in a separate brochure: Let me add that the "unifiers," just like the accomplices in Stolypin's agrarian policy, did not have long to celebrate their triumph, triumphs that were to the detriment of Russia.

My relationship with the Poles took an entirely different turn. In our faction, we had one unconditional defender of the Poles: F. I. Rodichev. A warm admirer of Herzen, he completely shared Herzen's point of view, his politics, and his enthusiasm. I could not go quite that far. I already mentioned my cool attitude toward the Polish demands at the Paris Congress in 1904.[32] Perhaps the Poles' cool attitude toward me stems from that congress. At the Moscow congresses, on the other hand, I defended the idea of Polish autonomy with full sincerity and conviction, even against our immediate party interest. Both then and later, I went hand in hand with the representative of the democratic tendencies in Poland, A. P. Lednitsky. But the Polish kolo in the Duma had different attitudes. In the Second Duma, the Poles introduced their own project for autonomy without consulting us, while in the Third Duma, they openly marched together with Stolypin's government and only rarely supported the opposition with their votes. As I already mentioned, it was on this combination that Kramář built his "Neo-Slavism." In the Fourth Duma, Deputy Garusevich emphasized the insincerity of their attitudes toward us with the cruel verse from Lermontov:

There was no joy in love
There'll be no sadness in parting.

It would never have occurred to any of us to come to such a conclusion: we were too sentimental. We had experienced both "sadness" and "happiness". . . . Nevertheless, I must admit that I could not sympathize with the Polish social system as I did with the Finnish. Each system left its stamp on the national character of the people. The peasant-like simplicity and straightforwardness, the folklore and the poetry of nature, and the reflection of both characteristics in literature, all attracted me. On the contrary, the aristocratic "honor" and the attitude of the landowner toward the "khlop" (Polish peasant) repulsed me. Of course, I understood that, in the Polish question, we were dealing with a more complicated social organism, a higher level of intelligence, the old tradition of a lost state, the mysticism of national dreams, and complicated international relations. It was precisely this awareness that led me to be extremely cautious. In Moscow we had agreed on the restoration of the ethnographic borders—those same borders which the Versailles Conference later offered to the Poles (the Curzon Line), and which the Poles rejected. I knew that the Poles still had not repudiated the slogans "from sea to sea" and "the borders of 1772" (that is, before Catherine partitioned Poland), and I could not but realize that the Poles' refusal to have their independence restored was only temporary and conditional. Moreover, I myself wanted their independence restored, as did a few Russian Slavophiles; but I also knew that Poland could only be restored as a whole, that is, as a result of a general European agreement or European conflict. Finally, I knew that the Polish patriots excluded Russia from Europe and presented themselves to European public opinion as defenders of Europe from Russian "barbarism"—in the past, the present, and the future. Of course, all of this could not exactly foster a closer rapprochement between the two intelligentsias—and Mickiewicz's own true story showed this. In the second session (18, III), I had occasion to defend the Polish nation against the statements of the minister of justice. In general, however, this mission belonged to F. I. Rodichev.

Of course, the nationalists of the Third Duma, following Plehve, raised the Jewish question. The "kike-freemason" formula was already current, and Kadets in particular were denounced as "kike-freemasons." However, the systematic persecution of the Jews did not begin until the third session when the signal was given by the Congress of the United Nobility and a speech by Panchulidzev. They decided to bring up the Jewish question at every opportunity. Purishkevich, Zamyslovsky, and Markov II specialized in this task. If the army was being discussed, they proposed to exclude the Jews from the army; if projects for city and Zemstvo self-government were under discussion, they proposed to exclude the Jews from that area too; on the occasion of the debates over the school system, they demanded that the Jews be barred from admission, and Jews were to be excluded also from the liberal professions of law and medicine. One could object to such attacks only in passing, which is what the opposition did. Both the center and the presidium, however, behaved sympathetically toward them. The question was also raised concerning the use of Christian blood by the Jews in connection with the murder of Yushchinsky, and in the fifth session (6/3), I spoke specifically against the pogrom agitation being stirred up around that case.

I also protested to the Resettlement Department against the removal of the so-called "surpluses" from the land allotments of the seminomadic aliens. The transfer to a higher cultural level—agriculture—was entirely a natural, and predictable, process; but it was carried out with great arbitrariness and inconsideration, which, naturally, evoked the extreme irritation of the minority peoples who were being harassed in their age-old way of life. Finally, I defended the rights of the national minorities to receive instruction in their native language (fourth session, 12/7 and 11/12).

As has been mentioned above, we were artificially barred from questions of state defense by Guchkov in his committee. However, this did not prevent us from speaking about these questions at the general meetings. I spoke twice on this theme in the first session 11/29; 5/24) and twice in the last session 5/7; 6/6). Bypassing the Duma, young naval officers came directly to us with reports on the necessity of strengthening the navy. It was here that I met Kolchak for the first time, and he made a very favorable impression on me.

I had to spend an unexpectedly great amount of time both in committee and in the Duma, discussing the bill concerning copyrights. As a Russian writer and journalist, I defended the interests of the Russian reader against the monopoly powers of his own and foreign writers. Nevertheless, the foreign point of view prevailed and neither of the main questions concerning this matter—translation rights and the period during which a book is considered the author's property —was decided by the Duma in the sense of reducing these rights. Still, the bill was not a political one, and doubtlessly made a number of important improvements in the existing law.

In conclusion I should mention yet another area of our faction's work which I did not participate in, despite its importance, since I could thoroughly rely on a young member of our faction, V. A. Stepanov, who specialized in this area. This was the labor question. There was already the precedent of liberal factory inspectors, and the government introduced serious projects for workers' insurance, accident compensation, hiring of commercial employees, normal rest periods for shop assistants, and so on. V. A. Stepanov had to fight both the Duma and the State Council to preserve the initial spirit and possibly improve the above projects. To the question, "What did the Third Duma do about all these important questions of labor legislation?", Stepanov himself answered, "Almost nothing." He was modestly silent concerning his own work and the fact that his activities had at least kept the initiative in our faction's hands for future improvements in labor legislation.

Disintegration of the Duma Majority

I ORIGINALLY PLANNED to call this chapter "Evolution of the Third Duma," because an evolution really did take place, which prepared for the "evolution" of the Fourth Duma. This was a secondary effect of a fundamental process—the disintegration of the political idea responsible for the very convocation of the Third Duma. In the chain of events following the October Manifesto and the dispersal of the first two Dumas, the disintegration of the Third Duma represents a new link—a new section in the same descending political curve. Its sources must be sought outside of the Duma, outside the representative body; they must be sought in the same place that they were found earlier: the corrupting influence emanating from the Court and the Russian nobility. Both groups continued to strive for a complete return to the "historical principles," assuring their own dominance under the aegis of "autocracy." They could never reconcile themselves to the existence of a representative institution, and they continued the struggle essentially along the same line within the Third Duma. Thus, the "disintegration" represented the basic descending line, while the "evolution" was scarcely noticeable for the time being even though it was the undeniable beginning of a new political ascent. The ascent was not represented by the unsuccessful majority of that Duma which had been somehow precariously slapped together; it was represented by the opposition, namely by the Duma's moderate wing. For the time being, the left wing remained away from the scene of the everyday struggle.

The chief ferment for the disintegration of the Third Duma was precisely the Third Duma's creator: P. A. Stolypin. This may seem strange, but it was perfectly natural. Stolypin had built the house of his short rule, not on a solid foundation, but on the unstable, shifting sands of the political cave-in still underway. He was not only helpless to stop it but, on the contrary, only accelerated the process, thanks to his own personal traits.

P. A. Stolypin belonged to that group of people who imagined themselves to be the saviours of Russia, protecting her from "momentous catastrophes." To this task he brought his great temperament and stubborn will. He had faith in himself and in his purpose. Of course, he was a greater man than many of the high officials who sat in his place both before and after Witte. For the honored officials in the State Council, he was an alien, an upstart, a newcomer from the sidelines—and Stolypin was painfully aware of his isolation. He was not called for a quiet routine administration, but to display firm authority and power. He loved power and he strove for it, and he was ready to go a long way and sacrifice much in order to have it in his hands. He was no stranger to ideologies, traditional in his family; nor was he a stranger to intrigue. He was inclined to treat his allies as mere instruments in his own advance to power, and he was ready to change allies according to his needs. In view of his impatience to achieve victory and the short period of his rise, this rapid change could easily convert yesterday's friends into rivals and enemies, and his suddenly changing whims would annoy his guardians and protectors. His chief protector was the tsar, who did not like being ruled by another's will. Such is the story of Stolypin's rise and fall, which at the end, thrust him back into the isolation which he had left and which brought him to a tragic climax. Called forth to save Russia from revolution, he ended up in the role of Thomas Becket.

Let me mention here the first stages of Stolypin's rise to power. I spoke about Kokovtsov's suspicion before the Duma was dissolved that Stolypin "at that time smiled upon the idea of forming a cabinet from people enjoying the public's confidence." I caught a glimpse of this idea in his discussion with me on Aptekar Island. However, when he became convinced that he would never be part of such a cabinet, and when he finally agreed with Goremykin and Kokovtsov on the necessity of dissolving the Duma, he entered the second stage. The dissolution was decided upon—but it was to be a "liberal" dissolution. The Kadets were not suitable for this; it was the turn of the Peaceful Reconstructionists. In a previous chapter, I mentioned Stolypin's direct statement to D. N. Shipov on this matter: "The dissolution of the Duma should be carried out by a new government with a public figure at the head who enjoys the confidence of the public at large." For my part, I have no doubts whatever that this plan was suggested to the tsar by Stolypin, and not by Kokovtsov or, even less, by Goremykin. The tsar agreed—and not only because he had not yet dispelled his own doubts about dissolving the Duma (which I discussed earlier). Another, more realistic reason can be found in the contemporary correspondence between Izvolsky and Benckendorff. They were afraid of dissolving the Duma both because of Europe and because of Russia.

In Benckendorff's letter of June 14 (27), 1906, we read: "It seems to me that this cabinet (of Goremykin's) is doomed; the Duma, in its present composition, sooner or later, will also be doomed. However, the present cabinet cannot dissolve the Duma. The mere fact that this cabinet will take the responsibility for such an act will entail, in the first place, physical danger, and in the second place, elections with still worse results. . . . It seems to me that a cabinet must be formed from the liberal but moderate minority of the Duma; it would have infinitely more moral authority. Such a cabinet would be left in the minority on the very first vote and could then undertake to dissolve the Duma with far greater chances of success. I see no other way of avoiding both a red Duma and military repression." This prototype of a parliamentary decision of the question was simplified in Petersburg to mean a cabinet with Shipov at the head but with Stolypin's participation, while Stolypin's own newspaper, *Rossiia,* tried to scare the public, even in those early days, by warning of German and Austrian interference.

I reported Shipov's refusal of this ignoble role, in his remarkable conversation with the tsar on June 28, 1906. With that conversation, the second stage of Stolypin's tactics came to an end. Then began the third stage, which can only be called intrigue. It is interesting to note that Stolypin removed even his intimate accomplice, Kokovtsov, from direct contact with the tsar. It was decided that Stolypin would replace Goremykin as premier, and the tsar even approved all the practical steps to be taken for the dissolution, including fixing the date of July 9. The tsar "blessed Stolypin with an icon" (see my detailed account above). Stolypin then deceived the Duma as to the day of dissolution, Sunday, by scheduling his own speech in the Duma for Monday, thereby disarming his still dangerous adversary.

And thus, in the third and decisive stage, Stolypin made himself the hero of the dissolution of the First Duma, although his political evolution could not end with that. The fourth stage, dissolving the Second Duma, was much easier. As sensible people had foreseen, this Duma turned out to be "red" and very vulnerable. A victory over it was therefore much cheaper, and did not require any heroes. From the indispensable saviour, Stolypin was reduced to the role of executor of other people's orders. The "black cross" which Purishkevich placed over the Second Duma was the first signal to ring out from the vanguard of masked conspirators. The electoral coup d'etat, prepared by Kryzhanovsky on orders from the nobility, was a shot from long-range artillery; while the agrarian bill of Gurke & Co., was a banner unfurled on the site of victory. But where was the real victor? Amidst these forces, Stolypin, with his already habitual treachery, marched along a well-trodden path, without any risk whatsoever. Nevertheless he still felt out of place among such allies. He had to keep at least a "tint of nobility"; the idea of a "liberal" dissolution, not yet dead, was expressed in the alliance between Stolypin and Guchkov. We saw, however, that the allies were split, from the very beginning, over the most fundamental question of the Russian state system. Their alliance reminded one of Krylov's fable about the swan, the crab, and the pike,[33] the only difference being that the Octobrist "clouds" were hanging too low, the crab turned out to be the strongest of the partners, and Stolypin, himself, was forced to play the role of the pike and drown himself. This alignment of forces constituted the "original sin" of the Third Duma. Then began the fifth and penultimate stage of Stolypin's tactics: his future retreat toward the right.

Stolypin could hardly have expected the disintegration of his majority to begin so soon, especially on the grounds of the—for him— most dangerous struggle concerning the limits of the monarch's prerogatives and those of the legislative institutions; nor could he have expected that it would be his chief ally, Guchkov, who would drag him onto this shaky ground. After his sporting trip to the Boers and the Far East, Guchkov considered himself an expert on military matters and specialized in the Duma on questions of Russia's military rearmament. This was both patriotic and expedient. He thus monopolized the military questions in his own committee, from which he excluded his rivals from the opposition under the pretext of preserving state secrets. I protested, in the name of our faction, against such methods of guarding state secrets and monopolizing those rights which belonged to the Duma as a whole (first session, 29, XI and 24, V). An occasion for conflict soon presented itself. The state of affairs of the Naval Department was the talk of the town in Petersburg; naval officers had come to us and to others pleading for reform and waiting for speeches on the subject from the Duma. Guchkov learned the department's secrets through a more direct route. Together with the Octobrists, we refused to grant credit to the Naval Department for the construction of four new battleships. This did not hurt the Naval Department any, since they were given credit by the State Council. An impression had been made, however. It was strengthened even further by Guchkov's effective speech during the discussion of the budget. He hinted quite clearly that the grand dukes were the source of all the department's troubles.

Stolypin quickly sensed the danger, and on June 13, 1908, in a speech to the State Council, he gave the first warning cry to his ally. He drew a "line of demarcation" between what was allowed and what was not allowed for "insiders and strangers" alike. The rightists hastened to take advantage of this occasion. At the Christmas Congress of the "united nobility," it was decided to go over to the offensive with the definite goal of again changing the electoral law and restoring the old order. The rightists watched for every opportunity to accuse the Duma of violating the rights of the monarch. Guchkov was branded with the nickname "Young Turk," which evoked all sorts of unpleasant associations at the Court and which marked the beginning of the Court's hatred of Guchkov. Suddenly, another circumstance emerged. At the end of the spring session of 1908, the State Council rejected a rather minor bill which the Duma had adopted concerning the composition of the Navy's General Staff. They rejected it on the grounds that the Duma can decide only the monetary appropriations and not approve or disapprove personnel. In the fall of 1908, the personnel bill was passed on for a second time—both in the Duma and the State Council; and the government affirmed that there had been no infringement on the monarch's prerogatives. Then higher circles became involved. In the summer of 1909, a bill was not honored with the emperor's approval, and a rescript was published in Stolypin's name, demanding that rules be established which would definitely delineate the competence of the government and the legislative chambers in the areas of military and naval legislation.

Meanwhile, in March and April of 1909, P. A. Stolypin underwent medical treatment in the Crimea. During his absence, the first rumors were heard that he would not return to his post. For his part, Stolypin took steps to defend himself. *Novoe Vremia,* which carried articles by Stolypin's brother, reported somewhat later that Stolypin "had been morally weakened by the affair concerning naval personnel," and at that time had even moved "cautiously away from the Octobrists" and had begun "to look for safe ground in new Duma combinations." More precisely, these combinations had already formed by themselves in anticipation of his retirement and he had only to accept them. The right wing of the Octobrists had already rebelled against Guchkov and had formed a separate group (the "bareheaded" [*gololobovtsy*]). Balashev's "moderate-rightist" faction was renamed the "National party." In one way or other, at the price of moving to the right, Stolypin managed to stay in power. The "rules" which had been demanded for demarcation of the Duma's legislative competence were published on August 24, 1909. In direct violation of Article 96 of the Fundamental Laws, these rules left the legislative establishments with only the right of discussing budgetary appropriations—and even then, only if there was nothing left over in the budgets which could be used, without turning to the Duma at all, for creating new government agencies.

This clear violation of the law almost evoked the first spark of

protest from among the ruling center of the Duma. The S. D.'s introduced an interpellation concerning the irregular issuance of the rules
of August 24, which interpellation Guchkov supported on the very
first day of the third session, recognizing the necessity of a public explanation from the government. In session on February 22, 1910, he
frankly expressed the reason for his impatience, admitting that the
Octobrists "both here and in the country feel themselves somewhat
isolated." Moreover, while searching for a way out of this position of
"isolation," he declared to the government that the "deplorable necessity" for Stolypin's system of "pacification" had passed, and that, "under
the present conditions, he and his friends no longer see the obstacles
which previously justified the delay in introducing civil liberties." He
defined his faction's stance with the impatient cry: "We are waiting."
To tell the truth, we Kadets were not waiting for anything, but on
March 31, 1910, in the name of our faction, I too supported the interpellation introduced by the leftists.

The Octobrists had good reason to feel "isolated in the country."
Public opinion understood their ambiguous role in the Duma and
turned away from them. In the by-elections for the first curia in the
three main cities of Moscow, Petersburg, and Kiev, the big bourgeoisie
—the Octobrists' private domain—sent Kadets to the Duma instead of
Octobrists. S. A. Muromtsev died during the summer of 1910 and a
vast crowd of people turned out to accompany his body to the grave.
This scene engraved itself in my memory. Late in the evening the
crowd reached Novodevichie Monastery and, despite the prohibition,
they trickled past the fence. In the light of the torches, I spoke over
the open grave, trying to describe the majestic image of this leader who
had calmly opposed the people's will to the arbitrary rule of the
sovereign power. In December and January, for the first time after a
long interruption, the academic year opened with student disorders—
the first symptom of the rising curve of the public mood.

For his part, Stolypin, too, did not "wait." From the very beginning
of the third session he had already composed his right-wing majority
of 151 members, including the right-wing Octobrists, a majority whose
dominant sentiment was one of militant nationalism based on the
slightly refurbished old formula: autocracy, Orthodoxy, and nationality.

Precisely during this time a furious antisemitic campaign was
started in the Duma, accompanied by pogrom agitation in the country.
The Octobrists' facade of decency began to crumble, and N. A. Khomiakov began to feel uncomfortable in his chairman's seat. His friends
were saying: You'll see, one of these fine days, he'll just get up and
walk away, saying: I don't want it any more. I remember how the

young Nikolai Alexeevich had once spared himself from the heat of the Caucasus and the worries of the medical brigade by lying on the couch in Surami. And he did, in fact, walk away when things got too hot in the Duma. Guchkov had no choice. Even apart from his vanity and his desire to bolster his fallen influence, he had to assume the post of chairman. He arrived at a bad time, however, because now he had to compete with the nationalists and fight with their weapons. First of all, he had to cover over all the controversial issues. The Octobrists had come into the Duma thanks to government support, but Stolypin had just declared in *Novoe Vremia* that he conceived of the future Fourth Duma as having "a strong stable center with a national tint to it." Such calculations on receiving support from the voters were bad.

Under these conditions, the interpellation concerning the illegality of the rules of August 24, 1909, was also eliminated. In his answer to me and Maklakov, Stolypin spoke about all sorts of things—the struggle against the revolution, capital punishment, the political situation, but essentially he limited himself to reading excerpts from the journal of the Council of Ministers which recognized the rules of August 24 to be only "instructions" for the ministers. The Octobrists, too, led by their obliging speaker Shubinsky, adopted this point of view, and the interpellation was rejected 161 to 100. The majority thus repudiated its own right to legislate.

According to Stolypin's interpretation, the Council of Ministers, which was created in place of the previous Committee of Ministers at the time the October Manifesto was issued, would henceforth serve as a sort of guardian over the legislative institutions. Until the "Fundamental Laws" were issued, the Council of Ministers could issue acts having the force of law. This was only its temporary function, however. After the Fundamental Laws were issued, the legislative powers were formally transferred to the Duma and the Council of State. Nevertheless, the Council of Ministers continued the old practice of the Committee of Ministers. For example, even such an exceptionally important act (which legalized Russian lawlessness) as the statute of 1881 concerning intensified and extraordinary police powers, continued to be renewed by the Council of Ministers at the beginning of each new year; and it was only after Stolypin's death that the Third Duma turned its attention to that statute. Even the change brought in by the special regulations of 1911, which took away the rights of citizens in 37 provinces and 21 districts and turned the population over to the arbitrary rule of the administration, was introduced by the ministers. In addition, the notorious Article 87 of the Fundamental Laws threatened to eliminate the recently drawn boundary between law and administrative measures. In many constitutions the possibility was foreseen of issuing regulations having the force of law as an extraordinary measure in case of urgent necessity and the absence of the representative body. Only in Russia, however, was this article used to issue acts of crucial importance in the interval between two Dumas and for a definite political purpose. Stolypin went even further by attempting to convert this exceptional provision into a normal part of the legislative process. He even invented his own special theory for the occasion. The Council of Ministers, in his interpretation, had become a sort of independent body between the monarch and the legislative institutions. In addition to the rights of the sovereign power to veto a bill adopted by those institutions, or to dissolve the institutions themselves, the Council of Ministers issued its own legislation in accordance with Article 87 without any concern for the conditions imposed by that article. This is how Stolypin reasoned in his speech on April 1, 1911, in the State Council: "The legislative bodies discuss and vote, while the government must act and bear the responsibility." This was almost a return to the "consultative" Duma of Loris-Melikov and Bulygin.

It is characteristic that, in the case about to be discussed, Stolypin appeared in a double mask: that of a liberal and that of an extreme nationalist. As a liberal, he wanted to conquer the resistance of the State Council, and apparently he made an agreement with Guchkov, since the latter would hardly have announced on his own in the fourth session of the Duma that he "is taking the State Council into consideration." As the most orthodox nationalist, Stolypin made as the object of struggle has own plan for pursuing a nationalistic policy in Russia to the end. He had a very high regard for the measures he dreamed up, and he declared before the State Council that his policy would lead precisely to the "turning point" in Russian history. It was here that Russia's "national future was to be decided," and the law which he passed was the "lawful expression," the "lawful bearer of Russian hopes." On the contrary, Stolypin's opponents in both the Duma and the State Council saw his self-styled national-radicalism as the beginning of Russia's disintegration.

What has been said is enough to show that it was no accident that Stolypin at this point displayed the strongest of "his willful impulses." Stolypin entered the fifth and last stage of his political evolution. He was playing for keeps, staking on one card everything that was left of his personal influence in his role as saviour of Russia. It is a problem for psychologists to determine whether Stolypin overestimated his influence and made a mistake, or whether, on the contrary, he saw his influence already teetering and preferred a risky tour de force to an ambiguous and uncertain position.

Again I must draw on the help of that same source which helped me reconstruct the picture of the preparations for dissolving the First Duma: the memoirs of V. N. Kokovtsov. The only information about what was going on at the "summit" which reached our opposition circles was that contained in more or less obscure and incomplete rumors. In the hands of the tsar's offended servant (Kokovtsov was very sensitive and quick to take offense), these rumors are turned into tangible facts, shedding light on the darkest corners of what, in the Aesopian language of that time, was called "the secrets of the Madrid Court."

We knew more or less that the Court was shutting itself off ever tighter into a close family circle, which gave rise to the fluctuating influences of the tsar's weak will—first his mother, then his uncle, and, finally, his own wife. A long time had passed since the first stage when Maria Fedorovna, born Dagmar of Denmark, exerted influence on him. Through her, at least, some sort of liberal strains filtered through from Fredensborg. Then there followed a period, which had also come to an end, of the "Slavic" influences of the Montenegrins— the "dark women" in the hostile words of Alexandra Fedorovna.[34] This period was marked by spiritualist séances and a switch from Monsieur Philippe, to homegrown, God's fools like the fanatic, Iliodor, or that little imbecile Mitya Kozelsky, or—the last of the series—that Siberian "fugitive," as Kokovtsov called him, or the "holy devil," as Iliodor nicknamed him in his incriminating pamphlet—Grigorii Rasputin, who completely dominated the will of the tsarina. Stolypin turned against Rasputin, refused to subordinate himself to him, and was gradually assigned to the category of enemies of "our Friend." We shall see that the same fate lay in store for Kokovtsov; but, stranger as he was to "bigtime politics" and proud as he was of his financial office, Kokovtsov preserved a neutral stance for the time being and, on the grounds of merit, considered himself Stolypin's inevitable successor.

Such was the situation when Stolypin, in agreement with the nationalists, submitted his project to the Duma for introducing the Zemstvo system into the nine western provinces. This project was supposed to make Russia happy by bringing a new nationalist principle into the legislative process. He said that he "had carried the idea in his soul since the time of his early youth" as a landowner from the northwestern region "where he had spent his best years." The idea was to "prevent the Polish element from absorbing the Russian peasantry at electoral meetings." The method for doing this was based on an "idea" of that adept master, Kryzhanovsky: shuffle the voters by "curiae" into arbitrary groups in order to give the advantage to a particular candidate. In this case, however, the class or group "curia" was to become "national." Stolypin seriously maintained that "next to the peasant land reform" this would be his greatest innovation. He made this his personal project and carried it through the Council of Ministers by himself and then through the Duma, which was so obedient to him. Much to his surprise, however, he met with resistance in the State Council: the "Russian curia" was rejected and the whole project fell through.

Stolypin was "shocked." He made inquiries, and it turned out that Council members V. N. Durnovo and V. F. Trepov had run to the tsar and explained Stolypin's project to him as a "revolutionary invention" in favor of the "petty Russian intelligentsia" which wanted to force out of Zemstvo activities "the cultured and conservative" (Polish) elements and "enrich themselves on the Zemstvo pie." Stolypin immediately went to Tsarskoe Selo and gave the tsar an ultimatum: either he would resign or . . . his enemies would be punished and the bill passed under Article 87 (for which purpose both the Duma and the State Council would be prorogued for three days). The tsar was "overwhelmed" and would not agree to dismiss his minister over a disagreement with the legislative bodies, for that would have been "parliamentarism." He likewise did not want to accept Stolypin's conditions, and decided to "think it over." He "thought it over" for a whole week. The situation grew extremely tense. The public believed that Stolypin's dismissal was imminent. In the press, and especially the rightist press, there were heard voices of sharp condemnation. Stolypin "has taken the glove off his mailed-fist policy," wrote Komarov's *Svet*. It was "an enormous conspiracy against Russia," added Prince Meshchersky, the mentor of two tsars. Even *Novoe Vremia* had to declare that "until the last minute, we refused to believe what people are saying today about the event which has taken place, namely, the departure of P. A. Stolypin. . . . But the facts are stronger than our wish. This unexpected event, has apparently really happened."

Apparently, an episode told to V. N. Kokovtsov by a certain Sazonov belongs precisely to this moment. Sazonov was one of the Black Hundred volunteers who made their way into the Court during such situations. In the spring of 1911 (that is, just at the time of Stolypin's disagreement with the tsar), under instructions from Tsarskoe Selo, this Sazonov was given the task of going, together with Rasputin, to Nizhny Novgorod to look over the governor of that area, A. N. Khvostov, for the post of minister of internal affairs. Khvostov did not consent because Witte had been nominated to be premier. Rasputin at that time sized up Khvostov as "bright but very young" and "let him wait a while more." Kokovtsov adds that after six months, in Kiev, this same Khvostov was suggested for the same post, as a replacement for the murdered Stolypin. . . .

The difficulty of the tsar's position, of course, was recognized by others as well. At that time, Kokovtsov told Stolypin directly that the tsar "would never forgive" the pressure which Stolypin had put on him. Maria Fedorovna, condemning the actions of the tsar and his informers, nevertheless remarked to Kokovtsov: The tsar "does not know how to get out of the situation. . . . After much hesitation, he will end by giving in." But, "having lived through the crisis together with the Empress" and "having made the decision which Stolypin wanted, the sovereign will still feel long and intensely the whole weight of the decision"; and "there will be those who will remind my son that he had been forced to make that decision. . . . How highly he values Meshchersky! As time passes the sovereign's dissatisfaction with Stolypin will continue to grow ever more and deeper. I am almost certain that poor Stolypin has won for the moment, but not for long, and we will soon see him out of power." Stolypin, for his part, answered Kokovtsov's advice to take it easy with: "It is better to cut the knot at one stroke. . . . You are right; the sovereign will not forgive me if he has to fulfill my request, but it is all the same to me, since even without that I know quite well that I am being attacked from all sides and that I will not be here for long."

That is just what happened. Nicholas II conceded and bore a grudge against Stolypin for it. Stolypin's enemies were given a holiday until 1912. Even though the Octobrists immediately reintroduced the bill into the Duma which the State Council had rejected, Stolypin preferred "to cut the knot" by proroguing the legislative chambers for three days and passing the law under Article 87. The tsar's prediction to Stolypin came true, namely, that the State Council and the Duma would never reconcile themselves to that fact. Guchkov demonstratively cast off from himself his obligation to act as an "intermediary" between the Duma and the government, and based his departure from the chairmanship on the fact that his role had been predicated on mutual trust, which had now been violated. Of course, the mutual trust had been violated much earlier, but that had not prevented the Duma from remaining obedient. Once the precise date for the formal personal break had occurred, Guchkov had to get out of the hypocritical situation. On March 14, the very day of the decree proroguing the Duma, the four opposition factions submitted interpellations concerning the illegality of the decree, and it was my job to justify our faction's interpellation. Stolypin's explanations at the April 27 session were proclaimed unsatisfactory and his act was recognized as illegal. By a majority of 202 against 82, the Duma adopted a statement of no-confidence which was worked out with our direct participation. The State Council, especially in the speeches given by Witte and M. M. Kovalevsky, acknowledged the division into national curiae as an anti-Russian and antistate idea.

It was still a long way, of course, from the demonstration to real action. This was reflected above all in the elections for A. I. Guchkov's replacement: the right-wing Octobrist, Rodzianko, was elected by a Duma majority. The Duma's obedience was shown by the fact that the Duma session was forcibly broken off by the new chairman just before the end of the period in which, according to law, Stolypin was required to introduce into the Duma the law which he had passed under Article 87. The Third Duma thereupon simply forgot about its right to reexamine the law. . . .

Here for the first time we met the personality of M. V. Rodzianko in the leading post of Duma chairman, and that personality accompanied us right up to the onset of the revolution. By itself, his personality was insignificant, but as Duma chairman, it took on an unexpected interest. The question naturally arises in the first place, how could it happen that this person, whose advancement to chairman symbolized the low point on the political curve of the Duma, could ride this curve to its highest point?

Indeed, M. V. Rodzianko could have applied the old Russian proverb to himself: They married me off in my absence. The first thing that struck us when he appeared on the chairman's tribune was his imposing figure and his stentorian voice. These traits were coupled with a rather comic impression made by the newly elected chairman. For his pealing voice, the jokers compared him to a "drum," while his massive figure gave him the nickname "samovar." Behind these traits was hidden a natural goodwill, while the flashes of affected importance, which quickly died down, gave occasion to repeat the ancient line: "When Bullion boiled over, Bullion flowed to temple. . . ." "Bullion" with a capital letter, of course, meant Godfrey Bouillon, a leader in the Second Crusade.

Mikhail Vladimirovich was basically a fine person. His early career in the Guards Cavalry cultivated patriotic traditions in him and gave him some reknown as well as connections in military circles; while his material circumstances assured him a feeling of independence. He suffered from no great ambition; he had no inclination or ties to any particular "policy," and he was not capable of intrigues. He was obviously out of place in this critical post; he would find himself at a loss at the slightest complication and could commit any sort of gaffe. He could not be left alone without guidance, and it was this fact which probably determined his election. Behind him stood a small group of Octobrist "leaders." headed by the chief oracle, Nikanor V. Savich, who played the role of the *éminence grise*. When it came to Savich's mind, his knowledge of people, and his ability to find a way out of difficult situations while preserving the faction's "general line," the Duma's gossip was perhaps exaggerated. Savich kept to the sidelines, remained silent and smiled, while cunningly retaining his political anonymity. In exceptional cases of *Haupt-und-Staats Aktionen*, it was Guchkov (who had still not lost his political authority) who came forward to speak. The entire Octobrist combination, however, was clearly on the decline, and the faction's members awaited the approach of the elections with anxiety, not knowing whom they would have to rely on as insurance against losing the support of the next chief. The nationalists, headed by Balashev, felt themselves to be the real masters of the situation, and they continued their antisemitic and antipopular orgy. Nevertheless, since Stolypin had begun to stagger and since his stay in power was considered to be only short and temporary, both the nationalists and the purebred Black Hundreds had to assume a temporizing position, awaiting the coming changes. In the sharp words of Purishkevich, the Duma "rotted on the vine."

Der Mohr Kann Gehen: The Assassination of Stolypin

As KOKOVTSOV SHOWS, Stolypin became "unrecognizable" after the March crisis. He "sort of shut himself up in his own shell." "Something broke inside of him; his previous self-confidence vanished, and he apparently felt that everyone around him, either silently or openly, was set against him." From what he revealed to Kokovtsov, "everything that happened after the beginning of March completely upset him: he lost sleep, his nerves were on edge, and the slightest trifle irritated and excited him. He felt the need of a prolonged and absolute rest, preferably in his favorite village Kovenskaia." He received the tsar's permission to turn over all the business of the Council of Ministers to Kokovtsov. He only asked Kokovtsov to come to Kiev without fail where a monument to Alexander II was going to be unveiled and where a reception was planned for the Zemstvo representatives from the western region who had just been elected under Stolypin's new law.

Arriving in Kiev on August 28, Kokovtsov found Stolypin in a gloomy mood, which was expressed in his phrase: "We are entirely superfluous persons here." Indeed, during the preparation of the program for the festivities, they were ignored to such an extent that no means of transportation had even been arranged for them. On the next day, Stolypin ordered that Kokovtsov's carriage always follow his own, and on the 31, he requested Kokovtsov to sit in his closed carriage, reasoning that "he is afraid that some sort of attempt on his life is being prepared" and that "he (Kokovtsov) should yield to this demand." Kokovtsov was "greatly surprised" that Stolypin, as it were, was asking him "to share his fate. . . ." One cannot miss the comparision between this and Stolypin's earlier "presentiments" that he would fall at the hands of a tsarist police agent. For two days, both ministers rode around the city in this manner and arrived together on September 1 for the gala performance at the city theater. Kokovtsov sat at one end of the first row, while Stolypin sat at the other end, "right next to the Tsar's box." During the second intermission, Kokovtsov went up to Stolypin to say good-bye, since he was leaving for Petersburg, and he listened to Stolypin's request to take him along: "It is miserable for me here with nothing to do." The intermission had not yet ended and the tsar's box was still empty when Kokovtsov, who had not yet left the auditorium, heard two muffled shots. The assassin, the "Jew" Bogrov, half-revolutionary, half-police agent, freely went up to Stolypin, who was standing by the orchestra railing, and just as freely shot him point-blank. A great bustle ensued, while Stolypin, turning to the tsar's box with a bitter smile on his face, cast his broad shadow over it in the form of a cross, and then slowly sank into his seat. The tsar appeared in his box, with General Dediulin standing nearby, saber drawn. The orchestra struck up the national anthem, the public shouted "hurrah," and the tsar, "pale and agitated, stood alone at the very edge of his box and bowed to the public." They carried Stolypin out on his chair. The crowd brought the criminal to the floor and the police took him away. The departure began. . . . Instead of going to the station, Kokovtsov went to the clinic and automatically assumed Stolypin's duties. They informed him that a Jewish pogrom was being prepared, and he ordered three Cossack regiments to return to the city instead of being reviewed on the following day as planned, since the program of festivities had in no way changed. This was the first political act of the new president of the Council of Ministers. At the church service in the cathedral scheduled for noon of September 2, "no member of the Tsar's family was present and no one from the sovereign' suite turned up either." One member of the Third Duma approached Kokovtsov and expressed his regrets that Kokovtsov had missed "a fine opportunity to answer Bogrov's shot with a nice little Jewish pogrom." Kokovtsov found the tsar "perfectly calm," his only "remark was that it was unfortunate that the regiments would not be inspected after the maneuvers." Hearing Kokovtsov's misgivings regarding the outcome of the attack on Stolypin, Nicholas reproached him for his "usual pessimism" and was "surprised" by Kokovtsov's report that "according to the preliminary investigation, General Kurlov had already been linked to the assassination by his incomprehensible activities." He also rejected the automatic replacement of the minister of internal affairs by the deputy minister, Kryzhanovsky, saying: "I have no grounds for trusting this person." Evidently, the Court already had another candidate in mind.

On the evening of September 4, in keeping with the program, Nicholas sailed for Chernigov, where another candidate was being prepared. This was N. A. Maklakov, the governor of Chernigov, whose

manners made him a favorite of the tsar's family. Stolypin was still
alive, though he had already lost consciousness; but the tsar did not
go to see him. Stolypin died on the night of September 6, notwithstanding the reassuring prognoses of Doctor Botkin, whereupon the tsar went
straight from the dock to the hospital and bowed to Stolypin's remains.
Returning to his palace, Nicholas summoned Kokovtsov and formally
offered him the post of chairman of the Council of Ministers. Kokovtsov thanked the tsar for his confidence, but added that "in the difficult conditions of governing Russia," he must know who is to be
appointed the minister of internal affairs. "I already thought of that,"
answered the tsar . . . and named Khvostov. Then Kokovtsov, warning
the tsar of the "harm" to come from such an appointment, asked him
"to relieve him of his high appointment." Nicholas "lost his patience
and the door twice opened part way" (that was a signal from the
empress). Nicholas hastily announced that he considered the appointment made and the cortege started for the train. Arriving in Petersburg, Kokovtsov gave the tsar a negative description of Khvostov, and
in his letter were the following comments which characterized his
general point of view: "(Khvostov) is a man whom everyone knows
for his extremist convictions, which are in complete contradiction to
the system of government nurtured by the mighty will of your Highness. Most important of all, his appointment would be received by the
entire public, and especially by our legislative institutions, with complete bewilderment and even distrust, against which he would be
helpless to fight because of his lack of skill, talent, knowledge and
experience." Kokovtsov apparently also had some basis in character-
izing the other likely candidate, N. A. Maklakov, as a man "who is
insufficiently educated or even-tempered, who is easily influenced by
people having no responsibility, but an abundance of prejudiced
ideas" (here, of course, he meant Prince Meshchersky), and who
"could hardly win respect for himself either in his department or in
the legislative bodies." For his own part, Kokovtsov recommended the
state secretary, Makarov, laying special emphasis on Makarov's "knowledge of police affairs" and his "respect for the law." Makarov was, in
fact, appointed, and in his answer, the tsar stressed also his other
qualities: under him the ministry will be "kept within its proper
bounds" and will introduce "a businesslike calm" where "politics have
developed too much and where passions have been set loose among the
various parties who are struggling, if not for a seizure of power, then
at least for influence over the Minister of Internal Affairs." Kokovtsov
correctly detected in these hints "a clear disapproval of the policy of
Stolypin who had just left the stage in so tragic a manner." He could
not hide from himself the fact that this was a disapproval also of his

own policy as far as that policy was reflected in the above-mentioned quotations and characterizations. If the tsar expressed himself in hints, then the tsarina expressed herself more directly and more categorically. In Livadia on October 5, the name day of the heir to the crown, Alexandra Fedorovna had a special hour-long talk with Kokovtsov in which she laid her cards on the table, a conversation which Kokovtsov "recorded word for word." The talk began with a repetition of the sovereign's words: "We hope that you will never take the road of these terrible political parties which dream only of seizing power or of making the government subordinate to their will." Kokovtsov tried to answer that he had always been outside of all political parties and that he sensed a weakness of his position precisely in that fact, that his position was "much more difficult" than Stolypin's as far as working with the legislative establishments was concerned. Either he did not understand or he did not want to understand that the tsarina's thoughts went exactly in the opposite direction. She became more frank: "I see that you are still comparing yourself to Stolypin. It seems to me that you honor his memory very much and that you ascribe too much significance to his activities and his personality. . . . Believe me, you need not be sorry for those who are no more. . . . I am certain that each person performs his own role and fulfills his own appointment, and if someone is not among our circle, then that is because he has already played his role and has had to retire to the background, there being nothing more for him to do here. Life always takes on new forms, and you ought not try to continue blindly what your predecessor was doing. Be yourself, and do not look for support among the political parties; they are utterly insignificant in this country. Rely on the Sovereign's trust—and God will help you. I am sure that Stolypin died in order to give you his place, and that this will be to Russia's good."

> Der Mohr hat seine Schuldigkeit getan,
> Der Mohr kann gehen.

What was this: mysticism or a concrete political program? Kokovtsov was supposed to understand that he had been appointed to the role of the next "Moor," who after finishing his part, would also cease to be needed "for the good of Russia" and would be subjected, in one form or other, to Stolypin's fate, which, "one month after his demise, few people even remembered." "One month later" the following happened. When Kokovtsov made his report, the tsar told him with some embarrassment that, desiring to commemorate the "good deed" of the heir's recovery, he decided to stop the case against Kurlov, Kulyabka, Virigin, and Spiridovich—the Kiev police agents who were accused of "negligent" behavior on the day of Stolypin's assassination. Kokovtsov became disturbed and began pointing out to the tsar that Russia "will never reconcile itself to the fact that the culprits in this crime have gone unpunished and everyone will be at a loss as to why those people who did not guard the sovereign are not persecuted. . . . God knows whether an investigation might have uncovered something bigger." . . . The tsar was unmoved. On the evening of September 1, he himself had not been subjected to any danger.

When he began to discharge his duties, Kokovtsov soon found himself under an examination which was to reveal to him the source of the threads of these high-level politics. He was put to the test of Rasputin.

Since Kokovtsov, despite strong insistences, refused to see him, Rasputin, apparently on orders from Tsarskoe Selo, invited himself to a meeting. He tried to hypnotize Kokovtsov with his intent gaze; he remained quiet and he played the Divine fool, but when he saw that this had no effect whatsoever on the minister, he began to speak about the main object of his visit. "What then, should I go away, or something? And why are they muttering nasty things about me?" "Yes," answered Kokovtsov, "you are harming the Tsar by telling people about your intimacy with him and by giving food for the most incredible inventions to whomever you please." "All right, I'll go, only don't let them call me back if I'm so bad that the Tsar feels bad because of me." The next day, he told "dear one" about his talk in Tsarskoe Selo and reported his impressions: "They are getting angry; whose business is it where I live? I'm not under arrest after all." On the following day in his report to the tsar about the conversation, Nicholas asked him, "You didn't tell him that you're sending him away?" and, hearing a negative reply, said, "I'm glad" since it would have been "extremely painful if someone was harassed because of us." In answer to the negative opinion about "that muzhik," the tsar said that "he has almost no acquaintance with him personally" and "saw him for a short time not more than two or three times over a very long period." He was hardly being honest. On the same day, Kokovtsov was informed that Rasputin was aware of the unfavorable report Kokovtsov had given to the tsar and that he responded: "So that's what kind of a guy he is; well, let him be; everyone knows his own business." When Kokovtsov showed surprise at the speed of the report from Tsarskoe Selo to Rasputin's apartment they explained that "there is nothing surprising about it at all. It was enough to tell it at breakfast to the Tsarina who would hardly wait long before telling it to Vyrubova, who would immediately get on the telephone, and the business would be done." The entire organization of contacts was right here, on the palm of a hand.

Nevertheless, Rasputin went away one week later—but then the matter became complicated by the fact that Guchkov laid his hands on a letter which the empress had written to Rasputin, containing, among other things, the phrase cited by Kokovtsov: "It seems to me that my head bows when I listen to thee and I feel the touch of thy hand." Guchkov had copies made of the text of the letter and decided to make a case of it, giving a copy to Rodzianko as a subject for a report to the emperor. This more or less coincided with Nicholas' action of sending the Duma chairman the case on Rasputin's Khlystovstvo[35] which had been started by the Tobol Ecclesiastical Consistory. The whole case was absurd, and these rumors had to be refuted. Rodzianko, however, greatly priding himself on this assignment, set up an entire committee with Guchkov's participation and prepared a long report. When Bullion boiled over, Bullion flowed to temple.

Then Alexandra Fedorovna's letter got involved and Rodzianko became the hauty guardian of the tsar's honor. This whole matter was "secretly" divulged both inside and outside of the Duma, and Rodzianko began preparing himself for the report. Meanwhile, Makarov found the original letter and he had the imprudence to turn it over to Nicholas. Kokovtsov's report testifies to the impression thus created. "The sovereign went white, nervously took the letter out of the envelope and, glancing at the empress' handwriting, said, Yes, this letter is not forged! He then opened the drawer of his desk and with a sharp, untypical movement, he threw the envelope in the drawer." Hearing this story from Makarov himself, Kokovtsov told him: "Now your dismissal is assured."

The impression of a profound personal insult created by such uninvited interference in the intimate side of the tsar's family life spread to the whole of the State Duma because of Rodzianko and Guchkov. Rodzianko made his report to the tsar, and on his return, told with great animation about what a deep impression his words had made and what great prestige the State Duma was enjoying. Specifically concerning the report on Rasputin, however, the tsar had said only that he could invite him to a special talk about it. After waiting in vain, Rodzianko wrote the tsar, requesting an audience to discuss the current affairs of the Duma. There was no answer; again Rodzianko came to Kokovtsov to complain about the insult given to the people's representatives and threatened to send in his resignation. The tsar, in reality, returned Rodzianko's request to Kokovtsov with his resolution written in pencil: "I do not desire to see Rodzianko. The Duma's behavior is disgraceful." Kokovtsov concealed this resolution from Rodzianko and persuaded the tsar to replace it with a note saying that he would see Rodzianko after his return from the Crimea. Rodzianko was satisfied and demonstratively announced to the deputies surrounding him that "the sovereign was always favorably inclined" toward him personally "and would not decide to spoil his relationship with the Duma by showing a lack of attention to the Duma's elected representative." Departing, Nicholas said to Kokovtsov: "I simply suffocate in this atmosphere of gossip, lies and spite. . . . I will try to return as late as possible." As they were leaving, the empress walked past all those who had come to see them off without saying a word of good-bye to any of them. The tsar hardly managed to reach Livadia when Rasputin returned to Petersburg. In the Crimea, Alexandra Fedorovna gave clear signs of not paying attention to Kokovtsov. But even before this, and before his meeting with Rasputin, Kokovtsov felt that his "honeymoon" was coming to an end. The tsar demanded that the most resolute punitive measures be taken against the press which had responded to the rumors about Rasputin, but Kokovtsov and Makarov proved to him that it would be impossible to take such steps through the Duma, by the legislative process. On the occasion of the Duma debates over the synod's budget, Maria Fedorovna summoned him in order to speak about the Rasputin business. She "cried bitterly" upon hearing his explanations and promised to speak with the tsar. She ended the talk with the prediction that: "My unhappy daughter-in-law does not understand that she is ruining both the dynasty and herself. She sincerely believes in the holiness of some rogue and we are all helpless to avert misfortune." These few words contained a precise analysis of this very lamentable situation as well as a true historical prognosis which Kokovtsov could not help agreeing with. Somewhat later, during the festivities in honor of the three hundredth anniversary of the founding of the Romanov dynasty, Kokovtsov himself made the following, entirely correct diagnosis of the very roots of the state's disease. "In the intimate circle around the tsar, an understanding of government, of its meaning, has somehow become eclipsed. The personal character of the Tsar's rule stands out ever more sharply, while unnoticeably it is becoming more and more apparent that the government is seen as a 'barrier' between two factors (the tsar and the people—P.M.), preventing their mutual rapprochement. The recent halo which 'the head of the Government,' in the person of Stolypin, acquired during the moment of revolutionary danger, had faded completely (under Kokovtsov—P.M.) while the purely military circles stood ever closer to the tsar, surrounding him and developing in him the cult of 'autocracy,' which they understood in the sense of pure absolutism. The simplistic views of these military circles were gathering more and more force (this refers mainly to

Sukhomlinov's influence—P.M.). . . . The painful experiences of the revolutionary years 1905–6 were replaced by seven years of internal calm, thus making room for the idea of the tsar's personal majesty, for faith in an unlimited devotion to the tsar as the Lord's Anointed, the faith of the whole people, the blind faith of the masses. . . . In the circles immediately surrounding the tsar, there was undoubtedly an increasing sense that the sovereign could do everything without assistance because the people were with him. . . . The ministers, however, were not bound by any such idea of absolutism, not to mention the Duma, which was forever pestering the government with its criticisms, interpellations, faultfinding, its desire to rule, and its desire to limit the executive power—all of which was created, as it were, for the purpose of handling the commonplace and tedious current affairs and should be limited to the smallest possible scope. The further away from the tsar that this unpleasant apparatus could be held, the better it would be and the less probable it would be for all sorts of vexing objections to crop up along the way—objections which insidiously reminded him of what he should no longer be doing, which required him to adjust to some sort of new conditions, and which, in any case, reduced the erstwhile prestige and obscured the halo of the 'Muscovite Tsar,' ruling Russia as his own patrimony."

Kokovtsov did not share the opinion which is condemned here, and it was he who had to remind the tsar continually that "things must not be done as they used to be" and who continually had to restrain the paroxysms of "such absolutism." Incidentally, let me take the opportunity here to answer the remark from Kokovtsov's memoirs regarding my personal relations with him from the time of my first speech on the budget for 1908: "From that time, our meetings were filled with a sort of polite stiffness; we always restricted ourselves to refined, polite courtesies and even after we both became émigrés the character of our rather distant relationship changed little." I have already remarked that V. N. Kokovtsov was very quick to take offense. He did not detect in my "refined politeness" that element of personal respect which was my tribute to him as a political figure in spite of all the differences in our political roles and in our personalities. In Kokovtsov's character, there was a streak of inner self-esteem, coupled with an insistence that other people recognize it, and this streak was a basis for making fun of his vanity. I did not share this rather widespread opinion. The French expression *vanité* is perhaps more applicable than the Russian "vainglory" (*tshcheslavie*). I remembered La Bruyère's remark that *vanité* could be combined with the feeling of having fulfilled a duty, whereas vainglory is contentment with superficial success, even though that success may not be justified by its inherent merits. Kokovtsov obviously failed, but he remained true to himself and to his role, and that fact could not help but inspire respect for him, especially in connection with his understanding of that role as it is expressed in the above citation.

This session of the State Duma was coming to a close, and Kokovtsov had to render it a last service, which evoked the sovereign's great displeasure. Many of the members of the Duma majority wanted the Duma to be received by the tsar before their departure at the end of the session. Nicholas consented to this on condition that the Duma adopt his naval program. Kokovtsov had exaggerated the danger of Guchkov's resistance, since the program was adopted in spite of Guchkov's criticism. Only the tsar's promise remained to be fulfilled. But the tsar became evasive and in response to the insistent reminders about the promise he had given, he finally said in answer to Kokovtsov that he had "definitely no time for it." At renewed insistence, he tossed out the phrase with great irritation: "Then it means that I will simply be receiving the Duma?" "Yes, Your Highness," answered Kokovtsov, "or else I will have to bear the responsibility for this excess of your authority." The tsar conceded, but he warned that he would express his anger at the Duma members over their speeches. Kokovtsov then outlined a very complimentary draft of the tsar's address. The tsar consented to this too, but at the reception on June 12, Kokovtsov heard his compliments shortened and replaced by the phrase: "I am deeply pained by your negative attitude toward the church-parish schools— a matter which is very close to my heart." On the same day, the Duma answered this reprimand with a refusal by the overwhelming majority to grant credits which had remained undecided for the church-parish schools. On this dissonant note, the activity of the Third Duma came to an end. The opposition, of course, did not take part in the reception.

Sazonov's "Nationalist" Policy
and the Balkans

A. P. IZVOLSKY WAS CORRECT when he predicted to Sir Edward Grey that in Petersburg they would not forgive his failure on the Dardanelles' question and that he would be replaced by a "reactionary" minister. A protégé of Maria Fedorovna, a liberal and a "European," a candidate for a post in a Kadet cabinet, and appointed in place of the timid Lamsdorf in order to talk with the First Duma, Izvolsky simply did not suit the style of the Third Duma. Nicholas, who still remained faithful to his German ties, did not share Izvolsky's Anglophile tendencies. In reality, the achievements of 1907 were more profitable for England than for Russia, while the national humiliation of 1908–9 was explained not only by the difficulty of the problem but also by England's refusal to lend support. True, Izvolsky did not want to give up. If the "friends and allies" in London and Paris would not help, then he would have to turn to a member of the other alliance. Of course, he could not turn either to Austria or to Germany. That left only Italy. Izvolsky's inventive mind concocted a new alliance in place of the one with Austria which had failed. The new one, however, would serve the same purpose. Instead of Bosnia and Herzegovina, the cession of Tripolitania and Cyranaica to Italy was supposed to serve as bait, while Italy, in exchange, would agree to support the Russian demands in the straits. Should the status quo be broken in the Balkans, events were supposed to take shape around the recognition of the "principle of nationalities." All this was formulated in a secret document signed after a meeting between the tsar and the king of Italy in Racconiggi, October 22–24, 1909. After the war with Turkey in 1911, Italy achieved her aim by annexing Tripolitania and Cyranaica. I will return in just a moment to the realization of the "nationalities principle" in the Balkans. Regarding the straits, however, Charykov, the new ambassador in Constantinople, delivered a rather strange draft of a convention to the Porte on November 27. Russia promised Turkey to support the existing regime in the Dardanelles in the event of a foreign attack, under the condition that Turkey grant Russia free passage of military vessels through the straits and that Russian protection be extended to "neighboring localities." This poorly disguised plan of taking over the straits naturally evoked Turkey's resistance, which was supported by Germany, while evoking no sympathy whatever in England or France. It was up to Izvolsky's successor to rectify this clumsy move.

At any rate, Izvolsky's dismissal was decided, although the implementation of that decision was held up for more than a year, apparently for the reason that there was no one to replace him. In the end, on Izvolsky's own instructions (if we are to believe Witte), the choice came to rest on Stolypin's brother-in-law, S. D. Sazonov. At first, Sazonov was appointed assistant minister, and at the end of September 1910, he replaced Izvolsky who received the post of ambassador in Paris. In his Memoirs, Witte characterized the new minister as: "very sensible," "with average abilities," "untalented," "not very experienced," and, on top of it all, not in good health. His appointment took place at the end of September 1910 while the royal couple was visiting their Hessen relatives in Germany. This fact alone emphasized, as it were, his political goal: a new orientation of Russian foreign policy. The change in orientation, however, did not occur, and although Edward VII died on May 6, 1910, the goal which he had set, together with Izvolsky's hatred for Austria-Hungary, led Russian policy along its already well-beaten path. Izvolsky's influence on the poorly prepared and unoriginal Sazonov continued to express itself.

Sazonov's replacement of Izvolsky was received sympathetically by the Russian nationalists, and the new minister's first step fulfilled their expectation. The tsar ended his stay in Germany with a meeting between himself and William II in Potsdam. Sazonov was also present at that meeting (November 1910). German diplomacy wanted to take advantage of this meeting in order to reinforce the changes which had occurred, and immediately after Potsdam, Sazonov received from Berlin a clear and precise formula of the new direction which Germany desired for Russo-German policy. The first point of this formula stated that Germany "had received a most precise assertion from the Austro-Hungarian government that Austria-Hungary does not plan to pursue an expansionist policy in the East." For her part, Germany announced that she "did not assume any obligations and has no intention whatsoever of supporting such a policy, should Austria-Hungary pursue it." The second point proposed that Russia make reciprocal declarations to the effect that "she did not obligate herself to support and that she has no intentions of supporting a policy hostile to Germany which

England might pursue." This meant dotting all the i's and paralyzing the existing separation of Europe into two camps; in short, it was an attempt to return to the unsuccessful experiment at Björkö. Sazonov did not support this attempt; he delayed his answer and then made the excuse that the tsar had already given in Potsdam, his promise never to support any anti-German policy. Sazonov explained his evasiveness quite clearly to the German ambassador, Pourtales, by saying that such a secret document might compromise Anglo-Russian relations. Such a justification for avoiding an answer was itself an answer, and as far as the ripened European conflict goes, the situation remained unchanged.

Characteristically, German diplomatic attention in Potsdam focused on the concrete question of Russian-Persian relations. In the spirit of his "global politics," William had declared as early as the 1890's that he would not tolerate any global deals to be made without his consent and without his signature. But there, right in front of his face, was the Anglo-Russian Agreement of 1907, concerning Persia, which had taken the sting out of the old Anglo-Russian conflict. With Russia's consent, the Potsdam agreement had provided that neither side should hinder the construction of the Baghdad Railway and that the Russian-Persian line ("when it would be finished") should be connected to the German line at the border station of Khaniqin. It must be said that Russian interests were hardly affected by this linking of Russia's "national" needs to the "world" problems of England and Germany—other than the fact that the Agreement of 1907 gave Russia a carte blanche to pursue a policy which the English liberal press called the "suffocation of Persia." During the first year of his reign, Sazonov was ill and often absent, and this year of 1911 was marked precisely by Russian excesses which did not stand on ceremonies with the young and infantile Persian "constitution." These excesses even included punitive expeditions with death sentences and occupation by Cossack detachments, which created the gravest impressions in England.

Much more important for Russian interests was the strengthening of Russia's position in the Far East. Also in 1911, a revolution took place in China, and the Manchu dynasty gave way to a republic under President Yuan Shih-kai. The sovereign princes of Mongolia felt themselves freed from the Chinese bureaucrats, soldiers, and colonists, and they declared Mongolia independent. Mongolian delegations appeared in Petersburg to ask for Russian support. Here Russia's interests were touched directly, and the support was given. After long negotiations which lasted into 1912, an agreement was worked out on October 21, 1912, whereby Mongolia's wishes were satisfied, although the nominal sovereignty of China was still preserved. Mongolia became autonomous, with the right to maintain her own national troops and government. The Chinese were removed. On the other hand, the rights of Russian merchants and Russian subjects were precisely defined. The treaty was declared to be unalterable without the agreement of Russia. Thus, in Outer Mongolia, Russia established herself in the role of guardian, and her territory was expanded and consolidated. So-called Inner Mongolia went under the protection of Japan, and the "special interests" of Russia and Japan in Manchuria and Mongolia were demarcated more precisely. Here without doubt was a success for Sazonov's "nationalist" policy.

But the main interest of Russia's nationalist politics during the years of 1912–13 was focused on the Balkan question. Here, in their own peculiar way, "nationalist" ideas—that is, the old Slavophile attitude toward the "Slavic" question—fused with Slavic reality in the Balkans and with Russia's international position. For the historian, this period is of special interest in view of the fact that the intertwining of the tangled threads and influences are still not clarified. For the politician, the situation holds a burning and painful interest as a transitional stage leading to the tragedy of Russian participation in the World War of 1914–18. Of course, only the future course of events and the publication of documents unknown at that time provide the possibility of seeing the more or less complete picture. I must admit that many things remained in a fog at that time, even for me. Nevertheless, my double observation point, as a member of the Duma and as a person well-informed about the Balkan peoples, both free and unfree, placed me in a special position. I learned much on my own during these two years, and many remnants of my former illusions and exaggerations were left behind. I was gradually working my way toward a view of Russia's role in the subsequent events which I still consider correct.

It all began with Izvolsky's plan to take revenge for the failure of 1908–9 by uniting various conflicting elements. Such was his project of bringing together the Balkan peoples into a single "federation" with Turkey's participation, thereby paralyzing Austrian dominance. Given a better knowledge of Balkan affairs, this plan would not have been considered feasible even then; but it seemed perfectly natural at that time and was made the cornerstone of Russia's policy. Sazonov was supposed to be the executor of this policy, but Sazonov was a peculiar kind of executor. Lacking in proper training and deprived of real personal experiences, he was fundamentally indifferent to all tasks and dealt with them in a routine, departmental fashion. The nationalists considered him one of their own although he was not a nationalist: he feared extremes whether in politics or elsewhere. Accurately and precisely conducting routine affairs, he had no general view of them.

He was not a "functional part" of the department, as Izvolsky was, and he introduced no new ideas. From personal contacts I later convinced myself that on the Slavic question, he adhered to the official opinions of the time and found himself in the hands of old-time executives like our Belgrade representative, Hartwig, a fiery fanatic in the old Slavophile tradition. Sazonov, of course, shared the one-sided preference for the Serbs, Russia's old clients, over Russia's new clients, the Bulgars. Sazonov also shared the faith in the complete preservation of Russian prestige in the Balkans as well as the traditional view of Russia's providential role in Slavdom. My few attempts to bring new material to his awareness ran up against his ignorant self-confidence, his turgid thought and his lack of interest in anything that did not fit into neatly ordered patterns. Given such a limited understanding, together with Russia's still light weight in the Balkans, carrying out Izvolsky's anti-Austrian policy with the forces of Slavdom threatened Russia with the most unexpected surprises.

In the meantime, this policy had already begun to be carried out. At the end of January 1912, Nicholas Chernogorsky arrived in Petersburg with a definite plan of expanding Montenegro's territory at the expense of Turkey and the Albanians. In the eyes of the Petersburg Court, and in accordance with established tradition, he was considered a leader of the Slavic movement in the Balkans. On February 29, 1912, with Russia's assistance, a secret Serbian-Bulgarian defensive treaty was concluded which was supposed to remove the main obstacle to the participation of Serbia and Bulgaria in a general Balkan League, namely their dispute over Macedonia. This "secret," of course, became known very quickly. The basis of the agreement was the division of Macedonia between both states, but the middle strip between the Serbian and the Bulgarian shares remained in dispute, and the fate of this middle zone was to be decided by the Russian tsar.[36]

In contrast, Turkey's role in this "federation" was supposed to lead to a policy of strengthening Turkish influence in the Balkans. Turkey had been weakened by the war with Italy, and Sazonov's efforts were directed toward an immediate cessation of that war. These efforts, however, came to naught (the peace with Italy was concluded only after the start of the Balkan War), while Turkey's growing impotence was one of the main encouragements behind the Balkan peoples' efforts to win immediate liberation from Turkish rule. The bankruptcy of the Young Turk's policy had already become an incontestable fact, and the return to endless attempts of deciding the age-old argument by internal reforms only came up against traditional Turkish resistance. It had become clearly impossible by such means to reconcile the interests of the Christian population with the preservation of Turkish rule. It was clear that the Balkan peoples would not

march toward their liberation along the road that Izvolsky and Sazonov wanted them to take, since both of them believed that the *casus
foederis* would come about only "if some great power tried to annex
. . . some part of the territory of the peninsula."

Finally, there was an attempt to persuade Turkey to make concessions regarding the straits. It was equally clear, however, that this
was no way to attract Turkey to Russia. Charykov's above-mentioned
project, which in substance was bolder than previous ones, only clashed
with Germany's growing influence. The influential German ambassador in Constantinople, Marshal von Biberstein, sharply objected to
the project and Sazonov had to withdraw it, stating that it was a
purely "academic discussion" and sacrificing Charykov, who was transferred to the Senate.

In sum, Izvolsky's plan not only did not succeed but was converted into its antithesis. Izvolsky had planned to create the Balkan
federation with Turkey's participation as a counter weight to Austria-
Hungary. The Balkan nationals now directed their union *against*
Turkey as their bitterest enemy. All the later steps toward creating a
Balkan union were taken in the greatest secrecy, apart from the powers, including Russia. After October 1911, negotiations were carried on
between Bulgaria and Greece, and on May 16–29, 1912, another "defensive" agreement was concluded between them in which there was
no mention of territorial limitations, a question which had become
even more disputed. It was clear, nevertheless, that the immediate
aim of the agreement was military action. The agreement was extended to include Montenegro, too. Then the general staffs of the four
cosignatory states started to work out a plan for war against Turkey.
Each of them was to supply a specific number of troops and to occupy
that part of the territory which it claimed. By spring it was already
decided that the war would begin in the middle of September, after the
harvest. The uprising in Albania served as a prologue to the war.

The details of these preparations, of course, were known to those
persons who specialized in Balkan affairs. Rumors that something was
being prepared in the Balkans reached even higher places. The next
stage was the clarification of how the leaders of great European politics viewed what was going on. This was seen best of all by two
visits to Russia: Emperor William at the Baltic Port (June 21–22
O.S.) and the new French premier, Poincaré, in Petersburg (July 27–
31 O.S.). Starting from opposite points of view, both of them regarded
the sparks from an enkindled Balkan fire as a dangerous complication
in the world conflict then in the making. They had the identical aim
of separating their own interests from the Balkan argument by imposing their veto on it.

Sazonov was elated when he gave Kokovtsov the general sense of

William's talks with Nicholas in the Baltic Port. "We can be perfectly calm; the German Government does not want to let the Balkan fire ignite a Europeon conflagration, and it is only necessary to take steps to keep our half-baked politicians from dragging us into some kind of a Slavic adventure." The tsar was "in a wonderful mood" having received from William "the most definite assertion that he will not allow the aggravation of the Balkan situation to develop into world conflagration." This was all very fine and perfectly sincere, since the main nerve of German policy led elsewhere. Kokovtsov discovered this nerve when he spoke with Chancellor Bethmann-Hollweg, who accompanied William, about "the German rearmament program of 1911 and the extraordinary military tax voted by the Reichstag which was causing us great alarm; we see quite clearly that Germany is arming at a feverish pace, and I (Kokovtsov) am powerless to oppose such aspirations here in my own country." Indeed, the tsar finished the phrase quoted above with: "Nevertheless we must prepare; and it is good that we can carry out our naval program, and it is necessary to prepare also for defense on land." We shall see that these words were not accidental.

France, in turn, likewise had no wish to mix the struggle for her world position with the outcome of the Balkan conflict. Having acquainted himself in Petersburg with the military treaty of the Balkan League, Poincaré stated to Sazonov directly that "French public opinion will not allow the government of the Republic to decide on military action because of purely Balkan questions. Only if Germany takes part or if she provokes the *casus foederis* on her own initiative could Russia count on France to fulfill her obligations precisely and completely."

The line of differentiation between the conflicts leading to a world clash and the purely Russian national interests was drawn here quite clearly. In fact, it was precisely in 1912 that the clash between the global interests of the European democracies and the *Weltpolitik* of William II entered its last and decisive phase. In April and May of 1911 the entry of a French detachment into Fez again placed the Moroccan question high on the agenda. William announced that this act had violated the Algeciras convention and he sent his cruiser "Panther" to Agadir. Edward Grey then laid down his cards for the first time, announcing to the German ambassador in London that in the event of an armed conflict between Germany and France, England would have to fulfill its obligations toward France on the Moroccan question. The argument was settled by conceding a part of the French Congo to Germany. However, this in no way eliminated the possibility of a "world conflagration." William only eliminated the possibility of a second front, while holding in check Austria-Hungary, the only link between the "global" and Russian interests. Austria, in her turn, was supposed to tie down Russia; this was a sort of surrogate for the "Three Emperors' League" which was not renewed in 1890. England's position also became clear in Russia when on January 25–28, 1912, the reciprocal visit of English public figures and naval officers took place. As a Duma member, I was present at the breakfast and dinner which were given in honor of the guests. I was thus a witness to the heated speeches and reciprocal toasts of our right-wing parliamentarians and the English military men. I do not know what was being said backstage, but the meaning of this public exchange of courtesies was clear enough. For her part, in no hurry to respond to our Balkan complications, France started negotiations for cooperation between the Russian and French navies in the Mediterranean. This made it easier for France to transfer her navy to the south, leaving the defense of her western and northern borders to the English navy. Meanwhile, England made a final attempt to persuade William to halt the rapid expansion of the German navy and to give up the idea of being England's competitor on the seas. The attempt met with a rebuff, and relations between the two countries took a turn for the worse. The Reichstag decided to take measures for increasing military construction and taxes, which Kokovtsov was "helpless to fight against" in Russia. This meant that the Russian Military Department, too, went its own way without asking permission from the chairman of the Council of Ministers. Sukhomlinov maintains in his memoirs that as early as 1912 Russian mobilization was so well prepared that he was given the power to give orders immediately for military action against Germany and Austria!

In September, the military preparations of the Balkan states and the discontent became so evident that Sazonov decided to take a trip around the European states in order to reach an agreement on common action for preserving the peace. The results were paltry. In London they were speaking more about the disgraceful Russian practices in Persia. On invitation from George V, Sazonov stayed in the residence of the king of Balmoral for about a week, but nothing at all, either positive or negative, came out of it. In Paris they took a somewhat more active interest in the question, offering to send a strong note by way of Austria and Russia, in order to prevent a Balkan war and promising in the note—reforms. If war should begin anyway, the Great Powers announced that regardless of the result, no territorial changes would be allowed and the sovereignty of the Sultan as well as Turkey's territorial integrity would be preserved. The Great Powers doubtlessly figured that the Balkan Allies would be beaten by the Turks and that the whole matter would be limited to a new attempt to introduce those reforms which were promised as far back as the

Berlin Treaty, but which had never been realized. The Balkan nationals had long ago lost faith in these reforms, but the note of October 7 gave them an unexpected advantage. At least during the period of military action, the note guaranteed the noninterference of the Great Powers (including Austria) and the struggle could be waged for the first time, one against one.

"L'Europe s'est retrouvé," Sazonov consoled himself while leaving for Berlin. At a banquet in the Russian embassy in Berlin, however, he announced that henceforth the great danger of a general uprising in the Balkans was eliminated. The nearsightedness of such predictions was exposed that very evening. On the evening before the note of October 7 was presented, Nikolai Chernogorsky, deliberately moving ahead of events, began military operations and declared war on Turkey. After a few days, Bulgaria presented Turkey with the collective demands of the Allies: administrative autonomy of the vilayets, Belgian and Swiss governors, proportional nationality representation, native gendarmes and militia, supervisory council made up equally of Moslems and Christians to oversee the reforms, under the control of envoys from the Great Powers and representatives from the four Allied states. On October 15, Turkey broke diplomatic relations and on October 17 declared war on Bulgaria and Serbia. That same day, Greece declared war on Turkey.

Then there followed something extraordinary and unexpected. Left to themselves, the Balkan Slavs, without the help of Russia or Europe, freed themselves from the remains of the Turkish yoke. Not only that but they did it with such rapidity that Europe did not have time to come to its senses before it was faced by a fait accompli. Europe's warning against permitting territorial changes or weakening the sovereignty or the integrity of Turkish territory was simply thrown away into the wastebin of history.

As was foreseen, the series of military actions against Turkey began with an uprising in Albania, on the Gregorian date of April 23, 1912, with a frank assumption of support from the Montenegrins. The government troops sent against the Albanians returned to oppose the Committee of "Unity and Progress," demanding a change in the cabinet, dissolution of the chamber, and the elimination of the committee from politics. A threat of a march against Constantinople had its desired effect, as it had in 1908: the new cabinet dissolved the chamber on July 23. Such a display of weakness on the part of the Young Turks encouraged their adversaries and aided the formation of a Balkan military alliance. Accidently or not, the Albanian uprising also provided the occasion for my next trip to the Balkans.

My Last Trips to the Balkans

My old friend, Charles Crane, an everlasting admirer of old cultures and a supporter of peoples struggling to liberate themselves, turned up in the Balkans. Later it was said that he gave the Albanians material aid; of course, he did not tell me about that. He wrote me inviting me to accompany him on his trip through the Balkans. Naturally, I accepted with pleasure. The interval between the dissolution of the Third Duma on June 8 and the convocation of the Fourth Duma on November 15 gave me a perfect opportunity to visit the Balkans, and from what I knew of the events going on there, this trip was necessary. I was in no special rush to go to any particular place. From Belgrade, I decided to go down along the Danube, across the famous Iron Gates to Turnu-Măgurele, and from there I would go across the picturesque mountain canyons of the river Isker, on to Sofia where Crane was already waiting for me. I found him in contact with Bulgarian artists; and while my attempt to turn his attention from Bulgarian life to Mitov's picture was not successful, he did obtain a life-size portrait of "the Tsar of the Bulgars" in magnificent Byzantine attire, which he later hung in his New York apartment. The ancient Slavic sacred objects also interested him. He knew Saint Afonsky's Mountain, and the picture of Pantaleimon's Monastery, which he ordered from a Czech historical artist, Mukha, stood conspicuously and beautifully in his apartment. We made the Rylsky Monastery the goal of our first trip, and we set off for it on horseback across the Samokov mountain plateau. I did not find anything especially remarkable in the monastery, perhaps because I did not really search. My head was filled with thoughts of politics. Like us, waiting for news, the famous journalist Dillon was also staying in the monastery. I had known him as a *Times'* correspondent since 1905. He had aged considerably since that time, but he preserved his lively temperament, his cool intellect, which was inclined to portray people and things in a black light, and his passion for sensational exposés, although they may not have been completely trustworthy. He considered me a dangerous competitor and carefully concealed his contacts with local informants who brought him news for a fee. Nevertheless, we were constantly arguing. Crane listened in silence, except to interject his venomous jokes, which he did quite successfully. Thus we whiled away several days under this monastic regime, and we returned to Sofia without anything sensational. Our second trip aimed at visiting the Shipka Pass—a monument to the heroic battles of the War of 1878. As we climbed to the top, I recalled General Gurko's bold crossing, his difficult retreat, and his winter encampment ("All is quiet on Shipka!"). Crane was more attracted by the Russian Orthodox church —a monument at the top of the pass. The clergymen greeted us affectionately. Adjoining the church lived a few Russian invalid-pensioners from the time of the war. We went up to the top and then came down along the path of the Russian offensive, from north to south, coming out into the "Valley of Roses" (Kazanluk). Aside from the name, there was nothing at all poetic about this valley: it was simply a large plantation of rose bushes from which rose essence was extracted—an expensive product. At the monument I got a small bottle of the essense. From Staraya Zagora we climbed up along the railroad tracks. It was October; in Russia, the elections to the Fourth Duma were already underway, and Sazonov had returned from his trip abroad. Bulgaria had begun military action against Turkey; the Bulgarian troops took the Mustafa Pasha station on the Maritsa River and quickly moved on to Adrianople. It was time for me to return, but Crane and I decided to travel to the south in the tracks of the Bulgarian army. We stopped in Mustafa Pasha, since it was forbidden to travel farther. While waiting for the return train, we took a walk around town, and a small incident happened which has remained strongly fixed in my memory. It was market day, and the sun shone brightly on the peasant crowd and on the women in their colorful local costumes. Crane lost himself in admiration of this oriental picture while I, with my Kodak in hand, went down to the banks of the Maritsa, which was spanned by a high railway bridge in the direction of Karaagach, a suburb of Adrianople. A beautiful view of the opposite shore opened up under the bridge, and I got in position to photograph it. I had completely forgotten that we were right in the middle of the war zone, and that what I was doing could lead to the firing squad. The gendarmes came up from behind, grabbed me, took away my camera and led me off to the police. Crane rushed up to meet me. We stopped at the bazaar; the crowd surrounded us; the policemen began their interrogation. Of course, my first explanations did not satisfy them, while my knowledge of Bulgarian showed only that I was not Bulgarian. The situation became unpleasant; they demanded to see my documents, and I took offense, even further increasing their suspicion. Crane looked at me mournfully, but he was helpless without the language. Finally I took out my passport; the police officer began to read it, and suddenly the situation changed. "Mister Miliukov? The friend of Bulgaria?!" The gendarme took a step back, saluted, gave me back my passport and camera, and apologized. I almost cried from joy. Here, at a small transit station, they knew me as a friend and believed me instantly! This was unexpected and—touching. . . . This was my reward for my years of work for the Bulgarian people. Crane was as surprised and touched as I was. In this mood we started on our return trip.

I had to hurry to get back in time for the elections and the opening of the Fourth Duma, so I stopped in Sofia only very briefly. It was during these few days that I had my first meeting with Tsar Ferdinand. The meeting, of course, was on his initiative, but he decided to arrange it in a conspiratorial manner. I was informed that we would meet in his private zoo where he kept his ornithological collections. I was in the appointed place at the appointed hour and Ferdinand came along the designated path in civilian clothes to meet me. Nothing has remained in my memory from our conversation; apparently our talk bore a predominantly complimentary character and Ferdinand did not show me his cards. And there was indeed something to show! I knew, but not from him of course, that the negotiations with Serbia and Greece were continuing between Malinov's more agreeable successor, Gueshov, and Venizelos and Milovanović. The conditions for agreement had not been worked out since the general atmosphere in the Balkans still wavered between "a war for liberation" and a "war for conquest." Those who favored ending the war in its "liberating" stage considered that the goal had already been reached by the Lulé-Burgas victories (October 31, 1912), and those in Salonika (October 27) and in Bitole Monastery (October 18). On the other hand, those who favored continuing the war strove for a complete victory over Turkey, which subsequently was made definite by the seizure of Adrianople by the Bulgarians (March 13, 1913), Janina by the Greeks (February 24), and Durazzo and Skutari by the Serbs and the Montenegrins (April 9). It was clear, of course, that Ferdinand was on the side which favored continuing the war and that the Austrians were encouraging him in this policy. The Bulgarian troops besieged Adrianople and moved on toward Constantinople. The prospects, however, were still not clear.

Before parting, Crane wanted to take a look at the beautiful mountain landscape on the Danube, not far from the Serbian border. As a result of the sandstone erosion, the cliffs there took on unusually fantastic forms. After staying for awhile, Crane and I parted on the Danube at Nikolai. From there, I went down along the river to Giurgiu in order to return by way of Bucharest, which I had never seen. I wanted to see the last trace of Kiselev's rule over the Danubian principalities in the time of Nicholas I. One such trace could be seen in the Russian cab drivers, who still wore their black velvet kaftans and their caps trimmed with a peacock feather. One of them gave me a ride along "Kiselevsky Prospect." Then I took the train to Jassy, where I became interested in the results of the archeological excavations of the so-called Tripolsky culture. A young university professor received me very courteously. At the university, I took photographs of decorated ceramic objects which were related to those of the Kievan period. I returned home by way of Tiraspol.

October was the decisive month in the history of the Balkan struggle. In the winter months, the struggle entered a new and dangerous phase. The incontestable became contestable. Europe's uneasiness grew as its predictions were frustrated. Not Turkey, but the Slavs were victorious; and their final liberation from the Turkish yoke became just as much an incontrovertible fact as the long-expected disintegration of Turkey. The whole question was pushed onto an international plane.

Let me mention the main facts of this turning point. The Bulgarians, as we noted, besieged Adrianople and almost got as far as Constantinople, stopping only at the strongly fortified line at Chatalja. The Montenegrins went to the Adriatic ports and planned to divide up the Albanian lands with the Greeks. The Greeks occupied Khalkidhiki Peninsula, the southern part of Macedonia and the island. Salonika remained a bone of contention between the Serbs, the Bulgars, and the Greeks, and here the main object of disagreement became clearer since the Serbs were in occupation of all Macedonia and were becoming ever less inclined to give it up. Tied down by the battle at Adrianople, the Bulgars were late by several hours or days (October 26–27) in reaching Salonika, and the Serbs beat them to it.

In November the threatening voices of Austria and Germany were heard. Austria protested against the Slavic occupation of the ports on the Adriatic Sea (San Giovanni di Medua and Alessio). Guarding her interests in Albania, Austria proclaimed the area independent on November 16. Immediately following this, Germany's first cry was heard from the lips of Chancellor Bethmann-Hollweg. If the belligerents did not manage to come to an agreement, he warned, if an open clash should arise between them, and if danger threatened the existence of Austria-Hungary as a result of an attack by a third party, then, in that case, Germany "would have to stand decisively on Austria's side in accordance with the obligations of the alliance."

Naturally enough, the opposite camp also became concerned. Poincaré and Grey hastened to warn of the danger which would arise from "an irretrievable step" by some separate state. Austria, of course, was the one that was meant. Austria hurriedly armed herself and prepared for mobilization. In November of 1912, the situation reached such a level of tension that William himself considered it necessary to call his "brilliant second" to order (November 11): "Germany must risk its existence," he wrote, "because Austria does not desire to see the Serbs in Albania or in Durazzo! It is evident that this is no basis for Germany to wage a destructive war. . . . To place the German army and people in dependence on the whims of another state would mean to go beyond the limits of the treaty obligations. A *casus foederis* would occur if Austria were subjected to attack from Russia only under the condition that the Russian attack was not provoked by Austria which in practice might happen because of Serbia. Austria is obligated to avoid this situation." If repeated in 1914, these wise warnings might have prevented the world war over the Balkans. But, alas, this was the last echo of the mood at the Baltic Port meeting; the opposite mood was soon to be dominant.

We shall see how Russia reacted to this November tension. However, I do not want to interrupt my story about the further Balkan complications at the end of 1912 and the beginning of 1913. Here the tense mood of late Autumn was temporarily resolved by a cessation of military activities. On October 22, Turkey turned to the Great Powers, requesting them to intervene. One month later, on November 20, a truce was signed between Turkey and Bulgaria, Serbia, and Montenegro (Greece refused to sign). At the invitation of England, the representatives of the Balkan Powers converged in London for talks (December 2) and the next day a conference of ambassadors began there as a sort of control commission. All disagreements were transferred to London—disagreements which were rapidly becoming sharper because of, and to the delight of, Austrian diplomacy. As the demands of the Allies grew, Turkey's obstinacy also grew. Bulgaria demanded the beseiged Adrianople. Turkey refused (January 6, 1913). The Allies then suspended the conference work. In Constantinople, a special "great meeting" gathered together to deliver an answer in a conciliatory spirit, when the members of the Committee of "Unity and Progress" broke into the meeting, murdered the commander-in-chief, Nazim Pasha, and obtained the resignation of the cabinet. The Allied delegates in London answered by "interrupting" the negotiations (January 16), and at the end of the armistice (January 21), military action was renewed. Turkey renewed her request for the Great Powers to intercede (February 16), but, in their answer, the Allies raised their demands even further (March 1). On March 13, Adrianople was taken by storm. I remember, as if it had just happened, the stupid look on the face of the Duma joker, Paul Krupensky, who leaped up to the rostrum, waved his hands wildly and roared at the top of his voice, "Hurrah" for the Bulgarians. The rightists' "Slavic" demonstrations took to the streets. On March 19, Nikolai Chernogorsky refused to give in to the demand of the Great Powers to end the seige of Skutari even though Russia had already agreed to leave Skutari within the boundaries of Albania. On March 25, Bethmann-Hollweg responded to these manifestations of Slavic independence by a speech in which the first hints of William's new mood were heard. The imperial chancellor spoke of "the rebirth and the aggravation of racial instincts," about the necessity for "Germandom" to struggle against "Slavdom," and about the destruction of the balance of power in Europe in favor of the Slavs. He used these excuses to prove the necessity of further armament, and declared, more definitely this time, that the assistance which Germany is obliged to render Austria "is not restricted to the limits of diplomatic intercession." In that same month of March 1913, a new *Wehrvorlage* was introduced into the Reichstag, demanding a billion marks for new armaments.

The idea of a struggle between "Germandom" and "Slavdom" was, of course, far from new. It was an indispensable part of the code of official Pan-Germanism. However, the Slavic victories in the Balkans gave this thesis a new, real content. Emperor William, a long-time supporter of Pan-Germanism, reacted very sensitively and nervously to this new application of an old principle. He did not have to change in order to do this. He simply brought the struggle against "Slavism," as personified in the eyes of the theoreticians by the eastern part of Central Europe, into his general program of "world politics." We even learned the name of his intermediary in assimilating this old but revived idea. He admits, "In particular, my confidence was gained by the Baltic professor, Schiemann, an author of works on Russian history and the publisher of annual collections concerning 'big power politics.' " In the eyes of the emperor, this man was a "penetrating politician, a brilliant historian and man of letters, a champion of Germanism against the Slavic impudence" with whom he "constantly consulted in political questions," and a man to whom he was "obliged for many explanations and interpretations especially regarding the East."

Still not realizing that William's mood had entered a new phase, that Austro-Hungarian policy was being conducted in a heightened

tone, and that the disagreements between the Allies had reached such
a serious level, I felt, above all, the need to learn the results of the
Balkan victories on the spot. I only had at my disposal the Duma's
Easter vacation (April 6–13, 1913), and I took advantage of it to visit
at least the main centers of the struggle. First of all I went to Sofia.
The military activities between the Bulgars and the Turks ended on
March 25, and the armistice conditions were published on April 5
(extended to April 21). The border between Bulgaria and the remainder of Turkish territory, which was agreed to also by Europe,
passed along the line Enos–Midia. However, the aspirations of the
military party went further. Rumors were heard in the capital, half-
jokingly, half-seriously, that Ferdinand had already ordered a white
horse prepared for his triumphant entry into Constantinople. True,
they added that having occupied the Turkish capital, Ferdinand
would turn over the keys of Constantinople to the Russian tsar. On
the other hand, the Austrians had already hinted to Premier Danev
that the Bulgarians could make themselves the "*gute Huter der
Dardanellen*," the good keepers of the straits. Be that as it may, I
personally observed these militant moods. Tsar Ferdinand again
desired to see me, but this time in entirely different surroundings: in
his palace, in a solemn audience.

He began our talk with the phrase: "I know that your Tsar hates
me. But why?" This was not far from the truth, but I prepared myself
to object and did manage to say that, apparently, the tsar did not
have a prejudiced opinion, and that if there were misunderstandings,
then they would be mitigated; that there was already evidence of a
conciliatory attitude. I saw, however, that his question had been, so
to say, rhetorical and that Ferdinand was not listening to my answer.
He had his speech all ready, well-arranged and thought out beforehand, and he started on it, listening only to himself. His speech flowed
in cascades, sparkled with flashes of wit, antitheses, and unexpected
saillies in the style of French eloquence, in brilliant French. I remember
that somebody once told me that should Ferdinand want to charm
somebody, he would certainly know how to do it. "Yes, I know that
they suspect me, that they consider me a foreigner. But I love that
people; they are a good, honest people. I want to merge with them.
And the people as well remember and love Russia. I am raising my
son in Orthodoxy and giving him a knowledge of the Russian language.
I want you to see him." Then he ordered Boris to be brought in. The
boy was brought in with his governor, a Russian priest. I greeted
him and spoke a few words in Russian. The confused Boris remained
silent and his governor hastened to answer for him. Then Ferdinand
turned toward Boris: "Here is your teacher. Remember, you must

follow his advice." The scene ended, the boy was led away and Ferdinand continued: "They accuse me because of the personal character of my regime. But I am a constitutional sovereign; the country is governed by a responsible cabinet which at this moment is made up of democrats and friends of Russia. True, the country is young, the parties are artificial, and I must alter them when they are in power. But they do represent the people. And now I am working precisely for the cause of the people. I will complete the unification of Bulgaria. It is a national task, but at the same time it is our common Slavic task. And you should help me in this cause. Persuade the tsar to concede Rodosto to me" (Rodosto is a city on the Sea of Marmora, halfway between Constantinople and Gallipoli). I was somewhat taken aback. Apparently, Ferdinand considered the role of "leader of the opposition" in the Duma as some sort of responsible post in the Bulgarian National Assembly, as a candidate for a future premier! I did not have to engage in polemics over this theme, however. The speech was finished, Ferdinand gave the sign; I thanked him for his trust and took my leave. It turned out that his request was more serious than I had thought. Late in the evening of the same day (I left early in the morning) Ferdinand's intimate minister, Khristov, came to me in my hotel on a secret mission confirming the request about Rodosto; and as a souvenir, he gave me a large frame portrait of Ferdinand with his autograph. . . . The demand of Rodosto had already been formally included in the Allies' general demands from Turkey (March 1, 1913), and was the subject of Ferdinand's special request to the tsar. This request, of course, was not received well in Petersburg. Understandably, I took no steps in this direction whatsoever.

My next goal was Salonika where the Bulgarian garrison was still stationed and where I had friends in the Bulgarian colony whom I was counting on to inform me about the situation in Macedonia, under Serbian occupation. Disagreements over interpretations of the partition treaty existed even at that time in the ruling circles, although they were unknown to me. The heir to the Serbian throne, the young Alexander, remained in Salonika in a car of his special train, and I was not surprised that he wanted to see me. Our talk made a most favorable impression on me. An alumnus of the Russian military academy, he spoke excellent Russian and was extremely amiable toward me. He knew that I was well acquainted with Macedonia and questioned me in detail about the situation there. I answered him willingly and gave special praise to the natural beauty of the country. We did not touch upon the delicate aspects of the question, and I did not know that Alexander was considered the chief advocate of annexation of the whole of Macedonia. Of course, I also did not know that on March 24, the Serbian envoy in Bucharest had relayed the Rumanian proposal to form an alliance against the Bulgars, while on April 19, the Greek envoy had made the same proposal. Finally, I also did not know that Prince Nikolai Grechesky, in his capacity as military governor of Salonika, had taken part in the negotiations on this matter which had been carried on in "special" trains. I do not recall now whether or not it was in a special or ordinary train that I got the opportunity to take a ride through Macedonia right up to Uskyub. The Bulgarian name of the city "Skopje" had already begun to give way to the Serbian "Skoplje," and the local Bulgarian colony, as far as I could learn, already began to feel rather uncomfortable in this city. I will return to this question again later. Here, too, the Serbs continued to give me special attention. I was invited to a meeting in honor of the *voivode* of Putnik just at the time of his trip to "inspect" Macedonia; and Alexander, who put in a personal appearance at the meeting, specifically ordered that I be brought to him for a personal talk. Of course, standing in the crowd, no serious conversation was possible. It was merely a sign of attention.

In Vienna, on the way back, I had the opportunity to speak with a man of another type, the minister of internal affairs, Milovanović, who had been, since 1904, one of the supporters and ideologists of Serbo-Bulgarian rapprochement. We stayed at the same hotel and our conversation was a very intimate one. Nowhere yet could I notice signs of a cooling off between the Allies. As late as March 21, Tsar Ferdinand sent a telegram to King Peter thanking him for the brotherly help in taking Adrianople.

The end of April saw another interruption in my personal contacts with the Balkan countries—until August 13 of that same year. (All the dates are given in Old Style.) And how many new and serious changes had occurred in the situation during these almost four months! Disagreements between the Allies had finally come out into the open and had led to tragic consequences. Again, in order to preserve the continuity of the story, I will exclude everything that is connected with Russia's role in the Balkans. I will return later to what I am omitting here.

In August and September of that same year, 1913, entirely unexpectedly, I had to make another trip to the Balkans—not in the role of politician and observer, but in the role of a judge. After having been amazed by the Slavic "glory," the entire world then began talking about Balkan "atrocities." Yesterday's Allies began to fight among themselves over partitioning the conquered territory. This new struggle, which was no longer diplomatic, but military, began to show traits, peculiar, it is true, not only to primitive peoples. Bulgaria was the country legally responsible for resorting to arms; and, as it turned out, Bulgaria was the first victim. Bulgaria was the first to turn to the Great Powers and to public opinion with a complaint against the "atrocities" which she had suffered. Formally, the main facts concerning Bulgaria's responsibility in raising the sword developed in the following way. In accordance with a secret order given to Bulgarian troops on June 15 and 17, they began offensive operations. The persons responsible for this action were Tsar Ferdinand, his intimate advisor, General Savov, and their associates. Danev's cabinet insisted on an immediate cessation of military actions, but the fateful step had already been taken. The Bulgarian troops were exhausted by the preceding struggle against the Turks and improperly placed for the improvised war in Macedonia. The Serbs, on the other hand, prepared themselves for the struggle ahead of time. Within three days, the Bulgarian offensive was repulsed. The Greeks met the Bulgars with four times as much force. The Rumanian troops crossed the Danube and moved in the direction of the undefended Sofia. Turkish troops also went over to the offensive and took away everything which the Bulgarians had conquered, including Adrianople (July 9). Bulgaria, without setting any conditions this time, made an appeal for either Russia, Austria, or Rumania to intercede. But the offensive from all sides continued. Finally, the Rumanian king, Carol (Hohenzollern), took it upon himself to intercede; and on July 18, a five-day armistice was concluded in Bucharest. Bulgaria was offered extremely harsh peace terms; but no longer in any position to object, she was forced on July 24 to accept these conditions. In accordance with the Bucharest agreement, both Adrianople and Eastern Frakia remained in Turkish hands; while the boundary, instead of Rodosto or the Enos-Midia, was drawn, in accordance with the treaty with Turkey on September 9, along the shore of the Maritsa as far as Demotiki. Western Frakia, with all the ports of the Aegean Sea which Bulgaria had claimed, including Salonika, went to Greece. All of Macedonia up to the watershed between the rivers Vardar and Struma (with the exception of Strumitsa) was awarded to Serbia. Rumania extended her boundary southward into Dobrudja, occupying Turtukaia and Balchik. As is already known, Austria was on the point of taking advantage of this situation by dealing a "final" blow to Serbia, and turned to her Allies for help. She was stopped only by Italy's and Germany's refusal.

So far, we have reviewed only the crude, bare facts here. But what, essentially, had happened? How did it happen that Bulgaria so rapidly shifted from the role of instigator to the role of victim of all the other Balkan ambitions? A not entirely accidental circumstance placed me in the position of investigator and gave me the opportunity of giving exact answers to these questions.

In July of 1913, the Education and Information Section of the Carnegie Endowment for International Peace decided to organize an "international investigatory commission" to study, on the spot, the origins and the methods of the Balkan Wars with the aim of fostering "the replacement of violence by conciliation and justice in the regulation of international disagreements." This task was entrusted to the senator Baron D'Estournelles de Constant, chairman of the French branch of the Carnegie Institute, participant in both Hague Conferences of 1899 and 1907 and a well-known pacifist. D'Estournelles did not take part personally in the trip to the Balkans but transferred the chairmanship and the roles of treasurer and speaker to a deputy from Lyon, Justin Godard. The international make-up of the commission was assured when various other persons agreed to participate, including Professors Pashkovsky and Schücking from Germany, Professor Redlich from Austria, Professor Datton from the United States, the journalist, Brailsford, from England, and the writer of these lines from Russia. We, of course, did not go as official representatives of our states, but as people capable of dealing with public opinion. The mishaps which befell this commission began even before it reached its destination. The German professors backed out under obvious pressure from above; Pashkovsky was forbidden from the outset to participate, while Schücking got as far as Belgrade and turned back, believing a report that the commission had broken up. The Austrian professor, Redlich, restricted himself to "advice," to which none of us listened. Four of us reached Belgrade: the old man, Datton, a respected pedagogue and professor at Columbia University; Godard, the acting chairman, a vivacious and energetic man of conviction; and Brailsford and myself, the only active participants on the commission who were acquainted with the aspirations and the languages of the Balkan peoples. It was the two of us who became the objects of future persecution. In Belgrade, Pašić refused to receive the commission which included such an *ennemi déclaré* of Serbia as Miliukov. The commission held a conference and decided that it was a single unit and that it could only work together. Then they suggested that we leave Belgrade, which we did, riding out on the early morning train to Salonika. In the evening, before our departure, I became the object of a specially arranged demonstration. Several of my Serbian friends came to me in our Hotel Rossiia to say good-bye. We were sitting downstairs in the restaurant when the demonstrators, mostly patriotic youth, took their places around us at separate tables. At a prearranged signal, crude shouts and sharp words rang out against the "enemy" of Serbia. To my great delight, my friends did not stand for it. The Montenegrin, Venovich, whom I knew from Petersburg, jumped up on a chair and delivered a heated speech, proving my tried friendship to Serbia by my protest over the annexation of Bosnia and Herzegovina. After him, Professor Liuba Jovanović got up and began explaining to the youths my position of political radicalism. A pause followed which my friends took advantage of to whisper to me that it was not safe to remain any longer; and they led me to my room. I felt the bitterness of the unwarranted insult and of the impossibility of explaining myself properly to the youths. Early in the morning, we all left for Salonika. This was my last visit to Belgrade.

We arrived in Salonika on August 14, 1913, where they left us in peace for a few days. This was, of course, inconsistent and I recalled the verdict from Krylov's fable: "drown the pike in the river." I now understood why Pašić had hastily proclaimed me "an enemy." Among the Bulgarian colony of Salonika I was a trusted friend, and from here, the threads of my contacts reached out to all the cities of Macedonia. From everywhere there came evidence from witnesses showing what means the Serbs were using to change rapidly, Bulgarian Macedonia into Serbia. Of course, the general picture was clear to me even before. Here, the picture blossomed out with a large collection of documents and evidence from witnesses which went far beyond the limits of our immediate goal: investigation of violations of the rules of war. My data testified to the fact that the war itself had gradually come to be inevitable. I summarized these data in the introductory chapter to the commission's report, and here I will dwell only on those main features, which make all the others comprehensible.

The original aim of the war was liberation from the Turks, and the Turkish population was the first to suffer at the hands of the liberators. Turkish villages were burned down; Moslems became the first victims of the atrocities; and those who survived, fled. The commission members saw thousands of them packed around Salonika, without shelter of any kind, under the open sky, without food and without any real hopes of resettlement. Then began the clashes between the Christians themselves. Since the main area of these clashes was Macedonia, it was the native Bulgarian population that became the victim of the atrocities, while the guilty parties were the Serbs and the Greeks. As soon as the upper lid of Turkish authority was thrown off, the age-old fight between the Christian peoples was uncovered—that same struggle which I had observed as early as the end of the nineteenth century. The only difference this time was that the troops which occupied Macedonia came to the aid of the Serbian and Greek minorities. There was a moment of elemental, common enthusiasm for the liberators. The Bulgarian revolutionaries, the "Komitaji," came down from the mountains into their villages and summoned the population to greet the liberators "with laurels of victory" and "to strew the path of their glory with flowers." Alas, this moment passed quickly, and the "Komitaji," the members of the secret Bulgarian "inner organization," were the first to be subjected to persecution. In almost every Bulgarian village there was some kind of a "Serboman" or "Grekoman" who knew the inner Bulgarian relations much better than the previous Turkish authorities. These were the numerous patriot-informers. Later, the struggle became more difficult; it was directed against the village teacher and priest, who were always suspected of having contact with secret organizations. The Bulgarian schools were closed and used as lodgings for the occupying troops. The priests and bishops were forbidden to perform services in Bulgarian, and, in general, they were prevented from keeping in touch with their flocks. As the occupying troops moved further into Macedonia, all of this became systematized by the occupying authorities. The task of converting the Bulgarian population into Serbian or Greek was openly announced. Unacquainted with the local propaganda, the officers and soldiers were surprised when they had to explain themselves in a foreign tongue to the Bulgarian population. They assured them that these "Bulgarophones" had previously spoken Serbian and Greek and that they had only recently learned Bulgarian under the influence of Bulgarian propaganda in the schools and churches. The conclusion directly followed: namely, to force them to return to their previous language and nationality. Such orders were, in fact, given, and since disobedience was threatened with violence, the occupied localities gradually adopted the new official appearance. This metamorphosis took place especially in 1913.

But where were the Bulgarians? According to the treaty—which was, it is true, little known to the public—the Bulgarian troops, numbering 100,000, were supposed to take part in the liberation of Macedonia and in the "co-dominion" over it. In actual fact, they were not in Macedonia, but in the main theater of the war with the Turks. Even the fifteen thousand-man corps of Macedonian volunteers, instead of preserving the rights of their compatriots, were billeted on the Gallipoli Peninsula. From there, complaints were heard that Bulgaria had switched from a war of liberation to a war of conquest. There was an element of truth in this, but it should still not be forgotten that the common aim of the war was victory over Turkey, and the main role in this struggle, for geographical and strategic reasons, was played by Bulgaria. True, the Serbs also sent an auxiliary force. Was Macedonia completely forgotten during this time? The Bulgarians, above all, had assumed the inviolability of the treaty which had been made with the tsar's arbitration. But as the Serbian and Greek occupation force became stronger, the situation changed. The new occupiers began to demand changes in the treaty and, later, simply did not bother about the treaty at all. They argued: Bulgaria had taken possession of Adrianople, while Serbia and Montenegro had been deprived of an exit to the Adriatic. Since this matter is linked to Russia's role, we shall return to it presently. At any rate, neither the one side nor the other wanted to repudiate voluntarily what it had already managed to gain. The knot was tied, and it could only be cut by force. Both sides prepared to do just that.

The whole course of this process became clear to me in detail precisely during the days of the commission's stay in Salonika. Brailsford and I divided up the work between us: I collected the data on Serbo-Greek-Bulgarian relations in Macedonia, while he collected material on the Greek-Turkish relations. He managed to visit several places where particularly notable atrocities had been committed. I had no great need to take these trips around the country, since at my fingertips, I had the central headquarters for collecting evidence and documents from witnesses. This situation of tense work continued only for a short time—for only as much time as was needed for the Serbian authorities to contact the Greek authorities. Already on August 18, the governor of Salonika transmitted an order to the commission to leave Salonika. I was mentioned in the order, but the main "enemy" of Greece turned out to be Brailsford, a participant in the struggle for the liberation of Crete, and persona non grata for the Athens government. We had to get ready to leave. Only two members of our commission, Godard and myself, took part in the next leg of our trip: Greece. In addition, we decided to split up. As a person, he was not formally under suspicion; and after our arrival in Athens, he was supposed to settle in one of the best hotels, befitting the dignity of the commission chairman. Disembarking from the boat, I decided to stay in Piraeus, in some small hotel so that I could go to him each day and confer with him.

Thus several days passed, and no one bothered us. I must admit that since it was impossible to continue our work, I devoted these days to purely tourist activities. I had never been in Athens before this, and it was with special freshness that I observed the magnificent colors of the Athenian sky, the view of Gimett and the spectacle of Salamin. I was mainly attracted, of course, by the Acropolis and the other remains of ancient Greece. Unexpectedly, in the Athens Museum I discovered a magnificent collection of sculpture, especially women's heads done in the Ionian style, a style with which I was not familiar. It was a real artistic feast.

It did not last long, however. One fine morning on the way from Piraeus to Athens, I stumbled across my own name in a Greek paper. The paper reported that the well-known "enemy of Greece," Miliukov, was now in Athens. In the evening, when I returned to Piraeus, the proprietor of the hotel announced to me that he could not keep such an "enemy" at his hotel, and he suggested that I find lodgings elsewhere. I wandered through the narrow streets of Piraeus, and I found somewhat poorer lodgings in a hole for sailors, where newspapers were not read. I could have stayed there longer, but Godard and I decided that there was nothing more for me to do there. I proposed traveling on alone to Turkey in order to make use of my former Young Turk acquaintances and then to meet Godard (and Datton) at the last point in our wanderings, Sofia. We decided to do it that way. I took the next boat, traveled the familiar route across the straits, and got off in Constantinople.

Talaat, to whom I was bound by memories of the heroic and triumphant months of the Young Turk revolution, was minister of internal affairs. He remembered our long talks in the "Crystal Hotel" in Salonika and received me in a very friendly manner. He knew the aim of my visit beforehand, and he offered me his own private automobile and his aide-de-camp for trips to wherever I would like to go. Perhaps this was an expression of the old Turkish custom of keeping a watch over one's guest. As it happened, the Turks had almost nothing to hide, and Talaat's gesture—in contrast to the Serbs and the Greeks—was intelligent and understandable. In addition, his Albanian aide-de-camp did not speak any of the local languages, and we somehow managed to make ourselves understood in French.

In Turkey, I was, above all, interested in clarifying the question of Bulgarian "atrocities" during the occupation of Adrianople. With the light hand of Mashkov, the former Russian consul of the old school, whom I knew personally, information about this matter reached the English press and was used by Pierre Loti to create a strong impression throughout the world. Mashkov got material from a Greek source, and it had to be verified on the spot. I was also interested in the question of the nationality of the population surrounding Adrianople. Finally, I had to take a ride to the borders of Eastern Frakia, about which the commission's information was inadequate. I began with the first question, the most exciting of them all. Of course, it turned out that the facts from the Greek source were greatly exaggerated. The city was genuinely a victim of universal plunder and murder in the first two days of the Bulgarian occupation, with the local population, including the Greeks, taking an active part in the plunder. Only on the third day was order restored. A very calm and even-tempered testimony of the days of Bulgarian rule over the city was given in a letter by V. I. Ikskul, who managed the Kaufman nurses' commune during those months. This testimony speaks in favor of the Bulgarians. I cannot remain silent about the one exception, however, concerning the headquarters' extreme negligence toward the prisoners. A large number of them were brought to a deserted island in the Tundzha River where they were left to the whim of fate, without any shelter, in the rain, dirt, and cold of the night. I took pictures of trees whose bark was gnawed away by the prisoners. Hundreds and perhaps thousands perished here from hunger and cholera. The plunder and killings were renewed after the Bulgarians' rapid departure from Adrianople. This time the role of plunderers and torturers was taken by the Turks, who were late in occupying the city and who followed the tracks of the retreating Bulgars. The famous mosque of Sultan Selim suffered a little from the Bulgarian bombardment. In the span of its cupola, this mosque was second only to the Justinian Saint Sofia, and was a creation of the Turkish architect Sinan from the sixteenth century. This time I was able to acquaint myself thoroughly with this remarkable historical monument.

I asked my aide-de-camp to arrange a trip for me through the environs of Adrianople when the people were working in the fields. No matter where I stopped and talked with the peasants, I always spoke with them in Bulgarian. My aide-de-camp pricked up his ears and asked me what we were talking about. I reassured him that it was not about politics.

I still had to visit Western Frakia, but I had no more time; Godard and Datton were already waiting for me in Sofia. I devoted several more days to Constantinople in order to visit my friends in the summer residence of the Russian embassy in Büyükdere and to acquaint myself with their political news. I will return to them later.

Talaat willingly granted my last request—to take me to the Bulgarian border in that same automobile. A telegram was sent to Sofia and it was arranged that a special train would meet me at an appointed place. I could not help noticing that as we approached that place, my aide-de-camp made notes about the location of the bridges we passed. Finally we stopped at the point where Bulgarian officers were waiting for me. They took my baggage and led me across a field to a train which was waiting right here in the field. I was in Bulgaria.

It was already rather late, and I wanted to find accommodations for the night. But there were none here: a sleepless night was in store for me. My arrival was known and a Bulgarian delegation was waiting for me at every big station. I had to get out of the train, listen to their speeches of welcome, and answer them. After everything I had experienced, this was especially touching but extremely tiring. They brought me half-asleep to the capital and settled me in the hotel "Bulgaria." It was August 31 (O.S.) when the abbreviated three-man committee met in Sofia and began its work—two weeks before the signing of the Bulgarian-Turkish peace treaty and a month and a half before the opening of the second session of the Duma. We used ten days of this period for our work in Sofia, and on September 10 the commission went to Paris.

Of course, our work in Sofia was arranged entirely differently than it was in the other three states we had visited. We were not only officially and festively received but the Bulgarians, who were the first ones to raise the question of "atrocities," did not wait for our arrival to prepare material for us. I must admit that all the preparation was done without prejudice and without partisan interest. We were already in a position to pass judgment on this matter because all the ends whose beginnings we had studied met here, and there were no contradictions between the beginnings and the ends. We arrived at the conclusion that in the struggle between the nationalities, not one of them was free from guilt in violating all the rules of the Hague Conventions or in displaying the most primitive savagery on a mass scale. Our work in Sofia only confirmed this conclusion; the only difference was in the extenuating circumstances due to different times and place. Our commission's sessions were open. A significant portion of the documents and testimonies from witnesses were prepared for us beforehand; the rest were delivered immediately on our demand. The preliminary work was done for the most part by my old friend, Professor Miletich; I could not have the slightest doubts of his disinterestedness and his unconditional conscientiousness.

The verdict of the Carnegie Commission had even more significance for the Bulgars, since we found Bulgaria oppressed and humiliated by the treaty of Bucharest. No matter how severe this verdict was, Bulgaria had reconciled herself to it beforehand, since, for her, this was still the voice of acquittal. Moreover, in spite of all the attempts to discredit the work of the commission, it was, after all, the voice of Europe. Of course, not everybody in Bulgaria saw it that way; but all who did see it this way were those who had earlier condemned the "imperialistic" enthusiasm of the higher Bulgarian circles which had made them forget the fate of Macedonia.

On the way to Paris, I sat in one section of the car with Godard, and we exchanged impressions. No matter how horrible these impressions were, I said, we ought at least to take one comfort from them. If a military clash should occur between the more civilized countries of Europe, we would not witness extremes like the ones we had studied. Godard remained silent; then he answered curtly: "I'm not so sure" . . . Alas, at that time I did not suspect that two years would not pass before I would have to summarize for *Rech's Year-book* the literature, which was growing under our light—or heavy—hand, concerning "violations of the rules of war" on the part of the civilized states of Europe. I did not suspect that I would again have to enumerate all the paragraphs of the Hague Conventions violated by the belligerents.

Nevertheless, the transition from the boiling cauldron of savage national passions, which had raised worse than animal instincts from the depths of the human soul, to the stale atmosphere of abstract pacifism was too abrupt. I do not want to call it "armchair" pacifism, but I must admit that the worm of doubt which had long been growing in me, received abundant food here. Faith in higher ideals seemed blind; pacifism's facile terminology—a willing delusion of ignorance; the fervor of the sermons—nothing more than professional hypocrisy. It seemed that a great abyss lay between the task we had been given and the report which we brought back. On the one hand, there was the "great step towards conciliation and justice"; on the other hand, there were hundreds of pages dotted with the names of persons and places which no one knew, with numbers, dates, half-literate accusations and confessions which nobody would ever read. . . . It was as if one of us was not entirely serious. Nevertheless, within one year, there appeared a gigantic volume of 500 pages of our *Enquête dans les Balkans*, printed on magnificent paper, with maps and photographs of the "atrocities." Half the volume was devoted to the documents we had collected. The seven chapters of the text were divided between the participants of the expedition. Brailsford, Godard, and Datton wrote one chapter each; the remaining four chapters were mine. We were all merged together and covered with flowers of praise for our lack of prejudice, and "profound gratitude" for our selfless work. On the shelves of the Carnegie publications, this thick volume occupied an outstanding place. My historical part, I think, was translated into Bulgarian.

Returning to Petersburg for the opening of the Duma session, I experienced a not-so-harmless flash of my own pacifism. While the train was stopped in Köln, I stumbled upon Professor Fried's book in the newsstand: *Der Friedenkaiser*. The book left an impression on me. Did not William concede in Algeciras? Did he not also concede in Tangeir? Wasn't his *Weltpolitik* really a policy of peace? And would he not concede now before the European tension which he had created? This possibility continued to confuse my mind right up to the declaration of war, although, of course, it contradicted everything that I am saying now.

Still, my conception of Russia's role in the Slavic question took final shape. I have already traced the process of the emancipation of the Balkan peoples from their traditional Russian tutelage. Now the process had reached the end. The Balkan peoples had freed themselves without Russian help and even in spite of Russia's policy. They showed themselves to be independent not only in the process of liberation but also in the struggle among themselves. Since that time, I found, Russia was freed of the burden of constantly worrying about the interests of Slavdom as a whole. Each Slavic state was now going its own way, protecting its interests as it deemed necessary. Russia, too, in its relations to the Slavs, had to guide itself by its own interests. Russia must no longer fight because of the Slavs. We will see how already in the following few months I tried to apply this conclusion in practice, in connection with those same Balkan events and with their direct continuation.

Before the end of 1913 I had to go abroad again in connection with the same question, the liberation of still another Christian people from the Turkish yoke. This time, the matter concerned the Armenians. In Paris on November 18, 1913, a conference of the Committees of Friends of the Armenian People was held to discuss the project of Armenian reforms and to turn the attention of European public opinion to the terrible plight of the Armenian people. I represented the Russian Committee there, and I had both moral and personal reasons for my action. In spite of the cruel insults which the old Russian administration dealt their national consciousness, the Armenians, of all the Caucasian peoples, remained the most loyal to Russia. They took an active part in all the Russian wars with Turkey; this was understandable, since a good half of the population of the Asia Minor peninsula was Armenian and generally Christian.[37] Also Armenians were politically closer to us than the others. The majority of the Armenian intelligentsia shared the convictions of the Kadets, and their representatives like Adzhemov and Papadzhanov even joined our Duma faction, while the mayor of Tiflis, A. I. Khatisov, represented the same political direction in the Caucasus. In contrast to the European Christians of Turkey, the Turkish Armenians lived far from the eyes of Europe, and their situation was comparatively little known. In the meantime, for forty years, the Turks and especially the Kurds, amongst whom they lived (the Kurds were a savage people living a primitive life, like the Albanians in Europe), systematically raided them as if following the principle that "the solution to the Armenian question lies in exterminating the Armenian people to the last man." The English philanthropists and consuls carefully compiled the numerical totals of the Armenian pogroms—after the pogroms had been carried out—while the English government, in its policy of protecting Turkey, looked at these pogroms through its fingers, as though encouraging them. In the last stretch of this long-suffered road, Russia interfered diplomatically in 1912, and in 1913 I saw the secretaries at the Russian embassy in Constantinople working out a project for uniting the six *vilayets* where the Armenian population[38] was settled into one autonomous province. For his part, the Armenian Katolikos, living in Russian Armenia (Echmiadzin), appointed a special national commission under the chairmanship of the leading Egyptian Armenian, Boğos-Nubar Pasha. The Great Powers, and especially Germany, intervened and the customary redoing of the Russian project was begun in the manner desired by Turkey, which again talked about introducing its law of 1880 concerning the *vilayet*. On the other hand, the representatives from seven powers, meeting in Paris on November 17 with the Committee Asie Française, discussed the question of pressuring Turkey by refusing loans. Our conference, under the chairmanship of Boğos, was supposed to work through all this material, and from this basis, the idea ripened for creating a "Greater Armenia" out of the six *vilayets*, with the exception of the northern, western, and southern slices, which were populated mainly by Turks. This idea was propagandized among the progressive circles of Europe.

Today it is hard to see how anyone could have defended that plan. It might have seemed that the war with Turkey would make the plan easier to put into effect, but Turkey prevented it with the horrible pogrom of 1915. A significant portion of the Armenian population of the six *vilayets* was annihilated by the Kurds; the rest—old men, women, and children—the Turks decided to resettle in Mesopotamia. A pitiful remnant of the Armenian population reached it; the majority died along the way from cold, exhaustion, disease, Southern heat, and dampness. Out of a million people, only a few hundred thousand saved themselves in Russian Armenia. The very idea of a "Greater Armenia" clashed with the claims of the Great Powers on parts of Asia Minor territory, while the outcome of the Great War buried the Armenian question altogether.

The Loss of Russia's Influence in the Balkans

IN THE PREVIOUS CHAPTER I described the tense situation into which Europe was led by the preparations of the Balkan peoples for a general war against Turkey, and then, after October 1912, by that war itself. As noted above, November was the moment of greatest tension—a tension which threatened to break out into a European crisis as a result of all the unexpected victories of the Christian peoples. I returned from my trip with Crane in time for the opening of the Duma on November 18, 1912, at the height of the struggle between the peaceful and militant camps in Petersburg. The peaceful attitudes were strengthened by echoes from the meeting between the tsar and William in the Baltic Port. The militant attitudes emanated from Sukhomlinov's department which the tsar supported in questions of Russian armament. The most striking episode in this internal conflict is related in Kokovtsov's memoirs. At the time we had no way of knowing about it, but I will make use of it now. On November 9, Sukhomlinov decided to take advantage of his carte blanche (which I mentioned before) and carry out a mobilization. Let me mention that in accordance with the idea behind this carte blanche, mobilization was equivalent to a declaration of war by Russia against Austria and Germany. Everything was ready and the telegrams had been sent when Nicholas II began to doubt the very possibility of undertaking such a grave measure without even informing the ministers. He scheduled a special session under his chairmanship for November 10. Sukhomlinov was supposed to forewarn the participants of the session, but he did not do this, and his enterprise, already underway, was disclosed only at the session itself. Naturally, Kokovtsov, the chairman of the Council of Ministers and an eternal adversary of Sukhomlinov, sounded the alarm. Nicholas tried to calm him down. "This is not a matter of war, but a simple precautionary measure involving the reinforcement of the ranks of our weak army on the (Austrian) border. I do not plan to mobilize our units against Germany, with whom we maintain the most friendly relations, and Ger-

267

many causes us no alarm at all, while Austria is definitely hostile towards us." Kokovtsov tried to show that a separate step on the part of Russia violated the military convention with France, thereby freeing France from her obligations; while in the war which would result from Russian mobilization, Germany, of course, would support Austria as part of her treaty obligations. He proposed, as a way out, to extend the length of military service by half a year without canceling the next recruitment; thus the size of the army would be increased without a declaration of mobilization. It was discovered that Sukhomlinov, having declared the mobilization, planned to take a leave of absence and travel abroad to visit his sick wife, and that armament orders had been given to factories inside the Austrian boundaries. Such a degree of carelessness horrified Sazonov who turned to Sukhomlinov after the session with bitter reproaches. Sukhomlinov was not perturbed. He answered in his "infantile prattle," and with his usual "nonchalant tone," that there was "no harm at all" in mobilization since "we cannot escape war in any case, and it is better for us to begin it earlier. . . . It is your (Sazonov's) and the Council chairman's (Kokovtsov's) belief that we are unprepared, while the sovereign and I have faith in the army and know that only good can come to us from war."

In the Duma we had no idea that the situation was so acute; but we knew well that the disagreement over funds between the minister of finance and the minister of war had begun as far back as the end of the Third Duma. Given his view on the royal prerogative in military affairs and in diplomacy, the tsar had not informed either Kokovtsov or Sukhomlinov of his intentions, and even in his memoirs, Kokovtsov was unable to reconstruct the situation completely. The events in the Balkans alone raised the question of war and peace; and among the rightist ranks, extreme nationalistic attitudes were coming to the fore. Some of the ministers—Rukhlov, Krivoshein, Shcheglovitov, and, later, N. Maklakov—shared these extreme nationalistic views, and in the Council of Ministers, speeches were heard on the necessity "of having more faith in the Russian people," whom Kokovtsov did not know, and in "the age-old love of the people for their motherland." Kokovtsov could counter them all he pleased with facts about the army's poor supply system and the lack of preparation of the army's leaders. For the Duma, Sukhomlinov's personality was clear—his senile slackness, his complete lack of information in practical questions, his extreme carelessness in using the funds which had been generously extended to his department. All this was cloaked by demonstrations of patriotism and servility before the tsar. Kokovtsov himself was forced to admit that the tsar was on the side of those ministers named above. The tsar continued to maintain that "the matter concerns only Austria" and "there is every reason to rely on the support of Emperor William"!

The thoughtlessness, lack of information, and the conceit of this obscurantist nationalism, disclosed in the almost unbelievable episode recounted by Kokovtsov, apparently were typical not only of Sukhomlinov but of the entire ruling clique and the tsar himself. They simply did not take note of the impressions made by the Christian victories over the Turks or of Emperor William's new mood. The sobering-up was to take place when the peaceful negotiations began in London, where Austria's resistance was displayed. Regarding Russia, this resistance was expressed in Austria's definite proposal for demobilization. On February 26, 1913, an agreement was made, according to which Russia was to release 350,000 of the soldiers called up in 1910, while Austria was to disband part of her mobilized army not needed for "internal" difficulties. In a characteristic manner the Russian communication on this agreement appeared with an addition: "from the discussions with the Vienna cabinet, it has become apparent that Austria-Hungary has no aggressive intentions towards her southern neighbors (that is, Serbia)." This was the same formula which Germany had proposed after Potsdam and which Sazonov did not want to use. Now Austria herself did not wish to repeat it: apparently, Austria was indeed "entertaining aggressive views."

Now, at last, they understood in Petersburg, too, what Kokovtsov had vainly been trying to make them understand in November 1912: that it was impossible to wage a struggle with Austria without the risk of dragging in Germany, thereby turning the Balkan dispute into a European conflagration. Russia's Balkan policy had to adjust to the new situation. She had to retreat. The first experiment in this kind of retreat involved Nikolai Chernogorsky. On March 29—four days after Bethmann-Hollweg's speech, and eleven days after the Montenegrin "hero's" refusal to submit to the demand of the Great Powers—there appeared a government communication, sharply condemning his behavior. The Montenegrin prince, it said, "clearly bases his calculations on dragging Russia and the Great Powers into a European war." This was, perhaps, overdoing it. Nicholas Chernogorsky's "calculation" was more childish. It was naïvely expressed by his daughter, Militsa, who, mediating through Kokovtsov, said that the tsar should leave Skutari to her father: "Well, why should we pose the question so one-sidedly? If Russia states her desire insistently . . . , then Austria wouldn't dare threaten war." By then, this kind of objection had lost its force. Russia, it said further in the communication of March 29, "did not stint on aid and sacrifice for her brothers; but she is not obliged always and in all cases to fulfill all their wishes and demands. . . . The government must carefully weigh its decisions so that not one drop of Russian blood should be spilled except as the interests of the motherland demand it." The Montenegrin "eagle," however, would not bend even before this suggestion. He continued the struggle and, on April 10, obtained the surrender of Skutari. Only in the face of a direct threat from Austria-Hungary and the collective demand of the Powers did he finally retreat and, on April 23, pull out of the fortress.

Also in March of 1913, the tsar at last withdrew Sukhomlinov's power to begin war with Austria whenever he would take it into his head to send his 1912 order for mobilization. In his memoirs, Sukhomlinov mentions this with his usual ingenuousness and shamelessness: "The order was canceled because the Tsar feared leaving the final word to the military commander, when at the last moment diplomacy might still be able to find a way out and prevent a catastrophe. From the technical point of view we made a concession to diplomacy, introducing the idea of a preparatory period for war." One reads and cannot believe one's eyes: how close this was to what Sukhomlinov actually did before the catastrophe of 1914.

At any rate, during the spring of 1913, Nicholas II was greatly frightened by William's new mood. In complete secrecy (from everyone except Prince Meshchersky), he decided to retreat along the whole line of his Balkan policy. We now know, from documents which have been published recently, the belated and by then entirely useless step which he took. In May 1913, the three monarchs, Russian, English, and German, were supposed to get together in Berlin for a family festivity: the wedding of William's daughter, Louise, to the duke of Braunschweig. William recorded the tsar's statement in the following words: "He will not put forward any claims to either Istanbul or to the Dardanelles. The Sultan will become the doorkeeper of the Dardanelles, and the English King (George V) will adhere unconditionally to the Tsar's view, which also coincides with the policy of the German Emperor."

But . . . William no longer believed Nicholas! During those same days, (May 6, 1913) he inscribed on Pourtales' report: "*Der Kampf zwischen Slaven and Germanen ist nicht mehr zu umgehen. Er kommt sicher. Wann? Das findet sich.*" On another report from Purtales (May 17) we find an appraisal of the behavior of Nicholas II: "*Halbeiten und Flachmacherei! Es wird nichts zwischen uns mehr werden.*"

Under such influences, the Balkan peoples spent months fighting for their interests, no longer on the battlefield, but around the green tables of the London Diplomatic Conferences. It was comparatively easy to be rid of the "eagle" of Black Mountain (Montenegro), who had nourished himself on Russian subsidies and Russian armaments. It was much more difficult to support the claims of Serbia, the chief protégé of Russian diplomacy, proud of its independence, and evoking Austria's special hatred. In both controversial issues—concerning the territory of Albania and an outlet to the Adriatic Sea—Russia refused to risk offering Serbia any kind of strong support. In rapture over the victories of 1912, Serbia was already planning to share this mountainous country with Greece, this country without any definite borders, populated in the center by warlike tribes who preserved their prehistoric way of life, but in the north and south merging with the mixed population of Old Serbia and the pure Greek settlements of Epirus. According to Pašić's "minimal" formula, the approximate border of annexation was to run along the strip between Diakovo and Alessio in the north and Ohrid-Durazzo in the south. In London, however, Austria, together with Italy, cut out of this conglomeration an "autonomous" and, then, an "independent" Albania—a fictitious state with artificial borders. The commissions charged with establishing the borders set about their work but got all tangled up in it; and the borders had to be cut at random. Serbia and Greece protested and mobilized their troops; and Serbia appealed to Russia (September 1913). Austria then presented its ultimatum by demanding the withdrawal of Serbian troops from the north (October 20) and of Greek troops from the south (October 30). Not supported by Russia and only weakly supported by England, both states had to submit to the coercive London decisions.

The saddest thing of all, and leading to a direct loss of Russian prestige, was the resolution of the Serbo-Bulgarian argument over the division of Macedonia. We already know that, having occupied all of Macedonia in 1912, the Serbs did not want to share it with the Bulgarians and demanded a revision of the Treaty of February 29, 1912. On April 17, 1913, the Bulgarians appealed to Russia, requesting the tsar to mediate as provided for in the treaty, but only within the boundaries of the disputed zone. Russia immediately agreed but advised the Bulgarians not to stand on an "irreconcilable and formal" interpretation of the treaty; rather, the Russians advised the Bulgarians to give the Serbs some small additional plots of land from their own part, over and above the "disputed" zone. This spoiled the fruits of the tsar's arbitration beforehand, and Bulgaria stepped up her military preparations. Then, on May 26, the tsar appealed directly to the Bulgarian tsar and to the Serbian king, warning them against "a fratricidal war which could darken the glory that both of them had jointly won" and threatening that "the state which begins the war will be responsible to all of Slavdom for it." The tsar "reserved for himself complete freedom in determining the consequences of such a criminal struggle." But . . . the tsar's word was left hanging in air. Bulgaria agreed—on the condition that the mediation be carried out within the limits of the treaty. Serbia's answer was such that it was not allowed to be printed. Nevertheless, it was taken as a consent to arbitration, and the premiers were invited to come to Petersburg. Bulgaria then demanded that the business be resolved within a seven-day period; and, after the demand was refused, Bulgaria announced on June 12 that she was stopping all negotiations. There followed several days of internal struggle between the supporters of war and peace in both countries. Those favoring peace—Premiers Pašić and Danev—won and prepared to go to Petersburg. In Bulgaria, however, Tsar Ferdinand and General Savov decided behind the cabinet's back to present diplomacy with a fait accompli and began military operations. We already know the sad consequences. The absence of Russian support for Bulgaria in this decisive moment led Ferdinand to disclose openly his pro-Austrian policy. Danev's pro-Russian cabinet was replaced by a cabinet under Radoslavov-Gennadiev, who had only recently and publicly advised Ferdinand to turn away from Russia and to look for support from Austria. In answer to the request for help, Russia only expressed her regrets that Bulgaria had placed herself in a difficult situation, and limited herself to the promise that "excessive humiliation and weakening of Bulgaria will not be allowed." The Bucharest Treaty showed that this royal promise, too, remained merely empty words. Never before had Russian prestige fallen so low in the Balkans. Russia's place in Bulgaria's policy passed to Germany and Austria.

The loss of Russian prestige among the Balkan Slavs was not slow, of course, in having an effect on our position in Turkey. Again I will break the chronology of the story in order not to break the continuity of events. William decided to take advantage of the new turn of events in order to take into his own hands, control of Turkey's military organization. The German general, von der Holtz, was already there as an instructor to the Turkish troops. Now it was decided to replace him by General Liman von Sanders in the role of commander of the First Turkish Corps, quartered in Constantinople. The tsar decided to protest this appointment as an act "equivalent to transferring the entire authority over the Turkish capital and over the Straits to Germany." This protest was supposed to be passed on to the German Government and to William by Kokovtsov, who was returning from Paris to Russia by way of Berlin. Bethmann-Hollweg reacted to Kokovtsov's statement rather sympathetically and promised to change the form of the appointment. The emperor, however, was crude and sharp at the reception in Potsdam on November 19, 1913; he even contended that the tsar had already agreed to the measure which had been taken, during the Potsdam meeting in November of the year before (Nicholas later denied this). "Is this an ultimatum or a friendly transmission of the views of your emperor?" asked William. Kokovtsov, of course, tried in all possible ways to soften the form of his statement. This, however, did not prevent William from making the following announcement during breakfast (he did not announce it directly to Kokovtsov, but to the director of the credit office, Davidov, who was sitting next to him): "I must tell you directly: I see an imminent conflict between two races—the Romano-Slavic and the German—and I cannot help but warn you about it. . . . You assume that Germandom will be the first to begin hostile actions. If war is inevitable, then I consider it totally unimportant who begins it. . . . I am very concerned by events and I am telling you quite definitely that war may become simply inevitable. . . . Believe me, I am exaggerating nothing." The tsar listened rather indifferently to Kokovtsov's report of this matter, for during the interval he had already decided to part with his minister. Kokovtsov's pessimism coincided with Nicholas' already well-known mood—and at the very end of December 1913, the tsar instructed him to examine Sazonov's special note on the Turkish question together with the ministers of internal affairs, army, navy, and the head of the General Staff. I learned about this conference only in 1916, in a distorted form, from our allies. Both the note and the conference are very interesting as a finale to the peaceful attitude on the Balkan questions which, as I noted earlier, prevailed throughout 1913. In a typical manner, the minor and major keys became interlaced here—so difficult was it to move away from the traditional view. As before, a compromise decision was formulated such that the preservation of a weak Turkey would be favorable to Russia, but only until Turkey's final collapse. Until that time (this was the new part of the formula), Russia was to prepare herself by means of negotiations with France and England and by making an outline right now "of realistic measures" to be taken from our side. Sazonov even made casual mention about launching an invasion of the Bosphorus—about which much had then been written and spoken in the Naval Department—the only stipulation being that the operation was a complex one and required a long preparation. Sazonov, however, laid special stress on the necessity of occupying "strategic points" on the border with Turkey—Trabzon and Bayezit. Chairman Kokovtsov categorically declared that in the given situation, any exacerbation of the Turkish question was ex-

tremely dangerous in view of "the closeness of an armed clash, for
any reason at all," on the part of Germany. He put to a vote the
blunt question: Do we or do we not want to draw nearer to war?
The question being posed in that way, everyone, including Sukhomlinov, answered negatively. It was decided not to raise any questions
or conduct any negotiations with our allies on these themes, but to
wait out "the general course of events in Europe." Documents published later describe the course of the conference and its results in a
somewhat less smoothed-over form. If Kokovtsov considered war "the
greatest catastrophe for Russia," then Sukhomlinov and Yanushkevich "categorically declared that Russia is completely ready for a
fight, one against one, against Germany, not to mention a clash with
Austria." The conclusion, recorded in the minutes of the conference,
reads: "In the event that France's and England's cooperation with
Russia in joint operations cannot be assured, then it is not considered
possible to resort to measures of compulsion which might lead to
war with Germany." Given such a formulation, the initiative for
"operations" is assumed to belong to Russia, while "cooperation" is
expected from her allies. The "operation" referred to the occupation
of several points in Asia Minor (for England and France—Smirna and
Beirut), while the immediate aim of cooperation was put forward as
the liquidation of the still undecided question concerning the "command" of General Liman von Sanders in Constantinople. It was foreseen, however, that as a result of Germany's intervention, there was
a possibility that "the solution to this problem will be transferred to
our western border with all the consequences that derive therefrom."
. . . Shrouding all these plans in secrecy was evidently the result
of Kokovtsov's objections, and not Sazonov's; probably the tsar himself strove for this outcome, scheduling this conference under his own
chairmanship. Only a few weeks separate the conference of December 31, from Kokovtsov's dismissal on January 29, 1914. The Russian
battle chariot entered the new and decisive year with dimmed lan-
terns, but also with the chief factor for peace removed from government.

The Fourth Duma

The Position of a Historian Memorist

WHEN MY YOUNGER BROTHER AND I were very small children, we, like all children, grew very rapidly, unaware of our own growth. A certain time interval was necessary in order to notice it; and in order not only to notice but to measure the difference, we were taught to stand by the wall on some annual holiday and to make a notch marking our height. The years passed, and the notches rose higher and higher; we grew a part of an inch, an inch and more, without much outward change in appearance. Then our growth became slower, while the changes were greater. At first, old acquaintances who saw us from time to time said: "My, how much you have grown!"; later, they began to say: "You haven't changed at all"; and finally, when the changes went the opposite way, they consolingly remarked: "You look younger." This comparison comes to me now that, in the course of my story, I turn from the Third Duma to the Fourth. In public life, especially when you take part in it yourself, the changes from day to day seem negligible—all the more so if you do not know where they are leading. Only later, from the heights of what has already been achieved, you notice that the changes were going on all the time without stopping, and you mark the growth— or the decay. The observer on the sidelines—especially if he is an inveterate historian—connects the notches and traces the curve, either ascending or descending, or both, as we saw in the Third Duma. But, did he notice the course of these curves at the time they were unfolding from day to day, or only when he marked and then connected the points into one continuous line, perhaps many years after the changes had occurred?

In this respect, the position of a historian memoirist necessarily differs from that of an ordinary observer. With the latter, the notches are either not made or are more or less forgotten, and fresh events come unexpected. The former might say that he foresaw everything.

Conscientiousness, however, requires him to admit that in his time there was much that he did not know, and his notches, far from merging into a continuous line, seemed to him a broken row of dots. How are these dots distributed along the final curve after everything, or at least everything important, has become known? With the depth of understanding he has achieved over time, does he not, himself, see these past events in a different light than he saw them when they were occurring—even though these events were the object of his observation at that time, or even the reason for his actions?

Here we come to the real *cas de conscience* for the historian memoirist. Does he not introduce a subjective element into his evaluation? Or was it only in the past that he introduced it, while now he desires to be objective? He necessarily sees many things more clearly, but does he see them in the same light as before? If he takes it upon himself to describe the past in which he was not only a witness but also a participant, then should he or should he not bring into the present description his clearer understanding? Or should he veil his story under the cloak of his previously incomplete knowledge?

For the sake of complete objectivity I have not wanted to conceal either from myself or from the reader the difference between the one and the other. I have purposely tried to stress the horizons of my previously limited outlook which gradually broadened as the overall curve was traced. To the extent that these limits existed, I made myself an object of my narrative. It was easier for me to do this because, in general, my understanding of the events which were occurring did not change. Precisely for this reason it far from always coincided with the general understanding, and gave me in my time a certain freedom of choice and decision, which was not always favorable for actions in all varieties of circumstance, as behooves the politician. In this sense, even acting like a politician, I remained faithful to my calling as a historian. That is why, now, at a great distance from these events, I am not forced to change my positions; I have merely to enlarge my understanding of them and to make my explanations of them more precise. I must confess to the new elements in my description; I can not deny them. Nevertheless, I think I am correct when I maintain that this is a deeper understanding and not a denial of the past. It is only a result of the habit of linking facts into one whole and searching for the casual relationships.

I am forced to make this admission by the fact that, now, turning away from all these descending or ascending curves, the very contour of the curves breaks sharply, and the difference between my understanding of events then and now runs the risk of becoming greater than before. In this stage, too, I shall attempt to render an account to myself and to the reader of that abrupt change from possible "evolution" to actual "revolution," in the confines of which I, as a political figure, remain, but as an historian would not want to be confined. Was I successful in this? It is not for me to judge; I have frequently been treated as a memoirist desiring to introduce his subjectivism into history. I have written much about this latest period, perhaps more than about anything else, adopting my own positions here, too, in my efforts to remain true to myself, and, therefore, objective. They will judge, whose task it will be to trace the curves of the future.

From the Third Duma to the Fourth

STOLYPIN'S MURDER on September 2, 1911,[39] was the natural climax to that stage in the history of our domestic politics represented by the Third Duma. If we cannot place a sufficiently distinct notch here, it is above all because the short intermezzo of Kokovtsov's chairmanship somewhat obscured the political significance of the new change. It may have seemed that the transition from the Third Duma to the Fourth was a simple continuation of what had been established during the preceding five years. We already know, however, that nothing had been "established"; and it was only the internal struggle between the supporters of the old and the new order that "continued." With the appearance of the Fourth Duma, this struggle entered a new phase. At first, one could not predict that this stage would be the last, for there was still no evidence of that third factor, which bent the outcome of the struggle in a direction opposite to the one pursued by the government. This factor, which decided the argument between the country and the government, was the war.

Setting this aside for a moment, it was, nevertheless, possible to foresee that in the Fourth Duma the struggle between the autocracy and the people's representatives would be waged under different conditions from those of the Third Duma. The Third Duma saw the last attempt to establish at least the appearance of some sort of balance between the opposing forces. In the Fourth Duma, this facade disappeared, and the struggle moved out into the open. In the Third Duma, the government took the offensive; society was weakly organized and could only defend itself, barely holding the positions it occupied and seeking a compromise with the government. The essence of the change in the Fourth Duma was the fact that compromise turned out to be impossible, and lost all meaning. Together with it, the middle currents representing it also disappeared. The "center" vanished, and with it the fictitious government majority. Two opposing camps now stood openly against each other. The members of the representative institution divided themselves between the two camps, which became more differentiated as time went on. It is difficult to say how this struggle would have ended had the adversaries been left to themselves. It was not impossible that the party desiring to return to the old order might have won and achieved its plans. But then the third factor, the war, interfered and, most important above all, carried the struggle beyond the walls of the Duma. This is the fundamental difference between the transitional role played in the social conflict by the Third Duma, and the role of the Fourth Duma. In the Third Duma, the struggle was carried on mainly within the limits of the representative institution. The country listened attentively to it, drew conclusions, and united around its slogans, in theory though not in practice. In the Fourth Duma, the struggle went beyond these limits. The country got the opportunity to organize itself independently. It put forward its own slogans, supported the militant attitudes of the Duma community, and together with the Duma, went over to the offensive. The government, in its blindness, let the moment slip when, for the price of substantial reforms, it might still have been able to effect a new compromise—no longer in the interests of victory, but in the interest of its very existence. Such is the complex political picture which developed in the Fourth Duma and which excludes any comparison between this Duma and its humble predecessor.

It may be that the war was not a deciding factor, since the process of political differentiation which had begun earlier ("ascending curve") continued by itself. It was the fundamental trait which, from the very beginning, distinguished the Fourth Duma from the Third, irrespective of the future events. This was reflected above all in the course and the outcome of the elections to the Fourth Duma.

It was more or less known that the question of government influence on the elections amounted, primarily, to the question of government subsidies. V. N. Kokovtsov subsequently reported the precise figures. Stolypin had begun the preparations as early as 1910 by demanding from the minister of finance four million rubles for the elections. "All that I could do," said Kokovtsov, "was to hand over the sum in installments, having reduced it indiscriminately by ordinary haggling to a little more than three million. I was able to stretch this figure over the three years 1910–12." After he became chairman of the Council of Ministers, Kokovtsov became interested in finding out where these sums were going. "Everyone came here," he remarks, except for the Kadets and some of the Octobrists. But it was the right wing that predominated "indivisibly and peremptorily." "There was Markov II with his *Kurskaia Byl'* and *Zemshchina* swallowing up 200,000 rubles a year; the notorious Doctor Dubrovin with his *Russkoe Znamia*; there was also Purishkevich with the most varied sorts of undertakings—includ-

ing even the Academic Union of Students; there were representatives
from the Assembly of Nationalists, Zamyslovsky, Savenko, a few
bishops with their enlightenment unions, the *Listok Pochaevskoi
Lavry* and finally, the leading representatives of the Nationalist party
in the Duma." The minister of internal affairs, Makarov, agreed with
Kokovtsov regarding the "pointlessness" of these expenditures but he
did not want to stop them only eight months before the elections.
True, the Nationalists refused the subsidies after December 1911—
after the opposition had raised the question of "shady money." Others,
however, demanded even more. In 1912 the demands increased.
Markov II and Purishkevich promised Kokovtsov "to surpass his bold-
est expectations" regarding the future composition of the Duma, if he
would not be stingy and give them . . . a million (the precise figure
was 960,000 rubles—in order to flatter the minister's thriftiness). When
he was refused, Markov II threatened: "You'll not get the sort of Duma
we would have given you for such an insignificant sum." In September of that year (1912) the question was discussed at a meeting of
fourteen to fifteen governors who had come to Petersburg. Their information was far from pleasing, which was all the more reason for
giving them more freedom to exert local influence. Kokovtsov only
insisted on their not resorting to Kryzhanovsky's old device of arbitrarily shuffling the electoral congress. He split once and for all with
Makarov, who entrusted the conduct of the elections to his bureaucrat,
Kharuzin. And what a campaign this was! Everyone who was the
least bit suspect politically was unceremoniously eliminated from
participation in the elections. Whole categories of people were deprived of their electoral rights or of the possibility of participating in
the elections. The land captains were present at the elections. Undesirable elections were annulled. Preelection meetings were not permitted and it was forbidden even to speak, write, or print the names of
undesirable parties. The electoral congresses were divided into arbitrary groups in order to create an artificial majority. The entire first
period of the election of the first-stage representatives was passed in
the dark. The small landowners were absent almost to a man; on the
other hand, on instructions from the clerical authorities, the clergy
was mobilized and turned out to be the masters of the situation. In
forty-nine provinces, out of 8764 representatives, 7142 were clergymen, and only for the sake of avoiding scandal, it was forbidden to
send more than 150 clergymen to the Duma; moreover, they had to
vote for the government candidates everywhere.

The next stage, that of electing the electors, was carried out more
rationally although all the devices of political pressure were employed. Only in the cities—and especially in the five big cities with

their separate representation—was open public influence on the elections possible. Here deputies came through who were famous for their oppositional views, and the Octobrists were outvoted (at the same time they were also outvoted on the right). It would be absolutely impossible to draw anything near a complete picture of the organized coercion at these elections. But what were the results? Let us glance at the comparative table of party groupings in the Third and Fourth Duma.

At first glance, the difference was not so great—with the exception of the transfer of votes from the Octobrists to the rightists (thirty-five to forty) and the enlargement of both opposition parties at their expense (plus fifteen). In reality, not only the moral significance but also the actual significance of these changes are quite great. Together with the Octobrists, the rightists still comprised a majority (283 instead of the 278 in the Third Duma). But would these groups work together? In the election for Duma chairman, they immediately came to grips with each other. The rightists demanded political agreement on all Duma questions. The Octobrists refused and made an agreement with the opposition to put up Rodzianko as a candidate. Rodzianko was elected 251 to 150. The political significance of this choice was underscored in Rodzianko's introductory words: "I have always been and always will be a convinced supporter of the representative system of government based on the constitutional principles granted to Russia by the Great Manifesto of October 17, 1905. Strengthening the foundations of that manifesto should be the first and indisputable concern of the Russian people's representative institution." The same reference to the October Manifesto was inserted by Kokovtsov in the government declaration and repeated once more in the concluding formula of the Progressivists, which was adopted on December 15, 1912, by 132 (Octobrists plus opposition) to 78.[40] After Rodzianko was elected, the rightists and the Nationalists demonstratively got up and left the room. Thus the differentiation toward the left was immediately countered by a differentiation toward the right.

The other outstanding result of the election—the strengthening of the opposition despite all the government pressure—was no less significant. The leading role in the opposition was still reserved for the People's Freedom party. The second curiae of the main cities became inalienable Kadet property. Our list in Petersburg far surpassed all the others, and I could be proud of the fact that I received the largest number of votes in all of Russia—22,700 for the Third Duma, and 18,455 for the Fourth Duma, despite the Poles' demonstrative vote against me, and despite the forcible reduction of the number of voters. The Octobrists received eight to nine thousand votes for the Third

Duma and four and one-half thousand for the Fourth Duma; while the Social Democrats raised themselves from three to five thousand to six to seven thousand, and the Union of Russian People went down from four thousand to one thousand. The preelection struggle against the left competition was extraordinarily easy: we came out armed with full knowledge, and our program did not exclude the practical interests of urban populace; whereas our opponents on the left got wound up in abstractions and verbal rhetoric. In Moscow, the chief sensation of the elections was the defeat of Guchkov in the first curia and the increase of the percent of votes for the Kadets from fifty-five to sixty-two; in the grand total, instead of 75 percent, 88 percent of the voters turned up on the side of the opposition. The rightists were elected only in Odessa and in the first curia in Kiev.

The first victim of the above-mentioned split in the composition and the tasks of the Fourth Duma was the head of government himself, Kokovtsov. On January 29, 1914, he received a rescript secretly prepared long ago announcing his dismissal. Kokovtsov himself realized that his retirement had become inevitable from the moment of his unsuccessful meeting with Rasputin and that it was the fruit of some crafty "intrigue." But this explanation is too personal. Kokovtsov understood that the roots of the change lay deeper than mere intrigue, but he did not wish to dwell on this explanation. His premiership was simply not suited to the task now placed upon the chairman of the government from above. The new "Moor" did the job he was supposed to do, and now he too had to leave in order to make room for the next one. The tsar parted with Kokovtsov with kisses and tears. The first words of the rescript of January 29 read: "not a feeling of hostility, but my long and profound awareness of state necessity" forced the tsar to remove his Moor at this new stage. Then there followed a precise chronological statement. "The experience of the last eight years (that is since 1906) has thoroughly convinced me that the union in one person of the posts of chairman of the Council of Ministers and Minister of Finance or Minister of Internal Affairs is incorrect and inconvenient in such a country as Russia." This date marked the beginning of the tsar's struggle against the "constitution of October 17." This is exactly what the chief inspirer of "intrigue," Prince Meshchersky, the publisher of *Grazhdanin*, had been saying, and these were the same accusations from *Grazhdanin* which Kokovtsov brought to the tsar with a complaint against Meshchersky: "The chairman of the Council is overshadowing the person of the Tsar and is awarding to himself the position of the Grand Vizier." "It is time to put an end to this Western European innovation; it is time for the sovereign to recognize who is his servant and who is the servant of the

Young Turks, the Rodziankos and the Guchkovs." And what does Kokovtsov do? This "Duma lackey," suborned "by applause in the Duma," demands that the "unity of the cabinet" be preserved, creates obstacles to the tsar's will at every step through some sort of legislative rights for the Duma, and refuses all "illegal" demands! Kokovtsov defined two fundamental traits in the empress' character: belief in the inviolability of the autocracy and an inclination toward mysticism. He did not stress, however, that the first was a goal, while the second was only a means. He ignored Alexandra Fedorovna's original advice not to imitate Stolypin. The empress had turned from him, no longer wanted to see him, and deliberately displayed her disregard of him. Already in the summer of 1912, Nicholas had shocked Kokovtsov by suggesting that he change his post to that of ambassador in Berlin, since he would probably not like the new candidate for minister of internal affairs, the governor of Chernigov, N. Maklakov, who had amused the heir to the throne with his famous "leap of an enamoured panther" and who had pleased the royal couple with his talent for mimicking the ministers. Kokovtsov immediately understood that this was "the Empress' wish to get him out of Petersburg." Alien to "big-time politics," he nevertheless considered himself protected and infallible in his own department—finance. But the shadows of the "Rodziankos and Guchkovs" persecuted him. The French ambassador conveyed to his government the rumor that Kokovtsov's dismissal "has been decided on for a long time, because the tsar finds that he subordinates the interests of internal policy too much to his narrow financial considerations." This meant apparently the struggle with Sukhomlinov and the preservation of peace, which interfered with the military and diplomatic prerogatives of the monarch. They deliberately kept Kokovstov away from both areas, for more was involved than a mere struggle against Sukhomlinov's thoughtlessness or against delays in fulfilling military supply orders. The tsar was deceiving Kokovtsov when he told him that he hardly knew the "muzhik," Rasputin, that he did not read Meshchersky's newspaper, that he did not approve of Sukhomlinov. Whether by necessity or willingly, he pursued his line of "the needs of the state" and with a growing impatience endured Kokovtsov's reprimands. His revenge came with the intrusion of the rescript of January 29, 1914, into Kokovtsov's sacred preserve: the Department of Finance, "which can be managed only by a new person" since "it cannot continue any longer in this manner." The reason for this was the same one which Kokovtsov used to explain the success of his financial policy: "the rapid pace of domestic life and the striking increase in the country's economic forces"—"uprecedented prosperity," in Kokovtsov's words. Then there followed tears and kisses and "we part friends."

I have combined here the revelations of Kokovtsov's memoirs with what we knew and at once understood even at that time, but what the tsar's faithful servant either did not completely guess or did not wish to discuss candidly. The choice of his successor exposed once and for all what he left unsaid. The next "Moor," chosen by Meshchersky and "brought out of moth-balls," was I. L. Goremykin.

If it was necessary to conceal the seething passion of prerevolutionary society behind a mask of peace and tranquillity—with the sole aim of deceiving the eyes of the supreme authority and of extending the time of waiting for something to happen by itself—then a better choice than Goremykin could not have been made. Decrepit, not only in years but also in his senile indifference to everything, Goremykin was not looking for power. After his appointment, he himself told Kokovtsov: "I completely fail to understand why I was needed; I resemble an old raccoon fur coat which has been packed away in the trunk long ago and sprinkled with camphor. . . . Nevertheless, they will put the coat back in the trunk just as unexpectedly as they took it out." It was Krivoshein, a very intelligent man who understood the situation better than the majority of those around him, who dreamed up the idea of Goremykin. Subsequently, I was able to convince myself personally of the breadth of his outlook. Kokovtsov was right in his description of Krivoshein: while wishing to direct events, he did not want to bear the responsibility and deliberately remained in the back rows. Goremykin was convenient for him in that he was a vacuum, inert, and would not interfere in any future plans that might be needed. As I had the occasion to find out later, it was absolutely impossible to surprise Goremykin with anything or to rouse him to action. He waved his hand at everything, called it "nonsense," and then settled down on the road like some heavy stone. The greatest mistake in appointing him was that one could not make up the lost time. In the absence of any creative program at all, an interregnum of chaos set in.

There was another feature of the new situation which characterized the transition from the Third Duma to the Fourth—just the opposite of the change in government. Not only the new "Moor" but also the new form assumed by the representative institutions "had done its job" and had to depart from the story into history. Russian society felt the need of stronger excitement than the everyday, routine work of the Duma which was apparently condemned to sterility. The whole of 1913 passed with displays of new independent social activity. The public was not the least interested in the question of how to handle the legislative rubbish left over as a legacy from the Third Duma. On the contrary, society's attention was attracted by public congresses meeting in Kiev, at the same time that the nationalists were vainly trying to raise a fuss over the festive unveiling of a monument to Stolypin. There was an agricultural congress, an urban congress, and finally, the Octobrists' conference which had been long postponed while Guchkov was carrying on so pompously in the Duma. Drowned at the first curia of Moscow, he swam out here and scratched his political itch. Among his faithful followers, he coined a new and effective formula for denying his previous activity: "We are forced to defend the monarchy against those who are the natural defenders of the monarchical principle; we are forced to defend the church against the church hierarchy; the army against its leaders; the authority of government power against the bearers of that power." He even dictated to the congress its concluding resolution about grave upheavals and disastrous consequences which would threaten the country as a result of further delay in realizing the reforms of October 17. We saw a reflection of these attitudes among the Octobrist faction in the Duma; but, alas, they soon came to naught. Rodzianko's second speech at his reelection was colorless; the Duma's legislative activity was equal to that of the State Council.

The high point of public indignation was reached when all the falsehood of the regime, all its personal violence, was embodied in an attempt to level at the innocent Jew, Beilis, the medieval slanderous accusation against a whole people, that of using Christian blood. A nervous excitement gripped even the remotest corners of Russia, when, for thirty-five days, with the encouragement or the direct assistance of the authorities, there unfolded in Kiev a vile picture of perjury, bribed experts, and obliging efforts on the part of the procurator to wring out a verdict of "guilty" from the specially selected, semi-literate peasant jurors. I remember how a group of friends and co-workers gathered late in the evening at the offices of *Rech* and anxiously awaited the verdict. I remember our exultation when the ignorant Russian peasants brought Beilis a verdict of "not guilty."

Of course, all manifestations of public sentiments were accompanied by the police scorpions. During the Beilis trial, 102 penalties were meted out to the press, including the arrest of six editors. One hundred and twenty professional and cultural-educational societies were either closed or declared illegal. In Petersburg, Shingarev and I were forbidden to give a report about the Fourth Duma to the voters, while in Moscow the same kind of meeting, led by the reelected Kadets, Shchepkin and Novikov, was closed by the police. The police also closed down the jubilee session and banquet in honor of the fiftieth anniversary of *Russkie Vedomosti*. I was forbidden to speak on the Balkan question in Ekaterinodar and Mariupol. These are only a few individual episodes from a whole ocean of similar ones. All of it together resembled the prerevolutionary atmosphere and the police reaction to it in 1905.

It was natural that the behavior of our Duma faction, and my behavior in particular, should now take another direction. Given the complete hopelessness of the Duma's legislative work, the preliminary work in the committees was pushed far into the background. Our speeches concentrated on what the country was interested in, that is, on questions of a general political significance and on criticism in the form of interpellations on the government's behavior in Russia's domestic life. I am speaking here of the first two sessions of the Fourth Duma, from the time it was opened on November 15, 1912, to the only meeting of a "special session," that of July 26, 1914, in which the Duma was invited to say its word on the war that had just begun. The following period of Duma activity bears an entirely different character and it must be discussed separately.

First of all, we decided that the time was appropriate for introducing as part of the Duma legislation, the Kadet projects for civil liberties which bore the "stamp" of October 17. This was not difficult since our jurists had prepared excellent texts, which were supposed to have been introduced into the Second Duma, and these texts had been printed. This time, however, introducing them was not a mere demonstration; it was a direct consequence of the above-mentioned demands made by the Octobrists and the opposition together. We were not mistaken: the bill for freedom of the press which I had defended in two meetings of the first session (8, II and 13, II—see the table in Appendix 3) was recognized by the Duma as "desirable" and turned over to committee to be worked out. The same thing happened with the bills for freedom of conscience, unions, and assembly. Only our bill for introducing universal suffrage, which I defended in detail, and which included extending suffrage rights to women, turned out to be indigestible for the Octobrists. After the project was debated at three meetings (27,II; 8,II; and 18,II) it was rejected 206 to 126. Our interpellation on the most important themes of interest to the country met with less success; these themes included abuses at the elections, the Lena events, Rasputin's influence on the Holy Synod and so on. Most of the time they applied the old tactic of putting off the ministers' explanations for many months.

The second part of these sessions of the Fourth Duma passed under Kokovtsov's successor, Goremykin. The new government went over to a direct offensive against the legislative rights of the Duma, and our role, sometimes together with the Octobrists, consisted of defending these rights. Their attacks were usually petty, technical, and not very comprehensible to the country; the session seemed colorless. In the general course of events, however, this struggle itself reflected a heightened tension. We were especially agitated over the infringement of the deputies' freedom of speech when Chkheidze was persecuted, in accordance with Article 129. The Kadet party introduced a proposal not to begin budget discussions until the bill concerning the deputies' freedom of speech was confirmed. I defended this proposal on April 21, 1914. For the first time we had a majority ready to refuse confirmation of the budget; and the Octobrists spoke in a tone unusual for them. Together with Goremykin, N. Maklakov, who openly announced that he was a member of the "Union of Russian People," also pursued this line of struggle. He tried to sneak through a clever theory, according to which the Duma and the Council of Ministers were merely two coordinated organs, above which stood the tsar with complete legislative authority. I spoke against him on May 2, 1914, demonstrating that a whole series of his statements coincided with the Bulygin Duma Act of August 6, 1905, that is, with the decree on a legal-consultative Duma which preceded the October Manifesto.

I will not dwell on my other speeches from this part of the session that I gave in response to statements by the ministers of foreign affairs, justice, public education, and by Goremykin himself. All of it seems so terribly insignificant in the light of the events that followed. I will dwell only on my speech of February 19 in defense of Ukrainian national self-determination—a speech which the famous separatist A. Shulgin subsequently called "beautiful"—only in order to contrast it with my views in 1939. I gave the speech at the request of the Ukrainians themselves to defend them from the attacks of the Kiev Russian Nationalists, who had prohibited the jubilee celebrations in honor of Shevchenko. In order to prepare for this speech, I made a special trip to Kiev where I had long conferences with a group of honored Ukrainian "progressivists." My tactic was to focus on their comparatively moderate demands for "Ukrainianizing school instruction, the right to use the Ukrainian language in judicial and governmental establishments, elimination of restrictions on the Ukrainian press, and improvement in conditions for the legal existence of Ukrainian national establishments." The leaders of the T. U. P.[41] were satisfied with this and agreed to set aside in the future their demand for a "federation" and to exclude "separatism" completely. Only Professor Hrushevsky tried to deceive and hide his real intentions. For my part in the Duma, I maintained that "the true separatists are the Russian nationalists" who deny an independent Ukrainian language and Ukrainian literature and who encourage the government persecutions which have already made the Ukrainian movement shift its center to Austrian territory, where the creation of Ukrainian separatism is a real possibility.

Between the first and second sessions, the Duma's business was interrupted from June 25 to October 15 (O.S.). As related above, I devoted a large portion of this interval to my trip through the Balkans with the Carnegie Commission. In July, I experienced a sorrowful event. My younger brother, Alexei, lay dying in Kislovodsk. We had not seen much of each other, as he lived in Moscow, but we were bound until the very end by the most tender friendship. He joined the Kadet party; and only a short time before that, I had to free him from arrest as a result of an incident which occurred at my Moscow lecture and which testified to the fact that he preserved to the end all the vivacity of his character. He was well-known in Moscow as a specialist in building construction, but even more so as a passionate hunter of fine game, which reputation gave him extensive connections in the leading circles of the old capital. He arrived in Kislovodsk for a rest but caught streptococcus and within a week the disease brought him to the grave. He was consumed rapidly before my eyes, and this change from a state of flourishing health to a coma was terrible to see. In the last days he was interested only in the Balkan questions and asked me about them in detail. Surrounded by friends and relatives, he died in the hands of our mutual friend, Doctor M. S. Zernov.

War

As we have seen, the thirteenth year of the new century ended for Russia with a series of failures in her Balkan policy. Russia left the Balkans, and left consciously, aware of her impotence in supporting her old clients with either her weapons or her moral force. Nevertheless, only half of the fourteenth year had passed when a signal rang forth from the Balkans which caused the rulers of Russia to remember her old, played-out role and return to it regardless of the obvious risk. Instead of the mighty defender of the interests of the Balkan co-religionists, Russia ended up in the second ranks of the defenders of European political interests which were alien to her.

It is impossible to explain by logic alone this blatant contradiction between the task and the fulfillment. Psychological reasons are involved here. The very same Balkan "lessons" made some people march briskly forward; others did not sufficiently understand or appreciate these lessons, and their psychological state lagged behind events.

Austria and Germany, of course, must be placed in the first category. In all the secret information which I made use of above, there was no need to evaluate the significance of the changes which had occurred here. The Austrian position was strengthened in 1913 by Austria's influence over Ferdinand of Bulgaria and Carol of Rumania, as well as by her bloodless victories over Serbia on the Adriatic and in Albania. Her principal and most dangerous enemy was still Serbia, which had become stronger by its acquisition of Macedonia and which, in spite of the obligation of 1909, had not refused to support the aspirations for Serbian unification in the Austrian provinces. "We" or "they" became Berchtold's final policy, and we saw that in 1913 he had already tried to use his alliance with Italy and Germany to settle accounts "once and for all" with the Serbian kingdom. Giolitti refused, and the German ambassador in Vienna, Tschirschky, called Berchtold's policy *unklug and kleinlich:* "stupid" and "petty."

Everything depended on Germany's role; but even the German ambassadors did not immediately notice that William's psychological state had changed, as we have already pointed out. From Bethmann-Hollweg's speeches cited above, however, it is possible to detect the idea behind this change. The victory for "Slavdom" in the Balkans had disrupted the "balance"; the "balance" would have to be restored by a victory for "Germandom" over "Slavdom." In William's inscriptions in the margins of his ambassadors' reports, in 1914, we can continue to trace the character of this change: it included both Nicholas II and Russia. On the twelfth (twenty-fifth) of February 1914, Purtales reported to William on Sazonov's conciliatory attitude. With exclamation marks and question marks, William writes: "Enough! He (the tsar) at any rate does not want and is not able to do anything in order to change (the situation). Russian-Prussian relations, once and for all, are dead. We have become enemies (*Wir sind Feinde geworden*)." The reader will recall the conversation between the emperor and Davidov. In his report dated March 11, Purtales assures the emperor that Nicholas' peace-loving attitude "does not raise the slightest doubt." William sarcastically inscribed: "Just like his complete inconstancy and weakness in the face of any influence at all." Purtales notes that there are militant generals in every army, but it is impossible to predict what will happen in two years unless you possess the gift of prophecy. Now quite angry, William answered: "That gift exists—often with sovereigns, rarely with statesmen, and almost never with diplomats. . . . Better that dear Pourtales had not written this report. . . . We are in that border region between war and politics, that difficult and vague region where diplomats usually get lost. As a military man, according to all my information, I do not doubt in the slightest that Russia is systematically preparing for war against us; and I carry out my policy in conformity with that fact." Twice in that same inscription, he repeats: This is "a matter of race."

And so, William's decision remained unalterable: he is ready to do battle with Russia, and the Russian "racists" and chauvinists gave him plenty of supporting material for his arguments. I mentioned the "Slavic" demonstrations in the Duma and in the streets. In addition, there were Bashmakov's "Slavic dinners," prayer services in the cathedral, etc. We recall that after the meeting in the Baltic Port, Sazonov said, "We have only to take all the necessary steps to prevent our half-baked politicians from dragging us into some kind of a Slavic adventure." Did he keep this line to the end? At any rate, William understood "Slavism" to mean not only the Balkan Slavs, but also the Russian Slavs—precisely at the moment when Russia was repudiating the Slavic "adventures" and was experiencing one defeat after another in her traditional "Slavic" policies. This "question of race" was put forward when the European conflict was ripening, not on the grounds of "race," but on the grounds of William's *Weltpolitik*. I stated the assumption that he tried to reconcile the one with the other, but this reconciliation was obviously artificial. William also had another reason for war against Russia: "Russia is systematically preparing for war against us." In the first place, Russia was not the only one who was preparing: these were the years of a general "armament race." In the second place, William knew the price of the Russian preparations. When on March 12, 1914, Sukhomlinov, in an anonymous article in *Birzhevye Vedomosti,* repeated his boast that Russia was "ready," Pourtales called it "a fanfaronade." All of Russia saw it just the same way and was indignant toward the minister for this provocation. This deliberate confusion of "world" and "Slavic" can be explained only by Germany's calculation of settling accounts with Russia in private—precisely when Russia was "not ready." We shall see that that is just the way it was.

On the other hand, the democratic camp of Europe, counting on Russia's help in case of a world conflict, drew a careful distinction between Russia's Balkan interests and her general European interests. We saw Poincaré's definite statement that France would not fight for these Balkan interests regardless of her treaty obligations. England behaved especially cautiously. Apparently a definite line was drawn between European interests and specifically Russian interests, and this policy, in a certain sense, went along with William's calculation of dealing with Russia, one against one. There was no logic on either side; psychological motives were dominant instead.

Be that as it may, the fourteenth year of the new century did not end happily. The smell of gun powder was in the air. Even people who were not well informed were waiting for something to happen.[42] The Duma session ended and I moved to my Finnish cottage for a summer's rest. On the morning of June 16 (29), I went out to meet the postman, got my mail, unfolded the newspaper and read the report about the murder in Sarajevo of the heir to the Austro-Hungarian throne, Archduke Franz Ferdinand, and his wife. I could not help exclaiming, "This is war!", repeating it to my family when I got back to the house. I vividly imagined the place where the crime occurred, the place where I had taken lonely walks during my visits to Sarajevo. I saw the newly built canal, bordered by narrow quays, always deserted. A hot and cloudless day. The archduke's cortege approached along the outside quay to the narrow bridge which I had often walked across. No crowd of people; two conspirators are walking freely along the parapet of the quay. There is no bodyguard. The archduke's carriage, without hurrying, turns onto the bridge. The conspirators approach from the other side. Two shots, two fatal wounds. . . . Who are they? For me it is clear immediately. They are Serbian patriot-terrorists, whether from Serbia or from Bosnia makes no difference: there are no geographical boundaries for conspiracy. The crime could not have been entirely unexpected. The archduke was disliked at Court, and his trip to the demonstrative maneuvers in Bosnia was not popular. They should have expected, not displays of loyalty from the population, but rather hostile demonstrations. Nevertheless, the heir's bodyguard was left only to the local police. It goes without saying that neither Pašić nor Hartwig arranged the conspiracy; and the honest Austrian bureaucrat, Wiesner, who was specially entrusted with the investigation, could conscientiously report that "there is no evidence indicating the participation of the Serbian government." (Subsequently, some threads were found—Colonel Dimitrievich—but they still did not lead to the top governmental circles.) The removal of the heir to the throne, however, did not meet with any special regret in Vienna. Soon after the beginning of the war, Paul Rohrbach, the famous Russophobe and Slavophobe, candidly stated: "They made us a present of this war, and we can only consider the mortal sacrifice of the Archduke Franz Ferdinand as a stroke of good fortune." It was even greater good fortune for Count Berchtold. At last he got the chance to take care of Serbia once and for all—before Europe's very eyes and with the sympathy, if not the assistance, of Germany. For me, this consequence of the Sarajevo murder was absolutely indisputable and inevitable.

I hurriedly returned to Petersburg. The staff of the Ministry of Internal Affairs was also on vacation; but in that department I was on good terms with Gregory Nikolaevich Trubetskoy, a knowledgeable and thoughtful person and the brother of Sergei and Eugene. We agreed on our impression of the phrase "localization" of the war. The word was dangerous and soon became heretical. It naturally coincided with Count Berchtold's intentions and Emperor William's approval. For the ministry it soon became awkward—and psychologically impossible. Nevertheless, I continued to consider it the only correct word and the only means of preventing Russian intervention in a European war, even if, in spite of us, the war turned out to be inevitable at that moment.

For myself, this outcome—localization of the Austro-Serbian conflict—was the natural conclusion of all my previous observations, which I have summarized above. After all the Balkan events of the preceding years, it was already too late to speak of Russia's moral obligations toward a Slavdom which had begun to stand on its own legs. Russia had to guide herself only by Russian interests, and these, as they were understood in 1913, differed from the interests of the Balkan nations.

After the Carnegie investigation, the horrors of war were especially clear to me. This matter concerned not just the "hundreds of thousands" of Russian people whom Yanushkevich and Sukhomlinov were ready to sacrifice. I do not know whether Izvolsky really wanted his "little war" as they were saying, as Plehve, in his time, had wanted the Japanese war. I did not want to believe it. Given Russia's obvious unpreparedness for war and her internal situation, it seemed to me more than probable that Russia would be defeated; and the consequences of defeat were incalculable. No, no matter what might happen to Serbia, I was for "localization."

Berchtold, of course, grasped at the word. He still needed support from Germany, and given William's mood, which we well knew, he received that support in the first days of the fighting. However, making his promises, William, in his turn, was also counting psychologically on the possibility of localization. At the farewell dinner in Potsdam (before his vacation trip through the Norwegian fjords), he promised the representative from the Austro-Hungarian Government unconditional support, even in the event of Russian intervention, and he told him that "Russia is not at all prepared for war, and she should think it over for a long time before she takes up arms." "Think it over for a long time"—assuming that Russia had the ability to think—this was wise advice which William unintentionally gave his enemy. But, so that there would be no time to think, William gave another piece of advice to his ally: "act at once"—in order to get results as soon as possible and place before both Russia and Europe a fait accompli.

We know now, no matter how hard Berchtold tried, he was not able to follow this advice to the letter. Konrad von Hetzendorf had warned him that Austria would still have to prepare herself even for crushing Serbia. And for the first week after Sarajevo, when everything, in effect, had been decided, there followed another two or three leisurely weeks of diplomatic preparations.

I took advantage of the interval in order to wage my campaign against the war—or rather against Russian participation in the war—in my newspaper, Rech. I do not have the complete set of articles at hand now, and I cannot cite evidence of it. My position, however, was well known. When Poincaré (also on vacation) arrived in Russia, this time as president, I as well as many others, understood this trip as an encouragement to enter the war. In Petersburg, the arrival of this "herald of war" was, in general, unpopular, and Poincaré even had to be protected from unfriendly demonstrations. I was wrong, since Poincaré's second trip to Russia, like his first, was rather a precautionary measure against any warlike surprises on the part of Russia. Nicholas II, however, had reason for writing his Danish relatives on the occasion of this second visit: "Poincaré needs peace, not, like me, for the sake of peace. He believes that good wars do exist." Apparently, private conversations between the tsar and the president of the Republic went beyond the public declarations of alliance friendship.

During these weeks of "calm before the storm," in my articles I continued to warn that the danger had not passed and that Austria was secretly preparing to deliver a decisive blow. Indeed, in deep secret even from Germany, Berchtold was preparing his notorious "ultimatum" to Serbia. His task was defined completely: "fix such far-reaching conditions that we can be sure they will be refused. That will open the way for a radical solution by means of military intervention." On June 27 (July 10), Berchtold told the German ambassador: "It would be very unpleasant if Serbia were to agree. I am planning to pose such conditions that Serbia's acceptance will be absolutely inconceivable!"

Such was the document presented to Serbia on July 10 (23), after waiting for Poincaré's departure from Petersburg. How did Russia react to this? I must admit that Sazonov's first statements were not inconsistent with the possibility of localizing the war. Sazonov immediately telegraphed Belgrade: "The situation is hopeless for the Serbs; the best thing for them is not to try to resist, but to appeal to the Great Powers." He told the French ambassador: "I think that even if the Austro-Hungarian government begins actions, Serbia should permit the attack without a fight and show Austria's shamelessness to the whole world." No matter how unacceptable the Austrian ultimatum was, Sazonov advised the Serbs to accept its demands; a reservation was made only for Serbia's sovereignty. Austria, however, without going into a substantial analysis and not giving the other powers a chance to discuss the Austrian demands, called the answer unsatisfactory and broke off diplomatic relations with Serbia. On the very next day (July 25), Germany urged the Austrians on: "Every delay in military operations runs the risk of intervention by the other powers." On July 28 Austria declared war on Serbia. The bombardment of Belgrade began on July 29. After delaying a whole month from the time of the Sarajevo murder (June 28–July 28), only four days (July 29–August 1) were left for diplomatic negotiations, which were totally useless since Austria-Hungary systematically rejected all forms of mediation suggested by the other powers (Sazonov and Grey). Bethmann-Hollweg was on the point of reminding his ally that Austria should at least make the appearance of making concessions, so that "the responsibility for the European conflagration would fall on Russia." In a typical fashion, this telegram (No. 200, July 17) was immediately canceled: William had changed his mind. After his first acquaintance with the content of the ultimatum, he wrote that Austria had won a victory and could be satisfied—even though this did not exclude "teaching Serbia a severe lesson." This view was still compatible with "localization." However, after Austria declared war on Serbia (July 28), William's tone immediately changed in his telegraph exchanges with the tsar. Nicholas, "in the name of our old friendship," asked William "to prevent your ally from going too far" in "this ignoble war against a weak country." William placed two exclamation marks after the words "ignoble war" and noted in the margins: "A confession of weakness and an attempt to saddle me with the responsibility for the war. The telegram contains a veiled threat and a demand, similar to an order, to stay the hand of our ally." William's next telegram recalled the Austrian point of view and the right to deliver a "just punishment" to the perpetrators of this "foul murder." He condescendingly recognized the difficult situation facing Nicholas, who would have to "reckon with the direction of public opinion" (Slavism). He promised to exert influence on Austria in the spirit of a "satisfactory agreement" with Russia. But the next day the conflict widened. On July 17 Pourtales brought Sazonov a telegram from Bethmann-Hollweg stating that if Russia did not cease its military preparations, even though she had not even begun to mobilize, then "Germany herself would have to mobilize and immediately go over to the offensive." Sazonov, greatly agitated, answered that now he understood Austria's stubbornness—and made a sharp protest to Pourtales. Reporting Pourtales' statement to the tsar, and learning from him about William's conciliatory telegram, Sazonov pointed out the contradiction. Then at 8:30 in the evening, Nicholas asked William to "explain the contradiction" and added that "the correct thing to do would be to turn over the Austro-Serbian problem to the Hague Conference." William placed yet another exclamation mark after the reference to the Hague, and Bethmann cabled Pourtales a request to explain to Sazonov the "imaginary contradiction," adding that "of course the idea of the Hague Conference in the given situation must be excluded."

Since during these last two days the Russian generals began arguing about a "partial" (against Austria) vs. a "general" mobilization and since the tsar did not want to allow a "general" mobilization under any condition, Sazonov asked permission to take part in the discussions of this question. Having convinced himself after Purtales' visit that war with Germany was unavoidable, he wanted certainty as to the inevitability of a general mobilization. His conference with the generals convinced him that it was inevitable, and the tsar also inclined toward this opinion. Nevertheless, on that same day, July 17, at 9:40 in the evening, William's telegram arrived with a new pro-

posal to arrange direct negotiations with Vienna. In order to avoid
the catastrophe which Russian armament threatened, William was
ready to take the role of mediator upon himself. We know the price of
this last concession, the aim of which was, not to prevent war, but to
throw the responsibility for war off of Austria and onto Russia. The tsar
did not understand this perfidy; he became excited and ordered Yanushkevich to cancel the "general" mobilization which had just been
scheduled for the next day (July 18) and to limit himself to merely
"partial" mobilization. At 12:30 A.M., another telegram from William
arrived, written in the tone of an ultimatum: "If Russia mobilizes
against Austria (that is, if Russia begins "partial mobilization"), then
my role as mediator, which you have so kindly given me, will be
placed in danger, if not entirely destroyed. *The whole weight of the
decision now lies only on your shoulders, which now bear the responsibility for war or peace.*" William's secret plans were thus exposed;
but the tsar continued to believe in the possibility of preserving peace
and was disturbed by the direct threat of responsibility. Sazonov, who
had just prepared a conciliatory formula for negotiations with Austria
("if Austria recognizes that the conflict has become a European conflict, and preserves the rights of Serbian sovereignty, then Russia promises to cease military preparations"), understood the futility of negotiations which threatened merely to delay the decision. They were
caught in a dilemma: the tsar again refused to permit Yanushkevich
to carry out "general" mobilization; Sazonov, meanwhile, was convinced of the "technical" necessity of such a mobilization and undertook to defend the views of the Military Department in an audience
with the tsar in Peterhof at three o'clock in the afternoon. Both were
extremely agitated; the final decision was impending. Sazonov used
the same argument that Joffre used to convince Viviani: it is senseless
to delay the preparations when Germany is preparing to start military
operations. The tsar agreed and Sazonov switched to a sentimentally
patriotic tone. "Russia will not forgive the Tsar" for a capitulation
"which covers the good name of the Russian people with shame";
"the historical influence on Russia's natural allies in the Balkans will be
destroyed" (but it was already lost); Russia "will be condemned to a
pitiful existence dependent on the arbitrary will of the Central Imperial Powers. . . . The Tsar's conscience may rest at ease before God
and future generations." Silence followed. Sazonov saw on the tsar's
face signs of an inner struggle. Finally, in a constrained voice, the tsar
said: "You are right; we have only to wait for the attack," and he gave
the order for general mobilization. In a new telegram on July 18
(31), William continued to mask his intentions by a reference to "his
continuing peaceful mediation." Sazonov was ready "to negotiate

with him to the end" on the basis of his formula which had been improved by Grey. The tsar gave William his word of honor that his
army would not move while negotiations were going on. However,
before receiving this telegram, Bethmann-Hollweg had already cabled
Pourtales an ultimatum with a demand to cancel the mobilization,
which Pourtales handed over to Sazonov at midnight on July 19
(August 1). The period of the ultimatum was supposed to expire at
noon, but already in the morning, *Kriegsgefahrzustand* (war alert) was
announced in Germany; at 5:45 in the afternoon, Pourtales received a
document declaring war on Russia, and with a slight delay, he passed
the document on to Sazonov. The most curious thing of all, was that
several hours after war had been declared, the tsar received a telegram from William demanding that he not cross the border. The
Russian border had already been crossed. Thus ended the clumsy
game of transferring the responsibility to Russia.

It is interesting to note that William was so enthused over the idea
of war with Russia, that he forgot, as it were, that the war would be
linked to a European war. Having received the false information that
France would not interfere in this war, he told Moltke: "Wonderful.
Then we'll simply move our whole army over to the East." Moltke
almost had a fit. "Absolutely impossible, Your Majesty," he reminded
him, "the operation cannot be carried out except according to plan: a
strong force in the West and a weak force in the East." This was the
general staff's ABC. Nevertheless, William made a hopeless attempt
to obtain French neutrality. As for England entering the war, William
simply ignored it. When he learned that England had finally declared herself, William went berserk. "That notorious encirclement
has become an accomplished fact after all! The game was well-played,
and admiration must be shown even for those who threaten us with
ruin. Edward VII, even dead, turns out to be stronger than I, alive! We
have been made fools of in our touching hope of pacifying England!!!
All our precautions and requests were in vain. There it is, that so-
called English gratitude. The dilemma of our loyalty to the aged and
venerable emperor (Franz Josef) has placed us in a position which
gives England an excuse to crush us. . . . We must expose these
machinations, sparing nobody's feelings! Our consuls, our agents in
Turkey and India must rouse all Mohammedans to a fierce uprising
against this odious, hypocritical, unscrupulous, shameless nation of
merchants. We may sacrifice our own skin, but England, at least,
must lose her India!"

As is known, the Allies tried in vain to persuade Grey to declare
England on the side of France and Russia, believing that this was the

only way to prevent war. At that time I was much taken by Grey, and I understood his motives—to manipulate disagreements in the cabinet and among the English public. I remember the anxious expectations with which I followed his two speeches in Parliament. In the first he announced that England was free to dispose of her own fate, while in the second, after an interruption, he argued that the duty of honor required this freedom to be sacrificed for a struggle against the violators of Belgian neutrality. Grey's voice always seemed to me to be the voice of wise statesmanship, inner honesty, and nobility. In addition, I was convinced that England's neutrality would not have changed William's plans. For those four anxious days, I rid myself of the illusion of the *Friedenkaiser* once and for all. Not everything, of course, but much of what I have recounted above reached me during those days from our Ministry of Foreign Affairs. I accused Sazonov of not knowing how to carry out his "localization" of the war when it was still possible; but I understood the indefensibility of this position after Berchtold managed to attract William to his side, and after the kaiser's resolution to fight became clear. It was clear even before the decisive conversation between Sazonov and Pourtales; I understood the "technical" meaning of general mobilization—especially where mobilization must be carried out in a tremendous, roadless, poorly governed, and illiterate Russia. This time I did not condemn our Military Department at all for undertaking defensive measures well in advance. But alas, these measures turned out to be too late anyway. I felt not only a personal disappointment in William but outright hatred from that moment when my impressions of him were deceived. On the day Germany declared war, we prepared the July 20 issue of *Rech* with sharp articles against Germany. At night the proofs had already been sent to the military censors when we learned that, with the appointment of Grand Duke Nikolai Nikolaevich as supreme commander, our paper had been banned because of its well-known opposition to the war. No less than William, we knew, of course, about the tsar's weak character, and we sympathized all the more with the firmness and persistence of his intentions to preserve peace. This time it was not his weakness in the face of alien influences that could explain his resolution to run the risk of war. I could not have agreed with Sazonov's sentimental-nationalistic arguments (which, by the way, I learned of only from his memoirs), but the tsar had already been convinced by military and technical considerations. Nevertheless, even after Russia's entry into the war, Nicholas II continued to consider his decision as something like betrayal of his love for peace. Baron Taube recounted his talk with the tsar which took place on December 28, 1914. Earlier, Taube had read in the tsar's presence an historical report with pessimistic conclusions. Recalling this, Nicholas confessed to him: "Hearing your gloomy predictions, I said to myself: there is a theoretician and professor who does not take into account the peaceful intentions of his sovereign. I thought then: if we should sometime get into a mess with Austria, then it will be under Alexei Nikolaevich (the heir to the throne). Now, four months later, they forced me to get myself mixed up in this terrible war." Given William's disposition, the war would have occurred all the same, whether Russia mobilized or not. It was too late to reach an agreement with Austria after the events which had already taken place and which had been approved by Germany—even had Grey continued to insist on such agreement. Nevertheless, Nicholas' "they forced me" continued to sound like an awareness of his own guilt, an awareness of some sort of responsibility which he had taken upon himself. . . . It may be appropriate to recall —and not in jest—that as for "alien influences," Nicholas had allies. These were Prince Meshchersky and Rasputin. The latter lay bedridden at the time, gravely wounded by one of his lady admirers, Guseva, and maintained that were it not for his illness, there would have been no war. Or rather, it might have occurred, but would not have taken on the character of a war over Russian claims in the Balkans and over Russian "Slavic racism."

Rech's proofs were turned over to the proper authorities, who were convinced that our patriotism was sufficient. The ban was lifted from our paper, and the issue appeared—on the following day or two days after war was declared, I do not recall—with the articles that had been either written or set before the ban. I. V. Hessen recalls that among the caustic statements of my editorials in those days was a phrase about "the lack of correspondence between the reason for and the prospects of the European war," and that when the other editors objected that this phrase was irksome, I answered: "There will come a day when we will have to refer to the fact that we said this in time and that we tried to avert misfortune." That day came sooner than I expected.

How the War Was Received in Russia

How WAS THE WAR of 1914 generally received in Russia? To say simply that it was "popular" is not enough. This question should be discussed now in order to avoid misunderstandings in the future. Especially at the beginning, of course, there was no lack of displays of enthusiasm, and not only government sponsored enthusiasm. Even our émigrés like Burtsev, Kropotkin, and Plekhanov regarded this defensive war favorably. Workers' strikes ceased—for the moment—not to mention street and public demonstrations. As for the popular masses, their attitude, in proportion to their increase in literacy, was more conscious than the attitude of the enserfed peasants toward the wars under Nicholas I, or even of the emancipated peasants to the war of liberation in 1877–78, which had fascinated part of our intelligentsia. In general, however, our poet's picture was still true of life: "orators thunder" in the capitals, while in the depths of Russia "eternal silence" reigns. In the war of 1914, the "eternal silence" was summed up in the common phrase: "we are from Kaluga," that is, William will never reach Kaluga. In this sense Kokovtsov's statement to a foreign correspondent that one hundred versts from the big cities all political struggle lapses into silence was justified. It was this statement that provoked protests against Kokovtsov from colleagues like Rukhlov or even Krivoshein, protests that appealed to the tsar: it is necessary "to have more faith in the Russian people," in its "age-old devotion to the motherland" and in its "unlimited devotion to the sovereign." The pitiful failure of the "Romanov Jubilee Celebration" clearly showed the absurdity of all those protestations. Of course, the Russian soldier from the time of Suvorov had shown his steadfastness, his courage, and his selflessness at the front. Nevertheless, after deserting the front for his village, he displayed with no less energy his "age-old devotion" to his land which he had rid of Russian landlords. Consequently, there were general traits manifested at one time or another which force the historian to throw out of his calculations this Russian "ballast" which the tsar's flatterers had mistakenly counted on in questions of high policy, just as Witte had been mistaken in the elections to the Duma. Saltykov, the Russian satirist, once coined the official formula for the peasant's attitude toward the taxes which were weighing down upon him: "he will have enough." But "he" did not "have enough," just as "he" at the front could not fill Sukhomlinov's empty arsenals with his own body. The "eternal silence" harbored within itself unspent forces and waited, according to Joseph de Maistre's prediction, for its "Pugachev from a Russian university" . . . .

Passing from the Russian "Sphinx" to Russian "public life" we have to admit that its attitude toward the war in 1914–18 was incomparably more complex than the attitude of those same circles to wars in the 1850's and the 1870's. The intelligentsia's ideology regarding the war was subject to foreign pacifist and socialist influences in a much greater degree. Above all, the realistic problems of defense, and then, the use to be made of the victory, if that would be the outcome, were somehow placed in the background and under suspicion by public circles. Defense was left to the knowledge of the military, while the use to be made of victory was left to the diplomats. Of course, the public circles could not refuse to take part in the work of defense, but they took part in the discussion of the fruits of victory only in a limited sense, condemning the positive goals as a manifestation of illegitimate "imperialism." A positive attitude toward war and its realistic problems was left to the attacker, that is, Germany. In Germany, however, the conception of the war took on a mystic coloring. War was considered some kind of a superhuman phenomenon which elevated the spirits and bolstered the strength of the people. Such were the teachings of the Pan-Germanists and the German generals in the style of Bernhardy. War was not to be discussed; it must be accepted like any other phenomenon of nature, like life and death, or like a command from above for accomplishing the mission which had been given to the people by a divine protector for the realization of its historical fate.

Our attitude toward the war, of course, did not approach either extreme. From a realistic point of view, our immediate task was to explain the war we had been saddled with, to explain its origins and its possible aftereffects. Russian society had to be united around this general understanding of the war, its significance for Russia and its connections with Russian interests. This task fell to me in particular as some sort of recognized expert. They turned to me for explanations and for articles, and I did my best to meet the need by gathering data which were little known to the Russian reader and drawing conclusions from them about possible gains for Russia. My printed explanations in journals, special anthologies, and finally in *Rech's Year-*

book might easily fill several volumes. It is natural that I became an object of criticism for those who would not agree to view the war realistically, or those who did not accept the war at all. As an example of this criticism, let me mention one epithet against me which was quite widespread in leftist circles at that time. They called me "Miliu-kov-Dardanelsky"—an epithet of which I could have been justi-fiably proud had it not contained an indubitable exaggeration created out of ignorance by hostile propaganda. In *Rech's Yearbook* for 1916 one can find a proposal for solving this problem in a way which I had accepted until the 1915 agreement between Sazonov and the Allies.[43] At that point the proposal had not yet been made to take possession of Constantinople, both shores of the straits and the nearby islands. Of course it was recognized that "Germany's very position" "created exceptionally favorable circumstances for Russia to realize her most important national goal." At the same time I noted the admission of the French writer Gauchillière that my view "is based not on the old Slavophile mystic ideology, but on the tremendous fact of the rapid economic development of the Russian South which can no longer remain without free access to the sea."

The public at large did not take these concrete considerations into account. Though accepting the war, they considered it necessary to justify the war on a higher level and searched for a compromise be-tween their pacifist convictions and sad reality. In these attempts to reconcile mass killing with the voice of human conscience, it was im-possible not to accept some basic idea. Thus, various slogans appeared and became widespread, such as "the war against war," "the last war," "the war without conquerors and conquered," "without annexation or indemnities," and the particularly acceptable and comprehensible formula was for the liberation of the small enslaved peoples. All these slogans cleared the way for Wilsonism, Versailles, and the League of Nations. With some delay these slogans reached Russia in transla-tion from the French.

Generally speaking, tsarist Russia was suspected beforehand of not accepting the democratic slogans. The European pacifists felt burdened by the alliance with Russia, as by an unavoidable evil. After the war, even such a realist as Clemenceau who understood France's national interests perfectly and who had fought desperately for them, welcomed the liberation of France's ally from the ideology of the old Russian regime even though that liberation had occurred through the mediation of the Bolsheviks. He wrote, "The shameful peace of Brest-Litovsk immediately freed us from supporting our ally-oppressors (Russia.—P.M.), and now we can restore our high moral forces in an alliance with the enslaved peoples of the Adriatic in Belgrade—from

Prague to Bucharest, from Warsaw to the northern countries. . . . With the military defeat of Russia, Poland was immediately liberated and restored; the nationalities all over Europe raised their heads, and our war for national defense was transformed by events into a war of liberation." We can now criticize Clemenceau and show that inadequacies in the war for national defense harmed the goal of liberating the "small peoples." At that time, "liberation" was still in the future and justified national defense as a goal of a lower order. The Allied governments might conclude "secret treaties" with Russia, but public opinion demanded a rejection of "secret diplomacy" and public discussion of the "goals of the war." These goals, outlined in Wilson's program, included the liberation of the "small peoples" "who were enslaved" not only by Austria-Hungary and Turkey, but also by their ally, Russia, which the Russian émigré separatists already called "the prison of peoples." Only the Russian socialists, members of the Second International, were not suspected, while the Russian intelligentsia of the liberal type was placed in a rather difficult situation in democratic Europe.

A third group of attitudes toward the war had already become apparent: complete nonrecognition. Those socialists who accepted the war, even in a noble form, received the derisive label "social patriots" from those who repudiated it. The first example of "betrayal" here was provided by the German Social Democrats who, from the very first days of the war, supported their government. After them came the moderate socialists from the democratic countries. The socialists from neutral countries like Switzerland and Scandinavia took the position of mediators between the two camps of acceptors and nonacceptors, with a tendency to lean in the direction of the latter. Their task was to review the "aims of the war" in the most radical sense of a "liberation" from them—for the quickest possible end to this "last" war.

Then there followed the evolution of nonrecognition. On the extreme wing a tendency emerged which used war not for ending war, but for converting it into a war of liberation from governments, in favor of peoples. The external war between states was supposed to turn into an internal war between classes. Essentially, the entire Social Democratic movement of the Second International before 1914 stood for creating an international situation which would serve to turn the political war into a social war. However, after the "social patriots" "betrayed" the decisions of the congresses by taking a nationalist stand, the extreme wing still remained, sticking to its previous "defeatist" position and striving to turn the war into a struggle between the proletariat and the capitalists. At first there were not many of them; they were found only in isolated revolutionary circles. They were led by the Russian émigrés, the socialist "Bolsheviks," who set as their goal the separation of these elements out of the Second International and their unification into a new "Third International" and placed before them the new international goal of "world revolution." At two secret congresses in Switzerland (Zimmerwald and Kienthal) the original steps for the achievement of this goal were taken under the influence of the Russians. The kernel of a permanent organization was created in Bern—until circumstances would allow it to be transferred to Moscow.

I will have occasion to return to various separate stages of the process which I have described here in brief. It is important to stress that this process comprises a single whole, that it penetrated into Russia from Europe, and that, in both places, the war was an indispensable prerequisite. Why was it only in our country that it found the most favorable soil and unfolded without hindrance to its logical end? This is a special question, and for the time being I will not discuss it. The subsequent events will give a partial answer, but it is substantially a question of our particular Russian philosophy of history.

The "Sacred Union"

BE THAT AS IT MAY, at the moment war was declared all these differences faded into the background before a general display of healthy
patriotism in the face of the enemy invasion of Russian frontiers. The
explosions of nationalist sentiment occurred simultaneously and everywhere identically. The French called it *union sacrée* "the sacred union."
Even William considered it necessary to arouse this sentiment, deceiving German public opinion and passing off his offensive war as a
defensive one. Russia did not have to do this. The Russian opposition
bore a particular obligation—to display this feeling triumphantly
toward the very government it was struggling against. There was no
disagreement on this matter within the ranks of our party. In that
same issue of *Rech* which had been first banned then permitted, the
Central Committee published an appeal, hastily composed with my
participation:

"No matter what our attitude toward the government's domestic
policy, our first duty is to preserve the unity and integrity of our
country, and to defend its position as a world power—a position
which is now being contested by the enemy. Let us postpone our
domestic disputes; let us not give our adversary even the slightest
excuse for relying on the differences which divide us; let us remember,
and remember well, that at the present moment our first and only
task is to support our soldiers and to inspire them with faith in the
rightness of our cause, with calm courage, and with hope for the victory of our arms."

On that same day, a tsarist manifesto was published expressing
the wish "that in this year of terrible trials, internal disagreements be
forgotten, that the union of the tsar with the people be strengthened,
and that all of Russia stand united to repel the enemy's criminal attack." Appreciating the significance of a unified stand on the part of
the people's representatives, the government scheduled a one-day
special session of the Duma on July 26 (August 8). After Rodzianko's
speech, three ministers, Goremykin, Sazonov, and Bark, spoke at this

meeting, and statements were given by representatives of the national minorities—the Poles, the Latvians, the Lithuanians, the Jews, the Moslems, the Baltic Germans, and the German colonists on the Volga. All of them, of course, spoke the same thoughts of defending the motherland, of devotion to the tsar and the nation. Then there followed the statements of the "responsible opposition," the Progressivists and the Kadets. Our statement was written by me and approved by our faction, the Central Committee, and especially by I. I. Petrunkevich. "We are fighting for the liberation of the motherland from foreign invasion; for the liberation of Europe and Slavdom from German hegemony; for the liberation of the whole world from the unbearable weight of ever-increasing armament. . . . We are united in this struggle; we set no conditions and we demand nothing. On the scales of war, we simply place our firm will for victory." Such a statement, emphasizing our solidarity with our allies, identified our own unique role in the war, stressed its defensive character, stated the pacifist goal of disarmament and stipulated only one condition for our collaboration with the government—victory.

Presented to the government voluntarily, in spite of apparent misgivings, the "sacred union" lasted only a short time. And it was not the fault of the Duma that the union was destroyed. The session on July 26 was the only Duma session; but we had nothing against that in view of the gravity of the moment. On the eve of that meeting, we had learned that, in accordance with N. Maklakov's project, the Duma would not be convened until autumn of 1915, that is, not until more than a year from that time. This was not only an insult to the Duma, but a direct violation of the Fundamental Laws. The Duma had to be convened at least once a year in any case in order to pass on the budget. The Council of Elders decided to announce this to Goremykin without delay. He refused to see us. As representatives of all the Duma factions, we then turned to Krivoshein who understood the situation better than the rest of them and who was secretly planning to replace Goremykin. I remember that I ended up in the same taxi with A. N. Khvostov who represented the right wing of the Duma. As if to underscore the unanimity of the whole Duma, we appeared as the first two speakers. Krivoshein agreed that it was necessary to push up the convocation of the Duma in order to preserve the atmosphere that had already been created; and he reported as much to the Council of Ministers. Goremykin yielded, and the Duma's convocation was set for "not later than February" of 1915. This was the first time that such an indefinite formula was used here. Nevertheless, the Duma was not absent by any means during this interval: its Budget Committee continued to function; and contact with the ministers was not interrupted.

Incidentally, we learned then that N. Maklakov and Shcheglovitov had given the tsar a note stressing the necessity of an immediate end to the war and a reconciliation with Germany, since Germany was kindred to Russia in its political system; while, on the contrary, they considered it dangerous for Russia to become too intimate with her allies. During the budget review for the Ministry of Foreign Affairs I posed the question directly to Sazonov whether or not this was true. Sazonov pleaded ignorance, while N. Maklakov and Shcheglovitov, who were also present, remained silent and smiled embarrassed smiles. According to other rumors which perhaps coincided with the first ones, a similar note was passed on to the tsar by the circle of the "united nobility." This note, too, pointed to the danger of revolution if the war were continued and to the necessity of concluding a separate peace with Germany without delay.

The promised session of the Duma was scheduled for January 27, 1915. Goremykin stipulated that it would last three days in all and that it would be devoted exclusively to discussing and accepting the budget. There were to be no objections, all the more so as the budget had already been discussed in committee and our common attitude was to support the spirit of the "sacred union." Nevertheless, since the session on July 26, events had occurred greatly changing the substance of this attitude. These events were related to Sukhomlinov's conduct of the war as well as to the course of internal politics under Maklakov, and in part, to foreign policy under Sazonov.

Russian society, of course, did not believe Sukhomlinov's assertions that Russia was ready for war. Just before the outbreak of the war, Baron Taube asked a leading representative of the Military Department what these assurances meant, and received the following answer: "We are prepared to fight for six months; the war will be short." In December 1914, the tsar told Ruchlov: "Here everybody is falling upon General Sukhomlinov, but look and see how brilliantly things are going under him." And, in fact, the military operations at the end of 1914 still provided no opportunity for verifying in fact Russia's lack of preparedness. Mobilization was carried out calmly though with some delay. The deployment of troops along the German and Austro-Hungarian borders went according to plan, and the first offense into enemy territory corresponded to the agreement with the Allies. The catastrophe which befell General Samsonov's army in the region of the Mazurian lakes could be explained by the incomprehensible sluggishness of General Rennenkampf. On the other hand, the Russian offensive on the Austrian front was successful. Lvov was taken. The Germans' attempt to come to the aid of the Austrians was successfully held up by shifting the Russian front to the north, with the threat of surrounding the Germans at Lodz. The army spent their shells without count, which partially explained the Russian successes. In a word, there were apparently no grounds for argument with the government. True, people who were more familiar with the technical aspect of military affairs foresaw danger even at that time. Guchkov had sounded the alarm before the war had begun. As befitted his temperament, and, moreover, irritated by the fact that he had not been elected to the Duma, he spoke at an Octobrists' conference in 1913 and made the extreme proposal of "shifting to better opposition and struggle"—not against the impotent government, but against those "dark," irresponsible forces standing behind the government. He warned that otherwise, Russia would be plunged into "prolonged chaos," etc., by "an inevitable and grave catastrophe." When the war began, he immediately declared that it "would end in failure," and in December 1914, he gathered the "representatives of the legislative establishments" (I was not present) and "painted a perfectly hopeless picture for them." His gloomy mood, however, was not shared at that time either by his faction or by ours.

N. Maklakov's internal policy created an entirely different impression. Under his administration, the practice of extra-Duma legislation by Article 87 immediately blossomed forth into a magnificent flower. All changes in the management of the state caused by the war were hurriedly carried out by decisions of the Council of Ministers and decrees from the tsar. A rivalry began between the cabinet and the military command over the bounds of authority between the front and the rear. Inside the country, persecutions were stepped up against all displays of public activity. The uncontrolled orders of the chief of staff, General Yanushkevich, who had the grand duke, the supreme commander, "in his pocket," violated the most elementary rights of the population, and gave the people plenty of reason to struggle. Persecutions were also carried out against the national minorities; in particular, the promises given to the Poles were not kept. And when Rodzianko passed the Poles' complaints on to the tsar, the tsar answered him only by saying: "It seems that we have been hasty."

On this issue, discontent had already spilled over into the area of international relations. After the struggle was carried onto the territory of the kingdom of Poland, the Polish question really did threaten to become international unless some concessions, even minimal ones, were made.

The seizure of Eastern Galicia by Russian troops and the crossing of the Carpathians by Russian troops also did not result in the benefits which the old-Slavophile circles had counted on. Our rightist nationalists, like Count Bobrinsky, who occupied administrative posts in the "Piedmont of Ukrainianism," began to persecute the Ukrainian nationalist movement and to convert forcibly the Uniates to Orthodoxy. A painful impression was made by the arrest of the Uniate Metropolitan, Sheptitsky—a man who enjoyed great respect and influence in the region. All of this engendered a hostile attitude among the population toward the victors.

In such a situation, while not desiring to destroy the "sacred union," we still wanted to have it out with the ministers. For this purpose, on the day before the Duma session of January 27–29, 1915, was to open, a private conference was held between the Duma Defense Committee and the ministers. It was mainly Shingarev and myself who spoke at this conference. With a series of concrete examples, Shingarev brilliantly summarized Maklakov's domestic policy. For my part, I dwelled on Maklakov's attitude toward the press, toward the national minorities (the Poles and the Jews), and on his policy in Galicia; and I requested the government to introduce a bill for Polish autonomy in the Duma. In conclusion we demanded the dismissal of Maklakov as a violator of the sacred union.

With the exceptions of Maklakov and Sukhomlinov, the ministers' explanations went rather peacefully. Sukhomlinov reassured us: everything is favorable, everything has been foreseen, and our idea of the situation is incorrect. Purishkevich, having just arrived from the front, where he saw the situation as it really was, answered him with a sharp rejoinder, and we told Sukhomlinov to his face that he was deceiving the Duma. Maklakov, in his answer to Shingarev, was crude and caustic. He also pounced on me with irritation—not daring to give concrete answers, however. His tricks made a disgusting impression not only on us, but also on the other ministers present. They threw over to Goremykin Rodzianko's note with a request to tone down the unpleasant picture. He uttered a few conciliatory words and promised, among other things, that the bill for Polish autonomy would be introduced into the Duma. The closed session ended with this single promise (which was not fulfilled).

In the open sessions the budget passed without hindrance. We announced that we maintained our previous attitudes toward the war and that we would not join the struggle against the government. However, we added in cautious phrases, that the government, for its part, was not abiding by the truce, but was using it to bolster its position on the domestic scene.

After the January session, the relations between the government and the Duma and society at large began to deteriorate rapidly. Between this and the next Duma session another half year passed; the government not only did not use this postponement to smooth its relations with society, but on the contrary, it shattered them once and for all. Two fundamental traits characterize this period from January to July. In the first place the Russian bureaucracy showed itself to be totally incapable of organizing the country on the scale which was demanded in order to fight the mighty enemy; and it was forced to turn to society for help. In the second place the bureaucracy continued to suspect society of revolutionary intentions and embarked upon an open struggle against it. The consequences of the division of Russia into two camps developed at an increasing rate—as Russian failures followed one after another in the theater of war. We will deal with these first of all.

As is known, the French victory on the Marne, won with Russian help, put an end to the German hopes for a "Blitzkrieg" and turned the mobile struggle into trench warfare. In addition, the Germans had to turn their attention to the serious danger on the Russian front. Russian troops stood in German territory and had penetrated deeply into the territory of the weakest enemy, Austria-Hungary. The first task was to drive them out of there. According to the data from our Military Department, fifty enemy infantry divisions and thirteen enemy cavalry divisions stood on the Russian front at the beginning of the war. Gradually transferring their troops from the Western front, the Austrians and Germans brought their numbers to 137 infantry divisions and twenty-four cavalry divisions by September of 1915. The Russian front first penetrated into eastern Galicia, the kingdom of Poland, and East Prussia in an arc, the summit of which was located somewhere west of Warsaw. In three steps, the German-Austrian forces straightened out the arc. First, Mackensen broke through the Carpathian front at Görlitz and by the end of June freed eastern Galicia. Then he came from the south while Gallwitz came from the north to force the Russians out of the "Polish sack." They reached the line Narev-Bug by the beginning of August. At the same time, the Germans seized Courland and the middle stream of the Niemen (Kovno-Grodno). Finally, in September and October, with separate blows, Hindenburg raided both Minsk and Pinsk, while Konrad raided Rovno—all of this in the rear of our straightened-out line of trenches— at the end of 1915. July and August were decisive months during which the enemy's threat was felt to be very close.

It was along this route of suffering that I lost a grave which was very dear to me and which I had never seen. My younger son, Sergei, was killed around Cholm. He was a talented boy, and I had great hopes for him. After his death they gave me his correspondence with his Moscow cousin, the daughter of my late brother. From that correspondence, I saw that he idolized me, and at the same time suffered much from the lack of intimacy between us. Nervous, with a delicate spiritual balance, he gave the impression of one condemned, rushing uneasily from one thing to another in his transition from childhood to youth. He wanted to follow in my steps, but he soon dropped his philological studies at the University, moved in with a Moscow family, and entered the Petrovsky Academy, where he carefully concealed his relationship to "Miliukov," painfully preserving his own individuality. The war began; in spite of my insistence to the contrary, he volunteered, passed the abridged officers' course, and came in his brand new uniform to say good-bye. (My older son Nikolai was already serving in the army as an artilleryman and, later, as a pilot.) We accompanied him to the Nikolaevsky Station—he had only a short leave—embarrassed and proud of his rank and of the orderly accompanying him. Later, just as briefly and unexpectedly, he came on foot to our Crimean cottage in order to ask my advice. Having finished near the top of his class, he had the right to choose between two assignments: on the southern front or in the Far East. He seemed to hesitate. I told him where the real struggle was, and with a heavy heart I accompanied him as far as the Baidarsky road. . . . I received his first letter from the front, vividly describing his first attack; he was delighted with his soldiers who taught their newly baked leader the elementary ways of war. The tone of his letter was excited and joyful. A short time later I received the first news of his death. General Irmanov was famous for his unbending severity. He sent the freshly baked officers first to the dangerous places, thus preserving his own cadres. My son's detachment was heading for a rest after sitting out the required time in the trenches. The Austrians attacked rapidly, and his division was turned around en route in order to stop the attack. On that day, thirty such young officers perished in that improvised skirmish. But the attacks did not stop the offensive. . . . His assistant later brought me a small suitcase with everyday articles I had given Sergei for the road; his new shoulder straps were there, and I preserved them like a sacred relic. . . . I never forgave myself for not advising him to go to the Far East. This was one of those wounds which do not heal. . . . It is bleeding even now. . . .

I ask my future reader's forgiveness for this digression; I will now return to the main theme.

The first news that not everything was going favorably at the front began to reach us as early as the end of January 1915. It was only in April, however, that we felt the gravity of the situation at the front in eastern Galicia. The cannon shells and arms prepared to last for "six months" were gone. The soldiers suffered intensely, clambering up the steep ice-covered slopes of the Carpathians; and when it came their turn to make the most of success, they were caught without shells and cartridges. Foreseeing that the war would be a long one, our allies took pains beforehand to create a large-scale war industry. What about Russia?

The main Artillery Department, headed by Grand Duke Sergei Mikhailovich, had no means whatsoever of replenishing Russian armament. He had to turn for military supplies to those same Allies. The Allies, however, were busy with their own problems and did not worry much about filling the Russian orders on time. It was also difficult to deliver those orders across the far north. Deals with private agents gave rise to rumors about abuses, bribes, high commissions, etc. Russian industrialists were offered unacceptable conditions. In view of the obvious necessity of relying on the forces of the country after the May and June failures at the front, the tsar at last agreed to organize hastily, under Article 87, a Special Conference on Defense under government leadership. He opened the conference personally, announcing that in this difficult time, he himself would guide the work of the conference. Members of the legislative chambers were brought into the conference, as were representatives from industry and the financial world, and representatives of the corresponding government departments. Of course, the promise of the tsar's leadership remained unfulfilled, and the original atmosphere of trust was replaced by the opposite mood. The time came when Nicholas was asked by the conference to listen personally to a report on the situation, and Nicholas refused to visit the conference.

Medical services at the front were headed by the "supreme" commander, Prince Oldenburgsky, a capricious, stubborn, and extremely limited person. The services were deplorable. Medical personnel were insufficient; even the most necessary medicines were lacking; the wounded were dumped on the floors of freight cars without medical care and died there, in the trains, by the hundreds. This was the area least defended against public participation, and it was in this area that the public most quickly scrambled over the obstacles which had been placed in its way.

Between the front and the rear stood an impenetrable wall. Maklakov reigned in the rear, which was even less adapted to waging a long and serious war than the front. There was no system at all for supplying provisions for the army, and the transport of recruits as well as of supplies suffered not only from an inadequate railroad network, but also from the inability to organize railway movement efficiently. Transport of goods was carried out from one incident to the next, and bottlenecks choked the railway junctions, paralyzing all movement. Railway cars had to be burned or taken off the tracks in

order to clear the way. As a result, the army suffered, the local population suffered, the passenger movement suffered, and freight transport
suffered.

The government was clearly in no condition to work all this out
and organize Russia for war. The funds were available, but not the
people. The government could send bureaucrats to the provinces, but
the country was strange to these people, these bureaucrats who knew
office work with its red tape, but who were not accustomed to live
action which they inevitably slowed down and messed up. Meanwhile, there were people, right on the spot, who knew the country
from the inside, who were familiar with the country's needs, and who
were accustomed to satisfying them. These were the people of the
land, the Zemstvo people. Without waiting for orders from above,
they began to do what had to be done. They did not act separately,
but together. In order to organize Russia, they had to have their own
organization, and so they created it. However, Kadetism had arisen
from this same Zemstvo organization during the liberal years of 1904–
6, and the government instinctively mistrusted it and considered it an
enemy of autocracy and the breeding ground for future revolution.
Maklakov was particularly fired by this idea. But there was nothing
he could do. The Zemstvo organization already had its own tradition.
Neither legitimized nor officially legalized, it had already worked "to
help the sick and wounded" during the Japanese War, and it did this
on its own, without the "O.K." from above. Fourteen provincial
Zemstvo boards, with their center in Moscow, put forward a man who
became the soul of this organization: Prince Georgii Evgenievich Lvov.
He became indispensable at this post, and it was impossible to accuse
him of "politics." "Politics" and "action" were two different areas of
lifetime activity for him and he chose the second. He was distrustful
of "politics" and of all abstract ideas. On the other hand, he knew
"action" from its roots, from the land, from the Russian village; he
performed it magnificently, sparing no effort, and knowing how to
unite similarly active coworkers around himself. In the fields of Manchuria, with all the confusion there, they could not do much; but
what they did manage to do stood above all office work and earned the
public's love. Kuropatkin became Lvov's friend and recommended
him to Nicholas II; Lvov's name thundered through the liberal circles
of Russia, and the press carried it everywhere, perhaps even more
than was deserved, as his biographer, Polner, admitted. He was tied
to "Kadetism" by more personal relationships; while the "leftists"
scowled at him because of his readiness to communicate with anyone
at all, with Stolypin, with the Red Cross, if it was necessary for his
cause. After the Manchurian detachments were liquidated, Lvov did

not disperse his cohort, but transferred his activity to the service of other national calamities. In Petersburg in 1905 it was expected that there would be a bad harvest in 138 districts of twenty-one provinces, and it was feared that the number of victims might reach eighteen million. G. E. Lvov made an alliance with the government Red Cross and received a significant amount of funds. In 1906–7 aid to the starving continued. In 1908 Lvov directed the Zemstvo Union toward organizing the movement for resettlement in the Far East, and he personally investigated the backwoods river routes of the unknown region. In 1909 he took a trip to Canada in order to study the ways of American colonization and sought out the Dukhobors. During these years of "pacification," Stolypin formally declared the Zemstvo organization illegal, and it was forced to disband. After Stolypin's death, the question of a famine campaign (1911–12), was again raised. Kokovtsov announced to the Zemstvo delegates that "an all-Zemstvo organization cannot be allowed to enter the struggle against famine." Nevertheless, the last (closed) congress of twenty representatives from twelve provinces was held for the purpose of allocating funds, and aid from the individual Zemstvos to the starving continued.

Thus, the Zemstvo Union reached 1913, the time of the Fourth Duma. Under Lvov since 1905 it had long renounced "politics" and had continued to busy itself exclusively with charitable activities. At the beginning of the war the Union possessed a firm base of sympathy among the public at large. In government circles, however, it was considered all the more suspect of "Kadetism" and dangerous as a hotbed of social ferment. The Union shared this role with the Duma and leaned on the Duma for support. Such was the situation when at the very beginning of the war the Moscow Zemstvo Board raised the question of creating an "All-Russian Zemstvo Union for aid to the sick and wounded soldiers." Under the spell of the "sacred union" it was impossible to repudiate this initiative. Lvov was received by the tsar, who expressed his "sympathy" for the undertaking; and on August 25, 1914, an announcement was made by imperial order concerning the existence and activity of the Union, analogous to the Red Cross. True, a part of Russia, along the line from Moscow to Kiev, was separated from the rear, and here the "supreme" chief of the Medical Division was still Prince Oldenburgsky. The tireless Zemstvo activity, however, soon broke through this border and came into direct contact with the urgent needs at the front. Even more obviously than the rear, the front ended up being run by the Zemstvos. The quality of the Zemstvo's work was higher than the government's; but more important, it came to the soldiers' aid more quickly. Personal ties grew up between the military authorities and the sections of the Zemstvo

Union. From surgical instruments and dressings to evacuation trains, distribution centers, medical personnel, and hospitals—all of these were provided in time and staffed by the Zemstvo organization. Besides the twelve million rubles from the Zemstvo funds, tremendous additional amounts were needed; and the government was forced to provide them. By the end of 1915, the government had granted the Zemstvos seventy-two million; and by January 1, 1916, the total sum of credits advanced grew to 187 million. By the end of 1916, the number of Zemstvo establishments of various sorts scattered throughout Russia and on the front amounted to about eight thousand, and the people working in them numbered in the hundreds of thousands. Clearly, it was impossible for the government not to take into consideration an organization of such large scope.

Nevertheless, in spite of G. E. Lvov's political neutrality, the political antagonism between society, as represented by the Zemstvo, and the government not only did not diminish but continued to increase as the Zemstvos scored new successes. The main role in this aggravation of affairs was played by Maklakov in his capacity of minister of internal affairs. When in November 1914, Rodzianko came to Maklakov from General Headquarters with a written certification from the Grand Duke Nikolai Niklaevich and with a request to permit a congress of public organizations, Maklakov answered, literally: "I cannot give you permission for convening such a congress; it would be an undesirable and universal demonstration to the effect that there exist disorders in supplying the army. Besides, I do not wish to give permission, since under the guise of delivering boots (a special request from the commander-in-chief) you will begin to make a revolution." The Duma chairman recalls, "We parted in bitterness against each other." In his testimony before the Extraordinary Commission, Maklakov reported this conversation differently: he, it seems, suggested that Rodzianko, as chairman of the Duma, should not lead the Congress of Zemstvo Boards, but should turn the chairmanship over to the minister of the army or his chief commissary. This sounded ironic, however, and Maklakov's true thoughts were exposed before the same commission in a series of his letters to the tsar written from October 14, 1914, right up until the time of his dismissal on July 7, 1915. "The Duma is paving the road for freedom of revolution." "I am struggling against the tendency which is irrepressibly growing in everyone, to forget the tsar and to consider public opinion as the beginning and the end of everything." "Rodzianko is only a pompous and stupid executor, while behind him stand his guides, Mssrs. Guchkov, Prince Lvov, and others, systematically moving toward their own goal." Finally, already after his dismissal and on the eve of revolution: "The Duma and the

Unions are without doubt inciting a part of the population to temporary disorders. . . . The (tsarist) authorities must . . . be certain of victory over the internal enemy, which has long been more dangerous and fierce and brazen than the external enemy" (February 9, 1917). "Essentially," remarked the commission chairman, "you are declaring all of Russia the internal enemy."

This all happened subsequently, while at the beginning of the war, Maklakov stood alone in the Council of Ministers. Then came the whole process of gradually isolating the tsar's family from the "internal enemy," and a series of attempts on the part of public circles to avert this road to revolution.

In May 1915, after Rodzianko's arrival from the Galician front, the general picture of the Russian retreat became clear. From that moment we decided to insist in the Duma on the immediate reopening of the Duma sessions, and this time for a prolonged period. At that time only a small number of deputies were working in the Duma. We asked the chairman to summon all the members, and they came together in the first week of June. In the Council of Elders we then introduced our proposal concerning the session. The entire second half of June was spent on negotiations with Goremykin. But the old man refused to give in; he evaded fixing either a definite date for convening the Duma or the term of the session. The situation had changed so much after January 1915, however, both in the theater of war and in the area of public organizational activity, that it was no longer possible to support Maklakov's line (which the tsar had first agreed with). It was likewise impossible to ignore the Duma, which had reminded everyone of its existence by the work of its Budget Committee. For his part the chairman of the Duma did not cease pestering the tsar with his reports on the difficult situation inside the country and at the front. The tsar did not like him; Maklakov hated him. In his post as chairman, Rodzianko came to the forefront as spokesman for the Duma and for public opinion. Maklakov called him "pompous and stupid." "Pompous," Rodzianko was not; he played his role simply and honestly. We know him, however: he "boiled over," swelled up in the awareness of his great mission, and "flowed to temple." "Stupid" he was; in his reports, as in his memoirs, he simplified and exaggerated the situation—probably under Guchkov's influence. Alarmism was part of his nature. It was ironic that, frightening the tsar, he confirmed Maklakov's prognosis, though from the opposite side. Nevertheless, in spite of all that, it was impossible not to pay attention to him. The back-stage kitchen was unknown to us, but there, apparently, they decided to make a concession, and Goremykin received the tsar's sanction to convene the Duma "no later than Aug-

ust." This did not satisfy us, and in the Council of Elders we decided
to get the date pushed up. This time Goremykin did not refuse to
receive our delegation; I was given the task of speaking with him,
apparently in order to give the conversation a sense of urgency. I
really did raise the tone of the meeting; and I spoke without inhibi-
tion, referring to both factors of the changed situation: the failures at
the front and the public discontent created by the government's policy. I pointed out the impossibility of finding the chief culprits of this
discontent in the Duma, and I stressed the necessity of dismissing
Maklakov and Sukhomlinov. I spoke for a long time; Goremykin heard
me in silence; but it could be seen that even before our meeting he
had reached some kind of decision. He did not say, as he usually did:
"That's a mere trifle; everything will be all right in the end." He stuck
to the letter of the decree: "no later than August," and he pleaded the
necessity of preparing bills to be introduced in the new session. He
was answered, of course, that the Duma has its own bills, and the
government's bills can be introduced later. After our long insistence,
Goremykin made a small concession and pushed up the date for convening the Duma to July 19. The decree was published ten days before—on July 9. In private conversations with Rodzianko and with us
he hinted mysteriously that, given the present situation of public
opinion, a "change in circumstances" must precede the convening of
the Duma. The meaning of this hint soon became apparent. On July
7, unexpectedly for himself—that is how the tsar usually acted with
his ministers—Maklakov was fired. His successor was Prince Shcherbatov, an impersonal but respectable man. On July 11 Sukhomlinov
was dismissed—just as unexpectedly as Maklakov. The third member
of this solid trio, Shcheglovitov, who had earned the special indignation of the Russian public, received his retirement somewhat later,
being replaced by A. A. Khvostov. Sabler also left, and his post of
chief procurator of the Synod was taken by A. D. Samarin. Samarin
had pleased the tsar with his cooperation during the time of the
Jubilee trip in 1913. At the same time he was popular among the
nobility and especially in the Moscow circles. This personal appointment of the tsar turned out to be unfortunate for the ruling power,
because Samarin, a man of right-wing convictions, was too honest
and unbending in his religious convictions, and interfered with the
twisting and shady church politics, the roots of which led through
Rasputin to the empress.

The way to opening the July session of the Duma was now clear.
The most hated names had disappeared from the stage and could no
longer serve as a target for the Duma's attacks. Nevertheless, the Duma
could not be satisfied with the new appointments except for General

Polivanov, who had drawn near to Guchkov and the Duma circles in general during the time of the Third Duma. The retention of Goremykin continued to cast a special shadow on the government. This man was an immovable stone weighing down upon government policy, and his person symbolized the absence of any substantial change in the direction of that policy. Although a new "liberal" group appeared among the renovated government, whose leadership actually belonged to Krivoshein, this was far from sufficient for the Duma, which had managed to unify itself and find its majority. The struggle against the government was, apparently, hopeless and lost its interest. First in the order of business was the Duma's appeal directly to the supreme authority. The session opened with a whole series of statements to the effect that it was impossible to come to an agreement with the existing government—and that it was not even worth the trouble. The Duma felt that it had the power to make such statements, above all, because of its own solidarity in the form of the so-called Progressive bloc.

The Progressive Bloc

THE CREATION AND THE FATE of the Progressive bloc doubtlessly comprises a separate chapter in the history of the development of the prerevolutionary atmosphere. Its political significance lay in the fact that it was the last attempt to find a peaceful way out of a situation which from day to day was becoming ever more threatening. The means used to do this consisted in forming, within the limits of the legislative institutions, a majority of representatives which would take the direction of future events into its own hands. As one can see from what has been said, the time for that attempt was quite favorable. The mood in both chambers became identical in spite of the differences between the political parties. In its own way this was a "surrogate" of the "sacred union" between the government and the country after the latter had been destroyed. This mood still had to be transformed into a political fact.

That turned out to be my special mission. They called me "the author of the bloc," the "leader of the bloc," and they waited for me to give it its political direction. Returning my thoughts to that moment, I can say now that this was the culmination of my political career. I did not reach that point by accident. Such titles as "party leader," "leader of the Duma opposition," "leader of the Duma" (as I was symbolically chosen for the last conversation with Goremykin), themselves showed the route by which I became "leader of the bloc." This role was thus not a result of my personal choice: it was given to me, so to say, automatically—and just as with the previous stages, I did not go out of my way to seek it. Perhaps I could have done more if I would have been a real political "seeker." I did not create situations; I took them ready made, as I found them, and within the limits of those situations I tried to do the maximum possible. Perhaps, for this reason, the curve of my political life never fell too low, though, on the other hand, never rose too high, either.

Moreover, I could not be especially proud of my role, because I understood its inevitable limitations. The Duma gave itself up to me;

but this was the Duma of June 3. Now the center, normal for its predecessors, shifted to the left; and I ended up in the center. The way events were developing, this center might be shifted further—even beyond the bounds of the Duma; and this was precisely what the Progressive bloc wanted to avoid. But could it? In addition to the danger from above, from the dynastic monomania of the royal couple, was not danger also threatening from below—that same danger which had constantly threatened both from the right and the left, although it was not yet the order of the day? I was still a historian—and I studied the history of social movements. I could not help knowing that a certain dynamism existed in these movements which was independent of personal will. Even if I had not known this, my own experience of 1905 would have taught it to me. At that time I had sensed the vanity of my own personal efforts to direct the impulsive current of revolution into a channel for conscious utilization. And now, what was in the making threatened to take on much greater dimensions than before. It was precisely in these months that I reread Taine—with a different attitude than when I had compared him to Michelet during my student years. Our Russian experience was sufficient to snatch the halo from "revolution" as such and to destroy its mystique, in my eyes at least. I knew that my place was not there.

True, next to me stood people—and their numbers were rapidly increasing—who were hoping to prevent the spontaneous revolution by a palace revolution, dethroning the royal couple. Of those people, I have already named Guchkov. In his testimony before the Extraordinary Commission, Guchkov, using hindsight, very confidently developed his thesis—and even turned it into an indictment of those who had let the opportunity slip by. He considered that the "historical guilt of Russian society" lay in the fact that it "did not take this revolution into its hands", but "left it to spontaneous forces." I am not sure that this accusation does not apply in some degree to Guchkov himself, who loved to create spectacular situations which ended in failure. He remained faithful to his ideas to the very end, and as far as I know, his accusation was aimed at me personally. Without getting into polemics, I will say for the moment only that during the period of the formation of the Progressive bloc of 1915, the atmosphere which would have suited Guchkov's plans simply did not exist. That atmosphere arose and spread itself everywhere only one year later, in the second half of 1916 and only as the result of the bloc's failure. We shall see what use the "bloc" then made of it. It should be made clear that, essentially, the period of "exaltation and decline" of the "bloc's" great political activity belongs to the short interval between May and September of 1915; it is connected with the preparation, the activity and the postponement of the "prolonged" Duma session. However, the political consequences of the later existence of the "bloc" had their effect right up to the February revolution of 1917.

Returning to my role in the "bloc" in this period, let me add also that I cannot ascribe my success to my own personal qualities, since these qualities derived from my political position. For the "bloc" I represented, so to say, the limit of possible achievements for this Duma and the frontier against future threats. Thus, V. V. Shulgin, who was obsessed by the Jewish question, did not hide the fact that he considered me some sort of guarantee against Jewish world "domination." The Octobrist landowners, like Shidlovsky, had to admit that the Kadet agrarian program, in spite of "forced expropriation", was the nearest reasonable limit of their concessions and a means of keeping the transfer of lands to the peasants within the framework of the law. All of them waited for me to give a rebuff to the social and political demands of the extreme parties. Finally, even the nationalists of the Fourth Duma could convince themselves during the war of the sincere patriotic feelings of the People's Freedom party. The time had passed when Guchkov in the Third Duma did not allow us to take part in the Defense Committee under the pretext of preserving state secrets. Now in questions of defense, Shingarev and myself had the first say, and it was we who had to preserve state secrets from the rightists.

After this necessary personal digression, I will now switch over to the detailed story. Since we were petitioning for a prolonged session of the Duma, the first step in preparing the Duma's work was to elaborate the program of business. I busied myself with this more than anything else, and as early as May, when I was preparing my report for the forthcoming party conference (June 6–8), I composed a list of urgent projects for Duma legislation, concerning the most important domestic questions. Of course, we would not wait for government bills to be introduced and limit ourselves to "questions of the war," as Goremykin would have liked. On the other hand, we had to choose those projects which would unify the Duma. First on the list were important bills concerning municipal self-government and the formation of a Zemstvo unit on the volost level. Then there followed measures for a renovation of the administration and a reconciliation with the national minorities of the empire. The party conference discussed and accepted my project, and I introduced it for discussion in the Council of Elders. The discussion went along party lines, and disagreements from both the right and the left came to light. I considered that my project was the minimum that we could accept at the given time. The Progressivists and the leftists wanted to include as well bills on political liberties which we had already introduced and discussed in the Fourth Duma. I refused to do this. The rightists did not consent to include questions concerning domestic policy. The debates continued throughout all of June, and it was during this time that the nucleus of the future "bloc" was outlined. Thanks to the separating out of the two extreme flanks, it was possible to preserve the content of the program in the form I desired.

It was more difficult to solve the second problem: by what methods would it be possible to implement this program, which had come out rather radical. It was perfectly clear that with Goremykin's cabinet, even though it had been renovated, it would be impossible to carry out this program in practice. Here began the main difficulties in both directions. In the first session where a desirable cabinet was discussed, Krivoshein's name was mentioned as premier. This, of course, changed the whole political meaning of the bloc, and we broke with these mediators, such as P. Krupensky. Other names were mentioned —Khvostov and even Guchkov; but this did not suit us. Then, parallel to our own bloc, the rightists began talking about forming a "black bloc," relying on support from the right wing of the State Council. The deputy nationalists like Balashov and Chikhaev attempted to counterpose their own idea of a bloc to ours: the creation of an information bureau among the rightist groups of both legislative chambers. In August this difference in intentions led to open conflict.

Our support in this struggle came from the public organizations which by that time had managed to grow up around the Duma, so to say. Since the time of the pre-bloc period their own attitudes had changed significantly. Even Prince Lvov's strictly business organization was being penetrated by political attitudes. This can be shown by the excited atmosphere of its congresses. At its first congress on March 12, 1915, which had closely followed the demonstration of the "sacred union" in the short Duma session of January 27–29, patriotic enthusiasm was displayed, most-faithful-servant telegrams were sent to representatives of the royal family and "hurrahs" were sounded in honor of the sovereign. Convoked by telegraph on June 5 during the days of our army's retreat and of our worries about opening the prolonged session, the second congress was pervaded by a different atmosphere. The congress declared that "the great national cause is not being pursued according to those principles which assure its success." "The final victory can be assured only by a total exertion of all the national forces, given complete mutual trust between the government and the country." The word had been spoken. The congress talked of a "complete agreement of the people, in the person of the Duma as the organ of the people's representatives, with the higher organs of State government." We received support and together with it, a demand. Lvov called upon the Zemstvoists "to implore the monarch to convoke the Duma without delay." This was in June.

Moscow went even farther than the Zemstvoists, thereby vindicating its old reputation as a center of opposition. Placed at the head of the Union of Cities as far back as the liberal years of 1904–5, Moscow not only brought purely businesslike work into the union, but also the political spirit of "Kadetism." As has been recounted in these memoirs, Russia's first capital was the birthplace of "Kadetism"; and thus it remained even after the center of political activity was transferred to Petersburg, following the Dumas. For all that, Moscow retained its freedom from the limitations which the Duma activity had placed on the Petersburg center. The Moscow City Duma was the arena for practical application of Kadet aspirations; and a struggle was concentrated around it in which "politics" was inextricably linked with "action." According to the old law of 1892 Moscow was ruled by a handful of town-councilors elected by the merchant class. Out of a population of one and a half million, only ninety-five hundred possessed the right to vote; and of those, not more than three thousand turned out at the elections. As a result, the group of "old Duma members," calling itself "moderate businesslike," or "moderate non-partisan," held a majority and bossed the show in the city Duma, while a small group of representatives from the Moscow intelligentsia, under the name "progressive," waged a struggle against them to democratize city government. The struggle turned out to be far from hopeless, and in 1913 the "Progressivists" elected Prince Lvov as mayor over N. I. Guchkov, the brother of Alexander Ivanovich Guchkov who had just failed to be reelected to the Duma in the first curia. But this was a "Kadet," antigovernmental demonstration! According to the law of 1892 the city mayor was appointed by the superior authorities from two candidates elected by the City Duma. Maklakov, who had become minister by that time, made use of this law not to confirm Lvov's election; and he systematically refused to confirm all the other candidates offered by the Moscow Duma, threatening to appoint by decree a government deputy to Moscow. At one time even Stürmer sailed out as a candidate for this post, seeking to worm himself into any lucrative den of depravity which opened up. This appointment, however, was just too indecent, and it fell through. With the beginning of the war, they were forced to confirm the candidate elected by the Duma, M. V. Chelnokov. In order to emphasize the businesslike character of the election, Chelnokov simultaneously refused to participate in the Kadet party. He was a true Russian, a person of natural gifts, organically linked to the soil on which he grew up. With his drawling, almost lazy "Maahscow" accent, he was not born to be an orator (much as Lvov, with his village slang was not), and he was not entirely at home in his role of deputy in the Second Duma. On the other hand, he was very much at home in the Moscow merchant circles. Everywhere he went he brought his penetrating mind, his worldly dexterity, and his slightly skeptical attitude toward things and people. Nevertheless, he was still not able to shed his coat of "Kadetism"; and, in general, he went along with us as part of our "chorus."

After the start of the war, the Union of Cities united, if not formally, at least in practice, with the Zemstvo Union in their mutual work of serving the wounded and, later, the refugees who were flooding the inner provinces in their massive exodus from the occupied provinces and the provinces at the front, and it, too, was subjected to identical obstacles and persecution from above. Influenced by the Moscow intelligentsia, however, the union experienced none of the conciliatory illusions that Prince Lvov did, and went farther in its political conclusions and reached them sooner. From this derived the unexpected (for me) leftism of the "Progressivist" Duma faction, which, as has already been noted, in part, suddenly jumped over us into the ideological neighborhood of the Duma's extreme left wing, and separated off from the "bloc." We shall now see the consequences of this move, which were so painful for me.

Before that, however, let me dwell for a moment on the third public union which also affected the atmosphere in the Duma: the Military-Industrial Committee headed by A. I. Guchkov. Given its connection with big Russian industry working on defense, this committee should have turned out to be the most moderate, and the government should have taken it into special consideration. But it also had another front, the factory workers, and here it turned out to be very far to the left. A "workers' group" was brought into the Military-Industrial Committee; representing the factories, this group was given special patronage by Guchkov. These workers' representatives were Social Democrats of the moderate tendency, and their leader was the very intelligent and sensible worker, Gvozdev. Among them, however, there appeared a certain Abrosimov, obviously a provocateur, who delivered fiery speeches and who egged the group on to revolutionary action. It was obvious that this was the work of the tsarist police (this was confirmed later) and more than likely its aim was the same as it was before the Bolshevik uprising in December 1905: to provoke an artificial revolutionary flare-up and then to shoot it down. All this would have been innocent enough if at the same time the workers' group had not been busy organizing its sections in the provinces, and if, on the other hand, a whole series of worker disturbances had not begun in the country, provoked, it is true, not by political, but primarily by purely economic reasons: the rise in food prices, the devaluation of the workers' wages, etc. Given the presence of these complications, the situation at the factories became quite alarming, and the government's suspicion toward the Military-Industrial Committee was aggravated.

It was under these circumstances that the "bloc" had to formulate its views on the question of insuring the passage of its program by the corresponding group in the government. I personally insisted on accepting the formula according to which the government desired by the bloc would have to secure "union with the entire country and enjoy its confidence." This formula was deliberately vague and did not indicate the composition of such a government; on the other hand, it could unite all parts of the bloc. The Progressivists were not satisfied with this and introduced their own formula "for a ministerial cabinet responsible to the people's representatives." This meant the realization of a parliamentary system, that is, a sort of revolution, with which neither the supreme authorities nor the right-wing section of the bloc could knowingly agree. I resolutely refused to support this formula. The City Union, however, adopted it, while the Zemstvo Union adopted mine and remained faithful to it until the very end. Because political knowledge was not widespread, the difference between these two formulas remained little noticed by the public at large. However, our adversaries from both the right and the left lost no time interpreting it—which threatened beforehand to produce untoward consequences for the bloc. I was thus bypassed and forced to defend a position I had chosen against dual pressure, but especially pressure from the left. In addition, the Duma's final stance was defined with respect to the social currents which had overtaken and passed it by.

I had no doubts about the choice. If the Duma were predestined to play an independent role, then it could do so only if it retained its own identity. The public organizations of that time had already recognized the Duma as it was, and had leaned on it for support as the truly popular representative body. On the other hand, I knew only too well that the Duma of June 3 was a Noah's Ark which contained each kind of animal in pairs, in expectation of the threatening deluge. The question inevitably arose: after the deluge was over, who in this ark would be spared for a new life? Would the various types of Black Hundreds with their government subsidies come out of it unharmed? Was it possible that the stupid landowner-aristocrats would blossom forth, like Markov II, who reigned in the Kursk gubernia, or the Krupensky family who owned Bessarabia as their own estate? It goes without saying that I thought this could not happen. In that case the Duma's role would turn out to be temporary and transitory. Nevertheless, precisely this position had to be strengthened. Here then, the trenches were dug and a regular struggle was waged around them. And this machinery of state was under my direction. I went about my task, and from it there followed certain consequences to which we will return shortly.

After working out its program and defining the character of the future government, the third step in the formation of the "bloc" was the strengthening of the bloc by bringing the Duma closer to other realistic forces (besides those with which this had already occurred), to the public organizations. Here, above all, we were faced with the task of strengthening our ties with the army. This problem, of course, had been solved by the previous activities of both the Duma and the public organizations. The rapprochement with the army by groups was achieved, essentially, over the head of the government; it was, in fact, a fait accompli. It turned out, however, that here too we were faced with a future choice. The army was headed by the supreme commander, the Grand Duke Nikolai Nikolaevich, whom the First Zemstvo Congress honored with the title "Russian Hero." It was precisely this that evoked opposition toward him from the royal couple. The empress was already afraid for her spouse; rumors began to be spread that Nikolai Nikolaevich was preparing his own candidacy for the royal throne. By this time, the tsarina had fallen out with the "dark women" (the Montenegrins) with whom she had previously occupied herself with spiritualist seances and mesmerism; and one of these women, Anastasia, was the wife of Nikolai Nikolaevich. From the other side the government, too, even in its renovated state, had a score to settle with the military authorities because of the latter's constant interference in the civilian area. Goremykin warned the Council of Ministers that this conflict would lead to the dismissal of the supreme commander and to his replacement by the tsar himself. When this finally happened, the right-wing part of the Duma with the chairman at the head, took the side of Nikolai Nikolaevich, against the tsar's decision. From my point of view, this was a stupid and unnecessary interference, and directly dealt a blow to the politics of the bloc. I was not able to counteract it, however. Fortunately, this episode by itself did not spoil the army's attitude toward the Duma: the Duma retained its authority vis-à-vis the army command. We will also come back to this point later.

Next came the fulfillment of one of the most important tasks: the rapprochement of the Duma bloc with the State Council. As has already been mentioned, opposition to the Duma bloc formation came from the right wing of the State Council. But here I had good luck. As it turned out, the political attitudes which had helped to unify the Duma reached even the upper chamber. Above all, the left-wing group of the State Council was of like mind with us: this group included such members as our Kadet Professor Grimm, Meller-Zakomelsky, and Count Olsufiev, who adhered to the bloc. Even the most right-wing members, like Gurko, turned up in our ranks—and even expressed themselves in the most radical manner. In a note which Trepov sent to the sovereign in November 1916 the State Council's leftward shift was also explained by political reasons. "For the last two years the series of appointments to the State Council of persons who do not belong to the right wing in their opinions, combined with the sharp reduction of the number of conservatively inclined elected members of the State Council, has been reflected very substantially in the numerical relation of separate groups in the State Council. The right-wing group, even when united with its nearest neighboring group from the right center, was not only disinclined to stand wholly on the point of view of the rightist group, in the sense of union with the government, but in its chairman's speech, it underscored its definitely negative attitude toward the head of the Ministry for Internal Affairs (A. D. Protopopov), and its lack of confidence in the government's attempts at unification. . . . Then, speeches by various representatives of groups in the State Council, who had joined with representatives from the majority of the Duma's parties to form a so-called parliamentary bloc, were substantially the same as the speeches of the members of the State Duma, in some cases even in the sharpness of their tone. Thus, the mutual relations between the government and the State Council likewise cannot be considered as assuring the mutual trust and the proper union."

Given such a situation, I brought in our program to be discussed jointly with the members of the State Council. We held several joint conferences in Meller-Zakomelsky's apartment under the chairmanship of the host. I unofficially took notes on the speeches of the participants; these notes were preserved among my papers and were later published by the Bolsheviks.[44] I much regret that I do not have the printed text in my hands so that I could summarize here the extraordinary character of this exchange of opinion. As a result of the discussion the bloc's program was adopted without any significant changes. This circumstance, of course, gave the bloc a special meaning, since it removed the obstacle to passing legislation through both legislative chambers at the initiative of the Duma. Such a profound change in the system which had been created by the Fundamental Laws of 1906, of course, was bound to evoke special concern in the ranks of the government.

The Offensive and the Struggle
Against the Bloc

THE BLOC was still in the discussion stage when the Duma began its
session on July 19—a session which we thought would be a long one.
Nevertheless, the spirit of the bloc was already evident, and this was
immediately reflected in the introductory speeches of the Duma
members. Even such a nationalist as Count V. A. Bobrinsky mounted
the tribune and demanded "a display of patriotic skepticism toward
everything that the government presents." The transition formula
which he introduced set forth the bloc's basic thesis: "union of the
whole country and a government which enjoys the country's complete
trust." This same demand was modified somewhat in the speeches of
V. N. Lvov and N. V. Savich (Octobrist). Only I. N. Efremov in the
name of the Progressivists demanded a cabinet responsible to the
people's representatives. To our formula of a "cabinet of confidence,"
I added also a list of reforms which had to be introduced without
delay. The bloc was finally ready in August, and its program was
publicized both in print and from the Duma tribune on August 21.
Goremykin tried to break up the bloc by summoning the representatives of the bloc's right wing to a conference on August 15 in order
to organize a counter bloc. But it was too late; the colleagues he invited informed him that the majority in the Duma did not wish to
negotiate with him. At that time opinion was divided in the Council
of Ministers. The minority of rightists agreed with Goremykin that
the Duma must be dissolved. We know, however, that there was a
"liberal" group within the Council of Ministers[45] which had a different view on this issue. It too was negatively disposed toward the
bloc as a whole, but it nevertheless decided to attempt to reach an
agreement. Even the wholly "illiberal" Prince V. Shakhovsky said in
the council: "It is impossible not to take into consideration the fact
that the defeats at the front have created a charged, revolutionary
atmosphere in the country." "We must tell His Highness that as long

as the public mood in general and the Moscow mood in particular still remain moderate and clothed in respectable forms, to sweep it all aside indiscriminately would be dangerous." Krivoshein, the leader of the group who had still not given up hope of becoming premier, posed the dilemma pointblank (August 19): "We must either react with faith in our power or we must openly start on the road of winning moral confidence for the government." He justly noted: "We are capable of neither the one nor the other." . . . No wonder he already felt this: if the government were to concede, then he already had a dangerous rival—Prince Lvov. "This prince is just about making himself chairman of some sort of government. At the front, they speak only of him; he is the savior of the situation; he supplies the army; he feeds the hungry; he cures the sick; he arranges barbershops for the soldiers. In a word, he is some kind of an omnipresent Miur and Meriliz (a Moscow department store). . . . We must either put an end to it or turn over complete authority to him. . . . If it is impossible to take away from the (Zemstvo) Union what it has seized thus far, then at any rate, we must not expand its activities any further."

Krivoshein's acumen was evidenced quite clearly here: Prince Lvov already stood behind the Duma bloc. Nevertheless, the liberal group of ministers decided to try, if not to reach an agreement with the bloc, then at least to talk to it. On August 27, at Kharitonov's apartment a "private conference" was held between this group of ministers and the representatives of the bloc. The bloc's program was read and discussed point by point. This is an opportune time to examine the content of that program.

The program rested on two basic principles: (1) the creation of a homogeneous government composed of persons enjoying the confidence of the country who have decided to carry out, in the shortest possible time, the program agreed upon by the two chambers; (2) a radical change in the present mode of government which was based on distrust of any independent political activity; in particular a strict observance of legality in administration, the noninterference by the military and civilian authorities in questions which do not directly concern military operations; a change in the local administrative personnel, and the adoption of a reasonable and consistent policy capable of preserving internal peace and of avoiding clashes between the social classes and between the various nationalities. The bloc's program then indicated a whole series of measures for carrying out the enumerated tasks. These included mainly administrative measures: a general amnesty for political and religious crimes and offenses, the return of political exiles, the cessation of religious persecution, granting of autonomy to Poland, abolition of legal restrictions against Jews, prohibition of persecution of Ukrainians in Russia and in Galicia, and the restoration of professional labor unions. Then there followed a series of legislative measures including: equalization of peasants with other classes before the law, the creation of a Zemstvo organization on the volost level, and a reform of the city and Zemstvo institutions.

Of course, for the existing government, this program was unacceptable. It was no whim, seriously based on a "ministry of confidence." It was understood in just that way—mainly between me and Kharitonov. He admitted that although several of the points in the program were impractical and unessential, five-sixths of the program was acceptable—except that the given composition of the cabinet would not be able to carry it out. They were not empowered to speak about a "ministry of confidence"; for this they had to make a report to the tsar. On the next day this conclusion was delivered to the conference of the Council of Ministers. Krivoshein did not hide his skepticism: "No matter what we promise, no matter how much we flirt with the progressive bloc and the public, all the same, they will not trust us for anything. The demands of the State Duma and of the whole country are not a question of program, but one of people." And he concluded: "Let the monarch decide how he wants to direct the future internal policy—by ignoring such desires, or by reconciliation." In the second case "he will select a person enjoying the public sympathy and will entrust him with the formation of a government measuring up to the hopes of the country." This sounded a bit ironic coming from the lips of the old courtier; while for Goremykin, the very possibility of placing the monarch before such a choice was already a crime. "As long as I live, I will fight for the inviolability of the tsar's authority"—such was his immovable thesis. In the given case, however, he had another conflict with the ministers which violated this thesis and which, from the dynastic point of view was infinitely more important than the question of ministerial confidence. "When the enemy penetrated deeply into the territory of the empire," it was announced in a rescript of August 4, the tsar felt the need to take over the command of the army himself. The empress thus got the chance to settle accounts with "Nikolasha"; both she and Rasputin supported the tsar in his conviction that this was his religious and "sacred" duty. There could be no argument about that; but the ministers began to argue all the same. At the conference of the Council of Ministers held at Tsarskoe Selo on August 20, under the chairmanship of the tsar, they disagreed with Goremykin who supported Nicholas in the decision, which the latter had already made, to take over the post of commander-in-chief. After the conference, eight "liberal" ministers gave the tsar a written statement insisting that Grand Duke Nikolai Nikolaevich keep his post, admitting their "fundamental difference of opinion" with Goremykin and declaring that "under such conditions they lost their faith in the possibility of usefully serving the tsar and the motherland." The Duma too was dragged into this hopeless conflict through the intervention of Rodzianko who raised a fuss, became all excited, and went to persuade Nicholas to cancel his decision. Rodzianko, of course, did not change Nicholas' mind, but only angered him. Naturally, the subtlety of both the bloc and the "ministry of confidence" was drowned in the question which touched upon the Court, and Goremykin could kill both birds with one stone. On August 29, immediately after the conference on the bloc, he departed for General Headquarters (where the tsar had already moved) without reaching an agreement with his colleagues; and he returned from there with prepared decisions. In Goremykin's words, "all of them got a good scolding for that August letter and for their behavior during the August crisis." The tsar decided: "The Duma must be closed no later than September 3, and all the ministers are to remain at their posts." Nicholas, of course, could not accept their "constitutional" resignation. The tsar "will arrive and settle everything personally." On September 16 a conference was held at the General Headquarters for which Nicholas was carefully prepared by the empress and Rasputin. "Do not be late for the ordeal; the Lord will glorify you with his appearance," thus telegraphed the "old man" on September 7. On the fifteenth, on the eve of the conference, the empress reminded him, "Do not forget to hold the icon in your hand and to comb your hair several times with *his* comb before the conference of ministers." The comb was set in motion, the tsar was "deliberately impolite" with his ministers, and one day later, after his arrival in Petersburg, he signed the dismissal notice for two of the eight minister-protestors who were especially detested by the tsarina's circle: Shcherbatov and Samarin. The same fate was in store for the remaining six. Thus began the new course.

The sharp leap to the right, after the visible successes of the progressive bloc which had, it seemed, opened prospects for a reconciliation between the tsar and the people's representatives, created a tremendous impression in the country. This impression was strengthened and deepened as the consequences of the change became evident. With his departure to General Headquarters in the seclusion of Mogilev, the tsar's personality somehow faded into the background. He was probably satisfied with this change as he began to lead a life more to his taste. Nicholas was not a strategist, and he could not, of course, guide the military operations. His workday was monotonous

and peaceful. Until ten o'clock in the morning, he was left to himself; he was not bothered either by the intrigues and gossip of the
Petersburg Court or by the cannon shots from the front. At ten
o'clock he went to the chief of staff, General Alexeev, and remained
there until eleven. With the aid of a large wall map and little flags,
Alexeev informed him about the shifting of troops the day before and
gave his opinions about future operations. This was more of a briefing
session than a conference, and the tsar could do nothing but agree. The
report finished by breakfast time, and after breakfast came tea. After
seven o'clock the mail came from Petersburg with letters from the
empress, who day after day informed him of political events, gave
him advice, and dictated decisions to him which in their definiteness
and insistence were not surpassed even by Alexeev's plans. From this
time on, at the tsar's expense, the tsarina came forward into the
limelight. The only "man in trousers," she received the ministers' reports and, ever more confidently, began to relish ruling the state.
Rasputin flattered her by comparisons with Catherine II. It goes without saying that in matters of state she understood even less than the
emperor did in military affairs. Her "rule" amounted to personal
preferences for some persons over others, depending on whether or
not these persons were friends or enemies of "our friend." The
Court was secluded within the confines of the tsarina's apartment and
the "little house" of her faithful but stupid friend, Anna Vyrubova.
Rasputin reigned over both of them, and around this central luminary
gathered circles of rogues and swindlers who fought for influence
over Rasputin and squabbled among themselves. There was Bardu-
kov's circle, which had been spared by Prince Meshchersky; the circle
of Prince Andronikov, who showed off with his informal manners and
his imaginary connections; the circle of Manesevich-Manuilov, a swin-
dler of the highest order, connected to the banks and to the secret
police; the circle of Doctor Badmaev, a specialist in Tibetan medicine
and the occult arts. All of them created a barrier which had to be
crossed in order to gain the favor of the tsarina's associates and to land
in the high posts—regardless of personal knowledge or merit. The
matter did not stop merely with the high posts, however. Petty, fast
dealers did their petty business, made appointments to various posts,
freed people from military service and judicial persecution, and so on
—all for appropriate price. Rasputin's apartment served as cover for
shady deals, and his letters of recommendation with the standard
formula "darling, help" were manufactured by the batch; all of this
was done for a fee, while Rasputin received the usual trifles which
were enough to assure him his cheap debauchery and his tavern exploits. This scandalous picture took shape gradually; but only at this

time, when crisis was threatening both the bloc and the government simultaneously, was the domestic front of the camarilla exposed to the public at large—that camarilla which, until this time, had been hidden behind the responsible executive authority. As the country became aware of who was really ruling it, the prestige of the supreme authority fell. In place of the traditional respect for the throne, indignation and contempt spread through the country toward that handful of people who were really responsible for the situation which had come about. It was from them, and not from the government puppets who were changed in a "ministerial leapfrog" (to use Purishkevich's apt expression), that the country now demanded a direct answer for what was going on.

The existence of the Duma with its bloc was, of course, the main obstacle which interfered with this whole concoction. On September 3 they almost freed themselves of the Duma, but not quite. It was impossible to dissolve the Duma, for then new elections would have to be scheduled. It was only possible to recess the Duma. It was recessed until November 15. Before this period was over, however, the activity of the extreme rightist organizations was aroused. The "United Nobility" held their congresses more frequently and spoke in a more militant tone. The various sections of the "Union of Russian people" were restored. Shcheglovitov chaired the Union's congress on November 21, and he delivered a speech declaring the act of October 17 to be "a defunct political instrument" and proposed a return to the instrument by which Mikhail Fedorovich had been elected tsar; that is, a return to a consultative Duma. He was a little too much in a hurry, though. True, in November, the convocation of the Duma was again postponed, for an indefinite period—which was a clear violation of the law: the reason devised was that the Duma committee had still not finished examining the budget. The bloc decided to hurry things up, and the Duma finished examining the budget by the end of December. Rodzianko reported this to the tsar and demanded that the Duma be convoked without delay. As before, Goremykin took a firm stand. He finally agreed to convoke the Duma for only five days and only in order to confirm the budget of 1916. Then began the intrigues aimed at shoving Goremykin aside. In connection with this intrigue, an interest in convoking the Duma was suddenly renewed in the higher spheres. Several days before the tsar's arrival in Tsarskoe Selo (January 18, 1916), Metropolitan Pitirim came to see Rodzianko and informed him in secret that it had already been decided to develop friendly relations with the Duma, to get rid of the implacable Goremykin and to appoint in his place—Stürmer! Stürmer apparently was the champion of this new turnabout. He was backed

by Rasputin, who called his candidate "a little old man on a leash."
In November this keen-witted little man solemnly uttered his Sibylline
prophecy: "If we are victorious, then the Duma will not have to be
convoked; if not, then it will." There was no victory. A replacement
had to be made.

Stürmer was not such a decrepit old man as Goremykin. Nevertheless, he displayed all the signs of old age and could walk "on a
leash." He was totally ignorant of everything he undertook; he was
unable to connect two words to express any kind of a serious thought:
for his speeches he had to write down or have someone else write
down on paper a few words or phrases. In serious questions he preferred to maintain a mysterious silence, as if to hide his decision. On
the other hand, he knew very well how to preserve his own interests
in all appointments. It was not difficult to persuade the tsar of the
impossibility of convoking the Duma only for a short period and only
for the budget. It was on this point that Stürmer was able to overthrow Goremykin. But what would be done with the bloc and with
the bloc's policy, which inevitably would be put forward in a Duma
uninhibited by a narrow framework?

As a mediator between Stürmer and the bloc, another minister
appeared who had also come through Rasputin and had also been
appointed unexpectedly: the "boring" Shcherbatov was replaced as
minister of internal affairs, by the "happy" A. N. Khvostov, another
figure from an operetta—or Guignol. Khvostov was a bright young
man, energetic and enterprising—only not when it came to activities
of state. When Nicholas II asked A. N. Khvostov's uncle, the minister
of justice, A. A. Khvostov, what opinion he had of the candidate, the
tsar received the answer: "Absolutely ignorant of the matter, unsuitable character, very sensible but unable to criticize his own motives
and thoughts; no stranger to intrigue. . . . His entire activity in service
will not be devoted to business, but to considerations alien to it." The
candidate was nevertheless appointed. Nicholas gave the appearance
that he was very interested in A. N. Khvostov's Duma speeches on
German dominance. In reality he was obliged to accept this candidate
put forward by Rasputin. We saw that on an assignment from Tsarskoe
Selo, Rasputin had earlier "felt the soul" of Khvostov (who was then
governor of Nizhny Novgorod), and had found him "unripe"; now he
admitted that "God ordains Khvostov even though he lacks something," and he turned the favor of the empress toward his protege.

At the request of Prince V. M. Volkonsky, the former deputy
chairman of the Duma and now deputy minister of internal affairs, I
went to a meeting with A. N. Khvostov at the apartment of Barun-
Sekret, the deputy chairman of the Duma. I found that a whole group

had gathered there to learn what the "leader of the bloc" thinks of
the Duma's new meeting with the government. A. N. Khvostov told
me that it had not yet been decided to convoke the Duma, and it
would not be decided until it became clear whether or not the bloc
would refrain from attacking Rasputin. The threat was artificial, and
the condition set for convoking the Duma seemed too strange. I
answered that the Duma had much more important accounts to settle
with the government than such gossip. The Duma had come to an
abrupt end on the question of the bloc's program and the creation of
a government enjoying the public confidence. It was with this question
that the Duma would have to begin again. In the Duma there was a
leader, and this leader had a definite opinion. I was then asked
whether or not it was at all possible to have more friendly relations
between the bloc and Stürmer. It was proposed to bring about this
rapprochement in the form of a large evening reception to be given
by Stürmer. They then reminded me that the Duma had gone to a
reception given by Goremykin. I answered that there was a difference
between January 1915 and January 1916; we raised the question of
"confidence"; we have no confidence in Stürmer, and at any rate, I
said, my faction would not go to the reception; we are waiting for a
clarification of the fundamental questions which have been raised by
the majority. They tried to persuade me, saying that Stürmer was a
new man, that he did not know politics and that his attitude toward
the bloc might depend on a friendly reception. In answer to this I
declared resolutely that the situation has become too aggravated for
such an experiment, that we would have to express ourselves definitely,
and that we would do this not at a reception, but at the very first
session of the Duma: it was there that Stürmer would find out our
wishes and our attitude toward the government. On this point our
talk ended. Later on, Stürmer met with Rodzianko, and there were
attempts to speak with representatives of the individual factions. In
the documents later made public by the Extraordinary Commission,
the hesitation regarding the date on which the Duma was to be convoked, the length of the session and a discussion of the guarantees for
a peaceful meeting were all made clear. But all this remained on the
sidelines: I insisted on the Duma being convoked by February 5,
1916, and I conceded only postponing it until the ninth in view of
the technical difficulties of arranging the convocation. On the eve of
that day it became known that the tsar personally planned to visit the
Duma. This, apparently, was yet another means of influencing the
Duma—and it originated from that same clique. At least it is known
that Rasputin praised himself before his protectors: "They said to me:
how will things go with the State Duma. I have no idea at all. . . .

But do you know what? I'll send him to the Duma himself; let him go and open the Duma and nobody will dare say anything." . . . This was still in December 1915.

The royal visit actually did take place, on February 9, the day the Duma was opened. It was the only such visit in the entire existence of the Duma. The ritual of "enthusiasm," of course, was observed. Before his entrance into the session hall, a public prayer service was improvised in the columned hall of the Taurida Palace. The deputies surrounded the tsar. I stood far away from the dense nucleus and did not hear the tsar's short speech; they said that it was colorless but well disposed. Then Rodzianko, who had been informed of the tsar's visit only an hour beforehand, led Nicholas into the hall, and the public in the gallery joined in the ovation. He showed the tsar the Duma's other rooms, and the tsar made some insignificant remarks. In the round hall (next to the entrance of the palace) the Duma Elders gathered; and Rodzianko introduced them to Nicholas as the tsar was leaving. Rodzianko called everyone by name, and the tsar shook each person's hand. This introduction remained in my memory because of one small incident. Moving several steps away from our group, Nicholas suddenly stopped and turned around, and I felt his intent gaze on me. For several instants I held out, then unexpectedly even for myself, I smiled and lowered my eyes. I remember that in that moment, I felt sorry for him as for a condemned man. Everything happened so quickly that no one noticed the incident at all. The tsar turned around and left.

Nicholas' visit changed exactly nothing. Politics remained the same. Simultaneously with the announcement of the decree convoking the Duma, another one of the "eight" was dismissed—Kharitonov. Krivoshein, feeling that he had nothing to wait for, humbly had already left, at his own request, in November 1915. In September, the tsar refused to receive the delegation elected by the Third Congress of the Zemstvo organization (September 7-9) which had joined with the members of the City Union under the chairmanship of Prince Lvov. And no wonder: Lvov stated once and for all at the congress that "the mighty union of government activity with public activity, so much desired by the entire country, has not taken place"; and the congress' resolution repeated the formula of the bloc, from the Duma which had just been closed: "The threat of disastrous destruction of internal unity can be eliminated only by a renovation of the government; and the government can be strong only if it has the confidence of the country, only in a union with the country's legal representatives." The congresses of the union, scheduled for December 5, were banned.

As it desired, the bloc met Stürmer for the first time only in the Duma session. The new premier made the impression of total failure. In a weak voice which could not command even the peaceful and silent audience, Stürmer read his introductory speech from his notes. His speech included a categorical statement about the inflexibility of the historical foundations on which the Russian state had grown and become strong; and this was enough. Before us stood a new variation of Goremykin. The bloc finished the session with the statement that had been prepared for the opening of the Duma in November, which never took place. For this new session the statement had been revised and strengthened. We pointed out that the six months delay in convoking the Duma had aggravated all the problems and that it was now impossible to find a way out of the difficult situation. Our demands, which were essential and fundamental, remained unsatisfied, and we retained our previous position. We had prepared the country for victory, but now, because the old order of government had been preserved, we considered that victory to be impossible. We did not see any way out of the situation by means of the Duma's own forces. In the name of the bloc I finished this statement on a note of pessimism: "I do not expect an answer from this government"; and I left the rostrum without an answer.

Stürmer, however, did not immediately refuse to come to an agreement with the Duma about refraining from verbal attacks on Rasputin. The tsar was afraid of debates over the budget for the synod. Rodzianko had been promised that Rasputin would be removed if there would not be any "undesirable speeches." On February 24, Rodzianko invited the representatives of the bloc to his place and attempted to persuade them not to take the rostrum themselves and to support the chairman in case of excesses from the extreme right or left. He heard the answer that promises to eliminate the "old man's" influences had been given more than once, but that this "terrible ulcer on Russian life" continued to exist. It was impossible to shut the mouths of the deputies, especially "in the excited atmosphere reflecting the collective conscience." Nevertheless, on the next day, Rasputin was ordered to go to Tobolsk.

In the next few days, the career of A. N. Khvostov, the minister of internal affairs, was cut short, although this can in no way be laid to the efforts of the Duma. Khvostov fell victim to his own thoughtlessness, and Stürmer picked up the spoils. The detailed testimony of the director of the Police Department, later Deputy Minister Beletsky, lighted the lamp in that filthy kitchen where this scandal was cooked up. It all began when A. N. Khvostov, feeling that his position was sufficiently consolidated thanks to his ties with the rightists, decided that the time had come to do without the help of the Vyrubova-Rasputin circle which had brought him to power; and he set himself the goal of "liquidating" Rasputin. As his accomplice, he chose Beletsky who used all possible means of postponing the crime. At the same time, noticing that Goremykin's position was tottering, Khvostov found it an appropriate time to put forward his own candidacy for chairman of the Council of Ministers—a post for which Rasputin had pegged him from the very beginning. But he was too late. Stürmer's candidacy had already been urged on the tsar by that very same circle. Beletsky, saving himself, left Khvostov and went over to Stürmer's side, maintaining his relations with Vyrubova. Then, at his own risk, Khvostov returned to his plan of killing Rasputin. He thought to take advantage of the services of that violently fanatic monk, Iliodor, an old friend of Rasputin who had later argued with the "old man" and fled Russia. Once abroad he published a pamphlet against Rasputin ("The Holy Devil") with a supplement of letters which the empress had written him. Two missions were equipped and sent abroad by the Ministry of Internal Affairs: one with the aim of "ransoming" Iliodor's manuscript, the other—specially sent by Khvostov without Beletsky's knowledge—in order to make an agreement with Iliodor concerning the plan to kill Rasputin. Khvostov's go-between, the journalist Rzhevsky, turned out to be unreliable. The matter was made public. Khvostov threw the blame onto Beletsky; Beletsky proved that this was Khvostov's affair and told about the previous plans. Both sides resorted to the press and the scandal became public. In the Duma, my fellow faction member, Adzhemov, christened the scandal a "cheap novel." It all ended with both Khovstov and Beletsky being forced to abandon their posts (March 5, 1916). Stürmer had long considered it natural to combine the title of premier with the power of minister of internal affairs, and now he achieved his goal. This whole business gave society the impression that the political and personal morals in government circles had taken a profound plunge.

The Duma nevertheless continued its business, and, in spite of the wishes of the rightists, the Duma session could not be cut off as long as discussion of the budget continued. Both sides, as I said elsewhere, ensconced themselves in their trenches and went over to a positional war. Still, manifestations of this war on the part of the rightists continued. It was at that time that we learned that a campaign had been started against Count Ignatiev, whom they accused of antistate activities and subordination to the bloc. The struggle against Polivanov was waged even more energetically, however. It was aggravated in connection with labor disturbances which were beginning at that time in the factories. Debates on this matter were held in the meetings of the Conference on Defense. On the occasion of a strike at the Putilov Works, I pointed out that the reason for the strike was purely economic and lay in the fact that the wage rate lagged behind the increase in prices of essential items. Polivanov agreed with us. We then decided to transfer these debates to a closed session of the Duma (March 7), where I was able to develop my argument in more detail. My speech was considered so dangerous that the verbatim report was held up and appeared together with Polivanov's speech only on March 13. On March 15 Polivanov was dismissed and replaced by General Shumaev. A new low level of government was reached. As chairman of the Conference on Defense, the decrepit old man, Shumaev, made a pitiful impression: he absolutely could not follow the reports and lead the discussions, for he possessed neither knowledge nor the least bit of cultivated psychology. He was simply impossible in the role of minister of war.

The budget was finally discussed by the Duma and adopted by the end of March. The session was closed on April 5, and a break was announced until May 16. For the time being I will stop on that date, because on April 16 I had to leave Petersburg, as a member of a delegation to our allies from our legislative institutions.

The Duma Delegation Visits Our Allies[46]

THE IDEA of sending a Duma delegation to our allies arose in obvious connection with the attempts at reconciliation with the Duma at the beginning of 1916 and with the tsar's visit to the Duma. The idea was picked up first of all by the English circles in Petersburg and approved by the English Government, which hastened to send an official invitation to Rodzianko in March. Hearing of these proposals, Izvolsky, after much trouble, obtained a similar invitation from the French Government, and this was later extended to include the third Ally, Italy. In England they wanted to show the new military factories to the representatives of Russian public opinion, while in France they wanted to show the Russians the front. Besides the military aspect, a political idea was also doubtlessly behind this venture: namely, to rehabilitate Russia in the opinion of the Allied countries whose public circles regarded Russia with little sympathy. The existence of the Progressive bloc offered the possibility for the first time of showing off abroad the representatives of the Russian legislative institutions as a whole in the spirit of the "sacred union." For me, personally, this was an opportunity to reinforce the Russian Progressive tendencies through public European recognition and thereby to open a new door for our influence just at the moment when another door was being slammed in our faces.

The delegation consisted of seventeen members representing the State Council (6) and the State Duma (11). Of these, one from the council and three from the Duma belonged to the Kadet party; two from the council "adhered" to the Progressive bloc. Two belonged to the "center," one was an Octobrist, three called themselves "nationalists," and two were definitely "rightists." Separately, one of them represented the united Polish groups, while one represented the Belorussian-Lithuanian group. The defeatists—the extreme leftists and the extreme rightists—were absent.

Of course, given such a composition, the delegation could not command the respect of the European democracies. In the Allied countries to which we were traveling, the *union sacrée* was represented in both public and government circles by the socialists, whom their leftist colleagues had dubbed, as was mentioned above, "social patriots." Only the left wing of our delegation came in contact with their views and could speak the common, democratic language. Our left wing was put forward in all public and official demonstrations of a general character: Shingarev and I were the political face of our delegation.

True, the assistant chairman of the Duma, A. D. Protopopov, was placed above us in the role of governor. This name falls under my pen for the first time here, and I ought to dwell upon it if only because one year later he was destined to play the role of gravedigger of the tsarist regime. His role in the delegation was totally insignificant and we were forced to control his public appearances. He was a typical Russian nobleman from the era of "impoverishment." People from this stratum, ruined by the abolition of serfdom, attempted to switch to speculation, to commercial operations, or to exist at the expense of remortgaging their lands in the Nobles' Bank. They usually lacked sufficient business experience, and they were forced to compensate for this deficiency by the privileged position of their class. This explains their political and material dependence on the government. The result was a peculiar mixture of the old-fashioned gentleman and the external features of the gentry's noble breeding with the psychology of one who uneasily seeks favor from the strong. With Protopopov this degenerate psychology was masked by a traditional aristocratic air of culture—the fruit of domestic rather than higher education. As was typical of the nobility, he had a mastery of the French language; English he had picked up more from hearing it than studying it, while his knowledge of Italian did not go beyond the operatic arias. Also, as was typical of the nobility, he was not backward when it came to drinking; he loved good eating; and when overcome with feeling, he would take to kissing just anyone at all. In general, his manner was comradely and easygoing. Those who knew him more closely, however, found signs in him of progressive paralysis; and his absurd speeches seemed to confirm this diagnosis. I was rather inclined to explain these peculiarities as a variation of the psychology of the dying class.

The remaining members of the delegation abroad more or less straggled and faded into the background. I had the impression that they simply took advantage of the trip abroad in order to occupy themselves with their own individual business. Above all, the representatives of the various nationalities acted this way. The most outstanding of them, Count Wielopolski, told us that he would not have come if he had not counted on reaching an agreement with us (Kadets), and he said that in the delegation he would demonstrate solidarity with Russia. Naturally, he sought contact everywhere with Poles of various currents, promising to keep us informed. Another solicitor, the young deputy Ichas, who was nearest to us politically and a member of our faction, was swallowed up by his contacts with fellow Lithuanians. He explained their political aspirations as being somewhere between autonomy and independence. Above all, he came into contact with the opposition circles of the Catholic clergy. He did not tell us everything about his political work, but he did show us his other side. Sociable and cheerful, he called himself jokingly "the youngest and the most unmarried" member of our delegation, and in our meetings he performed his role with vigor.

I will not discuss the other members of our delegation whose activities escaped me; instead I will talk about our trip. Our time was measured out precisely. We left Petersburg on April 16, 1916; from the seventeenth to the twentieth we were in Sweden, the twentieth–twenty-first in Norway, April 22–May 7 in England. After England we also visited France and Italy and returned home one day before the close of the summer session of the Duma on June 19, 1916. The roundabout route via the Scandinavian states was the only one which the war had left free. The dismal landscape of the littoral Finnish plains covered by sparse pine growth led us to the border station of Torneo by evening, where I had the pleasure of taking a picture of the midnight sun at eleven o'clock at night. Crossing the marshy plain on a wooden raft with our luggage in our arms we reached the clean town of Gaparanda and found ourselves in Sweden, where we immediately sensed that our reception was far from friendly. In this neutral country, they did not wish to receive a delegation to the Allies and our emissary in Stockholm, A. V. Nekliudov, even tried to surround our train by some sort of secrecy. Of course, I knew the deeper reasons for this attitude toward Russia. The Court, the aristocracy, and the army suspected Russian diplomacy of expansionist plans. Not far from the Russian border we passed the Boden station where a secret underground fortification had been constructed, and from the neighboring Liuleo, the strategic railroad line led to the nearby Norwegian border, to Narvik with its magnetic ore on which Russia supposedly had some weak designs. Besides that, there was the question of Russia's arming the Aland Islands for the duration of the war. All of this was blown up by the chauvinist press and German propaganda. This was the only passage free from blockade for the goods we needed, and it was subjected to all possible constraints and restrictions.

The public attitude, however, was different from Sweden's official one; and I immediately came into contact with Swedish socialists and pacifists. I made the acquaintance of Branting, the "social-patriot," and found that we had several points of view in common. Even earlier, I was taken over by the pacifist circle headed by the burgomaster of Stockholm, the socialist Lindhagen, who was pursuing the special task of questioning the visiting Russian politician about the "aims of the war." After the Central Bureau of the Second International was liquidated in Brussels, Branting gave it refuge in Stockholm, and it was there that the idea arose of calling a conference of the International on the question of bringing the war to a rapid end by means of clarifying the aims of the war and the conditions of peace. A committee was formed for preparing the conference, and Lindhagen's circle gathered the preliminary information. I had to answer negatively to the questions which were put to me. I could not agree with their abstract statement of the problems which were being decided by the force of arms. The opinions of the "neutrals" could not influence the aspirations of those who were fighting. At this point I brought up the questions which were close to Russia's interest: the "liberation" of the nationalities in the areas occupied by the Germans; "free access" for Germany to the Near East, and so on. In general the German tendencies shone through here quite clearly. I noticed that my answers were being recorded—for the future. I saw the dissatisfied faces of my questioners, and I understood the meaning behind their insidious questions. Here for the first time, I came face to face with the differences in views between Russian radical-democrats and the left wing of public opinion among our allies.

Immediately upon our arrival in Norway, we breathed rather more freely. The landscape itself, flooded with sunshine, the neat and clean little homes, suddenly, after the unpopulated wild border, the precious valley of Grommen, and, finally, Christiania, which at that time had not yet been christened Oslo. Then there was the affectionate reception of our emissary, K. N. Gulkevich—a very different type from Nekliudov in Stockholm. Of course, Nekliudov, too, displayed society politeness and Russian hospitality and was even liberal in the contemporary fashion. But that was still not the same. A career diplomat, here today, there tomorrow, he sat out his term in Stockholm for his advancement, but he had little interest in the country and depended on chance informants, who brought him the "most reliable" secret news. From the start, Gulkevich gave me the impression of a vital person, directly interested in the milieu which surrounded him and bound to that milieu by simple and sincere human sympathy. The country itself won us over. Here, from our window, we did not see the heavy historical building of the royal castle; there were no old memories connected with it; there was no military-aristocratic class surrounding the Court; there was no prejudiced suspicion toward Russia. Pacifism itself looked different here, more acceptable: since the time of the first Duma we had been organically linked to this kind of pacifism by our contacts in the "interparliamentary union." Here I met the principle activist in this union, Lange, and I could speak with him calmly about the idea which I shared myself—the juridical organization of postwar Europe and the sanctions necessary to give it force. Lange carefully began speaking about disarmament, about the opinions of Schücking and Quidde, the German professor-pacifists who preferred ending the war in a draw. I made the objection that without a decisive victory, armaments would be increased even more than now. I advised him to continue constructing the international edifice of peace from that point at which the building had stopped and to leave aside the demands for international organizations while the actual conditions of peace were being worked out.

Before our departure from Christiania we learned that the secret of our trip was traveling with us. Some "Prussian" had informed a lady acquaintance that the Germans were perfectly well-informed of our route and that they were planning to "catch Miliukov"; they advised against traveling on the English vessel, "Jupiter" which was waiting for us near Bergen. Our "lords," as we called the members of the State Council, were deeply disturbed: Prince Lobanov-Rostovsky and Gurko even sent a telegram ordering a special train and asking that the "Jupiter"'s sailing be delayed for two and a half hours. The delegation decided to proceed without delay.

A railroad line, a remarkable monument to the art of engineering, leads to Bergen across a mountain pass. I will return to that later. We found Bergen in a sad moment of its existence: half the city had been destroyed by fire. We managed somehow to spend the night there and early the next morning moved on. The royal Norwegian yacht took us to the English cruiser—not to the "Jupiter," but to the "Donegal"—which was waiting for us, as agreed, in a secluded spot in the reefs twenty kilometers away. We were cordially met, and each person was given his own cabin. They fed us well, and after dinner the captain invited the diplomat Rosen, Protopopov, Count Wielopolski, myself, and Shingarev for further drinks. He turned out to be a very jovial fellow; he was already tipsy and struck up a song in a furious voice insisting that we join in with him. We sent for Ichas to lend us support and broke up late at night. Early in the morning, a surprise was in store for us. We were scheduled to get off in Cromarty (northern Scotland); but during the night the captain had received orders to change course, since the approach to Cromarty was strewn with enemy

mines. Apparently, our entire route had been discovered. They put us
off at the very tip of Scotland, in Thurso, in direct proximity to the
Orkney Islands, where the English squadron was based. Although it
was not on the program, the sailors decided to show us the squadron—a deep secret of the English admiralty. We, in fact, did see—in
the area which was later made famous by the name Scapa-Flow—five
dreadnaughts headed by the "Queen Elizabeth." The remaining vessels, under the command of the Admiral Jellicoe, were supposed to
return after them. We had to wait however, and the vice-admiral was
not at all prepared for an official reception. We preferred to return to
Thurso and to board the royal train which was waiting for us. We
had to pass through rather deserted places, across the entire island to
London. We were rewarded by a bountiful breakfast and dinner which
had been prepared for us. At nine o'clock in the morning on April
23, we were in London. They settled us in the Hotel Claridge which
had been specially leased by the government for receiving foreign
delegations—especially from the East. My first visit was devoted to my
old Russian friends, Dioneo-Shklovsky and Kropotkin (in Brighton).
I found the old man in good health but in a state of anxiety over the
success among the Social Democrats of the manifesto published by
the Zimmerwald Conference (against the "imperialist" war). Then
there came a series of all sorts of invitations, so plentiful that the
delegation could not satisfy them all—and there was no reason to do
so anyway. The majority of them dealt with performances, plays,
sports—none of which were scheduled especially for the delegation.
Those of us who wanted to go to them, signed up for them. Next
there came invitations to breakfasts and dinners with ministers and
political figures. There was a special invitation for dinner arranged
for the delegation by the Cabinet in the aristocratic Lancaster House,
a reception in the House of Commons, and, finally, to top it all, an
audience with the king in Buckingham Palace.

Actually, it all began with the audience in Buckingham Palace.
We were given a short course in Court etiquette, and for the first time
in my life I had to buy a top hat which I later left with Shklovsky as a
memento, since I had good reason to suppose that I would not need
it again. Special carriages drove us to the Palace; they arranged us in
a semicircle receiving line facing the entrance with our "lords" in
front; and they introduced us by list. King George V came out of that
door with his queen; and I was shocked: before me stood Nicholas II.
The king bore an amazing resemblence to his cousin, except that he
limped somewhat after a recent fall from a horse, and his movements
were looser. The king, who had been briefed beforehand, tried to
say some polite words to each of us judging by our positions. Appar-

ently, I had been especially recommended as an expert in foreign policy, and he lingered over me a while. I told the king that I had had the honor of being presented to his father (Edward VII) and that even at that time the knot of our present relations had been tied. George had prepared a secret for me which testified to a special trust in his allies. He recounted how, four years before, William's brother Prince Heinrich had come to see him with the definite aim of finding out confidentially how England would behave in the event of war between Germany, France, and Russia. In his words, George V answered: "England would probably stand on the side of the latter." (I later asked through our ambassador whether it was all right to give publicity to this important communication, but I was told that this was a private conversation.) The king then expressed his conviction that the struggle had to be carried to the end; otherwise (and I agreed perfectly) it would be necessary to fight again after ten years. He spoke of the necessity for a rapprochement between England and Russia in order to eliminate mutual misunderstandings. (Mutual accusations of insufficient support were being made in the press at that time.) I answered that these misunderstandings were greatly exaggerated, laid the responsibility to an article in the *Times*, and remarked that, although the masses generally know little about other peoples, the cultured class in Russia was better informed about England than that class in England was about Russia.

To the Pole Raczkowski, George V said that the shipment of wheat to occupied Poland would be arranged. He expressed his hope to Ichas that the Lithuanian nation would be reborn, and he expressed his satisfaction that the tsar had visited the Duma.

The queen also took part in the conversation. I recounted to her the plan of our trip and expressed the desire to become more closely acquainted with London and with the English statesmen—topics which for her were apparently not very interesting. With others she spoke about the weather, the landscape, and the birds.

Upon parting, the royal couple again went around and shook everyone's hand. That same evening we had dinner with the government in Lancaster House. The palace was filled to overflowing with the fashionable public. The delegation chose me as their speaker, and I found myself in an embarrassing situation. Dinner speeches in England were not supposed to be too serious, and they were usually sprinkled with English humor, which was way beyond me. The compulsory theme of Alliance relations was too dry and trite. I was supposed to answer Asquith, who was a master of parliamentary eloquence. But I was saved by a fortunate accident.

Asquith read his speech, which had been reported beforehand, dryly and from his text, filling in extemporaneously the part on the Near East. Gurko spoke in a taut excited tone; his pronunciation was indistinct. I was able to answer Asquith's general statements with equally general phrases. For the finale, however, a spectacular and unexpected theme presented itself. Through the dark rain clouds and through the large window opposite the wall, a ray from the setting sun broke in and lit up the allegorical fresco right next to our table which portrayed Mars, conquered by Venus. Around the figures was written: *Veritas vincit, justicia vincit, Mars opprimatur.* Finishing my speech, I raised my hand towards the ray of sunshine and greeted the heavenly prophesy. Yes! Truth will conquer, justice will conquer, and Mars will be crushed! Captivated by the spectacle, the public rose from their seats, followed the movement of my hand, looked at the sun ray and at the fresco—and broke out in thunderous applause. Asquith came up to me from the nearby table, congratulated me and said: "What a pity I did not notice it. I envy you very much." The effect was stronger than I had anticipated. Some Englishman even remembered that Pitt in one of his speeches made use of the very same effect.

The official series ended with a reception and a breakfast in the chambers of the House of Commons. The speaker of the House spoke; and Protopopov and I answered. On that same day (April 27) Gurko and I were at the home of Lloyd George who, by the way, shared my opinion that we must wait with the offensive, not only until autumn as I had said, but even until the next year when it would be possible to deliver the blow all at once, from all sides, with full armament. As an illustration of English armaments, Lloyd George ordered that we be shown the tremendous armament factories in Enfield and the even more tremendous construction for the production of explosives, which used female labor exclusively. The impression was a strong one indeed. However, I could not help being convinced that there was no correspondence between the armament minister's energetic initiative and his technical knowledge. At the breakfast which was arranged by the Ministries of the Army and Foreign Affairs I sat next to the head of one of Lloyd George's departments who bitterly complained about his chief. Lloyd George, he said, does not understand practical matters, he impedes the work, and with his improvised appearances in the House, he creates false impressions. "We prepare the most detailed reports for him, with precise figures, dates and conclusions. But he, when he begins to speak, lays aside the information, gets all enthused over his eloquence and lets his imagination run away with him. Then they reproach us for not giving him the correct information." In general, as can be seen, people feared Lloyd

George as the "coming man." And in fact, very soon after our arrival, he really did replace Asquith as premier and justified the misgivings of his political adversaries by switching from decayed classical liberalism to laborism. My old friend Gardiner gave me a reprint of his article in which he openly accused Lloyd George of becoming a Napoleon.

Of the numerous private meetings, acquaintances, breakfasts, and dinners, I will mention only a few. Bryce and Noel Baxton arranged a dinner for me at which the main topic of discussion was the Armenian question; both Bryce and Baxton were defenders of Armenia. Myself being a defender of Armenia, I nevertheless contrasted the autonomy of a Greater Armenia under Russian sovereignty to their aspirations of Armenian independence under the protectorate of the Great Powers. On the question of the territory of the future Armenia, I denied that we were aspiring to Mosul, limiting our aspirations to Diyarbekir—the border of mountains and plains separating Little Armenia (Kilikia) and Alexandretta. They knew and showed me a translation of my Duma speech on Armenia (II, 1916). Concerning the question of William's responsibility for the war, they, like Branting in Stockholm and Lange in Christiania, exonerated the German emperor, alleging that he was forced to fight under pressure from the militarists in Potsdam.

I had a very businesslike conversation with Runciman, the minister of supply. He was buying up cold meat and sugar throughout the world, and considered himself, with certain reservations, a free trader. I had to defend our own interest, namely the imposition of tariffs on foreign materials with the aim of producing and exporting semimanufactures ourselves, instead of giving this opportunity to Germany. Runciman then questioned me about the state of affairs in Russia, and I did not hide the danger that was threatening the dynasty and the old order. In conclusion, Runciman invited me for the weekend to his suburban estate. For me this was my first old-time aristocratic weekend of which we read in English novels, and with great curiosity I became acquainted with the ritual of English hospitality and with the public significance of a free exchange of opinions between intellectual colleagues in a friendly circle during leisure hours. The great local squires gathered here—people of rather conservative outlook. The breakdown of the old Whiggism after the defeat of home rule was already evident in the transition to new political groupings. The radicalism of the military cabinet intensified the course of socialpolitical differentiation. They simply hated Lloyd George here and could not forgive him for his radical budget of 1909. They went farther in speaking of him, accusing him of aspiring to become a "second Cromwell." They had little interest in Russia and even less knowledge about that country; I was thus spared having to answer elementary questions.

My conversation with Sir Edward (Lord) Grey stands out by itself. I assured him that our conversation would have a private character and that I would tell only Sazonov. As the basic topic for discussion I took Russia's interests after the conclusion of peace. Of course, I understood myself that it was possible to judge the conditions of peace only after military success, and Grey also appreciated this. However, this did not preclude preliminary agreement between the Allies. Coming to the point directly, Grey listed the mutual concessions which he considered incontestable. "We are bound by honor to Belgium. Then, we desire a route from Egypt to India. We have no desires on the European continent. The question of German colonies is the affair of our dominions. For France, the first necessary condition is Alsace and Lorraine. For you—Constantinople and the straits (this conversation took place after the official agreement of 1915). Anything in addition to this will depend on the extent of our success in the war." Nevertheless, a great deal was already indicated "in addition to this," and I quickly posed the question: "Further, at the head of the list, stands the question of the partitioning of Austria-Hungary without which it is impossible to solve the Polish, Serbian, and Rumanian questions." I added that Sazonov personally thought that it would be dangerous to destroy Austria-Hungary because the Austro-Germans would then strengthen Germany (the Anschluss was understood here), and that it would be better to link Austria-Hungary to the Slavs. I, of course, did not share this point of view. Grey immediately objected: "Germany never wanted the adherence of the Austrian Germans since that would weaken Prussia." He gave the Serbian question the highest priority in the partition: "Serbia will receive Bosnia and Herzegovina." Naturally, I reminded him then of the "Yugoslav" aspirations: "what about the question of the adherence of the Croatians and the Slovenes?" Grey answered: "It is a matter primarily of Russia raising this question at the right time, and it is a matter of an internal agreement between these peoples." As is known, such an agreement was already in the works at that time. We had to return to the Serbian question later: I was mainly interested in the Polish question since that was the closest to Russia's interests. When I mentioned this, Grey answered quickly: "That is Russia's business; we, of course, would like to see Russia give the Poles autonomy, but we cannot interfere." I then stressed: "in our opinion, too, this is an internal Russian question. We insisted (in order to maintain that position) that the government, without waiting for the military events to develop, should itself place the question of autonomy on the agenda." I could say that "Sazonov is now in agreement with our (Kadet) project for autonomy based in general on the model of your home rule. But we are against mentioning an internal Polish constitution in an international act. At most, only the borders of the Polish (liberated) territory should be indicated. The Poles are now insisting on independence and on international recognition, but we cannot go that far." Grey repeated that here they were following Russia. "To bring something unpleasant for our ally into an international act would mean to weaken the act itself. In the international act, only that should be mentioned which is in the interests of all of us." Going on to other questions connected with the partition of Austria-Hungary, I touched upon, first of all, Bohemia, and I asked whether or not Grey had been informed about the desires of the Czechs from Masaryk. Russia's position in this matter was easy because there was no question here of any strategic border. Grey did not recall Masaryk's memorandum from February 1916, but he answered that in this area, too, the jurisdiction should belong to Russia. I then asked about Rumania, which was continuing to bargain with both sides over its entrance into the war. Grey answered: "Rumania will get Transylvania when she joins our side, and she certainly will join us when the military situation becomes clear." (Rumania did join only on August 27, 1916—and she did so unsuccessfully.) To my question whether or not the Turks were attempting to conclude a separate peace, Grey answered: "Yes; but through an intermediary; we suggested that they turn to Russia since the war began with an attack on you. We cannot come to an agreement because of the risk of offending our allies." The hint was clear: how was it possible to make an agreement with Turkey when you have been promised the straits? In connection with this I raised another delicate question—Armenia. Grey countered my question by reminding me of my speech in the Duma (II, 1916) which "made quite a noise here" (the matter concerned Greater Armenia). He admitted that Sazonov too had "written him of his desire for annexation" and repeated anew: "This is Russia's affair; we must conform to your desires." Apparently, however, he did not look favorably on this matter. I asked him about the boundary of our spheres of influence in northern Mesopotamia (I hinted at the boundary between the mountains and the plain, that is, Diyarbekir), and he answered, "Without a map, I cannot say anything." Regarding "the claims of the other Allies," he remarked: "In eastern Asia Minor you will meet only the French; in the western part—the Italians." Regarding Persia, the other country where our spheres of influence came into contact

with each other, he merely pointed out the force of the German influence and welcomed a Russian offensive in that area.

In addition to all these questions which were close to Russia's interests, I, of course, brought up one question that was important for us
both: the fate of Germany after the war. Grey's remarks were interesting and fraught with consequences for the future. He was optimistic
on this fundamental question. To my anxious question: "How do you
plan 'to crush Prussian militarism?'" he gave the answer: "I hope
that after the first unsuccessful war, following three wars won by Bismarck, Germany herself will understand that Prussian leadership is
not profitable for her; I expect profound changes in her internal
moods." I expressed my doubts on this score "because of the extreme
difference between us and the Germans in our views on the role of
the state and the individual." Grey repeated that "signs of the great
change are already evident," and that "having erred in counting on a
rapid victory, the Germans would rather end it now than continue a
fruitless two-year war." This was true, but it was not an answer to my
theoretical objection. I then posed the next question: "Does Grey hope
to bring Germany after the war into the family of nations on the
principles of new international law?" Grey replied with conviction:
"I aspired to this before the war, and I will return to it just as soon as
our victory becomes clear. I hope that it will be possible to oblige
the nations to hand over their disagreements for discussion by the
Great Powers which will agree to this." "And what will be the sanctions in the event of disagreement," I asked. With no less assurance,
Grey replied: "The sanction will be a declaration of war against any
state which does not obey." Here, of course, was the embryo of the
League of Nations, but without the numerous limitations which enfeebled the basic principle put forward by Grey at Versailles. Regarding the reduction of armaments, Grey was likewise optimistic: "I
am relying here not so much on direct proposals, which were not
successful, as on indirect circumstances which will lead to it," namely,
"the general exhaustion after such a war as the present one." We know
that these circumstances did lead the victors to such a conclusion, but
not the defeated. The future, however, was hidden by a curtain, and in
my heart I shared Grey's noble aspirations, which were based on his
apparent realism which, in turn, was alien to all utopias.

The time set aside for our conversation came to an end. I was
preparing to take my leave when Grey stopped me: "You asked me
about everything, now let me ask you a question. What do you think
about Bulgaria?" This was a painful subject for me. In the fall of
1915, after long hesitation, Bulgaria went over to the side of our
enemies and Serbia was crushed. It was as if I bore some kind of

responsibility for this volte-face and it was difficult for me to answer him without becoming inwardly excited. I accepted the challenge. "I am considered a Bulgarophile," I began, "but I know the situation. We made a mistake. The Bucharest Peace Treaty showed the Bulgars that we cannot bring about their national aspirations. Germany and Austria, on the other hand, promised it to them, and have now made their promise good. In essence, they have carried out the Russian program of 1878, the program of Count Ignatiev for a Greater Bulgaria." Grey objected: "But it was impossible to get Serbia to agree to this." My agitated reply was: "It was necessary to force her. We did this in the fall, but it was too late." Grey insisted: "Serbia did not agree even then. It was difficult to force her when the war had begun over her in the first place." I could not stand it any longer: "Listen, the war occurred as a result of Serbian megalomania! Austria might really have thought that she was being threatened by a serious danger. Serbia represented, no more and no less, the issue of the partition of Austria." . . . Avoiding an answer, Grey made a concession to my Bulgarophilism. "In England people are convinced that Ferdinand is more to blame than the Bulgarian people." I picked up this theme. "The people are with him, as long as his policy is successful (for the nation's cause). I do not doubt, however, that at the first failure, the Russophile feelings of the Bulgarian people will win out." I suggested that this should be taken advantage of in order to bring Bulgaria back into our camp. "We can bring back Bulgaria if we promise to let her keep Macedonia—even with the boundaries of 1912, plus Üskup, but minus Nish, Vranje and Pirot." I continued: "You have two authorities on the Bulgarian question: Baxton and Seton-Watson. Ask them. Baxton traveled to Sofia to come to an agreement, but he received no authorization from you to make concessions. If concessions could have been made at that time, my influence in Bulgaria would have been given force, and Bulgaria would not have gone against us." I added that I had also pleaded for this in Petrograd. . . .

The time set aside for our meeting had long since elapsed. I pointed to my watch. Grey thanked me for an interesting conversation, and we went out together. He went into his office while arranging for me to be driven to Claridge's.

They took us from England to France with the same precautions with which they had brought us to England. We traversed the short distance from Dover to Calais between military vessels, and, in addition, were accompanied on both sides of our ship, by two torpedo boats.

In Paris they placed us—a rank higher—in the Hotel Crillon on the Place de la Concorde. The delegation immediately seemed to feel itself at home here, and split up, each person attending to his own business and acquaintances. The traditional Franco-Russian intimacy was expressed in the more careless manner in which the delegation was received. Here there was none of that solicitude and fine organization which marked our official reception in London. I do not recall even a single official breakfast or dinner here in the delegation's honor. The variety of ways we spent our time here testified to the improvised character of our meetings with official circles. I will mention one example. We were scheduled to have a reception in the Ministry of Foreign Affairs at the Quai d'Orsay. The delegates gathered together, and we were led in groups through the "Hall of Clocks." Nobody was there to meet us. After waiting a while, those who were standing at the right saw a group of ministers hurrying, in order, from the inner rooms to the entrance, as if after a good breakfast. I heard shouts from the crowd: "Aristide, Aristide, speak: the Russian delegation has arrived." They pushed Briand forward in a disheveled appearance to meet us. Apparently, he himself did not know who was here and what he would say. I then witnessed his outstanding oratorical gift. His first phrases were incoherent and incomprehensible. It was as if Briand was groping for his theme. After a few moments he found it. A smooth and beautiful speech flowed forth. I am not speaking of the content of the speech, which was difficult to remember, but the form of the speech was what captivated us and created the mood. Stormy applause broke out at the end and the reception was over. The delegates talked for a while in their places and gradually went their ways.

Our private conversation on special topics were more concentrated. It was my lot to have a conversation with the socialist deputies on the subject of foreign policy—something like the examination which had been arranged for me in Stockholm—and in the same spirit of distrust and concealed disapproval. Such leading leftist deputies took part in the conversation as Renaudel, Lafon, Moutier, Longué, Brisson, Sembat, and others. Here too the question of the straits evoked special interest. In Parliament they had probably heard something about our agreements, and my silence on the subject sounded like intentional evasiveness. From the pacifist side, I was later wearied sick of this theme by D'Estournelle-de-Constant, who referred to "reliable" information on the December session of 1913—information which was then completely unknown to me (and which turned out to be false). We could not get by, of course, without an interrogation on the intentions of the Russian liberals regarding the liberation of the "small nationalities." In a word, there was no ideological contact between us. As in London (with Seton-Watson), I found more identity of views here with the young local historians. They knew these questions better (Ernest Denis, Fournolle, Eisenmann, and others), and we could discuss the details and not only the general principles.

The highpoint of the official welcomes in Paris turned out to be the triumphant reception in the Sorbonne, which was not so much political as it was cultural. Only the left wing of our delegation was honored here, that is, Shingarev and myself. The celebration took place in the great hall of the Sorbonne, which was packed from top to bottom with members of the public. Herriot appeared as speaker. He had given himself the task of collecting information about our biographies and political activity. The speech was very interesting, and, of course, Herriot delivered it with his usual animation. Having warmed up the audience, he finished with a direct appeal to us both and brought forth a genuine ovation both for himself and for us. The response was sincere, and we could chalk it up in our favor. Shingarev, incidentally, found work in Paris to his liking: with the assistance of our military agent, Count Ignatiev (who later served the Bolsheviks), he gathered data on the fulfillment of our military-industrial orders.

The main distinctive feature of our sojourn in France was not the official gatherings or the political meetings, but our acquaintance, as Allies, with the course of the war at the front. The Military Department showed us a piece of the actual war. Of course they did not show us the mad slaughterhouse at Verdun, the Germans' desperate effort to force a success. They took us to the more peaceful front at Champaign. From there we could see the war *au ralenti*, as it were, and acquaint ourselves more closely with its components. We asked them to show us a cross section of the war, from the rear of the operations to the trenches, and the military command ably carried out this program. Above all, we saw the organization of supply of shells and food to the place of battle. The system worked with the precision of a watch mechanism, and with chagrin we compared what was going on before our eyes to the disorders in supply on our section of the front. We saw companies of soldiers changing shifts in the trenches, and we were surprised by their well-fed appearance, the state of their clothes, and their cheerful mood. Then they acquainted us with the arrangement of observation posts and the unusually ingenious forms of camouflage at the front, with the aerial reconnaissance work over the front and with the photographs of the whole front taken at short-time intervals. Going out onto the highway, which was located right behind the net of trenches, of which they showed us the plan, we saw an unusual spectacle. In the air were hanging balloons, "sausages," observing the enemy and reporting the precise spots for aiming the guns; in the distance we could see that the enemy was using the very same device. The enemy's airplanes were soaring in the air, while white clouds of the French shells were bursting around them. From above, the enemy noticed our group moving along the highway, and the officers who were accompanying us insisted to their general that we go no farther. Nevertheless, we went forward, hiding ourselves in the shadows of the forest which surrounded the highway. The enemy did not lose sight of us, however, and gave the signal to their artillerymen down below. Soon the whistle and explosion of shells began to come closer to us. The last shell which we waited for to strike fell nearby and showered us with fragments: one of these hot fragments hit Gurko in the face and fell at his feet. We then decided that our program had been fulfilled completely and prudently left the scene, changing our direction and thanking our guides.

I did notice signs of fatigue in the surrounding population. It was after all the third year of war. This vicinity had suffered little so far; but when, in a patriotically excited voice, I struck up a conversation with a servant in the small hotel where we were staying, I met with no sympathy. One of the woman clerks scornfully threw out the phrase: *ah, ces polissons-la!* Thus, we came in contact with the other side of the war, and Barbusse's books held no surprise for me later.

It was time to depart for our third ally—Italy. A part of the delegation decided to go there directly from Paris. A few of the members followed up an invitation to stop in Lyon, where we went accompanied by the boisterous and courteous deputy Franklin Buillon, who had combined leftism with high quality patriotism and who was involved in foreign policy thanks to his knowledge of foreign languages. I in no way expected that my impression from this last trip would turn out to be the strongest of them all. It seemed to me that the entire population of Lyon came out to meet us, full of enthusiasm for their allies. Nowhere in my life have I ever seen such a purely popular reception. There were no speeches, no parades; we were conquered by the force of this collective feeling which poured forth spontaneously. . . . I will not dwell on the individual episodes of this short trip: the individual impressions were drowned in the general impression.

We were left with two or three days before the official receptions in Italy. The delegation which remained in Paris was supposed to go directly from there to Rome. I decided to move ahead of the delegation in order to spend these two days in Switzerland. A classical country with centers of emigration and nationalist propaganda from everywhere; the center where political influences of the belligerent countries crossed; the cradle of Bolshevism and the Third International; the source of back-stage information which was impossible to get in the capitals of the Allied states—neutral Switzerland promised to give me much more of the material I needed than neutral Sweden. I had to include it in my itinerary even if only for a preliminary reconnaissance. The Polish question stood before me at the top of the list of vital questions concerning Russia's interest. I stopped in Lausanne, where friends arranged meetings for me with Polish émigrés. Piltz was a comparatively moderate representative of the "Russian orientation," and my talk with him was especially useful. Grand Duke Nikolai Nikolaevich's well-known appeal to the Poles, timed for the beginning of the war (1–14 August 1914), contained a program uniting the majority of Poles from the various areas but at the same time casting the Polish "left wing" of the S. D.'s into the hostile camp. "May those borders be obliterated which cut the Polish people into separate parts" promised the appeal. It was only possible to achieve this by the victory of the democratic bloc together with Russia. But then there followed: "May it be united under the scepter of the Russian tsar." At this the Poles split into various "orientations." The Austrian Poles had had it rather well under the Austrian regime and were merely striving, by means of partial unification, to create a basis for converting the dual Austro-Hungarian Empire into a "triune" ("trialist") empire. In the Polish kingdom, Russian troops, instead of fulfilling their promises, irritated the population by continuing the old restrictive policies. When they had to retreat and abandon Warsaw, the Germans came and laid the beginning, even though a weak one, of the "German" orientation. The third section of the grand duke's program proclaimed: "Under this scepter (of the Russian tsar) Poland shall be reborn, free in its faith, its language and in its self-government." Nobody believed this any more. The word "autonomy" was not uttered, and it remained a forbidden word. The government commission which had prepared the project for the future Polish system in the summer of 1915 consisted of right-wing members of the State Duma and the State Council, with the addition of the Polish representatives; and, of course, it split into two parts, after which the question died down for a whole year. At the same time the Kadet party in May 1915 worked out its own project, which was much more radical: this was a new project for Polish "autonomy," and the Poles borrowed several features from it. There the matter rested up to the time of my arrival in Lausanne. There was a solid basis here for talks with Piltz. The leftists, of course, went much further, and I also met with several of their representatives in Lausanne. For them, our program was not even the minimum. To my surprise, however, I found that the demands of the nationalities, given the still indefinite outcome of the war, were comparatively moderate and restrained in their form. During these very days the congress of nationalities took place in Lausanne.

Opening a whole series of cautious statements by the numerous Russian nationalities, the Swiss chairman, Otlet, warned against the "dismemberment of Europe and the return to the medieval fragmentations in the name of a falsely understood principle of nationality." The appeal to Wilson by the radical representatives of the Russian nationalities (at that same time, in May 1916) did not even formulate definite demands, but limited itself to the request: "Come to our aid; save us from destruction." Apparently, the time had not yet come for solving within the limits of moderation questions of this type concerning Russia. Later, the situation changed rapidly.

I understood quite clearly at the time that for my purposes the visit to Switzerland could not be limited to this short stay. The prospect of a second trip to England for the Cambridge lectures opened up the possibility of stopping in Switzerland for a longer period. Now, however, I had to hurry in order to make the first gala reception for the delegation in the Italian Chamber of Deputies. I took the express train to Rome thinking over my impending role along the way. Of course, they would again put me forward as the chief speaker.

It took it in my head to surprise the public by delivering my speech in Italian. I spoke Italian well and without an accent; my knowledge of the language was sufficient so as not to have to subordinate my thoughts to my verbal expression; the defects in style would be corrected by my émigré friends on the spot. I started writing the text of my speech in the train. That did not stop me from enjoying the beauties of Lago Maggiore while traveling across the Simplon. This was the first time I had come to Italy by this route.

My expectations were realized: I was met at the station by Al. Amfiteatrov, a famous writer, who had moved to Italy to get away from the Russian censors.[47] He took me to the hotel which had been prepared for the delegation. We went over my speech together, and he volunteered to make the necessary corrections. Soon afterward they drove us to the Parliament building, where the deputies and several ministers had gathered in the semicircle of the amphitheater. The Italians spoke in Italian and in mediocre French. My Italian speech created a furor. Unfortunately, I do not remember the contents of the speech. I hardly brought glory to "eternal" Rome by my references to the worldwide problems of the Roman Caesars and the medieval popes, but for a long time I had had a deep respect for the secular culture—the first in Europe—of the Italian Renaissance. I deeply felt the experience of the Italian Risorgimento and the triumph of the national principle in the years of Italian unification. There was enough material here for me to be able to tell the Italians what we value in Italy and why we love the country. The Italians vied with each other in thanking me, and Sonnino had the kindness to say that this was the best speech. I was content, as I rarely am, with my oratorical success.

They took us to the Quirinal and presented us to the queen, who in contrast to the king, was tall, portly, and beautiful. I had the pleasure of exchanging several words with her in a sort of half-Slavic language (I speak Serbian poorly). The king was at the front, and the last stage of our sojourn in Italy was to be a trip there. In farewell the municipality gave us a bountiful dinner—and without speeches. However, by the end of the meal, a crowd of people gathered by the city hall building in order to greet the delegates. They suggested that we show ourselves in the window, and when we appeared friendly cries and applause broke forth. Italy is a country of inspiration, and again I became inspired, improvising some sort of greeting. I was very proud of my recollections of Rome: in this very place, thirty-five years before, I, an unknown student, had been detained by the museum attendants on suspicion almost of theft. Now, I, a representative of the people, was delivering a speech from the Capitol to the Roman people —two steps away from the statue of Marcus Aurelius and right next door to that same museum! But here I was punished for my pride. Protopopov, flushed from libations to Bacchus, elbowed his way to the window and in a hoarse voice began to yell out some kind of French words, breaking them on an operatic tune and imagining that he was speaking Italian. I strongly tugged at his coattails; his purse was soon spent and he fell silent, guessing that he ought to be ashamed of himself. The Roman people did not notice the humor of the scene and continued to clap their hands.... They gave us a chance to rest after the filling meal and then, directly from the city hall, they drove us to the front.

Because of the drawn-out negotiations over the conditions for entry into the war on the side of the Entente, Italy lost the opportunity of entering when Austria was most distracted by the Russian offensive and came into the war under comparatively unfavorable conditions. The advance of Italian troops into Austrian territory went very slowly. Only in the eastern section of the front, in the direction of the Isonzo River and Gorizia, did the Italians manage to occupy the frontier strip, and naturally, they took us there. By way of Udino we arrived at the king's Headquarters not far from the front. Everyone here was delighted by the behavior of the king, who displayed unusual courage. He stubbornly remained in buildings while enemy airplanes flew overhead; he led a simple life on a level equal to that of his soldiers, and so on. They invited us to his plain breakfast, and there we could see for ourselves the extreme simplicity of his way of life. Several officers sat at a simple wooden table, the food was less than sparse and cheap, and there was no wine at all. They honored me by placing me next to the king, and he fascinated me with his free and easy manner. We conversed in Italian; there was nothing artificial, nothing prepared beforehand in the topics of our talk. We spoke of the events of the day, and from time to time the officers joined in. Two trips were outlined for us here: through the occupied territory of the Isonzo Valley and in the mountain fortifications, on the very threshhold of military action. The aim of the first trip was to give us a picture of the pacified population in the strip of territory which had just been conquered; the aim of the second trip was to familiarize ourselves with the latest improvements in mountain warfare. Both trips were very interesting and instructive.

With these favorable impressions, we left Italy.

At home we were met by news which was in no way favorable. First of all, we had to hurry back to be in time for the closing of the Duma's summer session. The news reached us that the government planned to dissolve the Duma before our arrival, and we sent a telegram to Rodzianko asking him to try to drag out the session. Later, we learned that he had been to see Stürmer about this matter—and achieved his aim. Nevertheless, the very possibility of compressing or dragging out the session by the will of the chairman of the Council of Ministers was itself a violation of the law. At that time, it had already become customary for the premier to use blank forms which the tsar gave him for fixing the length of the session, or recess (or even dissolution) of the State Duma. This matter will be discussed later.

For our return trip, the delegation broke up into three groups. I was in the second one, and Protopopov was in the last. Thus traveling via Stockholm, I could not know that Protopopov who was traveling right behind me got himself involved in an adventure, either through thoughtlessness or with more serious intentions, which turned out to be fraught with important consequences. He agreed to a meeting with Warburg, a representative from the German ambassador, Lüzius, and had a talk with him concerning German conditions for a separate peace. As was his wont, he did not conceal this upon his return; but trumpeted it through the lobbies, and I, already in Petersburg, learned about the conversation and its content. My first impression was that the incident amounted to nothing, that it was merely Protopopov's arrogant bragging. I invited Protopopov to come and see me, and in the presence of V. V. Shulgin, I tried to convince him that he should not lend any significance to that meeting, that he should explain it as a chance tourist adventure. The matter turned out to be much more serious, however. Immediately after his conversation with Warburg, Protopopov had gone into action. He was invited to Headquarters by the tsar in order to give his impressions of his trip abroad—and also for another reason. I will subsequently come back to this, too.

As already mentioned, we arrived just before the end of the Duma's summer session, and on the next to the last day Shulgin gave his general report in the Duma—in the spirit of the "sacred union" of Russia with her allies. Rodzianko's answer was followed by a "stormy ovation" for the ambassadors who were present in the diplomats' boxes. For more serious reports, a closed session of the defense committee was scheduled. A large number of deputies gathered for this session; the Duma's semicircular hall (behind the chairman's place) was full. Several ministers also attended. Shingarev gave a report on the fulfillment of military-industrial orders, while I reported on the attitudes and the moods of public opinion in the Allied countries, and especially on the state of the Polish question. Lieutenant Colonel Engelhart spoke about the military affairs of our allies; and Demchinsky, it seems, reported on military production.

Stürmer's "Dictatorship"

I USED THIS IRONIC TITLE in order to characterize the period which elapsed between Stürmer's appearance at the head of government on January 20, 1916 and his dismissal on November 10 of that same year. The two words of the title have nothing in common, of course, and I could just as well have titled this pre-revolutionary year "the paralysis of authority." There is an inner connection between the two headings: "paralysis of authority," was a result of Stürmer's claims to "dictatorship." One might object that both headings could be applied as well to 1915, the year of "Goremykin's dictatorship." The process which unfolded in both years of the war was, of course, the same. The stages of the process, however, were different. In 1915 the main concern of Russians was directed toward correcting the military failures, and this was achieved with the collaboration, albeit unfriendly collaboration, between the Defense Committee, the public organizations, and the government. In 1916 this collaboration was already inadequate, for concern was now directed not toward the front but toward the rear. It was not the retreat of the troops and the lack of ammunition that was worrying the Russian people, but the profound functional dislocations within the country itself. It was precisely this dislocation which created the dilemma: dictatorship or surrender of the government. With pride, Prince Lvov now said at the congress of the union: "We are carrying out the business of the state." He might have said: "We are taking the place of state authority."

In 1915 the country lived on the momentum for prewar prosperity. Economic and financial difficulties were concealed in the tradition of the Kokovtsov budgets, while the additional expenses had been satisfied even earlier apart from the budget confirmed by the State Duma. Much money suddenly appeared in the country, and the first impression was that the countryside had immediately struck it rich. The first waves of recruitment had not yet weakened national production; the land under cultivation was almost the same as before; deposits in the savings banks grew; billion ruble credit operations of the State Bank were marvelously successful; and emission of short-term promissory notes added new issues of paper money to the unbacked old money. . . . The dark side of this apparent prosperity, it is true, had already begun to express itself: increase in prices for consumer products, devaluation of wages and salaries of the administration, falling-off of export trade with the closing of the borders, etc. Transportation also was beginning to be disorganized; but in general, the distributive apparatus of the country was still not paralyzed.

In 1916 the picture was entirely different. In order to emphasize the contrast from the start, I will resort to a quotation: a concise summary of the situation made for the Extraordinary Commission by none other than A. D. Protopopov, the former minister of interior affairs: "Finances were in disorder, exchange of goods was disrupted, the productivity of the country took a tremendous drop, . . . the communication routes were in total disorder. . . . The dual authority (Military Headquarters and Government Ministry) on the railroads led to terrifying disorders. . . . The recruitment levies depopulated the countryside (they were taking their thirteenth million—P.M.), and stopped agricultural industry; there was a tremendous shortage of labor, the labor force had been supplemented with prisoners, Persian and Chinese hired labor. . . . The general harvest in Russia exceeded the demands of the army and the population, but the system of prohibitions against exports (complex and many-staged), the requisitions (abused by some people), and the dislocation of exports created local famine, high prices for goods, and general discontent. . . . Many people thought that only the countryside was rich; but goods did not go to the countryside, and the countryside did not let go of its grain. The village without husbands, brothers, sons, and youths was also miserable. The cities starved, and trade, constantly in fear of requisitions, was stifled. Competition, the only method of establishing prices, did not exist. . . . Statutory prices led to the development of "under the table" sales; speculation resulted, not as a fundamental sickness, but as a manifestation of insufficient production and exchange. . . . The army was tired; shortages of everything lowered its morale; and this does not lead to victory."

What were the obstacles? Our former fellow member of the Duma and of our travel delegation, in a gush of repentance, saw the reason distinctly: "There was no one to put things in order. The authorities were everywhere, supposedly giving orders, and there were a lot of them. But there was no directing will, no plan, no system; and there couldn't be any, given the general discord among the executive authorities, and given the absence of legislative work and genuine control over the work of the ministers. The supreme authority . . . was impris-

oned by harmful influences and harmful forces. It provided no moti-
vating force. The Council of Ministers had decrepit chairmen incapable
of giving direction to the work of the Council. . . . The public organizations seized the work: they stood for (that is, instead of) the government, but they could not invest their full labor in the form of law."

Such was the situation in which the idea of dictatorship thrust
itself forward. The question was posed in Headquarters by the chief
of staff, General Alexeev, in the interests of the Military Department.
Supply and provision of the army suffered from lack of agreement
between the dimensions of the task and the condition of transportation, and Alexeev considered it necessary to concentrate these three
departments in one person—a "dictator" who would combine civilian
authority with military authority. The dictator would have to be a
military man. This question was discussed in a session of the Council
of Ministers at Headquarters under Stürmer's chairmanship on June
27 and 28, 1916. The Duma was also informed of the project, and
Rodzianko set out for Headquarters with the aim of persuading the
tsar to refuse permission to create a "dictatorship of the rear." His
reasoning was quite bold and sweeping, and it was summarized in his
famous article. But, as often happened with him, he overshot his
target. In the above-mentioned session, Stürmer quickly felt that this
"superpower" might be given to him and would have to be expressed
in his right to decide the question in his own way "when the ministers
quarrel with each other." In the interrogation, Stürmer told how
someone "uttered the word 'dictator,'" while "someone else" asked
him: "Why bring in some new personality? Why can't you (Stürmer)
do it?" The tsar asked "whether or not I could take it," and Stürmer
felt himself to be at once the chairman of the Council of Ministers and
dictator. But, "on the evening of that very same day," he "had time
to think it over" and telephoned the tsar that he could not combine
these two posts with the third, the minister of internal affairs. The
matter could be explained simply: just at that time a new vacant place
turned up—the tsar decided to dismiss Sazonov. The Ministry of Internal Affairs is "tedious . . . at all times of the day and night there
are inquiries, telegrams, phone calls, orders" . . . The Ministry of
Foreign Affairs is easier: one merely sits and listens how, at a particular
time, Neratov converses with the ambassadors. Stürmer got the tsar,
who had no candidate of his own, to give him the Ministry of Foreign
Affairs, while he passed on Internal Affairs to another unexpected
candidate, A. A. Khvostov. Thus on July 7, this appointment which
shocked both the Russian public and the Allies, became official. The
"dictator" in internal politics now became the leader of foreign policy.

It goes without saying that nothing came of all this. Instead of the

Council of Ministers, Stürmer commanded only separate ministries, convened as desired for each separate question. And how could he command anyway? When he was asked by the Extraordinary Commission what "program" he had when he took power, Stürmer was extremely embarrassed. "Program? How should I tell you? One thing followed from another. . . . I believed it was necessary . . . without clashes, without quarrels (with the State Duma) to support that which was. . . . Tomorrow it would be clear what would come next." . . . And what about internal affairs in this vast state?—asked the commission. Stürmer took a firm stand: "A series of reforms . . . required by realities, for example, the *volost* reform, the small Zemstvo unit." . . . By the next session Stürmer had "thought through the question" and returned to it. "It was impossible for me to have a program . . . , because we do not do things here like they do in Europe!" Well, and what about foreign policy?—continued the commission with interest. That was easier: "The program" here was to get the straits from the Allies and to put the brakes on the Polish question which had led to Sazonov's downfall. . . . To that must also be added: to sit with the ambassadors and be quiet, not understanding what they were speaking about with Neratov—that walking encyclopedia of the Ministry. As we see, there was no "dictatorship" at all. There was inertia in the government which was occupied with a hidden struggle against the Duma and an open struggle against the public organizations. "Perhaps I was shortsighted," Stürmer allowed in his answer to the insistent reproaches by the chairman of the Extraordinary Commission, but . . . "I served the old regime, while I do not consider myself capable of serving the new one."

We did not have all these colorful facts, published only after the revolution. Nevertheless, in our appraisal of the personality and activities of this hapless "dictator," we were not mistaken, and this gives me grounds for refreshing the portrait of Goremykin's successor without resorting to personal recollections.

I was not in Russia from April 16 to June 19, 1916, and, naturally, I was unable to follow the events and the changes of moods in the course of these two months. My first concern was to fill in this blank, and my first impression was of Sazonov's dismissal and Stürmer's seizure of the Ministry of Foreign Affairs. Sazonov had been dismissed unexpectedly during vacation very soon after I had given my detailed report to the closed session of the Duma Defense Committee concerning the Polish question, the report being based on impressions I had received abroad. I do not know whether or not there was a direct link here, but I just remembered that I was in agreement with Sazonov on this question. Like him, I considered that the German occupation of Poland had changed the situation and that it would be necessary for us to assume a new and more progressive stance on the Polish question in order to get the jump on the German promises and keep the decision of this question in Russia's hands. For his part, soon after his return, Count Wielopolski, our fellow traveler abroad, presented himself to the emperor on June 17, told him of the necessity of issuing a new act concerning Poland, and obtained the promise that the act would soon be issued. On July 22 (i.e., after Sazonov's dismissal) his brother visited the empress; and, after their conversation, the latter sent a telegram to the tsar requesting him "to hold up the decision on the Polish question until her arrival at Headquarters" (after June, her visits to Headquarters became more and more frequent). A delay followed, and on August 19, Wielopolski, having received new information from Paris, demanded a definite answer from Stürmer once and for all. This time, in view of the expected German statement, the Poles presented the demand no longer for "personal union" but for Polish independence. After his report at Headquarters on August 26, Stürmer again tried to pacify Wielopolski by saying that "everything will be done." He attempted to distort Wielpolski's telegraphed answer to Paris, in the direction of conciliation, and then fell silent. Only after the German document was issued on November 6, did Wielopolski receive a new audience with the tsar (December 23), who promised him that "Poland will be granted its own state system with its own legislative chambers and its own army." Nevertheless, this time, too, the matter did not get beyond the creation of a new (Russian) commission which continued to hold conferences in February 1917, expecting an invitation from the Polish representatives. Stürmer's "patriotic" excuse, he said, consisted of the following: "When the Polish question began, when the Poles asked that they be given certain rights," he "insisted that the Russian people first be given" (the straits). It was the Provisional Government that had to decide the question.

Another important question for me was how the summer session of the Duma (May 16–June 20) passed. Stürmer had apparently permitted this session à contre-coeur—anxiously waiting to see whether it would occupy itself with "business" or "politics." The Extraordinary Commission discovered that in the event the Duma should choose "politics," i.e., "undesirable" speeches, the tsar, on the eve of the opening session, gave Stürmer a carte blanche to close the Duma. This time the Duma occupied itself with "business." Now, however, "business" smelled of "politics." The Duma began discussion of the bills which were put on the agenda by the bloc. Some of them, especially the city reform, the Duma even managed to prepare. "Politics" was in fact concealed here. There was no longer a "stopper" to plug up Duma legislation, because the bloc had a majority in the State Council. It was later calculated that the rightist party lacked fifteen votes for a majority. As early as June 7, Stürmer announced in a note to the tsar that the passage of all of the bloc's bills together "would place the country in an absolutely desperate situation." I already mentioned that the session managed to be dragged out until the day the Duma delegation returned. Only after the Duma was closed and after a new postponement until November 1 did Stürmer breathe freely: a little more than four months were at the complete disposal of the "dictator."

The public at large knew nothing about this hidden side of Stürmer's struggle; I myself learned the details recounted here only from Stürmer's interrogation before the Extraordinary Commission. Nobody understood at all why, after the stormy clashes of the bloc with the government in 1915, the Duma suddenly, at the beginning of 1916, grew quiet and busied itself "with beating the air." I already said that the Duma "ensconced itself in the trenches" waiting for a new conflict. I tried to persuade the impatient ones that the mere existence of the bloc was important, that the bloc's existence had "driven the government into a corner and is holding it there in a deadlock." If the bloc were to be broken up, the government would regain its freedom of maneuver. The Duma is not, I said, a weapon for extraparliamentary struggle; but when the struggle becomes necessary, the Duma will be ready in place. We maintained the link with the public organizations, but, while waiting, we reconciled ourselves to the temporary calm. The bloc would wait for its hour to come. The more leftist currents could not have known my reasoning, and they would not have agreed with it even if they had known. Their impression was that the Duma was lagging behind events; the Duma was only "talking" when it was necessary to "act." Just how it should "act" remained their secret.

From I. V. Hessen's memoirs I later learned that this same criticism was directed at me personally in the journalistic and literary circles from which I had been removed by my political activities. Dissatisfaction with our tactics found its way even into our faction, which was usually friendly and which usually shared our opinions. Nekrasov, a young engineer and teacher at the Tomsk Technological Institute, came forward as the leader of the leftist currents. I scheduled a special session for reviewing our tactics. The debates were heated, but in the final total, only two or three protestors came out in favor of the leftist tactics. In any case I could not make a concession in this matter: I knew the material we had to deal with in order to move the whole Duma machine forward.

The third circumstance which troubled me and which had to be clarified was the rise of A. D. Protopopov in my absence. Rumors concerning the Germans' attempts to make contact with the Court on the question of concluding a separate peace had been circulating for some time. Besides the rumors, however, there were concrete facts; Fräulein Vasilchikov's attempt to raise this question in the spring of 1915 was well known. She wrote the tsar about the proposal made to her by von Jagow in Berlin, and she brought the empress letters from her Hessen brother and sister. True, she was sent out of Petersburg and deprived of the title fräulein; and it was clear that the tsar regarded this attempt very negatively. Nevertheless, rumors about the empress' contact with her German relatives, and about her concern for the German prisoners, continued to be spread—together with her reputation of being a "German." The arrest of Sukhomlinov and his imprisonment in the fortress on the charge of treason disturbed the royal couple. A. N. Khvostov made himself a reputation with the tsar on the question of German espionage. It was natural that Protopopov's summons to the tsar, immediately after his return from abroad, and his affectionate reception in Headquarters should have evoked intense interest in his conversation with Warburg in Stockholm. Shulgin and I heard Protopopov tell his story about this discussion as it was written down roughly in his notebook. (He refused to reconstruct the German proposal exactly and the book itself later disappeared.) At any rate, perfectly concrete proposals were included: the annexation of Lithuania and Courland to Germany, revision of the borders in Lorraine (Alsace was left aside), and finally, the return of Germany's colonies. Poland should be restored only from two parts—the Russian and the Austrian, since "there are no Poles in Germany"; the borders should be geographical and not ethnographic; Belgium would be restored; England, the main culprit in the war, would deceive Russia—Germany would give Russia more (Jagow, through Vasilchikov, promised both the straits and Constantinople). Protopopov enthusiastically related how, after this reception, he "grew fond" of the tsar and how the tsar "grew fond" of him. I am ready to believe that this was not a mere pose with the aim of self-justification. I already remarked on the capacity for sentimental attachments in Protopopov's decadent nature. In this case, he really was deeply touched. He also "grew fond" of the empress. In contact between the royal couple and outsiders, such sentimentality did not often appear. Apparently, it was appreciated immediately, and on this basis was created Protopopov's unusually rapid intimacy with the right circle of "friends."

Of course, there was also an element of more worldly calculations in this. Protopopov's unscrupulousness was known to me; nevertheless, his sharp switch from the comparative leftism which he displayed on our trip abroad to the directly opposite set of ideas was something I did not expect. At that time I did not suspect that Protopopov's contacts with Rasputin and Vyrubova (through Badmaev) had begun even before our trip and that Rasputin had already promised him a ministerial post when he would meet with the tsar upon his return. Protopopov was aiming at the Ministry of Trade and Industry, which was more suitable for him, but was appointed to the Ministry of Internal Affairs, "temporarily" occupied by Khvostov's uncle after Stürmer had preferred to transfer from Internal Affairs to Foreign Affairs. The only motive for the appointment, it seems, was that in his conversation with the tsar, he had expressed an interest in the food supply question. Just at that time however, the food question had been turned over to the Ministry of Agriculture, still under Krivoshein, and Protopopov vainly tried to bring it back out of that ministry. Protopopov's appointment as chief of the Ministry of Internal Affairs took place on September 18. I remember that when I met him later in the Duma, I expressed my amazement and asked him whether or not he intended to carry out Stürmer's program. His answer was inconsistent, and the conversation broke off. Of Protopopov's "liberalism," three points remained: "judicial" responsibility of the ministers, extension of rights for Jews, and salary for the clergy. The fourth point—reform of the Zemstvo—was rather hazy. The Zemstvo should be reformed, but how? Before the Extraordinary Commission Protopopov declared: "I saw perfectly clearly that there was no government" . . . "the public had seized power, and was doing what the government should have been doing"; "it seemed to me that the government should do what the public institutions were doing." We shall see the consequences of this change of key presently.

Before this change occurred, however, our tender calf wanted— and was sure that he was able—to suck two cows. He did not give up his title of Duma member, and he even endeavored to make speeches as such. He wanted to justify himself before his fellow members, and he asked Rodzianko to arrange a meeting for this purpose with the Duma Elders and party leaders. The meeting was held, and Protopopov's hopes were dealt a cruel blow. He was pitiful, but we did not pity him. He then complained that "they beat him, spit on him, lashed him and chopped him"—and with this he explained his final switch over to the rightists. I participated actively in this; I wrote down his incoherent babble from memory, and my record was circulated among the public. He was sure that a stenographer was sitting behind the wall: the exact record sounded like a caricature. Rod-zianko later refused to shake hands with him in the tsar's antechamber. He also found no support forthcoming from his new colleagues. Both premiers, Stürmer and, later, Trepov, demanded his dismissal and called him "a madman" when speaking to the tsar. In the more ac-ceptable nomenclature of the Court, he was probably chalked up as a "divine fool"—and in this capacity the royal circle retained some sort of exceptional trust and affection for him; they almost brought him into the tight circle of "their own," and kept him in his post, con-firming his title of minister (December 20, 1916), right up to the climax. We will come back to him at that time.

I must admit now that, in spite of all the tenseness of the situa-tion, I left my post for a second trip abroad without great misgivings. This, apparently, was due to my belief that in the developing drama, the Duma would not be a decisive factor—and it was also due to the role which I had accordingly marked out for myself. I will speak about this trip briefly—insofar as it was still related to Russia and to events in Russia.

During my first trip I had received two invitations which it was now too late to turn down. One of them was to England. Our friend and sympathizer, Professor Pares, had the idea of combining with a political celebration of the Allies, a Slavic cultural celebration. From this he developed the theme for the following summer's congress of the University Extension in Cambridge. Struve, Dmowski, and I were invited to give lectures there. The other proposal, after a short time, came from Christiania: I was invited to give a few lectures at the Uni-versity there on my way back to Russia. Above all I was attracted by the opportunity of spending the intervening period in Switzerland, where I wanted to gather data from sources, unavailable in Russia, on secret contacts between the Germans and Russian circles re-garding the conclusion of a separate peace. First of all, in passing through Stockholm I tried to question Nekliudov on this matter. His answer was complete ignorance about Protopopov's talks, and he maintained that the very fact of the meeting with Warburg became known to him only after the meeting had taken place.

Gulkevich met me in Christiania like an old friend and arranged an interesting meeting for me with King Haakon. I was perfectly charmed by the king's reception. Though no longer young, he met me with the air of a student wanting to show respect for his professor. Our talk was lively and easy. He wanted to find out from me details of the political situation in Russia. I had nothing to hide from him, all the more so as he turned out to be well informed. In gloomy colors, I drew a picture for him of Russia's internal disorder, which threatened to produce not only military failures but also immediate danger to the state system. I laid special stress on the fact that the very existence of the dynasty was in danger, that the royal couple completely isolated itself from the population, that they were fighting against imaginary enemies without seeing the real ones, that they were in no way prepared to understand the situation, and that they did not know how to choose their advisers. I then turned to him with the question: How is it possible that other, kindred dynasties of Europe can passively regard such a situation and not do anything at all to inform the sovereign Russian power of the real state of affairs? Haakon answered that nothing can be done by exchange of letters; that personal influences are necessary, but are difficult to achieve in the absence of personal meetings. He added incidentally, that such a meeting was actually under consideration, and he personally hoped to use it for the purpose indicated above. When I left the king, I was aware of having attained a positive result.

In Cambridge I was met by the familiar surroundings of the summer session of the University Extension: a university center filled with teachers who had arrived from various places, who ran from one lecture to another, and who hastened to get everything they could from the professors. For my lectures I outlined two themes related to current events yet within an academic framework: "The awakening of the nationalities in the Balkans," as an introduction to the war which was going on; and "The Russian Constitution" with its tricks and pitfalls, as an introduction to understanding the political struggle in Russia. Both lectures evoked a series of questions from the audience, and the atmosphere was animated. Dmowski was correct and loyal to us in his account of the Polish question: since 1908, he had declared his "turn towards the East." Struve was very scholarly and not on very good terms with the English language; this, however, did not prevent the audience from regarding him with due respect. The main festivities were still ahead: the Cambridge University senate decided to raise us to the rank of honorary doctor. The ritual was conducted with the customary solemnity, which included also the right of the students to react to the scholarly promotion with cries from the gallery—either friendly or unfriendly. On this occasion we made it through without such interference. As was the custom, a special speaker delivered a speech before each promotion in Latin on the merits of the candidates for the doctor's degree. With interest I listened to how I was the descendant of that "Paul who at one time came from a far-away country to the river Cam" bringing enlightenment with him. After the promotion, they dressed us in previously fitted gowns of red velvet and matching berets, and led a triumphant

processional through the streets of the city. I thus received the right
to place the letters LL.D. (Legum Doctor) alongside my name; and
if I had valued titles I could have with satisfaction contrasted this
latter recognition with my Moscow vow to remain forever a Russian
"master" and not seek the title of "doctor."

Much more sentimental for me was the banquet, specially arranged for me by the professors and "selected public." The welcome
speech was delivered by Sir Paul Vinogradoff who had made a worldwide name for himself with his lectures at Oxford on medieval law—
after he, together with M. M. Kovalevsky and S. A. Muromtsev, had
been forced to leave Moscow University in order to escape government persecutions. The highly emotional speech of my old teacher
and friend restored relations, as it were, which had been spoiled by
the cooling of our friendship and, later, by the divergence in our
views (P. G. [Vinogradoff] was closest of all to the Octobrists). They
introduced me to the professors, including the son of the famous Dar-
win. There were also Russians there to witness my exultation.

Before my departure from England, I met with the aged Count
Benckendorff and listened to his description of the impression made
on the Allies by Stürmer's appointment to Sazonov's post. Benckendorff had previously enjoyed the Allies' unconditional confidence,
and they used to let him in on all sorts of secret information. Now, he
told me, when he arrived, they hid all the secret papers from him in
the desk, explaining: "We are no longer sure that the major secrets
would not reach the enemy; we have information that these secrets,
ever since the appointment of Stürmer, have somehow become known
to the enemy." More than once I had the occasion to cite this testimony of our ambassador in London.

At last I made my way to Switzerland and stopped in Lausanne,
where I had some connections with the old Russian émigrés. In this
circle, everyone was sure that the Russian government was in contact with the Germans through their special agents. I was showered
with a whole bouquet of facts—authentic, doubtful, and unlikely. It
was difficult to sort them out. I received information about the Russian Germanophile salons run by ladies in leading public position.
One of them belonged to Naryshkina (whom I confused with the aged
lady-in-waiting, E. K. Naryshkina, one of the empress' intimates). Another salon, which had moved from Italy to Montreux, was especially
interesting in that, so they told me, Stürmer in order to keep in touch
had sent a special bureaucrat who became a constant visitor of the
salon. The purpose of this bureaucrat was either to make observations
or contacts—it was not clear which. A note from a certain Rey which
accused Izvolsky of Germanophilism was delivered to me personally

in my capacity as representative of the Kadet party. On my way back I stopped in Paris, and Izvolsky, at my request, made an inquiry and found out from Briand that this Rey was an intimate of William. True, a relative of Izvolsky's wife was staying with the Izvolsky family, and she did not hide her Germanophile sympathies, thereby giving the embassy the reputation of being a nest of Germanophilism. For his part, Izvolsky told me of Manisevich-Manuilov's complicity in an attempt to bribe *Novoe Vremia* with German money. Let me repeat that it was very difficult to comprehend and interpret all this in connection with the data I had gathered in Russia. Nevertheless, I used a part of the material from Switzerland for my speech on November 1.

On the trip home I stopped in Christiania to deliver my lectures. The theme they gave was the description of the "Russian soul." In its Slavophilic sense, this topic contradicted my views, and, beginning with a criticism of the popular understanding of this term so current abroad, I focused the attention of my listeners on the main organ of Russian national self-consciousness—the Russian intelligentsia. I summarized the history of the development of this "school of national feeling." The auditorium was filled, the public "select," and the sympathy undoubted. We left satisfied with each other.[48] This time I widened my knowledge of Norway by asking the son of the famous writer Arne Garborg to give me a few lessons in Norwegian. I learned that after separation from Sweden, the Norwegian literary language was rapidly moving away from the influence of the Court strata and upper class, toward the popular level; that is, the literary language was shifting from literary Danish to peasant Swedish, which I knew. This fact strengthened my sympathies for this democratic country even more.

Before the Climax

I SPENT ALL OF AUGUST and part of September on this second trip. The first question upon my return, was, naturally enough, whether or not I was late for what had been happening in Russia during this time. The answer was both yes and no. With regard to Russia's internal situation as described above, I was not late. That situation had remained essentially unchanged, and I have almost nothing more to add to what I have already described. In another respect, however, I was doubtlessly late. Everything previously known only to the more or less tight circle of the devoted, became, during this time, the property of the public at large including the rank and file citizen. The barometer of the domestic mood rose accordingly. That mood was still not expressed in drastic forms and had still not been poured into molds of definite political plans and prospects. As before, the word still belonged to the Duma and to the public organizations, but with growing impatience, people were waiting for some new word from both the one and the other. It had to be decided just what this new word was to be. The answer had to be given within a definite time; the Duma was to meet and begin discussions on November 1. It was clear, a priori, that the tone of the discussion would be different from what it had been in the summer session of May–June.

I will dwell on several of these transitional attitudes which were leading to revolution. The first of these was the evolution of the view concerning the composition of the ministry of "confidence" or the "responsible" ministry—a question which, as we have seen, evoked disagreements among the bloc itself. Essentially, with all the difference of principle between the two formulas, it was an argument over words, given the conditions which prevailed at that time. A ministry of "confidence" in the country offered more prospects than ministerial "responsibility" before the Fourth Duma. This becomes clear just as soon as we move from formulas to personalities. At that time, many people occupied themselves with preparing lists of future ministers. Usually, these lists merely varied the same names which had become popular thanks to the Duma opposition and to the activities of the public organizations. There was no one to be "responsible" to; it was a question of "confidence."

I will compare three of these lists in chronological order; this will show their evolution and their limits. The first list was composed in the apartment of the big industrialist P. Riabushinsky ("the bony hand of hunger" in revolutionary terminology) on August 13, 1915— at the very same time the "bloc" was formed. The second list was made at a meeting of representatives of the leftist parties at the apartment of S. N. and E. D. Prokopovich on April 6, 1916, for the Kadet congress. The third list, for comparison, represents the composition of the Provisional Government, formed on March 2, 1917.

Ministry	Aug. 13, 1915	April 6, 1916	March 2, 1917
Premier	Rodzianko	Prince Lvov	Prince Lvov
Interior Affairs	Guchkov		Prince Lvov
Foreign Affairs	Miliukov	Miliukov	Miliukov
Finance	Shingarev		Tereshchenko
Communications	Nekrasov		Nekrasov
Trade and Industry	Konovalov	Konovalov (Tretiakov?)	Konovalov
Agriculture	Krivoshein	Shingarev	Shingarev
Army	Polivanov	Guchkov	Guchkov
Navy	Savich		Guchkov
State Controller	Efremov		Godnev
Chief Procurator of the Synod	V. Lvov		V. Lvov
Education	Count P. Ignatiev	Gerasimov (Manuilov)	Manuilov
Justice	V. Maklakov	V. Maklakov (Nabokov)	Kerensky
Labor		Lutugin	Chkheidze[49]

In the first list, three of the liberal ministers of that time were included; in the subsequent lists, the tsarist ministers no longer appear. The influence of the moderate part of the bloc (the Octobrists) could be seen in the first list, although the popular names from the Duma opposition were not excluded. These latter names are repeated in the second and third lists, except for Rodzianko who was replaced by Prince Lvov. Except for Guchkov, the second list is silent with regard to Octobrists and includes a Ministry of Labor. The third list returns to a conscientious government of the Duma factions of the bloc and also brings in nonbloc leftists.

It is characteristic that the second list, composed by the party leftists, does not deviate from the general line and does not contain the names of party leftists. Meanwhile, E. D. Kuskova, at the request of our Kadet D. I. Shakhovsky, gathered at her house a whole bouquet of leftists in order to compose this list which Shakhovsy then brought to the Kadet congress. At that meeting were the S. R., Gerkenheim, the S. D., N. K. Muraviev, and even the Bolsheviks, I. I. Skvortsov, and E. L. Gurevich-Smirnov. There were only two Kadets, Avsarkisov and Maksimov-Olgin. L. I. Lutugin, the good-natured cynic and "nonpartisan leftist" whom we remember from 1905, arrived only at the end: he ridiculed the purpose of the meeting: "Your bourgeois cabinet cannot simply brush aside the old galoshes of the autocracy and peacefully in brand new uniforms ensconce itself in their places." Nevertheless, the S. R.'s and the S. D.'s named a "bourgeois cabinet"! In her letter to me, E. D. Kuskova explained this seeming contradiction perfectly correctly. Then, as in 1905, the general opinion of the leftists was that the revolution in Russia must begin with the bourgeois revolution. The socialists refused on principle to take power at the very beginning, leaving this for the next "stage." They magnanimously gave us a reprieve, and our whole problem was how to take advantage of it. I also shared this opinion on the psychology of all revolutions, only I did not intend to fold my arms while waiting for the next "stage."

In connection with this, let me speak for a moment about Prince Lvov's replacement of Rodzianko in the post of premier. It is sufficient to read Rodzianko's memoirs in order to understand to what degree this man was not suited for the role the Duma was to play in the impending revolution. He continued to think of himself as leader and savior of Russia in this transition stage, too. He had to be removed from that place; and I was given the task of removing him—a mission which was in agreement with my own intentions. It was not easy to replace the chairman of the Duma by the chairman of the Zemstvo organization in the bloc's plans, but I managed to do it. It was made easier of course by Prince Lvov's nationwide reputation: at that time he was indispensable. I cannot say whether Rodzianko resigned himself to this decision. He continued a secret struggle, manifestations of which we will see presently. He later came out in printed polemics against me, accusing me of degrading the Duma after the revolution. I had nothing against this accusation. The political role which the Duma had been playing with the public's tacit consent, should be transferred to the Russian public if this public could serve as a bulwark against the onset of the next "stages." In this respect Rodzianko's replacement by Prince Lvov was the first revolutionary step and a necessary inoculation against further aggravation of the disease. This did not fit into Rodzianko's view of things, and I did not at all regret that it was my lot to perform this surgical operation. I will make one reservation, however; much later I had moments of doubt as to the correctness of replacing the old cavalryman by the Tolstoyan. Nevertheless, I found there was no other way.

Next on the agenda was the revolutionizing of the public organizations as a result of the open struggle the government had been waging against them. On April 7, 1916, Stürmer labeled as inopportune permission for congresses of any organization. Later, on September 21, that is, already under Protopopov, this interdiction was interpreted in the sense that all meetings attended by persons outside of the institution organizing the meeting, were to be considered public meetings. Representatives of the bureaucracy could thus attend these meetings (as well as the closed meetings) and prohibit them if they went beyond the framework of their immediate tasks. This was motivated by the "ripened necessity to guard the Zemstvo and City Unions and the Military-Industrial Committee from all excesses of a political character in order to preserve their highly valued specialized activity." This bit of hypocrisy was apparently Protopopov's doing. He stated to Prince Lvov directly: "I am aware that the Kadets have a plan to kidnap the tsar from Headquarters, take him off to Moscow, and force him on bended knees to swear allegiance to a constitution"! A storm of protests was raised, and the mood of the unions became much more tense. Just before the opening of the Duma on November 1, the chairman of the Duma received an appeal to the Duma from a meeting of the representatives of the provincial Zemstvo boards and from the plenipotentiary of the Union of Cities; this appeal was signed by both Lvov and Chelnokov. Prince Lvov wrote that those at the meeting "arrived at the unanimous conclusion that the government presently in power is openly suspected of being dependent on dark influences hostile to Russia, that this government cannot govern the country, and that it is leading the country down the road to ruin and shame." "The members of the meeting unanimously authorized (him) to bring it to the attention of the members of the Duma that in the Duma's decisive struggle for the creation of a government capable of uniting all vital national forces and of leading our homeland to victory, Zemstvo Russia will stand together with the people's representatives." Among the reasons given were "the sinister rumors about betrayal and treason," the "laying of the groundwork for a shameful peace," and the necessity "for an unbending continuation of the war to final victory." In the appeal from the Union of Cities, the same reasons were repeated, together with the accusation of "criminal delay in the Polish question," and the Duma was informed that "the decisive hour has come—delay cannot be tolerated; all nerves must be strained to create, once and for all, such a government which, together with the people, will lead the country to victory."

The topic of the speech I prepared for the opening of the Duma coincided with these indications, which confirmed its timeliness and necessity. I used all the material for that speech which I had collected in Russia and abroad, and I decided to go even farther. It was obvious that a blow at Stürmer would no longer be sufficient; it was necessary to go farther and higher than theatrical extras from this "ministerial leapfrog," to expose the "dark forces" to the public, and to touch upon those "sinister rumors" without sparing the subject toward whom they ascended. I recognized the risk to which I was subjecting myself; but since the "decisive hour" had really come I considered it necessary not to take this into account. I spoke about the rumors concerning "treason," which were spreading through the country without restraint, about the actions of the government which roused the public's indignation; and in each case I left it to my listeners to decide whether or not this was "stupidity" or "treason." By its approval the audience resolutely supported the second interpretation—even in those aspects where I myself was not entirely sure. These points in my speech were especially remembered and widely circulated not only in the Russian, but also in the foreign press. The most forceful, central part of my speech I masked by a quotation from *Neue Freie Presse*. The quotation mentioned the name of the empress in connection with the names of the camarilla which surrounded her. This saved my speech from attacks by the chairman, who did not understand the German text, but, of course, it was immediately deciphered by my listeners. It was as though a pus-filled sack had burst: such was the impression. The basic evil known to all and waiting for a public exposure was placed out in the open for all to see. Stürmer, at whom I had directed a personal accusation, tried to raise the question of sanctions against me in the Council of Ministers, but he met with no sympathy. It was suggested that he start a libel suit, but he wisely restrained himself. He did not even achieve an interruption in the work of the Duma. At the next session the attack continued. V. V. Shulgin delivered a venomous and furious speech—and drew practical conclusions. More cautiously, but quite clearly, V. A. Maklakov supported me. Our speeches were forbidden to be printed, but this only increased their echo. They were mimeographed in millions of copies on the machines of the ministries and staffs, and they were scattered to all parts of the country. My speech acquired the reputation of an attack signal for the revolution. I did not desire this, but the pervasive mood of the country was a tremendous multiplier of the impression which had been made. As an indication of the impression made on the government, Stürmer was immediately dismissed. On November 10, A. F. Trepov was appointed to Stürmer's post and the session was interrupted until the nineteenth in order to give the new premier an opportunity to get his bearings and prepare his speech.

It seemed that we had won some sort of a real victory here. But . . . it only seemed that way. The very choice of the new head of government showed that the ruling authorities did not want to come out of their trenches, continuing to seek its servants in that same old circle of aged high officials. We waited for some steps to be taken regarding the Duma, to prepare a peaceful meeting. No steps of any kind were taken during those days, however, and both sides met each other as enemies. . . . At least we wanted to wait for the new premier's speech in order to judge his intentions, but the leftists decided to create obstructions for Trepov. Three times he tried in vain to speak— and three times he was drowned out by shouts from the benches of the socialists and the Trudoviks. Even his prepared trump did not help him: the public announcement of the secret treaty concerning the Allies' concession to Russia of Constantinople and the straits.

During the next few days, the situation became even more complicated by the events in Moscow. Our speeches on November 1 raised the tone of the Zemstvo Union even more. The Union decided to answer the government's ban by convening an open congress under what in 1905 had received the name *iavochny poriadok*, that is, without prior permission from the authorities, totally ignoring the government interference. Prince Lvov prepared a speech for the opening of the congress which completely broke with the previous "businesslike" traditions of the Union.

"What we wanted to tell the leader of the Russian people in private fifteen months ago," declared Lvov (he was referring to the delegation which was not received), "what we spoke in a whisper at that time, has now become the general cry of the whole people and has taken to the streets." "Must we mention the names of the secret Magi and sorcerers of our national government? Must we dwell on the feelings of indignation, contempt and hate?" "When the authorities have become totally alien to the interests of the people, we must take the responsibility into our own hands." "We can only appeal to the State Duma, which legally represents the whole of the Russian people, and we do appeal to it: do not go away!" "Forget further attempts to harmonize your work jointly with the present authorities; they are doomed to failure, they only separate us from our goal. Do not succumb to illusions; turn away from phantoms! There is no authority!"

. . . "The country needs a monarch protected by a government responsible to the country and the Duma."

This speech was not delivered due to the fact that the congress, as expected, was closed by the police. It was replaced by a resolution of equal sharpness, adopted unanimously by the fifty-nine attending representatives from twenty provinces, and it was adopted in surroundings which genuinely recalled 1905. The meeting was divided into two parts. The plenipotentiary Prince Lvov remained in the building which the police entered. While the police were preparing the protocols for closing the meeting, a part of the members went into another room and, under the chairmanship of the assistant plenipotentiary, the young D. M. Shchepkin, they adopted the resolution.

The Duma immediately reacted to these Moscow events of December 9–11. On December 13–16 we put an interpellation on the agenda concerning the attitude of the government toward the public organizations, and in spite of Protopopov's attempt to close the session we delivered specific and substantive speeches. In particular, I said that, once the struggle takes on a conspiratorial form, which does not take the law into consideration, then this fact alone restores the united front which existed before the October Manifesto. Until that time the leftists had tried to separate themselves from the bloc. Now we were faced by common tasks and a common enemy. The only difference lay in the fact that the dimensions of the struggle were not the same as they were in 1905. I finished my speech with a hint which was not understood until the following day. I said that the air was highly charged and that it was uncertain when the blow would fall. I knew where it would fall, however. A few days before that, V. A. Maklakov told me an attempt on Rasputin's life was being prepared and that he had been told this by Purishkevich. He then gave an account of the information which he had given me in print. On that very night of December 17 a decree appeared announcing the postponement of the Duma sessions until February 19. On the next day Rasputin was murdered. The session began and ended with events which would have been impossible in the normal life of the state.

It was interesting to learn subsequently how these fateful days were reflected in the mind of the empress, as seen from her letters to Nicholas at Headquarters. On December 10, 1916, she writes as if she has just won a victory: "Thank God the meetings in Moscow have been stopped. Six times Kalinin (Protopopov's nickname) was at the phone until four in the morning, but Prince Lvov managed to read his paper (the resolution of the Congress—P.M.) before the police found them in one place. You see, Kalinin is working hard and well, and he does not flirt with the Duma; he thinks only of us." On December 14, the empress already draws conclusions: "With a clean conscience before all of Russia, I would calmly send Lvov to Siberia; I would strip Samarin of his rank (he signed this paper in Moscow), and I would also send Miliukov, Guchkov, and Polivanov to Siberia. A war is going on, and in such a time, an internal war is state treason. Why you do not see it that way, I truly cannot understand. I am only a woman, but my heart and mind tell me that this would be the saving of Russia." She tries to strengthen the basic thesis of their whole reign in the mind of her husband. "We have been enthroned by God, and we must guard that throne staunchly and pass it on intact to our son. If you keep this in mind, then you will not forget to act like the Sovereign. And this is much easier for an autocratic sovereign than for one who has sworn allegiance to a constitution." What should an "autocratic sovereign" do? "Be Peter the Great, be Ivan the Terrible, be Emperor Paul," counsels the empress. "Crush them all under yourself"! In answer to this, Nicholas II wrote down as a matter of form: "Poor old huzy—with no will."

"There is no authority," wrote Prince Lvov. "There is no government," affirmed Protopopov. From opposite camps, both recognized that the public organizations intended to take the place of governmental authority. These admissions determined the political substance of the next, prerevolutionary segment of time.

Before getting myself buried in the New Year's atmosphere of Petersburg, I took a trip to the Crimea for the Christmas holidays in order to see I. I. Petrunkevich who lived in Gaspre, the estate of S. V. Panina near Yalta. S. V. was admitted to the world of the grand dukes and princes, and their mood was thus able to reach us. It was a mood of complete triumph for the heroic action of "Felix" (Yusupov-Sumarokov-Elston) who had risked himself in order to free Russia and the dynasty from the malignant plague. I must confess that for me, the deed of Felix and Dmitri Pavlovich, in cooperation with Purishkevich, did not present itself in such a romantic light. The disgraceful drama in Yusupov's residence was repulsive in its essence and in its details. The saving of Russia turned out to be illusive; the murder of Rasputin could change nothing. I anticipated the judgment of the Russian peasant concerning the death of his fellow peasant: "So, at last there came a time when a peasant made his way to the royal palace—to speak truth to the tsars—and the gentry killed him." Indeed, it happened just that way. The collective Russian peasant was preparing to repeat this operation on the "gentry." However, in the princely villas surrounding Gaspre, nobody was thinking of such things. I must admit that in my conversations with I. I. Petrunkevich about what was in store for

Russia during the next two months, there was more guesswork than concrete judgments.

On the way back I stopped in Moscow, and there I found more definite attitudes. Prince Lvov had just returned from Petersburg, and in Chelnokov's apartment he secretly told the latest news from the capital. In the very near future we could expect a palace revolution. Military circles, the grand dukes, and various political figures were to take part in this scheme. Apparently, they were planning to remove Nicholas II and Alexandra Fedorovna. We must be ready for the consequences. A few of those present were in agreement that Lvov himself could not avoid becoming the head of the government. Chelnokov later described this conversation by saying that "nobody thought seriously of this, and they made idle talk about how nice it would be if only someone would arrange it." I was grieved to learn that V. A. Maklakov, who was present at this conversation, made a more definite report in a Kadet circle at the home of Prince P. D. Dolgorukov, concerning the impending revolution. It seemed to me that the more one sees the real image of the revolution, the less one should "gossip" about its inevitable coming and, so to say, popularize it. I remember, however, that in Moscow they asked me the perfectly concrete question: why doesn't the State Duma take power? I well remember what I answered: "Bring me two regiments to the Taurida Palace, and we will take power." I had intended to set an impossible condition. In fact I involuntarily uttered a prophecy.

The Petersburg situation replaced all this fortune-telling with real substance.

Self-Liquidation of the Old Order

AFTER THE BATTLE of the bloc and the public organizations against the government in November and December of 1916, January and February of 1917 passed somewhat colorlessly, leaving no vivid memories. Nevertheless, these two months were full of political substance which could be appreciated only after the revolution. Different opinions are possible as to whether this was an epilogue to what had already occurred or a prologue to what was about to begin. At any rate, it was a separate historical moment deserving special description. The basic characteristic of this period was that everybody, including the "street," was now waiting for something; and both sides, having embarked upon an open struggle, were preparing themselves for something. This "something," however, remained somewhere behind the lowered curtain of history, and neither side displayed sufficient organization or will to be the first to raise the curtain. As a result, a third "something" happened which nobody had expected to happen in this particular form: something indefinite and amorphous which, as a result of propaganda from both sides, immediately received the name of the beginning of the great Russian revolution.

The State Duma was again adjourned but not dissolved. At the end of 1916, there was talk about dissolution and about elections to a new Fifth Duma. But no decision was made to hold new elections, and even less did there appear a readiness to abolish the Duma entirely or to remake it with the aid of a new coup d'etat. The tsar, it is true, summoned N. A. Maklakov in order to entrust him with composing a manifesto for complete dissolution; and the former minister urged the tsar to take measures while there was still time, "to restore state order, no matter what the cost might be." "God reigns over the bold," Stolypin's successor urged Nicholas, but Nicholas, "in a hurry to go" somewhere, put aside the letter and "said that he would look into it." In the Council of Ministers the argument concerned only the duration of the new adjournment. In the January 3 session, five ministers came out in favor of January 12 in accordance with the decree of December 15 concerning the adjournment, while a majority of eight (including Protopopov) favored delaying it until January 31, in order to avoid "undesirable and inadmissable speeches." Finally, three ministers adhered to Protopopov's proposal to extend the adjournment until February 14. The premier, instead of Trepov, was Prince N. D. Golitsyn, a complete nonentity as far as politics goes, but personally known to the empress in his role as manager of her "committee for aid to Russian prisoners of war." A more outstanding man in this decisive moment could not be found in the ruling circles, and Golitsyn put down February 14 on the blank form which had been lying around Stürmer's office since November 7. This blank form ordered the Duma to be convened in what was fated to be its last session. With this adjournment of one and a half months, the ministers partially achieved their aim of forestalling "undesirable speeches." However, it was no longer a question of "undesirable speeches." It was neither Golitsyn nor Protopopov who had to be fought. In November and December, the bloc had taken definite positions. As we shall see, the bloc was now faced with another problem. In the sessions of February 14 and 15, the nonbloc opposition from both the left and the right spoke very sharply, although the press of the time testifies to the fact that their speeches were pale in comparison with the general mood of the country. I also spoke; and I honestly do not remember what I said or what I talked about. In those days, the leading role did not belong to the Duma.

Was that role transferred to the public organizations? Prince Lvov's Zemstvo organization was in the same position we were in. They too had spoken their last words. The Military-Industrial Committee could assume a more active role, partially in view of their connections with the workers' group, partially as a result of A. I. Guchkov's chairmanship. We know that the idea of a palace coup ripened in Guchkov's plans, but what he himself essentially did in order to realize those ideas, and what exactly the coup would be like, nobody knew. In any case, the idea of a palace coup came into the foreground and had to be dealt with as the first order of business, and thus it was also put forward for discussion among members of the bloc. It was clear to everyone that it was not the business of the Duma to arrange the coup. It was extremely important, however, to define the role of the Duma once the coup would be arranged. The bloc started with the assumption that, given the coup, Nicholas II would be removed from the throne, one way or another. The bloc agreed on transferring the authority of the monarch to the legal heir, Alexei, under the regency of Grand Duke Mikhail Alexandrovich until Alexei would reach maturity. The grand duke's gentle character and the young age of the heir seemed to be the best guarantee of a transition to a constitutional system. Of course, conversations on these themes were also carried on in those days outside of the bloc. Unfortunately, I do not remember exactly on what day we were invited by M. M. Fedorov to take part in a conference held in the building of the Military-Industrial Committee. I remember only that we arrived there with our decision ready and that after an exchange of opinions, our proposal was adopted; Guchkov was present at the discussions, but he kept mysteriously silent; and this silence was taken as evidence of his complicity in the impending coup. It was said in private that the fate of the emperor and the empress was still undecided—right up to the intervention by the grenadiers of the Preobrazhensky Regiment as happened in the eighteenth century. It was likewise said that Guchkov had ties with the officers of the guards' regiments which were quartered in the capital, etc. At any rate, we left without complete assurance that the coup would take place, but with the firm decision that, in the event the coup did take place, we would take it upon ourselves to arrange the transfer of power to the heir and the regent. Whether this could be achieved by the decision of the whole Duma or in the name of the Duma or in some other way, remained, of course, an open question—since the very existence of the Duma and the Duma's session at the moment of the coup could not be certain beforehand. Be that as it may, we were sure, after the conference in the building of the Military-Industrial Committee, that our decision would meet with support of the non-Duma public circles.

Before the awaited moment came, we had to come into contact with the Military-Industrial Committee on another question—the question of the fate of the committee's labor group. Agents of the tsarist secret police were planted in that group in order to follow any activities which they considered especially dangerous. We have seen, however, that this was a comparatively moderate group. According to Guchkov, the aim of that group in joining the committee was to "achieve legal forms for workers' organizations." According to the tsarist police's own admission, the socialist organizations, such as the Bolsheviks, the unity party, and the internationalists, remained aloof from the group's propaganda. They accused the group of preparing a welcome demonstration at the Taurida Palace for the day of the opening of the Duma —and this was entirely probable. It was only the provocateurs, like Abrosimov, who was planted in the group, who maintained that the aim of the demonstration was "an armed uprising and overthrow of the government." Nevertheless, Protopopov decided to deliver a blow to the workers' group, and on January 27, he arrested its members. This act caused great alarm. On January 29 Guchkov and Konovalov convoked a meeting of the public organizations with the aim of making a protest; and they complained to Prince Golitsyn, who admitted that the arrest was a "mistake" on Protopopov's part. Excitement among the workers grew: in the next few days (January 31–February 5) a whole series of meetings and strikes took place at the factories and plants. Then the Petersburg military district was separated from the northern front and placed under the command of General Khabalov, who was given wide-ranging powers, independent even of the minister of the army. Protopopov's hand could be seen here too: the empress approved his plan of combating the popular disturbances. Nevertheless, from February 7–13, the strikes continued and clashes with the police began. Rumors of a procession to the Duma on February 14 took on concrete form, and it was not difficult to detect police provocation behind these rumors. Protopopov, apparently, was preparing to follow the Moscow model of 1905 by artificially provoking a "revolution" and then shooting it down. The whole plan of dividing Petersburg into parts with the aim of crushing the expected uprising was ascribed to him. The rumor was spread that Protopopov had supplied the police with machine guns to be placed on the rooftops at various strategic points throughout the capital. My own name was mentioned as instigator of the workers' demonstration, and I had to become involved in this business. On February 9 my appeal to the workers appeared, urging them not to yield to the clear provocation and not to fall into the obvious police trap of the procession to the Duma on February 14. My appeal, placed together with Khabalov's, evoked criticism from the left, but it achieved its aim: the workers' procession of February 14 did not take place.

Manifestations of popular discontent along this political, yet non-partisan, line were somewhat checked, but they burst through in a much more mighty torrent, along economic lines. The "intelligentsia" circles of the capital could dream of a palace coup which was not materializing and of terroristic acts directed against highly placed persons—but nobody could be found to carry them out—and the secret police could use rumors about this to fill the reports of their spies to their superiors. In actuality, the danger lay elsewhere. Everyone admitted it, but no help was anywhere forthcoming. A police report from January 10 already linked both political and economic themes: "The adjournment of the Duma continues to occupy the center of all opinions" . . . but "the rise in the cost of living and the repeated failures of the government's measures in the struggle against the disappearance of products provoked a sharp wave of protest even before Christmas. . . . The population openly (in the streets, on the streetcars, in the theaters, in the stores) criticizes all government undertakings in an impermissibly sharp manner." Or, in a report from February 5: "With each passing day, the food question becomes more aggravated and forces the average citizen to curse everyone having anything at all to do with food, and to curse them in the most uncensored expressions." "The new explosion of discontent," because of the new rise in prices and the disappearance of urgently needed articles from the market, has taken hold of "even the conservative strata of the bureaucracy." "Never before has there been so much cursing, scenes and scandals as at the present time. . . . If the population has not yet made hunger mutinies, that is no guarantee they will not do so in the very near future. Resentment is growing, and there is no end in sight." And the secret police "has no doubts" about the onset of "anarchic revolution"! What was being done to prevent it?

On February 23, when 87,000 workers from fifty enterprises went out on strike over the bread shortage, Protopopov asked Khabalov to announce to the population that "there is enough bread." "The disturbances were caused by provocateurs." On February 24, 197,000 workers were out on strike. Khabalov announced that "there ought to be no shortage of bread for sale." . . . Evidently, "many people are buying up bread for reserve, for dry biscuits." The government decided to "turn over the food problem to the municipal authorities." The minister of the army ordered the speeches of Rodichev, Chkheidze, and Kerensky not to be printed, while Khabalov, on February 25, threatened to draft new recruits into the army before the recruitment levy was scheduled to take place—this announcement was made when 240,000 workers had already gone out on strike. Protopopov sent a telegram to Headquarters saying that there was not enough bread because the "public is increasingly buying it up for reserves," and that "measures are being taken to put an end to the disorders." The City Duma considered the question of bread cards, while the State Duma discussed an extension of the powers of the local governments in the area of food supply. The "measures" consisted of arresting about one hundred members of revolutionary organizations on the night of February 26.

It was obvious that all these efforts came hopelessly late and were misdirected anyway. There remained only—a call to the troops and suppression by force. On the night of February 25, the tsar sent a telegram to Khabalov: "I order that the disorders in the capital be stopped tomorrow; such disorders are impermissible during this difficult time of war against Germany and Austria!" What could be further from a realistic understanding of what was going on?

And so the last recourse was the troops. But where were the troops? What troops? Before the Extraordinary Commission, Protopopov showed that he "was uninformed in this matter also." He counted on the troops being "more reliable" than they really were. "I did not expect to find strong revolutionary currents in the army, and I was sure that in the event of a workers' uprising, the government would find a bulwark in the troops"; and "I did not doubt that the general mass of troops was faithful to the tsar," and "I reported this to the tsar." "The tsar was pleased with my report." In reality, things were different. If the police and the gendarmes could still manage to control the crowds on February 23, then on February 24 it was necessary to bring in the army—although Khabalov did not want to fire into the crowd. After the tsar's order on February 25, it was decided to open fire; and on February 26, the troops began shooting in several places. However, one company of the reserve battalion of the Pavlovsky Regiment demanded that the shooting be stopped and itself opened fire on the mounted police. On February 27, individual sections of the troops were declared to be in a state of siege. By evening, those troops who remained "faithful" amounted to only an insignificant minority, and they had to be concentrated around the government institutions: the Admiralty, the Winter Palace and the Peter and Paul Fortress.

Where were the representatives of the ruling circles during these fateful days of February 23–27?

To the surprise of "many" on February 22, the eve of the disturbances, the tsar left Tsarskoe Selo for Headquarters maintaining only telegraph and, as it turned out, the even less reliable railroad connections between himself and the capital. He was satisfied with Protopopov's comparatively reassuring telegrams and did not pay attention to the alarming telegrams from Rodzianko. He told Fredericks on February 27: "Again that fat Rodzianko wrote me all sorts of nonsense which I will not even bother answering." "Nonsense" referred to Rodzianko's proposal "to entrust someone enjoying the confidence of the country to form a new government immediately."

The Council of Ministers met each day, having transferred their sessions to the Marinsky Palace for safety's sake. Their meetings were not so much for the purpose of undertaking decisive measures as they were for exchanging information on the events taking place. They did take one decisive measure, however. On the night of February 26, Golitsyn raised the question of "dissolving" or of "adjourning the work of the State Duma." The majority inclined toward "adjournment," but on Protopopov's testimony it was decided that an attempt should first be made "to win the progressive bloc over the reconciliation." Two ministers, N. N. Pokrovsky (appointed to replace Stürmer as minister of foreign affairs on November 10, 1916) and Rittich (minister of agriculture, who introduced measures into the Duma in connection with the food question), took it upon themselves to hold talks with me, V. A. Maklakov, and N. V. Savich. I do not at all remember what they actually spoke about with me. The answer, however, appeared the next day: "Reconciliation is impossible; the deputies demanded a change in the government and the appointment of new ministers from people enjoying the public confidence." The demand was considered unacceptable, and it was decided to publish the decree announcing the "adjournment." Prince Golitsyn had only to write in the date on one of the three blanks which the tsar had placed at his disposal; and in the evening of that very day, Rodzianko found the decree on his desk announcing the recess as of February 26 and stating that the Duma sessions should be resumed "not later than April 1917, depending on the extraordinary circumstances." On February 27, however, even the members of the Council of Ministers "walked around lost, expecting to be arrested," and, as a "sacrifice," they offered up Protopopov's resignation. He agreed, and from that moment he went into hiding. The Council of Ministers petitioned for the appointment of a military commander with a popular name, to lead the "troops which have remained faithful," and they also petitioned for a responsible cabinet. The tsar agreed to the "military leader" (Ivanov) but declared that "changes in the composition of the cabinet under the given circumstances cannot be allowed." He also rejected Grand Duke Mikhail Alexandrovich's proposal to name himself regent and Prince Lvov premier. The tsar sent word through Alexeev that "he thanks the Grand Duke for his attention," that he "will leave tomorrow," and that he "will make the decision himself." The next day (February 28) the Council of Ministers itself sent in its resignation and ceased to exist. The Marinsky Palace was occupied by "outsiders," and the ministers were forced to go into hiding. At that moment in the Russian capital, there was no tsar, no Duma, and no Council of Ministers. The "disorders" assumed the appearance of a regular "revolution."

The Creation of a New Order

WAS THERE ANY LEGAL CONTINUITY between the old order which liquidated itself, and the new order, created on March 2, 1917? A revolution occurred between them, and this circumstance alone, it seems, implies a negative answer. Nevertheless, people have attempted more than once to find ties of succession between them. Some derived the authority of the Provisional Government from the tsar's orders given before his abdication, appointing Prince Lvov as premier and giving him the right to form his own cabinet. Others searched for the ties in that act by which Nicholas II, abdicating, transferred his authority to his brother the Grand Duke Mikhail Alexandrovich. Those who consider this act illegal, point to the conditional character of Mikhail's abdication (until the decision of the Constituent Assembly) and to his reference to the "complete authority" of the State Duma. In all probability, apparently the chairman of the State Duma wanted to establish his succession, and polemicized continually with the Kadet party (and with its leader) which was preventing this. As the story continues, we shall see that none of these attempts are sufficiently justified. It is another matter how the provisional government viewed its own authority. Did it believe that all sovereign power had been transferred to it, and that it in turn would have to turn over this power to the Constituent Assembly? Or were there elements of sovereignty which it did not possess? There were decisions which the provisional government refused to take, considering them an infringement on the rights of the Constituent Assembly (for example, the question of the form of the future government). On the other hand, a real dictatorial group emerged from among its membership which did not stop short of even that decision. All of these were questions for a legal expert. For a historian, and even more so for a memoirist, some evidence is contained in the very name "Provisional"—a modest self-determination which was maintained until the very end of the existence of that government.

I am mentioning all of this briefly here, in connection with the transition to a new historical phase, because, among the possible and impossible interpretations, I had to pursue my own line which had been successful right up to the creation of the Provisional Government although it was no longer the line of the Progressive bloc. The others subordinated themselves to the circumstances which had come about, and went even further. My starting point at that time was the position which the German jurists define by the concept *Rechtsbruch*—"interruption in the law." My starting point assumed that this interruption was unique and temporary (until the Constituent Assembly). The circumstances which came about while the Provisional Government was in power did not correspond to this concept. The *Rechtsbruch* turned out to be a prolonged phenomenon because the revolution continued: it entered a new "stage," one which continued the reformation of the law. And it was here that my tactics were wrecked. Let me repeat that all this will become clearer as my story continues: only the most important tendencies are outlined here.

On the morning of February 27, I was awakened by the bell of the doorkeeper who had come to tell me that there was something wrong going on in the barracks of the Volynsky Regiment. The window of my apartment—on the corner of Bassein Street and Parade Lane—overlooked a short lane at the end of which were the gates of the regiment. The gates were open; in the courtyard handfuls of soldiers were shouting something, acting excitedly, and waving their arms. There was nothing unexpected in all this given the events of the last few days. I suddenly felt, however, that events were entering a new stage.

The bell was sounded from the Taurida Palace. The chairman was convening the members of the Duma for a session. Since the night before, the Duma Elders and party leaders had known that the decree announcing the recess of the Duma had been received. The ritual of holding a session had also been decided upon the night before: it had been decided to heed to the decree, make no demonstration and close the session immediately. Of course, they knew nothing of this in the barracks of the Volynsky Regiment. The disturbances there were entirely independent of the fate of the Duma.

I walked to the Duma taking my usual route along Potemkin Street. My wife accompanied me. The street was deserted, and bullets from stray shots smacked against the trees and the walls of the palace. Nobody was around the Duma yet; the entrance was clear. Not all the deputies gathered there had been informed of what was about to take place. The session was held as planned: the decree was read while the deputies maintained complete silence except for sporadic shouts from the rightists. The Duma's suicide was committed without protest.

What came next? After a silent session, it was impossible to break up and depart in silence! Without any previous arrangement the members of the Duma straggled from the session hall into the adjoining semicircular hall. This was not a meeting of the Duma which had just ended, nor was it a session of one of its committees. It was a private conference of the Duma members. The solitary individuals who had loitered in the other halls, began to approach the group which had gathered. I do not remember whether Rodzianko acted as chairman; the meeting was amorphous; heated speeches sounded forth from the group in the middle. Proposals were made to return and reopen a formal session of the Duma, refusing to recognize the decree (M. A. Karavalov); to declare the Duma a Constituent Assembly, and to turn over authority to a dictator (General Manikovsky); to take power with those gathered there and create our own body—in any event, not to disperse and leave Petersburg. I proposed to wait awhile until the character of the disturbances became clearer, and, in the meantime, to create a temporary committee of Duma members "for restoring order and maintaining contact with various persons and institutions." This awkward formula had the advantage of meeting the problem of the moment without determining anything for the future. Limiting itself to the minimum, it created a working body but did not lead the Duma members into criminal action. Stormy protests rang forth from the left, but the meeting as a whole did not waver. After long arguments my compromise proposal was adopted, and the election of a "Temporary Committee" was entrusted to the Council of Elders. This meant transferring it to the bloc. At three o'clock in the afternoon, the Elders carried out their task, nominating representatives of the bloc parties to the committee. It should be added that this choice partially determined the composition of the future government. First of all, the members of the Duma presidium entered the committee (Rodzianko, Dmitriukov, Rzhevsky); then there came the representatives of the factions: Shulgin (from the nationalists), V. I. Lvov (from the center), Shidlovsky (from the Octobrists), Miliukov and Nekrasov, the deputy chairman, (from the Kadets); the leftists Kerensky and Chkheidze also adhered to the project. The Elders' draft was aired among the factions and reported to the gathering in the semicircular hall. By evening, when the composition of the Temporary Committee became clear, the revolutionary character of the disturbances had also become clear; and the committee decided to take the next step: take power into its own hands. The members of the government were also named, but since Prince Lvov was named as premier in the bloc's list, the formal creation of the government was postponed until his arrival in Petersburg; and an urgent telegram to that effect was sent to him. In the meantime, the Temporary Committee busied itself with the restoration of the administrative apparatus and sent the Duma commissars around to all the higher governmental institutions.

While all these measures for the creation of a new order were being taken, the physiognomy of the Taurida Palace changed completely. The gates of the palace were locked, but from morning on, the Duma building was infiltrated mainly by the "pure public," the intellectuals who had something to do with politics. I remember my first impressions. I was standing by the main entrance, and my old acquaintance, Charnolussky, marched by me at the head of a small group. He had the air of one who held power, who had come here, not as a spectator, but as a participant. He had a tense and concentrated look, and in his hands he held a rifle tilted forward. He did not notice me even though I was but two steps away from him. "Here is the first competitor for power, armed with the symbol of rule," the thought flashed through my mind. "This is that very revolution which everyone was talking about but which nobody was planning to make." At that moment a shot rang out and from the guard room they carried the officer of the Duma guards by his hands and legs. He was guilty of having worn a uniform. Not long before that, the chief of the guards, also in uniform, dashed into the semicircular hall begging us to protect him. They had asked him whether he was for the people or against the people and he did not know how to answer. A little later, in the circular Catherine's Hall, a more peaceful group of intellectuals came up to meet me. The head of the group was also an old acquaintance of mine, Tatiana Bogdanovich, Korolenko's niece and the wife of my fellow editor from *Mir Bozhi*. In an excited and pleading voice she asked me: Is it really true that even now the State Duma will not stand at the head of the people's movement? Is it really true that the Duma will not take power? I had a thousand grounds for explaining to her that the Duma no longer existed and that I personally did not want the Duma to take power. The conversations about taking power had already begun in the semicircular hall, and I hurried over there, telling her only that the question had already been raised and would be decided when the movement going on outside would become clearer.

After noon, a large crowd piled up before the gates of the palace, crushing against the iron bars. Here was the "public," and the workers, and the soldiers. We had to open the gates, and the crowd gushed into the palace. By evening time we felt that we were no longer alone in the palace, and in general that we were no longer masters of the palace. At the other end of the palace, the other pretender to power had already gathered: the Soviet of Workers' Deputies hurriedly convened by the party organizations which until that time had refrained from leading the revolution. At that time, the composition of the Soviet was rather amorphous—in addition to the representatives which had been called from the factories, anyone who wanted to join—and by the end of the day, the name of the "Soviet of Workers' Deputies" had to be changed to the "Soviet of Workers' and Soldiers' Deputies." The soldiers were the last ones to appear, but they were the real masters of the situation. It is true that they themselves did not admit this; they rushed into the palace, not as conquerors, but as people afraid of taking responsibility for committing a breach of discipline, for the murder of the commanders and officers. They were even less sure than we were that the revolution had won. Like the officer of the guard, they too wanted protection, not recognition, from the Duma. By night time, the Taurida Palace had turned into a fortified camp. The soldiers brought with themselves boxes of machine-gun cartridge belts and hand grenades; and, I think, they also dragged in a cannon. When shots were heard somewhere around the palace, some of the soldiers began to run, broke the windows in the semicircular hall, and jumped out of the windows into the courtyard. Later, when they had calmed down, they spread themselves around the rooms of the palace for the night. Radical, aristocratic young ladies appeared and treated the soldiers to tea and sandwiches. The entire meeting hall, the gallery, and the adjoining hall were filled with soldiers. Then, in the meeting hall, sessions of the Soviet of Workers' and Soldiers' Deputies were convened right among the soldiers. The Soviet had its own worries. While we were taking measures to keep the higher governmental institutions functioning, the Soviet fortified its position in the capital by dividing Petersburg up into districts. In each district the troops and the factories were to elect their representatives; district commissars were appointed "in order to establish the people's power in the districts," and the population was invited "to organize local committees and to take into their own hands the government of local affairs." The Temporary Committee of the Duma was pushed aside into a far corner of the palace, next to the chairman's office. Nevertheless, for the necessities of the day, both organizations, the Duma and the Soviet, were forced into immediate contact with each other. The rooms of the Duma factions were occupied by joint committees. A. I. Shingarev became chairman of the Food Committee appointed by the Soviet; our traveling

POLITICAL MEMOIRS

companion, Colonel Engelhart, was co-opted by the Duma's Temporary Committee and sat down together with the leftists Palchinsky and
Fedorovsky in the Army Committee. A whole series of other committees were organized with the help of the Kadet, Ichas; these included
a Judicial Committee, a committee to deal with those who were
arrested and a committee for handling internal rules and order in the
palace. Former ministers either came to the Duma by themselves (like
Protopopov) or were taken there under arrest. Then there occurred
a typical episode with Kerensky who hurried to appear in his dual
role of assistant chairman of the Soviet of Deputies and candidate
for the post of minister of justice. Students with sabers in hand led
Shcheglovitov to the palace, and Rodzianko, apparently, wanted to let
him go. Called forth by the students, Kerensky, overriding Rodzianko's
objections, declared him under arrest "until the creation of the Duma's
Provisional Committee" and ordered him to be taken away to the
ministers' pavilion of the Duma to spend the night The next day,
all the arrested ministers and other persons were taken from there
to the Peter and Paul Fortress.

The following day, February 28, the situation had finally cleared
up. We were the victors. But who were "we"? The masses could not
tell. The State Duma was the symbol of victory and became the object of a general pilgrimage. Was this the Duma as a building, or the
Duma as an institution? Of course, Rodzianko wanted to understand
it in the latter sense, and he already considered himself the chief
and the leader of what had been accomplished. In answer to his last
telegram to the tsar that "the fate of the homeland and the dynasty
is being decided," he received the reply on February 28 permitting
him personally to form a responsible cabinet. Right up to March 2, he
stuck to this proposal in his telephone conversation with General
Ruzsky and declared that "until this time the people believe only
him and fulfill only his commands"—although at the same time he
admitted that "he himself is hanging by a hair, that power is slipping
away out of his hands and that he was forced to appoint the Provisional Government on the night of March 2." It was only as a matter
of information that he had told Ruzsky about the "threatening demands for the Tsar's abdication in favor of his son, under the regency
of Mikhail Alexandrovich." Right up to 3:45 A.M. of March 2 the tsar
was ready to send a telegram to this effect, giving way to the advice
of the leaders at the front. Events unfolded rapidly and this whole
mess was left behind. Nevertheless, during these days, the fiction of
the victory of the State Duma as an institution was supported by the
Duma's chairman.

In fact the whole day of February 28 was a day of triumph for the State Duma as such. To the Taurida Palace came entire regiments which had gone over to the side of the Duma, expressing their subordination to the State Duma. The chairman of the Duma went out to meet them, alternating with the deputies; and I had to perform a significant portion of these triumphant receptions and speeches. The officers from one of the regiments came to me with a special request to go with them to the barracks and deliver a speech of triumph. I went. They put me up on a tower surrounded by the whole regiment. I had to shout from above so that they could hear me. I congratulated the regiment on the victory but I added that the victory must still be reinforced; that in order to do this it was necessary to preserve their unity with the officer corps without which they would crumble into dust; that they should refrain from being carried away by all sorts of festive celebrations. Our time to celebrate was still before us. I was received most warmly and the officers were satisfied. Of course, it was not so much my speech which produced the effect as it was the fact that a leading member of the Duma had come to visit the regiment. My voice suffered much from this and other such efforts.

In the Duma building, the ambiguity which Rodzianko had permitted still had to be eliminated. The Temporary Committee existed independently of the chairman's sanctions; and just as independently, it was the committee, and not the chairman, who selected the provisional government. Not Rodzianko, but Prince Lvov was supposed to head the government, not "appoint" it. The roles of the bloc, the chairman, and the intended premier were defined once and for all —as a solution to the dynastic question. The plans only remained to be carried out. But how could this be reconciled with the position of the chairman which was supported by our recognition of the role of the Duma as an institution? This was a disturbing problem which had to be solved without delay, before the arrival of Prince Lvov. Rodzianko was obviously dragging things out and vacillating, apparently counting somehow on outwitting us.

It was necessary to clarify as soon as possible his attitudes toward the steps already taken: toward the rights and powers of the Temporary Committee and the composition of the Provisional Government. For this purpose I decided to take advantage of the moment when Rodzianko would return from his trip to the Marinsky Palace with the news that the Council of Ministers had resigned. The following scene occurred, and I remember it in all its details. "Mikhail Vladimirovich," I told the chairman, "the time has come to decide." I meant, of course, to decide once and for all to recognize the revolution as an accomplished fact. Rodzianko asked for a quarter of an hour to think it over and went up to his office. We sat in a group by the door of his office, waiting for his answer. In these minutes of anxious waiting, the telephone rang out. The call was for Colonel Engelhart. Our colleague went to the phone. From the Preobrazhensky Regiment: "The Preobrazhensky Regiment places itself at the disposal of the State Duma." The members of the committee felt relieved. "Colonel, pass this report on immediately to Mikhail Vladimirovich." Engelhart went into the office. The committee was waiting tensely to see what sort of impression this news would make on the old guardsman. At last Rodzianko came out and sat down at the table. "I consent," he said raising his voice and trying to give it a maximum of significance. "But —only on one condition. I demand—and this refers especially to you, Alexander Fedorovich (Kerensky)—that all the members of the committee (no mention about the government) unconditionally and blindly subordinate themselves to my command. . . ." We were dumbfounded. Both the tone and the substance of Rodzianko's ultimatum were so out of place in the given situation. Even Stürmer had not demanded such a degree of subordination from his Council of Ministers . . . . We were being spoken to by the dictator of the Russian revolution! The future dictator, Kerensky, restrained himself and modestly reminded Rodzianko that he (Kerensky) was still assistant chairman of the Soviet of Workers' Deputies. The rest of us kept silent. We knew Rodzianko: "When Bullion boiled over, Bullion flowed to temple!" His agreement was, nevertheless, given and the next day, March 1, Prince Lvov was to arrive and everything would be put in its proper framework.

Georgii Evgenievich [Lvov] did, in fact, arrive, and in the afternoon he made his way to the Taurida Palace. At last we felt ourselves *au complet;* the Temporary Committee and the government gathered together for a preliminary exchange of opinion. I do not remember the substance of the talks: it could hardly have focused on specialized questions. On the other hand, I do remember the impression made on me and probably on others too. We did not feel that a leader was standing before us. The prince was evasive and cautious: he reacted to events in a gentle, diffuse manner and talked his way out with general phrases.

At the end of the conference I. P. Demidov bent over to me and whispered in my ear: "Well, what do you think? How is he?" With disappointment I answered him in one word, also in a whisper: "A wet rag!" I am not sure that this expressed what I felt.

At any rate, I was greatly disappointed.

I had known the prince only superficially. The others knew him even less than I did; and they had faith in my choice, sight unseen. I was, in a way, responsible for this choice. V. V. Shulgin wrote later:

Prince Lvov "unquestionably moved on to the minister's pedestal in Miliukov's list." My friend Nabokov also wrote later: "He sat in the driver's box but didn't even try to pick up the reins." When his friends asked him how he could have agreed to accept the post, he answered with his eyes lowered: "I could not do otherwise. . . ." What sort of a man was this who formerly had been indispensable when it came to "business," but who now turned out to be unfit for "politics"?

Of course, it would be absurd to blame Prince Lvov for the failure of the revolution. The revolution was too large and complex a thing. Nevertheless, it seems that I do have the right to blame him for the failure of my policy in the first stage of the revolution. Or, in the last analysis, should I blame myself for a bad choice of the executor of this policy? But, just as he "could not do otherwise," so I could not choose otherwise. V. V. Shulgin asked himself: Well, was Rodzianko better? And he answered correctly, as I did: No, Rodzianko was impossible; "the leftists would not have allowed it"! Would they have "allowed" us, Kadets, who still possessed "some sort of force"? Stripped to its essentials, the whole question amounted precisely to this. My answer will become clear from the following.

In any case, I do not wish to be unjust to Prince Lvov. Before writing the following lines, I read Lvov's detailed biography written by his intimate co-worker, T. I. Polner, and written with love and deep respect for the person of its hero. He, too, looks for explanations, and not justifications. I will allow myself to cite a few traits from that book which previously were unknown to me.

Prince Lvov spent the first ten years of his life in the countryside, in an atmosphere of family love and favorable disposition toward the peasants. During this time he learned the rural way of life, from the inside, one might say. He was able to speak with the peasants in the peasant's own language; he knew the peasant's peculiarities and his needs. Lvov spent the next twenty years of his life in the service of the Zemstvo establishments and thus gave meaning to his childhood impressions. In the style of the Slavophiles, he valued the "people's soul," and he reconstructed Russian history in his mind in agreement with Konstantin Aksakov. His attitude toward the peasant was expressed in the old formula: "we are yours and you are ours." His attitude toward the state was expressed in Aksakov's formula: power to the monarch, but opinion to the "land." He was not able, nor did he want, to see the evil in Russian life; and he pushed it away from him whenever he came in contact with it. He accepted the given reality and drew the maximum good from it, not through struggle, but through adaptation. "Everything will be all right in the end" thanks to the people's wisdom: this is what his philosophy amounted to. Those who are on top only prevent it from happening that way. It was sufficient to have a heart-to-heart talk, to joke, to laugh, and the matter would be done better than by giving orders. The person you talk to will be yours.

Formal learning was of no use to the prince. He came to hate Classicism; and he sat through two years in two classes at the gymnasium. He chose the law faculty as the "easiest one" and came from the village to the university only to take exams. On the other hand, the practical, applied knowledge which was needed in the village, he assimilated in all its details in order to apply it to life in the village as well as in his "aristocratic nest" at Popovka. Under the father, Popovka had passed through the terrible ordeal of the impoverishment of the nobility, but it was restored by the businesslike efficiency of the son. In urban circles and in cultured society, Lvov withdrew into himself; he did not shine forth with eloquent speech, did not join in arguments, and gave the impression, even to the closest friends of his youth, like Count D. Olsufiev, of being a clever man and nobody's fool. In others as well as in himself, he appreciated the quality of being purely "businesslike"; he did not like orders from above and he did not like "statistics." He regarded the bureaucracy with distrust, as he did official legislation. The people would arrange everything for themselves; the people know what they need.

Prince Lvov approached public activity through the Zemstvos and put into it all the traits of his personality. At that time Zemstvo work was carried out under the banner of liberalism; but Lvov remained aloof from politics, concentrating his activity on work which our satirist cruelly and unjustly ridiculed as "plating the washstands." Lvov was at home in this practical work and displayed himself fully in it. He showed unusual inventiveness, inexhaustible energy, knowledge of life, and ability to gather the youth around him, acting not by giving orders, but by setting an example, with gentleness and humor. He was extraordinarily simple and well-mannered; he never used a bossy tone. Then came the open struggle against the government. Lvov was elected to the first two Dumas on the Kadet list, and he used his position of deputy, not for militant speeches but for advancing those same businesslike undertakings. For me, he was a pale shadow and left no memorable impressions whatever. It is true, he recalled that in Vyborg we had spent the night in the same bed, but this was hardly unusual since the bed was the floor and everyone was lying side by side. He left Vyborg without signing the appeal; and they did not sentence him. He transferred all his habits to the leadership of the Zemstvo organizations when the war began. "Politics" was then the affair of the government; while he defended from "politics" his prac-

tical work. When, in addition to the practical obstacles, political persecutions were stepped up, the tone of the public organizations, as we
have seen, became more excited. Lvov's own speeches became more
excited: it was becoming difficult to distinguish politics from practical
work. While speaking of "taking responsibility on myself," Lvov continued to place his hopes on the "soul of the people" which "always
led the country out of danger." "Only a lofty ascent of the people's
spirit, only a national feat can save our perishing fatherland," he wrote
in an undelivered speech. Events, however, surpassed Slavophile lyrics.
"With some bewilderment," Prince Lvov said, "I feel that events are
going on over my head." From all sides he was put forward as the
savior of the homeland. He let the moment slip when he could say:
"definitely not." "By the middle of 1916, he 'finally gave in'," says his
biographer. "He was not thinking of revolution," but conceiving of
Russia's fate in the form of a monarchy with a cabinet responsible to
a legally elected body of people's representatives. This was the position of the "bloc," but Prince Lvov had absolutely no idea about how
to achieve that goal or what methods to use. The bloc's tactics, on the
other hand, were already planned out. Thus, we invited him to be
premier. He "could not do otherwise. . . ." Once arrived, he began to
get acclimated, as was his custom. From this followed his indefiniteness which at the first meeting caused my disappointment. We did
not know "whose" he would be, but we felt that he would not be
"ours."

There was no time to wait, however. The new ruling authority
had been created. In those moments it was too early to theorize; but
the realities of the situation were apparent to everyone. He had to begin ruling the state immediately, and if even roughly, to define his
attitude toward the other factors of the situation: the Duma, the
Soviet of Workers' Deputies, and the tsar. From his cramped corner
in the Taurida Palace each minister began making contact with the
personnel of his ministry. People from the Ministry of Foreign Affairs
came to see me. N. N. Pokrovsky asked to be allowed to stay in the
building until he found an apartment. I agreed all the more willingly
since I was, in any case, not planning to move. The French ambassador, Paléologue, came and firmly insisted that in our declaration
we express our faithfulness to our allies. I promised him that we would
do so. They brought me a paper signed by four grand dukes: they
agreed to a responsible cabinet. They were too late; I told the person
who brought the paper: "This is an interesting historical document,"
and I put the paper in my briefcase. The grand dukes were very offended by my lack of attention.

Rodzianko was left out of the new government, although he continued as president of the Duma, which had not been dissolved, but merely adjourned by the tsar's decree. He tried to consider the Duma not only as in existence but as standing higher than the government. This was the Duma of the "Third of June"—clamped in a vise by the prerogatives of the "autocratic" authorities, by the Fundamental Laws of April 1906, and by the "bottleneck" of the State Council, which had become the "cemetery" for Duma legislation. Could this institution really be considered a factor in the current situation? The Duma was but a shadow of its past. Moreover, its term of office ended that very year. The Provisional Government later decided to pay the deputies' salaries until the end of the term and did not object against the chairman's convoking the Duma members who were present. This was all that remained of the Duma after it had served as the symbol of the revolution in the first days of forming the new government. Of course, it was difficult for Rodzianko to see it from this point of view. I do not know when it was that he composed his own theory which he later recounted in his memoirs. He relates the basic features of that theory to the period just described, maintaining that his plan was to convoke the Duma immediately as an institution. "The State Duma would have been the bearer of supreme authority and the body to which the Provisional Government would have been responsible. Such was the plan of the chairman of the State Duma. This plan was resolutely opposed primarily by the members of the Kadet party." Rodzianko, of course, had the "leader" of the Kadet party in mind, and my objections have just been given. I do not remember whether or not I stated my objections to Rodzianko personally; he knew my views, however, and these views were adopted by the bloc. Prince Lvov merely adhered to them.

Rodzianko made a great mistake in attributing the weakness of the Provisional Government to the fact that the Provisional Government was not led by the State Duma. He himself recognized that this would only have been a source of further weakness. His error went even farther. He did not understand the socialists' basic principle which I have already mentioned more than once: according to their theory, the Russian revolution was supposed to be "bourgeois"; and, preserving the "purity of the holy vestments," they refused on principle to join the new government. We included them in our government as representatives of the leftist factions in the Duma, and we highly valued their participation. However, Chkheidze, the chairman of the Soviet of Workers' Deputies, refused. Kerensky, the assistant chairman of the Soviet, who was personally invited, valued a ministerial post as a trump in his own game, and one might say, forced the Soviet to agree. This "Trudovik" who declared himself a Socialist Revolutionary when it was necessary, was now preparing for the role of "hostage of revolutionary democracy" in the camp of the "bourgeoisie"; and he adopted the corresponding poses. He was desperately in need of this post, but the Soviet had decided not to send the representatives of democracy to the government. In the memoirs of Sukhanov, Mstislavsky, and a certain "Count V. V.," it is described how Kerensky overcame this obstacle. He delivered an incoherent speech recommending himself, demanding "confidence" and support, declaring his "readiness to die," and promising to liberate "with honor" the political prisoners from Siberia "not excluding even the terrorists." "Comrades, the representatives of the old order are in my hands, and I am not about to let them out of my hands . . . I cannot live without the people, and when the moment comes that you have doubts about me, then kill me!" Having delivered this speech, "now in a dying whisper, now in gripping notes with a quiver in his voice," Kerensky dashed out of the meeting without waiting for the vote, but with his prepared decision to "announce to the government that he would join it with the permission of the Soviet and as a representative of the Soviet."

Apart from viewing the government on principle as a "bourgeois" government, there was also another reason explaining why the socialists refrained from participating in the rule of the country. I already mentioned that the socialist parties held themselves aloof from the broad workers' movement during the last days before the revolution. They had been caught unaware without having had time to organize their ideological allies in the country. Rodzianko, who lumped all the leftists into one pile, ascribes a preconceived and premeditated plan to them. No such plan existed, and it was precisely for that reason the government was strong. It was precisely on this idea of a bourgeois revolution that Kerensky built up his role as mediator for seven months. Until July, even Lenin held to this idea, and his disciples Zinoviev and Kamenev based on it their belief that the October revolution was premature. Returning to the first days of the revolution, speakers at the Congress of Soviets on March 30 openly recognized this "psychological" reason for their refusal to take power. "We did not yet have anything to lean on for support. We had only the unorganized masses before us," said Steklov. "During the first days of the revolution, we did not feel that we had the ground under our feet for taking power," repeated the military doctor, Esipovsky. In the absence of this ground, stressed Sukhanov (Himmer), the socialists "would have to carry out the bourgeois business with their socialist hands, and this would have meant destruction of the trust of the people and of the socialist parties in their leaders." The "bourgeois" government was, thus, given a period of grace and had, therefore, to be recognized as the legitimate governing power.

The Soviet, however, did not want to repudiate its share of actual power. It was necessary to establish a definite agreement between these two most important factors. The need for this was felt no less by the Soviet than it was by the Provisional Government. The initiative for the negotiations, at least, belonged to the Executive Committee of the Soviet of Workers' and Soldiers' Deputies. Late in the evening of March 1, a delegation from the Executive Committee, consisting of Chkheidze, Steklov, Sukhanov, Sokolov, Filippovsky, and others, came to the Temporary Committee of the Duma and to the government with a proposal to discuss the conditions under which the democratic organizations would support the government. They brought with them a prepared text of these conditions which they intended to have published in the name of the government. For the left wing of the bloc, the majority of these conditions were entirely acceptable, since they were a part of the leftists' own program. These included: all civil liberties; abolition of all restrictions based on class, religion, or nationality; convocation of a Constituent Assembly which would establish the form of government; elections to the organs of self-government based on universal suffrage; and a complete amnesty. There were also points of substantial disagreement, entailing a protracted argument which ended in agreement only at four in the morning. Prince Lvov was absent. During this night of March 1–2, Guchkov went to the Warsaw and Baltic stations in order to forestall the arrival of the troops which the tsar had sent to Petersburg to quell the uprising. It must be explained that as late as February 28, Headquarters viewed the disturbances in the capital as a mutiny which could be suppressed. For this purpose, some of the troops from the northern and western fronts were sent; General Ivanov was appointed dictator; martial law was declared in Petersburg; and the tsar left Headquarters on March 1 for Tsarskoe Selo. At the same time, our engineers, Nekrasov and Bublikov (a Progressivist), together with the leftists, made contact with the Railway Workers' Union and came out in control of all movement along the entire railway network. The Executive Committee of the Soviet of Workers' and Soldiers' Deputies was also impressed by these events, and perhaps it was this threat that explains the mood of the delegates and their comparative tractability on the night of March 2.

V. V. Shulgin gave a very picturesque description of the external aspect of our conference with the delegates. "It went on for a long time, endlessly . . . Chkheidze was lying down. . . . Kerensky jumped up from time to time, ran away somewhere and again appeared . . .

I do not remember how many hours this lasted. I was thoroughly exhausted, and I stopped helping Miliukov, as I had tried to do at the beginning . . . Kerensky was lying to my right, . . . apparently in a state of complete exhaustion. The rest of them, too, were completely worn out." Shulgin bent over Chkheidze to ask why they were so insistent on an elected officer corps. Chkheidze "raised his thoroughly tired eyelids, rolled his eyes and answered in a whisper: 'In general everything has failed . . . a miracle is needed in order to save. . . . We must try it. . . . It cannot be any worse . . . because, I tell you, everything has failed. . . . Only Miliukov sat straight and fresh.' "

Alas, I too, was not "fresh." This was already the third sleepless night I had spent without leaving the Taurida Palace. I spent snatches of the night on a corner of the large table in the room of the Budget Committee, covering myself with my fur coat; next to me was lying Skobelev, who likewise did not display a very cheerful mood. I was aware of the importance of the talks, which apparently was by no means clear to all of them, and this awareness sustained me. Step by step I won over the delegation on those points in their text which were unacceptable. Thus, I did not agree to consider "the question of the form of government as an open question" (they wanted to introduce a republic at once). They also agreed, as Shulgin, half-awake, heard, to strike out the demand for election of the officer corps. I held the soldiers' civil liberties "to the limits allowable under the military and technical conditions," and I defended the "retention of strict military discipline in the structure and the carrying out of military service," while introducing equality for soldiers "in civil rights." I could not object to "not disarming and not sending out of Petrograd those troops which had taken part in the revolutionary movement" and which had just assured our victory. At that moment it was still uncertain whether or not they would have to fight against those "loyal" troops which had been sent to the capital. I have already spoken about the mood of the soldiers.

When at last we had agreed upon everything in the text which was supposed to appear in the name of the government, I raised the question as to what compensations the Soviet could give in exchange. The question was an unexpected one for the delegates, but they recognized its fairness. N. D. Sokolov outlined a plan on the spot for a similar statement in the name of the Soviet. I did not consider this acceptable, and I wrote my own. My draft was adopted, and in it was the Soviet's obligation to restore order. "We cannot allow disunity and anarchy. We must immediately put a stop to all excesses, thefts, breaking into private apartments, plundering and damaging of all sorts of property, and purposeless seizures of public institutions.

The breakdown of discipline, and anarchy, will ruin the revolution and the people's freedom. The danger of a military movement against the revolution has not yet been removed. In order to prevent it, it is extremely important to assure that the soldiers act in a friendly and conciliatory manner with the officers. . . . The army can be strong only if the two are united." This is almost the same thing that I had told the soldiers from the tower of the regiment barracks. And it was accepted for publication in the name of the Soviet! The agreement was signed and declared final. But at that moment Guchkov returned from his circuit of the railway stations. He began to object—and wrecked the agreement. The decision was postponed until the following day, and in the interval, the conciliatory attitude of the delegation changed. At Rodzianko's insistence, the talks were renewed on the evening of March 2 and the support promised to the government was set in confined limits. The Soviet emphasized that "the new government had been created from the moderate public strata of society" and that, consequently, it had to be watched carefully. "To the extent" that the new government fulfilled these (their) obligations, "the people would offer it their support." This was the famous "to the extent that." The government was also to obligate itself not to use the wartime conditions as an excuse for delaying reforms which it had recognized as necessary. All correlation between our obligations, formulated by them and voluntarily accepted by us, and their obligations, formulated by me and accepted by them, was thus pushed into the background and changed in the direction of class suspiciousness. Here already was the embryo of future difficulties between us, "the propertied elite" and "revolutionary democracy." Both declarations appeared next to each other in the press: their statement, edited by us in the name of the government, and my statement, edited and supplemented by them in the name of the Soviet of Workers' and Soldiers' Deputies. For amicable resolutions of future disagreements, while the mutual obligations were being fulfilled, a special "Contact Committee" was formed. I will presently come back to how it functioned. At any rate, everything that could be done on paper, was done.

The last of the big questions concerning the formation of the new government had yet to be decided: how to define the position of the tsar. That Nicholas II would no longer reign was so obvious for the Russian public at large that nobody even thought about the technical means for carrying out this general decision. Nobody, that is, except one person: A. I. Guchkov. From his testimony before the Extraordinary Commission, it can be seen that he himself did not know how this would be accomplished, since he did not know the final form the expected revolution would take. He did not exclude even the most extreme methods of removing the tsar if the revolution were to be accomplished in the form which for him recalled eighteenth-century, Russian history, that is, in the form of murder. However, if the revolution were accomplished in the form he personally preferred—a military pronouncement—then he desired that the tsar be removed in the "gentlest" manner—abdication of the throne. He admitted to the commission that he and his "friends" (whom he refused to name) had a "plan to seize the Emperor's train on the way from Headquarters to Tsarskoe Selo, to force the Tsar to abdicate, arrest simultaneously the existing government, and only then announce the revolution and the persons who would head the new government." As is already known, the first half of the plan was realized with a few variations, independently of Guchkov. The new government had been formed earlier, also independently of Guchkov, and had invited him to take part in it. In any case, he considered himself the principal candidate for getting the tsar to abdicate; and after it became clear that Rodzianko's candidacy would not meet with support from either the government or the leftists, Guchkov put forward his own candidacy almost as an ultimatum. On the evening of March 1, he "announced that being convinced (for a long time already) of the necessity of this step, he decided to undertake it no matter what, and if the Duma committee would not authorize him to do it, he was ready to do it on his own, at his own risk." It seems to me that the account given here is somewhat retouched; but the unbending determination and a temperament which the Germans call *Schadenfreude* are well known from Guchkov's political career. The dethronement of the tsar was the highpoint of that career. The government did not object, and at his request, sent V. V. Shulgin to witness the triumphant act. The committee and the government gave the travelers the assignment in the form previously arranged by the bloc. The tsar was to abdicate in favor of his son and appoint the grand duke Mikhail Alexandrovich as regent. The succession of the dynasty would thus be assured.

However, during the day of March 2, the atmosphere in Petersburg continued to change, and the bloc's plan became threatened with danger from the left. At about three o'clock in the afternoon I was asked to come out to the public which had gathered in the columned hall of the palace and to make a formal announcement about the newly formed government. I accepted the proposal with pleasure: this was the first semiofficial act which was to give the new government, so to say, a public investiture. I went out to the crowd which had filled up the hall; I was aware of the importance of the task and was in a very exultant mood. The subject of my speech was a report on the fulfillment of our program of creating a new government. My words somehow strung together by themselves; my speech finished, I wrote it down and gave it to the journalists. It was printed in the next issues of the papers, and marked a historical stage which, alas, in its turn, had already slipped away into the past. . . . The mood of the majority of listeners was sympathetic and even highly enthusiastic, but there were among the public some convinced opponents. Before me here, was a meeting of leftists. Straight away someone tossed out the venomous question: "Who elected you?" I could have read a whole dissertation as my answer. The Duma did not "elect" us. Nor did Rodzianko choose us on the belated instructions of the emperor. Nor did Lvov choose us in agreement with the new decree prepared by the tsar at Headquarters—an agreement which we could not even have known about. We consciously thrust aside all these sources of legitimate succession for our government. Only one answer remained—the clearest and most convincing one. I answered: "We were chosen by the Russian revolution!" This simple reference to the historical process which had brought us to power shut the mouths of the most radical opponents. They even referred to it later as the canonical source of our power. I then had to make one reservation. "Not for one minute will we retain this power after the freely elected people's representatives tell us that they desire to see people in our places who are more deserving of their confidence." Alas, we did not succeed in establishing the succession of our government until that time, until the Constituent Assembly. Our governmental power was pulverized by myriads of future changes and adjustments —until it was finally drowned in a new revolution.

I then had to recommend to the gathering, those chosen by the revolution. I began: "At the head we have placed a man whose name is synonymous with organized Russian society so implacably persecuted by the old Russian Government." Immediately there followed an objection from the same side: "rich society." I answered in the same spirit as the protestors: "Yes, but the only one which will later allow the other strata of Russian society to organize themselves." The answer was really to my own detriment, but it could not help satisfying the most convinced adherents of the "development by stages" of the Russian revolution. I then switched over to recommendations of individual members of the government. Kerensky, who had telephoned me in the morning about his final agreement, went without mention. The nationally famous names of the leaders of the Duma opposition were met with applause. Silently the public swallowed the names of the less well-known Duma opponents of the old govern-

ment, opponents from the right on financial and church questions—
Godnev and V. Lvov. The most difficult of all was to recommend the
newcomer into our ranks, Tereshchenko, who was known to no one
and who was the only "minister-capitalist" among us. By what "list"
did he "get into" the Ministry of Finance? I did not know then that
the source was the same as that from which Kerensky had been
thrust forward, from which our Nekrasov's republicanism derived,
and from which emerged the unexpected radicalism of the "progressivists" Konovalov and Erfemov. I learned about this source
long after the events. . . .

Then came the thorniest question, concerning the tsar and the
dynasty. I had foreseen objections, and I began with excuses. "I know
in advance that my answer will not satisfy all of you. But I will give
it anyway. The old despot who led Russia to complete ruin will
voluntarily renounce the throne—or else he will be deposed. Power
will be transferred to the regent, Grand Duke Mikhail Alexandrovich. Alexei will be the heir." The hall became noisy. Shouts were
heard: "That is the old dynasty!" I stated the bloc's position with
assurance, but those shouts somewhat disturbed me. I continued in
a more excited tone. "Yes, gentlemen, that is the old dynasty, which
perhaps you do not like, and which perhaps I do not like either. But
at the moment we are not concerned with who likes what. We cannot
leave the question of the form of the state system without an answer.
We conceive of that system as a parliamentary and a constitutional
monarchy. Perhaps others imagine the state system differently. But,
if we are going to argue about it now, instead of reaching a solution
immediately, then Russia will find herself in a state of civil war, and
the regime which has just been destroyed will rise anew. We do not
have the right to do this." I spoke with an awareness that I was
right; and my argument apparently had its effect. Again I appealed
to a higher judge. "Just as soon as the danger is passed and a firm
peace established, we will begin preparations for the Constituent
Assembly on the basis of direct, equal, secret and universal suffrage. The freely elected representatives of the people will decide who
better reflects Russian public opinion, we or our adversaries." I must
confess, there was little logic in this finale. Nevertheless, the mood of
a significant portion of the gathering was still on my side. They sent
me off with deafening applause and carried me on their shoulders
to the ministerial offices.

The following scene occurred in the very same hall at dusk. I saw
Rodzianko trotting toward me accompanied by a handful of officers
smelling of liquor. In a halting voice, he repeated their words, that
after my statements about the dynasty they could not return to their

soldiers. They demanded that I take back my words. Of course, I could not take them back, but, seeing the behavior of Rodzianko, who knew very well that I had spoken not only in my own name but in the name of the bloc, I agreed to announce that I was expressing my own personal opinion. I knew Rodzianko's peculiarity of losing himself in a difficult situation, but such a display of cowardice I had never observed before. In the same mood, that very evening, he insisted that I conclude our agreement with the Soviet as quickly as possible, the agreement having already been spoiled by Guchkov's interference. The next morning, he displayed the same characteristics in an incomparably more significant situation. . . .

Only at three o'clock in the afternoon did our delegates, Guchkov and Shulgin, leave to meet the tsar, and did not reach Pskov until ten in the evening. During that time a significant change took place in the tsar's attitude. Leaving Headquarters on the night of the twenty-eighth of February, he still counted on suppressing the uprising. He gave General Ivanov wide powers even though General Alexeev had already persuaded him to grant a "constitution." In view of the danger of a clash with the rebellious troops, he stopped for the night of March 1 in Malaya Vishera, where he agreed to a "constitution." Nevertheless, after deciding to return to Pskov, under the protection of General Ruzsky, he wavered between suppression and concessions depending on the course of events. Arriving in Pskov at 8:00 P.M. on March 1 and learning that the revolution was victorious, he heeded Ruzsky's advice to "make all the necessary concessions" and entrusted Rodzianko with forming a "responsible" cabinet. By the morning of March 2, Ruzsky told him that this concession was already insufficient and that all the troops had gone over to the side of the rebels. After breakfast, Ruzsky brought the tsar seven telegrams from Grand Duke Nikolai Nikolaevich, General Alexeev, and from the commanders at the front. All of them insisted that the tsar renounce the throne in accordance with the formula of the bloc, which Alexeev had communicated to him: abdication in favor of his son with Mikhail as regent. Nicholas consented to this too, and composed the appropriate telegram to that effect; but, as mentioned above, the telegram was not sent until 3:15. Later he learned of the impending arrival of Guchkov and Shulgin, and his attitude changed. Instead of transferring the throne to his son, he decided to give it to Mikhail and composed the text of his abdication accordingly. When the deputies arrived, he met them "calmly" and gave them his latest decision already prepared. In his rather verbose testimony before the Extraordinary Commission, Guchkov explained why he had deviated from the task which the Temporary Committee had given him. Come what may, he wanted to carry away some kind of prepared statement of abdication, and he did not want to be insistent. After the act had been signed, Shulgin mentioned Prince Lvov, and the tsar wrote out a paper appointing Lvov premier. In this way, Shulgin desired to establish a legitimate succession of power, and he proposed that the date of abdication be inscribed, until which time Nicholas would still have the right to command. Guchkov wanted to obscure this fact before the committee, but he did not succeed: the committee certified that Lvov's appointment was made entirely independently of the tsar's decree.

In anticipation of the tsar's abdication, the night of March 3 passed with great anxiety in Petersburg. At about three in the morning, we received the first news in the Taurida Palace that the tsar had abdicated in favor of the Grand Duke Mikhail Alexandrovich. We did not have a copy at hand of Emperor Paul's manifesto on succession to the throne, and we had no idea at that time that the tsar's very action was illegal. He could renounce the throne for himself, but he had no right to renounce it for his son. Several days later I attended a breakfast given for us by the Department of the Army, and next to me sat Grand Duke Sergei Mikhailovich. In our conversation he told me that, of course, all the grand dukes immediately understood the illegality of the emperor's act. If that is so, then we must assume that the law concerning the succession to the throne was well known also to the monarch. The inescapable conclusion is that by substituting his brother for his son, the tsar knew what he was doing. He appealed to his paternal feelings, thereby even touching deeply the delegates. These were the same paternal feelings, however, which guided the royal couple in their plans to safeguard the throne intact for their son. In the empress' letters there is one place in which the tsarina approved of the tsar's decision as a means of not betraying the vow which he made at his coronation. Comparing all these things, it is impossible not to come to the conclusion that Nicholas II was being cunning here, just as he was when he issued the October Manifesto. The difficult days would pass, everything would calm down, and then it would be possible to take his promise back. It was not for nothing that Rasputin promised the son a happy reign. . . .

Regardless of all these considerations, which came later, the substitution of the brother for the son was without doubt a heavy blow which the tsar himself gave to the fate of the dynasty at a moment when the continuation of the dynasty was still open to question. The public had more or less become used to the idea of the young Alexei inheriting the throne; they linked this idea, as I mentioned earlier, with the possibility of evolving a parliamentary system under the weak Mikhail. Now the whole question was reopened, and everyone's attention was focused on how the grand duke would regard his appointment. Rodzianko and Lvov waited for the precise text of the manifesto in the Ministry of the Army in order to determine the possibility of changing it. The ministers and the Temporary Committee in the Duma's quarters took measures to contact Mikhail Alexandrovich and to arrange a meeting with him in the morning. Two sides were apparent from the beginning: for and against the grand duke's accepting the throne. Of course, there was a question of principle behind this disagreement which concerned the Russian state system. One nocturnal episode thoroughly convinced me of this. Three of us were sitting in the corner of the room: Kerensky, Nekrasov, and myself. Nekrasov handed me a crumpled paper with a few lines written on it in pencil: it was a proposal for introducing a republic. Kerensky convulsively clutched at my wrist and tensely waited for my answer. Irritated, I tossed the paper away and uttered some sharp words at Nekrasov. Kerensky roughly pushed away my hand. That very evening in the Soviet of Workers' and Soldiers' Deputies he had declared himself in favor of a republic and stressed his role as the "hostage of democracy." A nervous exchange of opinions began. I told them that in the morning I would defend the grand duke's accession to the throne. They stated that they would insist on his refusal. Having made it clear that none of us would keep silent, we agreed that only two opinions would be expressed at the meeting: Kerensky's and mine—and then we would leave the choice up to the grand duke. We agreed that, no matter what the decision would be, the other side would not interfere and would not join the government. In the morning, the delegates from Pskov returned. I managed to warn Shulgin by telephone at the station of the atmosphere in Petersburg. Guchkov went directly to the railroad workshops, made an announcement to the workers about Mikhail— and just barely managed to escape getting beaten or killed.

The meeting with the grand duke took place on Millionnaia Street in Prince Putiatin's apartment. Members of the government, Rodzianko, and several members of the Temporary Committee gathered there. Guchkov arrived later. Entering the apartment, I bumped into the grand duke, who turned to me jokingly with a not very coherently improvised phrase: "Well, what do you think? It's not bad to be in position of the King of England! Well?" I answered: "Yes, Your Highness, one can rule very peacefully by observing a constitution." With this remark, we both went into the meeting room. Rodzianko took the chairman's place and gave the introductory speech—arguing the necessity of renouncing the throne! Apparently, he had already been propagandized—and by no means in the ideological sense, of course. After him, Kerensky spoke in the same spirit. Then came my turn to speak. I showed that in order to strengthen the new order, a strong governmental authority was needed, and that it can be strong only when it relies on the symbol of authority to which the masses are accustomed. The monarchy serves as just such a symbol. The Provisional Government by itself, without the support of this symbol, will simply not survive until the opening of the Constituent Assembly. It will turn out to be a fragile boat which will sink in the ocean of mass disturbances. The country will be threatened by the loss of all sense of state organization and by complete anarchy. In spite of our agreement, a whole torrent of speeches poured forth after our speeches—and all of them were for renunciation of the throne. Then, in spite of Kerensky's passionate resistance, I asked for the floor to give my reply. I was terribly disturbed by the unexpected agreement among the opponents who represented all political colorings. Guchkov, who had just come in, defended my point of view, but he did it weakly and lifelessly. Shulgin wrote an impressionistic description of the scene, and I will permit myself to cite a few lines from it. "This was obstructionism, in a way . . . Miliukov did not want to finish, was not able to finish, and was afraid of finishing. This man who was usually so polite and self-restrained would not allow anyone to speak; he interrupted those who were objecting to him, he interrupted Rodzianko, Kerensky, everyone. . . . White as a sheet, with his face bluish-grey from lack of sleep, completely hoarse from his speeches in the barracks and at meetings, he croaked away raspingly." Then there follows a selection of fragmentary phrases taken partially from my first speech. "If this can be called a speech, then his speech was tremendous. . . ." The external aspects are captured faithfully here, but, of course, Shulgin exaggerated a little. There was, nevertheless, a method in my "croaking." I was shocked by the fact that my adversaries, instead of presenting considerations of principle, tried to intimidate the grand duke. I saw that Rodzianko was continuing to play the coward. Others, too, were frightened by what was going on. All of this was so petty in comparison with the importance of the moment. . . . I admitted that those who had spoken might be right. Perhaps danger was threatening the participants and the grand duke himself. But we were playing for big stakes—for all of Russia— and we had to take the risk, no matter how great it may have been. Only then would we be relieved of responsibility for the future which we had taken upon ourselves. And what did this risk consist of? I was still influenced by the impressions of news from Moscow, reported to me by Colonel Gruzinov, who had just arrived from there:

in Moscow everything was calm and the garrison maintained its
discipline. I suggested that we should take automobiles immediately
and go to Moscow where we could find the organized force necessary
to back up the grand dukes affirmative decision. I was sure that this
solution was comparatively safe. But, even if it was dangerous, and
even if the situation in Petrograd really was that bad, then, we still
had to take the risk: this was the only solution. These considerations
of mine were subsequently much disputed. I was, of course, improvising. Perhaps, given agreement, my proposal would have been
altered, and more thought out. Perhaps, Ruzsky himself would have
regarded defense of the emperor, who would be installed under his
command, differently than he had regarded defense of the old
emperor. . . . But there was no agreement; and there was no desire
to discuss the question further. This threw me into a state of complete
despair. . . . Kerensky, on the contrary, was ecstatic. In an exalted
voice he proclaimed: "Your Highness, you are a noble person! I
will say this everywhere now!"

The grand duke, who had kept silent the whole time, asked for a
few minutes to think it over. Leaving the room, he turned to Rodzianko with the request to talk with him in private. The result, of
course, could be predicted. Returning to the deputation, he said that
he would accept Rodzianko's proposal. Pulling me aside, he thanked
me for my "patriotism," but. . . , etc. Before leaving, both sides
agreed to support the government, but I decided not to participate
in it.

Guchkov and I went out together and drove back in the same
sleigh. He declared to the Extraordinary Commission that, on leaving,
he had agreed with his friends who were trying to persuade him
to remain in the government "temporarily"; to me, however, he said
that he would leave the government. I thus considered that our
decision was mutual. After five sleepless nights in the palace and
after the ruin of my hopes which had just taken place, I was in a
state of utter exhaustion. Arriving home, I threw myself into bed
and fell fast asleep. In the evening, five hours later, I was awakened.
Before me stood a delegation from the Central Committee of the
party: Vinaver, Nabokov, Shingarev. All of them tried to persuade
me that at such a time I did not have the right to quit the government, thus depriving it of that portion of authority which was connected with my position. The public at large would simply not
understand it. I myself already felt that it was impossible to refuse,
and I went to the evening session of the ministers, where I found
Guchkov, too.

In the apartment on Millionnaia Street, the jurists who were invited, Nabokov and Nolde, wrote the Act of Abdication. Of course, there was no mention of the illegality of the tsar's act, and I think that even they themselves were not aware of it. Mikhail's renunciation was made conditionally: "I have taken the firm decision to accept supreme authority only in the event that such is the will of our great people" as expressed by the Constituent A· sembly. The form of government thus remained an open question. As for the Provisional Government, the absence of the succession of power from the monarch was emphasized, and the grand duke merely expressed a request for subordination to the government, which "at the initiative of the State Duma has arisen and has been invested with complete authority." These ambiguous expressions contained a small concession to Rodzianko: there had been no "initiative" of the Duma as an institution, nor, even less, had there been any "investment" with complete authority.

Rodzianko saw to it that the emperor's abdication and Mikhail's renunciation were published simultaneously. For this purpose, he delayed the publication of the first act. Apparently, he had already foreseen this outcome and, perhaps, had made arrangements in advance concerning publication.

The Provisional Government entered upon a new phase in Russian history, formally supported only by its own "complete authority."

The Provisional Government
(March 2, 1917—October 25, 1917)

INTRODUCTORY REMARKS

IN NO WAY do I intend to write a history of the Provisional Government here. To this topic I already devoted three parts of the *History of the Second Russian Revolution,* taking up eight hundred pages. Thus, for reasons of size alone, it cannot be reproduced in my personal memoirs.[50] Step by step I followed the activity of the Provisional Government, often day by day, according to the printed documents and memoirs of the participants in the events. Of course, my personal impressions were reflected both in the account and in the criticism of what had been accomplished, but I spoke of my own role in the events only in connection with the basic thread of the story, and, as far as possible, without naming myself. Nevertheless, my political adversaries who, naturally enough, did not agree with my evaluation of events, accused me of describing the events like a memoirist, and not like a historian. Having foreseen that, I made the reservation in the preface that I refuse in principle to make a subjective appraisal, and that I "forced only those facts to speak which could be verified objectively," "not desiring to drive the facts towards conclusions." I am convinced that I have written "a history" and not "memoirs." They also accused me of presenting the views of my party in my criticism and of making them a sort of axis for my entire account. This accusation—if it can be considered an accusation—is partially correct; but it is invalidated by the very substance of views involved. I have already mentioned here more than once that, not only we, but also our adversaries, considered the February revolution a "bourgeois" and not a "socialist" revolution. The People's Freedom party was the most left-wing of the political parties to which this name might be applied. It was not a party of the "capitalists," nor was it a party of the "land-

414

owners," as hostile propaganda tried to portray it. It was a "supra-class" party which did not exclude even those supraclass elements which were found in socialism. It rejected only the exclusively class character of socialist doctrine and that which in the socialism of the time was antistate and Utopian. In this rejection, the party's views were, in effect, shared by the entire moderate socialist wing which, together with it (the Kadet party) made the "bourgeois" revolution. This internal contradiction continued throughout the whole existence of the Provisional Government. Only the Bolsheviks were free from this contradiction, and internally consistent. Our criticism of the behavior of the so-called "revolutionary democracy" was directed pre-cisely at this contradiction, at the inability of the moderate socialist parties to eliminate those antistate and Utopian elements contradicting the views they had in common with us. Such is the starting point for the criticism to which we—and in particular, I, in my *History*—sub-jected their political behavior. In no way can such criticism be called "subjective"; and the justness of the criticism was demonstrated at that time by the very course of events. It can be shown that the indicated contradiction could not have been eliminated, given the attitudes at that time; but it cannot be denied that the contradiction existed and that it was precisely this contradiction which caused the failure of all the tactics of the moderate socialist parties. We will see all this here in my brief summary, and we shall see its direct connection with my personal role in the struggle against that fundamental defect in the politics of the moderate socialist parties.

I soon had to return to the "historical" aspect of that same topic. In my second work, *Russia at Its Turning Point (Rosiia na perelome),* I described very concisely this same process of disintegration of the Provisional Government. I had the opportunity there to check and confirm the objectivity of my account. During the interval, there appeared Sukhanov's seven-volume work, *Notes on the Revolution (Zapiski o revoliutsii).*[51] Together with my *History,* this is so far the only detailed and coherent account of events from February to October 1917. It was written from the point of view opposite to my own. Sukhanov, a consistent and thoughtful Marxist, in general, and a Zimmerwaldist, in particular, stood to the left of the ruling center of "revolutionary democracy," that of Kerensky and Tsereteli; he did not, however, go as far as the Bolsheviks. I stood to the right of this center, but not as far as the rightists of the State Duma. Our criticism was identically directed against the behavior of that center from the point of view of two opposing political criteria. In their essential features, however, our conclusions agree, and in *Rossiia na perelome,* the quotations from my *History* are always accompanied by references to corresponding passages in Sukhanov's *Notes*. His judgments and his conjectures are often unreliable; but he was a good observer and a talented writer. His characterizations are, for the most part, accurate; his descriptions are colorful. What we agree on is the criticism of the central stand of the Soviets, and for me, this agreement was supplementary evidence of the objectivity of my own judgments. Thus, with even greater assurance I included a concise outline of the history of the provisional government in the third volume of *Histoire de Russie,* which was published under my editorship: I brought only facts into the account—facts which speak clearly enough by themselves.

Now I will exercise my rights as a "memoirist." The anonymous brackets which concern me personally will be removed here. The stands of the People's Freedom party which I have defended will be emphasized and supplemented with special commentary. The characterizations of persons who had some relation to my activity will be outlined more frankly here than was possible in an impersonal account. On the other hand, the course of events, on the basis of which my own activity developed, and which I must assume are sufficiently well known, will be given here in only the most general outline in so far as this is necessary for an understanding of my story. I do not fear that on the whole my role will be exaggerated, because this was the role of one who was defeated, and my only justification is that I was not responsible for that defeat which I had foreseen.

I am not speaking here of the first two months, March and April 1917, when I took part in the First Provisional Government and when I was forced to wage an active struggle on three fronts: against Zimmerwaldism in favor of maintaining our general foreign policy with our allies; against Kerensky's aspirations of strengthening his own power; and for the preservation of the complete authority of the government which had been created by the revolution. My efforts turned out to be in vain in all three directions, and I was forced to give up my membership in the government. My political activity did not cease there, however. My like-minded party comrades remained in power; and in view of the socialists' conviction that the Russian revolution was a "bourgeois" revolution, they were to remain in the government through all three of the later coalitions between the "propertied" elements and the socialists, changing only the personnel. As chairman of the party's Central Committee, I took part in the preparations and execution of all these changes, with the exception of the last one. In the same way, I took part in the public appearances of the political organizations surrounding the government, and also in two representative meetings, organized by the second and third coalitions in Moscow and in Petrograd for the purpose (which was not attained) of bolstering the declining authority of these coalitions. As Kerensky's adversary, I was forced to support him at those meetings as the only remaining fragment of the nationwide governmental authority created by the revolution.

In order to make the subsequent account clearer, I will mention here the chronological dates of the four ministries of the Provisional Government, which succeeded each other during the eight-month period of the government's existence. I will also give the dates of the government's prolonged crises separating the first coalition from the second and the second from the third.

1. The original government: March–April (3/2/17–5/5/17)
2. The first coalition with the socialists: May–June (5/6/17–7/2/17)
3. Crisis of the first coalition: July (7/2/17–7/25/17)
4. Second coalition with the socialists: August (7/25/17–8/26/17)
5. Crisis of the second coalition: September (8/27/17–9/24/17)
6. Third coalition with socialists: October (9/24/17–10/25/17)

As we shall see, July and September 1917 passed in a state of crises for the government: July—as a result of the first (unsuccessful) uprising of the Bolsheviks, and September—the Bolsheviks' preparation for their second (successful) uprising. Only the original government and the first coalition continued in power for two months each. The last two coalitions lasted for only one month each without crises. The two meetings mentioned above, which were supposed to strengthen the power of the second and third coalitions, met in Moscow from August 12–15 and, the second, in Petrograd ("Soviet of the Republic" or "preparliament") from September 24 to October 25—the day the Bolsheviks seized power. To the extent that his authority was failing, Kerensky, that "national" axis around which all these changes were occurring, gradually increased the titles of his power. He changed from the post of minister of justice, which he held in the original government, to the post of minister of the army and navy in the first coalition. In the second coalition, he became the premier, in place of Prince Lvov; and after the victory over General Kornilov, during the second crisis, he took the title of supreme commander-in-chief and surrounded himself with a "directorate" of his closest followers. Finally, in the third, and last, coalition he vainly sought support among the "propertied" elements and created an artificial representative body of parties. The struggle against Kornilov for the dictatorship was the culmination of his efforts to hang on to power—and the sharp transition to surrender to the Bolsheviks.

The Composition and Initial Activity
of the Provisional Government

INTO WHOSE HANDS fell the all-Russian power of the first government, "chosen by the Russian revolution"? Comparing the composition of this government with the lists drawn up by various public circles, we see that it was far from an accidental grouping. To a certain degree, an accidental element was brought in, in the form of representatives from the different factions of the Progressive bloc. At one time it might have seemed that the bloc "leadership" would take over the corresponding posts in the cabinet of ministers. This was a very brief period, however, and, indeed, it only "seemed" that way. This is perhaps reflected in the first pages of Sukhanov's *Notes*, in several of Shulgin's expressions, and perhaps also in our Central Committee. Those who know me well can certify that I never aspired to the highest post myself. If I sometimes turned up in that post, then that is the way circumstances took shape, and I accepted the accomplished fact as a fulfillment of my civic duty. The circumstances under which the Provisional Government was created took a very different shape; and in that government I accepted that share of influence and power given to me by a unanimous public opinion. In the last analysis, this share was not great: it turned out to be less than I would have liked. From the very beginning I tried to draw the appropriate conclusion from this, but I was able to do so only later, after the actual experience, and as we shall see, not without a struggle. It was not my fault that I left power.

But this frank explanation is merely incidental. I must begin the description of the Provisional Government with those persons to whom the post should have belonged by right, or who aspired to the top post and actually attained it. *A tout seigneur—tout honneur.* I will begin with the head of the government, Prince G. E. Lvov.

I have already mentioned my disappointment upon meeting Prince Lvov for the first time in the role of premier. No matter at what cost, we had to have a strong governmental authority, and Prince Lvov did not carry this authority with him. In the words of his biographer, he felt within himself, as within the Russian people, "that the following qualities were good and desirable: humility, pacifism, kindness, and a patient bearing of the cross." He "was not able nor did he desire to discern in the popular masses the followers of Pugachev or Stenka Razin. Envy, malice, cruelty, savagery, tendencies to anarchy and rebellion remained almost unnoticed for him; these traits slipped past his attention." "He brought just such attitudes with him to the post of chairman of the Council of Ministers." That these features had been part of him for a long time, can be seen from the above-mentioned excerpts of his biography. His biographer—an intimate assistant and enthusiastic admirer of Prince Lvov—described Lvov's impression upon visiting the Dukhobors[52] in Canada in 1909. He found himself before a gigantic collective economy created under American conditions by Peter Virigin, the tsar and god of that commune. The local authorities considered Virigin a charlatan who was fleecing his "slaves." Prince Lvov wrote: "Observing the Dukhobor commune among the Canadian farmers, one is involuntarily gripped by a feeling of pride in the Russian name, in the inner dignity of that people which could produce from among itself such a noble offshoot so full of energy and idealism." This is the commentary of Lvov's traveling companion: "Every coin has an obverse side, but when the matter concerned the Russian people, Prince Lvov was not able to see it. . . . The negative facts he observed here had no power over G. E. They slipped through his consciousness without leaving a trace."

With such traits of character as these, Prince Lvov did Russia a bad service. Neither premier nor minister of internal affairs was his proper place. In those roles, instead of his accustomed and favorite "practical business," the usual "business" was "politics"—which he hated. At first he was simply lost and grew melancholy before the immensity of the tasks which had fallen upon him; then he "became all fired up" with his perpetual faith, and resorted to lyricism. "I have faith in the great heart of the Russian people, overflowing with love for its fellow man. I believe in this primary source of truth, and right and freedom. The totality of its glory will unfold and everything else will follow." That is what he told the press. After nearly two months in office, at a session of the four Dumas on April 27, he ended his animated speech by quoting a poet: "Liberty, let others despair; I shall never doubt thee." This obstinacy of faith cost him, too, a great deal when disappointment set in. After his departure from the government, his biographer, Polner, met him on July 9. "I did not recognize G. E. immediately. Before me sat an old man, his snow-white head lowered; his movements, few and slow. . . . He seemed shabby and completely worn-out. Without smiling, he slowly gave me his hand" and said in a very serious tone, "there is nothing more for me to do. To save the situation we would have had to dissolve the Soviets and open fire on the people. I could not do that. But Kerensky can." Leaving the government, Lvov himself proposed that Kerensky succeed him (who, by the way, no longer needed this support at that time).

Incapable of displaying strong authority, he transferred this mission to a man who likewise was incapable of creating it, but who at least was capable of simulating it. In the first cabinet, Kerensky did this mainly by subjugating the will of Prince Lvov to his own.

We Duma members had known Kerensky for a long time, and we were familiar with the methods of his self-exaltation. He knew how to thrust himself forward at the right moment. What we did not know was that from a habit, this had become a system, and it was I who created a springboard for him by inviting him to take the post of minister of justice. I have recounted the episode of Shcheglovitov's arrest, in which Kerensky easily broke the will of Rodzianko, and another episode in which he slipped into power through the Soviet of Workers' Deputies. Once inside the government, he continued these exercises—on me. One such incident is told by V. D. Nabokov, who remembered it even more clearly than I did; and I will cite it here. In one of the closed nocturnal sessions of the government in Marinsky Palace I said that German money was one of the factors contributing to the revolution. "As was his habit, Kerensky was impatiently and angrily pacing the hall from one corner to the other . . . suddenly he stopped, and shouted out from the far corner of the hall: 'What? What did you say? Repeat that!' . . . Miliukov calmly and weightily, so to say, repeated his statement. Again Kerensky grew rabid. He grabbed his briefcase, and slamming it on the table, yelled: 'After Mister Miliukov in my presence has dared to slander the holy cause of the great Russian revolution, I do not desire to remain here one minute longer.' With these words he turned around and, straight as an arrow, flew out of the hall. Tereshchenko and another one of the ministers ran after him; but, on returning, they reported that they had been unable to restrain him and that he had gone home. . . . Miliukov maintained complete presence of mind; and in answer to my words: 'What a disgraceful, absurd stunt,' he said: 'Yes, that is Kerensky's usual style. In the Duma, too, he often pulled such pranks. . . .' None of the remaining ministers said even one word about the comment which had evoked Kerensky's indignation; but all of them thought that he should be calmed down and won over without delay. . . . Somebody, Tereshchenko it seems, said that Prince Lvov should go to Kerensky. The others agreed, Miliukov remained passive; of course this whole incident was deeply repugnant to him. Prince Lvov willingly agreed to 'have a talk' with Kerensky. Of course, it all ended in nothing." I recall another incident in which the cabinet could not remain passive and had to take my side. Kerensky, who often ran out into the adjoining room where the reporters were waiting for him, told them, for publication, that the Provisional Government was preparing to send a note to the Allies concerning the aims of the war. Since I had not prepared anything of the sort, I demanded that the Provisional Government repudiate this report to the press. The fiction was obvious, and the government's refutation was printed on April 14. Kerensky had not succeeded in forcing my plans, though his aim was precisely that. These two incidents of clashes between two wills were not the only ones, and they usually did not end favorably for Kerensky. It was probably from such incidents that Kerensky's attitude toward me was formed. Nabokov is a witness to this attitude: "Miliukov was his *bête noire* in the fullest sense of the word. He did not miss a chance to speak ill of Miliukov, to speak sarcastically and sometimes with genuine hate." As for my attitude toward Kerensky, I quickly learned to consider his ostentatious grandeur and his dictatorial pose as the greatest misfortune for the Russian revolution. V. D. Nabokov is correct when he says that "personal (my) feelings and attitudes were reflected in (my) political behavior to a negligible degree: it was never determined by those attitudes. In the case of Kerensky, it was quite the contrary. He was woven entirely from personal impulses. . . ." When matters reached the point where I had to leave the government, it was precisely Kerensky who, at a government session, gave himself the pleasure of announcing to me that "seven members" of the government had decided (in my absence) to transfer me to the ministry of education (a situation that was intentionally unacceptable to me). Who were these "seven"? Above all, there was the "triumvirate" of Kerensky, Nekrasov, and Tereshchenko. Then came the two rightists who were completely enslaved by Kerensky's authority, Vladimir Lvov and Godnev. I am sure that my Kadet friends, Shingarev and Manuilov, did not take part in this collusion. Who were the other two (not counting Guchkov, who had already left the government, and myself, the tenth member of the government)? There remains only A. I. Konovalov, Kerensky's personal and political friend who later became a Kadet, and . . . Prince Lvov who had subordinated himself to Kerensky's influence and who had left it to

Kerensky to announce the general decision to me. This distribution of votes indicates better than anything else the degree and limits of Kerensky's influence on the original members of the Provisional Government. Not having had time to become the "strong authority" in the state, he undoubtedly became the strong authority in the government.

Who else, besides the premier and Kerensky, could lay claim to "strong authority"? I expected Guchkov to do so. However, after Prince Lvov, Guchkov was my second disappointment. In the provisional government, Guchkov did not live up to his former reputation. I had hoped to find an ally in him, but, as has already been mentioned, he kept to the sidelines, did not often participate in the cabinet sessions, and, apparently, pursued his own policy, which was not such that I could rely on it for support. This is partially explained by his ill health. Several times the government had to hold its sessions at his bedside. The weakening of his will, however, must be explained mainly by his pessimism with regard to what had happened. Nabokov's observations in this respect are perfectly correct. "From the very beginning, Guchkov felt in the bottom of his soul that the cause was lost, and he remained in the government only *par acquit de conscience*. . . . On the question of the army and navy, no one sounded a note of deep disappointment and skepticism with such intensity as did Guchkov. When he began to speak in his soft and gentle voice, gazing slightly cross-eyed out into space, I was horror-struck by the sense of something like complete and utter hopelessness. Everything seemed doomed." With me, Guchkov was less frank—either because he was a reserved man in general or because at that time I was not possessed by such extreme pessimism. I considered that it was still possible to fight, but he did not support me in that struggle. Moreover, brushing off the final outcome and entrusting his work to his old friend, General Polivanov, he yielded, without particular resistance, those views on the fundamental issues of war and peace that I still believed could be defended. Concealing from me what was going on in his ministry, and contrary to our agreement, he had a surprise in store for me: his premature departure from the government. In a word, I met with no "strong" authority or any authority at all from that corner.

I did not expect anything special from the remaining members of the government. Of my three like-minded political colleagues, I had grounds even at that time to consider N. V. Nekrasov a simple traitor, although there had been no formal break between us. I would not express myself in such strong terms if the matter concerned only political disagreements. We have seen that he was pursuing essentially a republican line. That was his business. I also will not mention the "underground" war against me in the faction, which remained unknown to me and about which Nabokov told Shingarev. It was worse that Nekrasov, seeing the rapid increase in Kerensky's influence, deserted to Kerensky's side for obviously personal reasons. He was, of course, smarter than Kerensky, and he cultivated Kerensky, so to say, in his favor. The impression he made on Nabokov, who knew him slightly at the beginning, was of a man whose "external manners won people over by their apparent goodnaturedness": "he knew how to appear sincere and ingenuous," but "he left an impression of duplicity, of a mask that hid his real face." Contrary to Nabokov, Nekrasov could not "play the leading role"; and, not wishing to run the risk, he did not even "aspire" to it. He was more capable of playing the role of informer, of secret adviser, of some kind of éminence grise. He tied himself too long to the chariot of the temporary victor, and himself brought his political career to nothing when the time came to hide from the success achieved. With these qualities, he was suitable for secondary roles under the Bolsheviks as well.

As for the remaining members of the government, I refer the reader to the striking and accurate descriptions given by V. D. Nabokov.[53] It is difficult to argue with them even when they seem not entirely just. Thus, from the heights of his cultural level and his strict scholarly background, Nabokov analyzes Shingarev's provincialism and dilettantism, and differs from me in the fundamental question of war and peace. Nevertheless, he treats my closest friend so well and warm-heartedly, and he appraises me personally with such exaggeration, that one cannot detect anything in these characterizations except the desire "to tell the truth." His appraisal of Godnev and V. Lvov—figures who were put forward exclusively by the Duma—are cruel, but just as true. I only wanted to stress again the link between Kerensky and Nekrasov and the two unnamed ministers, Tereshchenko and Konovalov. The four were very different in character, in past background, and in their political roles; but they were united by more than their radical political views. They were also linked by some sort of personal intimacy, not only in their purely political character but in their political-moral character. They were united as if by mutual obligations arising from a single source. In politics, both of the last named ministers were novices, and their emergence into this group demands special explanation. A native of Kiev, Tereshchenko was known to Nabokov as a music-lover in the Petersburg circles; the other "minister-capitalist," a pupil of Sauer and almost professional pianist, came from a line of Moscow Maecenas. Tereshchenko, in connection with his capital, took the portfolio of the minister of finance; then, just as unexpectedly, he became a diplomat, without any previous background. His native intelligence and his good upbringing saved him. My antagonist and successor, he quietly pursued my very policy, and successfully deceived the Soviet of Workers' Deputies; but toward the end he freed himself from his leftist hypnosis and even broke with Kerensky. The factories of the Konovalov firms were famous for the brilliant way in which they handled the labor question; and with good grounds, A. I. Konovalov took the post of minister of trade and industry. Even sooner than Tereshchenko, he broke with Marxist socialism, joined us, the Kadets —and at the very moment of extreme danger for Kerensky, suddenly turned up (in the third coalition) in the post of Kerensky's assistant, without having any personal or political qualifications for this post. Their friendship went beyond the limits of mutual policy. From the hints given here, the reader can conclude precisely what it was that linked this central group of four men. If I do not speak of the link more clearly here, that is because, observing the facts, I did not guess their origin at that time and learned of it from an accidental source only long after the Provisional Government ceased to exist.

Allow me to switch now from the composition of the provisional government to its activities during the first period. They have a double character. Guided, on the one hand, by the desire to give the country its first foundations for a democratic system, and bound by the agreement with the Soviet of Workers' and Soldiers' Deputies, the government hastened to publish the fundamental acts and declarations of the new order. In this respect, the government's work was made easier by the rich collection of legislative drafts worked out long before by the legal experts of the People's Freedom party and which had been lying around through all four Dumas. On the other hand, the government was drowned in a mass of questions arising daily and demanding immediate solutions. In the Dumas, this was called "vermicelli"; and the Dumas had been in no great rush to find the solutions. Now, in 1917, there was no time to lose, because these trifles were linked to the creation of the new order. The ministers held meetings every day, in the afternoon and in the evening; and there was no time to compose agendas and prepare reports. V. D. Nabokov took upon himself the difficult task of "business manager," but it took him some time before he managed to put the business in order. Prince Lvov turned out to be a failure as chairman: he was unable to guide the debates and for the most part kept silent, holding no opinion of his own. The only voice of authority in these sessions belonged to Kerensky, before whom the chairman receded completely into the background: "It often resembled something like timid flattery," remarks Nabokov.

My skirmishes with Kerensky usually brought the whole meeting to a state of confusion and indecision. Special efforts were needed to force the gathering to express an opinion. The debating and voting procedures were not carried on with a conscious intention of maintaining the fiction of governmental unity. Incidentally, the frequently heated debates revolved only around questions of principle at the end of the evening sessions when the office clerks had left. The ministers arrived at the afternoon sessions already exhausted from the work in their ministries; they came late and, half asleep, listened to the scheduled reports without knowing the subjects of the reports beforehand.

Of the Fundamental Acts issued during the first month of government activity, I will mention only the publication of the program, and the universal amnesty (March 6), the abolition of the previous administration (March 7), the abolition of capital punishment (March 12), appeal to the peasants (March 17), the abolition of all restrictions based on religion or nationality (March 20), the creation of a special conference to work out the electoral law for the Constituent Assembly (March 25). Then, on the nationality questions there was the abolition of all violations of the Finnish Constitution (March 6), the proclamation of Polish independence, and the first steps toward satisfying Ukrainian aspirations (March 19). I will have to come back later to a few of these acts. Here I will dwell only on one of them, which was linked to the activities of the Ministry of Internal Affairs.

In his own department, Prince Lvov was particularly depressed and lost. It was his task to change the entire system of administration in Russia, and it was obviously impossible to do this right away. Nevertheless, Prince Lvov decided to do just that. On March 5 he sent around a circular order by telegraph from the Provisional Government: "Relieve the governors and the vice-governors from the fulfillment of their duties," temporarily transferring the administration of the provinces to the chairmen of the provincial Zemstvo boards who were now to act in the capacity of government commissars. It had to be admitted from the start that this step was extremely rash and thoughtless—even from the political point of view. The chairmen of the Zemstvo boards were often reactionaries, while some of the governors were liberals. In addition, the abolition of local legal authority created a mess in all the lower administrative organs. Inquiries were sent to the ministry: How should this be done? The new authorities came for instructions as to what they should do. Prince Lvov was caught by surprise. He was unable to give any uniform instructions whatsoever. He concealed himself behind his ideology. The next day, March 7, he gave an interview to the press. "The government will not appoint anybody. . . . This is the old psychology. Such questions should be decided not in the center but by the population itself. . . . Let them decide in the provinces by themselves." Then there followed Prince Lvov's usual idealization. "We are all infinitely fortunate that we have lived to see this great moment when we can create a new life, not for the people, but together with the people. . . . In these historical times, the people have displayed their genius!"

What did this mean? In the provinces, following the example of the capital, the "people," in place of the authorities which had abolished themselves, had already created their own arbitrary organizations in the form of all sorts of "public committees," "Soviets," and so on. Lvov saw these as the "foundation" of future self-government and declared that the government "commissars" were not the "highest instance," but an "intermediate link" between the central authorities and these "organs." Such sanction from the government, of course, lent strength and legitimacy to the products of revolutionary law. Authority in the provinces generally disappeared, just as the gendarmes and the police had disappeared in Petrograd. Party organizations obtained a mighty means for propaganda and arbitrary action.

I very much suspect that these rash steps were taken under the influence of the young D. M. Shchepkin, who, from assistant to the manager-in-chief of the Zemstvo Union, had become assistant minister of the interior. Of course, things could not continue in that way. Next to D. M. Shchepkin, a more qualified worker, N. N. Avinov, labored to assist Prince Lvov. Through his wife Avinov was a relative of I. P. Demidov, as both men were married to the daughters of the influential Zemstvoist Novosiltsev, at whose mansion the first Zemstvo congresses of 1905 were held. At the end of the second month, on April 25, the government was able to report that "regulations for the elections to the City Dumas and for the militia have already been issued. In the very near future regulations concerning the *volost* Zemstvos will be issued, as will also regulations concerning the reforms of the provincial and district Zemstvos, provincial food-supply organs, provincial courts and administrative justice. . . ." Thus did the administrative system, prepared by the First Provisional Government, remain an unfinished structure.

My Victories and My Defeat

THUS, IN THE FIRST PROVISIONAL GOVERNMENT, I received the post of minister of foreign affairs, which had long been intended for me, both by the public and by my comrades. My position appeared solid, and indeed it was—at the beginning. People said that I was the only minister who did not have to learn his duties on the spot and who took his place in the ministerial cabinet on Palace Square as complete master of his business. It seems that I was also the only one who did not fire any of the former officials in the ministry. I valued the existing machine from the point of view of technique and tradition. I knew that among the officials in the ministry were people who did not share my views on the day-to-day questions of foreign policy; but I was not afraid of their influence on me, and I relied on their conscientious work.

Of course, I did not consider that my ministry was "an easy one," as Stürmer had done. I wanted to immerse myself in everything, and I spent a great amount of time familiarizing myself with current material, with daily correspondence, with deciphering the "secret drawer," not to mention the reception of necessary and unnecessary visitors and petitioners. Part of the day was spent in daily conversations with the ambassadors. I met with Buchanan, Paléologue, and Carlotti. Spolaikovich also took part in these meetings, but the "European" Allies wanted to speak with me in private, and I had to schedule separate meetings with the Serbs. I recall that twice a day I took part in the ministers' sessions, which I attended regularly, while each day I still found time to drop in at the editorial offices of *Rech* to inform my colleagues about the most important news of the day and to come to an agreement on pursuing our point of view.

With all of that, I did not consider my own position to be stable —later I will say why—and I did not plan to move into the plush apartment of the ministers' lodgings, which had been occupied by N. N. Pokrovsky. Since I was sometimes forced to work in the ministry long after midnight, I ordered a bed to be put in the small employees' room on the other side of the corridor, where I spent the night, having first assured myself of a morning glass of tea. Such was my daily schedule for these two months of my ministerial activity.

Now I will discuss the unstable elements of my position. All of us—and, clearly, in all aspects of our lives—inherited a painful and difficult legacy from the overthrown regime. Enough has been said about this earlier. To the former difficulties, new ones were now added, created by the special ideology of the new system. We were faced by very difficult problems in the areas of economics, finances, administration, and especially social and national questions. Not all of them, however, had to be solved immediately. On the contrary, the most urgent question facing us since the beginning of the revolution was that of war and peace—a question closest of all to my department and the Ministry of the Army. We know that the old government was overthrown because of its inability to carry on the war "to a victorious end." It was precisely this inability which assured the cooperation of the military leaders with the members of the State Duma in accomplishing the coup. It was thought that the liberation of Russia from the tsarist yoke would, by itself, evoke enthusiasm in the country and would be expressed in an increase in the fighting capabilities of the army. In the first few moments, this hope was even shared by our allies—at least by the left wing of their press and public opinion. However, this hope lingered for only a short time with them and for even less time with us. We knew that this drawn-out war, together with the dislocation of supplies, had exhausted and lowered the morale of the army. The last recruitment levy brought in material incapable of inspiring a new mood into the army. The so-called "reserve" battalions of new recruits, poorly trained and undisciplined, scattered themselves along the road to the front; those who arrived, did so in incomplete units; and in the opinion of the regular army, they would have done better not to arrive at all. Before they read the issue of *Okopnaia Pravda*—leaflets strewn into the trenches by German money for the purpose of disintegrating the army —and before native Russian agitators appeared in noticeable numbers in their ranks, the process of disintegration had already gone a long way among the soldiers. Ten days after the creation of the government, General Alexeev wrote to Guchkov that he was not in a position to fulfill the obligations he had accepted before the Allies at the conferences of Chantilly on November 15–18, 1916, and in Petrograd in February 1917: "We accepted the obligation to attack the enemy decisively not later than three weeks after the beginning of our allies' offensive. Now the matter comes down to postponing our accepted obligations or refusing to fulfill them entirely, with the least loss of dignity before our allies. . . . We had to report that we could begin active operations no earlier than the beginning of May. . . . We will now have to tell them that before July they cannot count on us." General Ludendorf, on the contrary, testifies in his memoirs that: "If the Russians had attacked us with even a small success in April and May of 1917, . . . the struggle would have been extraordinarily difficult for us. . . . If we suppose that the Russian successes of July had taken place in April and May, I do not know how the Supreme Command would have dealt with the situation. . . . Only the Russian revolution saved us from a difficult situation in April and May of 1917."

Naturally enough, the question arose as to whether or not Russia could continue the war at all. And if the answer was negative, then could Russia continue her former policies? Both questions, the military and the diplomatic, were closely bound together, but they had never before been posed so starkly. To pose them in that manner would have meant leaving the war by means of a separate peace. This solution was considered shameful and incompatible with the honor and dignity of Russia. At the end of the Provisional Government's eight months of existence, when the minister of the army, Verkhovsky, dared to hint at the possibility of a separate peace, he evoked the indignation of my successor, Tereshchenko, and was forced to resign immediately. Thus, it was deemed possible to stop the war only by concluding peace together with the Allies. But how could such a peace be insisted upon without forcing both ourselves and them to make a change in policy? This was obviously impossible and the defenders of such a solution inevitably wound up in a vicious circle. In this lay the strength of my position, and the futility of efforts after my departure showed the correctness of that position.

Such was the situation, and so the situation would have remained (in fact it did for a time remain that way) if a new factor, promising to cut the Gordian knot, had not intervened. This factor was the influence of Russian Zimmerwaldism.[54] Instead of the question "war or peace," the Zimmerwaldists (even Kerensky and Tsereteli considered themselves as such at the beginning) proclaimed the slogan "war—or revolution." It seems that it was the Zimmerwaldist, Martov, who first formulated this slogan in an appeal to the toiling masses of the whole world. This appeal had been adopted at a special meeting in Bern of all those ideological allies who happened at the time to be in Switzerland (the center of the future Third International had been transferred to Bern). "Either the revolution will kill the war, or the war will kill the revolution"—thus was the slogan developed. If the war kills the revolution, it would mean that reaction and "counter-revolution" would be victorious. If the revolution was victorious over the war—and this was possible only on an international scale—it would mean that the revolution would have achieved its final goal. Posing the problem in this way was just as unrealistic as "world revolution," but for the Russian half- or quarter-Zimmerwaldists, the unreality was hidden in the foggy distance, while in the meantime a new formula had opened up the possibility of a new solution. To convince the Allies of this possibility was the business of the international proletariat. It was necessary "simply" to change their views on the "aims of the war."

Phrased in that way the Zimmerwald slogan appeared in Petersburg during the first days of the revolution. In the first issue of the Soviet's paper, *Izvestiia*, in the manifesto of the Bolshevik Central Committee, we find the slogan in its developed form. "The immediate and urgent task of the Provisional Government (which had not yet been created)," *Izvestiia* dictated, "is to enter into relations with the proletariat of the belligerent countries for a revolutionary struggle of the peoples of all countries against their oppressors and enslavers, against the tsarist governments and the capitalist cliques, for the immediate cessation of this bloody slaughter of humanity which has been thrust upon the enslaved peoples." The Bolsheviks knew what they were talking about: this meant the conversion of the trench war into an internal civil war. Their imitators in Russia, however, did not know what was involved and toned it down. On March 14 the Soviet of Workers' and Soldiers' Deputies issued an appeal to the peoples of the whole world calling on them "to begin a decisive struggle against the expansionist aspirations of the governments of all countries and to take into their own hands the decision of war and peace." True, Chkheidze toned it down even further: "We make the proposal with weapons in our hands and the reason for this appeal is not all that we are tired and ask for peace. The slogan of the appeal is: down with William II." This was entirely loyal, and a corresponding proposal was introduced immediately in the "Contact Committee" of the Soviet and the government. They invited us to turn triumphantly and without delay to the country with the declaration that, first, we stand for "peace without annexations or indemnities," that we resolutely repudiate aggressive imperialist aspirations, and second, that we bind ourselves to take steps at once, before our allies, to achieve universal peace. Tsereteli, who had just returned from Siberian exile, assured everyone that such an appeal would cause an unprecedented uplift in the morale of the army and that "they will all follow us like a single man"; while, I, in particular, with my "subtle diplomatic devices" would be able to persuade the Allies to accept the directive of the Soviet. In vain did I try to persuade Tsereteli, who was a

Zimmerwaldist by misunderstanding, that the socialist patriots in the governments of the belligerent countries would never accept the Zimmerwald formula, and that to come to an agreement with them on this basis would be impossible. At that time, Zimmerwaldism had penetrated even into our ranks. With Prince Lvov, in particular, it appeared in his usual lyrical glow. On April 27, at a meeting of the four Dumas, he said: "The great Russian revolution is truly wonderful in its majestic serene procession. . . . The very essence of its guiding ideas is wonderful. The freedom of the Russian revolution is inspired with elements of a world and universal character. . . . The soul of the Russian people has turned out to be a world democratic soul by its very nature. It is prepared not only to merge with the masses of the whole world, but to stand in front of them and lead them along the path of the development of humanity, development based on the great principles of liberty, equality, fraternity." Tsereteli hastened to reinforce this unexpected amplification, contrasting it to the "old formulas" of tsarist and Allied "imperialism": "With the greatest pleasure I listened to the speech of Prince Lvov who phrased in a different way the tasks of the Russian revolution and foreign policy. Prince G. E. Lvov said that he looks upon the Russian revolution as more than a national revolution, that as a reflection of this revolution one can expect to see similar revolutionary movements throughout the entire world. I am deeply convinced that as long as the government formulates the aims of the war in accordance with the aspirations of the whole Russian people the position of the Provisional Government will be solid." Of course, the minister of foreign affairs was thereby excluded from the Zimmerwald insurance.

Simultaneously with the diplomatic aspect of the Zimmerwald slogan, the Bolshevik-Zimmerwaldists did not forget about the military aspect ("to kill the war") and even devoted special attention to that side of the issue. Here, in particular, I counted on Guchkov's assistance—and I made a mistake in so doing. The Bolshevik *Pravda* served as the organ of propaganda for this and was distributed in large number of copies. As early as the beginning of March, the Petersburg Committee of Bolsheviks recommended that the Soviet take measures to secure "free access to the front and the immediate rear for the transformation of the front" "by our party agitators" "with an appeal to fraternization at the front." On March 12 in the "Contact Committee" where Steklov reigned until Tsereteli's arrival, the Bolshevik committee demanded that the oath published by the government not be administered—which demand the government refused. This did not hinder him from reporting, at each meeting of the Contact Committee, a whole series of complaints from the army against the reluctance of the commanders to assimilate the principles of the new system and the corresponding attitudes toward the soldier. It even demanded that we declare as outlaws the "insurgent generals who do not desire to subordinate themselves to the will of the Russian people," and the right for "any officer, soldier or citizen to kill them." I had to oppose these and similar pranks by myself, since Guchkov, to the great irritation of the deputies of the Soviet, simply did not show up at these committee meetings. The Zimmerwaldists, of course, soon found other ways for their propagandists to penetrate into the army; and as early as April 1, General Alexeev complained: "A whole series of deserters from the enemy has shown that the Germans and the Austrians are relying on the various organizations inside of Russia, currently interfering with the work of the Provisional Government, to demoralize the Russian army." Finally, on March 14, there appeared in print "a declaration of the rights of the soldiers" which, in the words of General Alexeev, drove the last nail into the coffin of the Russian army. The soldiers' section which composed this plan, submitted it to the decision of the Soviet of Workers' and Soldiers' Deputies, and Guchkov passed it on to General Polivanov's committee which sanctioned it after a month and a half, by which time the entire substance of the declaration had already been realized in practice. "The disastrous slogan 'peace at the front and war in the country,'" to use Guchkov's expression, had already brought "the fatherland to the brink of disaster."

I still considered it possible to fight, since I was sure that "during the first month or month and a half after the revolution, the army was still healthy." Nevertheless, I had to carry on the struggle, not in this area, but in my own area. There, because of my "obstinacy," as they said, new obstacles kept appearing, some of them coming not at all from those quarters where I had expected them. Let me return to my story, in which Kerensky now assumes the leading role.

After Chkheidze's turnabout to the side opposing "William" and my refusal in the Contact Committee to appeal to the Allies with exhortations, they left me in peace, supposedly. But not for long. Kerensky soon brought our argument into the cabinet sessions. I would have forgotten entirely about the beginning of this campaign which was fated to unfold into a big story, if V. D. Nabokov had not mentioned it in his memoirs. It began when Kerensky printed an interview concerning the aims of Russian foreign policy. Then, as a counterweight to him, I printed my own report on that subject in *Rech* (March 23). I will now continue according to Nabokov's memoirs. "Of course, it was impossible to imagine any documents

more opposed to each other than these two documents. . . . Kerensky
was brought to a state of great excitement. . . I remember vividly
how he brought an issue of *Rech* to the meeting, and, before Miliukov's arrival, how he laughed unnaturally as was his manner; rapping
his fingers on the paper, he kept repeating, 'Oh, no, this issue will
not pass.'" He was apparently anticipating his victory over me with
pleasure, on the basis of the accusation, already being sounded among
the co-members, that I was carrying out my own independent policy.
This was indeed true, in the sense that no one who had faith in me
had been till then interested in the details of foreign politics. Now
Kerensky "very pointedly showed Miliukov that if the Minister of
Foreign Affairs under 'Tsarism' could not and was not supposed to
pursue his own policy, but was supposed to pursue the policy of the
Emperor, then, now, too, there was only the policy of the Provisional
Government. It is we, instead of you, Sovereign Emperor!" "Miliukov
(I continue to quote Nabokov) was outwardly calm but inwardly
extremely agitated; and he answered in approximately the following
way: 'I considered and I still consider that the policy I am pursuing
is indeed the policy of the Provisional Government. If I am mistaken,
then let it be said openly to me. I demand a definite answer, and depending on the answer, I will know what I should do next.'" In response to this "challenge," recalls Nabokov, "Kerensky paused. From
the lips of Prince Lvov it was certified that Miliukov was pursuing a
policy corresponding to the views and plans of the Provisional Government." Since I referred to the fact that my article was an answer to
Kerensky's interview, it was decided that "in the future, no individual
political interviews are to be given." Simultaneously, my colleagues
experienced an awakened interest in questions of foreign policy, and
they asked me to deliver a detailed report and especially to acquaint
them with the so-called "secret treaties." Of course I gladly agreed; I
dragged out the "treaties" from the ministry's archives and illustrated
my report with detailed maps. I remember that Tereshchenko displayed
a special interest in all these facts which had been unknown to him
until then. Vladimir Lvov, a long-legged hefty lad with the features
of a degenerate, who easily flared up in enthusiasm and anger and
who livened up the meeting with his absurd speeches, declared the
secret treaties to be treaties of "plunder" and "swindle" and demanded
that Russia repudiate them forthwith.

Returning to the session (March 24) at which it was decided not
to make individual declarations, I should note, finally, that it was at
this meeting that the question of a general declaration by the government on foreign policy was placed on the agenda, this question having
been raised previously by Tsereteli in the Contact Committee. Nabokov

recalls that as early as March 25, he and I together discussed the draft of this declaration in the Evropeiskaia Hotel upon returning from the Congress of the People's Freedom party, which had opened that day. That same day, the S. D. Committee printed a resolution proclaiming the slogan formulated by the leader of the Zimmerwaldists, Robert Grimm: "The most important and absolutely urgent task of the Russian revolution in the present moment is the struggle for peace without annexations or indemnities on the basis of national self-determination, the struggle for peace on an international scale." The S. D. Committee recognized the necessity of inducing the Provisional Government, first, "to repudiate officially and unconditionally all aggressive plans," and, second, "to take upon itself the initiative for preparing and publicizing a similar collective statement on the part of all the governments of the countries in the agreement." As in the Contact Committee, I had nothing against the first point, but I resolutely protested against the second. At that time I completely shared the ideological aim of the war of "liberation" but I considered it impossible to influence the official policy of the Allies. In this spirit I composed the demanded government declaration, which was published on March 28. I did not wish merely to introduce the Zimmerwald formula "without annexations or indemnities," and so I replaced that formula with descriptive expressions without excluding my own understanding of the problems of foreign policy. Reflecting a prolonged dispute with Nabokov, this passage took on the following appearance: "Leaving it to the will of the people (i.e., the Constituent Assembly—P.M.) in close unity with the Allies to make the final decision on all questions connected with the world war and with the outcome of that war, the Provisional Government considers it its right and duty to declare here and now that the aim of free Russia is not domination over other peoples, nor the deprivation of their national property, nor the forcible seizure of foreign territory, but rather the affirmation of a stable peace on the basis of national self-determination. The Russian people does not strive to strengthen its international power at the expense of other peoples, just as it does not set for itself the goal of enslaving or humiliating anybody." During the discussion of this draft in the government, F. F. Kokoshkin, to my delight, introduced the following reservations: "The Russian people will not allow its motherland to come out of this great struggle humiliated and undermined in its vital forces," and the government will "defend the rights of our motherland by observing fully the obligations which have been adopted with respect to our allies." These were the "secret treaties"! The representatives from the Soviet found this formulation unacceptable and threatened to begin a press campaign the very next day against the Provisional Government.

Nekrasov's resourcefulness calmed them down, however: it would be more advantageous for them to interpret the evasive phrases as a concession on the part of the government and to support the "declaration." For my part, I reserved for myself the right to interpret it in my own way in the event that the concluded compromise was interpreted unfavorably. This did not prove necessary, however. On March 29, the Congress of Workers' and Soldiers' Deputies announced that the Declaration of March 28 was "an important step toward the realization of democratic principles in the area of foreign policy"; and Tsereteli stated that although "everything has not yet been achieved," that which has been achieved "is a torch thrown into Europe where it will flare up with a brilliant flame." Thus, until the end of the existence of the Provisional Government, my declaration remained the starting point of my successor's further efforts.

In the eyes of "revolutionary democracy," the defect of the declaration was precisely the fact that I refused to throw this "torch into Europe," that is, to make this declaration a direct address to our allies. I insisted on directing the declaration to the citizens of Russia, that is, the declaration was meant for internal consumption. As we shall see, the future struggle was directed at this flaw. Before discussing this struggle, however, I would like to dwell upon that new factor which completely changed my personal position; and in connection with that, I will discuss my formal relations with the Allies in general. Here again, I will have to turn to sources which appeared later, and especially to the memoirs of the English ambassador, Sir George Buchanan and the French ambassador, Maurice Paléologue. Without them I would not have been able to disentangle the complex fabric of influences which led to the last phase of my diplomatic struggle and which played a role in my departure from the government.[55] Paléologue's diary is especially important. A diplomat of the old school, well-informed about Russia, and at the same time a talented writer wielding a skillful pen, Paléologue was more effusive than his reserved colleague, and his attitudes were more flexible and colorful and, day by day, better reflected the impression he received of the Russian revolution. He foresaw that the French press and public would regard the revolution with enthusiasm but he did not approve of this excessive jubilation. He himself was full of gloomy forebodings. In a private letter from Paris, he was already being accused of being too much of a "legitimist" and for not imitating Buchanan to whom the absurd legend was already being ascribed that he was—the author of the Russian revolution. The main reason for Paléologue's skepticism was the inevitable weakening of Russia's military might after the revolution. With distress he noted the fraternization of the Petersburg soldiers with the uprising, the "betrayal of the oath" of the Grand Duke Kiril Vladimirovich who led his detachment to the Taurida Palace, and the procession of the Tsarskoe Selo Garrison which abandoned the protection of the tsar in order to join the rest at the Taurida Palace. He was satisfied that at last a new government had been created, but he was disappointed with the members of that government. These were all fine people, these Lvov's, Guchkov's, Miliukov's: "they are serious, honest, wise and disinterested." But . . . "none of them has the political perspective, the spirit of rapid decisiveness, fearlessness, and daring needed in this threatening situation." Paléologue compares them to Mollet and Odilon Barrot in the July revolution of 1830 when "at the very least, a Danton was needed!" "However, they tell me that one of them, put forward by the Soviet, is a man of action: Kerensky." "It is precisely in the Soviet that one must look for people with initiative, with energy, with courage . . . the conspirators, the exiles, the convicts: Chkheidze, Tsereteli, Zinoviev, Axelrod. These are the real protagonists of the drama which is just beginning." All this was written on March 4 (17), two days after the appearance of the provisional government. Paléologue also attributes Mikhail's renunciation to the influence of the Soviet: "from now on, the Soviet is in command." Also, in my agreement with the Soviet, Paléologue detects one "shameful stain of the revolution": the rebellious troops will not go to the front.

At our first meeting, Paléologue asked me: "Before speaking officially, tell me frankly what you think of the situation." I answered: "Within twenty-four hours I have come from the deepest despair, to almost complete assurance." He then immediately demanded that the government triumphantly proclaim without delay its decision to continue the war *à outrance* and that the government declare its faithfulness to its allies. "The new forces must be oriented quickly" especially in view of the Germanophile tendencies of the Stürmers and the Protopopovs. I answered: "On this you will receive full guarantees." The next day, the government's appeal, dated March 6, was published. In that appeal, the government announced that its first task would be "to carry the war to a victorious conclusion," and promised "to preserve the sacred alliances that bind us to the other powers, and to fulfill unflinchingly the agreements concluded with the Allies." I thought that this would satisfy Paléologue, but I was wrong. On March 7 (20), Paléologue came running to me and pounced on me with "indignation" and bitter reproaches. "Germany is not mentioned at all! Not the slightest hint of Prussian militarism! Not the slightest reference to our aims in the war! . . . Danton in 1792 and Gambetta in 1870 spoke a different language!" I could not say in answer to

Paléologue that the phrases we had written were the maximum I was able to get out of the government, which did not want to mention the war at all in its manifesto. I told him only that the manifesto was intended for internal consumption and that political eloquence in general now employed a phraseology different from that in 1792 or 1870. "Give me time," I told him, "I will find another way to reassure you."

Paléologue's reports to Paris during those days show what was worrying him more than anything else. On March 5 (18) he telegraphed Briand that "the decisions of the last conference (see Gen. Alexeev's statement above) were already a dead letter"; that "disorders in military production and transport have begun again"; and that he does not believe in the "government's ability to carry out quickly the necessary reforms." "What can we count on, given the most optimistic assessment?" he asked; and he answered: "I would be relieved of a great burden if I could be sure that the armies at the front would not become infected by demagogic excesses, and that discipline would be quickly restored in the rear garrisons. I have still not given up this hope. I would also like to believe that the S. D.s will not turn their desire to end the war into irreversible actions. Finally, I would allow that in some areas of the country, a feeling of patriotism might be reborn. Nevertheless, there remains the weakening of the national effort which was already anemic enough. The crisis of restoration runs the risk of being a prolonged one." I too shared similar hopes, and within these limits, I was an "optimist." I should add that I detected the limits of this optimism, in the same place where Paléologue had indicated them in his next telegram to Ribot on March 10 (23). He found it impossible to foretell how the forces of the revolution would unfold, but he was sure that those forces "were fated to play the decisive role in the final result." Predictions made by people "whose judgment deserves our confidence," are directly contradictory. "For some, the proclamation of a republic is beyond doubt; others consider it inevitable that a constitutional monarchy will be restored." "Temporarily," as long as the war dominates everyone's thought, Paléologue conceived of the future "course of events" in the following manner: "Until now, the people have attacked the dynasty and the bureaucracy. Next on the agenda will soon come the economic, social, religious and national problems. From the point of view of war, these are terrible problems. . . . As long as they remain unsolved, the public will be preoccupied with them. We should not desire, however, that the solution to these problems be speeded up, because this cannot be realized without severe shock." Paléologue saw the reason for this shock in the fact that the "Slavic imagination" is not "constructive" like the Anglo-Saxon, but on the contrary, is "extraordinarily anarchic and destructive," and that fact augurs a "rather long period" of crisis.

The depth and perspicacity of these considerations cannot be denied. The course of the process, its tempo and its results did indeed turn out that way; and, given a knowledge of Russia, it was possible to predict them. Foreseeing them, was it possible to prevent them? The fundamental question of Russian domestic policy amounted essentially to just that. In this respect too, my views and plans closely resembled Paléologue's prognoses. The coincidence was real, since we had not spoken about these things with each other.

The immediate topic of my talks with Buchanan was the fate of the emperor who had just abdicated. From Pskov, Nicholas returned to Headquarters and lost several days hesitating about his future stay: should he go away to England or settle in Livadia. During those days the government decided, under obvious pressure from the Soviet, to hold him under arrest in Tsarskoe Selo. The decision was motivated by considerations of his safety, but the Soviet wanted, just as obviously, to prevent thereby any attempt at restoration. Kerensky? On March 7, Kerensky announced in Moscow: "At this moment, Nicholas II is in my hands. . . . I do not want and I will not allow myself to darken the Russian revolution. I will never be the Marat of the Russian revolution. . . . In the very near future, Nicholas II, under my personal supervision will be taken to the harbor, where he will board the boat and head for England." On March 10 (23), Buchanan answered my request for assisting Nicholas' departure, by saying that George, in agreement with the ministers, offered hospitality to the tsar and the tsarina on British territory, restricting himself only to the assurance that Nicholas II would remain in England until the end of the war. According to Paléologue's testimony, I had been very much moved by this information, but had added sadly: "Alas, I am afraid that it may already be too late!" In fact, Kerensky, upon learning that the Soviet was sending an armed guard to Tsarskoe Selo, immediately changed his good intentions and yielded to the Soviet. In connection with the events that followed, the English government, too, took back its agreement. Just before my resignation, Buchanan, with some embarrassment, informed me, in answer to my reminder about the cruiser which was expected, that his government "no longer insists" on its invitation. From the memoirs of Buchanan's daughter we know how difficult it was for him to bear this refusal himself.

Be that as it may, the gloomy prospects shared by informed people could not, of course, alter the most friendly attitude of the Allies toward the new Russian Government. There was even a certain amount of rivalry in this. The ambassador from the United States, the dear Francis (who was in no way a diplomat), clearly wanted America to be the first to recognize the Russian revolution, and I willingly entered a little conspiracy with him. On March 9, Francis was received by the government in a solemn audience. Two days later, March 11, we heard the announcement of recognition by our principal allies, France, England, and Italy; then, third in order, Belgium, Serbia, Rumania, Japan, and Portugal joined them.

When it was learned in Paris and in London that a conflict was arising between the "Socialist" Soviet and the "bourgeois" government, then, naturally enough, there were thoughts of arranging some kind of a "sacred union" between them with the help of foreign "comrades." This idea may even have originated in Petersburg. At least, as early as March 19 (April 1), we find a note in Paléologue's diary: "the socialists of the Allied countries must explain to their comrades in the Soviet that the political and social gains of the Russian revolution will be lost if Russia is not saved." They had probably talked this over with Buchanan too. Perhaps Danton and Gambetta were also recalled abroad. They forgot only—as I told Paléologue—that the political phraseology and ideology of the twentieth century were different. If the "social patriots" of the Allied countries were speaking one language, then the Russian "Zimmerwaldists" were speaking an entirely different one; and to teach them sense was impossible. Instead of an agreement, there might be a clash; and one of the sides would have to give in. Of the two themes in the Zimmerwald formula, the military one was, for the Allies, apparently much more important than the diplomatic one, even though both were closely bound together. Efforts had to be made to ensure that the "revolution" would not "kill the war," but would rather inspire it with new enthusiasm. The agreement took place—and at my expense.

But new sacrifices were now needed. On the next day, March 20 (April 2) Paléologue received news from Paris that a special mission, headed by the armaments minister, Albert Thomas, was being sent to Russia. He had already defined the mission's task as the desire to "bring home to the Provisional Government and the Soviet a few severe truths." In his diary, he added: "On the other hand, Thomas will see the Russian revolution more closely and will tone down the strange concert of flattery and praise which the revolution has evoked in France." Paléologue, however, guessed another reason also: he himself "had enjoyed the confidence of the old regime and does not have faith in the new one." Three days later, on March 23 (April 5), he telegraphed Ribot stating his readiness to yield his post to his assistant. He guessed right: Albert Thomas carried the order for

Paléologue's dismissal in his pocket. Somewhat later, a member of the British cabinet, Henderson, carried a similar order concerning the replacement of Buchanan.[56]

On March 27 (April 9), Paléologue learned that "between the Provisional Government and the Soviet—or more precisely, between Miliukov and Kerensky—a lively polemic has begun on the aims of the war." This is a reference to my appeal which on March 28 was adopted by the government. Paléologue tried energetically to persuade me that "the Soviet's demands are equivalent to treason against Russia, and if they are carried out, it will mean eternal disgrace for the Russian people." I answered him: "I agree with you so much that if the Soviet's demands triumph, I will resign immediately." It has already been mentioned that circumstances went favorably, and the Soviet recognized the appeal. Four days later the leftist deputies arrived: Moutier, Cachin, and Lafon from France, and O'Grady and Thorn from England. Paléologue was not aware of the extent of their leftism and the next morning (April 1/14) he spoke pleasantly with the newly arrived French socialists. "At first glance," wrote Paléologue, "one could not desire anything better. . . . They are mainly concerned over whether or not Russia can continue the war and whether or not there is reason to hope that her effort will allow us to realize our program of peace." Paléologue answered that the Russian army might still play an important role, if it gains the confidence of the Soviet and persuade it that the fate of the revolution depends on the fate of the war. "As for our program of peace, we will obviously have to adapt it to the new conditions. . . . In the West, there are no grounds for denying our claims or reducing our hopes. . . . In Eastern Europe and Asia Minor, however, we will doubtlessly have to sacrifice some of our hopes." As we see, the center of gravity was shifted here from the diplomatic to the military aspect: the hint at making concessions in the East, obviously, refers to the "secret treaties."

Alas, Paléologue made a mistake in his calculations. On April 2 (15) the French deputies were received by the Soviet "coldly—so coldly that Cachien lost his control and, in order to make negotiations possible, considered it necessary to 'jettison the ballast'." *Jeter le lest* since that time has become a classical phrase: the ballast was diplomacy and, above all, the Alsace-Lorraine, the return of which was deemed to be, not a right, but the result of a plebiscite! "If this is all the support that our deputies have brought me," exclaimed Paléologue, "it would have been better had they not taken the trouble to come!" "Miliukov tells me: How do you expect me to resist the claims of our maximalists, if the French socialists themselves are losing the game?" In vain did Paléologue try to persuade his compatriots that by "orienting the democratic policy towards internationalism," they were unbridling the Russian revolution, whereas, since the "movement is still only beginning, . . . it is still possible to slow it down, to maneuver, to win time: a postponement of only a few months could have a tremendous significance on the outcome of the war." But, "I soon noticed that I was preaching in the desert. I did not have the bombastic qualities of . . . Kerensky!"

During those days, Kerensky really did triumph. On April 6 (19), at a reception for the French deputies in the Marinsky Palace, he openly contrasted his own views to the government's official opinion, which I was defending. I argued that "despite the revolution we retained the main aim and idea of this war," and that "with still more force, the government will achieve the destruction of German militarism, for our ideal was to destroy the possibility of all future wars." To this pacifist view, Kerensky opposed his Zimmerwaldist view, openly stating, by the way, that he was "the only one in the cabinet" and that his opinion was not the opinion of the majority. "Russian democracy is the master of the Russian land," and "we have decided once and for all to put a stop in our country to all attempts at imperialism and seizure. . . . The enthusiasm of Russian democracy does not derive from the idea of the fatherland as that idea was understood by old Europe; rather it derives from the idea that the dream of brotherhood among peoples of the whole world will become a reality. . . . We expect you to exert that same decisive influence in your countries on the other classes of the population as we here have exerted on our bourgeois classes by proclaiming now our repudiation of imperialistic aspirations." What was most curious and most humiliating for me, was the fact that I was forced to translate Kerensky's speech into English for the British deputies!

It was at this time that the above-mentioned episode of Kerensky's falsification took place which I forced the government to repudiate on April 14. He forced the situation, promising in print that in the next few days the provisional government would publish a note to the Allied powers in which the government's views on the aims of the war would be developed in more detail than had been done in the declaration of March 28. At that time I was preparing no note whatsoever, but the smoke was not without fire. Apparently, Kerensky had already secured his rear and had not just sallied out blindly. The question of an address to our allies had been raised in the government itself as a pressing and predetermined question. Who was standing behind and encouraging Kerensky here? At that time, I could not know of this, but Buchanan's memoirs forced me to the conclusion that the source of it all was the talks which were going on behind my back in the British embassy. Buchanan arranged a number of conferences with Kerensky, Lvov, Tsereteli, and Tereshchenko. Excellently educated, having a perfect mastery of the English language, with a very kind and ingratiating manner of speaking, Tereshchenko gained Buchanan's favor. He even served as interpreter for others. The Allies needed Russia to continue the war; Paléologue doubted the feasibility of it; and Buchanan was no less pessimistic; but, why not try it? Kerensky promised to renew the army's "enthusiasm"! He made many such promises both before and afterwards. Why not make this promise, too, as long as it was on the agenda for the day anyway and as long as it served to advance his career and—he was so sure—suited his talents? I may be off by a few days regarding the date of this assurance, but that it was made by these conferees and that it was made precisely as a condition for changing the government, is shown by the subsequent events. In this change, Kerensky was slated to replace Guchkov as minister of the army, while Tereshchenko was slated to replace Miliukov in the Ministry of Foreign Affairs. Both of those ministers who despised "democracy" would have to leave their posts. It is difficult to say whether this was arranged only tentatively or finally; but it was arranged precisely during those two or three weeks in April.

On Sunday, April 9 (22), Paléologue, Tereshchenko, Konovalov, and I went to the Finland Station to meet Albert Thomas. I well remember this moment. The station was decked out in red flags. A tremendous crowd filled the courtyard and this platform: these were the numerous delegations which had come to meet—whom? Alas, not the French minister! On the same train, a few dozen Russian exiles were returning from Switzerland, France, and England. An ovation was being prepared for them. With difficulty we forced our way to the railway platform where we found Thomas and his suite. Although the ovation was not meant for him, he became ecstatic. "Here is a revolution in all its grandeur, in all its beauty," Paléologue reports Thomas' exclamation. When he took Thomas to the Evropeiskaia Hotel, he straight away began to inform the new arrival: "The situation has become more complex in the last two weeks. Miliukov is locked in conflict with Kerensky. We must support Miliukov because he represents the policy of the Alliance." Thomas quickly put a damper on the ambassador's ardor. "We must give serious attention to Russian democracy so as not to antagonize it. . . . I came here especially in order to find out about all of this. . . . We will continue the conversation tomorrow. . . ."

On April 10 (23) a breakfast was given for Thomas in the French embassy at which Tereshchenko, Konovalov, Nekrasov, and I were present. "Miliukov, with his usual goodnaturedness and breadth of views, explained his conflict with Kerensky. Albert Thomas listened, asked some questions, said little but rendered the Russian revolution a tremendous credit of confidence and a warm tribute of enthusiasm." After the breakfast was over, he led Paléologue to his office and gave him the letter from Ribot concerning his dismissal. . . . On April 11 (24), Paléologue gathered his colleagues, Buchanan and Carlotti, together at a breakfast with Thomas; an exchange of opinion took place here in which all the cards were laid on the table. I will cite Paléologue's report of this meeting in its entirety.

"Carlotti adheres entirely to my opinion that we should support Miliukov against Kerensky and that it would be a grievous error not to counterpose the political and moral authority of the Allied governments to the Soviet. I conclude: with Miliukov and with the moderate members of the Provisional Government, we still have a chance of checking the process of anarchy and of keeping Russia in the war. Kerensky means the certain triumph of the Soviet, that is, the unbridling of the popular passions, the destruction of the army, the rupture of ties binding the nationalities, and the end of the Russian state. And if Russia's ruin is inevitable, then at least we should not help it along with our own hands." Albert Thomas, supported by Buchanan, declared himself categorically for Kerensky: "The entire force of Russian democracy is on its revolutionary rise. Kerensky is the only one who is capable of creating, together with the Soviet, a government worthy of our confidence."

In the evening of April 12 (25) Thomas came to Paléologue to inform him of his lengthy talk with Kerensky. "Kerensky had firmly insisted on revising the aims of the war in accordance with the resolution of the Soviet; the Allied governments will lose all their credit with the Russian masses unless they openly repudiate their program of annexations and indemnities." Thomas stated that he, too, was impressed by Kerensky's arguments and the fervor with which he had defended them, and, also, repeated Cachien's phrase: "We will have to jettison the ballast." Paléologue tried to persuade him that Russian democracy was too young and ignorant to dictate its laws to the masses of the Allied countries. But Thomas only repeated his own argument: "That means nothing; we must jettison the ballast."

The next morning, I told Paléologue "dolefully": "Ach, your socialists are not making my task any easier for me." Now I see that at the very time I was preparing to wage the last battle with the Soviet over the inviolability of the general principles of our foreign policy, the leading representative of that policy was ready to betray me. It turned out that I also had enemies in the rear! True, Paléologue made a last attempt. He sent a telegram to Ribot insisting on the active defense of earlier agreements as to the bases for peace, should the Russian government demand a revision of them. Again he tried to defend my policy. Otherwise, he wrote in his telegram, "We will deprive Lvov, Miliukov etc. of all credit," and "we will paralyze those forces in the rest of the country and in the army which have not yet been affected by pacifist propaganda. These forces are reacting too slowly against the despotic domination of Petrograd because they are scattered and poorly organized; nevertheless, they comprise a reserve of national energy which could have a tremendous influence on the future course of the war." Paléologue and I had not come to any agreement, but this was approximately my own argument in favor of my policy. Thomas, however, found out about this telegram and announced to Paléologue that it would be his "last one." Thomas then sent a telegram to Ribot saying that from now on he himself would take the responsibility of informing the government. He summed up his quarrel with Paléologue in a single phrase: "You do not believe in the valour of the revolutionary forces, while I believe in them without reservation." It was apparently futile to argue any further. . . .

Coinciding with the arrival of the foreign socialists was the return from jail, from exile and from abroad—from Switzerland, Paris, London, and America—of the representatives of émigré Russia. They represented the tradition of the Russian revolution, and among them were famous names and people deserving of the greatest respect. We greeted them not only "respectfully" but very warmly. At first we had hoped to find useful allies among them; for Plekhanov, for example, we were holding the Ministry of Labor. When he arrived, however, we saw immediately that here was the past, not the present. The "old men" were silent and seemed to fade into the background. The leading roles were taken by representatives of the new Russian maximalism. At the beginning of April, Lenin arrived with his suite, via Germany, in the "sealed box-car." Before his departure from Zurich, he declared Kerensky and Chkheidze to be "traitors to the revolution," and on April 4, at a meeting of Bolsheviks, he invited the Social Democrats "to throw off their old linen" and assume the name "Communists." Even the Bolshevik *Pravda* was embarrassed, and on April 8, on the occasion of Lenin's demand of transferring power to the Soviet, wrote: "Comrade Lenin's scheme is unacceptable to us, since it is based on recognizing the bourgeois-democratic revolution as finished, and calls for the immediate transformation of this revolution into a socialist one." However, the calculation of many people that Lenin would discredit himself with his own speeches was far from correct. Trotsky arrived later, and, subsequently, I was severely blamed for "letting him through." Indeed, I insisted that the English, who had Trotsky on the "black list," not detain him. Those who blamed me, however, forgot that the government had already given a general amnesty. Moreover, Trotsky, although preparing himself for the future, was still considered a Menshevik. One could not be made to answer for one's past crimes. Nevertheless, when Lenin began delivering his criminal speeches before tremendous crowds from the balcony of Kshesinskaia's home, I insisted in the government on his immediate arrest. Alas, the Provisional Government did not decide to do this.

With the arrival of the Russian Zimmerwaldists, the pressure of their views on the Soviet was strongly increased. Agitation was carried over into worker and soldier circles, and extreme demands were presented to the Soviet in the name of factories, plants, sections of the garrison, post and telegraph workers, and so on. They put forward the same slogan I had refused to allow in the appeal to the citizens on March 28: The Soviet was to demand that the government send an address to the Allies without delay, proposing that they, in turn, renounce "annexations and indemnities." Only by this increased pressure can we explain, obviously, Kerensky's speech to the English socialists, his false report about the note supposedly being prepared, and, finally, the raising of the question of such a note in the government itself. A new campaign was begun against me, but this time on a broader front. It was obviously impossible to refuse all concessions, but I chose a path which still defended myself and my policy.

I consented to send our allies a note, not demanding anything from them, but informing them of our views on the aims of the war which had already been expressed in the address to the citizens on March 28. The government agreed to be satisfied with this. We had only to think up a pretext for this declaration to the Allies and to compose the accompanying note. The note was to serve as a subject for discussion in the government. My pretext consisted of refuting the rumors that Russia was preparing to conclude a separate peace with the Germans. I refuted them by saying that "the general principles already expressed by the Provisional Government (in the appeal of March 28) correspond completely to those high ideals—concerning the liberating character of the war, the creation of a stable foundation for the peaceful co-existence of peoples, the self-determination of the oppressed nationalities—ideals which have been constantly expressed by many leading statesmen in the Allied countries," especially America. Such ideas, I continued, could be expressed only by a liberated Russia, a Russia capable of "speaking the language that can be understood by the advanced democracies of contemporary humanity." Such statements not only gave no reason to think of a "weakening of Russia's role in the common, Allied struggle" but, on the contrary, they strengthened "the national aspirations of carrying the world war to a decisive finish"; the general attention here was focused on "the task which is immediate and urgent for everyone: to repulse the enemy who has invaded the very borders of our homeland." I then repeated Kokoshkin's insertion: "The Provisional Government, defending the rights of our homeland, will fully observe the obligations which it has accepted regarding our allies, as was said in the reported document." In conclusion, the note repeated, first of all, confidence in a "victorious finish to the present war in total agreement with our allies," and, in the second place, our assurance that "the questions raised by this war will be solved in the spirit of creating a solid foundation for a lasting peace, and that the advanced democracies, inspired by identical aspirations, will find the means to obtain those guarantees and sanctions necessary for the prevention of new bloody conflicts in the future." The words "guarantees and sanctions" were inserted by me at the insistent request of Albert Thomas, who, evidently, still did not want to thow away his Allied "ballast." These words were dangerous if they were understood, for example, in the sense of guarantees and sanctions for France from Germany upon conclusion of peace. However, they did secure me the French socialists' consent to my note.

On April 18, my note was ready and approved by the government; the following day the Soviet was informed of it. April 18 corresponded to May 1 New Style, and the Soviet prepared to celebrate the workers' holiday. The main celebration was held in Mars Field. Beginning in the morning, from all corners of the capital, processions of workers, soldiers, and others streamed to the field with placards and red banners. From my ministerial offices, I had the pleasure of seeing the inscription on the roof of the Winter Palace in huge letters: "Long Live the International." Included among the placards were such as "Down with the war," while a resolution of the factory workers had still earlier demanded the resignation of the Provisional Government and the transfer of power into the hands of the Soviet. These Bolshevik demonstrations, however, were drowned in the general character of the holiday: the Soviet printed in *Izvestiia*, that "they do not correspond to the views of the Soviet." The processions were well organized, and passed by in perfect order. The numerous speeches given by street orators, and the general mood of the crowd regarded the Leninists disapprovingly. Albert Thomas was delighted with the grandeur of the celebration and exclaimed: "What beauty, what beauty!" Here was a Soviet holiday.

The next day, April 19 (May 2), a "concert-meeting" was arranged in Mikhailovsky Theater, ·where Kerensky and I were scheduled to speak. At that time I paid no attention to the sequence of events, and again I must resort to Paléologue's powers of observation in his detailed and colorful description of that meeting. "After Tchaikovsky's symphonic prelude, Miliukov delivered a speech vibrant with patriotism and energy. From the gallery to the main floor he was applauded sympathetically." Then, after Kuznetsova's singing, a disheveled figure jumped out of the boxes with the shout: "I want to speak for peace, against war!" Who are you? The man hesitated, then, "as if throwing out a challenge to the audience," he shouted with anguish: "I am from Siberia! I am a convict!" "A political convict?" "No, but my conscience commands me!" "Hurrah, Hurrah, Speak, Speak!" The public carried him on their shoulders to the stage. "Albert Thomas was in raptures." With an ecstatic expression on his face, he seized Paléologue's arm and whispered in his ear: "This is incomparable grandeur! This is magnificently beautiful!" The convict began to read a letter from the front: the Germans want to fraternize with their Russian comrades. The public did not want to listen to him. At that moment, amidst the applause from the audience, Kerensky appeared (he always "appears"— P.M.). The convict was removed from the stage; Kerensky stepped out on the stage: "he was more pale than usual, worn out from fatigue." He answered the convict in a few words. "But, it seemed he has other thoughts in his head—and he suddenly formulated a strange conclusion." These are Paléologue's words, but we know that this was Kerensky's habitual manner: he fell into hysterics in order to express the intimate thought that was beating upon his brain. He exclaimed: "If they do not wish to believe me and follow behind me, I will step down from power. I will never use force to thrust my opinion on people. . . . When the country wants to throw itself into the abyss, no human force can stop it, and for those who are in power, there remains only one thing, to get out!" "With a disappointed look, he left the stage." Paléologue said in bewilderment: "I would like to answer him that when the country finds itself on the edge of the abyss, then the duty of the government is not to resign, but, at the risk of their own lives, to keep the country from falling into the abyss." He did not know, and I still did not know, that Kerensky's prank would reproduce the method of Boris Godunov. He "departs" before his rise. This was a repetition of the scene which he had made in the Soviet in order to force the Soviet's permission to join the government; it was a repetition of the scene of renunciation at the conference in Malakhitovy Hall; it was a repetition of the hysterical scene at the Moscow conference. . . . But all of this was hidden from observation for the time being, and I do not recall that I paid attention at that time to the statement about the necessity of the government's departure—or

Kerensky's arrival. . . . Only now do I see what it meant: the unwitting and premature exposure of the existing agreement (unknown to Paléologue). It establishes the date.

On the next day, May 3 (N.S.) the Bolsheviks took their revenge for the peaceful Soviet holiday of May 1. My note was published on that day, and it served as an excuse for the first armed demonstration in the streets of the capital against me and against the Provisional Government. By 3 or 4 o'clock in the afternoon, a reserve battalion of the Finnish Regiment marched to the Marinsky Palace with placards reading: "Down with Miliukov," "Miliukov, resign." Behind them came companies from the 180th Reserve Battalion and about one company from the Baltic naval depot. The majority of the soldiers did not know why they were being led. In a letter on April 23 (O.S.) to *Novaia Zhizn*, Fedor Linda, a member of the Soviet, admitted that he was "responsible." In addition to the troops, adolescent workers also took part in the demonstration without hiding the fact that they were each paid ten to fifteen rubles for doing so. The leaders of the Soviet could no longer be blamed, because the Soviet, limiting itself to applying "pressure," was in no way planning to take the place of the government. Indeed, the Soviet found itself in an embarrassing position, somewhere between my note and the Bolsheviks. The Executive Committee of the Soviet confined itself to a proposal to the Provisional Government for a joint decision of the events taking place. I will come back shortly to this unusual meeting which comprised about seventy people. Before doing so, however, I would like to relate the immediate results of the demonstration that affected me personally. For the majority of the Soviet and the public, it was still impermissible to attack personnel of the Provisional Government, which had obligated itself to guide the country until the Constituent Assembly. Behind the demonstrators, there appeared large processions with placards proclaiming: "Confidence in Miliukov!" and "Long Live the Provisional Government!" Conflicts even broke out in places, but by the evening of April 20 (O.S.) and throughout April 21, the mood prevailing in the streets was hostile to the Leninists. On April 21, at night, a crowd of many thousands filled the square of the Marinsky Palace expressing sympathy for me. They called me out of conference on to the balcony to answer their greeting. The public kept repeating one phrase from my emotional address to them: "When I saw the placards with the inscriptions 'Down with Miliukov,' I was not afraid for Miliukov. I was afraid for Russia." I pointed out the harm that would come from discrediting the governmental authority, and I indicated the impossibility of replacing this government by another one more authoritative and more capable of leading the country to the creation of a new democratic system. However, on April 21, the Bolsheviks attempted an armed struggle. From the workers' quarters to Mars Field, disciplined columns of workers marched behind detachments of Red Guards with placards "Down with War!" and "Down with the Provisional Government!" By evening there was shooting on the streets and victims fell.

The meeting between the Executive Committee of the Soviet and the government took place in this atmosphere on the evening of April 21. A whole series of ministers, including me, spoke at the meeting and gave our explanations of the difficulties in various areas of state life. The reports had an effect, and the attitude of the Executive Committee toward the government was conciliatory. Tsereteli, who by that time had assumed a leading role in the Executive Committee, consented, after my refusal to publish a new note, to limit himself to clarifying only two points which had caused especially furious attacks. The next day (April 22) the texts of the clarifications were discussed in the government and approved by Tsereteli. In one of them it was stated that "the note of the Minister of Foreign Affairs was the subject of careful discussion by the Provisional Government, and the text of that note was adopted unanimously" (Kerensky subsequently tried to deny this). Then followed the phrase "a decisive victory over the enemies means fulfillment of those tasks set forward in the declaration of March 28," while Thomas' reference to "the sanctions and guarantees refers to such measures as limitations of armaments, international tribunals and so on." By a vote of 34 to 19, the Executive Committee recognized the clarifications as satisfactory and the incident was closed. The Executive Committee's resolution proclaimed that the clarifications "put an end to the possibility of interpreting the note of April 18 in a spirit antithetical to the interests and demands of revolutionary democracy."

Upon returning to the ministry I was able to tell Albert Thomas about this result: "I was too victorious" (*j'ai trop vaincu*). Thomas was silent, and Tereshchenko disagreed. Buchanan reported to his government: "Tereshchenko told me that he does not share Miliukov's views that the result of the recent conflict between the Soviet and the government was a great victory for the latter. Of course, in the purely moral sense, it was a victory . . . but it may be that the government will have to bring into its membership one or two socialists." Elsewhere Buchanan wrote: "Lvov, Kerensky and Tereshchenko came to the conclusion that, since the Soviet was too powerful a factor either to be destroyed or ignored, the only means of putting an end to the dual government is to form a coalition."

This decision (for it already was a decision) placed an entirely new issue on the agenda, an issue incomparably more important than the arguments over individual expressions in the note or over the parties to which the statements of March 28 should be directed. From diplomacy, the argument switched to domestic policy. I might not have noticed the connection between this switch and my own personal fate, but I had to take a stand on the question of the fate of the whole cabinet, and this stand was negative. After the "unusual victory," I was faced with a new struggle, one completely beyond me.

I should add that the cabinet question came on the agenda simultaneously with another question—the direction of the nation's military forces. Perhaps from its own point of view, the Executive Committee was right when it responded to the armed demonstration of April 20–21 with the order "not to go into the streets with arms in your hands in these troubled days without a call from the Executive Committee." Nevertheless, the committee undoubtedly invaded the rights of the government when it added the following phrase: "Only the Executive Committee has the right to give you orders." On April 21, General Kornilov, acting in the capacity of commander-in-chief of the Petrograd district, had given the order to call out several sections of the garrison, but after an Executive Committee statement that calling out troops might make the situation worse, he canceled his order and instructed the troops to remain in their barracks. This was, perhaps, appropriate "in those troubled days" as a means of expediency, but it led to conflict after the above appeal from the Executive Committee of the Soviet. General Kornilov had to resign; even though the Provisional Government, in its turn, "explained" on April 26 that "the authority of the commander-in-chief remains in full force, and the right to issue instructions to the troops can be exercised only by him," Kornilov submitted his resignation a few days later and headed for the active army. Such was the conflict which promised to be no less menacing than the cabinet change.

It was Prince Lvov's lot to bring up the question of the ministerial crisis, and he did so at that same meeting with the Executive Committee, on April 21, which was discussed above. As far as I remember, the question took me by surprise, since I was not yet aware of the talks which were going on behind my back. Moreover, Prince Lvov introduced his proposal, as was his habit, in an indecisive and optional form. Of course, unlike Kerensky, he was not planning to make use of the crisis for himself personally, and one could argue with him only on grounds of principle—which, indeed, I had the occasion to do in the next few days.

In the April 21 session, Prince Lvov began right off with the statement: "The aggravated situation which has come about as the result of the note of April 18 is only a private affair. During the recent weeks, the government has generally been placed under suspicion. Not only does it find no support among the democratic masses, but it even meets with attempts to undermine its authority. In such a situation the government does not consider that it has the right to bear the responsibility. We (I exclude myself from this "we"—P.M.) decided to invite you here and talk the matter over. We should know whether or not we are fit for our responsible post at the given time. If not, then, for the good of the homeland, we are ready to lay down our authority and give our places to others." Prince Lvov was not referring here to an institution which had given us our authority. The Executive Committee was a party organization and did not represent the "will of the people" before which "we" were supposed to bend. It is true that the Temporary Committee of the State Duma represented that will even less, but except for Rodzianko, we never claimed otherwise. If the cabinet question had to be posed at the given time, we would address ourselves to the opinion of the country. But how could the country express its opinion? According to V. D. Nabokov, Guchkov was the first to begin speaking about the resignation of the government, and it was his idea to do this in the form of rendering an account to the country as a sort of "political testament." All Guchkov's behavior can be explained by this early intention of resigning from power as soon as possible. With the other ministers, however, the same idea had other motivations. In particular, Kokoshkin, who was entrusted with writing the draft of the appeal to the population, wanted to formulate a definite accusation against those who prevented the government from fulfilling its obligations. The original text of this "testament" took the form of an indictment against the Soviets—and, namely, against Kerensky. Kerensky later denied this, but he did not see the original draft reported to us Kadets. This draft was then subjected to a double rewriting, during which the caustic passages gradually disappeared, and the "accusation" was transformed into an "apology." For Prince Lvov, this final text, reviewed by the S. R.'s, was acceptable; but Prince Lvov personally was not planning to resign; rather, he planned to remain at the head of a "coalition." We have already seen Kerensky's intentions. The transition to a coalition with the socialists was supposed to return the confidence of the "revolutionary democratic masses" to the government and to create an excuse for changing the government's composition. Prince Lvov's practical suggestion was formulated in this latter sense: "to renew efforts directed at broadening the composition of the government."

I resolutely protested against publishing this accusatory—apologetic act and against bringing socialists into the government. I showed that the government would only discredit itself by admitting its failures and that the introduction of socialists would weaken governmental authority. Both of my protests were completely futile. In the spirit of Prince Lvov, the appeal itself acknowledged, on the one hand, that the government found its suport, not "in coercion and force, but in the voluntary obedience of free citizens" and, on the other hand, that the "impossibility" of overcoming the difficulties of its tasks was due to the fact that the government refused to use "the old violent methods of rule and the external, artificial means of raising the prestige of the governing authorities." This was very idealistic, but far too Tolstoyan. The appeal recognized that "among the less educated and less organized strata of the population," "violent and anarchic acts" were occurring in the country, which threatened "to bring the country to disintegration at home and defeat at the front." Nevertheless, the appeal did not indicate any measures to prevent those results except to say that the path "of civil war and anarchy, bringing disaster to liberty, should not be the path of the Russian people . . . the path from liberty to the return of despotism is well known in history."

At the session of April 21, I learned that my own personal fate had already been decided, once and for all. V. Chernov, Kerensky's dangerous rival in the party and the destined candidate for the post of minister of agriculture, declared "with his usual banal grimaces, his sugary smile and affectations" (in Nabokov's words), that "both he and his friends have unlimited respect for P. N. Miliukov, that they consider his participation in the Provisional Government necessary, but that, in their opinion, Miliukov could better develop his talents at any other post, even as Minister of Education."

The government's appeal to "the vital forces" was published on April 26, and Prince Lvov officially informed the representatives of the Soviet and the State Duma (Chkheidze and Rodzianko) about it. For his part, Kerensky forced the situation by publicly announcing his resignation from the Central Committee of the S. R. party, from the Soviet, and from the Temporary Committee of the State Duma. At the same time he dictated to the government a new means of composing a cabinet. In the first "propertied" cabinet, he (in his own words) "had to represent democracy at his own personal risk" (as we know, this was not true); now, "the forces of the organized laboring masses have grown," and "perhaps it is no longer possible to keep those masses from responsible participation in the rule of the State"; therefore, from now on, their representatives "can take the burden of power on themselves only through a direct selection and the formal authorization of those organizations to which those representatives belong." Thus, the government was now supposed to consist of representatives of parties and be responsible to those parties. This, of course, was a substantial change in the very source of governmental authority, condemning the government to subordinate itself to the struggle between the contending partisan currents. For the "revolutionary democrats" this new form of responsibility was inconvenient if only because, from their position of criticizing the government, they became those who would be criticized; and, sharing power with the "bourgeois" government, they would fall under the blows of their more left-wing adversaries. And, in fact, on April 29 the Executive Committee of the Soviet, after long arguments, refused by a majority of 23 to 22 to send its representatives to the government.

On this same day, Prince Lvov came to see me in the ministry. I already knew that the matter concerned my resignation; but he began the conversation with the phrase: "Things have gotten all messed up; help me!" For me, this was such a display of hypocrisy that I lost my temper—which happens only rarely. I answered him angrily that he knew very well what he was getting at and that it was useless to look for help when the question had already been decided. Before him was a choice that had already been made. On the one hand, there was the possibility of using the firm authority of the government. In that case, however, it would be necessary to part with Kerensky, to take advantage of his resignation, and to be ready to resist the Soviet's active steps toward seizing power. On the other hand, there was the agreement to form a coalition, which meant subordination to the coalition's program and, as a result, the further weakening of governmental authority and the disintegration of the state. In any case, I warned Prince Lvov that I would not agree to change my ministerial portfolio for a different one and that I would leave the question of my personal position to be decided in my absence. Shingarev and I arranged to leave for Headquarters that very day. As we were leaving, I asked A. I. Guchkov, who was already getting ready to resign, to postpone his own decision until the question had been decided about coalition and then to resign together with me.

Guchkov, however, pursued his own policy here too. We had hardly arrived at Headquarters when General Alexeev showed us A. I.'s telegram announcing his resignation and giving his well-known reason for it: "In view of the conditions which (he) has no power to alter and which threaten fatal consequences for the army, for the navy, for liberty and for the very existence of Russia." Such an admission from such a high post seemed to us excessive. Neither we nor General Alexeev were that pessimistic, and we would not have said it in the interests of self-justification even if we had been that pessimistic.

Guchkov's resignation forced the Executive Committee of the Soviet to reconsider its decision. On the evening of May 1 (O.S.), it was decided by a majority of 41 to 18 that the socialists would join a coalition government—with a definite program. Included here were "annexations and indemnities" and controversial points of social and agrarian policy; the paragraph on the army, however, proclaimed the "strengthening of the fighting force at the front"—apparently in view of Kerensky's obligations to the Allies to inspire the army with revolutionary enthusiasm. We hurried back from Headquarters, and beginning on the morning of May 2, I took part in the discussion of the Soviet's declaration. Similar declarations in addition to our objections were introduced by the People's Freedom party and the Temporary Committee of the State Duma. Together we demanded, above all, the formal recognition of the new government as the only organ of power. The Kadets then demanded recognition of the government's exclusive right to use force and command the army. In social, national, and constitutional questions, the Kadet party demanded that the government not anticipate the decisions of the Constituent Assembly. In the event that its demands were not satisfied, the party, acting on Kerensky's own principle, reserved for itself the right to recall its members from the government. This was all published in greater detail in the party's declaration of May 6—simultaneously with the government's declaration which made a few, but entirely unsatisfactory, concessions to us. Thus, the "coalition" from the very beginning was based, not on a full agreement, but on a rotten compromise which carried the struggle between the Soviet and the government right into the new cabinet. As before, I continued to protest against the very principle of a coalition, and it was on this question of principle, and not only on the question of the future conduct of our foreign policy, that I based my resignation. A typical scene followed when, upon leaving the session, I went around the table shaking the hands of my colleagues who remained. When I came to Prince Lvov, he grabbed hold of my hand, and, holding it in his own, incoherently babbled: "But what do you mean? What is this? No, don't go; but, no, you will come back to us." I coldly tossed him the phrase: "You were warned"—and walked out of the room. The next day, on instructions from the party Central Committee, Vinaver and Nabokov came to see me and insisted that I accept the post of minister of education and compromise with the cabinet—all the more so since it was assumed that special conferences would be organized within the cabinet on questions of defense and foreign policy: I could, thus, go to those conferences and continue to exert my influence. We had a long argument; finally, I broke it off, asserting that my behavior was dictated to me by my inner voice and that I could not act differently. I could exert my "influence," if anything was left of it, from the outside, too, as a member of the party. I knew what lay in store for me if I remained in the government—especially since Kerensky had begun his rise.

One day before my resignation (and unaware that I was about to resign), Paléologue left Russia. For the first and last time during my term as minister, I decided to give him a farewell dinner with all the formal ceremonies. Up to that time there had been only one such fête, when my fellow Kadets wanted to welcome me in the offices of the ministry. But, it had been arranged then that our Kadet wives would bring along their own refreshments, and the servants were quite surprised at seeing this home-style feast. This time they brought me two menus to choose from, and with the air of a connoisseur, I chose one of them. The servants were in shoes, stockings, and kaftans, as called for in the old tradition. Solemn speeches were delivered. . . . Thomas was also invited and he took me aside and said: "Ah ces cochons les tovaristch!" Paléologue praised me—also *a part*: for him, I was a minister *"comme il faut."* The general atmosphere, however, was funereal. . . .

From Governmental Unity to Coalition

THUS, MY INTENTION of preserving the unity of the First Provisional Government—the unity that existed when the government came into being—was frustrated. For me, the preservation of the original government was a vital matter of principle. Those who favored bringing socialists into the government were influenced by two factors: the weakness of the premier, Prince Lvov, and the exaltation of Kerensky. By attracting the socialists, Prince Lvov was searching for a means of strengthening the government with "vital forces," and Kerensky, meanwhile, had reached his agreement with the Allies regarding the conduct of the war. As we shall see, the difference in aims led to a difference in views as to how these aims should be realized. Practical considerations turned out to be stronger than considerations of principle, and the question of preserving governmental unity was decided negatively—even before I had the chance to pose the question formally. In vain I cited such advantages as our election, our ties with the masses via the Duma and with Russian society via the intelligentsia. In vain I recalled the promise we had given under oath to lead Russia to the elections for the Constituent Assembly; in vain I showed the prematurity of rendering an account (to whom?) of our weakness—when there was every ground to speak of our strength. All of these considerations which I deemed to be practically important were left aside. Either for internal or external consumption we wanted to be strengthened by support from socialists. But—which socialists? They were different for external, diplomatic goals, and internal, domestic politics.

A rapprochement between bourgeois governments and socialists was not, of course, peculiar to the Russian coalition. The "sacred union" of the parties in France against the common enemy served as a classic example. We must remember the difference in time, however. The French agreement took place at the very beginning of the war when the overwhelming majority of socialists were "patriotically" inclined.

Three years later, when these same "socialist patriots" arrived in

Russia to persuade the members of the Provisional Government not to stop the war in spite of our revolution, they found us in a different situation. In the "Soviets" sat opponents of further continuation of the war, Zimmerwaldists and even "defeatists." In the fourth year of war, the population, exhausted by the war's sacrifices, received defeatist propaganda warmly. For their part, the socialist intelligentsia was blinded by the revolutionary mirage of universal peace dictated to all governments by the proletariat of all countries. The classical socialism of the old parties was an object of fierce criticism. To which kind of socialism was the Provisional Government addressing itself? First of all, it must be noted that our homespun politicians were very poorly informed about the various socialist tendencies—especially the most recent ones. In addition, the choice itself was limited. Along with the revolution, a turbid stream of defeatism automatically filtered into Russia, as if by gravitational pull; and, with the assistance of the Germans, it soon became the theme of the most unrestrained propaganda. In Stankevich's memoirs, one finds the correct observation that none of the classical Russian parties can make any claim whatsoever to the honor of initiating the Russian revolution. It was not the Russian socialist parties that sent the first agents to incite Kronstadt to rebellion, that cut down, in accordance with German lists, the best naval officers at Helsingfors, that distributed *Okopnaia Pravda* among the soldiers, etc. Ideas about army disintegration, about stopping the war, and distorting the aims of Allied policy—all this became the property of the masses quite apart from intellectual socialism. And all these ideas penetrated, unhindered, to the front, into the first "Soviets," and elsewhere.

This was the kind of "socialism" that I had to struggle against in the "Contact Committee," when Steklov ruled there, and in the ministry, at a time when responses from the original staff of the Soviet were sent there. We were quite familiar with them in the government. At that time, Kerensky freely called himself a "Zimmerwaldist." I had to explain this theme more than once and to run up against objections taken from the same baggage. It goes without saying that I would have preferred to deal with traditional socialism, which was carrying on a struggle of principle against us, but which placed the struggle within the framework of historical theory. This socialism established a definite boundary between our "bourgeois" and their "socialist" revolution. And it was precisely this socialism that had no desire whatsoever to enter into an organic union with us.

We were first forewarned of this from the same person who later helped me make our union a reality: I. G. Tsereteli. Returning from Siberian exile with the reputation of a person of high moral standards and with great personal influence on his associates, Tsereteli first of all proved himself a good organizer. After March 20, he managed to bring order to the chaotic Soviet, to place his "Executive Committee" at the head of the Soviet and to put an end to the arbitrary and independent activities of the members of the Soviet. Invited at a session of the Contact Committee to join the Provisional Government, Tsereteli at first answered in bewilderment: "What good would that do you? We would make an ultimatum out of every controversial question and if you did not give in we would be forced to quit the cabinet with an uproar. This would be far worse than not joining the government at all." Other leaders expressed themselves, not in this form of a delicate declination, but by a categorical refusal. The S. D., Sukhanov, repeated: "We are now making, not a socialist revolution, but a bourgeois revolution; so, people from the bourgeoisie ought to stand at the head of that revolution and carry out their bourgeois affairs"; "otherwise, it would spell disaster for the confidence which the masses and the socialist parties have placed in their leaders." The S. R., Hendelman, expressed himself in a similar vein: "We must not lend authority to measures bearing a bourgeois character; we must not take power for ourselves either in whole or in part." From the opposite side: "We, too, must not give them power"—here was my formula in defense of the stability of the "bourgeois" Provisional Government. But what ideology could hold out against the agreement between Albert Thomas and Kerensky? The agreement was ready; now the task was to find someone to agree to it.

Tsereteli turned out to be just such a person, and he linked Kerensky's name with his to the very end of the coalition Provisional Government. From an orthodox Marxist and a natural-born peacemaker, he emerged a remarkable specialist on interparty technique, an inexhaustible inventor of verbal formulas extricating his hero and his party from the most impossible situations. The leaders of the most important socialist parties did not join the new bourgeois socialist government. Kerensky, however, was already inside that government, and this time he had the party's mandate without having to extort it. Tsereteli sacrificed himself, agreeing to join the cabinet in the minor post of minister of posts and telegraph. M. I. Skobelev, a simple soul and faithful executor of the party's instructions, was likewise sent by the party. My old friend, A. V. Peshekhonov, a temperamental intellectual with talent and knowledge, had long before settled down on the right wing of socialism and could only ornament the position with his collaboration. The fifth, V. M. Chernov, was thrust forward of necessity: he was the chief, whereas Kerensky was only a novice; and it was impossible to leave him behind the scenes. Thus there came

together "five minister-socialists": a rather motley socialist group. At
the beginning they could have appeared only as an appendage to the
basic, central constellation for which the coalition had been stuck
together in the first place. In fact, the central nucleus, which received
the name "triumvirate," held in its hands the entire direction of the
"coalition's" activities. The ministers of the army and of foreign affairs both joined the government in accordance with the agreement
with the Allies; as a third, our own Kadet, Nekrasov, joined them.
Nekrasov was a dextrous and agile person who knew the right time
to get close to the "favorite of the moment" and to occupy all manner
of positions under that person; he was adviser, secretary, informant,
go-between in contacts with the press, composer of drafts, assistant
—in a word, Nekrasov knew how to be everything and nothing, how to
become indispensable. Neither the weak premier, nor even A. I. Konovalov, a personal friend of Kerensky's, joined this exclusive circle. Of
course, the group of nonsocialist ministers adhered to them in their
former departments, which were preserved intact from the first composition of the Provisional Government, and temporarily, at least,
helped that institution retain its former character. Only the mutual
relations with the socialist group had to be defined.

Starting from the assumption that the coalition Provisional Government retained its complete independence and autocracy, the Kadet
Central Committee, in a statement on May 6, offered its own program
for government action. This program indicated measures to be taken
to prevent the socialists from violating the normal powers of government authority and outlined the limits of powers left to the Provisional Government of the first coalition as a whole. I will enumerate
these five points, which also provided the basis for future statements
of the Kadet party. The first point demanded a continuation of my
policy "of observing the obligations and defending the rights, dignity
and vital interests of Russia in close union with the Allies." The second
point prohibited all organizations whatsoever from encroaching on the
Provisional Government's sphere of legislation and rule. The third and
fourth points affirmed the right of the central government to use force
against violators of law and order, and also to support the discipline
and fighting power of the army. Finally, the fifth point forbade the
Provisional Government from anticipating the decision of the Constituent Assembly on the fundamental questions of state, including the
constitutional, social, and national structure of Russia. Until the Constituent Assembly would be convened, the program allowed only for
"urgent measures" in the areas of economic and financial policy,
the agrarian reform, local self-government, the courts, etc. The
program thus excluded unconditionally the socialists' attempts "to

extend the revolution" in all these directions before the convocation of the Constituent Assembly.

For their part, the socialists introduced their own program, which was broader than ours and which aimed in precisely the opposite direction. They, of course, were interested in the last-mentioned prohibited questions and not in the principles of state rule. In the debates, which I attended in the beginning, they made very few concessions to our program and limited themselves to a simple enumeration of general topics. Where it was impossible to dwell in detail on certain themes, they introduced elastic formulas, each of which entailed inevitable conflict in the future. For the time being these conflicts could remain hidden. The Zimmerwald formula for the democratization of war and peace was put forward in its entirety. Instead of resisting the disorganization of the army (our term for the danger "from the left"), the Provisional Government obligated itself to take "energetic measures" against the "counterrevolution" (the leftists' term for the military danger "from the right"). The leftists' text retained "the preparations for the transfer of land," the "transfer of the financial burdens to the wealthy classes," and "the organization of production in instances where such proves necessary." These left-wing formulas met with no objection from us. As for the main point—the recognition of "complete power" for the new government and "complete confidence" in that government on the part of the whole revolutionary people—both the one and the other rested on "the responsibility of the socialist ministers" before the Petersburg Soviet "until the creation of a nationwide organ of soviets," that is, until the creation of a supreme socialist body. Having taken this precaution, the Soviet itself admitted that the declaration, which had resulted from negotiations, "corresponds to the will of the population and to the tasks of fortifying the gains of the revolution and its future development." But to which part of the stated conditions did this broad recognition correspond: to those conditions which restricted or those that (conditionally) expanded the powers of the socialists? For the time being, the question was left unanswered. The political omnibus that was so haphazardly stuck together did not promise a very safe journey. Breakdowns were to be frequent and to become ever more frequent until the whole machine finally collapsed. But the socialists in the coalition had still not begun to participate. For an entire month, they were unconfirmed by the Congress of Soviets, and, apparently, displayed no particular activity. In May, only those two departments for which the coalition was created, the diplomatic and the military, began functioning— and furiously, at that. As early as May 3, Tereshchenko hastened to send around a note informing the Allies of the new course in Russian policy. Alas, he received unsatisfactory answers. He attempted to improve them through negotiations. Then there followed attempts to interpret the Zimmerwald formula. England and France made some concessions—verbally. America did not yield on a single word of Wilson's clearly anti-German position. On this occasion, *Den* wrote with irritation: "They spoke to democratic Russia as they would never have dared speak to Tsarist Russia." As long as the issue involved arguments within the limits of the position I had taken, Tereshchenko received only polite responses, but when the Soviet demanded a direct review of the treaties and the immediate convocation of a conference, the Allies published, on May 27-28, clear rejections. Tereshchenko retreated, and his policy came to be considered "a continuation of the policy of Miliukov." For its part, the Soviet continued to fortify itself on the Zimmerwald position.

In this area one could talk to one's heart's content, but in the area of military affairs, talk was impossible. General Alexeev understood that it was impossible for the army to take the offensive in its state of disintegration. Yet, Kerensky had promised an offensive.

As early as May 17 we hear N. Sukhanov's cry of discontent: "The new government (i.e., the coalition) has been in existence and has been functioning for ten days already. . . . What has it done with regard to war and peace?" The answer was unfavorable to Kerensky. "The Ministry of the Army, from top to bottom, with the cooperation of all the bourgeois and the majority of the democratic forces, is working with unusual energy on the restoration of discipline and the fighting ability of the army. Undoubtedly this work has already yielded results." The results, however, were negative from Sukhanov's point of view. "No one any longer has doubts about its aims—the unity of the Allied front and an offensive against the enemy." This was no positive achievement; it was a crime! It goes without saying, Sukhanov concedes, that "as long as the war continues, it is impossible to protest the function of the organization of the war as a whole." But, writes *Pravda*, the question "To whom will the full ruling power in our country belong?" is becoming "an ever more burning question. . . ." "Let all power be transferred to our hands"; "only then will we be able to propose a democratic peace, not in words but in deed." That was the first goal; that was the first action proposed by the coalition group of socialists—in the spirit of Zimmerwald.

These two "questions" were, in fact, mutually exclusive. And while, as to the first, work in the Ministry of the Army had been going on only "ten days," then, as to the second, this was not the first year that Russia had been inundated with defeatist propaganda. A conference of army and navy officers, held at Headquarters, drew dread conclusions from this propaganda. Kerensky knew this, of course, when, on April 29, he delivered his famous words to a meeting at the front: "Can the free Russian state really be a state of rebellious slaves? I am sorry that I did not die two months ago. I would have died with the great dream that we could rule our state without the stick and the whip." Now his hysterics were wrapped up in enthusiasm, the only means remaining at the disposal of the Ministry of the Army of the "revolutionary masses." At the very top of his voice he shouted to the crowds of soldiers from the tribune of liberty that he, who had never studied military affairs, had now taken command; that leading them "to an honorable death in the eyes of the whole world," he "would march at their head with rifle in hand" (with a reference to his "comrade S. R.'s"). In a heartrending voice he yelled out the words: liberty, light, truth, revolution—and forcefully reminded them of duty and discipline and of the fact that they were "free people." The soldiers shouted back their answer: "We will go"; "we will show them"; "we will not let you down." What was going on behind the line, reached only by some of the ministers' exclamations, remains, of course, unknown. However, it would not be fair to omit mentioning that between Kerensky's immediate associates and the crowd of curious people, a stratum of enthusiasts was created who really were fired up with the idea of an offensive. These enthusiasts came from among the officers as well as from leftist intellectual circles, and, generally, from among the youth. It was from these circles that Kerensky's "commissars" and "committee chairmen" came. In this connection, several organizations of officers sympathetic to the new regime took shape.

As we see, the two main questions occupying the central core of the coalition had already evoked sharp resistance from the Soviets, and through the month of May, both conflicts remained unresolved. The first of those conflicts, the diplomatic one, could simply be postponed, which is what Tereshchenko, in fact, did. The second one required further preparation, and disappeared from the stage for a month after Kerensky's May fanfaronades. Nevertheless, the depth of disagreement over this (military) question was already completely exposed and threatened Russia not only with conflict but with catastrophe.

An equally catastrophic situation was, in its essence, not only threatening but was actually at hand in the area of the national economy. Here, the conflict between labor and capital had been aggravated to the extreme. At a time when the national economy was already in a state of extreme dislocation, when industry could continue its illusory existence only by using up its capital or by living at the expense of government subsidies, when all the measures for the protection of labor had already been put into practice and when worker control was beginning to take coercive forms, when the "capitalists" as such were suspected of reaping "high profits" and were subjected to tremendous taxes, if not outright confiscation, the minister of trade and industry, A. I. Konovalov, a radical and the most liberal Russian manufacturer, was faced with the threat of total stoppage of all Russian industry as a result of the steadily growing demands of the "proletariat." He preferred to resign on May 18 without even finding a replacement for himself. In vain he was urged to remain at his post. . . . This was the first answer from the "bourgeois" members of the coalition to the unfeasible part of the coalition's program.

As if to stress the arbitrary and demagogic principle that had established itself in the economic rule of the state, Nekrasov, the third member of the "triumvirate," issued the well-known circular on May 27 nicknamed "order No. 1 from the railway department," which gave to the Railway Workers' Union control and supervision over all branches of the railroad with the right to remove any member of managerial staff for two months. It was explained to them that this did not mean "firm authority" . . . .

From the patch of comparative calm in May, we now move on to the changing weather of the beginning and middle of June and to the storm at the end of June and the beginning of July. The basic tensions for this accumulation of electrical charge came from the extreme left-wing mood of the capital; and the medium for spreading this mood was the workers' and soldiers' organizations. The focus of direct attack was the bourgeois part of the Provisional Government, while the aim for which the struggle was being waged was the organization of the socialist part of the coalition.

The "All-Russian Congress of Soviets" henceforth became the central organ through which the struggle was conducted. The "All-Russian Congress of Soviets" met for the first time in a plenipotentiary session and was authorized, as we know, either to provide official recognition of the socialist faction within the coalition or to create outright a separate socialist government.

The Congress of Soviets and
the Socialist Government

THE FIRST ALL-RUSSIAN CONGRESS of Soviets met in Petrograd in the Taurida Palace through most of June (from the third to the twenty-seventh). Naturally enough, this congress became the center of all political events in the capital. It represented 358 soviets, the army, the navy, other establishments in the rear, several peasant organizations, and individual socialist groups. The overwhelming majority at the congress was held by Russia's two main Socialist parties: 285 Socialist Revolutionaries, and 248 Social Democrats-Mensheviks, the party with the dominant ideology. The Social Democrats-Bolsheviks had only 105 but were the inflammatory element at the congress. About one hundred members represented small individual socialist circles which were more moderate in their outlook, and one member was proud of his provocative title "anarchist communist." Many of the congress members arrived from the provinces, and the congress' general atmosphere was rather moderate at the beginning. People came in order "to work" but were hindered by red-hot streams which burst in from the street. As early as the sixth of June and by a majority of 543 to 126, with 52 abstentions, both major parties approved the Executive Committee's decision to take part in a coalition government with the bourgeoisie. On June 8, the congress passed a resolution recognizing only the "socialist ministers" as responsible to the Soviets, on the grounds that "the transfer of all power to the Soviets in the present period of the Russian revolution would significantly weaken the revolution by prematurely repelling from it elements which are still capable of serving it." Such was Tsereteli's strictly Marxist position, but this line, evidently agreed upon by the coalitionists, immediately evoked a sharp reaction from the more leftist currents against the composition of the new Provisional Government. The Bolsheviks submitted the draft of a resolution stating that "the socialist ministers, by making promises binding them to nothing, serve as a cover for the same old imperialist and bourgeois policy" and slow down the unfolding of revolutionary conflicts. The Menshevik Internationalists, in the draft of their resolution, declared that the new composition of the Provisional Government was not "a valid organ of the revolution." Both resolutions were rejected by the congress, but in its combined resolution, the major parties demanded that the government act "more decisively and consistently" and adopted the "democratic" peace formula. The contradictions were only too clear. For example, the proposal was made "to carry out the further democratization of the army and to strengthen its fighting capacity"; or, to reconcile the "demands of the organized laboring masses" with "the vital interests of the national economy which has been undermined by the war." The latter was the contradiction which had led to Konovalov's resignation. In a word, given the embittered attitude toward the coalition, compromises were obviously no longer successful. The congress decided to exchange the partial contradictions for a single general one. Continuing to support the Provisional Government, the congress resolved to create simultaneously from the representatives of the congresses of workers' and peasants' deputies, "a single authoritative and representative organ for all of organized democratic Russia," "in order to provide a more rapid and resolute enactment of the indicated platform and to unite completely the democratic forces and demonstrate their will in all areas of state life." The socialist ministers would be responsible to this body for "all foreign and domestic policies of the Provisional Government"; it was assumed that the Soviet would lend the government active support and that "all of Russian revolutionary democracy would rally ever more closely" around the Soviet (and not around the government). The "indicated" platform was probably the one which had been agreed upon with the government; however, even if the original text of the socialists' demands was meant here, the difference is not great, especially since it was stressed that the matter concerned "future," "resolute" steps, that is, the development of the moderated demands and the disclosure of the conflicting regulations of June 8. Be that as it may, the congress apparently created a completely independent socialist section of the coalition, an independent socialist government.

However, the members picked by Tsereteli did not suit such a body. The honest Tsereteli picked moderate socialists for the coalition, while in Petrograd it was the street that was speaking. In their accounts and reports to the audiences of the capital, the "socialist ministers" spoke "like Kadets" at the congress! The members of the congress had to hear and approve a whole series of reasonable speeches. Tsereteli and Chernov together argued the Miliukov theses

here, saying that it was impossible to convene an international conference at that moment in order to review the aims of the war because the Western masses were not prepared; while the Allied governments could not be forced by means of "ultimatums" to adopt the
Zimmerwald or Kienthal point of view. As for the war, Tsereteli stated
that it was necessary to maintain the fighting ability of the army,
and that at same moment, which was a military secret, it might be
necessary even to take the offensive! Kerensky exposed German efforts
to encourage fraternization of the soldiers at the front. Skobelev and
Chernov pointed out the impossibility of the state undertaking to organize production. Chernov showed the absurdity of deciding nationality questions by stipulating separatism and affirmed that the
creation of a class rule would mean clearing the way for a general
on the white horse. Skobelev argued that the revolutionary measure of
compulsory loans was impractical since the "freedom loan" was supplemented from the surplus income of the wealthy classes. Peshekhonov maintained that wage increases would not achieve their aim,
since prices would also rise; there was only one way to raise productivity and that was increased labor, while removing income from
the capitalists meant destruction of capital itself.

A "Kadet congress"!? The Bolsheviks immediately spread this
rumor through the workers' quarters. On the Vyborg side, at the
Narva Gates, at the Putilov Works, they said that Tsereteli had been
bribed by Tereshchenko, who had given him ten million rubles. And
Kerensky? Kerensky collected forty thousand Cossacks just outside of
Petrograd. And the congress itself seemed to support this: "We know
that the counterrevolutionaries are eagerly waiting for the moment
when internecine struggle in the ranks of revolutionary democracy
would give them the chance to crush the revolution." Kerensky had to
appear at the congress in person to refute the rumors.

A week had not gone by since the opening of the congress when
it became known that an armed attack from the street was being prepared against the congress. On June 9, all the socialist newspapers came
out with anxious articles condemning the "anarchy" that was shat-
tering the gains of the revolution. In the evening, the chairman of the
congress, Chkheidze, informed the members that large demonstrations
were being prepared for the next day: "If the congress does not undertake the necessary measures, tomorrow will be a fateful day." Without
debate the congress adopted an appeal to the workers and soldiers,
telling them that "the Bolshevik party had called them into the streets
without the knowledge of the All-Russian Congress, without the
knowledge of the peasant deputies and without the knowledge of all
the socialist organizations," "in order to present demands for the

overthrow of the Provisional Government, the support of which the congress had just declared to be necessary." Their reasoning showed that the congress did not entirely understand what was being prepared. A blow was being directed against the congress itself—and not from the then imaginary "counterrevolutionaries" as assumed in revolutionary terminology. In any case, the congress' prohibition was passed: "Not one company, not one regiment, not one group of workers should be on the street." During the three days from June 11-13, all meetings and processions were forbidden and violators were declared to be "enemies of the revolution."

Having made their decision, the members of the congress went around through the workers' quarters to find out what was going on. Early in the morning of June 10 a special session was scheduled in the Taurida Palace where the members of the congress presented the results of their investigations. They had discovered two organizational centers of the supposed demonstration: Durnovo's notorious dacha and the barracks of the Izmailov Regiment. Durnovo's dacha served as a den for shady characters who had good grounds for fearing the police and the courts and who had disguised themselves by the party name "anarchist communist." One hundred and twenty-three delegates from factories and plants had met there to discuss action against the Provisional Government and the congress. In the barracks of the Izmailov Regiment, two thousand soldiers had held a meeting on the same double theme. The soldiers' section of the congress, however, had already managed to vote down that proposal. The Bolsheviks, of course, were in both places, but only to propagandize. They could not yet think about demonstrations for themselves. The general atmosphere was not Bolshevik, but anarchist; and it was directed against the congress. They did not even allow the congress delegates to enter their meeting places or talk with them, and they showered them with contemptuous abuse. "The congress is a bunch of people bribed by the landowners and the bourgeoisie." "The congress has sold itself out to the bourgeoisie; it aligns itself with the ministers, while the ministers align themselves with Prince Lvov, and Prince Lvov aligns himself with Sir George Buchanan." "And you, Mssrs. Imperialists, with your Kadet congress, will you soon stop fighting?" The mood was no better in the army. The ensign, Semashko, who had been put forward by the Bolshevik soldiers as the commander of the regiment, announced to the delegates that the soldiers do not recognize the congress, that they recognize the Central Committee of the Social Democrat party (Bolsheviks). "The socialist ministers have become the same as the old bourgeoisie, and are working against the people." "Even if the Bolsheviks cancel the demonstration, then, all the same, we will go out into

POLITICAL MEMOIRS

the street in a few days and crush the bourgeoisie." In one regiment, they even wanted to arrest the delegates, declaring that all of them should be hanged. In another regiment, the delegates were threatened with beating. In still another regiment, the soldiers announced they were going out "to cut down the bourgeoisie." The workers were saying that now the S. R. slogan should not be "in struggle you will find your rights," but "in theft you will find your rights." Such were the slogans advanced by the scum of the revolution who tried to organize the street demonstration on June 10. In the morning, the Bolshevik *Pravda* formally canceled the demonstration.

The demonstration, planned for June 10, was frustrated without street clashes, but what a price was paid in the loss of authority of the highest socialist body and of the groups which stood behind it! The demonstrators did not have to be dealt with as rebels. The troops did not join them this time, but seventeen military units which sympathized with them were counted in the capital. Tsereteli began to cut off useless tails. It cost nothing to announce the end of the existence of the State Duma and the State Council, which had angered the leftists. He then persuaded the government to agree to promise that the Constituent Assembly would convene by September 30, even though the conference concerned with the convocation of the Constituent Assembly had just made it known that the new organs of self-government necessary to ensure the rectitude and freedom of the elections would not start functioning before November. But this was not enough. On the following day it was decided to take the nascent movement in hand by announcing, in place of the canceled demonstration, "a peaceful demonstration of revolutionary Russia" on June 18. The demonstration was supposed to be in support of the program of the congress: the unity of the whole worker population, the masses, and the army around the Soviets; the struggle for universal peace, without annexations or indemnities, on the basis of national self-determination; and the convocation of the Constituent Assembly as soon as possible. The regimental committees from the Petersburg Garrison had already affirmed the exclusive right of the Soviet "to bring entire military detachments out into the streets," although each soldier was left to participate in any demonstration organized with the consent of the Soviet. One day Tsereteli changed his tactics by aiming his accusations in the opposite direction, against the "counterrevolutionaries" instead of the Bolsheviks. Invited to participate under slogans "shared by all," the Bolsheviks came with their own and were given good grounds to scoff: among "all" the slogans, one of them was evidently missing— there was no "support for the coalition government." *Pravda* wrote: "Down with the ten capitalist-ministers. All power to the Soviets. It is we (Bolsheviks) who say that. We are sure that the great majority of Petrograd workers and Petrograd soldiers will say it together with us. But, what about you, gentlemen? What do you have to say on the most important of all issues? You put forward the slogan: 'complete confidence,' but. . . . but only in the soviets, not in the Provisional Government. . . . One cannot find this slogan . . . Why? . . . Among the broadest circles of Petersburg workers and soldiers, the coalition government has hopelessly compromised itself for a month and a half. . . . To come out now with the slogan 'Confidence in the Provisional Government' would mean to arouse mistrust in ourselves as well."

This brought home to us the distance covered during the one-month period from the formation of the first coalition to its first political test. During that time: (1) the new Provisional Government had been discredited by left-wing propaganda; (2) a special "socialist government" had been formed which was responsible to the Congress of Soviets; (3) the socialist group in the coalition discredited itself by "Kadetism"; (4) the public masses in the capital had armed themselves and demonstrated against the Provisional Government and the Congress of Soviets itself; (5) Tsereteli made concessions to the demands put forward in the name of "revolutionary democracy." These concessions, in themselves, showed that neither the government nor the congress had the means to resist the demands of the street.

The government's impotence was so obvious that one can understand the temptation to attempt to do something more than merely postpone the demonstration of June 10. Two weeks after the "general" demonstration of June 18, we come upon an event which one might call the first Bolshevik attempt at revolution. The Bolshevik leaders denied that this was the meaning of the demonstration, and I think they are right. There was a moment, however, when the second-rank leaders and the crowd urged on by them wanted to believe this. On the anniversary of the uprising, Zinoviev explained the outbreak thus: "In the two-week period beginning with the demonstration on June 18, our party, whose influence was growing, not by the day, but by the hour, did everything it could to restrain premature action on the part of the Petrograd workers. We said jokingly that we had been transformed into firemen. We felt that the Petrograd vanguard had not yet merged sufficiently with the whole army of workers, that the vanguard had run too far in front, that it was too impatient, that the supporting columns had not yet arrived—especially the soldiers and peasants."

This was so, but, on the other hand, on the evening of July 3, Lenin had already occupied his famous balcony in the Kshesinskaia home where he welcomed the soldiers and gave them instructions. The entire military intelligence section of the Bolshevik party Central

Committee was housed in that building; military units were sent there and left from there. In a word, the military staff of the uprising was already on hand. Consequently, it was here that the aim of the uprising was to be indicated. There was an inconsistency, however. The Bolsheviks' usual slogan was "all power to the Soviets," but in the given moment the political composition and the mood of the Soviets under the guidance of Tsereteli did not suit Lenin at all. And, from the other side, Tsereteli himself in no way wanted to obtain "all" power for the Soviets, fearing the limitation of their influence. Finally, what relation did this slogan have to the "socialist republic," announced by Lenin to be the next stage? It was impossible to eliminate it, but it was futile to propagandize it further. The slogan was retained and became the official slogan of the uprising.

From the Kshesinskaia home and from other places in the city, military detachments and crowds of the public streamed day and night during these three days (July 3-5) toward the Taurida Palace where the Soviet was in session, and there they held the Soviet in an uninterrupted state of siege. Instances of the bloodless struggle flared up, while at times, real chaos threatened. Tsereteli bravely held the line: the sessions continued, delegations were received, proposals were heard and discussed, reports were delivered, decisions were made. At times the crowd demanded that the ministers come outside. They wanted to arrest Tsereteli but could not find him. They caught Chernov on the porch, and a strapping worker shouted out to him in a frenzied voice, shaking his fist in Chernov's face: "Take power, you son of a bitch, when they give it to you." The Kronstadt sailors dragged him into a car as a hostage so that the Soviets would take "all power," and only Trotsky let him go. When the situation became quite serious, Tsereteli's inventive mind thought up a way out and voted it through. He agreed to the power of the Soviets, but since the Executive Committee gathered here (after the congress was dissolved on June 27) did not have the right to do this, a "competent body" of the Soviets was needed; that is, a new congress which would meet in two weeks in Moscow where the work could be carried out more calmly.

The socialist faction of the coalition was thus deciding its fate, but where was the "triumvirate" which, until then, had been considered the center of the whole coalition? This "triumvirate" displayed its independence by simply walking away from the game. Prince Lvov, it is true, conscientiously remained and when shots were heard in the streets, moved the center of his activity to the Army Staff Headquarters. He composed the "appeal." Kerensky, appearing for a minute at Staff Headquarters, went off to the western front—just in time to avoid the trap which was being laid for him at the station. Two of the others arrived at Staff Headquarters, but when they saw that only a few invalids and Cossacks were defending it, they disappeared. So that there would be no doubts, Nekrasov sent an order the next day by which the government satisfied his own request to resign. When, on the evening of July 5, "loyal" troops called out by General Polkovnikov came to assist and the uprising stopped by itself, there was no more talk about resignation. All of them returned, and on the evening of July 6, Kerensky showed himself to the public from the window of the Staff Headquarters, proudly announcing to the crowd that the Russian revolutionary masses and he, who had been authorized by them to be minister of the army and who had been placed at the head of the army, would not allow any encroachments on the Russian revolution. Those who returned raised a storm of protest against the minister of justice, Pereverzev, who during those days had permitted secret intelligence documents to be made public; the documents showed how the Germans had bribed the Bolsheviks through the intermediacy of Swedish banks. Pereverzev was disavowed and dismissed even though the published documents greatly helped to discredit the mutinous Bolsheviks.

The behavior of Kerensky and his friends during the days of the Bolshevik uprising drew a much clearer boundary than had hitherto existed between the "triumvirate" and the Soviet. Nevertheless, during the days preceding the uprising, that same triumvirate, almost as a provocation, ousted the nonsocialist-ministers of the provisional government who had remained in the government from the beginning: except for Prince Lvov, and after Konovalov's resignation, there had remained a foursome of bourgeois ministers (the Kadet Shingarev, Prince D. I. Shakhovsky, Manuilov, and Deputy Minister V. A. Stepanov). They had occupied themselves with their own business, doing their best to avoid trouble. All the same, a conflict situation was created for them, as it was for the Kadets, over the nationality question.

The Congress of Soviets was supposed to be guided by Lenin's directive: "the right of nations to self-determination including separation." However, in its final decisions before closing, the congress displayed an awareness of the necessity to preserve the unity of revolutionary Russia, and it correspondingly softened its resolution with important reservations. Of course, this did not stop some nationalities, especially the Finns and the Ukrainians, from striving to take advantage of the Russian troubles in order to achieve complete separation from Russia. The Finnish jurists arrived at this more cautiously and subtly. The fanatics of the Ukrainian movement, headed by Professor Hrushevsky, chose the path of seizing de facto control of the main positions. Taking advantage of the fact that the Russian authorities were not familiar with the question, the Ukrainain politicians had already made significant gains, endowing their local institutions with the powers of state institutions. They already had their own government ("Rada"), their own ministry ("secretariat"), and even their own, first constitution ("universal"). All that remained was to convert actual possession into right. Since there were Russian experts on the situation (there were some in our Central Committee), it was difficult to achieve this, and the triumvirate busied itself with this delicate question. All of them, plus Tsereteli, arrived in Kiev on June 28-29 and in a few days drew up an agreement having the appearance of a bilateral state act. Fearing our criticism, the Kievites set as a condition the adoption of the final text without change. The document, however, betrayed Russia's interests and was juridically incompetent We demanded a revision and raised the question of the continuation of our members in the coalition. As evidence of the fact that we were not protesting the principle of self-government for the Ukraine, the Kadet ministers introduced our project for Ukrainian autonomy in a session on July 2. Because of the votes of Prince Lvov and V. Lvov, the Kadets found themselves in the minority and resigned from the government. The first coalition ceased to exist. Only a fragment of it remained: the triumvirate, with Chairman Prince Lvov, and "five socialist ministers" who at the same time composed a separate and independent entity.

These groups, so unrelated in their goals and their membership, were united by their leadership and were faced with a single common task: to eliminate the consequences of the Bolshevik uprising. Now, for the first time, a group had been separated from the general mass of revolutionaries which might appropriately be designated state criminals. Before his dismissal, Minister Pereverzev managed to arrest the Bolshevik intermediaries in the contacts with the Swedish banks[57] (Kozlovsky and Sumenson), and to begin an investigation of Lenin and his accomplices and clean up the Kshesinskaia residence, Durnovo's dacha, and the Peter and Paul Fortress. The order went out for the arrest and judicial investigation of all persons taking part in the organization and leadership of armed demonstrations; such persons were to be considered guilty of treason to the homeland and betrayal of the revolution. Arrests were, in fact, made—Trotsky, Kamenev, and Lunacharsky; Lenin and Zinoviev escaped arrest only by managing to hide themselves in time. Measures were taken against the instigators of the Kronstadt sailors' disorders and against suspected persons from the crews of the Baltic fleet; it was forbidden to bring into the army copies of Pravda, Okopnaia Pravda, and Soldatskaia Pravda. These were the actions of the minister of the army, authorized by the revolutionary masses; that is, they were carried out in the name of both groups of the coalition. This did not last long, however. After the elimination of the Bolshevik leaders, fear necessarily turned toward the government's repression—of the "counterrevolution." The "five socialists" remaining in the Socialist faction of the government, recognized the "inevitability" of repressive measures, but were even then fearful of "preparing the ground for counterrevolution" and demanded from Tsereteli that "the protection of revolutionary order" be carried out in collaboration with "the organs of revolutionary democracy." Returning to Petrograd, Kerensky gave "revolutionary democracy" a return bout. He freed Trotsky and Steklov from arrest, forbade the army staff to arrest more Bolsheviks, and stopped the compulsory disarmament of the Bolsheviks, changing this to a completely ineffective voluntary disarmament.

The Soviet went even further. It demanded compensation; it demanded a revision of the coalition program of May 6 with the aim of "immediately carrying out the tasks indicated in the decisions of the Congress of Soviets and directed toward the elimination of all vestiges of the old system, the establishment of a democratic republic, the introduction of urgent measures in the area of land and labor questions, the development of local self-government in order to prepare the elections to the Constituent Assembly, and also the regulation of life in the country, especially as it involved the food problem." Tsereteli attempted to assure everyone that this was in no way a new agreement but merely the realization of the agreement concluded on May 6. The May 6 Agreement, made when the first coalition was being formed, and the themes of the agreement reached on the occasion of selecting the new coalition government, were really the same; only the treatment was different. The new declaration, issued on July 8, extended the Declaration of May 6 which, as we know, was even then unacceptable to the Kadet participants. Above all, it turned out to be unacceptable to Premier Prince Lvov, both in general and in particular, as a result of V. Chernov's high-handed treatment of the agrarian question which "undermines the people's awareness of the necessity of preserving law and order." The chairman of the first coalition conscientiously remained until the end of that coalition's existence; he left, forgivingly, when his post was needed for a new elevation of Kerensky, and he obligingly recommended Kerensky as his successor. He was not answered very politely by Tsereteli, who, immediately after Lvov's departure, yielded on another demand which had been unacceptable to Prince Lvov—the demand for changing the state system to a republic before the Constituent Assembly. Of course, the promise of passing a series of sweeping projects on labor legislation in the "next few days" similarly remained unacceptable, and it was this legislation which forced Konovalov to resign. Plans for organizing the national economy and measures for controlling production were to be worked out "without delay" by the Economic Council and the Chief Economic Committee. There were many plans, but few possibilities after what had already been tried.

On the same day, the Temporary Committee of the Duma protested against the socialists' new means of creating a coalition. The committee defended its right to take part in the selection and emphasized that the coalition would bring "the people's general recognition of the government," only if it was founded on "balanced, mutual agreements of the constituent parts," and if it did not pursue the aims of particular parties. "These requirements for stability have not been observed," declared the Duma committee in complete accord with the ministers who had resigned. It was now a fact that the will of the Provisional Government was in the hands of "five socialist ministers," the authors of the revised and supplemented Declaration of July 8.

Only two days separate the mood of the Soviet in the days of the retreat at the front from the nearly total victory of the Bolsheviks over the Soviet. The impressions of both the one and the other were quite strong, and they sometimes got mixed up. However, I would like to keep them separated in the mind of the reader. For this purpose, I would like to make use of statements made by the leaders of both camps. Tsereteli defined the situation thus: "This is not only a government; this is a crisis of the revolution. A new era has begun in the history of the revolution." In his militant language, Lenin echoed: "On July 4 a peaceful transfer of power to the Soviets was still possible. . . . Now the peaceful development of the revolution in Russia is no longer possible, and history poses the alternatives of either complete victory for the counterrevolution or a new revolution."

Relating these conclusions, not to what happened afterward, but to what had already happened, I believe both leaders came to the conclusion that the struggle against the "bourgeoisie" was over, that a new act of the play was beginning: a struggle was being waged between two currents within socialism itself—the moderate and the extreme. It was a struggle which after July 4 could not end peacefully. Still more precisely, Lenin defined the Bolshevik experiment as the end of the peaceful evolution of socialism in Russia and the beginning of military relations. It is not entirely clear just what he understood by the victory of the "counterrevolution," but he hardly could have had in mind the return to a "bourgeois regime."

Notes

1. For translations and brief identifications of Russian periodicals, see the periodical glossary, pp. 495.
2. *Problemy Idealizma* (*Problems of Idealism*) (St. Petersburg, 1902).
3. The emancipation of the serfs in 1861 required a thorough reorganization of local administration. To meet this need, as well as to improve the quality of local government, Alexander II introduced a system of elected assemblies, the Zemstvos, in thirty of the thirty-nine provinces of European Russia. All classes participated both as electors and as delegates, although property qualifications and indirect electoral procedures for the peasantry decidedly favored the former serfowners. Elections were first held for the district Zemstvo, which, in turn, elected delegates for the higher, provincial Zemstvo. The Zemstvo assemblies met only once a year, leaving management of Zemstvo affairs to boards elected by the district and provincial Zemstvos. Zemstvo jurisdiction covered a wide range of activities, such as the provision of local schools, hospitals, orphanages, libraries, roads, postal service, and a variety of services aimed at improving the rural economy. The response of the population was mixed. Some resented the expense of all this, paid by local taxation. Others, including the liberal-minded landowners, regarded Zemstvo service as a noble enterprise in itself and as a vital step toward broader self-government in Russia. From the time of its introduction, the Zemstvo system came to represent a promising alternative to the traditional, arbitrary autocracy and its omnipotent and omnipresent bureaucracy. Besides providing thousands of provincial Russians with direct experience in self-government, the Zemstvo drew into its self-governing orbit large numbers of educated youth to serve as teachers, doctors, nurses, agronomists, librarians, clerks, statisticians, and in other such positions required by Zemstvo activites. Even the more conservative Zemstvo members found themselves in frequent conflict with the bureaucracy—and, implicitly, with the autocracy that stood behind it—in defense of Zemstvo rights. The conflict became increasingly serious after the government, fearful of this competing political force and principle, repeatedly restricted Zemstvo jurisdiction, limited its taxing powers, altered the franchise to assure the

dominance of the wealthiest landowners, and sharply increased the control of the tsarist bureaucracy over Zemstvo allocations and enterprises. Such restrictions, which became particularly severe during the reign of Alexander III, only intensified opposition among those directly and indirectly active in Zemstvo affairs and set the stage for the dramatic role played by the Zemstvo in the liberation movement and the 1905 revolution.

4. For brief descriptions of the political parties mentioned by Miliukov, see the political party glossary, pp. 493.

5. On the morning of January 9, 1905, a procession of workers advanced peacefully toward the Winter Palace, carrying religious images, portraits of the tsar and a petition for better working conditions and political reforms. Police and soldiers blocked the way and ordered the marchers to disband. When the workers refused to obey the order, the troops opened fire, killing about a hundred demonstrators and wounding several hundred more.

6. Miliukov's *Outlines of the History of Russian Civilization* is briefly discussed in the Introduction.

7. The Free Economic Society was founded in 1765 for the study of economic (mainly agrarian) problems and the dissemination of information on agriculture. During the reign of Nicholas II, it became a center of heated debates among liberals, Marxists, Populists, and conservatives as to alternative policies for Russian economic development.

8. The term "third element" refers to the people employed by the institutions of self-government, mainly the Zemstvos, as discussed in note 3 above. The other two "elements," to which this group made a third, were the tsarist bureaucracy and the elected representatives of local self-government. The "third element" became one of the most active and effective forces in the liberal movement.

9. The *World of Art (Mir Iskusstva)* was an immensely influential art journal founded in 1898. Its aims were to encourage modern trends in art, literature, ballet, and theater, to familiarize Russian readers with the latest currents in Western European art, and to promote the study of earlier periods in the history of Russian arts and crafts. After the journal ended, in 1904, its most prominent founder, Sergei Diaghilev (1872-1929), continued the work of the journal on a much more elaborate scale by arranging in Western Europe a series of Russian art exhibits and, after 1909, the enormously successful performances of his Ballet Russe.

10. D. N. Shipov was at the time a leading Zemstvo moderate. In contrast to the liberals in the League of Liberation, who wanted a truly legislative parliament, Shipov advocated only a consultative assembly, which he regarded as more in keeping with Russian traditions and more compatible with existing Russian conditions.

11. The "four tails" were the four essential requirements for a fully democratic election, as advocated by Miliukov and the League of Liberation: equal, direct, secret, and universal.

12. Faced, on the one hand, with defeat in the war with Japan and, on the other hand, with increasingly vehement and broadly supported demands for political reform, the government issued a manifesto and accompanying decrees establishing a central State Duma. This concession of August 6, 1905, however, fell far short of the liberals' demands, since the Duma it promised was to have only consultative rather than legislative powers and was to be elected by an indirect and unequal franchise. The later and more famous Manifesto of October 17, 1905, while still inadequate for Miliukov, at least improved upon the August 6 decree by granting a legislative assembly and a much wider franchise.

13. I later learned that V. O. [Kliuchevsky] had moved so close to our political position that he joined the Kadet party and ran as a candidate in the suburb of Sergei. (Note by Miliukov. Hereafter such notes are cited by the author's name).

14. At the time, I welcomed the emergence of the Octobrist party because it drew away elements from our party that did not suit us (Miliukov).

15. According to rumor, Grand Duke Nicholas Nicholaevich threatened the tsar with suicide. (Note by M. M. Karpovich and B. I. Elkin, editors of the original Russian memoirs. Hereafter such notes are cited by the editors' names.)

16. In an unsuccessful effort to quell the emerging revolution by timely concessions, the tsar ordered the Committee of Ministers to work out a set of economic, social, political, and religious reforms. In successive conferences with the committee and other advisors, however, the tsar showed himself unwilling to grant more than a vague reference to the participation of representatives of the public in the government's legislative action. He even rejected the proposal of the committee that these representatives be elected and insisted that he select them. In the end, the December 12 Manifesto was issued without any reference at all to popular representation and merely mentioned plans to improve the system of government.

17. Defeated in war and faced with revolution at home, the Russian government eagerly accepted President Theodore Roosevelt's offer to mediate the Russo-Japanese conflict. Witte was appointed chief Russian plenipotentiary in July 1905, and later that same month negotiations began at Portsmouth, New Hampshire. The treaty was signed on August 23.

18. The author is referring to notes he made a month and a half after the conversation (M. M. Karpovich and B. I. Elkin).

19. See p. 18.

20. Contrary to the aims of the Kadets, the elections to the Duma were neither direct nor equal. There were special qualifications as well as different electoral stages for the various classes—landowners, peasants, urban residents, and workers in mines and factories. There were even subdivisions within these categories; for example, with reference to Miliukov's "apartment qualification," urban residents were divided

into those who qualified by large tax payment and those who qualified by a required length of residence.

21. A fashionable St. Petersburg club, founded on March 1, 1770, by an
English banker, Cornelius Gardiner.

22. There is agreement among memoirists of the period that Tsarina Alexandra Fedorovna was estranged from prominent Court and capital
circles in St. Petersburg, whose members tended to favor the entourage of the dowager empress, Nicholas' mother. In part this was
because of Alexandra's foreign origin and up-bringing—she was born
Princess Alix of Hesse and raised at the Court of her grandmother,
Queen Victoria of England. A more important explanation, however,
was her personal preference for intimates who were obsequiously dependent on her, her adamant, indeed fanatic, dedication to what she
conceived to be the fundamental principles of the Russian state and
society, and her shy, melancholy temperament. The illness of her
son, Tsarevich Alexei, and her own chronic ill-health further ex-
acerbated these traits, narrowed her contacts to her most immediate
family, and fostered a paranoiac suspicion that everyone was con-
spiring against her and her family.

23. The congress took place September 24-28, 1906 (M. M. Karpovich
and B. I. Elkin).

24. At the last meeting of the Second Duma a bill concerning local courts
was discussed (M. M. Karpovich and B. I. Elkin).

25. Landowners sent to this meeting one elector per 230 landowners,
while the merchant-industrial class sent one elector per 1000, the
middle bourgeoisie one elector per 15,000, the peasantry one elector
per 60,000, and the workers one elector per 125,000 (Miliukov).

26. The owners of large amounts of immovable property and commercial-
industrial enterprises (M. M. Karpovich and B. I. Elkin).

27. This occurred in 1902 during Russian sea maneuvers near Reval, at
which Emperor William was present. As his yacht left, he signaled
his farewell: "The Admiral of the Atlantic Ocean sends greetings to
the Admiral of the Pacific Ocean" (M. M. Karpovich and B. I.
Elkin).

28. I gathered everything I wrote about this issue in a book, *Balkanskii
Krizis i Politika Izvolskogo* (*The Balkan Crisis and the Policy of
Izvolsky*), published in 1910. Since foreign affairs were the prerogative of the monarch, speeches by the foreign minister in the Duma
were rare. Almost the only time we could criticize the foreign minister from the Duma tribune was when we discussed the ministry's
budget (Miliukov).

29. In response to the dissolution of the First Duma, on July 8, 1906,
180 Duma members met in Vyborg, Finland, about twenty miles
from St. Petersburg. They denounced the dissolution as illegal and
called upon the Russian people to show their indignation by refusing
to pay taxes or fulfill military service. As punishment for this act, all
signatories to the "Vyborg Manifesto" were tried at the end of 1907,
imprisoned for three months, and disqualified from further Duma

participation. Since approximately two-thirds of the signatories were Kadets, this represented a severe blow to the party's leadership.

30. By the power of "interpelation" the Duma could summon tsarist ministers for questioning. This did not imply "ministerial responsibility" to the Duma, since the Duma had no power to remove, by a no-confidence vote, ministers whose policies it opposed. Nevertheless, it provided the Duma with one of its most effective channels for expressing its views on current legislation and influencing government policies. The very fact that ministers had to defend their programs before knowledgeable Duma representatives made them more responsive and sensitive to the Duma. But perhaps the most important consequence of this procedure was the gradual emergence of mutual understanding and cooperation between the more moderate Duma representatives and the more enlightened and progressive ministers.

31. The 1913 Jubilee commemorated the three hundred-year anniversary of the Romanov dynasty, which began with the election of Michael Romanov to the throne in 1613. Ironically, it was a quasi-parliament, the Zemsky Sobor, that elected the first Romanov to power, and it was a quasi-parliament, the Duma, that helped overthrow the last Romanov.

32. For comment on this conference, discussed by Miliukov in the first section of the memoirs, see the Introduction.

33. In Krylov's fable, a swan, a pike, and a crab join forces to pull a wagon, with little success: the swan took to the clouds, the crab went backward, and the pike chose the nearest waterway.

34. The "Montenegrins" were confidantes of Tsarina Alexandra Fedorovna. They were daughters of King Nicholas of Montenegro and had married two sons of the tsar's granduncle, Nicholas Nicholaevich, thereby becoming grand duchesses. Both "Montenegrins" were avid spiritualists who brought to the tsarina's attention a series of miracle workers and mediums and in other ways involved her in the bizarre occultism that pervaded the Court and high society at the time. One such seer was Philippe Vachot of Nizier, mentioned later in the paragraph, whom they introduced to the tsar and tsarina during the sovereigns' visit to France in 1900.

35. The "khlysty" were a religious sect established in the seventeenth century. They were flagellants, whence their name "khlysty" (whip), and were known for practicing other forms of self-torture as well. They became particularly numerous in the 1840's and, in 1842, were classified as one of the "most pernicious" sectarian groups.

36. See my introductory chapter in Carnegie's *Anketa* (*Questionnaire*) for a detailed account of the Serbo-Bulgarian negotiations (Miliukov).

37. According to the statistics of 1913, Christians occupied the six *vilayets* of Asia Minor and comprised 45.2 percent [of the population], Moslems comprised 45.1 percent. Of the total population here, 38.9 percent were Armenians (1,018,000, in contrast to 666,000 Turks and 424,000 Kurds, both settled and nomadic) (Miliukov).

38. Erzerum, Van, Bitlis, Diyarbekir, Kharput, and Sivas (Miliukov).
39. For the date and circumstances of Stolypin's death, see pp. 229-37, 278.
40. The opposition's general condemnation of the government's domestic policy was expressed in a formula regarding the budget of the Ministry of Internal Affairs proposed by the Octobrists and passed 164 to 117. "In view of the fact that the Ministry of Internal Affairs, which has continued its activities under special regulations after the reestablishment of order, evokes general discontent among the population as well as completely justifies feelings of indignation against uncalled for repressive measures; that the strong authority which is necessary in any state can be strong only by relying on the law; that, using its illegal activities to support a reign of arbitrary rule and judgment and refusing to allow the long-ripened reforms indicated in the October Manifesto to be examined by the legislative chambers, the ministry hinders the introduction of a system of law and order into Russia and destroys the people's respect for law and authority, thereby strengthening opposition attitudes in the country; that by applying present laws concerning nationalities, the administrative authorities divide Russian citizens and weaken the power of Russia—in view of all this, the Duma insists on the immediate introduction of far-reaching reforms" (Miliukov).
41. Tovaristvo Ukrainskikh Postupovtsiv [The Society of Ukrainian Progressives] (Miliukov).
42. In the newspaper published by the Ministry of the Army, *Razvedchik* (*Scout*), there appeared on New Years Day, 1914, one of Sukhomlinov's provocative articles, in which we read (I am translating from the French version): "We all know that we are preparing for war on our western border, primarily against Germany. . . . Not only the army but also the entire Russian people must be ready to accept the idea that we must arm ourselves for a war of annihilation against the Germans, and that the German Empire must be destroyed even if we have to sacrifice hundreds of thousands of human lives" (Miliukov).
43. Let me cite the following: "The writer of these lines has said more than once that a simple 'neutralization' of the Straits with international administration of Constantinople will not guarantee the interests of Russia. Without doubt, the rights of international trade on the Black Sea should be fully guaranteed as far as is possible, not only in time of peace but also in time of war. The report of the commission of the International Arbitration Union, presented to the Union's conference in 1913 (I myself prepared the report for the next conference—P.M.) might serve as the starting point for guaranteeing these rights. . . . These rights (the minimal ones—P.M.) did not include a denial of sovereignty over the shores of the Straits, or an obligation to destroy the fortification of the Straits, or an obligation to allow military vessels through the Straits. . . . Meanwhile, the right to sovereignty over the shores and the right to erect fortifications was fully recognized for the United States in the Panama Canal by the treaties of Hay-Pauncefote (1901) and Hay-Bunau-

Notes

Varilla (1904). The administration of that canal should serve as a model for the future administration of the Straits under Russian sovereignty. This is exceeded only by the demand to prohibit military vessels from crossing through the Straits. This demand follows inevitably, however, both from the entire previous history of Russian claims in the Straits, especially from the precedents of 1798, 1805, and 1833, and from the circumstance that the Black Sea is a closed body of water and not one of the world's interoceanic routes. The littoral states of the Black Sea, of course, should be given the right equal to Russia of free crossing for their military vessels" (Miliukov).

44. Soon after my departure from Petersburg, all my papers and my library were carried off by my old friend, Braudo, who worked in the public library. Part of my papers were hidden from the eyes of the victors, some in the Manuscript Section of the Academy of Sciences and some in the Petersburg Public Library. They remained there for fifteen years, were at last found, and were made into a so-called "Miliukov Archive," kept in the Special Section of the Moscow Central Historical Archive. Of these papers, the following were printed: the above-mentioned record of the conferences with the members of the State Council and the beginning of my diary covering the foreign trip of the delegation from the legislative institutions. The selection was made skillfully and the texts are accompanied by a commentary that indicates very careful study. The small errors and faults in the text do not prevent me from being satisfied with this selection of material; I only regret that the publication (in *Krasnyi Arkhiv*, Vols. 50-51, 52, 54-55, 56) was not continued, even though the documents were recognized to be extraordinarily important. About the "diary," see below [note 46] (Miliukov).

45. The composition of the "liberal" group was as follows: Of former members, there were Sazonov, Count Ignatiev, Krivoshein, Bark, and Kharitonov; and among the new appointments, Prince Shcherbatov, A. Samarin, and Polivanov (Miliukov).

46. During the two trips abroad in 1916, I kept a "diary" in three books, which were among my papers Braudo hid in the public library, and which the Bolsheviks found fifteen years later (see note 44). The Bolsheviks printed the first of these diaries in Volumes 54-55 of *Krasnyi Arkhiv* with a preface and comments which showed a careful study of my texts. The publication stopped with England, however, and I could use it only for this part. I had to write the rest from memory (Miliukov).

In addition, in Volume 58 of *Krasnyi Arkhiv*, under the title "The Russian Parliamentary Delegation Abroad," Miliukov's report to the Military-Naval Committee of the Duma on June 19, 1916, was published (M. M. Karpovich and B. I. Elkin).

47. He had made disrespectful comments about the Romanov family (Miliukov).

48. The lectures were published in the monthly journal, *Samtiden*.

49. Chkheidze was offered the post of minister of labor, but declined it (M. M. Karpovich and B. I. Elkin).

50. *Istoriia vtoroi Russkoi Revoliutsii (The History of the Second Russian Revolution)* was written soon after the events, in the period from the end of November 1917 to August 1918, then revised and expanded, first while I was in Kiev, during this same period, and again in Paris in December 1920. It was published in 1921-24 by the Russo-Bulgarian press in Sofia, incorporating new material on the subject that had since become available (Miliukov).

51. *Zapiski o revoliutsii (Notes on the Revolution)* was published in Berlin in 1922-23. My *Rossiia na perelome (Russia at the Turning Point)* was published in two volumes in Paris in 1927. For parallels between my account and Sukhanov's, see in particular Vol. I, pp. 48-49, 71-78, and 104-19, and also see *Histoire de Russie*, Vol. 3, pp. 1259-94 (Miliukov).

52. The Dukhobors were a religious sect founded in the eighteenth century. They were persecuted with particular severity because of their resistance to military service. With the aid of Leo Tolstoy and the Quakers, they emigrated from Russia in the 1890's to settle in Canada.

53. *Arkhiv Russkoi Revoliutsii (Archive of the Russian Revolution)*, Vol. I ("The Provisional Government"). V. D. Nabokov's richly substantive article is an indispensable aid in acquainting oneself with the members and the earliest activities of the first government of the revolution (Miliukov).

54. During September 5-12, 1915, at Zimmerwald, Switzerland, and during April 24-29 at Kienthal, another Swiss town, about forty European socialists gathered to express their opposition to the war. At both conferences, Lenin proposed a manifesto that would urge all soldiers to stop fighting among themselves and to turn their guns against their common enemy—the capitalist governments of both sides. The prevailing socialist opinion at the conferences, while opposed to the war, was nowhere near this radical: Lenin's proposals were defeated, and the conferences passed instead proclamations calling for an immediate armistice and "peace without annexations." The split between Lenin's Bolsheviks and the other delegates, the majority, was later to lead to the establishment of a separate, Communist "Third" International.

55. Sir George Buchanan, *My Mission to Russia*, Vol. II, and Maurice Paleologue, *La Russie des tsars pendant la grande guerre*, Vol. III (Miliukov).

56. After I had already resigned, Henderson asked my advice as to what to do about this. I told him that there were no grounds for dismissing Buchanan. He answered: "I am of the same opinion myself" (Miliukov).

57. According to Colonel B. V. Nikitin, director of counterespionage for the Provisional Government, Evgeniia Sumenson corroborated other evidence purportedly disclosing methods by which Germany pro-

vided funds for the Bolsheviks by way of Sweden. This cause célèbre has been heatedly debated ever since the Bolshevik revolution, and after World War II attracted particular interest because of disclosures in captured German secret documents. Two such documents, signed by Kühlmann, German state secretary at the time, state candidly that Germany supplied money to the Bolsheviks, although they do not indicate the specific channels. For the more recent discussions of the charges and countercharges, see Michael Futrell, *Northern Underground* (London, 1963), Chapter VII; George Katkov, *The February Revolution* (London, 1967); and Z. A. B. Zeman (ed.), *Germany and the Revolution in Russia 1915-1918* (London, 1958).

Glossary of Names

Miliukov refers to over four hundred persons in his memoirs. The following glossary represents, therefore, only a selection of those considered by the editor to be important enough for comment. Particularly well-known persons and those from countries other than Russia are not included.

Preparation of the glossary was facilitated by editorial notes in V. I. Gorko, *Features and Figures of the Past* (Stanford: Stanford University Press, 1939).

Aladin, A. F. Tried in 1901 for revolutionary propaganda, escaped to England. Returned to Russia in 1905, after the October Manifesto. A leading member of the Trudovik group in the First Duma, where he was known for his virulent attacks against the government.

Annensky, N. F. Economist, statistician, and publicist. Active in the Nizhny-Novgorod Zemstvo and a leading contributor to liberal Populist journals, particularly *Russkoe bogatstvo*. In 1904-5, an important member of the League of Liberation and, in 1906, prominent in the People's Socialist party, formed from moderate Social Revolutionaires and closely allied with the Kadets.

Axelrod, P. B. One of the founders of Russian Marxism in the 1880's. A leading Menshevik and, in the decade preceding World War I, one of the so-called liquidators who advocated substituting open and legal for underground and illegal activity by the Russian Social Democrats. Left Russia after the Bolshevik revolution, which he opposed.

Bulgakov, S. H. Economist and philosopher. Identified with the "legal Marxists," the revisionist, moderate wing of Russian Marxism in the 1890's. A Kadet during the 1905 revolution. Later turned increasingly to philosophical idealism and religion. Ordained an Orthodox priest in 1918. Exiled from Russia in 1922.

Bulygin, A. G. Governor of Kaluga, 1887, and Moscow, 1893. Minister of the interior, January-October 1905. Best known for his relatively moderate policies during the revolutionary year and for the Bulygin Duma, the plan for a consultative assembly elected on a highly restricted franchise, announced in August 1905.

Burtsev, V. L. Arrested and imprisoned in the 1880's as a Populist revolutionary. Escaped to Switzerland, thence to England, where he continued publishing Russian revolutionary propaganda. Imprisoned in England. A Social Revolutionary until the 1905 revolution, then more closely associated with the Kadets. Famous for exposing tsarist secret agents in the opposition parties and for publishing *Byloe* (*The Past*), an important journal for information on the Russion revolutionary movement. Active in anti-Bolshevik organizations abroad after 1917.

Chelnokov, M. V. Wealthy manufacturer and property owner. Participated in the foundation of the Kadet party. Mayor of Moscow, 1914-17, and active in the urban and Zemstvo organizations formed during World War I to improve the war effort.

Chernov, V. M. A leader and principal theorist of the Social Revolutionary party. Editor of the party's journal, *Revoliutsionnaia Rossiia*. Minister of agriculture in the Provisional Government, May-August 1917. Active in the struggle against the Bolsheviks. Emigrated in 1920.

Chkeidze, N. S. Social Democrat, Menshevik. Elected to the Third and Fourth Dumas from Tiflis province and leader of the Menshevik faction in the Duma. After the February 1917 revolution, chairman of the Petrograd Soviet of Workers' and Soldiers' Deputies. Head of the anti-Bolshevik, socialist government in Georgia after the October revolution. Emigrated to Paris in 1921 when the Bolsheviks took Georgia.

Dolgorukov, Prince Pavel D. Member of the League of Liberation, a founder of the Kadet party, and first chairman of the party's Central Committee. Elected to the Second Duma. Active opponent of the Bolsheviks both before and after his emigration in 1920. Arrested when he returned to Russia on a forged passport in 1927, and shot.

Dolgorukov, Prince Peter D. Long participant in Zemstvo affairs, and a founding member of the League of Liberation and Kadet party. Elected vice-chairman of the First Duma. Signatory of the Vyborg Manifesto.

Dubrovin, A. I. Founder and head of the extreme right-wing Union of Russian People, and particularly active in campaigns against Russian Jews. Executed by the Bolsheviks after the October revolution.

Durnovo, P. N. Minister of interior, 1905-6. Author of a famous memorandum opposing Russia's entry into an alliance against Germany and predicting with remarkable accuracy the consequences of such an alliance.

Efremov, I. N. Member of the First, Third, and Fourth Dumas, founder of the Party of Peaceful Reconstruction, and a leader in the "Progressist" group in the Fourth Duma. Member of the Provisional Government after the February 1917 revolution.

Ermolov, A. S. Official during the reigns of Alexander II, Alexander III, and Nicholas II. Specialist in agrarian affairs. Minister of agriculture and state domains, 1894-1905.

Erogin, M. M. Prominent landowner and conservative member of the First Duma. Provided special boardinghouses for peasant deputies in the Duma in an effort to win them over to conservatism.

Fredericks, Baron V. B. Minister of the Imperial Court and one of the small circle attending the royal family.

Golovin, F. A. Zemstvo activist and a founder of the League of Liberation. Member of the Kadet party and chairman of the Second Duma.

Prominent in the work of the Union of Towns, organized to help meet military and economic needs during World War I.

Goremykin, I. L. Minister of interior, 1895-99. Chairman of the Council of Ministers, May-June 1906 and 1914-16. Notable for his opposition to liberal tendencies among tsarist Cabinet ministers during World War I.

Guchkov, A. I. Wealthy manufacturer and leader of the Octobrists. Chairman of the Third Duma, 1910-11. Minister of the army and navy in the first Provisional Government.

Heiden, Count P. A. High official in the tsarist judicial system under Alexander II and Alexander III. Chairman of the Free Economic Society, 1895. Also prominent as a moderate liberal in the Zemstvo movement of 1904-5. An Octobrist and later a founder of the Party of Peaceful Reconstruction.

Hertsenstein, M. I. Economics and professor at Moscow University. Active in the Moscow Zemstvo and City Council. Kadet member of the First Duma. Specialist in agrarian affairs. Murdered by the right-wing Union of the Russian People.

Hessen, I. V. Jurist, publicist, and political activist. A founder of the Kadet party and a Kadet representative to the Second Duma. Coeditor with Miliukov of the party's main journal, *Rech*. In emigration he edited *Arkhiv russkoi revoliutsii*, a valuable collection of materials pertaining to Russian political history.

Ignatev, Count P. N. Official in the Department of Agriculture from 1909 and minister of education, 1915-16.

Izvolsky, A. P. Career diplomat assigned to various Western European capitals. Minister of foreign affairs, 1906-10. Russian ambassador to Paris, 1910-17.

Kharitonov, M. M. Social Democrat, Bolshevik. Prominent among émigré Bolsheviks in Switzerland during World War I. Active in the Petrograd Bolshevik party organization after his return to Russia in April 1917.

Khomiakov, N. A. Official in the Ministry of Agriculture and well-known Zemstvo leader. Member of the Second, Third, and Fourth Dumas and chairman of the Third Duma. Associated with the liberal wing of the Octobrists and member of the Progressive bloc in the Fourth Duma.

Khvostov, A. A. From 1890 an official in various ministries, mainly Justice and Interior. Minister of justice, July 1915-July 1916. Minister of interior, July-September 1916.

Khvostov, A. N. Official in the Ministry of Justice and governor of Vologda, 1906-10, and of Nizhny-Novgorod, 1910-12. A leader of the rightist groups in the Duma. Minister of interior, 1915-16. Imprisoned by the Provisional Government. Shot by the Bolsheviks after October.

Kizevetter, A. A. Historian and professor at the Women's University, Moscow. Member of the League of Liberation and, in 1906, of the Kadet party's Central Committee. Elected to the Second Duma. Exiled from Russia in 1922.

Kliuchevsky, V. O. Distinguished historian and professor at Moscow University, where Miliukov was his student. For a short time, a member of the Kadet party.

Kokoshkin, F. F. Professor of constitutional law, Moscow University. Kadet member of the Provisional Government, August-September 1917. Imprisoned with other Kadets after the October revolution and killed.

Kokovtsov, Count V. N. Government official from 1873 to World War I. Assistant minister of finance under Count Witte, 1896-1902. Minister of finance, 1904-14, and chairman of the Council of Ministers, 1911-14.

Konovalov, A. I. Wealthy merchant and vice-chairman of the Moscow Stock Exchange. Member of the Fourth Duma and minister of commerce and industry in the Provisional Government.

Kornilov, L. G. Army General of Cossack origins. Served with distinction in the Russo-Japanese War and World War I. Commander of the Russian armies under the Provisional Government. Attempted an unsuccessful coup d'état to remove Kerensky as head of the Provisional Government in September 1917. Organizer of anti-Bolshevik forces after the October revolution. Killed in 1918.

Kovalevsky, M. M. Eminent jurist and historian of legal institutions. Dismissed from his position as professor of constitutional law, Moscow University, in 1887. Emigrated, but returned to Russia in 1905. Elected to the First Duma and, later, to the State Council. Member of the Party of Democratic Reform.

Krivoshein, A. V. From 1884 an official in various departments, including Justice, Interior, and Agriculture. Minister of agriculture, 1908-15.

Krupensky, P. N. Prominent and immensely wealthy landowner from Bessarabia province. Member of the Second, Third, and Fourth Dumas.

Kryzhanovsky, S. E. Official in judicial institutions and, later, in the Ministry of Interior. Helped prepare the laws covering the so-called "Bulygin Duma."

Kuskova, E. D. Participant in the first Russian Marxist group, the Liberation of Labor. Famous as a leading advocate of moderate, trade-union policies for the Russian working class and, for this, bitterly attacked by Lenin. Joined the League of Liberation and took an active part in the left-wing of the Kadet party. Exiled from Russia in 1922.

Kutler, N. N. Official in economic and financial departments under Alexander III and Nicholas II, specializing in agrarian affairs. Kadet member of the Second and Third Dumas. After the Bolshevik revolution remained in Russia and worked in government finance departments until his death in 1924.

Kuzmin-Karavaev, V. D. Jurist and professor, St. Petersburg University. Prominent in the Zemstvo congresses of 1904-5 and elected to the First and Second Dumas. A founder of the Party of Democratic Reforms.

Lvov, Prince G. E. Long career in Zemstvo affairs. Directed Zemstvo medical and relief work in the Russo-Japanese War and again in World War I. Moderate Kadet in the First Duma. Chairman of the Council of Ministers and minister of interior in the Provisional Government, March-May 1917. Imprisoned by the Bolsheviks. Escaped to Paris.

Lvov, N. N. Zemstvo activist. Kadet member in the First, Third, and Fourth Dumas. A founder of the Party of Peaceful Reconstruction.

Lvov, V. N. Member of the Third and Fourth Dumas. Head of the Holy Synod under the Provisional Government. Emigrated after the October revolution, but returned in 1922.

Makarov, A. A. High official in the judicial system and Ministry of Interior. Minister of interior after Stolypin's assassination in 1911. Minister of justice, July 1916-January 1917.

Maklakov, N. A. Governor of Chernigov, 1909, and minister of interior, 1913. Shot by the Bolsheviks.

Maklakov, V. A. Eminent Moscow and St. Petersburg attorney. Kadet member of the Second, Third, and Fourth Dumas. Ambassador to Paris for the Provisional Government. Engaged in prolonged polemics with Miliukov in emigration over the tactics and programs of the Kadets and the reasons for the failure of Russian liberalism.

Manuilov, A. A. Economist, prominent Kadet and an editor of *Russkie vedomosti*. Rector of Moscow University, 1905-11, and a member of the State Council, 1907-11. Minister of education in the Provisional Government.

Markov, N. E. (Markov II) Engineer, and active in large, private railway companies. A leader of the extreme right-wing factions in the Third and Fourth Dumas.

Martov, Lev. Social Democrat, leading Menshevik opponent of Lenin, editor of the moderate Marxist journal *Golos Sotsial-Democrata* (*The Voice of the Social Democrat*). Emigrated to Germany in 1920 and helped found the influential Menshevik journal, *Sotsialisticheskii vestnik* (*Socialist Courier*).

Meshchersky, V. P. Prominent right-wing publicist. Editor of the influential conservative journal *Grazhdanin*, 1872-1914, as well as other similar journals, all heavily subsidized by the government.

Muromstev, S. A. Professor at Moscow University. Zemstvo activist, a founder of the Kadet party and a member of its Central Committee. Chairman of the First Duma. Signatory of the Vyborg Manifesto.

Naumov, A. N. Well-known provincial Zemstvo official and member of the State Council. Minister of agriculture, November 1915-July 1916.

Nekrasov, N. V. Professor, Tomsk Technological Institute. Member of the Third and Fourth Dumas and vice-chairman of the Fourth. Minister of finance in the Provisional Government.

Nosar: Khrustalev-Nosar, G. S. Attorney. Elected chairman of the St. Petersburg Soviet of Workers' Deputies, 1905. Social Democrat, Menshevik. Exiled to Siberia in 1906, then escaped and lived abroad until his return to Russia in 1914. Again arrested, and imprisoned until 1917. Supported the anti-Bolshevik forces in the Ukraine after the October revolution. Shot by Bolshevik soldiers.

Peshekhonov, A. V. Moderate Populist in the 1890's and an editor of *Russkoe bogatstvo*. Member of League of Liberation and contributor to its journal, *Osvobozhdenie*. Closely affiliated as well with the Social Revolutionary party and its journal *Revoliutsionnaia Rossiia*.

Petrunkevich, I. I. One of the most prominent early Zemstvo liberals. A founder of the League of Liberation and the Kadet party. Floor leader of the Kadets in the First Duma and signatory of the Vyborg Manifesto.

Plehve, V. K. Minister of the interior, 1902. Famous for his reactionary policies, his "Russification" campaigns in Poland, Lithuania, and Finland, and his support of pogroms against the Jews. Assassinated in 1904.

Plekhanov, G. V. A founder and principal theorist of Russian Marxism in the 1880's and 1890's. Opposed the revisionist trends in the Russian labor movement at the turn of the century and in this conflict joined Lenin. Split with Lenin after the Second Congress of the Russian Social Democratic Workers' party, 1903, and thereafter a leader of the Mensheviks. Supported Russia in World War I and opposed the Bolshevik October revolution.

Pobedonostsev, K. P. Professor of Russian civil law, Moscow University, and tutor of the sons of Alexander II, 1860-65. Head of the Holy Synod, the highest church office, 1880-1905. Best known for his defense of Russian conservatism and criticism of liberal ideas and institutions.

Polivanov, General A. A. Editor of the main military journals, *Voennyi sbornik* (*Military Symposium*) and *Invalid*. Assistant minister of war, 1906-12. Minister of war, 1915. Continued to serve with the army after the Bolshevik revolution. Soviet military expert during Soviet-Polish negotiations.

Purishkevich, V. M. Member of the Second, Third, and Fourth Dumas. A founder of the right-wing Union of Russian People. Participant in the assassination of Rasputin. Joined Deniken's anti-Bolshevik forces after the Bolshevik revolution.

Rodichev, F. I. Long one of the most famous of the Zemstvo leaders and prominent in the movement for constitutional government since the 1880's. A founder of the Kadet party, member of its Central Committee, and one of its representatives in all four Dumas. After the February revolution, represented the Provisional Government in Finland. Left Russia after the October revolution.

Rodzianko, M. V. A wealthy landowner and Zemstvo leader from Ekaterinoslav (now Sverdlovsk) province. After the 1905 revolution, an Octobrist and, later, elected member to the State Council. Chairman of the Third and Fourth Dumas and of the Provisional Committee of the Duma after the February 1917 revolution. After the October revolution, participated in the civil war against the Bolsheviks until the defeat of the "White" forces in 1920. He then emigrated to Yugoslavia, where he died.

Sabler, V. K. Official in the Ministry of Justice, 1873, and in the Holy Synod from 1881. Head of the Holy Synod, 1911-15.

Sazonov, S. D. Career diplomat from 1883, serving in London and Rome. Minister of foreign affairs, 1910-16. After the Bolshevik revolution, joined Kolchak's anti-Bolshevik government as minister of foreign affairs.

Shakhovskoi, Prince D. I. Zemstvo leader and a founder of the League of Liberation and Kadet party. Member of the Central Committee of the Kadet party. Minister of social welfare in the Provisional Government, May-July 1917. Active in the Soviet cooperative movement.

Shcheglovitov, I. G. Official in the Ministry of Justice from 1890 and minister of justice, 1906-15. Arrested and killed by the Bolsheviks after the Bolshevik revolution.

Shcherbatov, Prince N. B. Marshal of the nobility, Poltava, 1907. Director of Chief Administration of State Stud Farms, 1913-15. Minister of interior, June-September 1915.

Shidlovsky, S. I. Liberal landowner and Zemstvo activist. Left-Octobrist, and vice-chairman of the Third Duma, 1907. A leader of the Progressive bloc in the Fourth Duma. Member of the Provisional Committee of the Duma, the predecessor of the Provisional Government. Emigrated in 1920.

Shingarev, A. I. Zemstvo leader and Kadet member of the Second, Third, and Fourth Dumas. Minister of agriculture in the Provisional Government, March-May 1917, then minister of finance, May-July 1917. Arrested and killed after the Bolshevik revolution.

Shipov, D. N. Prominent Zemstvo leader, chairman of the Moscow Provincial Zemstvo Board. A leading Octobrist and member of the Party of Peaceful Reconstruction 1908. Elected to the State Council, 1907-9. Died in prison after the Bolshevik revolution.

Shulgin, V. V. Zemstvo activist. Member of the Second, Third, and Fourth Dumas and of the Progressive bloc, 1915. Joined Deniken's anti-Bolshevik forces after the October revolution. Emigrated, but later returned to the Soviet Union.

Stolypin, P. A. Chairman of the Council of Ministers, and minister of the interior, 1906-11. Combined ruthless repression of revolutionaries with a willingness to cooperate with moderate Duma representatives. Most famous for his agrarian program through which he sought to replace the traditional Russian communes by individual peasant farms.

Struve, P. B. Economist and the most prominent of the moderate, "legal" Marxists in the 1890's. A founder of the League of Liberation and editor of *Osvobozhdenie*. Member of the Central Committee of the Kadet party and elected to the Second Duma. Joined Deniken and, later, Wrangle against the Bolsheviks in the Civil War, following the October revolution. Edited two of the main émigré Russian journals— *Russkaia mysl* (*Russian Thought*) in Prague and *Vozrozhdenie* (*Renaissance*) in Paris.

Stürmer, B. V. Entered the Ministry of Justice in 1875. Governor of Novgorod, 1894. Official in the Ministry of Interior after 1902. Chairman, Council of Ministers, February-November 1916. Minister of interior, March-July 1916. Minister of foreign affairs, July-November 1916.

Sukhomlinov, V. A. Governor-General of Kiev, 1904-8. Minister of war, 1909-15. Imprisoned after dismissal in 1915 on the charge of treasonable negligence for inadequately maintaining the Russian armed forces. Released and placed under house arrest. Tried and sentenced to hard labor for life by the Provisional Government. Released by the Bolsheviks. Escaped to Finland.

Trepov, D. F. Chief of Police, Moscow, 1896-1905. Governor-general of St. Petersburg and chief of police, St. Petersburg, 1905. Commandant at the Imperial Court, October 1905.

Trubetskoi, Prince E. N. Professor of legal philosophy at the University of Kiev and, later, Moscow University. Member of the Kadet party until 1906, then a founder of the Party of Peaceful Reconstruction.

Trubetskoi, Prince S. N. Professor of philosophy, Moscow University. Elected rector, Moscow University. Spokesman for a delegation of Zemstvo and town dignitaries who pleaded the cause of reform before the tsar, June 6, 1905.

Yanushkevich, General N. N. Chief of General Staff, 1914, then chief of staff for the supreme commander in chief, 1914-15.

Vyrubova, Anna A. Confidante of Tsarina Alexandra, and friend of Rasputin, whose wishes she communicated to the tsarina.

Witte, Count S. I. Began his government service with the Odessa State Railway in 1877 and rapidly rose in private and public railway management. Head of the Railway Department under Minister of Finance Vyshnegradsky, and succeeded Vyshnegradsky as minister of finance in 1893. By a variety of fiscal policies, he succeeded in stimulating a rapid advance in Russian industrial development in the 1890's. Chief Russian delegate at the Portsmouth, New Hampshire, negotiations ending the Russo-Japanese War, 1905. Played a leading role in drafting the Manifesto of October 17, 1905. Chairman of the first Council of Ministers, following the 1905 revolution, until his dismissal in 1906.

Glossary of Parties

Black Hundreds The name given to groups of self-appointed vigilantes regarding themselves as defenders of the Russian state, church, and traditional society against what they considered foreign influences. While active in anti-Jewish pogroms from the turn of the century, such as the Kishinev pogrom of 1903, they became particularly significant after the October Manifesto, when there was a wave of attacks on Jews, students, and liberals. In this later period, they were part of the organized rightist movement that centered around the Union of the Russian People and its journal, *Russkoe znamia.* Among its leaders were A. I. Dubrovin and V. M. Purishkevich and its membership included government officials, members of the Orthodox clergy, and conservatives from the landed gentry and lower middle class. It was known to have the approval of the Court and received government subsidies.

Black Partition The group opposing the emphasis on terror at the Voronezh meeting of revolutionary Populists in 1879 (see the *People's Will* party). Among its leading members were G. V. Plekhanov and others who were soon thereafter to shift from Populism to Marxism and form the first Russian Marxist party, the Liberation of Labor.

Holy Brigades Secret organization formed in the summer of 1881 by aristocratic courtiers to oppose the revolutionary movement. Grand dukes, cabinet ministers, and military generals participated in the direction of the organization. Dissolved at the end of 1882.

Octobrists Moderate liberal participants in the 1905 revolution who accepted the political system as established by the October Manifesto. Led by A. I. Guchkov and M. V. Rodzianko. The majority party in the Third and Fourth Dumas. Cooperated with the Stolypin government, but became increasingly antagonistic to the Court and the Cabinet after 1912 and especially during World War I. Active in the Provisional Government.

Party of Democratic Reform Formed in early 1906. While liberal, it was more moderate in its program and tactics than the Kadets. Its founders included Professors M. M. Kovalevsky and V. D. Kuzmin-Karavaev.

Party of Peaceful Reconstruction Formed in 1906 among liberals favoring a constitutional monarchy. Politically more conservative than the right Kadets, but to the left of the Octobrists. Its leaders were Count P. A. Heiden, M. A. Stakhovich, and D. N. Shipov.

Party of People's Freedom   Another name for the Constitutional Democratic party, the Kadets, founded in October 1905 under the principal leadership of P. N. Miliukov and I. I. Petrunkevich.

People's Rights   Illegal organization formed in 1893 by former revolutionary Populists. Led by M. A. Natanson. Attempted to unite the different opposition groups into a concentrated political struggle against tsarism. Suppressed by the police in the summer of 1894. Most of the members later entered the Social Revolutionary party.

People's Will   The Populist revolutionaries of the 1870's had different views on the role of terror. At a congress in Voronezh in the summer of 1879, a split occurred between those stressing terror and those opposed to its emphasis. The terrorists adopted as their party name, *People's Will*. It was this party that assassinated Tsar Alexander II on March 1, 1881. The party was crushed by the police in the following reign. The last issue of its journal, *People's Will*, appeared in 1885.

Social Democratic   Founded in 1898 as the Russian Social Democratic Workers' party. Split into Bolshevik and Menshevik factions at the Second Congress of the party in 1903. Nominally united again between 1906 and 1912, the party continued to be rent by factional polemics. In 1919, the Bolsheviks ceased using the title Russian Social Democratic Workers' party.

Social Revolutionary   Established in 1902 by revolutionary Populists, including among its leaders Victor Chernov. Called for socialization of the land and approved of terror as a political weapon. The radical wing of the party, the left socialists, accepted the Bolshevik revolution and participated in the government until their exclusion when they opposed the Brest-Litovsk Treaty, March 1918. The Social Revolutionaries won a majority of delegates to the Constituent Assembly of January 1918 and elected Chernov chairman of the assembly. The assembly was disbanded by the Bolsheviks after a single session, on January 18, 1918.

Trudovik   The so-called labor group (*Trukovaia gruppa*) formed during the First Duma, in 1906. It was led by Populist intellectuals, but included most of the peasant delegates elected to the Duma. While more radical than the Kadets, the group generally allied with them and joined the Kadets in the Vyborg Manifesto. Its most prominent leader in the Third and Fourth Dumas was A. F. Kerensky. Its largest representation was in the Second Duma, where it had 104 delegates.

Union of the Russian People   See *Black Hundreds*.

Glossary of Journals

Bez zaglaviia (Untitled) Weekly political journal published in St. Petersburg, January-May 1906, under the editorship of E. D. Kuskova, V. I. Bogucharsky, and S. N. Prokopovich. Represented a merger of moderate, "revisionist" Marxists and Kadets.

Birzhevye vedomosti (Stock Market Gazette) St. Petersburg newspaper founded in 1880 by S. M. Propper, who also edited the paper. In 1885, it became a daily, and from 1903 appeared twice daily. In 1905, it became a Kadet organ, with contributions from P. N. Miliukov, I. V. Hessen, and P. V. Struve, and twice changed its name, to *Svobodnyi narod (A Free People)* and *Narodnaia svoboda (The People's Freedom)* It resumed its former name in December, when it ceased being the voice of the Kadets. In September 1906, it became the organ of the Party of Peaceful Reconstruction.

Den (Day) A liberal daily published in St. Petersburg, 1912-17. It came under the control of Menshevik socialists after the February 1917 revolution. During the revolutionary year, 1917, under the editorship of A. N. Potresov, it became increasingly opposed to the Bolsheviks.

Grazhdanin (Citizen) A weekly (1872-87), then biweekly (1887-1914). F. M. Dostoevski was one of its early editors. From its founding, it was edited by the conservative Prince V. P. Meshchersky and received a large annual subsidy from the government.

Izvestiia (News)—Izvestiia Petrogradskogo Soveta rabochikh i soldatskikh deputatov (News of the Petrograd Soviet of Workers' and Soldiers' Deputies) A daily, published by the Central Executive Committee of the Soviet in 1917, after the February revolution. Mainly expressed views of the Mensheviks and Social Revolutionaries and in May and June 1917 was attacked by Lenin in *Pravda (Truth)*.

Kurskaia byl (Kursk Life) Kursk daily, 1906-16. The organ of the Union of the Russian People, the reactionary Black Hundreds, in Kursk.

Mir Bozhii (World of God) A literary and popular science, St. Petersburg monthly for youth. In the 1890's, became a vehicle for "legal" Marxist polemics against the Populists, particularly *Russkoe bogatstvo*. Published from 1892 to 1906.

Narodnaia svoboda (The People's Freedom) A Kadet political and literary journal edited by P. N. Miliukov and I. V. Hessen. Published in St. Petersburg for a short time in December 1905.

495

Novaia zhizn (New Life) The first legal paper of the Bolsheviks. Published daily in St. Petersburg, October-December 1905. De facto organ of the Central Committee of the Bolsheviks. Another daily with the same name appeared in Petrograd from April 1917 until June 1918, reflecting the views of Social Democrats less radical than the Bolsheviks.

Novoe vremia (New Times) A St. Petersburg daily established in 1868. After 1896, under the editorship of A. S. Suvorin, it became a widely read conservative paper, with contributions from eminent literary figures.

Okopnaia pravda (The Trench Truth) Published for the soldiers by the Bolsheviks in Riga in 1917. At first published by the soldiers themselves, it became, in May, the organ of the military section of Riga Bolshevik party. Repressed by the Provisional Government in July, but continued to appear under the name, *Okopnyi nabat (The Trench Tocsin)*.

Osvobozhdenie (Liberation) The main journal of the liberals. Published bimonthly, first in Stuttgart, July-October 1902, then in Paris, from October 1902 to October 1905. Its principal editor was P. B. Struve. The organ of the League of Liberation, it was persistently hostile to Bolshevism, but conciliatory with regard to the Mensheviks.

Poliarnaia zvezda (Polar Star) Weekly political and theoretical journal reflecting the views of the more conservative wing of the Kadet party. Published in St. Petersburg, December 1905-March 1906 under the editorship of P. B. Struve. It was replaced during April-May 1906 by *Svoboda i kultura (Freedom and Culture)*.

Poslednie novosti (Latest News) A leading organ of émigré Russians, published in Paris, 1920-40. After March 1921, edited by P. N. Miliukov.

Pravda (Truth) (1) Published in Moscow, January 1904-February 1906, as a Social Democratic monthly, including both Menshevik and Bolshevik participants but reflecting in the main Menshevik moderation. (2) A Bolshevik daily, published legally in St. Petersburg, April 1912-July 1914. Covered a wide range of political, economic, and cultural topics. The major organ for the party's Central Committee during these years. Published 265 articles by Lenin. (3) From March 1917 the organ of the Central Committee of the Petrograd Committee of the Russian Social Democratic Workers' party (Bolsheviks). Directed by Lenin after his return to Russia in April.

Pravitelstvennyi vestnik (Governmental News) Official government daily published in St. Petersburg, 1869-1917. After the February revolution, continued as *Vestnik vremennago pravitelstva (Provisional Government News)* until October 27, 1917. Included material on history, science, biography, and general news, in addition to official government information.

Rech (Speech) The central organ of the Kadet party, appearing as a daily paper in St. Petersburg from February 1906-17. The principal de facto editors were P. N. Miliukov and I. V. Hessen. Most of the leading members of the Kadet party, such as V. A. Maklakov, P. B. Struve, and I. I. Petrunkevich, contributed to it.

Rossiia (*Russia*)   Political and literary daily, published in St. Petersburg, November 1905 to April 1914. After 1906, regarded as the organ of the Ministry of Internal Affairs.

Rus (*Russia*)   St. Petersburg daily, December 1903-5, then intermittently, 1906-8. Liberal position, close to that of the Kadets.

Russkoe bogatstvo (*Russian Wealth*)   St. Petersburg monthly, 1876-1918. In the 1880's, became leading organ of the moderate, "legal" Populists, under the direction of N. K. Mikhailovsky. In the 1890's, carried on persistent polemics with Russian Marxists. The organ of the People's Socialist party during the 1905 revolution, merging the views of the Kadets and the Social Revolutionaries.

Russkoe gosudarstvo (*Russian State*)   Government publication, St. Petersburg, February-May 1906. Established during the brief period of Witte's chairmanship of the Council of Ministers. Ended with Stolypin's rise to power.

Russkoe znamia (*Russian Banner*)   Organ of the Union of the Russian People (the Black Hundreds), published daily in St. Petersburg, November 1905-17. After 1906, edited by the arch-reactionary, A. I. Dubrovin. Critical of Stolypin's government as too liberal.

Severnyi golos (*Northern Voice*)   (1) A Social Democratic daily published legally in St. Petersburg from December 1905. Reflected the union of Mensheviks and Bolsheviks, after the repression of their former organs, the Mensheviks' *Nachalo* (*Beginning*) and the Bolsheviks' *Novaia zhizn* (*New Life*). Closed by the government after the third issue. (2) Menshevik weekly, published in Petrograd, January-March 1915.

Svet (*Light*)   St. Petersburg daily, covering political, economic, and literary topics, 1882-1917. Strongly nationalistic.

Svobodnyi narod (*Free People*)   Organ of the Party of People's Freedom, published in June 1917 by Prince B. A. Obolensky.

Volga   A conservative daily published in Saratov, 1906-17.

Zemshchina   The title is taken from the name used during the reign of Ivan IV to refer to the area of Russia supposedly outside the direct control of Ivan's special military-police government, his "oprichnina." A daily, published in St. Petersburg, 1909-17. Reflected the views of the right-wing Duma representatives.

Index